QUID GLORIARIS IN MALITIA

D. DIONYSIVS CARTHVSIEÑ
DOCTOR EXTATICVS.

BENEDIC
TVS DEVS
IN SECVIA

QUID GLORIARIS IN MALITIA

DENIS THE CARTHUSIAN

COMMENTARY
on the
DAVIDIC
Psalms

VOLUME III
[PSALMS 51–75]

*Which are most learnedly explained, to the degree able,
in their multiple senses, namely* LITERAL, ALLEGORICAL,
TROPOLOGICAL, *&* ANAGOGICAL, *with nothing except
the most sound Scriptures of both Testaments.*

Translation & Introduction by
ANDREW M. GREENWELL

AROUCA
PRESS

Commentary in Latin taken from
Opera Omnia, Vol. 6
(Montreuil: Typis Cartusiae S. M. de Pratis 1898)
English Translation & Introduction © Andrew M. Greenwell
Copyright © Arouca Press 2022

ISBN: 978-1-990685-00-2 (pbk)
ISBN: 978-1-990685-01-9 (hardcover)

Arouca Press
PO Box 55003
Bridgeport PO
Waterloo, ON N2J3G0
Canada
www.aroucapress.com
Send inquiries to info@aroucapress.com

Book and cover design by
Michael Schrauzer

DEDICATION

To my children,
Elizabeth Grace, Mary Abigail, and Christopher Michael

Ecce haereditas Domini, filii; merces, fructus ventris.
Sicut sagittae in manu potentis, ita filii excussorum.
Beatus vir qui implevit desiderium suum ex ipsis:
non confundetur cum loquetur inimics suis in porta.
— Psalm 126:3-5

Ἐν ἐκκλησίᾳ παννυχίδες, καὶ πρῶτος καὶ μέσος καὶ τελευταῖος ὁ Δαυΐδ; ἐν ὀρθριναῖς ὑμνολογίαις, καὶ πρῶτος καὶ μέσος καὶ τελευταῖος ὁ Δαυΐδ; ἐν τοῖς σκηνώμασι τῶν νεκρῶν προπομπαὶ, καὶ πρῶτος καὶ μέσος καὶ τελευταῖος ὁ Δαυΐδ; ἐν ταῖς οἰκίαις τῶν παρθένων ἱστουργίαι, καὶ πρῶτος καὶ μέσος καὶ τελευταῖος ὁ Δαυΐδ; ... ἐν μοναστηρίοις χορὸς ἅγιος ταγμάτων ἀγγελικῶν, καὶ πρῶτος καὶ μέσος καὶ τελευταῖος ὁ Δαυΐδ; ἐν ἀσκητηρίοις παρθένων ἀγέλαι τῶν τὴν Μαριάμ μιμουμένων, καὶ πρῶτος καὶ μέσος καὶ τελευταῖος ὁ Δαυΐδ; ἐν ἐρημίαις ἄνδρες ἐσταυρωμένοι προσομιλοῦντες τῷ Θεῷ, καὶ πρῶτος καὶ μέσος καὶ τελευταῖος ὁ Δαυΐδ.

In the church during vigil, David is first, middle, and last; in the hymns of the morning, David is first, middle, and last; in the funeral processions of the dead, David is first, middle, and last; in the homes, where maidens ply the woof, David is first, middle, and last; ... in the holy monasteries, among the holy choirs of angelic warriors, David is first, middle, and last; in the convents of gathered virgins, who are imitators of Mary, David is first, middle, and last; in the deserts, where men crucified to the world hold converse with God, David is first, middle, and last.
—St. John Chrysostom

CONTENTS

ABBREVIATIONS

DS Heinrich Denziger, *Enchiridion Symbolorum Definitionum et Declarationum de Rebus Fidei et Morum* (*Compendium of Creeds, Definitions, and Déclarations on Matters of Faith and Morals*) (P. Hünerman, ed.) (Robert Fastiggi and Anne Englund Nash, eds., Eng. ed.) (43rd ed.) (San Francisco: Ignatius Press 2012).

PG *Patrologiae cursus completus. Series Graeca.* Ed. J.-P. Migne. Paris: Migne, 1857–1886.

PL *Patrologiae cursus completus. Series Latina.* Ed. J.-P. Migne. Paris: Migne, 1844–1864.

ST St. Thomas Aquinas, *Summa Theologiae* (corpusthomisticum.org)

CCC Catechism of the Catholic Church

INTRODUCTION
to
DENIS THE CARTHUSIAN'S
Commentary on the Psalms

PART 3
[PSALMS 51–75]

FAC QUOD IN TE EST! DO WHAT IS IN YOU!

N MY INTRODUCTION TO THE FIRST VOLUME of Denis's *Commentary on the Psalms*, I addressed the general schema of the *Commentary*. Then I discussed the characteristics of the Dionysian *Commentary*, namely, its ecstatic nature, its Dionysian/Thomistic character, its use of Scripture to interpret Scripture (*analogia Scripturae*), its Christocentric focus, and its emphasis on practical instruction, especially as it relates to the use of Psalm in one's prayer and practical life. In the introduction to the second volume, I concentrated on a cardinal theological tenet underlying the Dionysian *Commentary*, namely, Denis's notion that Jesus, in his human nature—specifically, in his human soul—enjoyed, from the first moment of his human existence, the beatific vision and infused knowledge. Therefore, from the first moment of his existence, the human soul of Jesus knew, as St. Thomas put it, "all things in the Word."[1] Denis's belief in this then-settled doctrine developed from the dogmatic teachings of the Council of Chalcedon, and it allowed him to understand the Psalms, as well as the Prophets, as being voices of Christ and Christ knowing it. This belief is an intrinsic constituent of the *Commentary*.

There is no need to repeat what was said in the first two introductions here except that they ought to be always kept in mind when reading the Carthusian. What I do want to address in this introduction is another feature of Denis's *Commentary* that a general reader might not readily detect or be familiar with. It is encountered anytime Denis says

---

1 ST IIIa, q. 10, art. 2, co.

something like "do what is in you." These words point to a theological principle or axiom known as the *facientibus* principle. It is a principle which underlies the *Commentary* and informs Denis the Carthusian's understanding of God and man's relationship with God, and the interplay of human nature, free will, and grace. This principle is a particularly important practical component when Denis discusses how the Psalms apply to the spiritual life, for he frequently exhorts the reader to "do what is in you," in which case, Denis assures the reader, he can be assured of God's favor, that is, God's grace.

DENIS AND THE *FACIENTIBUS* PRINCIPLE

The *facientibus* principle takes its name from the first word of the medieval maxim, *facientibus quod in se est Deus non denegat gratiam*, "God does not deny grace to those who do what is in them." The principle is sometimes found stated in a singular form: *facienti quod in se est, Deus no denegat gratiam*, "God will not deny grace to one who does what is in him." On occasion, it is found in the imperative form. For example, in the *Imitation of Christ* by Thomas à Kempis (*ca.* 1380–1471), one finds the maxim in the imperative: "Do what is in you and God will be with your good will," *Fac quod in te est; et Deus aderit bonae voluntatis tuae.*[2]

At the heart of the principle is the view that a man of good will who does his best—who does that which is in him, *quod in se est*—can be assured that he will be met (or better anticipated) by the merciful God, not unlike the prodigal son returning to his father, with the cloak of *supernatural grace.* The question is, what does "do what is *in* you" mean?[3] But this is to get ahead of ourselves. Let us first review the axiom as used by Denis in his *Commentary.*

In his commentary on Psalm 31:5, Denis states affirmatively: "[S]o long as the sinner does what is possible for him (*quod in se est*), the Lord immediately infuses grace, and so confession and penance begin to spring forth out of charity." Here, Denis is not particularly clear as to whether the act of good will on the part of the sinner is, or is not, elicited by

---

2 *Imitatio Christi*, I, 7, 1. The *facientibus* principle was very popular with the followers of *devotio moderna*, such as Thomas à Kempis.

3 Most fundamentally, there is a lack of clarity as to whether the axiom, in reference to the human act (what is in you), refers to a purely natural act of good will (what is in you by nature) or whether it refers to a natural act of good will be elicited by prevenient, antecedent, or operative grace. The former is clearly open to accusations of Pelagianism or semi-Pelagianism, which is condemned by the Church, most expressly in the Second Council of Orange (529), particularly DS 373–380.

prevenient actual grace or is one of nature alone. The subsequent grace that is "infused," since it stems from "charity," must be sanctifying grace.

In his commentary on Psalm 42:1, in the context of God's judgment, specifically, the merciful, patient judgment of discretion of God while we are *in via*, Denis states: "You, therefore, *judge me*, that is, do what I am unable to do: and as you promised to those seeking you, that you would immediately come to their aid, so long as they have done all that was in them (*quod in se est*), as much as possible applying their minds, in the manner that Samuel admonished, *Prepare your hearts unto the Lord, and serve him only, and he will deliver you*; such, I ask, O Lord, that you do to me." Again, Denis is silent about whether this doing all that is in you includes a response to a prevenient or exciting grace or not or whether this is some natural effort only.

In his commentary on Psalm 52:3, Denis states the following: "God from heaven and his holy dwelling looks down *upon the children of men*, that is, he gives consideration to all of the sons of the first parents, *to see*, that is, he may cause some to know, or show himself to know; *if there were any that did understand or did seek God*, that is, either anyone perceiving God in a right way, or knowing him by a formed intellect and by faith, or performing good works, or requiring himself to do that which is within his power to do (*quod in se est*)." Here, Denis suggests that the *facientibus* principle applies broadly to those in a state of sanctifying or habitual grace and those that may not be in that condition. But again, Denis is not clear on whether a purely natural act by one with unformed faith or an unbeliever could elicit grace, or whether a prevenient grace of God is involved in "doing all that is in you."

In his commentary on Psalm 66:5, Denis states: "*Let them be glad* with interior gladness, *and let them rejoice* with outward signs expressing their internal rejoicing, *the nations* called to the faith of Christ, *for you judge the people with justice*. For at present God daily judges the people with the judgment of discretion: of which the Savior said: *Now is the judgment of the world.* For God gives faith and grace without respect of persons to all who are so disposed and who do that which is within them (*quod in se est*), and he forsakes all others." Here, Denis appears to understand the *facientibus* principle as applying to an unbeliever of good will, and such might be assured, so long as he does what is in him, that he will enjoy grace by the unfathomable mercy of God and not through any intrinsic merit of his. But again, Denis is here not clear about whether doing "all that is in you" refers to an act of nature alone or an act elicited by prevenient or antecedent grace.

In his commentary on Psalm 68:33, Denis seems to apply it to the context of justification, though it is not absolutely clear if he does so:[4] "*Seek God*, doing all that is in you (*faciendo quod in vobis est*), and directly attend to him with faith and works, *and your soul shall live*, that is, it will receive grace which is the life of the soul, just as the soul is the life of the body. This is what the prophet Isaiah said: *Seek the Lord, while he may be found: call upon him, while he is near*." As in the other instances, Denis does not expressly enunciate whether "doing all that is in you" is a purely natural act of good will, or an act of good will elicited by, and cooperating with, prevenient grace.

In his commentary on Psalm 36:3, Denis states the *facientibus* principle to exhort the reader not to neglect it: "*Trust in the Lord*: according to that which we read elsewhere: *Have confidence in the Lord with all your heart* (Prov. 3:5), *and do good*, that is, live in a praiseworthy way. It is as if he were saying, 'Do not so hope in God that you neglect to do that which is in you (*quod in te est*).'" Again, Denis is utterly silent on whether this is a purely natural act or one elicited by some prevenient, operative grace with which the recipient cooperates.

Similarly, in his commentary on Psalm 69:5, Denis states the following: "*Let . . . them rejoice*, that is, let them show a sign of joy externally, and let it spring forth out from them from an interior cheerfulness, and *let them rejoice* with an interior joy, *in you*, and not in the vanities of the world, all that seek you with faith and in deed, or doing all which is in their power (*quod in se est*), so that they might acquire, preserve, and possess your grace and the contemplation and delight in your goodness." Here, the *facientibus* principle appears to apply to those in a state of sanctifying grace striving for perfection, for the contemplative life.

Denis understands the *facientibus* principle therefore broadly—it includes the unbeliever, the baptized Christian in a state of mortal sin, and the baptized Christian in a state of grace seeking additional graces or seeking perfection. This is clear from the various contexts of the sections of the *Commentary* listed above, but it is also clear from Denis's extensive treatment of the *facientibus* principle in his *Commentary* on Proverbs 16.1: *hominis est animum praeparare*, "it is the part of man to prepare his soul." Because of its importance to the issue treated here, I will translate it:

---

4   There seems to be inconsistency in that he supposes "faith and works" (which implies grace) but speaks of receiving grace "which is the life of the soul," which suggests sanctifying or justifying grace. But perhaps he is referring to *an increase* in sanctifying or justifying grace.

It is the part of man to prepare his soul, that is, to dispose himself to the grace of God, doing what is in him *(faciendo quod
in se est)*, that is, to do that which he is able to do by nature
and by gift given to him, and that so long as with all his effort
makes the attempt, God most certainly will pour grace upon
him. Now God in different ways anticipates [the needs of]
men,[5] and sometimes with great kindness, so that even when
a man is intent upon vicious acts, he draws them forcibly and
completely mercifully towards him, as he did to Paul as he
was going to Damascus to persecute the Christian faithful.[6]
Yet always in the case of adults consent is required, and some
cooperation of the free will: for, as Augustine asserts, he who
created you without you will not justify you without you.

And so, by free will and natural reason, man disposes
himself to grace by withdrawing from evil, by adhering to
good works, according to the dictates of natural reason to the
extent such is possible by his natural powers: and so unbelievers can dispose themselves. Yet believers, though living in
mortal sin, still by unformed faith,[7] and by the remnants of
the virtues they have otherwise lost by sin, and the knowledge
of the commandments, can and should prepare themselves
[by doing all they can] for the infusion of the divine gift [of
grace]. Similarly, acquiescing to hidden angelic and divine
promptings by which men, even vicious and perfidious men,
often draw back from evil and are mercifully incited to do
good. And so not only is in *the part of man to prepare his soul*
for the infusion of grace in the manner already touched upon,
but also they who are in a state of grace, adorned with the
virtues, ought [to prepare themselves] for the perfection of
charity, to the increase of grace, and an ardent devotion, by
invoking the Lord, reflecting on the Scriptures, attentively
listening to sermons, and duly using the goods that have been
granted them. Indeed, man ought to prepare himself for such

---

5   In other words, God *praevenit homines*, "he prevents men," meaning he "comes
before" the act of man, he anticipates men's acts with prevenient or exciting grace.
6   Acts 9:1–22.
7   So long as a Catholic does not sin mortally against the faith, he retains the
supernatural virtue of faith, even though he may have lost sanctifying grace and the
theological virtue of charity. Even though he has not lost the gift of faith, it will
avail him nothing unless he repents, for so long as his faith is unformed by charity
and he persists in a state of mortal sin, he runs the risk of damnation.

prayer recollecting his heart, as is written in Ecclesiasticus: *Before prayer, prepare your soul.*[8] However, to that preparation just touched upon, that contained in Job can be applied to it: *If* man *turn his heart to God, he shall draw his spirit and breath unto himself*; and the Lord will say this, *Who is this that sets his heart to approach to me?*[9]

Since in the *Commentary on the Psalms* Denis is silent with respect to the role of prevenient or antecedent grace when it comes "doing what is in you," we might reasonably ask the question what he intended when he used the principle. Before addressing this, we should spend some time in reviewing the genesis of the *facientibus* principle. Following that, we will review the treatment of the *facientibus* axiom given by Denis's main theological guide — St. Thomas Aquinas.

THE *FACIENTIBUS* PRINCIPLE ITSELF

This introduction is hardly the place to investigate the axiom's Scriptural seeds[10] or its obscure Patristic roots with the Greek or Latin Fathers, an issue that has been recognized both as important as it is knotty.[11] Though certainly the axiom is not found in Scripture *in haec verba*, it can find as sufficient Scriptural support and warrant as can St. Augustine's "love and do what you will," *dilige et quod vis fac*,[12] or the famous commonplace phrase *omnia in confessione lavantur,* "all is washed in confession," a phrase that Denis — with many others — uses as a summarization of Scripture.[13]

In terms of Patristic pedigree, some have seen the principle as early as in the Apostolic Father, St. Irenaeus of Lyon (*ca.* 130–*ca.* 202).[14]

---

8   Ecclus. 18:23.
9   Job 34:14; Jer. 30:21. Doctoris Ecstatici D. Dionysii Cartusiani, *Opera Omnia*, Vol. 7 (Montreuil: 1898), 105–06.
10   *E.g.*, Acts 10:1–48 (Cornelius receives the spirit prior to baptism due to his virtuous behavior); 1 Tim. 2:4 (God wills all men to be saved); John 14:15–16 (keeping the Commandments results in receipt of the Holy Spirit). Denis himself finds a source of the *facientibus* principle in Proverbs 16:1: *It is the part of man to prepare the soul.* As Jean Rivière puts it: "The idea that God never refuses grace to a soul of will is one which imposes itself upon all Christian consciences." Rivière, 94.
11   Jean Rivière, *Quelques antécédents patristiques de la formule : «Facienti quod in se est»* Revue des Sciences Religieuses (1927), pp. 93–97.
12   *In Epistolam Joannis* ad Parthos, tr. 7, s. 8.
13   Volume 1, Article LVIII (Psalm 25:5) and footnote 25-89.
14   "If you offer to him (i.e., God) what is yours, that is [natural] faith in him and subjection, you shall receive his [i.e., grace], and become a perfect work of God."

Others have found it in Origen (*ca.* 184–*ca.* 253).[15] Others, such as Louis Capéran (1884–1962), claim to have found it in inchoate form in St. Gregory Nazianzen (*ca.* 329–390), St. Gregory of Nyssa (*ca.* 335–*ca.* 395), St. John Chrysostom (*ca.* 347–407), and St. Nilus of Sinai (d. 430).[16] Others such as Friedrich Loofes (1858–1928) in St. Jerome (347–420).[17] It is found in an anonymous sermon falsely attributed to St. Augustine.[18]

But though its seed may have come from the East, the provenance of its development is most certainly in the West. Yet how the axiom developed the way it did and from what sources it came is shrouded in the vagaries of an opaque history. Despite the difficulties in discovering its precise source and its subsequent development, however, it is doubtful that the *facientibus* principle arose spontaneously and fully-formed in the Middle Ages, like Athena sprung fully-formed from the head of Zeus; so it must reach backward. In any event, whatever its genesis and developmental history might have been, by the Middle Ages the axiom was fully formed, and it was viewed as being a veritable "dogma," as being "part of the received western tradition concerning justification."[19] In the 18th century, the Jesuit Johannes Rupp who wrote a monograph on the axiom called it a "most celebrated theological axiom."[20]

Against Heresies, IV, 39, 2. See Alister E. McGrath, *Iustitia Dei: A History of the Christian Doctrine of Justification* (Cambridge: Cambridge University Press, 2020), 135. Rivière rejects the words of Irenaeus as a source of the *facientibus* principle. Rivière, 95.

15 Rivière, 95–96; Origen, *Contra Celsum*, VII, 42: "For ourselves, we maintain that human nature is in no way able to seek after God, or to attain a clear knowledge of Him without the help of Him whom it seeks. He makes Himself known to those who, after doing all that their powers will allow, confess that they need help from Him, who discovers Himself to those whom He approves, in so far as it is possible for man and the soul still dwelling in the body to know God." PG 11, 1481.

16 Rivière, 94 (citing Louis Capéran, *Le problème du salut des infidèles. Essai historique*, Paris, 1912, pp. 91–93, and 158). The proof texts are St. Nilus's Letter 154 to Maximiano, PG 79, 145; St. Gregory Nazianzus's funeral Oration No. 8.6, PG 35, 992; St. Gregory of Nyssa in his Great Catechetical Oration, II, 30, PG 45, 77; and St. John Chrysostom's Homily on Romans, Hom. 26.4, PG 60, 642.

17 Rivière, 94-95 (citing F. Loofs, *Leitfaden zum Studium der Dogmengeschicte*, 4th ed. (Halle: 1906), p. 545, 435). Rivière points to St. Jerome's *Dialogue with a Pelagian*, III, 6, PL 23, 601-02, as a text often proposed as seminal. "Our will which offered all which it was able (*quae obtulit omne quod potuit*), and did that labor it strove to do, and the humility which always looked for the aid of God." However, he interprets it as applying to one looking towards reward in heavenly glory, and not as applying to justification.

18 Sermon XVII, PL 40, 1262.

19 McGrath, 135. "Dogma" is too strong a word. It is more a theological principle, axiom, or rule.

20 Ioannes Rupp, S. J., *Exegesis Axiomatis Theologici Faicenti Quod Est In Se, Deus Non Denegat Gratiam* (Heidelberg: 1765), 2.

The axiom is an apothegm, and like most apothegms, it is vague, and it does not arrive and persist at the theological scene without a train of difficulties following from its vagueness.[21] Among the various variants as to its meaning, we might focus on the watershed distinction in interpretation:

> To the one who does what is in him [by nature alone], God does not deny [actual or justifying] grace.

> To the one who does what is in him [elicited by efficacious, or at least sufficient prevenient grace] God does not deny [actual or justifying] grace.

The first version of the axiom is clearly problematic and bears the badge of Pelagianism or semi-Pelagianism. The second version is consonant with the Catholic doctrine of grace. Which one does Denis hold? In answering this question, it is useful first to look at the treatment of the *facientibus* axiom in Denis's central theological influence: St. Thomas Aquinas, since it is most probable that Denis followed his master.

THE *FACIENTIBUS* PRINCIPLE IN ST. THOMAS AQUINAS

According to most commentators, St. Thomas shows a rather remarkable change in his view of the axiom.[22] In his early work, specifically is *Commentary on the Sentences*, it appears that St. Thomas harbored something suspiciously close to a semi-Pelagian view of the axiom. However, clearly in his later works, St. Thomas completely scrubbed the principle or axiom from any appearance of semi-Pelagianism. We can be assured that it was St. Thomas's mature views that provided Denis with his understanding of the axiom.

In his *Commentary on the Sentences*, St. Thomas states the *facientibus* principle in a manner that could be interpreted — as a result of its silence on the issue of prevenient or antecedent grace — as suggesting that grace is elicited by a human's purely natural acts to remove obstacles to it. The only grace mentioned is consequent grace, and whether the will of man is moved or elicited by prevenient or antecedent grace is not mentioned.[23]

---

21   Jean Rivière suggests it is universally accepted modernly "as a sort of controlling axiom," although he agrees that "the schools conceive it in different ways." Rivière, 93–94.
22   McGrath calls the early and late understandings of the axiom as "radically different interpretations." McGrath, 138. I think it might be more a matter of stating in the *Summa* something expressly which was not stated expressly in the *Commentary*.
23   According to Richard Rex, this view "permeated all the main schools," including "the early Thomas Aquinas, . . . Giles of Rome, Scotus, and Ockham." *The Theology of John Fisher* (Cambridge: Cambridge University Press, 1991), 112.

God, who gives abundantly to all, refuses grace to no one who does what is in him to prepare himself for grace [*nulli gratiam denegat qui quod in se est facit ut se ad gratiam praeparet*]. But . . . this preparation is done by the movement of the free will, and so as long as the use of the free will remains to a man in this life, when he cannot yet be confirmed in evil, he can prepare himself for grace by his sorrow for sins, and he obtains the grace of the remission of sins.[24]

Later, St. Thomas, though he by no means repudiates the *facientibus* axiom, certainly expands upon it in his *Summa Theologiae* where he addresses the question of whether man, by himself and without the external aid of grace, can prepare himself for grace (q. 109, IaIIae). St. Thomas here expressly is in the camp of those who say that the *facientibus* principle presupposes cooperating with antecedent or prevenient grace.[25] The axiom is not a principle that refers to a pure natural act unaided by grace. It is not Pelagian or semi-Pelagian in the least.

Now to prepare oneself for grace is, as it were, to be turned to God; just as, whoever has his eyes turned away from the light of the sun, prepares himself to receive the sun's light, by turning his eyes towards the sun. Hence it is clear that man cannot prepare himself to receive the light of grace *except by the gratuitous help of God moving him inwardly*.[26]

To the first objection, which is stated:

[M]an prepares himself for grace by doing what is in him to do, since if man does what is in him to do, God will not deny grace [*quia si homo facit quod in se est, Deus ei non denegat gratiam*], for it is written (Matthew 7:11) that God gives his good Spirit "to them that ask him." But what is in our power is in us to do. Therefore, it seems to be in our power to prepare ourselves for grace.[27]

---

24 Sent., lib. 4 d. 20 q. 1 a. 1 qc. 1 co. https://aquinas.cc/la/en/~Sent.IV.D20. Q1.A1.Q1.
25 Rex states that this was the view of a "substantial minority" of the schools, and shows "a more authentic Augustinianism." 112. As a result of John Capreolus and Cajetan, the latter view in the *Summa* "won general acceptance." Rex, op. cit., 112.
26 ST IaIIae, q. 109, art. 6, co. (Translation here and elsewhere in the introduction is by Fathers of the English Dominican Province).
27 ST IaIIae, q. 109, art. 6, arg. 2.

St. Thomas answers:

> Man can do nothing *unless moved by God*, according to John 15:5: "Without me, you can do nothing." Hence when a man is said to do what is in him to do (*facere quod in se est*), this is said to be in his power according as he is moved by God.[28]

St. Thomas here clearly understands the *facientibus* principle to mean that for a man to do what is in him (*quod in se est*) necessarily implies prevenient or antecedent grace with which he cooperates and by which he is freely moved by God.

Similarly, to the objection:

> Further, it is written (Proverbs 16:1) that "it is the part of man to prepare the soul." Now an action is said to be part of a man, when he can do it by himself. Hence it seems that man by himself can prepare himself for grace.[29]

Thomas responds:

> It is the part of man to prepare his soul, since he does this by his free-will. And yet he does not do this *without the help of God moving him*, and drawing him to himself, as was said above.[30]

In the *sed contra* to article 6, St. Thomas enunciates the following principle under which any *facientibus* axiom must be understood:

> It is written (John 6:44): "No man can come to me except the Father, who hath sent me, draw him." But if man could prepare himself, he would not need to be drawn by another. Hence man cannot prepare himself without the help of grace [*absque auxilio gratiae*].

The *facientibus* principle also finds itself the subject of another question in the *Summa*, namely, in treating the question of whether grace is necessarily given to whoever prepares himself for it, or to whoever does what is in him (q. 112, IaIIae).

The first objection specifically recites the *facientibus* axiom:

---

28 ST IaIIae, q. 109, art. 6, ad 2.
29 ST IaIIae, q. 109, art. 6, arg. 4.
30 ST IaIIae, q. 109, art. 6, ad 4.

It would seem that grace is necessarily given to whoever prepares himself for grace, or to whoever does what he can [*facienti quod in se est*], because, on Romans 5:1, "Being justified . . . by faith, let us have peace," etc. the gloss says: "God welcomes whoever flies to Him, otherwise there would be injustice with him." But it is impossible for injustice to be with God. Therefore, it is impossible for God not to welcome whoever flies to him. Hence he receives grace of necessity.[31]

To this argument, Thomas interposes a *sed contra*:

Man is compared to God as clay to the potter, according to Jeremiah 18:6: "As clay is in the hand of the potter, so are you in my hand." But however much the clay is prepared, it does not necessarily receive its shape from the potter. Hence, however much a man prepares himself, he does not necessarily receive grace from God.[32]

In responding to the objection, Thomas clearly rejects any Pelagian or semi-Pelagian interpretation of the *facientibus* principle:

This gloss [on Romans 5:1] is speaking of such as fly to God by a meritorious act of their free-will, already "informed" with grace; for if they did not receive grace, it would be against the justice which He Himself established. Or if it refers to the movement of free-will before grace, it is speaking in the sense that man's flight to God is by a Divine motion, which ought not, in justice, to fail.

In summary, we might rely on Alister McGrath's recapitulation of the issue:[33]

Whilst Thomas continues to insist upon the necessity of a preparation for justification, and continues to discuss this in terms of man's *quod in se est*, he now [in the *Summa* as compared to the *Commentary*] considers that this preparation lies outside man's purely natural powers. As he now understands the matter, man is not even capable of his full

---

31 ST IaIIae, q. 112, art. 3, arg. 1.
32 ST IaIIae, q. 112, art. 3, s.c.
33 Again, whether this is a change in understanding or a clarification of his understanding is debatable.

natural good, let alone the *supernatural* good required of him for justification. The preparation for justification is itself a work of grace, in which God is active and man passive. For Thomas, the axiom *facienti quod in se est* now assumes the meaning that God will not deny grace to the man who does his best, in so far as he is moved by God to do this: *Cum dicitur homo facere quod in se est, dicitur hoc esse in potestate hominis secundum quod est motus a Deo* [Hence when a man is said to do what is in him to do, this is said to be in his power according as he is moved by God].[34]

Denis accepts St. Thomas's understanding of the *facientibus* axiom. Indeed, this is what Denis appears to state in the conclusion of his treatment of Proverbs 16:1, part of which was quoted above, since he echoes therein St. Thomas's treatment of it in questions 109 and 112 of the *Prima Secundae Partis* of the *Summa Theologiae*:

> Moreover, it might be asked in what way can man so prepare the soul, since the Savior said, *Without me you can do nothing*;[35] and elsewhere, *Take no thought how or what to speak*.[36] The response to this is that without infused grace and the actual motion and aid of the Holy Spirit, we are unable to do so, indeed even to think, anything meritorious.[37]

Denis thus followed St. Thomas's mature doctrine, and so it would seem that Denis understands the *facientibus* principle as follows. First, in terms of justification, Denis would hold that the *facientibus* principle does not state that a man, through acts of natural virtue alone, and without any aid of prevenient grace, elicits or obtains or causes God to respond with sanctifying grace even *de congruo*, much less *de condigno*. Man simply cannot merit, by an natural act — even doing all that is in him in unaided nature — the "first grace,"[38] the grace of justification.[39] Accordingly, in the context of justification, Denis would have subscribed to a *facientibus*

---

34   Alister E. McGrath, *Iusitia Dei: A History of the Christian Doctrine of Justification* (Cambridge: Cambridge University Press1986) (2nd ed.), 86.
35   John 15:5b.
36   Matt. 10:19; Luke 21:14.
37   Doctoris Ecstatici D. Dionysii Cartusiani, *Opera Omnia*, Vol. 7 (Montreuil: 1898), 105–06.
38   ST IaIIae, q. 114, art. 5, s.c. & c.
39   This necessarily means there are no acts of supernatural merit in *any* natural acts, since sanctifying grace is the principle of merit.

principle that—expanded to express its implicit terms—states that to the one who does what is in him, God, who foresees all things, will not deny antecedent or prevenient actual grace by which that man, cooperating with it, might obtain the grace of salvation or sanctifying grace. Now, for those acts of man done while he is in a state of habitual or sanctifying grace, the *facientibus* principle would still require antecedent actual graces with which the recipient who does all that is in him cooperates. In sum, we might state the *facientibus* principle as understood by Denis the Carthusian and St. Thomas and the majority of his commentators: For a man to do what is in him (*facere quod in se est*), it must not be understood as doing what is in him without the help of grace, but rather as doing all that is within him in cooperation with God's prevenient, exciting, operative, or antecedent grace.

In a certain way, this is answered by the very formulation of the axiom. As Matthias Scheeben observes, the axiom is not formulated as a positive relationship between the natural man and effort and grace, but is expressed negatively, so as to implicitly negate any *quid pro quo* or intrinsic relationship between what man does by nature and what he achieves through the grace of God:

> The only thing that the natural use of freedom can achieve through grace is that the creature, through its good use, preserves and develops that receptivity which is given in nature itself, *i.e.*, the simple *capacitas* or ability to receive grace, and keep obstacles away which, through a wrong use of freedom, make the subject positively unworthy of grace and make it difficult to turn to God to allow the communication of grace and its easy and gentle effectiveness. This preservation and development of natural receptivity can, however, also be viewed as a disposition or preparation for grace, and, in relation to making the effectiveness of grace easier, it is even a positive preparation. But in relation to the actual reception of grace it is purely negative and indirect, like the preparation of a field so that it may be seeded, or the cutting of a tree to make a stock for the grafting of bud or scion. It therefore in itself (or *per se*) bears no intrinsic relation to the reception of grace, but can at most be brought into relation to it in a purely external and *per accidens* way through God's gracious will, in that it is pleasing to God to occasionally consider it. For that reason, however, the only possible connection of

grace to [the natural use of freedom] must by no means be expressed positively: *facienti quod in se est, Deus superaddit or subiungit gratiam*,[40] but only negatively: *facienti quod in se est, Deus non denegat gratiam*.[41]

CONCLUSION

This sure hope of grace that the *facientibus* principle propounds is not one founded on justice — for grace is a gift, something gratuitous, and not something one is entitled to demand from God in strict (condign) justice, especially in exchange for mere natural acts. The natural coin alone, which bears the image of man, is simply not accepted as a supernatural currency, for the supernatural currency must bear the image of the Son of God.

The *facientibus* axiom directs us into ourselves, into our hearts, it exhorts us to enter into the *homo abyssus* — what is "in" the abyss of man, and "to do" what is "in" the abyss of man.[42] It exhorts us: *fac quod in abyssum tuum est!* The abyss that is in man, the principle states, must with all that is within it strive toward the abyss that is God, the God who made him, the God whose image his abyss bears, the God who desires to share his life with him. *Homo abyssus abyssum invocat*.[43] "The infinite God is an abyss in whom there is no bottom, whose greatness is without end. Our soul is an abyss of infinite capacity, and it craves the most noble God, and its greatest good."[44] Only God, the abyss of infinite magnitude, suffices to fill the soul of infinite capacity. Thus it is our bounden duty, our salvation — indeed our beatitude — for us to do what is in us. It ought to be part of the scrutiny, the *examen* we make of our lives: do I do what is within me? *Facio quod in me est?*

Yet we should be aware that this is not a facile formula, for the moment we go "within us," we enter into an inscrutable mystery analogous to the Trinitarian relationship eternally existing between the Father, Son, and Holy Spirit. As there is an eternal perichoresis or circumincession within the Trinity of Persons that is God, so there is an analogous, subordinate

---

40   God will superadd or adjoin grace to them that do what is in them.

41   Matthias Joseph Scheeben, *Handbuch Katholischen Dogmatik* (Freiburg in Breisgan: Herder'sche Verlagshandlung, 1878), § 171, p. 411

42   *See* Ferdinand Ulrich, *Homo Abyssus: The Drama of the Question of Being* (Washington, DC: Humanum Academic Press, 2018) (trans., D. C. Schindler) and D. C. Schindler, *A Companion to Ferdinand Ulrich's Homo Abyssus* (Washington, DC: Humanum Academic Press, 2019).

43   *Cf.* Ps. 41(42):2.

44   Saint Antonius, O. P., *Summa Theologica* (Verona: 1740), IIa, 730.

perichoresis or circumincession between the Trinitarian God — the "I am who am" — and the human soul — the "she who is not."[45] This reciprocal relationship between the abyss that is God and the abyss that is man begins from the moment of the latter's creation, one where God seeks to woo that human soul, without offending its free will, with actual graces into the justifying grace that might assure him the salvific, eternal life to which God wills, at least antecedently, all men to come, but to which — alas — all men do not.[46] And where nature begins and ends, and where grace begins and ends, and how they work hand-in-hand is a mystery we cannot hope to unravel *in via*, though we know — given God's great mercy — that *facientibus quod in se est Deus non denegat gratiam.*

---

45   As revealed to St. Catherine of Siena. *See* Jordan Aumann, *Christian Spirituality in the Catholic Tradition* (London: Sheed & Ward, 1985), 174.

46   1 Tim. 2:4; ST Ia, q. 19, art. 6, ad 1.

ACKNOWLEDGMENTS

As in the prior two volumes, I thank Alex Barbas and Arouca Press for their support in continuing to publish this great work of the Carthusian, and to take the dusty tomes off from library shelves, to open up their shining contents, and to make them available to the English-speaking public for their edification. I thank my wife, Betsy, for her enduring patience. I thank my legal assistant Cindi for her proofreading of this text. I thank those kind clergy and religious who have given their support in recommending this text to the reading public, including Bishop Daniel Flores of Brownsville, Texas, Deacon Keith Fournier of Tyler, Texas, Dom Hugh Knapman, OSB, of Douay Abbey in Berkshire, England, Dom Pius Mary Noonan, OSB, of Notre Dame Priory in Tasmania, Australia, Abbot Philip Anderson, OSB, of Our Lady of Clear Creek Abbey in Hulbert, Oklahoma, and Dom Alcuin Reid, Prior of the Monastère Saint-Benoît in Brignoles, France. May the Lord bless them all.

—Feast of St. Francis Xavier (MMXXI)

PREFACE

to

DENIS THE CARTHUSIAN'S
Commentary on the Psalms

PART 3
[PSALMS 51–75]

God, *giving testimony of David, said: I have found David, the son of Jesse, a man according to my own heart, who shall do all my wills.*[1] Acts 13:22.

O HOW MUCH PERFECTION AND HOW SUB-lime a declaration are attributed to the holy man, excellent among the Prophets, in these words of introduction! For what can be so lofty as to be in unanimity with the divine mind and to have one's heart or will in concord with God? Moreover, where there is one affection and like hearts, there friendship is greatest, and where friendship is greatest, there is the height of communion, intimate union, and a special familiarity. For friends are entirely in communion; and to the degree one loves a friend more, to that degree he regards his good, and shares with him boundlessly, whether he is in need or it is profitable to him. Therefore, as the most blessed David was the more greatly conformed to the divine will, so he stood more loved by God, and so he revealed his mysteries to him more fully and more clearly, especially those which pertained to Christ and his spouse, the Church. Because of this, he humbly glorified in and truly confessed: *The uncertain and hidden things of your wisdom,* he said, *you have made manifest to me.*[2] Whence also it is believed that the book of Psalms is both more expressive and more full of the mysteries of Christ than the other books of the Prophets.

Since therefore in an earlier book the first fifty of the Psalms were expounded (as the Lord gave me the ability), it is now time to commence

---

1 Ps. 88:21 (according to LXX).
2 Ps. 50:8b.

[the exposition of] the second fifty of them. And as was there stated, this is my intention in the elucidation of the book of Psalms: that I might avoid difficulties of style and opinion, and that I might explain those Psalms in a four-fold way (as long as the matter allows and it seems desirable); and so now also I promise to do. And in handling all these things it behooves to understand what the distinction is between the literal, allegorical, tropological, and anagogical senses of Scripture: which, because they were explained in the first book,[3] I believe they ought not now be repeated.

But I, with all my heart invoke the Holy Spirit, in order that he may deign to direct me in the elucidation of the divine Scriptures. And so that he may be able to do this more completely, I pray to his goodness, so that he may fill my soul with such kind and quantity of grace, whereby I might be so lovingly conjoined to God, that I may be found worthy to be instructed in all things by him. For truly the holy and blessed God singularly and marvelously is accustomed to enlighten and instruct his chosen friends. For this reason it is written: *For the Lord God does nothing without revealing his secret to his servants the prophets.*[4] And Christ said to his disciples: *I will not now call you servants.... I have called you friends: because all things whatsoever I have heard of my Father, I have made known to you.*[5]

---

3   *E. N. See* Volume I, Article IV.
4   Amos 3:7.
5   John 15:15.

COMMENTARY
on the
DAVIDIC
Psalms

PART 3
[PSALMS 51–75]

Psalm 51

ARTICLE I

LITERAL EXPOSITION OF THE FIFTY-FIRST PSALM:
QUID GLORIARIS IN MALITIA? ETC.
WHY DO YOU GLORY IN MALICE? ETC.

51{52}[1] *Unto the end, understanding for David,*

> *In finem. Intellectus David,*

51{52}[2] *When Doeg the Edomite came and told Saul: David went to the house of Achimelech,*

> *Cum venit Doeg Idumaeus, et nuntiavit Sauli: Venit David in domum Achimelech.*

HE PSALM NOW BEING EXPLAINED HAS THIS title heading it: **51{52}[1]** *In finem. Intellectus David. Unto the end, understanding for David.* **51{52}[2]** *Cum venit Doeg Idumaeus, et nuntiavit Sauli: Venit David in domum Achimelech; When Doeg the Edomite came and told Saul: David went to the house of Achimelech.* According to a literal understanding, the sense of this title clearly is derived from the history of the book of Samuel. For we read in that very place the manner in which Saul, pained at the escape of David, said to his servants: *Hear me, you sons of Benjamin,* for there is none among you *that pities my case,* or that *gives me any information* of David, the son of Jesse. *And Doeg the Edomite...who was the chief among the servants of Saul,* and the most powerful of his herdsmen *answering said: I saw the son of Jesse in Nob with* the priest *Achimelech,* who gave him food and the *sword of Goliath.*[1] On account of this Saul ordered to have Achimelech (or Abimelech, for he was called by both names) and all his father's house killed.[2] Doeg was the executor of this deed, as we read in that same place: *Doeg fell upon the priests and slew in that day eighty-five men that wore the linen ephod. And Nob, the city of the priests, he smote with the edge of his sword, both humans and beasts. But Abiathar, the son of Achimelech, escaped, and he went to David, and recounted to him all that had happened.*[3]

---

1   1 Sam. 22:7–10.
2   1 Sam. 22:16, 17.
3   1 Sam. 18-21.

Regarding this, therefore, David wrote this Psalm, which literally can be explained as dealing with this historical occurrence, although it is more fruitful and fitting to expound upon the thing that is signified or figured by it. For since this Psalm is literally understood to be of Christ or the Church, the literal sense is sweet and full of devotion, and diligently to be examined. But if [this Psalm] is understood literally of David, or something along those lines, the literal sense confers little devotion and sweetness. Whence, few of the devoted [commentators] apply themselves in explaining it in this manner. Therefore, of such an explanation I will say but little. So according to this exposition, the sense of the title is: *Understanding for David*, that is, in this Psalm is found the instruction of holy David, directing us *unto the end*, that is, toward true happiness and toward Christ, to whom we will arrive if we follow the directions of this Psalm: *the understanding*, I say, prescribed by David, *when Doeg the Edomite came*, that is, after Doeg the Edomite came. For the rest [of the verse] is already sufficiently clear.

51{52}[3] *Why do you glory in malice, you that are mighty in iniquity?*

Quid gloriaris in malitia, qui potens es in iniquitate?

51{52}[4] *All the day long your tongue has devised injustice: as a sharp razor, you have wrought deceit.*

Tota die iniustitiam cogitavit lingua tua; sicut novacula acuta fecisti dolum.

Speaking in a rebuking manner to Doeg, David says: **51{52}[3]** *Quid gloriaris in malitia? Why do you glory in malice?* That is, for what advantage and utility do you rejoice in your evil works and the perpetration of sin, that you betrayed me, an innocent man, and the priest Abimelech, and killed him along with those of his own blood?[4] But Doeg gloried in this, for by this he had obtained for himself the great friendship of the wicked king. But this sort of glorification, and this evil of the soul, was noxious: and so David argued against Doeg saying, *Why do you glory in malice* that was not profitable to you? *You that are mighty in iniquity*, that is, you were powerful in killing innocent men, and you have abused the power conferred upon you, oppressing those that are your betters. **51{52}[4]** *Tota die, all the day long*, that is, incessantly, *iniustitiam cogitavit lingua tua, your tongue has devised injustice*, that is, you have conceived with the tongue of your heart unjust work, deceit, and traps against me

---

4   1 Sam. 22:9, 18.

and my friends, namely in the intellect, where interior words or thoughts are formed; or [alternatively], the tongue of the mouth devised, that is, it spoke out of the interior thoughts. For Doeg assiduously lay in ambush for David and his companions. Whence David said to Abiathar: *I knew that day when Doeg the Edomite was there, that without doubt he would tell Saul.*[5] *Sicut novacula acuta fecisti dolum, as a sharp razor, you have wrought deceit.* A sharp razor, when it is used to remove hair, sometimes dreadfully and quickly causes injury. And so detractors and the ungodly — when they ought to inform the king and their lord well and rightly and they announce false things to him or do not reveal to things [they ought] — detract others, inflict injury, and procure death. And in this way Doeg sought to ensnare David and Achimelech, and the others, whom he had first defamed, and thereafter killed.

51{52}[5] *You have loved malice more than goodness: and iniquity rather than to speak righteousness.*

Dilexisti malitiam super benignitatem; iniquitatem magis quam loqui aequitatem.

51{52}[6] *You have loved all the words of ruin, O deceitful tongue.*

Dilexisti omnia verba praecipitationis, lingua dolosa.

51{52}[5] *Dilexisti, you have loved,* O Doeg, *malitiam, malice,* that is, a cruel deed, *super benignitatem, more than goodness,* that is, more than the work of mercy, because you cruelly slaughtered the priests, and you were unmerciful to the innocent; *iniquitatem magi quam loqui aequitatem, and iniquity rather than to speak righteousness,* that is, you loved more to speak iniquitous, deceitful, and invidious words than true and just ones. For Doeg, so that he might be more pleasing to Saul, falsely attributed many crimes against David,[6] and he said that Achimelech consulted the Lord on behalf of David, and Doeg said other things that were false and were fabricated by him, as is the habit of detractors, that while they state something true, they intermix with it false things.[7] For we do not

---

5   1 Sam. 22:22.

6   1 Sam. 22:10.

7   E. N. "Doeg bears a striking resemblance to another literary character, Iago in Shakespeare's *Othello*; between the two there are striking parallels. Nowhere are we told explicitly that Doeg is ambitious or hungry for power. Yet his actions clearly point in that direction. In Iago's case, he wants the place of distinction in Othello's retinue. He dislikes the young Cassius, who is favored by his master, as much as Doeg dislikes David. He skillfully and deceptively plants the seeds of suspicion in

find in the text of the book of Samuel that Achimelech consulted the Lord on behalf of David, but that he gave to him bread and a sword.[8] **51{52}[6]** *Dilexisti omnia verba praecipitationis, you have loved all the words of ruin*, that is, speech designed to cause the downfall and death, both from your own mouth, and to your lord Saul, whom you willingly heard speak severe things against me, *lingua dolosa, O deceitful tongue*, that is, O you, Doeg, who had a deceitful tongue. For it is customary to name a part to signify the whole, especially when it plays a significant part in something,[9] in the way the Apostle [Paul] said, *The Cretans are always liars, evil beasts, slothful bellies.*[10]

51{52}[7] *Therefore will God destroy you forever: he will pluck you out, and remove you from your dwelling place: and your root out of the land of the living.*

Propterea Deus destruet te in finem; evellet te, et emigrabit te de tabernaculo tuo, et radicem tuam de terra viventium.

51{52}[7] *Propterea, therefore*, O Doeg, *Deus, God*, the just judge, *destruet te in finem, will destroy you forever*, withdrawing from you, or not maintaining in you, all spiritual existence and the ability to earn merit,[11] and eternally condemning you, unless you repent. *Evellet te, et emigrabit te de tabernaculo tuo; he will pluck you out, and remove you from your dwelling place*, that is, he will permit you to be killed by your enemies, as in fact occurred. For in mount Gilboa you were killed with Saul: because, according to the Hebrews,[12] he was then

---

Othello's mind regarding a secret affair between Cassius and Othello's wife, Desdemona. In the same way, Doeg causally mentions to Saul that he observed a meeting between David and Ahimelech. Both Othello and Saul are enraged by the information they receive. Iago has succeeded in orchestrating the death of both Othello and his wife; Doeg, an entire city and its priests." Roland James Faley, T. O. R., *Biblical Profiles: Contemporary Reflections on Old Testament People* (Mahwah, NJ: Paulist Press, 2003), 75–76.

8   1 Sam. 21:6, 9.

9   E. N. In other words, the "deceitful tongue" is used as a synecdoche for the deceitful man because of the role the tongue plays in such deceit. For the role of synecdoche (where a part of something refers to the whole) in Scriptural interpretation, *see* Denis's discussion of the fifth rule of Tychonius, Volume 1, Article IV.

10   Titus 1:12b.

11   E. N. In other words, because of Doeg's mortal sin, God withdrew the principle of all supernatural life and merit: sanctifying or habitual grace.

12   E. N. Denis here and elsewhere where he refers to the "Hebrews," is referring to the non-Biblical traditions of the Jews.

the armor bearer of Saul,[13] who also fell upon his own sword when he saw Saul fall upon his sword. It was therefore then that Doeg was plucked out of his dwelling place, that is, that his soul and his body were separated, and he no longer dwelled in his home, but left it to others. *Et radicem tuam de terra viventium, and your root out of the land of the living,* that is, your seed or your children the Lord plucked out from the land of Judah. For David also killed Doeg's children, as the Hebrews say. For he who announced to David, telling him that Saul and his sons were killed in battle and adding that he had flung himself upon Saul [to kill him], is reputed to have been the son of Doeg.[14] For when David said to him, *From where are you?* He responded, *I am the son of a stranger of an Amalekite:*[15] whereupon David slew him because he had dispatched the Lord's anointed.[16] One can see from this that it is clear that David in the spirit foreknew the degradation and the punishment of Doeg.

51{52}[8]   *The just shall see and fear, and shall laugh at him, and say:*

Videbunt iusti, et timebunt; et super eum ridebunt, et dicent:

51{52}[9]   *Behold the man that made not God his helper: But trusted in the abundance of his riches: and prevailed in his vanity.*

Ecce homo qui non posuit Deum adiutorem suum; sed speravit in multitudine divitiarum suarum, et praevaluit in vanitate sua.

51{52}[8] *Videbunt iusti, the just shall see,* that is, they will diligently consider the just vengeance of God in Doeg, *et timebunt, and [they shall] fear* the divine judgment so that it does not similarly befall them. For *the wicked man being scourged, the fool shall be the wiser.*[17] *Et super eum ridebunt, and shall laugh at him,* that is, they shall rejoice at the just punishments of Doeg which conform to the divine justice, *et dicent:* **51{52}**

---

13   *Cf.* 1 Sam. 31:4–5.

14   2 Sam. 1, 4, 10. E. N. The anonymous man from David's camp told David that Saul was dead, but added that he came upon Saul after he tried unsuccessfully to kill himself, and when Saul asked to be put to death did so and took his crown and bracelet. This anonymous person was, in the tradition of the Hebrews, Doeg's son.

15   2 Sam. 1:13.

16   E. N. The Lord's anointed meaning King Saul. As David himself referred to King Saul: "The Lord be merciful unto me, that I may do no such thing to my master, the Lord's anointed, as to lay my hand upon him, because he is the Lord's anointed." 1 Sam. 24:7.

17   Prov. 19:25a.

[9] *Ecce homo qui non posuit Deum adiutorem suum, behold the man that made not God his helper,* that is, in what manner it befalls him who does not confide in God. *Sed speravit in multitudine divitiarum suarum, but trusted in the abundance of his riches.* For Doeg was rich, since he was a most powerful herdsman of Saul;[18] and he had amassed these [riches] by adulating wealth and by perverting justice, and he placed his hope in these more than he did in God. *Et praevaluit in vanitate sua, and prevailed in his vanity.* For Doeg was strengthened at the time against David and other good men, and he flourished, grew bold, and oppressed others in his vanity, that is, in pride and in vain riches.

51{52}[10]   *But I, as a fruitful olive tree in the house of God, have hoped in the mercy of God for ever, yea for ever and ever.*

Ego autem, sicut oliva fructifera in domo Dei; speravi in misericordia Dei, in aeternum et in saeculum saeculi.

51{52}[10] *Ego autem,* but I David *sicut oliva fructifera, as a fruitful olive tree* existing *in domo Dei, in the house of God,* that is, in the Synagogue or among the people of the Jews, whom I instructed by word and example, and made fertile with good works: and so by resembling the olive tree, I was fruitful among the people, whose leader I was, converting many to God, and encouraging those who had converted and those who were good to be better; *speravi in misericordia Dei in aeternum, I have hoped in the mercy of God, forever,* that is, the entire time of my life, *et in saeculum saeculi, yea, for ever and ever,* that is, without end: not that hope remains in the future life, namely, in the heavenly homeland; but, *I have hoped,* it says, *in the mercy of God, forever, yea for ever and ever,* that is, to this end, or because of this end, that I may arrive through it to eternal, not temporal, goods,[19] and obtain eternal happiness.

51{52}[11]   *I will praise you forever, because you have done it: and I will wait on your name, for it is good in the sight of your saints.*

Confitebor tibi in saeculum, quia fecisti; et exspectabo nomen tuum, quoniam bonum est in conspectu sanctorum tuorum.

---

18   1 Sam. 21:7.

19   *E. N.* Denis makes this distinction in Article XVIII (Psalm 4:1) in Volume 1; namely, that the word "end" can mean two things: either the consumption of something (*e.g.,* the candle is at an end) or the consummation or perfection of something (*e.g.,* the construction of the home is at an end).

51{52}[11] *Confitebor tibi, I will praise you,* that is, I will recount with the confession of praise and penance your good and my evil, *in saeculum, forever,* that is, daily and unceasingly, *quia fecisti, because you have done it,* [that is you have provided me] so much goodness and grace. *Et exspectabo nomen tuum, and I will wait on your name,* that is, I will patiently await your coming, the future resurrection, and the glory of the blessed in heaven; I will not abandon you in adversity, but whatever may befall me, I will have unwavering hope in you, or in your name; *quoniam bonum est in conspectus sanctorum tuorum, for it is good in the sight of your saints,* that is, because your name is sweet and good in the judgment of the elect, and in the contemplation and the experience of those devoted to you, who taste *how great is the multitude of your sweetness, O Lord,*[20] and so think well of you in the manner that Jeremiah attests to: *The Lord is good to them that hope in him, to the soul that seeks him.*[21]

ARTICLE II

ALLEGORICAL EXPOSITION, NAMELY OF CHRIST, OF THE SAME FIFTY-FIRST PSALM:

51{52}[1]   *Unto the end, understanding for David,*

In finem. Intellectus David,

51{52}[2]   *When Doeg the Edomite came and told Saul: David went to the house of Achimelech,*

Cum venit Doeg Idumaeus, et nuntiavit Sauli: Venit David in domum Achimelech.

THE ALLEGORICAL SENSE OF SACRED SCRIPture is when we understand those things we read of the old saints to be about Christ. *All these things happened to them in figure.*[22] And so according to this understanding, by David—which is interpreted as being "strong of hand" *(manu fortis)*[23] or "with a desirable countenance"

---

20   Ps. 30:20a.

21   Lam. 3:25.

22   1 Cor. 10:11a.

23   E. N. Although David in Hebrew means "beloved," Christians traditionally understood it as meaning "strong of hand," that is, David had *manu fortis,* a "hand of strength." So St. Jerome: *"David ... interpetatur fortis manu." Comm. in Is.,* 17, PL 24,

(*adspectu desiderabilis*)[24]—is understood Christ, *the power of God*,[25] who is *beautiful above the sons of men*.[26] But by Doeg, which is interpreted as "movement," is understood the traitor Judas, inflamed with avarice in the selling out of Christ.[27] But by Saul, which is interpreted "appetite" or "death," is understood the chief of the priests of the Jewish people thirsting for the blood of Christ.[28] And so it [this Psalm] is [to be understood allegorically] in this sense: **51{52}[1]** *In finem, intellectus David; unto the end, understanding for David*, that is, understanding this Psalm as directing us to God, it refers to Christ figured by David; **51{52} [2]** *Cum venit Doeg Idumaeus, when Doeg the Edomite came*, that is, the traitor Judas, greedy and worldly (for Edomite is interpreted as being "worldly"), *et annuntiavit Sauli, and told Saul*, that is, told the chief priest and his council, *et dixit, and told* them: *Venit David, David went*, that is, Christ, *in domum Achimelech, to the house of Achimelech*, that is, in the society of his disciples (since Achimelech can be interpreted as "the kingdom of my father," by which is designated the Church, in which God reigns by grace). But this announcement to Judas, telling him that he was to go to Bethany with his disciples to the house of Martha, was on a Wednesday, the day when Judas sold Christ; and so on Thursday, when after eating the morsel, Judas immediately departed,[29] thereby telling the Jews that Jesus had come to the cenacle wherein he celebrated the Last Supper, and that Jesus would be withdrawing to the place wherein he frequently accustomed himself to go. Whence it is written: *And Judas also, who betrayed him, knew the place; because Jesus had often resorted there together with his disciples*.[30] For diligently did Judas show the Jews the place in which Christ had come and among whom he would

---

585; *Comm. in Hos.*,1, 3, PL 25, 845. So also St. Augustine, *Enarr. in Ps.*, 32, 4, PL 36, 302, and St. Isidore of Seville, *Etymol.*, 7, 64, PL 82, 279. See Leo Steinberg, *Michelangelo's Painting: Selected Essays* (Chicago: University of Chicago Press 2019), 356 n. 63. This is why, for example, Michelangelo's famous sculpture David has an oversized right hand. Howard Hibbard, *Michelangelo* (New York: Harper & Row, 1974), 57.

24   E. N. Similarly, the name David was interpreted to mean having a desirable countenance. For example, Peter Lombard in his *Commentary on the Psalms* (Psalm 2) says: "David is interpreted to mean with a strong hand or desirable aspect, and he signifies Christ, who truly is of strong hand, subduing the powers of the air (demons) and he is of desirable aspect." *Comm. in Ps.*, PL 191, 69.

25   1 Cor. 1:24.

26   Ps. 44:3a.

27   John 12:6; Matt. 26:14–16.

28   Matt. 27:1, 25.

29   John 13:30.

30   John 18:2.

be: because, as it is written, *He sought opportunity to betray him in the absence of the multitude.*[31]

51{52}[3] *Why do you glory in malice, you that are mighty in iniquity?*

Quid gloriaris in malitia, qui potens es in iniquitate?

51{52}[4] *All the day long your tongue has devised injustice: as a sharp razor, you have wrought deceit.*

Tota die iniustitiam cogitavit lingua tua; sicut novacula acuta fecisti dolum.

Therefore, the Prophet [David] in the person of Christ, or Christ himself, refuting Judas the traitor, says: **51{52}[3]** *Quid gloriaris in militia, why do you glory in malice,* that is, in the sale and the betrayal of the innocent blood of your Master and your Lord, who conferred upon so many good things, and showed you so many signs of his love, *qui potens es in iniquitate, you that are mighty in iniquity,* that is, who were slow and powerless to the doing of good works, but fast and cautious in selling and in betraying? **51{52}[4]** *Tota die, all the day long,* especially on Wednesday and Thursday before the Preparation of the Pasch, *iniustitiam, an injustice,* that is, the unjust sale and the dishonest betrayal, *cogitavit lingua tua, your tongue has devised,* when you discussed with the Jews the manner by which you would betray me.[32] *Sicut novacula acuta fecisti dolum, as a sharp razor, you have wrought deceit,* for you have praised me to my face, yet hiddenly you have detracted me. And Judas caused the greatest deceit just like a sharp razor when he was before the cohort and ministers of the Jews and said to them: *Whomsoever I shall kiss, that is he; lay hold on him, and lead him away carefully.*[33] And so Christ said to him: *Judas, do you betray the Son of man with a kiss?*[34]

51{52}[5] *You have loved malice more than goodness: and iniquity rather than to speak righteousness.*

Dilexisti malitiam super benignitatem; iniquitatem magis quam loqui aequitatem.

51{52}[6] *You have loved all the words of ruin, O deceitful tongue.*

Dilexisti omnia verba praecipitationis, lingua dolosa.

---

31   Luke 22:6.
32   Matt. 26:14–16.
33   Mark 14:44.
34   Luke 22:48.

51{52}[5] *Dilexisti, you have loved,* O Judas, *malitiam super benignitatem, malice more than goodness,* for you were a thief, and, having had possession of the purse, you stole that which had placed in there: and so goodness, that is, the words of mercy, you have omitted, since because of your cupidity you held back from giving to the needy; *iniquitatem magis quam loqui aequitatem, and iniquity rather than to speak righteousness,* that is, you desired more to speak to the Jews regarding the unjust sale of Christ and death and to excuse yourself from your Teacher, whom you knew to be innocent. **51{52} [6]** *Dilexisti omnia verba praecipitationis, you have loved all the words of ruin,* that is, the words of the chief priest about Christ, speaking precipitously bringing about oppression and death:[35] O *lingua dolosa,* O *deceitful tongue,* by which you so deceitfully said to your Teacher: *Hail, Rabbi.*[36]

51{52}[7] *Therefore will God destroy you forever: he will pluck you out and remove you from your dwelling place: and your root out of the land of the living.*

Propterea Deus destruet te in finem; evellet te, et emigrabit te de tabernaculo tuo, et radicem tuam de terra viventium.

51{52}[7] *Propterea Deus destruet te in finem, therefore will God destroy you forever,* because you will eternally perish and be damned. For the heavens and the earth shall rise up against him and shall reveal the iniquity of Judas.[37] *Evellet te, et emigrabit te de tabernaculo tuo; he will pluck you out and remove you from your dwelling place.* This was fulfilled in Judas, since departing, he *hanged himself with a noose,* and *burst asunder in the middle, and all his bowels gushed out.*[38] For at that time God plucked out his soul from the body, and he separated Judas from his tabernacle, that is, from the house of Christ or the college of the Apostles, which had offered to him grace in the present and glory in the future. Whence also Christ before the Passion said to his Apostles: *Have not I chosen you twelve; and one of you is a devil?* And this (according to what the Evangelist adds) was asserted of Judas.[39] *Et radicem tuam de terra viventium, and your root out of the land of the living:* that is, God, inasmuch as he will destroy and pluck you, O Judas, from the land of the living, that is, from the Church of the elect and the region of the

---

35   Matt. 26:3–5.
36   Matt. 26:49b.
37   *Cf.* Job 20:27: *The heavens shall reveal his iniquity, and the earth shall rise up against him.*
38   Matt. 27:5; Acts 1:18.
39   John 6:71; *cf.* John 6:72.

living,⁴⁰ so that you will not be able to be restored nor to rise again to [eternal, heavenly] life. By the word "root," therefore, is understood the reparative power of grace, or the rising again to [eternal] life.

51{52}[8] *The just shall see and fear, and shall laugh over him, and say:*

Videbunt iusti, et timebunt; et super eum ridebunt, et dicent:

51{52}[9] *Behold the man that made not God his helper: But trusted in the abundance of his riches: and prevailed in his vanity.*

Ecce homo qui non posuit Deum adiutorem suum; sed speravit in multitudine divitiarum suarum, et praevaluit in vanitate sua.

51{52}[8] *Videbunt iusti, the just shall see*, that is, the holy Apostles and the rest of the faithful [shall see] the hanging and the damnation of the wretched betrayer.⁴¹ For which reason in the book of Acts, Luke says: *And it became known* (this news, namely the hanging of Judas) *to all the inhabitants of Jerusalem, so that the same field was called in their tongue, Haceldama, that is to say, the field of blood.*⁴² **51{52}[9]**⁴³ *Ecce homo qui non posuit Deum adiutorem suum, Behold the man that made not God his helper*, that is, he who does not build his foundation or support himself in Christ as his teacher and Lord; *sed speravit in multitudine divitiarum suarum, but trusted in the abundance of his riches*, that is, he placed his hope in earthly things which he amassed by stealing and by selling off Christ, *et praevaluit in vanitate sua, and he prevailed in his vanity*, that is, he confirmed his heart against Christ, and in the most vain desires he was allowed to prevail against Christ, whom he had sold and had betrayed. Not that strictly speaking someone can prevail against Christ; for *he was offered because it was his own will;*⁴⁴ and the wicked are said to prevail against him because they were given permission to kill him. Whence, in a Psalm above, Christ said: *But my enemies live, and are stronger than I.*⁴⁵ And to Pilate saying, *Do you not know that I have power to crucify you, and I have power to release you?* Christ responded: *You would not have any power against me unless it were given you from above.*⁴⁶

---

40   E. N. For the expressions "land of the living" (*terra viventium*) and "region of the living" (*regio vivorum*) as expressions of the Kingdom of Heaven (here referring to the Church, the Kingdom of God on earth), see footnote 24-33 in Volume I.

41   Matt. 27:5.

42   Acts 1:19.

43   E. N. Denis does not address the rest of Psalm 51:8 in his *Commentary*.

44   Is. 53:7a.

45   Ps. 37:20a.

46   John 19:10, 11.

ON THE JEWISH PEOPLE

ND SO, AS THIS PSALM THUS FAR HAS BEEN expounded about Judas, so is it also possible to be explained with regard to the Jewish people who were in a furor against Christ. For in this the people gloried in malice, deriding, blaspheming, persecuting, and killing the Lord and Savior. And every day, especially in the Day of Preparation before the Sabbath, their tongues devised injustice, that is, false accusations and the sentence of death against Christ, crying out to the leaders, *We have found this man perverting our nation;*[47] and, *Away with him, away with him; crucify him.*[48] But also as a sharp razor they wrought deceit, sending disciples of the Pharisees with Herodians so that they might ensnare Jesus with words.[49] They delighted to say words precipitously, crying out to the judge, *If you release this man, you are not Caesar's friend;*[50] and, *His blood be upon us and our children.*[51] By these words they impetuously threw themselves and their posterity down before Christ. For *the wrath of God is come upon them,* as the Apostle [Paul] says, *until the end.*[52] It is for this reason that it is added: *Therefore,*[53] that is to say, because of the wickedness committed against Christ, *will God destroy you forever,* that is, he will forsake you even until the end of the world: in the manner that is foretold by Daniel, *The end thereof shall be waste, . . . and the desolation shall continue even . . . unto the end.*[54] And Amos: *The house of Israel is fallen, and it shall rise no more.*[55] *He will pluck you out, and remove you from your dwelling place,* that is, from the land of promise he will cast you out: as we recognize was fulfilled by Titus and Vespasian, in accordance with that said by Daniel: *And a people with their leader that shall come, shall destroy the city and the sanctuary.*[56] *And your root out of the land of the living,* that is, the generative power in the land of your fathers will be taken from you: for after your foretold banishment they did not generate or did not multiply in their own land as they had

---

47   Luke 23:2a.

48   John 19:15a.

49   Mark 12:13.

50   John 19:12a.

51   Matt. 27:25b.

52   1 Thess. 2:16b.

53   E. N. Denis retraces back to Psalm 51:7.

54   Dan. 9:26b, 27b.

55   Amos 5:1b.

56   Dan. 9:26b. E. N. The reference, of course Vespasian (9–79 AD) and Titus (39–81 AD), the Roman emperors responsible for destroying Jerusalem and its Temple (70 AD) during the First Jewish-Roman War.

before, nor were they able to restore as before.[57] Or [alternatively], *your root out of the land of the living*, that is, he will completely blot out of the kingdom of heaven: as even Christ in the Gospels said, *But the children of the kingdom shall be cast out into the exterior darkness: there shall be weeping and gnashing of teeth.*[58] *The just shall see*, that is, those among the Jews converted to Christ [shall see] the foretold punishments of the unbelievers, *and fear* the Lord Jesus Christ, a judge so strict; *and . . . at him*, namely the unfaithful the people, *they shall laugh over*, applauding the divine justice; *and they shall say: Behold the man that made not God his helper*: that is, look upon Israel according to the flesh, who *not knowing the justice of God, and seeking to establish their own*, were not subject *to the justice of God*;[59] nor did they rely on the grace of Christ, but they placed all their hope in the Law. Thus it adds: *but trusted in the abundance of their riches*, that is, they glorified in their own merits, and they took pride in their race and in their law,[60] and did not wish humbly to give assent to the grace of God or the faith of Christ. Or [an alternative interpretation is that], they hoped in the multitude of their corporal riches: for the Jews were most avaricious.[61] For when Christ disputed against avarice, they said: *He has a devil, and is mad.*[62] *And they prevailed in his vanity*, that is, in the pride of their heart during that time they prevailed against the early Church, which the Jewish people frequently persecuted, as is narrated in the Acts of the Apostles.[63]

---

57   E. N. Presumably, as the Jews were able to do after their Babylonian captivity.

58   Matt. 8:12.

59   Rom. 10:3.

60   *Cf.* Matt. 3:9: *And think not to say within yourselves, We have Abraham for our father. For I tell you that God is able of these stones to raise up children to Abraham.* John 8:33, 39: *They answered him: We are the seed of Abraham, and we have never been slaves to any man: how say you: you shall be free? And: They answered, and said to him: Abraham is our father. Jesus said to them: If you be the children of Abraham, do the works of Abraham.*

61   Luke 16:9: *And I say to you: Make unto you friends of the mammon of iniquity; that when you shall fail, they may receive you into everlasting dwellings.*

62   John 10:1, 8, 10, 12, 13, 20. The quote is from John 10:20. E. N. It may be difficult to see how Jesus is speaking of avarice here. However, Jesus is railing against the "hireling" (in Latin *mercenarius*, the word from which we derive the English word mercenary). As Denis says in his *Commentary on John*: "The hireling (*mercenarius*) is a false shepherd, who — gazing toward temporal advantage or having a desire for his own profit, and who because of the riches and the delights or the honors and vanities of the world, and not from sincere love of the souls of his own flock that they might obtain eternal life — does that which he does in his pastoral office." Doctoris Ecstatici D. Dionysii Cartusiani, *Opera Omnia*, Vol. 12 (Montreuil: 1901), 464.

63   Acts chps. 4, 7, 8, *etc.*

51{52}[10] *But I, as a fruitful olive tree in the house of God, have hoped in the mercy of God for ever, yea for ever and ever.*

Ego autem, sicut oliva fructifera in domo Dei; speravi in misericordia Dei, in aeternum et in saeculum saeculi.

51{52}[10] *Ego autem sicut oliva fructifera in domo Dei; but I, as a fruitful olive tree in the house of God.* In a most full sense this refers to Christ, *who,* according to the Apostle [Paul],[64] brings *many children into glory.*[65] For he brought to God the most copious fruit, because by the merit of his Passion he redeemed all the elect, and *neither is there salvation in any other.*[66] Hence, of the fruitfulness of Christ we find written in Isaiah: *This says the Lord that formed me from the womb to be his servant, that I may bring back Jacob unto him, and may cause Israel to be converted; I have given you to be a light to the Gentiles, that you may be my salvation even to the farthest part of the earth.*[67] And this is what Daniel says: *All peoples, tribes, and tongues shall serve him.*[68] And so Christ is like *a fruitful olive tree in the house of God, which house we are,*[69] according to the Apostle, for by him *we were reconciled to God.*[70] Whence to the Ephesians the Apostle said: God re-established *all things in Christ, that are in heaven and on earth.*[71] *Speravi in misericordia Dei, in aeternum, et in saeculum saeculi; I have hoped in the mercy of God for ever, yea, for ever and ever.* Christ as man, and in a certain way a wayfarer (*viator*), always and most perfectly hoped in the Lord, not by the hope which is a theological virtue, for he did not have that, nor by faith, as we have sufficiently shown above;[72] but by a certain trust or expectation proceeding from charity and grace.

---

64   E. N. On Denis's belief that St. Paul was the author of Hebrews, *see* footnote 8-34 in Volume I.

65   Heb. 2:10b.

66   Acts 4:12a.

67   Is. 49:5a, 6b.

68   Dani. 7:14a.

69   Heb. 3:6a.

70   Rom. 5:10a.

71   Eph. 1:10b.

72   E. N. Since Christ in his humanity enjoyed the beatific vision from the first moment of his human existence, he saw God face-to-face even while in the wayfaring state; accordingly, he had no need for faith or hope (as ordinary wayfarers do while on earth) just as the blessed in heaven have no need for it. This was the common teaching of Catholic theologians even up to Pope Pius XII. Denis addresses this *passim*; however, one may look at the more methodological treatments of Article XIX (Psalm 4:9), Article XXXVIII (Psalm 15:9) and footnote 1-46 in Volume I. For a contemporary defense to this doctrine (though he concedes too much in my view on Christ's infused virtues) *see* Simon Francis Gaine, *Did the Saviour See the Father?: Christ, Salvation, and the Vision of God* (London: Bloomsbury T & T Clark 2015).

51{52}[11] *I will confess*[73] *you forever, because you have done it: and I will wait on your name, for it is good in the sight of your saints.*

Confitebor tibi in saeculum, quia fecisti; et exspectabo nomen tuum, quoniam bonum est in conspectu sanctorum tuorum.

51{52}[11] *Confitebor tibi,* I will confess you, O Lord, that is, I will praise you, *in saeculum, quia fecisti,* forever, because you have done a just discernment between the good and the ungodly. This of course is written: *He rejoiced in the Holy Spirit, and said: I confess to you, O Father, Lord of heaven and earth, because you have hidden these things from the wise and prudent, and have revealed them to little ones.*[74] *Et exspectabo nomen tuum, quoniam bonum [est in conspectus sanctorum tuorum],* and I will wait on your name, for it is good [in the sight of your saints].*[75] As hope is an expectation, so also to hope and to expect are the same thing, and both are fitting to Christ in that mode, namely, as a wayfarer (*viatori*). For he hoped and expected from God to be raised again from the dead, and to be glorified in body, and to ascend above all heavens.

And those things that are omitted can be seen sufficiently elaborated in the preceding exposition.

ARTICLE III

TROPOLOGICAL OR MORAL EXPOSITION OF THE SAME FIFTY-FIRST PSALM.

51{52}[1] *Unto the end, understanding for David,*

In finem. Intellectus David,

51{52}[2] *When Doeg the Edomite came and told Saul: David went to the house of Achimelech,*

Cum venit Doeg Idumaeus, et nuntiavit Saul: Venit David in domum Achimelech.

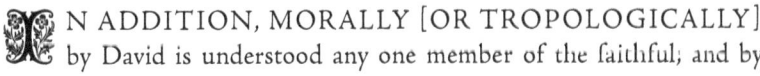 N ADDITION, MORALLY [OR TROPOLOGICALLY], by David is understood any one member of the faithful; and by

---

73   E. N. The Douay Rheims has already considered the fact that the Latin word *confitebor* can mean a confession (of sins) or a confession (of praise), and for this reason has already translated *confitebor* as *I will praise*. However, this would moot the commentary of Denis, so I have translated *confitebor* as "I will confess." This matter is further discussed in footnote 27-49 of Volume 2.

74   Luke 10:21.

75   E. N. I have added the part in brackets which are indicated in the text by "etc."

Doeg any envious and worldly man; and by Saul, unjust power or the reign of the reprobate; and by Achimelech, the Church of God. Therefore, according to the moral understanding, this is the sense of the title: **51{52}[1]** *In finem. Intellectus David. Unto the end, understanding for David.* That is, the doctrine of this present Psalm, directs us to the end, that is, the final retribution and of the just recompense, as befits David, that is, the faithful man; **51{52}[2]** *Cum venit Doeg Idumaeus, when Doeg the Edomite came* to Saul, that is, when a worldly man and detractor [comes] to an evil ruler or any other pestiferous and powerful man tyrannically oppressing the good, *et nuntiavit, and told* to him: *Venit David in domum Achimelech; David went to the house of Achimelech,* that is, a particular member of the faithful went in obedience to holy mother Church. And so the wicked are accustomed to persecute the just, because they despise their life and their precepts and because they submit to the just precepts of the Church.

51{52}[3] *Why do you glory in malice, you that are mighty in iniquity?*

Quid gloriaris in malitia, qui potens es in iniquitate?

And so he says: **51{52}[3]** *Quid gloriaris in malitia? Why do you glory in malice?* That is, why do you sin from choice and from the habit of doing evil and with purpose? For some men sin from weakness: and their sin is venial, or less grave.[76] But others sin from evil habit, and these glory in evil, and are corrected only with the most difficulty;[77] and this glorying is deadly and pernicious, for, according to the Philosopher [Aristotle], glorification or delight is annexed to operation,[78] and it is a sign of an interior habit. And also the Proverb states regarding such glorying persons: *They are glad when they have done evil, and rejoice in*

---

76   E. N. St. Thomas teaches that a sin from malice is more grave than a sin of passion (or weakness). ST IaIIae, q. 78, art. 4, co. He gives three reasons. First, since the will is an important component in sin, the more the will is involved in the sin, the more grievous the sin. Second, sins of passion are the result of a sudden impulse, and when the impulse passes, the man easily repents. This is not so when the sin becomes habitual as a result of malice. Third, a sinner that acts with malice is more directly fixed against the good.

77   *Cf.* Eccl. 1:15: *The perverse are hard to be corrected, and the number of fools is infinite.*

78   E. N. Denis: *gloriatio seu delectatio operationi annexa.* See Aristotle, *Nicomachean Ethics*, chapter 10, 1–5. In his commentary on Aristotle's *On the Soul* (I, d. 1, q. 1) Alphonsus Vargas of Toledo (1300-1366 AD), bishop of Seville, quotes a Latin translation of the Nicomachean Ethics which closely traces Denis's statement: "Aristoteles X *Ethicorum dicens quod 'cuilibet operationi est annexa sua propria delectatio.'*" http://textlib.thesis-project.ro/html/vargas/atv-lıdıqı.xml.

most wicked things;[79] and in the Gospel: *Woe to you that now laugh: for you shall mourn and weep.*[80] For this is the glorying of the world which transforms into eternal sadness; it is opposite to the sorrow of the elect which is changed into eternal joy, in the manner that Christ declared to his disciples: *Amen, amen I say to you, that you shall lament and weep, but the world shall rejoice; and you shall be made sorrowful, but your sorrow shall be turned into joy. So also you now indeed have sorrow; but I will see you again, and your heart shall rejoice; and your joy no man shall take from you.*[81] To be sure, no one glories in evil under the aspect of evil, but under the aspect of some apparent good:[82] for, according to Dionysius [the Areopagite], no one does something regarding it as evil,[83] since good is the object of the appetite, in which is the first root of sin.[84]

And so: Why do you glory in malice, *qui potens es in iniquitate, you that are mighty in iniquity?* According to Anselm,[85] with respect a person who can do something which is not to his advantage, to the extent he more able to do so, to that extent he is less powerful. For to be able to sin is more to be expressed as powerlessness than power, just like sin is better regarded as nothing than as something.[86] In what way, therefore, is something mighty in iniquity? The response is that man is said to be mighty in iniquity, not because he has the power to do evil, according to

---

79   Prov. 2:14.

80   Luke 6:25b.

81   John 15:20, 22.

82   E. N. See ST Ia, q. 82, art. 2, ad 1: *[V]oluntas in nihil potest tendere nisi sub ratione boni.* "The will is able to tend to nothing except under the aspect of the good."

83   E. N. See Pseudo-Dionysius, *De divin. nomin.* 4.1.304.

84   E. N. The appetitive power associated with the appetite is nothing other than the will, ST Ia, q. 83, arts. 3, 4. And the will is the root of sin, namely, malice in the will, is the root of all sin. ST IaIIae, q. 19, art. 4, s.c.

85   E. N. St. Anselm of Canterbury (1033-1109 AD), the famed Benedictine monk, abbot, philosopher, and theologian. Noted for his writings on the Incarnation (*Cur Deus homo*) and the controversial "ontological" proof of God's existence, he is sometimes regarded as the "father of scholasticism."

86   E. N. A reference to St. Anselm's *Proslogion*, where he argues that God, who is omnipotent, is nevertheless incapable of sinning, which would suggest that the omnipotent is "powerless" to sin. This further suggests that "power" of sinning is not, in fact, an addition to "power," but rather a detraction of true power. This also suggests that one who can do something to himself as disadvantageous as sinning (in other words one able to corrupt himself) should be said rather to suffer from powerlessness or impotence (*impotentia*) rather than enjoying true power (*potentia*). "So, then, when one is said to have the power of doing or suffering that which is expedient for him or that which he ought not do, by power is understood powerlessness; for the more he possesses this power, the more adversity and perversity are powerful in him and he is powerless against them." *Pros.*, VI, PL 158, 230.

being the origin and cause of it, as would be true power; but because the power given to him by God to do good is abused, and by it evil is violently and readily carried out. It is in this sense that it is written in Jeremiah: *They are wise to do evil.*[87] Not that doing evil is wisdom, as would be true wisdom, but because it is a certain perverse activity. Whence Wisdom says: *Wisdom will not enter into a malicious soul.*[88] But because some of the given dispositions and knowledge are abused, and the ways of sin are subtly traced out, so in that fashion the wise are described as doing evil.

51{52}[4]   *All the day long your tongue has considered injustice: as a sharp razor, you have wrought deceit.*[89]

Tota die iniustitiam cogitavit lingua tua; sicut novacula acuta fecisti dolum.

51{52}[4]   *Tota die, all the day long,* that is, unceasingly and with an obstinate spirit, *iniustitiam, injustice,* that is, deceit and detraction, *cogitavit lingua tua, your tongue has considered.* If we employ the word "tongue" as an organ of the body, and "has considered" to mean the interior act of reflection, then it is not fitting for the tongue to think, but the heart [is what ought to be considered as doing so]. The fact, therefore, that the two words "tongue" and "has considered" are associated together suggests that as soon as one thinks injustice, it is acted upon: as we find said in Ecclesiasticus: *The heart of a fool is like a broken vessel.*[90] And again: *The heart of fools is in their mouth: and the mouth of wise men is in their heart.*[91] This is the explanation of the venerable theologian Hugh [of St. Victor]. Yet because what is said in a Psalm above is justly said of a wise man, *And my tongue shall meditate your justice,*[92] where the words "to meditate" or "to consider" intend to express the tongues of the wise (whose mouth, as has been stated, is in their heart, because it awaits for the right time to speak, according to this, *A fool utters all his mind: a wise man defers, and keeps it till afterwards*[93]); and so the two explanations given above seem to be more acceptable [than others that may exist].[94]

---

87   Jer. 4:22b.
88   Wis. 1:4a.
89   E. N. I have substituted "considered" for *cogitavit*, replacing the "has devised" of the Douay Rheims. Otherwise, the argument by Denis is not easily followed.
90   Ecclus. 21:17a.
91   Ecclus. 21:29a.
92   Ps. 24:28a.
93   Prov. 29:11.
94   E. N. This paragraph is rather cryptic, but as I understand it Denis is trying to work out how a tongue can be said to think or to consider. He offers what he

Sicut novacula acuta fecisti dolum, as a sharp razor, you have wrought deceit, deceiving your neighbor; and so you are cursed: as we have in Malachi: *Cursed is the deceitful man that has in his flock a male, and making a vow offers in sacrifice that which is feeble to the Lord, for I am a great king, says the Lord.*[95] And another Prophet: *The vessels of the deceitful are most wicked: for he has framed devices to destroy the meek, with lying words.*[96] Faced with the opposite situation, Christ says about Nathanael: *Behold an Israelite indeed, in whom there is no guile.*[97] Therefore, we ought to take exceeding care to be wary of such a weighty vice if we wish to conform to Christ, of whom it is written: *No guile was found in his mouth.*[98]

51{52}[5] *You have loved malice more than goodness: and iniquity rather than to speak righteousness.*

Dilexisti malitiam super benignitatem; iniquitatem magis quam loqui aequitatem.

51{52}[6] *You have loved all the words of ruin, O deceitful tongue.*

Dilexisti omnia verba praecipitationis, lingua dolosa.

51{52}[7] *Therefore will God destroy you forever: he will pluck you out, and remove you from your dwelling place: and your root out of the land of the living.*

Propterea Deus destruet te in finem; evellet te, et emigrabit te de tabernaculo tuo, et radicem tuam de terra viventium.

51{52}[5] *Dilexisti malitiam super benignitatem,* you have loved malice more than goodness. All who sin knowingly love evil more than they do the good. Likewise, you have loved *iniquitatem,* iniquity, that is, forbidden words, *magis quam loqui aequitatem,* rather than to speak righteousness, that is, just, true, and instructive words. In opposition to this, Ecclesiasticus

---

believes are the two best explanations. The first: the "tongue" stands in place for any actual bodily member and the verb "consider" refers (implicitly or *sub silentio*) to the act of reflection (and therefore properly belongs to the heart or the mind, and not the tongue). So understood, the Psalm is chastising the man who says things or acts impulsively, leaving the mind or heart out of it. The second interpretation is that the tongue in question here is that of the unwise (and therefore the unjust) because it does not do what the tongue of a wise man does, namely, not speak or act on impulse.

95   Mal. 1:14.
96   Is. 32:7.
97   John 1:47b.
98   1 Pet. 2:22.

says: *Flee from sins as from the face of a serpent.*[99] And the Apostle [Paul]: *Let no evil speech proceed from your mouth;*[100] and *All bitterness, and anger, and indignation, and clamor, . . . be put away from you. And be kind one to another; merciful, forgiving one another, even as God has forgiven you in Christ.*[101] **51{52}[6]** *Dilexisti omnia verba praecipitationis, [lingua dolosa]; you have loved all the words of ruin, [O deceitful tongue]:*[102] this is contrary to fraternal charity, and, as a consequence, a mortal sin by which is merited eternal torment. Whence is added: **51{52}[7]** *Propterea Deus destruet te in finem, therefore will God destroy you forever.* The exposition of this verse is clarified from the preceding [expositions].

51{52}[8] *The just shall see and fear, and shall laugh at him, and say:*

Videbunt iusti, et timebunt; et super eum ridebunt, et dicent:

51{52}[8] *Videbunt iusti, the just shall see* the punishment of the evil in the present age and in the final judgment, *et timebunt, and they shall fear,* that is, they will be in dread of the divine justice, and there will be conceived in them a filial fear regarding God. And indeed in this way the holy angels receive the condemnation of the reprobate, as Job says of the devil under the appellation of Behemoth: *When he shall raise him up, the angels shall fear, and being affrighted shall purify themselves.*[103] And Christ in the Gospel: *The powers,* he says, *of heaven shall be moved.*[104] *Et super eum, and at him,* namely, the wicked and the reprobate, *ridebunt, they shall laugh,* as a later Psalm states, *The just shall rejoice when he shall see the revenge.*[105] For which reason, the Lord said of the just through Malachi: *You shall go forth, and shall leap like calves of the herd, and you shall tread down the wicked . . . in the day that I do this, says the Lord;*[106] and in Isaiah, *They shall go out, and see the carcasses of the men that have transgressed against me.*[107] And the just shall say of the of the ungodly:

---

99   Ecclus. 21:2a.
100   Eph. 4:29a.
101   Eph. 4:31-32.
102   E. N. I have completed the words in brackets; Denis inexplicably leaves them off.
103   Job. 41:16.
104   Matt. 24:29b. E. N. The "powers" are one of the nine choirs of angels. *See* footnote 9-12 in Volume I.
105   Ps. 57:11a.
106   Mal. 4:2b-3.
107   Is. 66:24a.

51{52}[9] *Behold the man that made not God his helper: But trusted in the abundance of his riches: and prevailed in his vanity.*

Ecce homo qui non posuit Deum adiutorem suum; sed speravit in multitudine divitiarum suarum, et praevaluit in vanitate sua.

51{52}[9] *Ecce homo qui non posuit Deum adiutorem suum; behold the man that made not God his helper.* This goes against the exhortation of Isaiah: *Who has walked in darkness, and has no light? Let him hope in the name of the Lord and lean upon his God.*[108] *Sed speravit in multitudine divitiarum suarum, but he trusted in the abundance of his riches,* either of the body or of the spirit, namely of merit, reckoning himself to be something, when he is nothing,[109] and glorying in himself of his own good works, as if he had not received them from elsewhere.[110] Let us not trust in our own righteousness, let us not place hope in the uncertainty of riches, so that we might have the ability to say with holy Job: *If I would justify myself, my own mouth shall condemn me. Although I should be simple, even this my soul shall be ignorant of.*[111] And again he says: *If I have thought gold my strength, and have said to fine gold: My confidence: If I have rejoiced over my great riches, and because my hand had gotten much.*[112] And this also the Apostle [Paul] says: *Admonish the rich of this world not to be high-minded, nor to trust in the uncertainty of riches, but in the living God.*[113] And elsewhere: *Let no man therefore,* he says, *glory in men,*[114] namely in himself; but *he that glories, let him glory in the Lord.*[115] Indeed any vain glory in our merits ought to be entirely excluded from us, since Christ said: *When you shall have done all these things that are commanded you, say: We are unprofitable servants; we have done that which we ought to do.*[116] *Et prevaluit in vanitate sua, and prevailed in his vanity,* that is, in the time of prosperity he flourished for a time, and strutted about in his own desires, and oppressed others.

---

108 Is. 50:10b.
109 Gal. 6:3: *For if any man think himself to be something, whereas he is nothing, he deceives himself.*
110 1 Cor. 4:7: *For who distinguishes you? Or what have you that you have not received? And if you have received, why do you glory, as if you had not received it?*
111 Job. 9:20a, 21a.
112 Job 31:24–25. E. N. Job later says that confiding in gold or riches "is a very great iniquity, and a denial against the most high God." Job. 31:28.
113 1 Tim. 6:17. I have changed the Douay Rheims "charge" to "admonish" for the Latin *praecipe.*
114 1 Cor. 3:21.
115 2 Cor. 10:17.
116 Luke 17:10.

51{52}[10]   *But I, as a fruitful olive tree in the house of God, have hoped in the mercy of God forever, yea forever and ever.*

Ego autem, sicut oliva fructifera in domo Dei; speravi in misericordia Dei, in aeternum et in saeculum saeculi.

51{52}[10] *Ego autem sicut oliva fructifera in domo Dei; but I, as a fruitful olive tree in the house of God.* This applies to any man who produces good works, but also instructs others in life and morals, which [instruction] bears fruit in eternal life, such as those of whom Levi was the patriarch, as Malachi attests, saying: *My covenant was with Levi, . . and he was afraid of my name; . . . he walked with me in peace and equity, and turned many away from iniquity.*[117] This also applies in the greatest degree to prelates or other teachers from whose hand God will require blood of those who perish.[118] *Speravi in misericordia Dei in aeternum, et in saeculum saeculi; I have hoped in the mercy of God for ever, yea, for ever and ever.* For I know I am not sufficient to think anything of myself, but my sufficiency is from God.[119] The rest might be clarified from what has been before.

Now we have regarded this brief and doctrinal Psalm, in which the distinction between good and evil is beautifully distinguished, and the divine judgment clearly recalled. Let us zealously apply ourselves, therefore, to flee the works of darkness,[120] and to procure a fruitful olive tree, spending all time fruitfully, scandalizing no one, lest we be to others a *stone of stumbling, and a rock of scandal;*[121] but let our life so be a light for our neighbor that they may be edified by us.[122]

---

117   Mal. 2:4b, 5b, 6.

118   *Cf.* Ez. 3:18: *If, when I say to the wicked, You shall surely die: you declare it not to him, nor speak to him, that he may be converted from his wicked way, and live: the same wicked man shall die in his iniquity, but I will require his blood at your hand.*

119   *Cf.* 2 Cor. 3:5.

120   *Cf.* Rom. 13:12b: *Let us therefore cast off the works of darkness, and put on the armor of light.*

121   1 Pet. 2:8a.

122   *Cf.* Matt. 5:16: *So let your light shine before men, that they may see your good works, and glorify your Father who is in heaven.*

PRAYER

O LORD, DEFENDER OF OUR LIFE AND OF our soul, oppose always our disordered inclinations, and do not permit us to grow strong in our vanity, so that, as fruitful olive trees in your home, we might hope for your name in in the sight of your Saints.

Defensor vitae et animae nostrae, Domine, pravis conatibus nostris semper obsiste, et ne sinas nos in nostra praevalere vanitate: ut sicut oliva fructificantes in domo tua, in aeternum exspectemus nomen tuum in conspectus Sanctorum tuorum.

Psalm 52

ARTICLE IV

EXPOSITION OF THE FIFTY-SECOND PSALM:
DIXIT INSIPIENS IN CORDE SUO.
THE FOOL SAID IN HIS HEART.

52{53}[1] *Unto the end, for Amalek,*[1] *understanding to David. The fool said in his heart: There is no God.*

In finem, pro Amalec, intellectus David. Dixit insipiens in corde suo: Non est Deus.

NOW THE TITLE OF THIS PSALM NOW BEING explained is: **52{53}[1]** *In finem, pro Amalec, intellectus David; unto the end, for Amalek, understandings to David.* Of this title many things can be said, for different persons understand it in different ways. But briefly passing over it, I say, as Hugh [of St. Victor] affirms, that this Psalm appears to be written on the occasion of the Amalekites, after they had seized and carried off David and his men's wives along with their children and their chattel, and set the city of Ziklag (Siceleg) on fire, which Achish the King of Gath gave to David who was fleeing Saul, in the manner that is written in the book of Samuel.[2] Not, however, that this Psalm addresses this history, but [that this is brought forth in the title] because of the things that are signified by the name Amalek, which is interpreted as meaning "feeling labor pains" or "giving birth." It [therefore] signifies the Mystical Body of Christ, namely, the Church lamenting for sins, and giving birth to children spiritually through the word of preaching, in the manner that the Apostle [Paul] says: *My little children, of whom I am in labor again, until Christ be formed in you;*[3] and elsewhere, *By the gospel, I have begotten you.*[4] But in this Psalm men rise up in protest against the Church. And the title is [thus to be understood] in this sense: *Intellectus David, understanding to David, that*

---

1 E. N. Denis's version departs from the Sixto-Clementine Vulgate which says, *In finem, pro Maeleth intelligentia. David,* "Unto the end, for Maeleth, understandings to David."

2 1 Sam. 30:1–5.

3 Gal. 4:19.

4 1 Cor. 4:15b.

is, this Psalm in which is set forth the knowledge of David, *in finem,* *unto the end,* that is, directing us unto Christ, is written about Amalek, that is, about that which is signified by him, namely, about the Church whose adversaries are here being rebuked. Therefore, this Psalm, both in word and in meaning, is very similar to the thirteenth Psalm. Because, however, it differs in title (for its title is *A Psalm of David*),[5] it is believed it differs in intention and sense, at least in part.

And so the holy Prophet [David] says: *Dixit insipiens in corde suo, the* *fool says in his heart,* that is, lacking the knowledge of God, he thinks within himself: *Non est Deus, there is no God.* This can be understood in two ways. The first is where someone holds that God does not exist because of an excessive blindness of mind, just like certain philosophers have denied first principles: still, however, neither for God not to exist nor the first principles to be false is able to be thought by someone [without absurdity], since both, according to probable opinion, are known *per se (per se notum).*[6] The second [way of understanding this verse] can be taken as follows: *The fool says in his heart: there is no God:* that is, anyone doing things foolishly and living sinfully holds himself out as if he considered God not to exist; indeed, whom he confesses by word, he denies by deeds, as the Apostle [Paul] says regarding some: *They say that* *they know God: but in their works they deny him.*[7] Whence also in the first epistle of John we read: *He who says that he knows him, and keeps not* *his commandments, is a liar.*[8] This is understood as pertaining to formed knowledge.[9] For the reprobate of God have unformed knowledge of God,

---

5   E. N. That is, Psalm 13 is denominated a "Psalm of David," and therefore differs from this one, which does not have that title.

6   E. N. Denis and St. Thomas agree on the self-evident (*per se nota*) status of the first principles of reason, but depart markedly on the issue of whether the knowledge of God is self-evident. Denis differs from St. Thomas Aquinas in this regard. Thomas taught that, contrary to the first principles of reason (the *principia* *per se nota,* e.g., the principle of identity, or the principle of sufficient reason, or the principle of efficient causality), the existence of God is not known *per se* (or known innately, or is self-evident), ST Ia, q. 2, art. 1, but is known only from the things that are made or known through the application of reason working from first principles (which are known innately or *per se*); that is, the existence of God is determined *a* *posteriori.* ST Ia, q. 2, arts. 2-3. Other theologians holding the existence of God to be self-evident (contrary to St. Thomas) are Sts. Augustine, Anselm, and Bonaventure. However, Denis labels his opinion only probable, not certain.

7   Titus 1:16a.

8   1 John 2:4.

9   E. N. As to this insidious form of practical atheism, Pope Benedict XVI observed in an Audience on November 14, 2012: "A particularly dangerous phenomenon for faith has arisen in our times: indeed a form of atheism exists which we define,

as the Apostle says of them: *When they knew God, they have not glorified him as God.*[10] In this second way, many say in their hearts, "There is no God": all, that is to say, who do not fear the judgment of God; for they go about doing things as if they reckoned God was not just. But few say there is no God in the first sense, for, as Augustine attests, just as great perfection is found in a few, so also great insanity is found in a few.[11]

52{53}[2] *They are corrupted, and become abominable in iniquities: there is none that does good.*

Corrupti sunt, et abominabiles facti sunt in iniquitatibus; non est qui faciat bonum.

Thereafter the Prophet [David] speaks many things concerning foolish men, saying **52{53}[2]** *Corrupti sunt, et abominabiles facti sunt in iniquitatibus; they are corrupted, and become abominable in iniquities.* The soundness of the mind arises from its turning towards (*conversio*) God; but its corruption is a turning away (*aversio*) from God and a turning toward (*conversio*) transitory things. For this reason, regarding those men turning away from the one great good, and turning toward this earth and toward vain things, we find written in Hosea: *Their heart is divided: now they shall perish.*[12] And of such persons, the Apostle [Paul] also says [in describing them]: *Men corrupted in mind, reprobate concerning the faith.*[13] Such men, therefore, are corrupt in mind, and they have become abominable, that is, irrational and hateful in their iniquities or because of their iniquities. *Non est qui faciat bonum, there is none that does good* meritorious of eternal life;

---

precisely, as 'practical,' in which the truths of faith or religious rites are not denied but are merely deemed irrelevant to daily life, detached from life, pointless. So it is that people often believe in God in a superficial manner, and live 'as though God did not exist' (*etsi Deus non daretur*). In the end, however, this way of life proves even more destructive because it leads to indifference to faith and to the question of God." http://www.vatican.va/content/benedict-xvi/en/audiences/2012/documents/hf_ben-xvi_aud_20121114.html.

10 Rom. 1:21a. E. N. Denis distinguishes between *unformed* knowledge of God (that is knowledge of God without charity — a *notitia informem* — and a knowledge formed by charity — a *notitia caritate formata*. He has made the same distinction formed and unformed faith and formed and unformed hope in prior articles.

11 E. N. The reference is to St. Augustine's Sermon 69, 2, 3, where, discussing this very verse, he says: *Dixit stultus in corde suo, Non est Deus. Insania ista paucorum est. Sicut enim magna pietas, paucorum est; ita et magna impietas, nihilominus paucorum est.* "The fool says in his heart, 'There is no God.' This insanity is of a few. For just as great piety is of a few, so also great impiety is nevertheless of a few." PL 39, 441.

12 Hosea 10:2a.

13 2 Tim. 3:8b.

[there is no good] that arises from [any of the activities] of these foolish men because they do not have grace and charity, without which no one has the power to merit or to be accepted by God.

52{53}[3]   *God looked down from heaven on the children of men: to see if there were any that did understand, or did seek God.*

Deus de caelo prospexit super filios hominum, ut videat si est intelligens, aut requirens Deum.

52{53}[3] *Deus de caelo prospexit super filios hominum,* God looked down from heaven on the children of men. In the manner that God in a special way is said to dwell in heaven, so he is said in a special way to look down from heaven, even though he fills heaven and earth, penetrates all things, and sees all things in himself.[14] And so, God from heaven and his holy dwelling looks down *upon the children of men,* that is, he gives consideration to all of the children of the first parents, *ut videat, to see,* that is, he may cause some to know, or show himself to know, *si est intelligens, aut requirens Deum; if there were any that did understand or did seek God,* that is, either anyone perceiving God in a right way, or knowing him by a formed intellect and by faith, or performing good works, or requiring himself to do that which is within his power to do. This is what Scripture says: *O most mighty, great, and powerful, the Lord of hosts is your name, . . . whose eyes are open upon all the ways of the children of Adam, to render unto every one according to his ways.*[15]

52{53}[4]   *All have gone aside, they are become unprofitable together, there is none that does good, no not one.*

Omnes declinaverunt, simul inutiles facti sunt; non est qui faciat bonum, non est usque ad unum.

52{53}[4] *Omnes,* all of the above-mentioned foolish men *declinaverunt, have gone aside* from right reason, from the way of justice, from the true God: by which going aside or withdrawing is not meant by a distance of place, but by a disobedience of mind, as is stated in Hosea: *They have forsaken the Lord in not observing his law.*[16] *Simul inutiles facti sunt, they are become unprofitable together,* that is, [they have become] incapable

---

14   Cf. Jer. 23:24: *Shall a man be hid in secret places, and I not see him, says the Lord? Do not I fill heaven and earth, says the Lord?*

15   Jer. 32:18b–19.

16   Hosea 4:10b.

of true happiness and unsuitable for the last end for which they were created. For sins impede men from the attainment of eternal life, and they cause separation between them and God. [17] *Non est qui faciat bonum, there is none that does good,* that is, from these foolish men a work that is acceptable to God; *non et usque ad unum, no not one,* that is, among them there is none doing any good whatsoever, because all of them lack grace.

52{53}[5]   *Shall not all the workers of iniquity know, who eat up my people as they eat bread?*

Nonne scient omnes qui operantur iniquitatem, qui devorant plebem meam ut cibum panis?

52{53}[5] *Nonne scient omnes qui operantur iniquitatem? Shall not all the workers of iniquity know?* That is, will not the sinners know God? It is as if he were saying, Indeed, at least after this life they will experience in punishment the divine justice, in the way that is stated about them in the book of Wisdom: *These seeing it, shall be troubled with terrible fear . . . groaning for anguish of spirit. . . . We have erred from the way of truth, and the light of justice has not shined upon us.* [18] And it continues: *Such things as these the sinners said in hell.* [19] *Qui devorant plebem meam, who eat up my people,* that is, who oppress, injure, and slay the innocent and the good, *ut cibum panis, as they eat bread,* that is, by chewing them like bread, which is food, by grinding them down and consuming them.

52{53}[6]   *They have not called upon God: there have they trembled for fear, where there was no fear. For God has scattered the bones of them that please men: they have been confounded, because God has despised them.*

Deum non invocaverunt; illic trepidaverunt timore, ubi non erat timor. Quoniam Deus dissipavit ossa eorum qui hominibus placent: confusi sunt, quoniam Deus sprevit eos?

52{53}[6] *Deum non invocaverunt, they have not called upon God,* that is, they have not called upon his mercy with an internal affection, because they did not come to know him, nor did they go out and seek him, nor did they hope in him, nor did they attend themselves to the necessary

---

17 Cf. Is. 59:2: *But your iniquities have divided between you and your God, and your sins have hid his face from you that he should not hear.*
18 Wis. 5:2a, 3a, 6a.
19 Wis. 5:14.

grace of God. *Illic trepidaverunt timore, ubi non fuit timor; there have they trembled for fear, where there was no fear*: that is, they feared things that were not fearful, and they did not fear the fearful things. They did not fear God, but [they feared] men; they feared temporal punishments, but not those of hell; they feared the loss of temporal prosperity, honor, fame, and glory, but not [the loss of] heavenly happiness. They feared to incur bodily diseases and discomfort, and to undergo the labors of penance, and to lay hold of the way of perfection; but they did not fear to lose the grace of God, to live in mortal vices, to displease the judgment of God. In this manner, therefore, they had a human, carnal, and disordered — and not a filial, divine, and chaste — fear. [All of] this is contrary to what Christ commanded his disciples: *Fear not, little flock, for it has pleased your Father to give you a kingdom.*[20] And again: *Fear not them that kill the body, and are not able to kill the soul: but rather fear him that can destroy both soul and body in hell.*[21] Whence also in Isaiah is contained this: *Fear not the reproach of men, and be not afraid of their blasphemies.*[22] Do you want to know, man, what fearful things to fear, and what fearful things not to fear? Listen to Job witnessing to himself about these things: *If I have been afraid at a very great multitude, and the contempt of kinsmen has terrified me.*[23] *I will not fear thousands of the people, surrounding me,*[24] nor will I dread to be despised by men. But whom should I fear? *I have* always, he says, *feared God as waves swelling over me.*[25] And again, he says: *God is alone, and no man can turn away his thought; and therefore I am troubled at his presence, and when I consider him I am made pensive with fear.*[26] To which holy fear Isaiah particularly exhorts us, saying: *Sanctify the Lord of hosts himself: and let him be your fear, and let him be your dread.*[27]

Quoniam Deus dissipavit ossa eorum qui hominibus placent, for God has scattered the bones of them that please men: that is, in the present life he will withdraw spiritual strength from them who please, or who desire to please, men according to the manner in which men live in this world; and also in the future judgment he will scatter their bones, pulverizing them

---

20   Luke 12:32.

21   Matt. 10:28.

22   Is. 51:7b.

23   Job 31:34. E. N. In other words, Job did not fear the multitude or even the contempt of his family.

24   Ps. 3:7a.

25   Job. 31:23a.

26   Job 23:13a, 15.

27   Is. 8:13.

into pieces, and casting their body and soul into eternal torment. For in this manner men in many ways depart from the path of righteousness on account of human favor, love, fear, or other similar affections. Whence it is written: *He that fears man, shall quickly fall.*[28] And to the Galatians the Apostle [Paul] asserts: *If I yet pleased men, I should not be the servant of Christ.*[29] And Christ says to his elect: *If you had been of the world, the world would love its own: but because you are not of the world, but I have chosen you out of the world, therefore the world hates you.*[30]

But this seems to be opposed to that which the Apostle [Paul] said: *Be without offense . . . to the Church of God, as I also in all things please all men, not seeking that which is profitable to myself, but to many;*[31] and elsewhere, *If it be possible, as much as is in you, have peace with all men.*[32] And of Samuel and also some others in the first book of Samuel and in Ecclesiasticus, the Scripture states in a greatly commendatory way, that they pleased both God and men.[33] In response to this, we can speak of men in two ways. The first way, according to those that are without charity, faith, and grace: and to wish to please such men is a sin, most especially as it relates to corrupt nature or in reference to the consent to its disordered desires. And so of these men the Apostle [Paul] says: *There is among you envying and contention, are you not carnal, and walk according to man?*[34] And again: *While one says, I indeed am of Paul; and another, I am of Apollo; are you not men?*[35] For speaking in this way of a man, he is always inclined to errors and vice and various fancies. For which reason the Apostle again says: *I beseech you, brethren, . . . that you all speak the same thing, and that there be no schisms among you; but that you be perfect in the same mind.*[36] But the second way we are able to speak of men is according to reason that is informed by the law and the grace of God; and in this way it is laudable to please men in God and for the sake of God. Whence the Apostle admonishes: *Let every one of you please his neighbor unto good, to edification.*[37] And

---

28 Prov. 29:25a.
29 Gal. 1:10b.
30 John 15:19.
31 1 Cor. 10:32–33.
32 Rom. 12:18.
33 1 Sam. 2:26: *But the child Samuel advanced, and grew on, and pleased both the Lord and men.* Ecclus. 45:1: *Moses was beloved of God, and men: whose memory is in benediction.*
34 1 Cor. 3:3.
35 1 Cor. 3:4.
36 1 Cor. 1:10.
37 Rom. 15:2.

in this manner also ought we to respect and to fear men, especially those who preside over us, because Christ says: *He that hears you, hears me; and he that despises you, despises me.*[38]

Confusi sunt, they have been confounded, [they, that is,] who desire inordinately to please men, *quoniam Deus sprevit eos, because God has despised them* on account of their sins, in the manner that is attested by Hosea: *I hated them: for the wickedness of their devices.*[39] Especially will they be confounded in the day of the Last Judgment, when they will perish in eternity.

52{53}[7]   *Who will give out of Sion the salvation of Israel? When God shall bring back the captivity of his people, Jacob shall rejoice, and Israel shall be glad.*

Quis dabit ex Sion salutare Israel? Cum converterit Deus captivitatem plebis suae, exsultabit Iacob, et laetabitur Israel.

52{53}[7] *Quis dabit ex Sion, who will give out of Sion,* that is, who among the number of the elect of God will render the spiritual examination, *salutare Israel, the salvation of Israel,* that is, the salvation and the liberation of the militant Church? Indeed, no one but Christ, who, insofar as he is man, has given satisfaction for us; and by his Incarnation he has made himself the brother and the friend of man, and so he is recognized as being among the number of the elect. Or [it can be understood] thus: *Who will give out of Sion,* that is, who from the heavenly city and the triumphant Church will give salvation to Israel, that is, the faithful people? Clearly, no one, unless it be God himself, sublime and blessed, who through Hosea says: *I am the Lord your God . . . and there is no Savior beside me.*[40] Of which Isaiah says: *Thus says the Lord your Redeemer, . . . I, the Lord your God, teaching you profitable things, governing the way that you walk.*[41]

Cum converterit Deus captivitatem plebis suae, when God shall bring back the captivity of his people, that is, at the time that Christ will have by his Passion redeemed his elect from the power of the devil and the bonds of sin, *exsultabit Iacob, Jacob shall rejoice:* that is, at that time the people overcoming vices and following the faith and works of holy Jacob will spiritually exult in such great benefits of Christ as is frequently narrated

---

38   Luke 10:16.
39   Hosea 9:15a.
40   Hosea 13:4.
41   Is. 48:17.

in the book of Acts as fulfilled;[42] *et laetabitur Israel, and Israel shall be glad*: that is, then men (*viri*) of contemplation and men (*homines*) of perfection, namely, true Israelites, will be glad, not only those who were wayfarers in the world, but also those who were detained in Purgatory and in Limbo.[43] Or [we can understand it] thus: *When God shall bring back the captivity of his people*, that is, since he will have redeemed the militant Church from corruption and the miseries of this life, and he will transform it to the society of the triumphant Church, which he will do in the last day; then *Jacob shall rejoice and Israel shall be* glad with an interior and exterior joy, consummate and perpetual, according to that which is prophesized: They who will have been redeemed by the Lord, shall return, and they shall come into Sion rejoicing, and eternal gladness shall be upon their heads, and sorrow and morning shall flee away.[44]

ARTICLE V

ALLEGORICAL EXPOSITION OF THE SAME FIFTY-SECOND PSALM, BY ITS RELATION TO CHRIST

52{53}[1]   *Unto the end, for Amalek,[45] understandings to David. The fool said in his heart: There is no God.*

In finem, pro Amalec, intellectus David. Dixit insipiens in corde suo: Non est Deus.

FROM THE DECLARATION OF THE THIRteenth Psalm, it is most easily apparent in which manner this Psalm can be applied to Christ. Therefore, touching upon this briefly, by the sons of Korah we understand the imitators and the sons of Jesus Christ crucified, because, in accordance with that which has been stated before, Korah is interpreted as Calvary, which is the name of the place at which the Savior

---

42   Acts chps. 2, 6.

43   E. N. Here, Purgatory and Limbo are used as synonyms, the word limbo being short for *limbus purgatorius*, the limbo of cleansing or purgation.

44   *Cf.* Is. 35:10. E. N. For more on the distinction between Jacob and Israel, the meaning of their names (Jacob = "supplanter" and Israel = "man seeing God"), and Jacob symbolizing a wayfarer (*viator*) and Israel one of the blessed in heaven (*comprehensor*), see Article XXXVI (Psalm 13:7) and footnotes 13-31, 13-64, and 21-12 in Volume I.

45   E. N. Denis's version departs from the Sixto-Clementine Vulgate which says, *In finem, pro Maeleth intelligentia. David*, "Unto the end, for Maeleth, understandings to David."

of the world hung upon the Cross; thus by Amalek, which is interpreted as suffering labor pains or giving birth, we are able to understand Christ, of whom it is written: *Surely he has borne our infirmities and carried our sorrows;*[46] and again, *He was wounded for our iniquities, he was bruised for our sins.*[47] Thus, the sense of the title of this Psalm will be: **52{53}[1]** *In finem, pro Amalec, intellectus David; unto the end, for Amalek, understandings to David:* that is, the knowledge of this present Psalm directs us to the end of eternal life; it was written by David for Amalek, that is, for the meaning of the interpretation of his name, Amalek, namely, for Christ.

And so he says: *Dixit insipiens, the fool said,* that is, the Jewish people and their speaking among themselves ridiculing, spurning, and persecuting Christ, the Wisdom of God incarnate; *in corde suo: Non est Deus; in his heart: There is no God,* that is, this Jesus of Nazareth is able to suffer similar to us, and so is neither God nor the Only-Begotten of God, but is a seducer and a blasphemer. Whence Christ exposed the blindness and the foolishness of the Jews' being contemptuous towards belief in him. *I speak to them in parables,* he says, *because seeing they see not, and hearing they hear not, neither do they understand; so that the prophecy of Isaiah is fulfilled in them, who says: By hearing you shall hear, and shall not understand: and seeing you shall see, and shall not perceive. For the heart of this people is grown gross.*[48] These words, or rather the sense of these words, we find in the book of the vision of Isaiah.[49] Moreover, when the Pharisees said to Jesus, *Master we would see a sign from you,*[50] he rebuked them for they had not paid heed to the time of his coming from the writings of the Prophets, especially the prophecy of Daniel, who in the book of his visions most clearly declared the time of the coming and Passion of Christ, when he said: *After sixty-two weeks Christ shall be slain.*[51] And it speaks of the weeks of years, not of days, so that one week contains seven years. And so, therefore, Christ responded to the Pharisees: *You know then how to discern the face of the sky; for when it is evening you say, it will be fair weather for the sky is red; and can you not know the signs of the times?*[52]

---

46   Is. 53:4a.

47   Is. 53:5a.

48   Matt. 13:13–15a.

49   Is. 6:9-10: *Go, and you shall say to this people: Hearing, hear, and understand not: and see the vision, and know it not. Blind the heart of this people, and make their ears heavy, and shut their eyes: lest they see with their eyes, and hear with their ears, and understand with their heart, and be converted and I heal them.*

50   Matt. 12:38b.

51   Dan. 9:26a.

52   Matt. 16:4, 2.

52{53}[2] *They are corrupted, and become abominable in iniquities: there is none that does good.*

Corrupti sunt, et abominabiles facti sunt in iniquitatibus; non est qui faciat bonum.

Thereafter the Prophet [David] expresses many things regarding these foolish men, saying **52{53}[2]** *Corrupti sunt, they are corrupted,* that is, they are destitute of all grace and [will be] bodily destroyed by the Romans; *et abominabiles facti sunt, and become abominable,* that is, they are hateful to both God and men, as the Apostle said about them: *They please not God, and are adversaries to all men.*[53] And that, *in iniquitatibus suis, in their iniquities,* that is, because of the sins by which they perse- cuted Christ, and because they denied him before Pilate and had him killed, as Christ attests through Jeremiah: *My inheritance is become to me as a lion in the wood: it has cried out against me, therefore have I hated it.*[54] And again, of the unbelieving Jews Jeremiah predicted: *They have denied the Lord, and said, It is not he.*[55] Whence in Hosea Christ most openly says: *They have departed from me, and I have chastised them, and have strengthened their arms, and they have imagined evil against me. They returned, that they might be without yoke, and I redeemed them, and they have spoken lies against me.*[56] *Non est, there is none* out of those foolish and perverse Jews, *qui faciat bonum, that does good* in a meritorious manner. For this reason, Christ says to them in the Gospel: *You shall die in your sin;*[57] and again, *You are of your father the devil;*[58] and yet again, *How can you speak good things, whereas you are evil?*[59]

---

53   1 Thess. 2:15b.

54   Jer. 12:8. E. N. As Denis explains in his *Commentary on Jeremiah,* St. Jerome applies this verse (which literally relates to the Jews and the Babylonian captivity) allegorically to the person of Christ and the Jews' rejection of him. The Jews (his inheritance) who rejected Christ were, according to Denis, "as a lion in the wood," "cruelly persecuting" Christ. And so, in response to this unjust persecution of him, "he hated it," that is, he hated his inheritance, "for, as the Apostle says, *the wrath of God is come upon them to the end* (1 Thess. 2:16b); and the Psalmist, *you hate all the workers of iniquity* (Ps. 5:7a)." Doctoris Ecstatici D. Dionysii Cartusiani, *Opera Omnia,* Vol. 9 (Montreuil: 1900), 117.

55   Jer. 5:12a.

56   Hosea 7:13–16. E. N. This is a patchwork of phrases taken from these verses in Hosea.

57   John 8:21a.

58   John 8:44a.

59   Matt. 12:34a.

52{53}[3] *God looked down from heaven on the children of men: to see if there were any that did understand, or did seek God.*

Deus de caelo prospexit super filios hominum, ut videat si est intelligens, aut requirens Deum.

52{53}[4] *All have gone aside, they are become unprofitable together, there is none that does good, no not one.*

Omnes declinaverunt, simul inutiles facti sunt; non est qui faciat bonum, non est usque ad unum.

52{53}[5] *Shall not all the workers of iniquity know, who eat up my people as they eat bread?*

Nonne scient omnes qui operantur iniquitatem, qui devorant plebem meam ut cibum panis?

52{53}[3] *Deus de caelo, God . . . from heaven,* that is, the Word of God, the Truth and the Wisdom of the Father, in the assumed humanity in which he dwelled as if in the most pure heaven, *prospexit super filios hominum, looked down . . . on the children of men,* that is, especially upon the Jews, first preaching to them the Kingdom of Heaven, as Christ in the Gospel confessed: *I was not sent but to the sheep that are lost of the house of Israel.*[60] *Ut videat si est intelligens, aut requirens Deum; to see if there were any that did understand, or did seek God* the Father, and his only Son, Jesus Christ. For Christ came into the world to save those seeking God, and to render acceptable [to God] those who would come to know him. **52{53}[4]** *Omnes, all* of the previously mentioned unbelievers, *declinaverunt, have gone aside* from the doctrine of Christ and the Catholic Faith, as the Lord said through Jeremiah: *They have turned their back to me, and not their face.*[61] **52{53}[5]**[62] *Nonne scient omnes qui operantur iniquitatem? Shall not all the workers of iniquity know?* That is, shall not the previously mentioned unfaithful Jews eventually acknowledge me to be the true Messiah? It is as if he were saying, "Indeed they will acknowledge," for in the day of judgment *they shall look upon me whom they have pierced.*[63] And in Revelation John says: *Behold, he comes with the clouds, and every eye shall see him, and they also that pierced him.*[64] *Qui devorant plebem meam, they who eat up my people,* that is, they who oppressed, afflicted, and in part killed and in part cast out the early

---

60   Matt. 15:24.
61   Jer. 2:27a.
62   E. N. Denis does not provide comment on the last part of Ps. 42:4.
63   Zech. 12:10a.
64   Rev. 1:7a.

Church first gathered together in Jerusalem from the boundaries [of Jerusalem], in the manner that is set forth by Luke in Acts: *At that time (when, namely, they had killed Stephen), he says, there was raised a great persecution against the church which was at Jerusalem; and they were all dispersed through the countries of Judea, and Samaria, except the Apostles.*[65]

> **52{53}[6]** *They have not called upon God: there have they trembled for fear, where there was no fear. For God has scattered the bones of them that please men: they have been confounded, because God has despised them.*
>
> *Deum non invocaverunt; illic trepidaverunt timore, ubi non erat timor. Quoniam Deus dissipavit ossa eorum qui hominibus placent: confusi sunt, quoniam Deus sprevit eos?*

52{53}[6] *Deum non invocaverunt,* they have not called upon God these unbelievers, for they did not truly know him, as Christ said to them: *Neither me do you know, nor my Father.*[66] And if they called repeatedly out to God with their lips, yet their hearts were far from him;[67] and therefore they did not call upon him. *Illic trepidaverunt timore, ubi non fuit timor; there they have trembled with fear, where there was no fear.* For they feared the coming of the Romans unless they killed Christ; as they put it, *The Romans will come, and take away our place and nation.*[68] And so they feared men and temporal punishments more than God and spiritual defeat. *Quoniam Deus dissipavit ossa eorum qui hominibus placent, for God has scattered the bones of them that please men,* that is, of the previously mentioned unfaithful Jews, who either fearing to displease the Romans or wishing to please the chiefs of the priests, procured the death of Christ. The bones of these men Christ scattered and will scatter, according to the meaning shown in the preceding exposition.[69] For Christ said to them: *How can you believe, who receive glory one from another: and the glory which is from God alone, you do not seek?*[70] *Confusi sunt,* they have been confounded, at the time of Titus and Vespasian,

---

65 Acts 8:1. *E. N.* The deacon, Stephen, is generally regarded to be the first martyr of the early Church, the protomartyr, being killed by stoning sometime *circa* 34 AD.
66 John 8:19a.
67 Is. 29:13: *Forasmuch as this people draw near me with their mouth, and with their lips glorify me, but their heart is far from me, and they have feared me with the commandment and doctrines of men.*
68 John 11:48b.
69 *E. N.* Article IV (Psalm 52:6).
70 John 5:44.

and they are daily confounded by the faithful; and finally, they will be eternally confounded by Christ, when Christ fulfills that which he foretold: *Hereafter you shall see the Son of man sitting on the right hand of the power of God, and coming in the clouds of heaven.*[71] Therefore, they are confounded in such a manner *quoniam Deus sprevit eos, because God has despised them.* Because they did not seek to inform themselves or to convert [to Christ], but remained incorrigible, so it might be verified in them that which is asserted by Solomon: *Consider the works of God, that no man can correct whom he has despised.*[72] The rest of the things are clear from the prior exposition.

See how great and salubrious warning can be drawn out of this Psalm, namely, that we not confess God with our mouth yet deny him in our deeds; and let us think about, revere, and love the God who considers all things; let us fear the future judgment, let us dread the torments of the ungodly: and above all let us bring to mind most diligently that verse which says, *For God has scattered the bones of them that please men* in order that we might seek to please God alone, and to avoid displeasing him alone, so that we might not be numbered among those of whom it is written: *For they loved the glory of men more than the glory of God.*[73]

PRAYER

RACIOUSLY LOOK OUT OVER US FROM heaven, we who are rendered unprofitable by our own vices, O God; stir up your grace in us, whereby we being enlightened might endeavor to please, not our own selves, but you.

Propriis vitiis inutiles factos, Deus, de caelo propitius prospice super nos; suscita in nobis gratiam tuam: qua illustrati, non nobis ipsis, sed tibi placere studeamus.

---

71 Matt. 26:64.
72 Eccl. 7:14.
73 John 12:42.

Psalm 53

ARTICLE VI

EXPOSITION OF CHRIST OF THE FIFTY-THIRD PSALM:
DEUS, IN NOMINE TUO SALVUM ME FAC.
SAVE ME, O GOD, BY YOUR NAME.

THE ARDENT LOVER CANNOT BE SATISFIED hearing, speaking, and thinking about the one whom he loves: and so the ardent worshippers of Christ, who together with the Apostle account all things as dung, because of the excellent knowledge of Christ, and so that they might gain Christ,[1] feast especially on the exposition of the words of the Prophets and of the Law and of the Psalms that savor of Christ. For he is the end of the Law and the salvation of all men: and as also the teachers of the Jews acknowledged, all of the Prophets have spoken of nothing other than the day of the Messiah. Whence, according to Augustine, unless the books of the Prophets are understood in Christ, they are as water, and without flavor or fruit. But if we understood them in Christ, they are as wine, and they refresh and intoxicate.[2]

And so, although one may frequently see explained the title of this Psalm with reference to the history which pertains to David, it does not follow from this that Psalms such as this are to be expounded of David in a literal sense, although at times there is merit in applying such a literal interpretation. For by these kinds of titles we are given to understand that such was the occasion for holy David to write the Psalms with such titles. But because David was full of the prophetic spirit, and he recognized most excellently the mysteries of Christ, and

---

1 Cf. Phil. 3:8: *Furthermore, I count all things to be but loss for the excellent knowledge of Jesus Christ my Lord; for whom I have suffered the loss of all things, and count them but as dung, that I may gain Christ.*

2 E. N. The reference is St. Augustine's Tractate 9 on the Gospel of John, where he speaks about how Christ has removed the veil from the law and the prophets: "The veil is taken away when you have passed to the Lord, and that which was water will become wine for you. Read all the prophetic books without understanding Christ in them, what do you find but so much insipidity and silliness? Understand Christ to be in them, and not only will you taste what you read, but you will also be intoxicated, moving your mind from the body, forgetting the past, and reaching forth toward those things that are before you." *Super Ioann.*, IX, 3, PL 35, 1459.

he knew he himself to be a figure of Christ—indeed, because he knew that the whole point of the Old Testament was to be a figure of the essential feature of the New Testament or the Law of Christ and grace, knowing without doubt that all things were contained in it in figure[3] (otherwise, in what way was he the most excellent of the Prophets?[4]); therefore, it is to be most certainly believed that holy David turned the eyes of his heart, in accordance with the illumination provided to him by the Holy Spirit, always toward Christ and the state of existence of the Church. And whenever in the Psalms we see him recite something regarding himself, it was also his principal intention to speak of Christ and his mysteries and the Church, just like he himself intimated: David the son of Jesse said: *The man to whom it was appointed concerning the Christ of the God: The Spirit of the Lord has spoken by me.*[5]

Moreover, if David in the Psalms was so often speaking of himself, and not rather more of Christ and the Church, as some people who superficially expound upon this book of Psalms in large part expounding these Psalms literally of David idly think, then these sorts of Psalms do not pertain to the Prophetic writings, but to historical narrative. For it would then seem that David was not prophesying of the future, but was producing a history of the past: and so [in this view] David prophesied very little of Christ. Indeed, if we were to consider this accurately [assuming that the Psalms are historical narrative as some think], then we would find Isaiah much more copious in describing the mysteries of Christ and the Church than the prophet David, which is something that no one concedes. Even more, the prophetic grace pertains to graces freely given (*gratias gratis datas*): for it is a common good or evil. For graces freely given (*gratiae gratis datae*) are ordered to the profit of others,[6] according to that which the Apostle [Paul] said: *And the manifestation of the Spirit is given to every man unto profit.*[7] And so the Holy Spirit, who bestowed such a grace of prophetic knowledge upon David, gave it to him for this reason: so that he might show forth to the whole Church information of the Christ.

---

3   1 Cor. 10:11: *Now all these things happened to them in figure: and they are written for our correction, upon whom the ends of the world are come.*

4   *E. N. See* Article III in Volume 1, where Denis addresses why David ought to be considered the most excellent of the Prophets. His conclusion: "David, therefore, is called the most excellent of Prophets . . . to this extent: that he prophesied most excellently and clearly of the mysteries of Christ." *Beatus Vir*, p. 12.

5   2 Sam. 23:1, 2.

6   *E. N.* On the distinction between these (freely given) graces and sanctifying or habitual grace (*gratia gratum faciens*), *see* footnote 44-40 in Volume 2.

7   1 Cor. 12:7.

I say this, therefore, so that it may be known how worthless are those comments which treat so superficially and literally the words of the Prophets and the Psalms, and why we always attempt, to the degree it can be done, to explain those Psalms of Christ or of his Mystical Body, which is the Church.

And although from the tenor of the title of this Psalm it seems to be understood as a Psalm about David, yet we ought not take the title of this Psalm historically, but it is to be taken in its mysterious signification. Nevertheless, this Psalm can be expounded of David, as it can be understood morally of any individual member of the faithful, which is something that will be made manifest in the explanation which follows this one.

53{54}[1] *Unto the end, in verses, understanding for David.*

In finem, in carminibus, intellectus David.

53{54}[2] *When the men of Ziph had come and said to Saul: Is not David hidden with us?*

Cum venissent Ziphaei, et dixissent ad Saul: Nonne David absconditus est apud nos?

But now, expounding it with respect to Christ, this Psalm, has this title: **53{54}[1]** *In finem, in carminibus, intellectus David,* **53{54}[2]** *cum venissent Ziphaei, et nuntiasset Sauli: Nonne David absconditus est apud nos? Unto the end, in verses, understanding for David, when the men of Ziph had come and said to Saul: Is not David hidden with us?*[8] The title of this Psalm is obtained from the first book of Samuel. For we read in that place the manner in which David, with his family, fled from the face of Saul and hid himself among the Ziphites.[9] But the Ziphites, though they were of the tribe of Judah as was David, also wanted to please their king, and so they betrayed David to him. For they are called Ziphites from Ziph, a village that belonged to the tribe of Judah. But David, hearing that he had been betrayed by the Ziphites, wrote this Psalm, desiring to be freed from such great danger.[10] The Ziphites, which is interpreted as "flowering," refers to the Jews who are rejoicing in their temporal prosperity; and David represents Christ; and Saul [represents] Pilate. Therefore, the Ziphites, that is, the Jews, announced to Saul, that

---

8   E. N. There is a slight variance between Denis's verse (Ps. 53:2) and the Sixto-Clementine Vulgate; however, it is of no material significance.

9   E. N. The Ziphites were the successors of Ziph, a man of the tribe of Judah (1 Chr. 4:16). Ziph was also the name of a town in the Judaean hill country (Joshua 15:55).

10   1 Sam. 23:13–20; 26:1.

is, Pilate: "Is not David hidden with us?" That is, have we not come upon Jesus seducing the people, and do we not already have him bound?[11] And so this title is [to be understood] in this sense: *Understanding for David*, that is, the meaning of this Psalm relates to Christ, *unto the end*, for the purpose of directing us to eternal life, *in verses*, that is, so that we always give thanks to the Lord both in adversity and prosperity: *understanding*, I say, written and addressed to those, *when the men of Ziph*, that is, the unbelieving Jews, *had come and said to Saul*, that is, Pilate: *Is not David hidden with us?* That is, is not this Jesus whom we have seized and bound and brought to you?

53{54}[3] *Save me, O God, by your name, and judge me in your strength.*

Deus, in nomine tuo salvum me fac, et in virtute tua iudica me.

53{54}[4] *O God, hear my prayer: give ear to the words of my mouth.*

Deus, exaudi orationem meam; auribus percipe verba oris mei.

The Prophet [David], therefore, speaking in the person of Christ, or Christ as man and in a certain sense a wayfarer (*viator*), and with the Passion already close-by, said to God the Father or to all the supermost-glorious Trinity: **53{54}[3]** *Deus, in nomine tuo salvum me fac; save me, O God, by your name*: that is, in you alone, above all things, and the true Savior, and to the glory of your name, raise me again from death, and in this Passion preserve and strengthen me against the natural horror and fear of imminent death. Whence we have in Luke: *There appeared to him an angel from heaven, strengthening him.*[12] *Et in virtute tua iudica me, and judge me in your strength*: that is, according to your justice restore to me, your beloved Son, separating and delivering me from this evil generation who do not believe in me and have persecuted me cruelly. For Christ implicitly asks for this when he says: *O incredulous generation, how long shall I be with you? How long shall I suffer you?*[13] **53{54}[4]** *Deus, exaudi orationem meam; O God, hear my prayer*, which I pray for my Mystical Body, namely for the Church of the elect, so that they might participate in the fruit of my Passion. For this Christ prayed for saying: *I pray not for the world, but for them whom you have given me.*[14] And again: *Holy Father, keep them in your name whom you have given me; that they may be*

----

11   Luke 23:1–2.
12   Luke 22:43a.
13   Mark 9:18.
14   John 17:9.

one, as we also are.[15] *Auribus percipe verba oris mei; give ear to the words of my mouth.* The ears of God, as all recognize, is the Wisdom of God, and the mercy which comes to the aid of those who pray. And so, O Lord Father, with your ears listen to the words of my mouth, which for myself I pray, namely for my bodily glorification and ascension: *Glorify me, O Father, with yourself, with the glory which I had, before the world was, with you.*[16] And elsewhere Christ prays: *O Lord, you know, remember me, and visit me, and defend me from them that persecute me.*[17]

53{54}[5]   *For strangers have risen up against me; and the mighty have sought after my soul: and they have not set God before their eyes.*

Quoniam alieni insurrexerunt adversum me, et fortes quae-sierunt animam meam, et non proposuerunt Deum ante conspectum suum.

53{54}[5] *Quoniam alieni insurrexerunt adversum me, for strangers have risen up against me:* that is, the unfaithful Jews were strangers to me — not in terms of race in accordance with the flesh, but by imitation of life; they were not [strangers] by nature, but, as a result of the lack of grace, have persecuted me: as John said, *Then the band and the tribune, and the servants of the Jews, took Jesus, and bound him.*[18] And so by strangers we can also understand the Gentiles who destroyed the Jews that had seized Jesus. *Et fortes quaesierunt animam meam, and the mighty have sought after my soul:* that is, the princes of the priests sought after my soul, that is, to extinguish my bodily life: as Wisdom asserts in their person: *Let us condemn him to a most shameful death.*[19] *Et non proposuerunt Deum ante conspectum suum, and they have not set God before their eyes:* that is, in committing such sins they did not fear God, but rather men, for they said: Lest perchance *the Romans will come, and take away our place and nation.*[20] For [so] also Pilate [did], since the Jews said to him, If you release this man, you are not Caesar's friend,[21] and he immediately *gave sentence that it should be as they required.*[22]

---

15   John 17:11b.
16   John 17:5.
17   Jer. 15:15a.
18   John 18:12.
19   Wis. 2:20a. *E. N.* Here, the Book of Wisdom is speaking in the person of the wicked, in other words, stating how the wicked think.
20   John 11:48b.
21   John 19:12b.
22   Luke 23:24.

53{54}[6] *For behold God is my helper: and the Lord is the protector of my soul.*

Ecce enim Deus adiuvat me, et Dominus susceptor est animae meae.

Consequently, Christ declared himself so that he would be heard, and they would be able to accomplish nothing. **53{54}[6]** *Ecce enim Deus adiuvat me, for behold God is my helper*: for the divinity of Christ in all things cooperated with his assumed humanity, and in all things it strengthened him and protected him, as that stated in Jeremiah: *But the Lord is with me as a strong warrior: therefore they that persecute me shall fall, and shall be weak.*[23] And the Savior said: *I am not alone, but I and the Father that sent me.*[24] *Et Dominus, and the Lord*, that is, God the Trinity, *susceptor est animae meae, is the protector of my soul*, that is, is the hearer of these prayers; or [alternatively], *the Lord is the protector of my soul*, that is, the Word or the Son of God is true God, and he has assumed my soul unto his divine personality, and he will not abandon it during the three days of death. For although during the time of the death and the sepulture of Christ the soul was separate from the body, both [body and soul] remained united with the Word. And this is what God says about Christ the man through the prophet Isaiah: *Behold my servant, I will uphold him: my elect, my soul delights in him.*[25]

53{54}[7] *Turn back the evils upon my enemies; and cut them off in your truth.*

Averte mala inimicis meis; et in veritate tua disperde illos.

53{54}[7] *Averte mala inimicis meis, turn back the evils upon my enemies*: that is, the evil and the punishments prepared for me by the Jews, and throw it back upon their heads; and deliver me, so that the snares which they have prepared for me shall cause their end: as is written in Ecclesiastes: *He that digs a pit, shall fall into it: and he that breaks a hedge, a serpent shall bite him.*[26] And again Solomon says: *The unjust shall be caught in their own snares.*[27] For every single wicked act returns back unto the actor himself; and the doer of evil

---

23   Jer. 20:11a.
24   John 8:16b.
25   Is. 42:1a.
26   Eccl. 10:8.
27   Prov. 11:6b.

is harmed more than is the one who suffers it. And this was fulfilled in the Jews because they sought to kill Christ and to entirely wipe out his name; but they achieved the opposite, because Christ rose again from the dead, and they, through the vengeance of the blood of Christ, were put to death and were dispersed. And therefore there is added: *Et in veritate tua, and ... in your truth*, that is, according to that which you said by the Prophets, *disperde illos, cut them off*, that is, ruin them with various plagues, namely, by the sword, hunger, and pestilence: in the manner that occurred during the time of Titus. Or [alternatively], *In your truth*, that is, in your justice, *cut them off*, that is, expel them from the land of promise and spread them and divide them throughout all the world, as it was predicted by Hosea: *My God will cast them away, because they hearkened not to him: and they shall be wanderers among the nations.*[28] This prophecy, as expressed by Hosea, is also to be fulfilled by the Jews: *Their own devices*, he says, *now have beset them about.*[29] One ought to be mindful that Christ here prays either conforming himself to the divine justice, or foretelling that which will be in the future, or making known that which they deserve, but not absolutely calling down evil upon his adversaries, especially since he has commanded us, *Love your enemies, ... and pray for them that persecute and calumniate you.*[30]

53{54}[8]   *I will freely sacrifice to you, and will confess your name, O Lord, to your name: because it is good.*[31]

Voluntarie sacrificabo tibi, et confitebor nomini tuo, Domine, quoniam bonum est.

53{54}[9]   *For you have delivered me out of all trouble: and my eye has looked down upon my enemies.*

Quoniam ex omni tribulatione eripuisti me, et super inimicos meos despexit oculus meus.

---

28   Hosea 9:17.
29   Hosea 7:2b.
30   Matt. 5:44. *E. N.* The maledictory verses are not to be understood in an optative sense, as is discussed in various places by Denis. *See, e.g.,* Article LVI (Psalm 24:4) and note 24-14 in Volume I.
31   *E. N.* I have translated the verb *confitebor* (which can be confession or sin or confession of praise) with the generic term "will confess," rather that the Douay Rheims' "will praise," since Denis makes clear in his *Commentary* that the confession in this Psalm is one of praise.

53{54}[8] *Voluntarie sacrificabo tibi, I will freely sacrifice to you*: that is, willingly and with the most ardent charity of God and neighbor I will offer myself in the altar of the Cross to you, Almighty God, for the salvation of the world, in the manner that is said about me in Isaiah: *He was offered because it was his own will; and he has borne the sins of many.*[32] Whence in the Gospel the Savior says: *I am the good shepherd . . . I lay down my life for my sheep;*[33] and again, *No man takes my life away from me: but I lay it down of myself.*[34] For this reason, the Apostle [Paul] says: *I live in the faith of the Son of God, who loved me, and delivered himself for me.*[35] And in this manner Christ sacrificed, that is, he gave himself in a salvific sacrifice out of a most fervent charity, both of God and neighbor, namely, so that he might restore the honor of God, and bring about the salvation of men, in the manner that is attested by the Apostle [Paul]: *The blood of Christ, who by the Holy Spirit offered himself unspotted unto God, will cleanse our conscience from dead works, to serve the living God.*[36]

Et confitebor nomini tuo, Domine; and I will confess your name, with the confession of praise, *quoniam bonum est, because it is good*, for he is by nature and in every possible manner good, and he is pure goodness, perfect and infinite. For which reason it is written: *None is good but God alone.*[37] And so you, O Lord God, you are to be praised for yourself, and you are eminently worthy of all praise. For Christ confessed the confession of praise to God the Father throughout all his life, and in the Passion, up to the time that he said, *In your hands I commend my spirit;*[38] and after death, when he said, *I ascend to my Father.*[39] For this reason he says, *I honor my Father;*[40] and *I do not seek my own glory;*[41] and *I do always the things that please him* (that is, the Father).[42] And so, O Lord, I will confess your name, **53{54}[9]** *Quoniam ex omni tribulatione eripuisti me, for you have delivered me out of all trouble* in the day of the Resurrection, when you raised me up unto an impassible life: as the Apostle [Paul] stated: *Christ rising again from the dead, dies now no more.*[43]

---

32 Is. 53:7a, 12b.
33 John 10:14a, 15b.
34 John 10:18a.
35 Gal. 2:20b.
36 Heb. 9:14.
37 Luke 18:19b.
38 Luke 23:46a.
39 John 20:17b.
40 John 8:49b.
41 John 8:50a.
42 John 8:29b.
43 Rom. 6:9a.

Two, therefore, are the reasons for praising God. The first is his goodness, for which reason it says, *I will confess your name ... because it is
good.* The second reason is the handing out of his benefits, for which it
says, *For you have delivered me out of all trouble.* But it is greater and of
more dignity, and of more merit, to praise, to honor, and to love God
because of his goodness than because of his benefits, for [the former]
arises from a more pure and more perfect divine charity. Now, we who
follow the path of Christ ought to praise and to love the Lord our God
because of both reasons: for this is the most perfect. Finally, that which
is said — *For you have delivered me out of all trouble* — can refer to that
which says, *because he is good;* but then this conjunction — *because* — does
not denote a cause, but a sign. For God is not good because he delivers
us; but he delivers us because he is good: and so the delivery by which
he delivers us is a sign of his divine goodness, and not its cause; or, if it
is said to be a cause, it is not a cause strictly so called (*simpliciter*) and
a prior cause (*a priori*), but with respect to us (*quoad nos*) and after the
fact (*a posteriori*), for by it the goodness of God is known by us, for he
most mercifully delivers us.

Et super inimicos meos, and upon my enemies persecuting me, *despexit
oculus meus, my eye has looked down:* that is, I have not feared them,
nor have I regarded their false happiness and malice for something else
[other than what it was], but in all things I have remained constant
and victorious.

ARTICLE VII

EXPLANATION OF THE SAME FIFTY-THIRD PSALM
MORAL AND AT THE SAME TIME LITERAL.

NOW MORALLY [EXPOUNDED], BY ZIPHITES,[44]
which (as has been shown) is to be interpreted as "flowering," are
understood the lovers of worldly things, things that are temporarily
in bloom: among whom David was hidden, that is, among those that
are faithful, living and lying concealed, despising temporal things, and
steadfastly enduring the persecution of worldly men. Also, by Saul is
understood the pestiferous princes and evil prelates, who accuse, display,
and abuse the just along with worldly and ungodly men.

---

44   1 Sam. 23:19.

53{54}[3] *Save me, O God, by your name, and judge me in your strength.*

Deus, in nomine tuo salvum me fac, et in virtute tua iudica me.

Whoever among the faithful, therefore, experiencing and suffering persecutions and various temptations, and finding himself unable by natural virtue to be able to resist, bear with, or prevail over them, but needing the help of the divine mercy, with the inmost part of his being[45] ought to flee to God, crying out and saying: **53{54}[3]** *Deus, in nomine tuo;* O God, by your name uncreated, in you alone, and not any other mere creature, *salvum me fac, save me,* taking away my fault and filling me with grace: *save me* from all past, present, and future evil; *save me* from the evil of punishment, from the evil of fault, from natural evil; *save me* from all enemies, visible and invisible, from all temptations, and all dangers. And so, O Lord, *save me* in the present by faith and grace and unceasing progress [in virtue], and in the future by the blessed enjoyment of your goodness. And this do, *by your name,* so that you are the efficient and final cause of my salvation. *For there is no other name under heaven given to men, whereby we must be saved,*[46] except for your name, as the prince of the Apostles testified; and as you yourself have spoken through Isaiah, *A just God and a Savior, there is none besides me.*[47] And I do not doubt, O Lord my God, that you will hear my prayers, provided I might pray perseveringly, because I believe that which is written to be true: *Everyone that shall call upon the name of the Lord shall be saved.*[48]

Et in virtute tua, and in your strength [which is] almighty, to which nothing is difficult, *iudica me, judge me.* Since the Apostle [Paul] says, *It is a fearful thing to fall into the hands of the living God,*[49] especially since man may not know *whether he be worthy of love or hatred,*[50] and it says in a later Psalm, *Enter not into judgment with your servant,*[51] O Lord; to which applies that which holy Job says of God, *I would not that he should contend with me:*[52] since, I say, things are so, does it not appear presumptuous and dangerous to dare to say this to God, *And in your strength judge me?*

---

45   L. *totis medullis,* literally with all the marrow of his being, that is, even unto the inside of one's bones. The expression comes from the Roman poet Ovid (43 BC — 17/18 AD). See *Metamorpheses* 9, 484 and 14, 351.

46   Acts 4:12b.

47   Is. 45:21b.

48   Joel 2:32a.

49   Heb. 10:31.

50   Eccl. 9:1b.

51   Ps. 142:2a.

52   Job 23:6a.

One ought to recognize that the judgment of God can be asserted in two ways: namely of discretion, which occurs in the present life; where the good from the evil, and the elect from the reprobate are severed and divided by grace, desire, and merit—not by place and reward. Of this judgment the Savior said: *Now is the judgment of the world.*[53] For although this judgment began from the beginning of the world, still with the coming and the preaching of Christ and the Apostles it especially began, for from that time the grace of God was poured out more copiously, and the faithful and the good were more abundantly and more evidently able to be separated from the unfaithful and the perverse. We ought, therefore, to wish this judgment, namely, that God in this world separates us from the flock of evil men, and counts us among the elect. Whence of this judgment it was said to blessed Job [by Elihu]: *Can he be healed that loves not judgment?*[54] On the other hand, entirely different is the judgment of God of strict examination and of just recompense: which indeed all of us ought to fear, and to pray that we may not be brought to it unprepared, or that we might not be judged by it based upon our evildoings, negligences, and imperfections, but rather that we might obtain mercy in this life, and we might receive the grace of satisfaction.[55] Whence, of the rigorous horror of this judgment, the blessed Job says: *I, who although I should have any just thing, would not answer, but would make supplication to my judge;*[56] and elsewhere: *And if I be wicked, woe unto me: and if just, I shall not lift up my head.*[57] And this ought to be held in the memory, for it recurs frequently in what follows.[58]

---

53 John 12:31a.

54 Job 34:17a.

55 E. N. The "grace of satisfaction" (*gratia satisfactionis*) is a synonym for sanctifying grace. As St. John Cassian discusses it: "Whoever, therefore, desires to obtain forgiveness of his crimes, should study and apply himself for it by these means, that the stubbornness of an obdurate heart not avert him from the saving remedy, the fount of so much goodness; for even if we may have achieved all these things, they will not be sufficient for the expiation of our faults, unless the goodness of the Lord effaces them at root, who when he sees the religious service offered by us with a suppliant soul, our small and inconsiderable efforts are accompanied by immense liberality, saying: 'I am, I am he that blots out your iniquities for my own sake, and I will not remember your sins.' Isaiah 43:25 To him, therefore, who desires to embark upon this state that we have mentioned, will seek the grace of satisfaction (*satisfactionis gratiam*) by daily fasting and mortification of heart and body." *Collationes*, 20, 8, PL 49, 1164.

56 Job 9:15.

57 Job 10:15.

58 E. N. For additional explication on the difference between the judgment of discretion or discernment and the final judgment, *see* also Article XXVIII (Psalm 9:1) in Volume 1 and footnote 1-39.

And so, O Lord, *judge me in your strength*, distinguishing me and separating me from the evil flock of which you say in the Gospel, *Many are called*; also placing me in that very small flock, of which you say thereafter, *But few are chosen*:[59] of which you also say, *Fear not, little flock, for it has pleased your Father to give you a kingdom.*[60]

53{54}[4] *O God, hear my prayer: give ear to the words of my mouth.*

Deus, exaudi orationem meam; auribus percipe verba oris mei.

53{54}[4] *Deus exaudi orationem meam*, O God hear my prayer already poured out; *auribus percipe verba oris mei*, give ear to the words of my mouth, that is, show yourself to listen to my prayers by a most kind hearkening. Especially in what pertains to the affections, it is the manner of sacred Scripture to repeat abundantly the same thought under other words, and so to make known the great desire of the heart, and more favorably to provoke the mercy of the Creator, so that the longing in one's self might be ignited and set aflame. For the more frequently words are brought forth, and that desire is more often repeated, the more the heart is amply inflamed, and the more ardently strengthened in the habit of charity.

53{54}[5] *For strangers have risen up against me; and the mighty have sought after my soul: and they have not set God before their eyes.*

Quoniam alieni insurrexerunt adversum me, et fortes quaesierunt animam meam, et non proposuerunt Deum ante conspectum suum.

53{54}[5] *Quoniam alieni*, for strangers from fraternal charity and from the fear and the justice of God, *insurrexerunt adversum me*, have risen up against me, resisting, detracting, or by similar means opposing me and my spiritual progress, tempting, injuring, and molesting me. For *all that will live godly in Christ Jesus, shall suffer persecution.*[61] *Et fortes, and the mighty* invisible or visible enemies, namely the demons and the secular princes, *quaesierunt animam meam*, have sought after my soul to make it depart from God, to draw it to fault, and to kill it spiritually, depriving it of charity and of grace, which is the life of the soul; or [we can understand it thus], *They have sought after my soul*, that is, to afflict

---

59 Matt. 22:14.
60 Luke 12:32.
61 2 Tim. 3:12.

or to extinguish my bodily life. This David could say literally regarding the Ziphites, and Saul, and their partisans. *Et non proposuerunt Deum ante conspectum suum, and they have not set God before their eyes,* considering the great evil they were doing, how they were gravely offending God, and how much punishment in the future they were acquiring for themselves, and so of such persons it is written: *You have stored up to yourselves wrath against the last days.*[62] He does not place God before the eyes of his heart, and neither does he believe in, nor does he pay heed to, divine providence; and he does not fear the judgment of God, and has no terror of punishment; or by the love of reward he does not turn away from sin, but without fear he transgresses against the law of the Most-High, and lives without reverence his entire life before the sight of the eternal perceiving Judge. Of such men it is written: *Distress shall surround him, as a king that is prepared for the battle. For he has stretched out his hand against God . . . and with his neck raised up . . . he has run against him.*[63]

53{54}[6] *For behold God is my helper: and the Lord is the protector of my soul.*

Ecce enim Deus adiuvat me, et Dominus susceptor est animae meae.

Now although so many adversities besiege the just man, he ought not for all that despair, because he has a helper who is insuperable. And so there follows: **53{54}[6]** *Ecce enim Deus adiuvat me, for behold God is my helper* strengthening me by grace and safeguarding me by angelic protection. Whence the Apostle [Paul] speaking of God: *He has said, I will not leave you, neither will I forsake you: so we may confidently say: The Lord is my helper, I will not fear what man shall do to me.*[64] And in another place: *He will make also with temptation issue, that you may be able to bear it.*[65] Therefore, we ought not to fear inordinately. *For, if God be for us, who can be against us?*[66] See how full of trust and love are these words, *God is my helper.* We should therefore be thankful and obedient to such a helper, and not unworthily be ungrateful in return for his help. For this reason Samuel said: *Prepare your hearts unto the Lord, and serve*

---

62   James 5:3b.
63   Job 15:24–26a.
64   Heb. 13:5b, 6; Ps. 117:6.
65   1 Cor. 10:13b.
66   Rom. 8:31b.

him only, and he will deliver you out of the hand of your enemies.[67] And
elsewhere: *Depart not from following the Lord,* he says, *but serve the Lord
with all your heart, and turn not aside after vain things which shall never
profit you, . . . for they are vain.*[68] *Et Dominus susceptor est animae meae,
and the Lord is the protector of my soul,* mercifully embracing it with
his arms of kindliness, speedily indulgent, preserving of goodness, and
providing always for all that which is necessary for salvation.

53{54}[7]   *Turn back the evils upon my enemies; and cut them off in
your truth.*

Averte mala inimicis meis; et in veritate tua disperde illos.

53{54}[7] *Averte mala inimicis meis,* turn back the evils upon my enemies, that is, remove from me the harmful things prepared by them for
me, and return them back upon them. It appears that this is contrary to
that warning given by the Apostle, who said, *Be not overcome by evil, but
overcome evil by good;*[69] and again, *To no man rendering evil for evil.*[70] But
from these words the solution is clear. For the just man does not say this
in an absolute sense, calling down some sort of evil upon his adversaries,
but [he says this] conforming himself to the divine justice and setting
forth what the ungodly may merit. For the ungodly man deserves that the
evil that he intends for another will be turned back upon him and harm
him, in the way that Solomon has confessed: *His own iniquities catch the
wicked, and he is fast bound with the ropes of his own sins.*[71] In just this
sense it is written in Genesis: *Whosoever shall shed man's blood, his blood*

---

67   1 Sam. 7:3b. *E. N.* Denis replaces "out of the hand of the Philistines," with "out
of the hand of your enemies."

68   1 Sam. 12:20b–21.

69   Rom. 12:21.

70   Rom. 12:17a.

71   Prov. 5:22. *E. N.* This brings to mind the Dantean notion of *contrapasso* (See
Inferno XXVIII, 142), where the punishment in hell is tied to the injury associated
with the sin. The notion of the *contrapassus* is biblical, *e.g.,* Matt. 7:2: "For with what
judgment you judge, you shall be judged: and with what measure you mete, it shall
be measured to you again." The term *contrapassus* is, however, the Latin translation
of the Greek τὸ ἀντιπεπονθός (*to antipeponthos*), the word used by Aristotle in his
Nicomachean Ethics roughly meaning reciprocity. *Nic. Eth.*, 5.5.1132b. It is the term
used by St. Thomas in his *Summa Theologiae*: "Retaliation (*contrapassum*) suggests
the equal recompense of passion to the preceding actions. That is, it is most properly
said in injurious passions where one injures the person of his neighbor; for example,
if he strike, that he be struck back. This kind of justice is laid down in the law (Ex.
21:23-24) *He shall render life for life, eye for eye,* and so forth." ST IIaIIae, q. 61, art.
4, co. It is an application of the Mosaic *lex talionis.*

shall be shed.[72] How many, whose blood was not shed, have poured out blood, but rested in peace—as Moses, who killed an Egyptian, and he said this very thing![73] What therefore does it mean, *whosoever shall shed man's blood, his blood shall be shed* other than that the malice of homicide first kills one spiritually as it does the other bodily. Also, that which the Savior said has a similar meaning: *All that take the sword shall perish with the sword.*[74] *In veritate tua disperde illos, and cut them off in your truth*, that is, destroy my enemies in your justice and just judgment and in accordance with your faithful promise, fighting them for me: destroy them (I say), impeding their malice from having its vicious effect, that they may not prevail over me. Not, however, that I desire that they be damned, but that in the present age they may repent. Yet the invisible enemies I desire to be entirely suppressed, as the Apostle [Paul] gave hope to: *And the God of peace crush Satan under your feet speedily.*[75]

53{54}[8] *I will freely sacrifice to you, and will confess your name, O Lord, to your name: because it is good.*[76]

Voluntarie sacrificabo tibi, et confitebor nomini tuo, Domine, quoniam bonum est.

53{54}[9] *For you have delivered me out of all trouble: and my eye has looked down upon my enemies.*

Quoniam ex omni tribulatione eripuisti me, et super inimicos meos despexit oculus meus.

53{54}[8] *Voluntarie, I will freely*, that is, of my own accord, and because of you yourself alone, and the glory of your name, and not in view of any temporal advantage, *sacrificabo tibi, sacrifice to you* a sacrifice of praise, a sacrificial victim of a virtuous manner of life, the Sacrament of the Altar, indeed my very self and all that I am, am able to be, and am able to do: for I owe this to you, as I have been chosen by you for it. For since all that my being is, is able to be, and is able to do has been bestowed upon me by you, I need to expend them in your honor and worship, and I am

---

72 Gen. 9:6a.

73 Ex. 2:12; Deut. 34:7. E. N. Denis views Moses the author of Genesis, and so observes that Moses—who said that one who sheds the blood of a man shall have his blood shed—himself killed an Egyptian and did not suffer the penalty of death. Denis sets out to explain this apparent antilogy.

74 Matt. 26:52b.

75 Rom. 16:20b.

76 E. N. *See* footnote 53-31.

obliged to give myself entirely over to the divine service, to the extent that all my substance, power, and life may venerate and bespeak of you, holy and blessed Creator. Of this sacrifice or victim the divine Apostle [Paul] also speaks: By Christ *let us offer the sacrifice of praise always to God.*[77] And of this sacrifice of a holy manner of life he adds: *And do not forget to do good, and to impart; for by such sacrifices God's favor is obtained.*[78] Of which sacrifice we also have this in Ecclesiasticus: *It is a wholesome sacrifice to take heed to the commandments, and to depart from all iniquity.*[79] And of this sacrifice wherein man offers himself, the writer of the Psalms says in an earlier Psalm: *A sacrifice to God is an afflicted spirit.*[80] Finally, of the Sacrifice of the Altar the Lord says in the Gospel: *Do this for a commemoration of me;*[81] and in Malachi also, *In every place there is sacrifice, and there is offered to my name a clean oblation.*[82]

Et confitebor nomini tuo, Domine; and I will confess your name, O Lord, my evil and your good, accusing myself and praising you, spurning myself and exalting you. **53{54}[9]** *Quoniam ex omni tribulatione, for... out of all trouble,* from which I have hitherto been freed, *you have delivered me* in reality, and also from the future tribulations you have already delivered me by hope. Not because I have prevailed from my own strength, but all my victory is from you: and so *super inimicos meos despexit oculus meus, my eye has looked down upon my enemies,* because of the great faith which I have placed in you, and because I have experienced so many times your grace. Here, therefore, I little regard the ungodly, and you alone do I fear, in the manner that the first book of Maccabees instructs: *And fear not the words of a sinful man, for his glory is dung, and worms. Today he is lifted up, and tomorrow he shall not be found.*[83]

See how this short Psalm includes such a remarkable flame of holy devotion. Let us learn from it, therefore, to offer ardent prayers to God, in all persecution and temptations to confidently turn to him, and to lovingly pray to him, and to speak affectionately and faithfully of him, and also most promptly to sacrifice ourselves to him, to give him thanks in all things, to praise him, and to recall to our minds his welcome benefits.

---

77   Heb. 13:15.
78   Heb. 13:16.
79   Ecclus. 35:2.
80   Ps. 50:19a.
81   Luke 22:19b.
82   Mal. 1:11b.
83   1 Macc. 2:62–63a.

PRAYER

OD, THE ONLY SALVATION OF THOSE
who hope in you, save us in your name, and powerfully help
us against the strong who are seeking our souls: so that delivered
from all tribulation by you, we might securely treat with disdain
all enemies.

Deus, in te sperantium salus summa, in nomine tuo nos salva,
et contra fortes quaerentes animas nostras nos potenter
adiuva: ut ex omni tribulatione erepti per te,
cunctos inimicos despiciamus securi.

Psalm 54

ARTICLE VIII

EXPOSITION OF CHRIST OF THE FIFTY-FOURTH PSALM:
EXAUDI, DEUS, ORATIONEM MEAM, ET NE, ETC.
HEAR, O GOD, MY PRAYER, ETC.

HE SAME REASON (IF I DO NOT ERR) WHICH established above that the fortieth Psalm—namely, [that Psalm that begins] *Blessed is he that understands*—could be literally explained to be of Christ,[1] is now also able to show that this Psalm ought to be explained as literally dealing with Christ. For there [in our commentary of Psalm 40] it was shown that that Psalm spoke of Christ, for the Savior asserted that the words written in the Psalm foretold of him: *But that the scripture may be fulfilled: He that eats bread with me, shall lift up his heel against me.*[2] For this fortieth Psalm says these words: *For even the man of peace, in whom I trusted, who ate my bread, has greatly supplanted me.*[3] Since therefore this [verse in Psalm 40] is what the Savior asserted foretold of him, to the degree that we have this same sense in this Psalm, the same can be said about it; thus we see this Psalm explaining of Christ, as also the former [Psalm 40], especially since in neither Psalm do we have the words of Christ other than in their sense;[4] and if we diligently think about this, we find the sense of the words of Christ in this Psalm more extensively pointed out [as relating to Christ] than the fortieth Psalm. For in this later [fifty-fourth] Psalm it says: *Quoniam si inimicus meus maledixisset mihi, sustinuissem utique, etc.; for if my enemy had reviled me, I would verily have borne with it, etc. Tu vero homo unanimis, dux meus, et notus meus, qui simul mecum dulces capiebas cibos; but you a man of one mind, my guide, and my familiar, who did take sweetmeats together with me.*[5] And so St. Gregory openly asserts that Christ referred to these words as applying to the traitor Judas.[6] Jerome and Cassiodorus also

---

1   Ps. 40:1

2   John 13:18.

3   Ps. 40:10.

4   *E. N.* In other words, neither Palm 40:10 nor Psalm 54:15 state the words of Christ *in haec verba*, in the exact words, but both share the sense or the meaning of what Christ said in the Gospel.

5   Ps. 45:13–15a.

6   *E. N.* Reference to Pope St. Gregory the Great and his sixth homily on Ezechiel. *Hom. in Ezech.*, II, VI, 42, PL 76, 1004.

expound this Psalm as being about Christ. They do not however negate that it also can be morally expounded with David as any just man disquieted by an adversary, and the Church (according to the manner that is expounded in the exposition after this one): for this exposition Augustine and Hugh [of St. Victor] amply develop. Therefore, I avoid the sterile expositions of those who explain this Psalm as pertaining literally of David.

After his resurrection, Christ appearing to his disciples said, *It is necessary that all things be fulfilled which are written in the law of Moses, and in the Prophets, and in the Psalms, concerning me.*[7] After Christ mentioned the law of Moses and the Prophets, why was it necessary to mention especially the Psalms, as if the author of the Psalms did not number among the Prophets? There is no other reason than because the Psalms especially — that is, more fully and more evidently than in the writings of the other Prophets — prophesy of Christ. And so, to the extent one is able, one ought always to take care that we understand the Psalms as being about Christ.

54{55}[1] *Unto the end, in verses, understanding for David.*

In finem, in carminibus. Intellectus David.

Now the title of this present Psalm is this: **54{55}[1]** *In finem, in carminibus, intellectus David; unto the end, in verses, understanding for David.* By David, the holy Prophets frequently understand Christ. Whence with Jeremiah we find written: *Strangers shall no more rule over Jacob, but they shall serve the Lord their God, and David their king, whom I will raise up to them,*[8] that is, Christ, as all interpret this [verse]. And so the title of this Psalm has this sense: *understanding for David,* that is, the sense of this Psalm relates to Christ: an *understanding,* I say, directing us *unto the end,* that is, unto God or eternal life; *in verse,* so that we return thanks to God always, whether in adversity or in prosperity, as also Christ did and taught.

54{55}[2] *Hear, O God, my prayer, and despise not my supplication.*

Exaudi, Deus, orationem meam, et ne despexeris deprecationem meam.

54{55}[3] *Be attentive to me and hear me. I am grieved in my exercise; and am troubled...*

Intende mihi, et exaudi me. Contristatus sum in exercitatione mea; et conturbatus sum...

---

7 Luke 24:44.
8 Jer. 30:8–9.

54{55}[4] *at the voice of the enemy, and at the tribulation of the sinner. For they have cast iniquities upon me: and in wrath they were troublesome to me.*

a voce inimici, et a tribulatione peccatoris. Quoniam declinaverunt in me iniquitates, et in ira molesti erant mihi.

Therefore, our Lord Jesus Christ who, as passible man and a wayfarer, *passed the whole night in the prayer of God* (as Luke said), and before the Passion said this: **54{55}[2]** *Exaudi, Deus; Hear, O God* my Father, or Trinity, one God, *orationem meam, my prayer,* which I pray for the accidental reward due to my manner of living, my humiliation, and my Passion. For Christ through his humiliation and death merited for himself an accidental, but not essential, reward, namely the judicial power, a quick resurrection, the glorification of the body, and the ascension. For this reason he himself, speaking to God the Father, said this regarding himself: *He has given him power to do judgment, because he is the Son of man.*[9] And the Apostle [Paul]: *He humbled himself, becoming obedient unto death, even to the death of the cross: for which cause God also has exalted him, and has given him a name which is above all names.*[10] This also is foretold of Christ in Isaiah: *Because his soul has labored, he shall see and be filled:*[11] not indeed with the joy of essential reward, for this Christ did not merit;[12] but [with the joy] of accidental [reward], which Christ has a part of, at least extensively, or to the degree manifested from the salvation for the elect.[13] Whence Christ is also promised as a reward the rulership over the militant Church, or the multiplication of the faithful, according to Isaiah.[14] *If he shall lay down his life for sin, he shall see a long-lived seed,*

---

9   John 5:27.

10   Phil. 2:8–9.

11   Is. 53:11a.

12   *E. N.* As Denis has said many times throughout this *Commentary,* Christ, as man, from the first moment of his existence had the beatific vision without foreseen merit (it was impossible to merit for oneself something humanly when one humanly does not exist). Since Jesus in his humanity enjoyed the beatific vision of God (which is the essential reward of the elect) while in a wayfaring state on earth, Jesus already had the eternal reward other humans hope for. Thus, Jesus did not merit *for himself* the essential reward for two reasons: first, he could not merit it because of when he received it, and secondly, because he had it from the very beginning of his existence. However, Jesus could and did merit — infinitely — *for others.*

13   Christ had grace intensively (internally as to himself) and extensively (as to the effect on others). While Christ's grace *intensive* could not increase, his grace *extensive* could (e.g., by more persons converting to the faith), which could cause him an accidental reward of the joy of the salvation of the elect.

14   *E. N.* Christ's reward here pertains to the increase of his Body, the Church, as

and the will of the Lord shall be prosperous in his hand.[15] And again, the
Lord says of Christ: *By his knowledge shall this my just servant justify many,
and he shall bear their iniquities; therefore will I distribute to him very many,
and he shall divide the spoils;*[16] that is, many of those converted to the
faith, and the spoils of the devil, that is, the souls which are under the
thrall of the devil through original or actual sin, will be delivered — not
all, but those of the elect — in the manner that is said by Hosea: *O death,
I will be your death; O hell, I will be your bite.*[17]

Et ne despexeris deprecationem meam, and despise not my supplication,
which I undertook for those for whom I became incarnate and suffered.
Whence Christ said to Peter in the person of the Church: *I have prayed
for you, that your faith fail not.*[18] **54{55}[3]** *Intende mihi, be attentive to me:*
that is, look upon me so as to fulfil the prayer which I have prayed for my
deliverance from death, or resurrection, saying: *Father, save me from this
hour. But for this cause I came unto this hour.*[19] *Et exaudi me, and hear* me
praying, and give honor to your name by glorifying it, so that all may know
you and worship you. For Christ prayed for this: *Father, glorify your name.*[20]

Contristatus sum in exercitatione, I am grieved in my exercise: that is, in
preaching and doing miracles, I suffered the blindness and the ingratitude
of the Jews, in the manner that is written, *for the blindness of their hearts
Jesus was grieved.*[21] Yet this sadness was not inordinate, but flowed out of
true charity, for it felt distress for the evil and the perverse. Hence, Solomon also asserted: *Whatsoever shall befall the just man. it shall not make
him sad.*[22] In addition this was foretold about Christ: *He shall not be sad,
nor troublesome,*[23] understanding this to refer to a worldly or inordinate
sorrow, which (as the Apostle attests) *works death;*[24] and of which is read
in Ecclesiasticus: *Drive away sadness far from you; for sadness has killed many,
and there is no profit in it.*[25] Also the Passion being at hand, Jesus began to

---

the Church — the *totus Christus*, the whole Christ — increases throughout history
with the addition of the elect and the increase of the Gospel until the end of time.

15   Is. 53:10b.
16   Is. 53:11b–12a.
17   Hosea 13:14b.
18   Luke 22:32a.
19   John 12:27b.
20   John 12:28a.
21   Mark 3:5a.
22   Prov. 12:21a.
23   Is. 42:4a.
24   2 Cor. 7:10: *For the sorrow that is according to God works penance, steadfast unto
salvation; but the sorrow of the world works death.*
25   Ecclus. 30:24b-25.

fear and feel repulsion and to say: *My soul is sorrowful even unto death.*[26]

Et conturbatus sum, and I am troubled 54{55}[4] *a voce inimici, at the voice of the enemy*: that is, I am troubled, not with an inordinate inner turbulence, but by a reasonable anger, for I am free from fear, or sorrow, or such similar vehement affections, because of the detractions and accusations and false interpretations with which the Jewish people regarded my works and doctrine, [finding them] as worthy of blasphemy, of contempt, and of being ascribed to Beelzebub: in the way that is stated in Mark, *And looking round about on them with anger, being grieved for the blindness of their hearts*, etc.[27] And also elsewhere: *Now is my soul troubled.*[28] And in the Last Supper itself, Jesus was troubled, as the Evangelist attests: *When Jesus had said these things, he was troubled in spirit; and he testified, and said: Amen, amen I say to you, one of you shall betray me.*[29] And I am also troubled *a tribulatio peccatoris, at the tribulation of the sinner*, that is, from the consideration of my most bitter Passion that is imminent before me: in the manner that we read, *Being in agony, he prayed the longer, and his sweat became as drops of blood, trickling down upon the ground.*[30] And in Hebrews the Apostle [Paul] says of Christ: *With a strong cry and tears he offered up prayers.*[31] And so in that Passion, Jesus was troubled in the manner stated, *at the tribulation of the sinner*, that is, by the persecution of the people spitting, flogging, piercing, and killing.

Quoniam declinaverunt in me iniquitates, for they have cast iniquities upon me: that is, the Jews placed upon me many sins, in the manner that is stated by the Evangelist, *And they began to accuse him, saying: We have found this man perverting our nation, and forbidding to give tribute to Caesar.*[32] And again: *And the chief priests and the scribes stood by, earnestly accusing him.*[33] But also before the Passion the Jews frequently calumniated him. For which reason it is written: *He is become mad.*[34] And again: *He has a devil, and is mad: why hear you him?*[35] Hence the Psalmist says of Christ in an earlier Psalm: *For they have intended evils against you: they have devised counsels which they have not been able to establish.*[36] And by Hosea, Christ

---

26 Mark 14:34a.

27 Mark 3:5a.

28 John 12:27a.

29 John 13:21.

30 Luke 22:43b-44.

31 Heb. 5:7a.

32 Luke 23:2.

33 Luke 23:10.

34 Mark 3:21b.

35 John 10:20.

36 Ps. 20:12.

says: *They shall be wasted because they have transgressed against me: and I redeemed them: and they have spoken lies against me.*[37] *Et ira molesti erant mihi, and in wrath they were troublesome to me*: that is, the perverse and unbelieving Jews out of the anger that they conceived against me, persecuted me: which persecution was to be troublesome, not because I might have put up with the adverse and troublesome things unwillingly and impatiently, but because I suffered with them for their blindness.

54{55}[5] *My heart is troubled within me: and the fear of death is fallen upon me.*

Cor meum conturbatum est in me, et formido mortis cecidit super me.

54{55}[6] *Fear and trembling are come upon me: and darkness has covered me.*

Timor et tremor venerunt super me, et contexerunt me tenebrae.

54{55}[5] *Cor meum conturbatum est in me, my heart is troubled within me*, out of great affection, not out of some kind of disorder, as has been explained. Whence in an earlier Psalm is stated: *My heart is become like wax melting.*[38] *Et formido mortis cecidit super me, and the fear of death is fallen upon me*, that is, the natural fear of imminent death was in me, especially when I prayed to the Father three times that, if it be possible, he take away from me the chalice of the Passion.[39] **54{55}[6]** *Timor, fear* of my soul or the interior appetite, *et tremor, and trembling* of the body caused by the interior fear, *venerunt super me, are come upon me*, not without predeliberation, but with reason leading the way. For the passions or sensitive appetites in Christ did not precede the reason, but they were voluntarily assumed by Christ, and at the command of the reason they ceased. And so in this way fear and trembling rushed in especially in Christ when from an immeasurable distress of his mind *his sweat became like drops of blood trickling down upon the earth.*[40] *Et contexerunt me tene-*

---

37   Hosea 7:13b.
38   Ps. 21:15b. E. N. As Denis's *Commentary* on this Psalm states: "*My heart is become like wax*, that is, my mind is spiritually loosened, softened, and is in a way spilling itself out confronted with so great an affection of divine honor and of human salvation, and also confronted with such violent of suffering nature, and confronted with the sadness arising from the ungratefulness of the reprobate." Article L (Psalm 21:15) in Volume I.
39   Matt. 26:39, 42, 44.
40   Luke 22:44b.

brae, and darkness has covered me: that is, great and most punishment-like adversities most profoundly burdened me, for I fully suffered in body and soul, for I suffered in all of the members of my body and powers of my soul. Or [we can understand it] in this way: *Darkness has covered me*: that is, sinners darkened with sins rushed in from all sides upon me. For regarding converted sinners, the Apostle [Paul] said: *You were heretofore darkness, but now light in the Lord.*[41] For which reason it was said of Christ earlier: *For many dogs have encompassed me.*[42]

54{55}[7] *And I said: Who will give me wings like a dove, and I will fly and be at rest?*

Et dixi: Quis dabit mihi pennas sicut columbae, et volabo, et requiescam?

54{55}[8] *Lo, I have gone far off flying away; and I abode in the wilderness.*

Ecce elongavi fugiens; et mansi in solitudine.

54{55}[7] *Et dixi*, and I said, mentally reflecting, or speaking with my mouth: *Quis dabit mihi pennas sicut columbae, et volabo, et requiescam? Who will give me wings like a dove, and I will fly and be at rest?* Christ possessed unceasingly the wings of contemplation and charity from the beginning of his Incarnation. So what wings is he suggesting he desires? None other than either the wings of the Resurrection and the Ascension, by which he flew from the tomb to hell,[43] and from hell to the believers upon the earth, and to the heavens, and rests at the right hand of the Father; or the wings of flight from the Jews, as long as the foretold time of his Passion had not been fulfilled, as is acknowledged by John the Evangelist, saying: *Wherefore Jesus walked no more openly among the Jews*; but he went into a place near the desert where *he abode with his disciples*, next to a city *that is called Ephrem.*[44] To this place, therefore, Christ flew with the wings of flight, that is, passed over to quickly, for *he passing through the midst of them, went his way*[45] (since they tried to

---

41 Eph. 5:8a.

42 Ps. 21:17a. E. N. The "dogs" are "detractors, angry and furious, who either by flattering or by deterring endeavor to bite my soul, that is, to divert it from meekness, humility, and tranquility, and to conform to their dog-like activities." Article L (Psalm 21:17) in Volume I.

43 E. N. This is not the hell of the damned, but the so-called limbo of the fathers.

44 John 11:54. E. N. Denis departs from the Gospel in the latter half of his quote, but not in any significant, substantive way.

45 Luke 4:30.

stone him and to throw him off a cliff, in the manner that is written⁴⁶),
that is, invisibly he slipped by the hands of the Jews. In this place he
also took refuge from the tumult and persecution of the Jews. And so is
appended: **54{55}[8]** *Ecce elongavi; Lo, I have gone far off* from the Jews
who were persecuting me, *fugiens, flying away* to a place in the desert;
et mansi, and I abode with my disciples *in solitudine, in the wilderness* or
the desert. Furthermore, of course, before Christ began to preach, *he was
led by the Spirit,* the Holy [Spirit] of course, *into the desert;*⁴⁷ and there
he was *with beasts, and the angels ministered unto him.*⁴⁸

54{55}[9]   I waited for him that has saved me from pusillanimity of
spirit, and a storm.

Exspectabam eum qui salvum me fecit a pusillanimitate spiritus, et tempestate.

54{55}[9] *Exspectabam eum qui salvum me fecit, I waited for him that
has saved me*: that is, I Christ anticipated the orders of God the Father,
so that I might fulfil them in me, in order that I might make myself manifest
at that time foreordained by him and might be put to death. For I did
not flee so that I might not die, for I came into the world that by dying
I might redeem the world; but not that I might lay down my life before
the foreordained time.⁴⁹ For this reason, the evangelist John often says:
*No man laid hands on him, because his hour was not yet come.*⁵⁰ And so, I
waited for him that has saved me, *a pusillanimitate spiritus, from pusillanimity of spirit,* that is, from an excessive fear of death and the world, *et
tempestate, and a storm,* that is, from impetuous movements of the soul
and turbulence of mind. Christ affirms this, since there was not ever in
him pusillanimity of spirit and storm, for both of these things are vicious,
and his soul was preserved by divine virtue from these movements.

54{55}[10]   Cast down, O Lord, and divide their tongues; for I have seen
iniquity and contradiction in the city.

Praecipita, Domine, divide linguas eorum; quoniam vidi iniquitatem et contradictionem in civitate.

---

46   John 8:59; Luke 4:29.
47   Matt. 4:1a.
48   Mark 1:13b.
49   John 18:5, 8.
50   John 7:30b; *Cf.* John 8:20a.

And Christ prays for the defeat of his enemies, according to the sense clearly set forth in the exposition of the previous Psalm;[51] and he says: 54{55}[10] *Praecipita, Domine; cast down, O Lord* Father, *et divide linguas eorum, and divide their tongues,* that is, confuse, falsify, condemn, and destroy the words of the Jews that are detracting of me, and their taking vain counsel for the purpose of capturing and killing me. Their tongues, that is, their words, cast down, destroy; and do not delay in preventing them from having their desired effect, not so that I might be delayed in dying, nor that I might be concealed from the knowledge of men, but raise me up, and glorify my name,[52] and cast them down for eternity and disperse them in the present life, so that, as they themselves prayed: my blood be upon them and their children.[53] All this we see fulfilled now in the Jews. For the Jews intended to kill Christ in this manner, so that he would not rise again, and would not remain from then on in the memories of men, in the way that they said in Jeremiah: *Let us cut him off from the land of the living, and let his name be remembered no more.*[54] But their opposition was shattered because Christ by his death merited to be glorified and honored in all sorts of ways, according to that of the Apostle [Paul]: *We see Jesus, who . . . for the suffering of death, crowned with glory and honor, that, through the grace of God, he might taste death for all.*[55]

And therefore this I pray, *quoniam, for I* Christ, who know all things, and who know *what was in man,*[56] *vidi iniquitatem, have seen iniquity,* that is, for the purpose of destroying me, *et contradictionem, and contradiction* against me and against my teaching, *in civitate, in the city,* that is, in the people dwelling in Jerusalem: or [alternatively], their contradiction amongst themselves,[57] for some resisted those wanting to put me to death. Whence Nicodemus said against the unbelieving Jews: *Does our law judge any man, unless it first hear him, and know what he does?*[58] And elsewhere it is written: Many out of the leaders *believed in him,* namely before his Passion.[59]

---

51 E. N. *See* Article VI (Psalm 53:7).

52 John 17:5a.

53 Matt. 27:25: *And the whole people answering, said: His blood be upon us and our children.*

54 Jer. 11:19b.

55 Heb. 2:9.

56 John 2:25b.

57 John 7:12: *And there was much murmuring among the multitude concerning him. For some said: He is a good man. And others said: No, but he seduces the people.*

58 John 7:41.

59 John 11:45.

54{55}[11] *Day and night shall iniquity surround it upon its walls: and in the midst thereof are labor,*

> *Die ac nocte circumdabit eam super muros eius iniquitas; et labor in medio eius,*

54{55}[12] *and injustice. And usury and deceit have not departed from its streets.*

> *et iniustitia: et non defecit de plateis eius usura et dolus.*

54{55}[11] *Die ac nocte,* day and night, that is, unceasingly, *circumdabit eam super muros eius iniquitas,* shall iniquity surround it upon its walls: that is, in the leadership of the Jewish people, who should have been the foundation and the walls of the others, confirming them in good, there existed great and extreme malice; for the chiefs of the priests instigated others toward the killing of Christ.[60] Or [we can see it this way], *iniquity shall surround it upon its walls,* for literally the guardians of the walls of Jerusalem, as if all singing one song, turned against Jesus Christ, incessantly deriding him, as a later Psalm sets forth more clearly: *They that sat in the gate spoke against me: and they that drank wine made me their song.*[61] *Et labor in medio eius* **54{55}** **[12]** *et iniustitia,* and in the midst thereof are labor **54{55}[12]** *and injustice,* that is, the evil of punishment and injustice was as though in all the people of the city of Jerusalem. Now, by labor is meant sin, because (as Augustine attests) the disordered soul is its own sin.[62] For it excludes true quiet and peace, and has, as an adjunct, the remorse of conscience. Great labor and the height of injustice was in the middle of the city of these people when, responding for the whole people, they said to the praetor [Pilate]: *His blood be upon us and our children.*[63] *Et non defecit de plateis eius; and have not departed from its streets,* that is, from the dwellers of the streets of Jerusalem, *usura et dolus,* usury and deceit. For the Judges were avaricious and deceitful: for which reason Christ cast out the buyers and sellers from the temple.[64] And in Micah we read: *Everyone hunts his brother to death;*[65] and elsewhere, *For from the least of them even to the greatest, all are given to covetousness.*[66]

---

60   Matt. 27:20; Mark 15:11.

61   Ps. 68:13.

62   E. N. Denis mentions this in Article XLI (Psalm 16:9) in Volume 1. The source of this is St. Augustine's *Confessions*, I, 12: *Iussisti, Domine, et sic est, ut poena sua sibi sit omnis animus inordinatus.* "You have commanded, O Lord, and so it is, that every disordered soul be its own punishment for itself."

63   Matt. 27:25b.

64   Matt. 21:12.

65   Micah 7:12b.

66   Jer. 6:13a.

54{55}[13] *For if my enemy had reviled me, I would verily have borne with it. And if he that hated me had spoken great things against me, I would perhaps have hidden myself from him.*

Quoniam si inimicus meus maledixisset mihi, sustinuissem utique. Et si is qui oderat me super me magna locutus fuisset, abscondissem me forsitan ab eo.

Consequently, Christ elaborates upon the sin of his betrayer. **54{55} [13]** *Quoniam si inimicus meus, for if my enemy,* that is, he who never before had been my friend, or he to whom I would have done something evil, or he to whom I would have failed to show so many signs of love, *maledixisset mihi, had reviled me,* selling me and surrendering me to my enemies; *sustinuissem utique, I would have verily borne it,* that is, I would have regarded it more tolerable, and I would have been less afflicted of heart; nor would I have taken vengeance so harshly as I punished the sin of Judas, whom I allowed to despair by just judgment, and whom I permitted to slay himself with a noose:[67] which was weighty vindication in the present, and one which was followed with the most heavy punishment in the future. Indeed, God more seriously avenges a sin, the more he permits the sinner to fall into yet graver sins. *Et si is qui oderat me, and if he who hated me,* that is, if he who was my enemy, would have clearly said so and shown it, *super me magna locutus fuisset, had spoken great things against me,* that is, would have spoken against me words of hypocritical deceit and cruelty to my adversaries; *abscondissem me forsitan ab eo, I would perhaps have hidden myself from him,* that is, I would not have so familiar and accessible to him as I was with Judas, from whom I did not hide myself as I hid for a while from the Jews who openly lay waiting for me.[68] Yet it is not to be supposed [by this] that Christ in some way would ultimately have remained hidden to the end because he did not wish to avoid death.[69]

---

67 Matt. 27:5.

68 John 8:59.

69 E. N. Denis states that he is not suggesting that, had Judas been more open with his deceit and betrayal, Jesus would have not befriended him or would have behaved differently (as if Jesus was ignorant of Judas's scheming). Denis is negating any suggestion that Jesus' hiding from his enemies was as a result of his fear of dying, but rather was a temporary expedient because his time had not yet come. What Denis is describing is how Jesus behaved when confronted by such a known — though deceitful — enemy as was Judas, who posed as a friend and received such benefits and love from Christ. This only serves to exacerbate the heinous nature of the sin of Judas against his master and against his God, justifying the vile manner of his death and his eternal damnation.

54{55}[14] *But you a man of one mind, my guide, and my familiar,*

   Tu vero homo unanimis, dux meus, et notus meus,

54{55}[15] *Who did take sweetmeats together with me: in the house of God we walked with consent.*

   Qui simul mecum dulces capiebas cibos, in domo Dei ambulavimus cum consensu.

54{55}[14] *Tu vero,* but you, O Judas, *homo unanimis,* a man of one mind with respect to me, both as to appearance and the profession of words, and also it would seem according to truth, and also for a time; *dux meus, my guide,* that is, whom I with the other Apostles assembled together as guides of my people, sending you before the Passion with them to preach the Kingdom of God and to heal the sick,[70] *et notus meus, and my familiar,* in the sense of dwelling and being familiar with me. **54{55}[15]** *Qui simul mecum dulces capiebas cibos, who did take sweet meats together with me,* during the time when you were my treasurer, eating bread with me at my table whereon I charitably and sweetly supped with you. But especially in the Last Supper, Judas received from Christ and with Christ *sweet meats,* that is, his Body and Blood. *In domo Dei, in the house of God,* that is, in the synagogue of the Jews and the temple of Jerusalem, or with the congregation of my faithful disciples, *ambulavimus, we walked,* that is, we lived and conversed, *cum consensus, with consent.* For in a way Christ and Judas walked with consent, since they were of one mind.

   But it is clear from this that those persecutions and injuries instigated by someone close and a friend or a familiar are more troublesome, especially when we presume on their love, and we deserve from them nothing but good things. For this reason, the Passion of Christ was more bitter, for he was sold by a disciple, and he was put to death by his own and the chosen people. And so by Micah he says: *O my people, what have I done to you, or in what have I molested you?*[71] And in another place: *What . . . ought I to do more to my vineyard, that I have not done to it?*[72]

54{55}[16] *Let death come upon them, and let them go down alive into hell. For there is wickedness in their dwellings: in the midst of them.*

   Veniat mors super illos, et descendant in infernum viventes: quoniam nequitiae in habitaculis eorum, in medio eorum.

---

70 Luke 9:2.
71 Micah 6:3.
72 Is. 5:4.

54{55}[16] *Veniat mors super illos,* let death come upon them, upon those who so seek to corrupt my disciples or appear as equal to them. Christ says this not desiring it, but foretelling it (unless it is understood to desire with the zeal of justice according to the order of divine equity, but not with an inordinate appetite for vengeance). *Let death come,* I say, death of the soul and body upon them, namely, that they might be deprived of the grace of God, and they might be slaughtered by their adversaries, in the manner that the Jews were killed by the army of the Romans. *Et descendant in infernum viventes,* and let them go down alive into hell, in the day of judgment with body and soul eternally condemned. For this they were deserving of. *Quoniam nequitiae,* for there is wickedness, that is, many and perverse maliciousness, *in habitaculis eorum,* in their dwellings, that is, in their hearts, within which men mull over thinking; or, *in their dwellings,* that is, in the dwelling of their tabernacle; *in medio eorum,* in the midst of them: so that all jointly do things evilly.

54{55}[17] But I have cried to God: and the Lord will save me.

Ego autem ad Deum clamavi, et Dominus salvabit me.

54{55}[18] Evening and morning, and at noon I will speak and declare: and he shall hear my voice.

Vespere, et mane, et meridie, narrabo, et annuntiabo; et exaudiet vocem meam.

54{55}[17] *Ego autem,* but I, Christ, the Son of God, *ad Deum clamavi,* have cried to God: as is openly expressed in the beginning of this Psalm; *et Dominus,* and the Lord, that is, God the Father or the holy Trinity, *salvavit me,* will save me from death, raising me to immortal life: according to that Apostle of Christ, *Who in the days of his flesh, with a strong cry and tears, offering up prayers and supplications to him that was able to save him from death, was heard for his reverence.*[73] **54{55}[18]** *Vespere,* in the evening, namely, in the night of the Last Supper, *et mane,* and in the morning, that is, in the Day of Preparation (*Parasceves*), *et meridie,* and at noon, hanging upon the Cross, *narrabo,* I will speak with my mouth: that is, I proclaimed the truth, taught saving wisdom, offered my cause and my prayers to the Lord, prayed for those who crucified me, and I commended my soul to the Father. For Christ in the evening of the Supper gave to his disciples most beautiful words,[74] and in the morning he confessed himself to be

---

73 Heb. 5:7.
74 John chps. 13–16.

the Christ,[75] and hanging upon the cross he cried out in a loud voice: *Father, into your hands I commend my spirit.*[76] *Et exaudiet vocem meam, and he shall hear my voice.* For Christ was heard in all prayer which he poured out with deliberate reason, in the manner that Martha said to him: *I know that whatsoever you will ask of God, God will give it you.*[77]

54{55}[19]   *He shall redeem my soul in peace from them that draw near to me: for among many they were with me.*

Redimet in pace animam meam ab his qui appropinquant mihi; quoniam inter multos erant mecum.

54{55}[20]   *God shall hear, and He who is eternal shall humble them.*[78] *For there is no change with them, and they have not feared God.*

Exaudiet Deus, et humiliabit illos, qui est ante saecula. Non enim est illis commutatio, et non timuerunt Deum.

54{55}[21]   *He has stretched forth his hand to repay. They have defiled his covenant.*

Extendit manum suam in retribuendo; contaminaverunt testamentum eius.

54{55}[22]   *They are divided by the wrath of his countenance; and his heart has drawn near. His words are smoother than oil, and the same are darts.*

Divisi sunt ab ira vultus eius; et appropinquavit cor illius. Molliti sunt sermones eius super oleum; et ipsi sunt iacula.

54{55}[19] *Redimet in pace, he shall redeem . . . in peace,* that is, redeeming he shall establish in true and stable peace, *animam meam, my soul,* that is myself, or my life, transferring me from mortal life to impassible life: and so he will redeem my soul *ab his qui appropinquant mihi, from them that draw near to me,* that is, from the Jews and the others who approach me so that they might capture me, bind me up, and kill me; *quoniam inter multos erant mecum, for among many they were with me:* that is, therefore God heard me, for these Jews so approached me, often they were present at my preaching among the many others who believed in me, and so they are without excuse. For which reason the Savior said: *I have always taught*

---

75   Mark 14:62.
76   Luke 23:46.
77   Jonn 11:22.
78   E. N. I have replaced the Douay-Rheims "eternal," with a little more literal translation of *Qui est ante saecula,* "He who is eternal (before all ages)."

in the synagogue, and in the temple, where all the Jews resort;[79] and again: *If I had not come, and spoken to them, they would not have sin; but now they have no excuse for their sin.*[80] **54{55}[20]** *Exaudiet Deus,* God shall hear my prayers, *et humiliabit illos,* and shall humble them, the proud, in the present and in the future. But the Jews are now humbled, for they are deprived of all the glory of the law of their fathers, and of kingdom, place, priest and prince; and in the future also with other proud people they will humiliatingly tumble down into the deepest hell. *Qui est ante saecula, he who is eternal,* that is, the eternal God, self-subsisting before all ages.

Non enim est illis commutatio, for there is no change with them from evil or unbelief to repentance and the Christian faith, in the manner we read in Jeremiah: *They have made their faces harder than the rock, and they have refused to return.*[81] And the Lord said to the Jews through Isaiah: *For I knew that you are stubborn, and your neck is as an iron sinew, and your forehead as brass.*[82] *Et non timuerunt Deum,* and they have not feared God, whose Son they killed. **54{55}[21]** *Extendit manum suam in retribuendo, he has stretched forth his hand to repay:* that is, God prepared the strength of his power, so that he might repay to them a just punishment.

Contaminaverunt testamentum eius, they have defiled his covenant, that is, the aforesaid Jews did not keep the law of God, but they defiled it by acting against it by doing evil and by understanding it in a carnal manner. **54{55}[22]** *Divisi sunt, they are divided* throughout the whole world *ab ira vultus eius, by the wrath of his countenance,* that is, by the just vindication of divine justice. For God expelled them from their own land, dispersed them throughout the world, and separated them from the charity and faith of Christ and from the number of the elect because of their sins. *Et appropinquavit cor illius, and his heart has drawn near:* that is, from the reprobate Jews the divine will or the kindness of God turned toward the Gentiles, as the Lord said through the prophet to the Jews: *I have no pleasure in you . . . for my name is great among the Gentiles.*[83] And the Apostle [Paul] said: *Blindness in part has happened in Israel, until the fulness of the Gentiles should come in;*[84] and again, *But by their offence, salvation is come to the Gentiles,*[85] that is, the occasion of the salvation of the Gentiles, because the Jews, having failed to believe, caused it to be fair to transfer

79 John 18:20.
80 John 15:22.
81 Jer. 5:3b.
82 Is. 48:4.
83 Mal. 1:10b, 11a.
84 Rom. 11:25b.
85 Rom. 11 :11b.

it to the Gentiles.[86] *Molliti sunt sermones eius super oleum, his words are smoother than oil,* that is, the doctrine and the preaching of Christ were and are more smooth than oil, because he preached the Kingdom of Heaven and the way of penance. Whence, it was said in a Psalm above regarding Christ: *Grace is poured abroad in your lips.*[87] And Luke said: *They wondered at the words of grace that proceeded from his mouth.*[88] *Et ipsi sunt iacula, and the same are darts:* that is, the unbelieving among the Jews opposed the doctrine and the works of Christ as if with arrows, piercing him with blasphemous words and finally puncturing him with nails.

54{55}[23] *Cast your care upon the Lord, and he shall sustain you: he shall not suffer the just to waver forever.*

Iacta super Dominum curam tuam, et ipse te enutriet; non dabit in aeternum fluctuationem iusto.

But you, O Christian, living among those who are so perishing, **54{55} [23]** *Iacta super Dominum curam tuam, cast your care upon the Lord:* that is, flee from disordered and superfluous concerns, and be vigilant in the Lord, having well-ordered care, namely, that you might with solicitude and fear live your life in a manner pleasing to God; but do not concern yourself with temporal things, either before due time or with exceeding anxiety, but according to what is necessary for spiritual advancement or profit.[89] Commit yourself to God, therefore, in this manner, but do not

---

86   E. N. As St. Peter says, the Gentiles "in time past were not a people," and yet after Christ, those among the Gentiles that turned to Christ "are now the people of God." 1 Pet. 2:10. "One enters into the People of God by faith and Baptism. 'All men are called to belong to the new People of God,' so that, in Christ, 'men may form one family and one People of God.'" CCC § 804 (quoting VII: LG, 13; AG, 1). At one time, one could say, *salus ex Judaeis est,* "salvation is from the Jews." John 4:22b. In the new dispensation, however, *salus est gentibus,* "salvation is come to the Gentiles" (Rom. 11:11b); more precisely, it is *salus ex ecclesia est,* "salvation is from the Church." As the Swiss theologian Albert Meyenberg (1861–1934) said: "*Salus ex ecclesia est* — ist nur die Fortsetzung dieses Grundsatzes." *Salus ex ecclesia est* is only a continuation of this principle of *salus ex Judaeis est.* Albert Meyenberg, *Homiletische und katechetische Studien* (Lucerne: Räber & Co., 1908), 132.

87   Ps. 44:3b.

88   Luke 4:22a.

89   E. N. Here, the Augustinian difference between "use" (*uti*) and "enjoyment" (*frui*) might be invoked. "To enjoy (*frui*) is to adhere to something in love for its own sake. However, to use (*uti*) is to refer to that which comes to you for the use of obtaining that which you love, supposing it is something that should be loved." *De doctrina Christiana,* I, 4, 4, PL 34, 20-21. Essentially, the *uti-frui* distinction is a distinction between ends and means. Thus, not only does the end that is loved have to be properly ordered, but the means to it must be used (*uti*), and not

neglect to do that which is in you,[90] and know that your own efforts and provision are insufficient. Therefore, trust in the Lord, and dispose and order your concerns in him: for as an earlier Psalm says, *The Lord is full of care for me*,[91] in the way that [the book of] Wisdom says.[92] *Et ipse te enutriet, and he shall sustain you*, that is, he will provide you with necessaries: as Christ promised, *Seek you therefore first the kingdom of God, and his justice, and all these things shall be added unto you.*[93] And again: *Be not therefore solicitous for tomorrow;*[94] *for your Father knows that you have need of all these things.*[95] This is what St. Peter says: *Casting all your care upon him, for he has care of you.*[96]

Non dabit in aeternum fluctuationem iusto, he shall not suffer the just to waver forever. This can be understood in two ways. First, in this way: God will never permit the just man to vacillate, that is, to withdraw from him or to remain unsteady, for by grace he will remain fixed in God through all temptations and all circumstances, and he will be conducted as the just man mentioned in a later Psalm: *His heart is ready to hope in the Lord, his heart is strengthened; he shall not be moved.*[97] Whence, the Lord says through Jeremiah: *If you will take away your stumbling blocks out of my sight, you shall not be moved.*[98] Unquestionably, sins make men irresolute and unstable, according to this: *Jerusalem has grievously sinned, therefore is she become unstable.*[99] And elsewhere: *The just man shall hold onto his way, and he that has clean hands shall be stronger and stronger.*[100] And yet again Scripture says: *A holy man continues in wisdom as the sun: but a*

---

inordinately enjoyed (*frui*) so as to detract from the very end to which it is to lead. In his *Confessions*, St. Augustine famously shows how difficult the balance is to maintain between *uti* and *frui* even in the context of liturgical music and the worship of God. *Conf.*, X, 33.

90   E. N. Denis has several times throughout this *Commentary* invoked the principle of *facere quod in te est*, "do what is in you." This has been called the *Facientibus* principle (from the maxim: *Facientibus quod in se est Deus non denegat gratiam*: If one does what is in one, God will not deny grace). This doctrine is an instance of a principle of the *devotio moderna* which Denis has incorporated into his Scholastic construct.

91   Ps. 39:18b. E. N. I have changed "careful" in the Douay Rheims to "full of care."

92   Wis. 12:13: *For there is no other God but you, who have care of all, that you should show that you do not give judgment unjustly.*

93   Matt. 6:33.

94   Matt. 6:34a.

95   Matt. 6:32b.

96   1 Pet. 5:7.

97   Ps. 111:7b–8a.

98   Jer. 4:1b.

99   Lam. 1:8a.

100   Job 17:9.

fool is changed as the moon.[101] All these things are not to be understood as if a just man is unable to sin; but that it behooves a just man, to the extent that he is just, to declare what is here said. Second, it may be understood in this way: *He will not suffer the just to waver forever*, that is, although at times God allows him to be tempted, to be troubled, and to be in anguish, there will also come a time when he will confirm in the good, and he will deliver from all instability and restlessness.

54{55}[24]   *But you, O God, shall bring them down into the pit of destruction. Bloody and deceitful men shall not live out half their days; but I will trust in you, O Lord.*

Tu vero, Deus, deduces eos in puteum interitus. Viri sanguinum et dolosi non dimidiabunt dies suos; ego autem sperabo in te, Domine.

54{55}[24] *Tu vero, Deus; but you, O God*, just Judge of all, *deduces eos, you shall bring them*, that is the Jews rebelling against Christ, *in puteum interitus*, that is, in the pit of hell, or you will allow them to be led into the most obstinate and most deep blindness in accordance with their malice: as it is written of them, *I will make to rot the pride* of this wicked people *that will not hear my words.*[102]

Viri sanguinum, bloody . . . men, that is, sinners, *et dolosi non dimidiabunt dies suos, and deceitful [men] shall not live out half their days*, that is, they will not live as long as they had reckoned; and often do not reach the middle of the time that they judged that they would remain alive: for immediately upon their performance of their iniquity they are taken away by the Lord. As the Savior said of the rich man who anticipated himself as having a long life: *You fool, this night do they require your soul of you.*[103] For which reason another scripture also says: *Wicked men . . . were taken before their time.*[104] Or [we can look at it] thus: These aforementioned men *shall not live out half their days*, namely, that, as their past time of their life was spent in pleasures and vices, so the time remaining they spend in penance and in the pursuit of virtue; but they have spent the given time, perseveringly in sin, of which kind of men the book of Job says: *God has given him place for penance, and he abuses it unto pride.*[105] For they are similar to the devil: for it is diabolical to persevere in evil.

---

101   Ecclus. 27:12.
102   Jer. 13:9, 10a.
103   Luke 12:20a.
104   John 22:15b–16a.
105   Job 24:23a.

Whence of such men the Lord laments through Jeremiah: *Why then is this people . . . turned away with a stubborn revolting?*[106] *Ego autem sperabo in te, Domine; but I will trust in you, O Lord.* Christ as man and so who is in a certain way a wayfarer, namely insofar as he is passible, trusts in God, expecting from him those goods which he does not yet have, but he prays to obtain them, that is, the glorification of the body, his ascension, etc.

See how pure, how true and properly this Psalm is expounded of Christ. Since, therefore, by evangelical and also apostolic authority we are compelled to expound certain Psalms literally of Christ, which still have certain things which in themselves do not befit Christ, such as the thirty-ninth Psalm or the fortieth Psalm,[107] namely, [those beginning with the phrases] *With expectation I have waited for the Lord,* in which among other things it says, *My iniquities have overtaken me, and I was not able to see;*[108] and, *Blessed is he that understands,* in which we read, *Heal my soul, for I have sinned against you:*[109] how much more should this Psalm and similar ones in which nothing is found in them that is not befitting of Christ be understood as literally referring to Christ?

ARTICLE IX

TROPOLOGICAL OR MORAL EXPLANATION OF THE SAME FIFTY-FOURTH PSALM, OF THE CHURCH OR ANY MEMBER OF THE FAITHFUL

54{55}[1] *Unto the end, in verses, understanding for David.*

In finem, in carminibus. Intellectus David.

NOW IT IS WELL-ESTABLISHED THAT BY David is designated the Church or any true member of the faithful, and so the sense of this title would be: **54{55}[1]** *In finem, in carminibus, intellectus David; unto the end, in verses, understanding for David:* that is, one is to understand this Psalm, *unto the end,* that is, directing us to Christ, conforming to David, that is, of the Church or its believers undergoing multiple tribulations, *in verses,* that is, in adversity by giving thanks and rendering praise.

---

106 Jer. 8:5a.
107 *E. N.* Psalm 39:6–8 is referred to in Heb. 10:4–7. Psalm 40:10 is quoted in John 13:18 as Messianic or Christological.
108 *E. N.* Ps. 39:2a, 13a.
109 *E. N.* Ps. 40:2a, 5b.

54{55}[2]   *Hear, O God, my prayer, and despise not my supplication.*

*Exaudi, Deus, orationem meam, et ne despexeris deprecatio-
nem meam.*

54{55}[3]   *Be attentive to me and hear me. I am grieved in my exercise;
and am troubled...*

*Intende mihi, et exaudi me. Contristatus sum in exercitatione
mea; et conturbatus sum...*

54{55}[4]   *at the voice of the enemy, and at the tribulation of the sinner.
For they have cast iniquities upon me: and in wrath they were
troublesome to me.*

*a voce inimici, et a tribulatione peccatoris. Quoniam declina-
verunt in me iniquitates, et in ira molesti erant mihi.*

And so he says: **54{55}[2]** *Exaudi, Deus, orationem meam; hear, O
God, my prayer.* Here, the same meaning under other words is repeated
four times, in order that the one praying might bring affection to a boil
within himself and might enkindle such a frame of mind as often as it
is repeated. And so, *Hear, O God, my prayer,* because of your goodness,
et ne despexeris deprecationem meam, and despise not my supplication, on
account of my imperfection and weakness; **54{55}[3]** *Intende mihi, be
attentive to me,* with your eyes of paternal kindness keeping me in view,
et exaudi me, and hear me praying for the removal of vices and all evil,
and the attainment of virtue and of reward.

Contristatus sum in exercitatione mea, I am grieved in my exercise.
The Apostle [Paul] speaking to Timothy teaches this exercise to be
twofold, namely, interior and spiritual but also exterior and corporal:
*Exercise yourself unto godliness, for bodily exercise is profitable to little:
but godliness is profitable to all things.*[110] But in both the exercise unto
the good is sorrowful, not from the exercise itself, but because of
the imperfections that accompany it and faults that are committed
[in its exercise], and because of being exiled in this *vale of tears*[111]
and on pilgrimage to the Lord,[112] aware of this world being replete
with its vices and errors: and so they sorrow from goodly compassion
for those partaking in error, yet most especially, having such zeal for
God, because of the wrongs and offenses levied against God. This is
a good sorrow which (according to the Apostle [Paul]) works towards

---

110   1 Tim. 4:7b–8a.
111   Ps. 83:7a.
112   *Cf.* 2 Cor. 5:6.

salvation.[113] Of this Solomon bears witness: *The heart of the wise is where there is mourning, and the heart of fools where there is mirth;*[114] and again, *It is better to go to the house of mourning, than to the house of feasting.*[115] For now is the time of mourning and weeping, in the manner that the Lord admonished through Joel, saying: *Be converted to me with all your heart, in fasting, and in weeping, and in mourning.*[116] For no one who now elects to take delight in the world will in the life hereafter be glorified with Christ.

Et conturbatus sum 54{55}[4] *a voce inimici;* and *I am troubled* 54{55} [4] *at the voice of the enemy,* that is, from the injuries of words, *et a tribulatio peccatoris, and at the tribulation of the sinner,* that is, at the injuries of lashings or of the damned. For twofold is this trouble, namely with good things, which was addressed in the preceding exposition; and with evil things, where someone is angered, afraid, or sorrowful more than is due, or is in a similar manner inordinately influenced so that it impedes an act of reason. And so to be troubled with a good trouble by the voice of the enemy and from the troubles of sinners is [an attribute] of the perfect, who endure adversity with equanimity, yet they are troubled, that is, they ardently suffer compassion for those doing evil or those in a similar way whose reason is afflicted, of the sort the Apostle had who said: *Who is weak, and I am not weak?*[117] And Job who said: *Before I eat I sigh: and as overflowing waters, so is my roaring.*[118] But to be troubled in the second fashion is something found with the imperfect who do not yet tranquilly endure all things and have not learned to praise [God] in adversity. James in his epistle instructs such as these: *My brothers, count it all joy,* he says, *when you shall fall into diverse trials.*[119] Whence also Christ says: *Blessed are you when they shall revile you, and persecute you, and speak all that is evil against you, untruly ... be glad and rejoice, for your reward is very great in heaven.*[120] We should not therefore be troubled

---

113   Cf. 2 Cor. 7:10: *For the sorrow that is according to God works penance, steadfast unto salvation; but the sorrow of the world works death.*

114   Eccl. 7:5.

115   Eccl. 7:3a.

116   Joel 2:12.

117   2 Cor. 11:29a.

118   Job 3:24. E. N. As Denis explains this verse in his *Commentary on Job*: "Before I eat, I sigh. The sigh is a sign of moderate sorrow; but a roar is a sign of an ardent sorrow: and so it continues, *and as overflowing waters, so is my roaring.*" *Commentary on Job*, Opera Omnia (Montreuil: 1897), Vol. 4, 359.

119   James 1:2. E. N. I have changed "temptations" to "trials," as this is how Denis appears to understand this verse in this context.

120   Matt. 5:11–12a.

because of adversities and injuries, nor should we be saddened because of harsh and harmful words directed to us, but [we should be troubled] only in grieving for sinners.

And so with merit do I call myself troubled, *Quoniam declinaverunt in me iniquitates, for they have cast iniquities upon me*, that is, evil men have levied upon me sins unjustly: for which the perfect are troubled with a virtuous perturbation, as has been stated, glorying in the fact that they are in some way conformed to Christ, who was most falsely accused of crimes by the Jews; but the imperfect sometimes are troubled with the perturbation of anger and impatience. *Et in ira*, and in wrath (not through zeal, but as a result of vice) which they have conceived against me, *molesti erant mihi, they were troublesome to me* with words, signs, or deeds, that is, they burdened me by avenging themselves on me: which troublesomeness I endured, not so much as a result of any injury to me, but rather because of their ruin and damnation. In this way, Paul endured evil that was directed against him:[121] for like a most indulgent father, who suffers so many painful beatings from his insane son, the more insane [the son] is, the more [the father] suffers; the greater the extent that ungodly men scourged Paul more severely, the more amply he sorrowed over their error.

54{55}[5] *My heart is troubled within me: and the fear of death is fallen upon me.*

Cor meum conturbatum est in me, et formido mortis cecidit super me.

54{55}[6] *Fear and trembling are come upon me: and darkness has covered me.*

Timor et tremor venerunt super me, et contexerunt me tenebrae.

54{55}[5] *Cor meum conturbatum est in me, my heart is troubled within me*: that is, my interior sensitive or intellectual appetite,[122] is vehemently or excessively moved by some passion or some affection, from which also the bodily heart is troubled, that is, is unnaturally agitated, because

---

121 Acts 14:18 (stoning); 16:23–25 (imprisonment, being put in stocks); 21:27–33 (capture in an effort to kill him, being beaten, and put in chains).

122 E. N. St. Thomas Aquinas distinguished the human appetite, which provides an inclination or tendency toward an object, into the natural appetite (*appetitus naturalis*), which was unconscious or involuntary, and the elicited appetite (*appetitus elicitus*). The elicited appetite was further of two kinds: the sensitive or animal appetite (*appetitus sensitivus* or *animalis*) and the intellectual or rational appetite (*appetitus intellectivus* or *rationalis*). See ST IaIIae, q. 8, art. 1, co.

passions give rise to bodily changes. *Et formido mortis cecidit super me, and the fear of death is fallen upon me,* that is, so gravely am I afflicted that I feared death. Or [alternatively], *the fear of death,* that is, the horror of sin, which is the death of the soul, fell upon me, for it is evident that from the perturbation that besets me I was afraid of impatience, anger, rancor, or some similar vicious movement and [feared] to fall into a mortal fault, or I feared to succumb either to the temptations of devils or the world and the flesh, which is spiritually to die and grow faint, according to this: *Now the scourge is come upon you, and you faint: it has touched you, and you are troubled.*[123] **54{55}[6]** *Timor,* fear in the soul *et tremor, and trembling* in the exterior, *venerunt super me, are come upon me,* because of imminent and future evil or torments or danger. For fear pertains to a future evil as sorrow pertains to a present evil.[124] And it is expedient for all of us to have such fear and trembling within ourselves because of the thousand impending dangers before us and because of the future judgment and the torments of hell: for we dwell in the middle of traps, and we battle against invisible and most wretched enemies. *Et contexerunt me tenebrae, and darkness has covered me,* that is, adversities and punishments or vices have surrounded me and have covered me completely so that my soul is filled with many evils: in the way the Apostle [Paul] said: *Combats without, fears within.*[125] *Through many tribulations we must enter into the kingdom of God.*[126] For this reason Job says: *I expected good things, and evils are come upon me: I waited for light, and darkness broke out.*[127]

54(55)[7]   *And I said: Who will give me wings like a dove, and I will fly and be at rest?*

   Et dixi: Quis dabit mihi pennas sicut columbae, et volabo, et requiescam?

54{55}[7] *Et dixi,* and I said, within myself: *Quis dabit mihi pennas sicut columbae,* who will give me wings like a dove? That is, how freeing it would be to have wings of virtue, namely, true and dovelike simplicity and innocence in order to evade the above-mentioned evils,[128] and to have the power to lead a pure life among the wicked! *Et volabo,*

---

123   Job 4:5.
124   E. N. *See* ST, IaIIae, q. 41, art. 1, co.
125   2 Cor. 7:5b.
126   Acts 14:21b.
127   Job 30:26.
128   E. N. *Cf.* Matt. 10:16: *Behold I send you as sheep in the midst of wolves. Be you therefore wise as serpents and simple as doves.*

and I will fly with the wings of contemplation, beholding the things of heaven on account of which I will despise earthly loves and freely endure adversities; *et requiescam, and I will be at rest* in God, through faith and charity and maintain an internal peace, [free] from the tumult of earthly things, and the disquiet of the passions and the concern with temporal things: as is said in an earlier Psalm, *In peace in the selfsame I will sleep, and I will rest.*[129]

54{55}[8]   *Lo, I have gone far off flying away; and I abode in the wilderness.*

Ecce elongavi fugiens; et mansi in solitudine.

54{55}[9]   *I waited for him that has saved me from pusillanimity of spirit, and a storm.*

Exspectabam eum qui salvum me fecit a pusillanimitate spiritus, et tempestate.

54{55}[8] *Ecce elongavi; Lo, I have gone far off* [separating] myself by affection or by place, life, and devotion from the sinner and restless men, *fugiens, flying away* from the dangers of this world, so that I might not be perverted with the perverted;[130] *et mansi in solitudine, and I abode in the wilderness,* that is, I attempted to empty myself only for God; or also in the desert place I paused, so that I might adhere more freely to God, and that I might more sweetly repose in him. For a solitary place (*solitarius locus*) directs most greatly to a quiet and contemplative life. For which reason, the Lord said to the soul devoted to him through Hosea: *Behold I will allure her and will lead her into the wilderness (solitudinem): and I will speak to her heart.*[131] And Jeremiah: *Who will give me in the wilderness (solitudinem) a lodging place of wayfaring men, and I will leave my people, and depart from them?*[132] Whence also Christ said to his Apostles as Mark attests: *Come apart into a desert place (desertum locum), and rest a little.*[133] **54{55}[9]** *Exspectabam eum, I waited for him,* that is, I endured for a long time, and I placed my hope in him, *qui salvum me fecit, that has saved me,* by his grace, *a pusillanimitate spiritus et tempestate, from pusillanimity of spirit and a storm* of adversities and dangers which I

---

129   Ps. 4:9.
130   *Cf.* Ps. 17:27b: *With the perverse you will be perverted.*
131   Hosea 2:14.
132   Jer. 9:2.
133   Mark 6:31a.

had, or which I could have had, except that the grace of God preserved me. We ought to be neither pusillanimous nor presumptuous, but magnanimous, humble, strong, always trusting in the Lord, saying with the Apostle [Paul]: *I can do all these things in him who strengthens me.*[134]

54{55}[10] *Cast down, O Lord, and divide their tongues; for I have seen iniquity and contradiction in the city.*

Praecipita, Domine, divide linguas eorum; quoniam vidi iniquitatem et contradictionem in civitate.

54{55}[11] *Day and night shall iniquity surround it upon its walls: and in the midst thereof are labor,*

Die ac nocte circumdabit eam super muros eius iniquitas; et labor in medio eius,

54{55}[12] *and injustice. And usury and deceit have not departed from its streets.*

et iniustitia: et non defecit de plateis eius usura et dolus.

54{55}[13] *For if my enemy had reviled me, I would verily have borne with it. And if he that hated me had spoken great things against me, I would perhaps have hidden myself from him.*

Quoniam si inimicus meus maledixisset mihi, sustinuissem utique. Et si is qui oderat me super me magna locutus fuisset, abscondissem me forsitan ab eo.

54{55}[14] *But you a man of one mind, my guide, and my familiar,*

Tu vero homo unanimis, dux meus, et notus meus,

54{55}[15] *Who did take sweetmeats together with me: in the house of God we walked with consent.*

Qui simul mecum dulces capiebas cibos, in domo Dei ambulavimus cum consensu.

Consequently, the Church or the faithful person prays for the extirpation of heretics, schismatics, tyrants, and persecutors, as well as the enemies of the common good and of just men. 54{55}[10] *Praecipita, Domine; cast down, O Lord,* that is, destroy *et divide, and divide,* that is, separate from one another, so that they are unable to unite in evil doing, *linguas eorum, their tongues,* that is, their words and efforts of

---

134 Phil. 4:13.

their preachers disturbing the Church, or of the detractors oppressing the innocent. The Church does not pray that they may perish completely, but that they may be corrected in the present, and that they may be held back from evildoing, or that they may be temporarily afflicted, or even that they might die if the Church is not otherwise able to obtain peace or to conserve the common good.

Quoniam vidi iniquitatem et contradictionem, for I have seen iniquity and contradiction, that is perversity, perfidy, schisms and attacks against the faith, *in civitate, in the city,* that is, in the Church militant, in which always the evil are mixed in with the good. *For there must be also heresies,*[135] and *it must needs be that scandals come.*[136] **54{55}[11]** *Die ac nocte, day and night,* that is, always even until the end of the world, *circumdabit eam, shall surround it,* namely, the Church, *super muros eius, upon its walls,* that is, in its prelates, pastors, and princes, *iniquitas, iniquity.* For some of the superiors among the Christian people infect, oppress, scandalize, or in a similar way pervert those who are inferior to them, as Daniel said: *Iniquity came out from Babylon from the ancient judges, that seemed to govern the people.*[137] So — unfortunately! — this is the way it is! For they who ought to be the protectors, the walls, or the supports of others have become corruptors of souls and plunderers of the wall, in the way the Lord says through Hosea: *Hear this, O priests, . . . because you have been a snare to them whom you should have watched over, and a net spread upon* the mountain.[138] *Et labor in medio eius,* **54{55}[12]** *et iniustitia; and in the midst thereof are labor,* **54{55} [12]** *and injustice,* that is, in the midst of the Church they come upon labor or violence, oppression, disorder, the fault of punishment, and laborious iniquity. *For many are called, but few are chosen.*[139] For this reason this evil abounds in the midst of the Christian people, according to that written in Hosea: *Cursing, and lying, and killing, and theft, and adultery have overflowed, and blood has touched blood.*[140] *Et non defecit de plateis eius, and . . . not departed from its streets,* that is, from particular churches or priests, who are on a path other than to God, *usura et dolus, usury and deceit.* For also this evil in the leaders of churches and

---

135   1 Cor. 11:19a.
136   Matt. 18:7a.
137   Dan. 13:5.
138   Hosea 5:1. E. N. Denis replaces (Mount) *Thabor* with the generic *montem,* "mountain."
139   Matt. 20:14, 16b.
140   Hosea 4:2.

those under them are found because *all* (as Jeremiah says) *are given to covetousness*,[141] and *all seek the things that are their own; not the things that are Jesus Christ's*,[142] according to the Apostle.

Consequently, the Church, or the faithful, shows how intolerable are the persecutions that are introduced from those who identify themselves as friends but are not. **54{55}[13]** *Quoniam si inimicus meus, for if my enemy* openly and evidently, *maledixisset mihi, had reviled me*, speaking out against, insulting, threatening, or cursing me, *sustinuissem utique, I would verily have borne with it* as more lightly or more acceptingly: for such not at all, or rarely, or tangentially has an effect upon me. *Et si is qui oderat me, and if he that hated me*, not only secretly, but also openly, *super me, against me*, that is, in opposition to me, *magna locutus fuisset, had spoken great things*, that is, words of animosity and severity, *abscondissem me forsitan ab eo, I would perhaps have hidden myself from him*. This accords with that which Christ on occasion sought to teach his disciples, saying: When you are persecuted in one city, *flee to another*.[143] For this is to be done sometimes, but not all the time: for if the faith, or the common good, or the salvation of the subjects is placed in danger, he who would be able to render aid by not fleeing should not flee from [persecution]. **54{55}[14]** *Tu vero homo unanimis, but you are a man of one mind*, confessing Christ with your mouth, as also do I; *dux meus, my guide*: that is, you who were the leader of others and were constituted leader of your brothers in the way of God by the Church; or you have in times past built me up, went before me, and led me in the divine service; *et notus meus, and my familiar*, having with me the same faith, or recognized as bodily [a member of the Church]; *qui mecum dulces capiebas cibos, who did take sweetmeats together with me*, hearing preaching and partaking in the sacraments of the Church before you so apostatized from the faith to heresy, from unity to schism, from love to persecution, and from a praiseworthy life to perverse morals; *in domo Dei ambulavimus cum consensus, in the house of God we walked with consent*, that is, we lived in a manner of life that is in accordance with the Church of Christ when you still were in the faith and the grace of God. For of such person John says: *They went out from us, but they were not of us. For if they had been of us, they would no doubt have remained with us*.[144]

---

141   Jer. 6:13a.

142   Phil. 2:21.

143   Matt. 10:23.

144   1 John 2:19.

54{55}[16] *Let death come upon them, and let them go down alive into hell. For there is wickedness in their dwellings: in the midst of them.*

Veniat mors super illos, et descendant in infernum viventes: quoniam nequitiae in habitaculis eorum, in medio eorum.

54{55}[16] *Veniat mors super illos, let death come upon them*: that is, they are worthy of spiritual death, namely, that in the present they lack the life of grace, and in the future the life of glory. Not, however, that we will that [to happen], but [we say this] as a foretelling or as conforming to the divine justice. It is in this sense that Christ or any just man says through Jeremiah: *You, O Lord, know all their counsel against me . . . ; forgive not their iniquity, and let not their sin be blotted out from your sight.*[145] *Et descendant in infernum viventes, and let them go down alive into hell*, that is, with their body and their soul, in the day of last judgment: whose descent is figured in the swallowing of Dathan and Abiron and Korah, who were devoured live by the earth.[146] *Quoniam nequitiae in habitaculis eorum, for there is wickedness in their dwellings*. In the preceding explanation the sense of these [words] is clear.

54{55}[17] *But I have cried to God: and the Lord will save me.*

Ego autem ad Deum clamavi, et Dominus salvabit me.

54{55}[18] *Evening and morning, and at noon I will speak and declare: and he shall hear my voice.*

Vespere, et mane, et meridie, narrabo, et annuntiabo; et exaudiet vocem meam.

54{55}[17] *Ego autem ad Deum clamavi, but I have cried to God*: for it is befitting to pray without ceasing[147] and in all necessity and danger to flee to God with one's entire affection. *Et Dominus salvabit me, and the Lord will save me*: for he does not forsake those who hope in him; for *everyone that asks will receive and he that seeks will find.*[148] For this reason the Lord says through Jeremiah: *Delivering, I will deliver you, . . . and your life will be saved for you, because you have put your trust in me.*[149] **54{55}[18]** *Vespere et mane et meridie; evening and morning,*

---

145 Jer. 18:23a.
146 Num. 16:32–33.
147 Luke 18:1: *And he spoke also a parable to them that we ought always to pray and not to faint.*
148 Matt. 7:8.
149 Jer. 39:18.

and at noon, that is, all day, from these hours constantly; or, *evening*, that is, in the state of the beginning, and *morning*, that is, in the state of the proficient, and *noon*, that is, in the state of the perfect; or, *evening and morning and at noon*, that is, in the end, the beginning, and the middle of my life; *narrabo, I will speak*, regarding myself, *et annuntiabo, and I will declare* to all the examples of the divine law and the works of the Savior, and other things pertaining to salvation; as the Apostle [Paul] teaches: *Be filled with the Holy Spirit, speaking to yourselves in Psalms, and hymns, and spiritual canticles, singing and making melody in your hearts to the Lord, giving thanks always for all things.*[150] *Et exaudiet, and he shall hear*, the Lord himself [shall hear], *vocem meam, my voice*, by which I praise and call upon him.

54{55}[19] *He shall redeem my soul in peace from them that draw near to me: for among many they were with me.*

Redimet in pace animam meam ab his qui appropinquant mihi; quoniam inter multos erant mecum.

54{55}[20] *God shall hear, and he who is eternal shall humble them. For there is no change with them, and they have not feared God.*

Exaudiet Deus, et humiliabit illos, qui est ante saecula. Non enim est illis commutatio, et non timuerunt Deum.

54{55}[21] *He has stretched forth his hand to repay. They have defiled his covenant.*

Extendit manum suam in retribuendo; contaminaverunt testamentum eius.

54{55}[22] *They are divided by the wrath of his countenance; and his heart has drawn near. His words are smoother than oil, and the same are darts.*

Divisi sunt ab ira vultus eius; et appropinquavit cor illius. Molliti sunt sermones eius super oleum; et ipsi sunt iacula.

54{55}[19] *Redimet in pace anima meam ab his qui appropinquant mihi, he shall redeem my soul in peace from them that draw near me* so that they might harm me, delivering me from their snares, and preserving in me interior peace. This is the word of loving trust. *Quoniam inter multos, for among many* called but not the elect, *erant mecum, were with me,* in

---

150 Eph. 4:18b–20a.

place, not in mind; bodily, not spiritually; in faith, not morals.[151] For the persecutors of the Church and of the just among those who are called (who are many) within the body of the elect, but by life and morals they are far away from them. **54{55}[20]** *Exaudiet Deus, God shall hear* my prayers, *et humiliabit illos, and shall humble them*, in the way that they who exalt themselves in this age will be humbled in the future. *Non enim est illis commutatio, for there is no change with them*: because they are disdainful of converting. Whence the Apostle [Paul] says: *A man that is a heretic, after the first and second admonition, avoid, knowing that he, that is, such a one, is subverted.*[152] Of such persons Isaiah also says: *For you have said: We have entered into a league with death, and we have made a covenant with hell.*[153] **54{55}[21]** *Contaminaverunt testamentum eius, they have defiled his covenant*, that is, they have transgressed the law of Christ, and they say *that they know God: but in their works they deny him.*[154] **54{55}[22]** *Divisi sunt, they are divided* from the society of the elect, and separated from the charity and the grace of God, *ab ira vultus eius, by the wrath of his countenance*, that is, by the just judgment of God; *et appropinquavit cor illius, and his heart has drawn near*, that is, God, as far as is in him, is always ready to be merciful, to render help, and to spare.

Molliti sunt sermones eius, his words are smoother, namely [the words] of God, *super oleum, than oil*: because sacred Scripture recommends to us his abundant love and his goodness: which indeed is more sweet than any honey or oil. For this reason, a later Psalm says: *How sweet are your words to my palate! More than honey to my mouth.*[155] Of these words we have also previously spoken above: *More to be desired than gold*

---

151   E. N. So long as one has not sinned against the faith, one can be in mortal sin (and therefore without sanctifying grace, without faith *formed in charity*), yet still a "dead" member of the Church. These are the ones to whom Denis is referring to. As St. Thomas makes clear, there are four "classes" of members of the Church, two of which are members incorporate of the Church *in act*, and two only *in potency* (potentially) or in an equivocal sense. ST IIIa, q. 8, art. 3, co and III *Super Sent.*, d. 13, q. 2, art. 2. The fully-incorporate members are members *through charity*. Underneath them are those members solely by faith (*per fidem*) but not charity, who are, from a supernatural perspective "dead." The remaining classes are potential members only and include all mankind, and among mankind are those who are only potential members, but will be actual members before their death and those who are potential members, but who never will be actual members before their death.

152   Tit. 3:10–11a.
153   Is. 28:15a.
154   Titus 1:16a.
155   Ps. 118:103.

and many precious stones: and sweeter than honey and the honeycomb.[156] Jeremiah experiencing this said: *I am become as a drunken man, and as a man full of wine, at the presence of the Lord, and at the presence of his holy words.*[157] For what can be as smooth and as sweet as that which the apostle Paul says, *For his exceeding charity wherewith* God the Father *loved us,*[158] he sent *his own Son, in the likeness of sinful flesh?*[159] And John: *God so loved the world,* he says, *as to give his only begotten Son.*[160] And again: *Behold what manner of charity the Father has bestowed upon us, that we should be called, and should be the sons of God.*[161] And so that which through Solomon, the eternal Wisdom, the most-high God, declares is exceedingly sweet: *My delights are to be with the children of men.*[162] *Et ipsi, and the same,* namely the heretics and the enemies of the Church and the persecutors of the just, *sunt iacula, are darts:* because they assail the truth and the deeds of the words of Scripture, and they diligently seek to injure the simple. And so the Apostle [Paul] says: *And their speech spreads like a cancer.*[163] Of which Job brings to mind: *They have been rebellious to the light; they have not known his ways,*[164] and God *does not suffer it to pass unrevenged.*[165] The rest [of the verses of this Psalm] are sufficiently explained.

From this Psalm we are taught how much Christ endured and how much it behooves us to carry out his example, since *the servant is not greater than his Lord.*[166] Let us therefore endeavor during this time on earth to bear with joy all difficult and bitter things for the love of Christ, keeping in mind that which the Apostle said: *A faithful saying: for if we be dead with him, we shall live also with him; if we suffer, we shall also reign with him.*[167]

---

156   Ps. 18:11.
157   Jer. 23 :9b.
158   Eph. 2:4b.
159   Rom. 8:3b.
160   John 3:16a.
161   1 John 3:1a.
162   Prov. 8:31.
163   2 Tim. 2:17a.
164   Job 24:13a.
165   Job. 24:12b.
166   John 13:16b.
167   2 Tim. 2:11–12a.

PRAYER

WE SUPPLIANTS PREVAIL UPON YOUR omnipotence, O God, who are before all ages, that you might hear our prayer and not reject our entreaty: so that we who are expecting you to save us, you might free from pusillanimity of spirit and from all turbulence of life and soul.

Omnipotentiam tuam supplices exoramus, qui es ante saecula,
Deus, ut orationem nostram exaudias, ac deprecationem
nostram ne despicias: ut qui te salvantem
nos exspectamus, liberes nos a pusillan-
imitate spiritus, et omni vitae et
animae tempestate.

Psalm 55

ARTICLE X

EXPLANATION OF CHRIST OF THE FIFTY-FIFTH PSALM:
MISERERE MEI, DEUS, QUONIAM
CONCULCAVIT ME HOMINE, ETC.
HAVE MERCY ON ME, O GOD, FOR MAN
HAS TRODDEN ME, ETC.

55{56}[1] *Unto the end, in verses, for a people that is removed at a distance from holy things, for an inscription of a title for David, when the Philistines (foreigners) held him in Gath.*[1]

In finem, in carminibus, pro populo qui longe factus est a sanctis, in tituli inscriptio ipsi David, cum tenerent eum allophyli in Geth.

HIS PSALM NOW BEING DISCUSSED HAS this title: 55{56}[1] *In finem, in carminibus, pro populo qui longe factus est a sanctis, in tituli inscriptio ipsi David, cum tenerent eum allophyli in Geth; Unto the end, in verses, for a people that is removed at a distance from holy things, for an inscription of a title for David, when the Philistines (foreigners) held him in Gath.* Some explain this Psalm as relating literally to David. Yet commonly it is explained as pertaining to the Church or any one member of the faithful facing multiple tribulations. But because Christ is the object[2] of all the Prophets, we ought (to the extent that we can) to expound the Psalms and all the prophetic Scriptures as referring to Christ: for the words that regard him are more sweet, more fruitful, and more instructive. Therefore, expounding upon this Psalm in such a manner, the sense of the title is: *For David,* that is, this Psalm by signification of David applies to Christ, and *unto the end,* the ultimate [end], which is eternal life, it directs us, *in verses,* so that in all things thanksgiving is to be rendered to God, written and published *for the people,* that is, about the people or against the people,

---

1 E. N. The text departs from the Sixto-Clementine Vulgate. I have retained Denis's reading.
2 E. N. The text has *opus* ("work"), but the editor suggests *scopus* ("goal" or "target") is proper.

that is removed at a distance, not in terms of place or space, but lacking faith and grace, *from holy things*, that is, Christ's faithful, *for an inscription of title* which Pilate placed over the head of Christ crucified, that is, against the Jews who denied this title, saying to Pilate: *Write not, The King of the Jews; but that he said, I am the King of the Jews;*[3] when [they] *held him*, namely, Christ, *the Philistines*, that is, the gentile subordinates of Pilate, those four that hung Christ upon the gibbet;[4] *in Gath*, that is, in the pressing of the Passion or the Cross.[5] By Philistine (*allophylos*) also one is able to understand the Jews themselves: for in the manner that the strangers (*allophyli*) or Palestinians (*Palaestini*) or Philistines (*Philistaei*) captured David in Gath,[6] leading him to Achis their king so that they might have him killed, [7] so did the Jews capture Jesus and bring him bound to Pontius Pilate so that he might put him to death.[8] And this they did in Gath, which is interpreted as wine press, that is, in Jerusalem, of which the Savior in the Gospel says: *Jerusalem, Jerusalem, you that kill the prophets;*[9] and again, *because it cannot be that a prophet perish, out of Jerusalem.*[10]

---

3   John 19:21b.

4   E. N. That there were four Roman soldiers at the crucifixion of Jesus is implied by John 19:23, in that the solders "when they had crucified him, took his garments (and they made four parts, to every soldier a part)."

5   E. N. Gath (or Geth) was one of the five city-states of the Philistines. *See* Joshua 13:3, 1 Sam. 5:7–10; 6:17. The Hebrew word Gath (גַּת) means a wine press. The motif of Christ's Passion and Crucifixion and the winepress (the so-called *torcular mysticum*, the mystical winepress) was frequent in Christian art in the Middle Ages and well into the 18th century. The ligature between Christ and the winepress is found, for example, in Is. 63:3 which prophesies of Christ ("I have trodden the winepress alone. . . .") and in Rev. 14:19–20 ("And the winepress was trodden without the city, and blood came out of the wine press. . . ."). An example of this theme rendered in art can be seen in the painting of Mary the Co-Redemptrix and the Mystical Press at the Church of San Gumberto (1511). The image with its Eucharistic suggestion wends its way even into the poetry of George Herbert (1593–1633): "Sinne is that presse and vice, which forceth pain / To hunt his cruell food through ev'ry vein. // Who knows not Love, let him assay / And taste that juice, which on the cross a pike / Did set again abroach; then let him say / If ever he did taste the like. / Love is that liquor sweet and most divine, / Which my God feels as bloude [blood] but I, as wine." "The Agonie," *The English Poems of George Herbert* (London: Dent 1974), 58. (ed. C. A Patrides).

6   1 Sam. 21:10–15.

7   E. N. The word *allophylos* (ἀλλόφυλος) is a Greek word meaning foreign or Gentile. By extension, it is used by the Jews to refer to the Philistines who lived in Palestine.

8   Matt. 27:1–2.

9   Matt. 23:37a.

10   Luke 13:33b.

55{56}[2] *Have mercy on me, O God, for man has trodden me under foot; all the day long he has afflicted me fighting against me.*

Miserere mei, Deus, quoniam conculcavit me homo; tota die impugnans, tribulavit me.

Therefore, Christ, as a man who is passible, at the approaching Passion, says to God, the Father: **55{56}[2]** *Miserere mei, Deus; have mercy on me, O God,* freeing me not from the misery of fault,[11] but of punishment, that is, from the state of passibility and death convey me by the blessed Resurrection to immortal life and the impassible state. And so I pray that you might be merciful to me, *quoniam conculcavit me homo, for man has trodden me under foot,* that is, Judas the traitor: of which an earlier Psalm states, *The man of peace, in whom I trusted, who ate my bread, hath greatly supplanted me.*[12] Here, I say, he tread on me with evil words and for the purposes of treading upon me he sold me out and betrayed me. *Tota die, all the day long,* namely, on the fourth day, when he sold me, or on the fifth day, when he betrayed me that evening,[13] *impugnans, fighting* me in a hidden manner, that is, withdrawing himself from me and inducing others to fight against me, *tribulavit me, he has afflicted me:* because, as was noted in the elucidation of the preceding Psalm,[14] Judas's persecution of Christ was the more grievous because Judas was so close to Christ. For since Christ was most just, so much the more did the sin of Judas and the Jews more greatly displease him the more unjust they were against him; and this holy and just displeasure is called the tribulation of Christ. It is also believed that Christ, as most loving, frequently felt distress about Judas, especially during the Passion.

AN ALTERNATIVE UNDERSTANDING

R THUS: *FOR MAN (HOMO) HAS TRODDEN ME,* that is, the multitude of men (*hominum*), namely, the Jews and the ministers of Pilate. For often in sacred Scripture a singular is put in place of a plural,[15] the way that Judah does his brother Simeon: *Come up with me into my lot,*[16] where by Judah and Simeon is understood the tribes

---

11   E. N. This is so because Christ had no sin, and so suffered no evil of fault (*mala culpae*), only the evil of punishment (*mala poena*). For more on the distinction between the evil of fault and the evil of punishment, *see* footnote 21-146 in Volume 1.

12   Ps. 40:10.

13   Matt. 26:14–16; 46-50. E. N. Judas made his pact with the chief priests on Wednesday and betrayed him on the evening of Thursday.

14   Ps. 54:13–15.

15   E. N. The word *homo*, a man, is considered plural under this custom, and so read as being *homines*, men.

16   Judges 1:3a.

or the people that were the progenitors of Judah and Simeon. And in Exodus, the Lord says to Pharaoh: *Let my son go* so that he might render sacrifice to me in the desert,[17] where by son is understood the sons of Israel. Here, therefore, they trampled upon the Son of God, reputing him to be as he were nothing, oppressing and vigorously trampling upon him with their bodily feet: especially in the night when the men that had him mocked him, beating him and spitting upon him.[18] For they most irreverently manhandled him and gratified themselves by tormenting him *tota die, all the day long* during the Day of Preparation (*Parasceves*). *Impugnans, fighting* with words and with whips, *tribulavit me, he has afflicted* me, [that is,] the man just mentioned, that is, the ungodly men, [have afflicted me] to death.[19] Of which it speaks more openly below:

55{56}[3] *My enemies have trodden on me all the day long; for they are many that make war against me.*

Conculcaverunt me inimici mei tota die; quoniam multi bellantes adversum me.

55{56}[3] *Conculcaverunt me, they have trodden on me*: in the manner already stated; *inimici mei, my enemies*, who *repaid me evil for good: and hatred for my love*,[20] *tota die, all the day long* as stated beforehand,[21] or [alternatively] *all the day long*, that is, the whole time when I dwelt among them preaching and performing miracles. For at the very beginning when Christ began to preach, the Jews opposed him, as is clear from the narrative of the Gospel.[22] *Quoniam multi bellantes adversum me, for they are many that make war against me*, namely, the chiefs of the priests with their partisans; but I through patience overcame them. For this reason one reads about me in an earlier Psalm: *The Lord who is strong and mighty: the Lord mighty in battle*.[23] Here also Christ [states] through Jeremiah: *I heard the reproaches of many, and terror on every side*.[24]

---

17 Ex. 4:23a.
18 Luke 22:63–65.
19 E. N. Again the singular (the pronoun "he" — referring to the object "man") is understood to refer to the plural ("men"). *See* footnote 55-15.
20 Ps. 108:5.
21 E. N. In other words, the Day of Preparation (*Parasceves*) before the Feast of the Passover (*Pasch*).
22 Matt. 9:3, 11, 14, 34; 11:19, 12:2, 10, 14, 24; 15: 1, 2, 12; 16:1; 21:15, 16, 23, 46; 22:15–17, 23–28, 34–36.
23 Ps. 23:8.
24 Jer. 20:10a.

55{56}[4] *From the height of the day I shall fear: but I will trust in you.*

Ab altitudine diei timebo: ego vero in te sperabo.

55{56}[5] *In God I will praise my words, in God I have put my trust: I will not fear what flesh can do against me.*

In Deo laudabo sermones meos; in Deo speravi; non timebo quid faciat mihi caro.

55{56}[4] *Ab altitudine diei timebo, from the height of the day I shall fear.* While some great torments are suffered on certain days, here it says to fear *the* day; the more one foresees a certain time of the day one will suffer more severely, to that extent that hour is asserted as more greatly to be feared. But the Passion of Christ, continuously increased and developed from the hour of night where, being taken hold of, he was first made captive and lasting even to the noon hour. Therefore, in the way that Christ by natural affection abhorred the approach of his Passion, so also he feared the day of his Passion: and all the more as that day ascended closer to the noon hour, because the punishment grew more burdensome for him as the day ascended. For this reason, he most feared the height of the day in which before the most immeasurable punishment he cried: *My God, my God, why have you forsaken me?*[25] Whence also *his sweat became like drops of blood, trickling down upon the ground.*[26] But this fear was in Christ, during the time of the three prayers we have previously tried to understand. *Ego vero in te, but I . . . in you* God, my Father, *sperabo, will trust,* trusting to be preserved, and raised up again, and glorified by you.
55{56}[5] *In Deo laudabo sermones meos. In God I will praise my words.* This is what Christ asserted in the Gospels: *My doctrine is not mine, but his that sent me.*[27] And again: *He that speaks of himself, seeks his own glory: but he that seeks the glory of him that sent him, he is true.*[28] *In Deo speravi, in God I have put my trust,* and so *non timebo, I will not fear* with an inordinate dread, *quid faciat mihi caro, what flesh can do against me,* that is, the Jews and whoever else [may be against me]. For however much Christ feared that hour, the Passion being imminent, nevertheless as he accepted this fear through the deliberation of reason, so at his command he made it to cease. Whence he also undaunted went to meet his enemies and said: *Whom do you seek?*[29]

---

25 Matt. 27:46.
26 Luke 22:44.
27 John 7:16b.
28 John 7:18.
29 John 18:4, 7.

55{56}[6]   *All the day long they detested my words: all their thoughts were against me unto evil.*

Tota die verba mea execrabantur; adversum me omnes cogitationes eorum in malum.

55{56}[7]   *They will dwell and hide themselves: they will watch my heel. As they have waited for my soul,*

Inhabitabunt, et abscondent; ipsi calcaneum meum observabunt. Sicut sustinuerunt animam meam,

55{56}[8]   *For nothing shall you save them: in your anger you shall break the people in pieces,*

Pro nihilo salvos facies illos; in ira populos confringes,

55{56}[6] *Tota die*, all the day long of my Passion, or all the days of my preaching, *verba mea execrabantur*, they detested my words, that is, they were condemned by the Jews, and they were interpreted badly. For they said as can be read in Matthew: *He has blasphemed*; and *He is guilty of death;*[30] and with John, *This man is not of God, who keeps not the sabbath.*[31] This is what according to Amos the Jews were led into: *They have hated him that rebukes in the gate: and have abhorred him that speaks perfectly.*[32] And also Christ said: *The world hates me, because I give testimony of it, that the works thereof are evil.*[33] *Adversum me omnes cogitationes eorum in malum*, all their thoughts were against me unto evil, namely, that they might falsely accuse me and unjustly put me to death.
55{56}[7] *Inhabitabunt, they will dwell*: that is, the unbelieving Jews dwelt with me and with my disciples in the Synagogue, or in the house of the Lord, at least with respect to the faith, for they declared themselves to worship God and to expect Christ the King: and so they dwelt in the Synagogue with those instructed in the faith and believing in God; *et abscondent, and they hide themselves*, that is, in a hidden way they sought to ambush me, testing me with deceitful words. *Ipsi calcaneum meum observabunt, they will watch my heel*, that is, they will scrutinize my works in order that they might unearth some pretext against me. For this reason it is written: *And they watched him whether he would heal on the sabbath days; that they might accuse him.*[34]

---

30   Matt. 26:65–66.
31   John 9:16a.
32   Amos 5:10.
33   John 7:7b.
34   Mark 3:2.

Sicut sustinuerunt animam meam, as they have waited for my soul **55{56}** [8] *pro nihilo, for nothing,* that is, as they sought to revile me, and awaited [to take] my life, seeing it for nothing, that is, as if it appeared to be nothing and was reckoned as nothing, it could be disposed of, and they would not judge themselves to be sinning by killing me; *Salvos facies illos? Shall you save them?* It is as if it said, "No." And as if it were also saying: How could those who persecute me in such a manner truly be doing good so that I shall truly save them? And so it adds: *In ira populos confringes, in your anger you shall break the people in pieces*: that is, by the redress of divine justice, you will totally destroy, with respect to the existence (*esse*) of grace and glory, the unbelieving and impenitent Jews persecuting me, not giving to them any existence (*esse*) of merit, but also in this life diminishing, dispersing, and humiliating them. For here is what Hosea says about them: *Their root is dried up, they shall yield no fruit.*[35] And through Isaiah, Christ speaks of them: *I have trampled on them in my indignation,*[36] *and I have trodden down the people in my wrath.*[37]

55{56}[9] O God, I have declared to you my life: you have set my tears in your sight, as also in your promise.

Deus, vitam meam annuntiavi tibi; posuisti lacrimas meas in conspectu tuo, sicut et in promissione tua.

55{56}[10] Then shall my enemies be turned back. In what day soever I shall call upon you, behold I know because you are my God.[38]

Tunc convertentur inimici mei retrorsum: in quacumque die invocavero te, ecce cognovi quoniam Deus meus es.

55{56}[11] In God will I praise the word, in the Lord will I praise his speech. In God have I hoped, I will not fear what man can do to me.

In Deo laudabo verbum; in Domino laudabo sermonem. In Deo speravi: non timebo quid faciat mihi homo.

55{56}[9] *Deus, vitam meam annuntiavi tibi,* O God, I have declared to you my life: that is, to the honor and glory of your name I have professed to others by the manner of my life, holiness, and all which I have done,

---

35 Hosea 9:16a.

36 Is. 63:3a.

37 Is. 63:6a.

38 E. N. The Douay Rheims does not translate *quoniam* (for/because); accordingly, I have added it.

I have done before you, and I have ascribed to you. In this way, Christ declared his life to God the Father, since he asserted: *I love the Father: and as the Father has given me commandment, so do I;*[39] and elsewhere, *I do always the things that please him* (that is, my Father).[40] And in Luke also, asserting fulfilled in him that which was foretold by Isaiah: *The Spirit of the Lord,* he said, *is upon me, because the Lord has anointed me: he has sent me to preach to the meek, to heal the contrite of heart.*[41] *Posuisti lacrimas meas in conspectu tuo, you have set my tears in your sight,* that is, you have accepted them, and for those tears that I have shed, you have been satisfied. Whence the Apostle [Paul] said: *with a strong cry and tears, offering up prayers . . . he was heard for his reverence.*[42] At the raising again of Lazarus from the dead, *Jesus wept,*[43] and said: *Father, I give you thanks that you have heard me.*[44] *Sicut et in promissione tua, as also in your promise,* that is, as you said through the Prophet: *Behold my servant, I will uphold him: my elect, my soul delights in him.*[45] **55{56}[10]** *Tunc, then,* that is, since you will have heard me by raising me up from the dead, *convertentur inimici mei, shall my enemies be turned,* namely, the Jews, *retrorsum, back,* departing from you and not believing in me, as is attested of them by the prophet Jeremiah: *They have turned their back to me, and not their face.*[46] Of which we elsewhere read: *After sixty-two weeks Christ shall be slain: and the people that shall deny him shall not be his,*[47] that is, the Jews who said, *We have no king but Caesar.*[48]

In quacumque die invocavero te, in what day soever I shall call upon you, praying for myself and for the Mystical Body, *ecce cognovit, behold I know,* by experience, or experiencing being heard in prayer, *quoniam Deus meus es, because you are my God* in a most special way, indeed also always ruling me and hearing me. **55{56}[11]** *In Deo laudabo verbum, in Domino laudabo sermonem; in God I will praise the word, in the Lord I will praise his speech.* One [part of the verse] explains the other [part]: that is, whatever I say or foretell, I refer ultimately to God, and I ascribe the illumination to him, and I do not seek my own glory. And so Christ says: *I receive glory*

---

39   John 14:31.
40   John 8:29b.
41   Luke 4:18–21 E. N. (quoting Luke 4:18 = Is. 61:1a). Denis's quote is from Isaiah, which is slightly different from the quote in Luke.
42   Heb. 5:7.
43   John 11:35.
44   John 11:41.
45   Is. 42:1a.
46   Jer. 2:27a.
47   Dan. 9:26a.
48   John 19:15b.

not from men;[49] and in another place, *I seek not my own glory.*[50] *In Deo speravi, non timebo quid faciat mihi homo; in God have I hoped, I will not fear what man can do to me,* [man] unjustly opposing me.

55{56}[12] *In me, O God, are vows to you, which I will pay, praises to you.*

In me sunt, Deus, vota tua, quae reddam, laudationes tibi.

55{56}[13] *Because you have delivered my soul from death, my feet from falling: that I may please in the sight of God, in the light of the living.*

Quoniam eripuisti animam meam de morte, et pedes meos de lapsu, ut placeam coram Deo in lumine viventium.

55{56}[12] *In me sunt, Deus, vota mea; in me, O God, are vows to you,* that is, in my heart are holy desires infused by you in me by which I desire your honor and the salvation of men; *quae reddam laudationes tibi, which I will pay praises to you,* that is, which I will offer to you both sacrifice of praise and matter of praise.[51] For God is praised and honored by holy desire. **55{56}[13]** *Quoniam eripuisti animam meam de morte, because you have delivered my soul from death* in the day of the Resurrection, uniting it with the body, from which it existed separated following death; *et pedes meos de lapsu, and my feet from falling:* that is, you have preserved from the ruin of sin all my operations by prevenient grace, so that I never fell, but I unceasingly did that which was pleasing to you. And this because you made it so, that I might also acknowledge openly this to be by your grace, *ut placeam coram Deo in lumine viventium; that I might please in the sight of God, in the light of the living,* that is, so that I might please you, and I might have pleasure in you and not in myself: *that I might please,*

---

49   John 5:41.
50   John 8:50a.
51   E. N. Everything ought to be offered to God or give rise to an occasion for praising God. As St. Thomas says in his work *De spiritualibus creaturis* (*On Spiritual Creatures*): "According to John of Damascus, the heavens are said to show forth, to praise, to exult, in a material sense, insofar as they are for men matters of praising (*materia laudandi*) or showing forth, or exulting." *De spirit. creat.*, a. 6, ad 14. As St. Francis de Sales (1567–1622) puts it this way in his *An Introduction to a Devout Life*: "Behold, Philothea, how one may extract good thoughts and holy aspirations from everything that presents itself amidst the variety of this mortal life! Unhappy they who withdraw the creatures from their Creator, to make them the instrument of sin; and thrice happy they that turn the creatures to the glory of their Creator, and employ them to the honor of his sovereign Majesty." St. Francis de Sales, *Introduction to a Devout Life* (New York: Frederick Pustet & Co. 1920), 92.

I say, before you, *in the light of the living,* that is, in the most splendid land of the blessed, where before God I stand interceding for the world, in the manner that the Apostle [Paul] expresses to the Hebrews, *Jesus is not entered into the holies made with hands, . . . but into heaven itself, that he may appear now in the presence of God for us.*[52]

Christ, therefore, did not please himself in himself, but in God, that is, in himself, since he was God, or in God the Father and the Holy Trinity.[53] [In light of Christ's example,] how then are we miserable and most vain and foolish men ever able do anything where we please ourselves, disdaining others, and glorifying in ourselves? Let us pay heed to the admonition of St. Paul: *We,* he says *who are stronger ought to bear the infirmities of the weak, and not to please ourselves. For Christ did not please himself.*[54]

ARTICLE XI

MORAL ELUCIDATION OF
THE SAME FIFTY-FIFTH PSALM:

55{56}[1]   *Unto the end, in verses, for a people that is removed at a distance from holy things, for an inscription of a title for David, when the Philistines (foreigners) held him in Gath.*

In finem, in carminibus, pro populo qui longe factus est a sanctis, in tituli inscriptio ipsi David, cum tenerent eum allophyli in Geth.

55{56}[2]   *Have mercy on me, O God, for man has trodden me under foot; all the day long he has afflicted me fighting against me.*

Miserere mei, Deus, quoniam conculcavit me homo; tota die impugnans, tribulavit me.

55{56}[3]   *My enemies have trodden on me all the day long; for they are many that make war against me.*

Conculcaverunt me inimici mei tota die; quoniam multi bellantes adversum me.

---

52   Heb. 9:24.
53   *E. N.* Christ's human nature—his intellect, his will, his body—did not seek its own glory or pleasure, but sought only to please Christ's divine person, God the Father, and the entirety of the Trinity.
54   Rom. 15:1, 3a.

OW, TROPOLOGICALLY EXPLAINING THIS Psalm, the previously mentioned title should be understood in this way: **55{56}[1]** *In finem, unto the end*, that is, this Psalm is directing us to Christ, and is written *pro populo qui longe factus est a sanctis, for a people that is removed at a distance from holy things*, that is, which in life and in morals are in discord from those of the elect, *in tituli inscriptione, for an inscription of a title*: for the title of the Crucified, namely, *This is the King of the Jews*,[55] whom those who are holy venerate with faith and works, and whom those with either a reprobate life or an unbelieving mind deny. The Psalm, let me say, *ipsi David, for David* in figure, *cum tenerunt eum allophyli in Geth, when the Philistines (foreigners) held him in Gath*, that is, those alienated from charity and a formed faith surround the Church or any Christian with troubles, temptations, and pressing matters. The Church, therefore, which is pressed upon by all manner of adversaries as if in a winepress, and any member of the faithful surrounded by many persecutors, cries out to God: **55{56}[2]** *Miserere mei, Deus; have mercy on me, O God*, that is, you, my Creator, Governor, Savior, and Judge, who are naturally kindly, and entirely merciful, show me consolation in my misery, not having a disposition towards punishment, but [a disposition towards] mercifully and quickly saving. For I am pressingly in need, *quoniam conculcavit me homo, for man has trodden me*, man the detractor, the harmer, the corrupter of souls, the persecutor of charity, the adversary of innocence, abusively oppressing me with the foot of pride. Of which foot an earlier Psalm said: *Let not the foot of pride come to me.*[56] **55{56} [3]** *Conculcaverunt me inimici mei, my enemies have trodden on me*, [my enemies] both domestic and foreign, visible and invisible, hidden and manifest, *tota die, all the day long*, [meaning during a] natural [day],[57] that is, during the daytime and nighttime, tempting, spurning, or by similar means opposing me. *Quoniam multi* sunt, *for they are many that bellantes adversum me, make war against me*, who attempt to try to turn me from you and to incline me to vice. For the world fights against us, that is, worldly men [fight against us], so that we might be perverted with the perverse; the flesh [fights us], that is the passions of the movements of sensuality, so that they might seduce men from the way of right reason; and demons [fight us]. Of this latter, the Apostle says: *Our wrestling is*

---

55   Luke 23:38.
56   Ps. 35:12a.
57   E. N. Here, and in the verses below, Denis speaks of a "natural day," *dies naturalis*, and an "artificial day," *dies artificialis*. A "natural day" is the normal 24-hour day. An "artificial day" is the day measured from the rising of the sun to its setting.

not against flesh and blood; but against principalities and powers, against the rulers of the world of this darkness, against the spirits of wickedness in the high places.[58] This [which is stated by the Apostle] is not to be understood as if there is not within us some battle against flesh and blood, since the Apostle says, *If you live according to the flesh, you shall die;*[59] and again, Whoever *are Christ's, have crucified their flesh, with the vices and concupiscences.*[60] But this is therefore said because it is not for us to fight only or principally against flesh and blood.[61]

55{56}[4] *From the height of the day I shall fear: but I will trust in you.*

Ab altitudine diei timebo: ego vero in te sperabo.

55{56}[5] *In God I will praise my words, in God I have put my trust: I will not fear what flesh can do against me.*

In Deo laudabo sermones meos; in Deo speravi; non timebo quid faciat mihi caro.

55{56}[4] *Ab altitudine diei timebo, from the height of the day I shall fear,* that is, by ascent or the course of time conceded me, I will fear because of the imminency of danger. For so long as I live, to that extent I will sin more frequently, especially when the just man falls seven times a day:[62] and so I fear time in the future, *because the days are evil*[63] for man often sins during them. Or [we might construe it] thus: *From the height of the day,* [of] any artificial [day],[64] in which I live, I fear: because more occasions for sin occur throughout the day than at night, especially when the day has reached its peak. For in the morning a man is more fit to toward devotion, but around noon the most burdensome needs of the body very seriously hinder it, for [at that time] we take in food and drink, which, once taken, make man less apt for devotion. For this reason, the devout fear this hour, namely, lest they burden their hearts with excessive drinking or drunkenness:[65] and so they draw near to the table as if it were a jail.

---

58   Eph. 6:12.

59   Rom. 8:13a.

60   Gal. 5:24.

61   E. N. Denis is suggesting that there is an implied limitation in Eph. 6:12, so that when St. Paul says that "our wrestling is not against flesh and blood," he implies an "only" or a "principally," but that a large part of the battle includes a fight against the world and against the devil and his minions.

62   *Cf.* Prov. 24:16a.

63   Eph. 5:16b.

64   E. N. For "artificial day," *see* footnote 55-57.

65   Luke 21:34a.

Ego vero in te sperabo, but I will trust in you: that is, though I am entirely encircled by evil, yet I do not despair; but I trust in you without ceasing that I will not succumb or be vanquished, but that in your name I will prevail, knowing as being of the utmost truth what is written, *Greater is he that is in you, than he that is in the world;*[66] and saying with the most blessed Elisha: *Fear not: for there are more with us than with them.*[67] *For with him is an arm of flesh: with us the Lord our God.*[68] Whence also it is said by Hosea: *Keep mercy and judgment, and hope in your God always.*[69] **55{56}[5]** *In Deo laudabo sermones meos, in God I will praise my words*, directing them to his honor; not in vain philosophy, or in sterile eloquence, or rhetorical speech, or with presumptuous, evil, or garrulous talk, will I praise him;[70] but I will rejoice by the word of confession, of prayer, and of divine praise. *In Deo speravi, non timebo; in God I have put my trust: I will not fear* finally, with an oppressive or disordered fear, *quid faciat mihi caro, what flesh can do against me*, that is, a worldly man. For I will not fear *them that kill the body:*[71] not at all — rather I will receive, I will embrace, and I will joyfully endure tribulations as if they were a gift of God, recalling that which the Apostle [Paul] said: *For unto you it is given for Christ, not only to believe in him, but also to suffer for him.*[72]

55{56}[6]   *All the day long they detested my words: all their thoughts were against me unto evil.*

Tota die verba mea execrabantur; adversum me omnes cogitationes eorum in malum.

55{56}[7]   *They will dwell and hide themselves: they will watch my heel. As they have restrained my soul,*[73]

Inhabitabunt, et abscondent; ipsi calcaneum meum observabunt. Sicut sustinuerunt animam meam,

---

66   1 John 4:4b.
67   2 Kings 6:16.
68   2 Chr. 32:8a.
69   Hosea 12:6.
70   Cf. Col. 2:8: *Beware lest any man cheat you by philosophy, and vain deceit; according to the tradition of men, according to the elements of the world, and not according to Christ.*
71   Matt. 10:28a.
72   Phil. 1:29.
73   E. N. I have rendered *sustinuerunt* from the Douay Rheims's "they have waited for my soul" to "they have restrained my soul."

55{56}[8] *For nothing shall you save them: in your anger you shall break the people in pieces,*

    Pro nihilo salvos facies illos; in ira populos confringes,

55{56}[6] *Tota die verba mea execrabantur, all the day long they detested my words.* This is what the Apostle said: *We are reviled, and we bless.*[74] For this reason also Christ said to his disciples: *If they have persecuted me, they will also persecute you.*[75] For the ungodly despise and disparage the words of just men; and as Job said, *The just man is laughed to scorn.*[76] *Adversum me omnes cogitationes eorum, all their thoughts were against me,* namely, [the thoughts of] heretics, schismatics, and the perverse, are *in malum, unto evil,* so that they might contradict me and harm me, and inflict upon me the evil of punishment and fault. **55{56}[7]** *Inhabitabunt, they will dwell* with me in the militant Church, wherein the good and the evil are mixed, and upon the earth and during this age the aforesaid will be my adversaries; *et abscondent, and they hide themselves,* that is, fraudulently and covertly endeavor to cause harm. Indeed, Christ foretold of such men: *Beware of false prophets, who come to you in the clothing of sheep, but inwardly they are ravening wolves;*[77] and again, *A man's enemies are they of his own household.*[78] *Ipsi calcaneum meum observabunt, they will watch my heel,* that is, they will scrutinize (*explorabunt*) all my works, not so that they might imitate them, but so that they might complain of them: in the way the Apostle spoke to the Galatians [regarding the] *false brethren brought in unawares, who came in privately to scrutinize (explorare) our liberty, which we have in Christ Jesus.*[79] Whence also in an earlier Psalm above: *The sinner shall watch the just man: and shall gnash upon him with his teeth.*[80]

Sicut sustinuerunt, as they have restrained, [that is, as] the ungodly [restrained], *animam meam, my soul* **55{56}[8]** *pro nihilo, for nothing,* spurning, offending, and persecuting it, *salvos facies illos, shall you save them:* that is, you will not save them,[81] because of the sins they have committed

74   1 Cor. 4:12b.

75   John 15:20b.

76   Job 12:4b.

77   Matt. 7:15.

78   Micah 7:6.

79   Gal. 2:4. E. N. I changed the Douay Rheims's "spy" which translated the Latin *explorare* to "scrutinize" so that it parallels Denis's *Commentary* where I translated *explorabunt* as "they will scrutinize."

80   Ps. 36:12.

81   E. N. This is a bit confusing, but Denis is understanding this verse as saying that, with respect to salvation, God will regard a soul's enemies just like they did the soul. In other words, God will save them like they treated the soul, *i.e.,* as nothing; hence, he will not save them at all (unless they repent).

against me: indeed, unless they will have done penance, I will perpetually
damn them, as they deserve.[82] But others explain this in a good way, so
that it reads in this sense: *As they have restrained my soul* from losing it,
for nothing, that is, graces or without their merit, *you shall save them.*[83]
In ira populos confringes, in your anger you shall break the people in pieces,
avenging their evil and damning them. Or [alternatively], *in your anger of
paternal discipline, you shall break the* sinning *people*, pressing down upon
their pride, and extirpating their vices: as we read in Isaiah: *The loftiness
of men shall be bowed down, and the haughtiness of men shall be humbled.*[84]

55{56}[9]   *O God, I have declared to you my life: you have set my tears
in your sight, as also in your promise.*

*Deus, vitam meam annuntiavi tibi; posuisti lacrimas meas
in conspectu tuo, sicut et in promissione tua.*

55{56}[10]   *Then shall my enemies be turned back. In what day soever I
shall call upon you, behold I know because you are my God.*[85]

*Tunc convertentur inimici mei retrorsum: in quacumque die
invocavero te, ecce cognovi quoniam Deus meus es.*

55{56}[9] *Deus, vitam meam annuntiavi tibi;* O God, I have declared
to you my life, [to you] or to your vicar, namely, the priest, humbly confessing my sins, and attributing good works. For Scripture states: *For
everyone that does evil hates the light, and comes not to the light, that his
works may not be reproved; but he that does truth, comes to the light, that
his works may be made manifest, because they are done in God.*[86] And
so also in an earlier Psalm it states: *Disclose your way to the Lord.*[87]
Posuisti lacrimas meas, you have set my tears, which I have shed for the
indulgence of sinners, or the delay of glory,[88] or a similar pious cause,

---

82   *Cf.* Luke 13:5: *I say to you; but except you do penance, you shall all likewise perish.*
83   E. N. Again, this is a bit cryptic. However, in this interpretation, Denis appears
to be saying that those who have prevented my soul from losing its grace and merits
will be saved.
84   Is. 2:17a.
85   E. N. The Douay Rheims does not translate *quoniam* (for/because); accordingly,
I have added it.
86   John 3:20–21.
87   Ps. 36:5a. *L.* The Douay Rheims has translated the imperative active verb *revela* as
"commit." But in this context (the confession of sins in auricular confession), *revela* might
better be understood in its other meanings: reveal, unveil, uncover, lay bare, disclose.
88   E. N. Like the souls suffering in Purgatory, *cf.* ST IIIa (Supp.), q. 4, art. 3, arg.
2, the souls on earth should lament the delay in glory (*i.e.*, the delay of death and

in conspectu tuo, in your sight, having received them and reserving for me a prize in the future on account of them. Hence the Lord by Hezekiah [says]: *I have heard,* he says, *your prayer, and I have seen your tears.*[89] And Jeremiah prays: *Turn not away your ear from my sighs and cries.*[90] *Sicut et in promissione tua, as also in your promise:* for God promised that he would hear the sighs, desires, prayers, and tears of his faithful.

55{56}[10] *Tunc convertentur inimici mei retrorsum, then shall my enemies be turned back:* that is, my visible and invisible enemies will lose heart when you hear my pleading. Whence also blessed James: *Resist the devil, and he will fly from you.*[91] *In quacumque die invocavero te, in what day soever I shall call upon you* with an internal, affectionate, and firm call, *ecce cognovit, behold I know,* by the reception of your goodness and grace, or the effect of devout prayers, *quoniam Deus meus es, for you are my God,* that is, you are in a special sense my God, providing to me and loving me. For this Christ affirms: *Amen, amen I say to you: if you ask the Father anything in my name, he will give it you.... Ask, and you shall receive; that your joy may be full.*[92]

55{56}[12] *In me, O God, are vows to you, which I will pay, praises to you.*

In me sunt, Deus, vota tua, quae reddam, laudationes tibi.[93]

55{56}[13] *Because you have delivered my soul from death, my feet from falling: that I may please in the sight of God, in the light of the living.*

Quoniam eripuisti animam meam de morte, et pedes meos de lapsu, ut placeam coram Deo in lumine viventium.

55{56}[12] *In me sunt, Deus, vota tua; in me, O God, are vows to you,* that is, the promises or affections by which I have obligated myself to serve you and by which I desire to honor you. For these vows are yours, that is, pleasing to you, and also mine, because they are conferred upon me by you. *Quae reddam laudationes tibi, which I will pay, praises to you,* fulfilling them, and so praising you by a good life. For while we are fulfilling the promise and the pious affections are led to their effect,

---

heavenly glory which follows) for it is death that separates us from the glory of the beatific vision and union with God.

89   2 Kings 20:5b.
90   Lam. 3:56b.
91   James 4:7b.
92   John 16:23–24.
93   E. N. Denis skips 55:11 in this article.

we praise God and we render a sacrifice of justice. **55{56}[13]** *Quoniam eripuisti animam meam de morte, because you have delivered my soul from death,* an eternal and infernal [death], by pouring out your Blood for me; by conferring also forgiveness from death from mortal sin; and by enlivening my soul, infusing it with charity and grace. *Et pedes meo, and my feet,* that is, my affections and my deeds, you have delivered *de lapsu, from falling,* that is, from the ruin of sin, directing my heart and my works according to the course of the divine law, in the manner you testified to regarding the people by the prophet [Hosea]: *I was like a foster father to Ephraim, I carried them in my arms.*[94] And this therefore you did to me, *ut placeam coram Deo, that I may please in the sight of God,* when I will have been brought to the tribunal of Christ and I will be saved, *in lumine viventium, in the light of the living,* that is, in the region of the living, and in the light of glory, participating in the divinity. Of this light a Psalm above says: *In your light we shall see light.*[95] And blessed Job writes: *Is there any numbering of his soldiers? And upon whom shall not his light arise?*[96]

See how truly full of feeling is this Psalm that we have heard: in which first, the tribulations of Christ and just men are recalled; and then the mind is strengthened by hope in God and by bringing out from the memory the benefits of God. Let us fulfill, therefore, the doctrine of this present Psalm, humbly fleeing to God in all tribulation, rousing true hope in him, and bearing a magnanimous and fearless heart, declaring our life to the Lord, ordering our words to his glory, returning the vows of promise and desire to him, and recalling intimately his benefits, so that we might choose in the future to please him alone, and not anything in this world.

---

94   Hosea 11:3a. *E. N.* "Surely Ephraim is an honorable son to me, surely he is a tender child; for since I spoke of him, I will still remember him . . . pitying I will pity him, says the Lord." Jer. 31:20. As Denis comments on Hosea 11:3: "'I was like a foster father to Ephraim.' I, the most merciful God, was like a kind caretaker or father to the people of Israel, preceding them in the wasteland during the day by column of cloud, lest they be burned by the heat of the sun, and by a column of light at night, lest they be afraid of the dark or go astray; 'I carried them in my arms,' that is, in the manner of a most kind foster father I sweetly conducted them, and led them by the desert, so that they might be sustained by my arms, that is, mercy and power." *Doctoris Ecstatici D. Dionysii Cartusiani, Opera Omnia,* Vol. 10 (Montreuil: 1900), 294.

95   Ps. 35:10b.

96   Job 25:3.

PRAYER

PLACE, O LORD, OUR TEARS BEFORE YOUR sight, and deliver our feet from a hopeless fall: so that proceeding forward cautiously, we might praise with proper ceremony, the Lord Christ, the Word consubstantial with you, and by him we might find favor in the land of the living.

Pone, Domine, lacrimas nostras in conspectu tuo, et erue pedes nostros a lapsu desperato: ut caute ambulantes, Verbum tibi consubstantiale Dominum Christum rite laudemus, et per eum in regione viventium placeamus.

Psalm 56

ARTICLE XII

EXPLANATION OF CHRIST OF THE FIFTY-SIXTH PSALM:
MISERERE MEI, DEUS, MISERERE MEI.
HAVE MERCY ON ME, O GOD, HAVE MERCY ON ME.

56{57}[1] *Unto the end, destroy not David, for an inscription of a title, when he fled from Saul into the cave.*

In finem, ne disperdas David in tituli inscriptionem, cum fugeret a facie Saul in speluncam.

HE TITLE OF THIS PSALM IS: 56{57}[1] *IN finem, ne disperdas David in tituli inscriptionem, cum fugeret a facie Saul in speluncam. Unto the end, destroy not David, for an inscription of a title, when he fled from Saul into the cave.* We read in the first book of Samuel that the holy David took flight twice from the presence of Saul in a cave; the first, in the cave of Adullam;[1] the second in the cave into which Saul descended so that he might relieve himself: in which David cut off the hem of his robe, and prohibited Abishai from killing Saul.[2] And this Psalm receives its title from this [latter] flight; and so one is able rightly to expound it regarding David, as in the subsequent exposition [where this Psalm] is expounded of any just man. Yet it also may be fittingly expounded of Christ who is signified by David, especially since David had not yet received his appointed title [as king]. And so the sense of the title [of this Psalm] is: *Unto the end*, that is, this Psalm is directing us to Christ, *destroy not David*, that is, that you may not deny Christ, the King and Lord of all, by word or deed, as it was signified *for an inscription of a title*, upon which Pilate wrote of Christ, *This is the King of the Jews;*[3] *when he*, David, *fled from the presence of Saul*, that is, when Christ withdrew from the knowledge of the Jews, and he hid himself in a cave, that is, in his mortal flesh, in which his divinity lay concealed, and so hid himself from the unbelieving Jews.

---

1   1 Sam. 22:1.
2   1 Sam. 24:4, 5, 8.
3   Luke 23:38.

56{57}[2] *Have mercy on me, O God, have mercy on me: for my soul trusts in you. And in the shadow of your wings will I hope, until iniquity pass away.*

Miserere mei, Deus, miserere mei, quoniam in te confidit anima mea. Et in umbra alarum tuarum sperabo, donec transeat iniquitas.

56{57}[3] *I will cry to God the most High; to God who has done good to me.*

Clamabo ad Deum altissimum, Deum qui benefecit mihi.

And so Christ, his Passion then imminent, on the part of the still-mortal man he had assumed, and having naturally an abhorrence towards death, prays to the Father: **56{57}[2]** *Miserere mei, Deus; have mercy on me, O God,* carrying me over from this state of possibility to the state of immortality, *miserere mei, have mercy on me* praying for my Mystical Body, so that it may obtain the fruit of the Passion; *quoniam in te confidit anima mea, for my soul trusts in you*: that is, I hope in your goodness, as a passible man and in a certain way a wayfarer (*viator*), [and] not as God and as *comprehensor*.[4] *Et in umbra alarum tuarum, and in the shadow of your wings,* that is, as a defensive plea for, and in need of, your mercy and your power, *sperabo, donec transeat iniquitas; will I hope, until iniquity pass away,* that is, until the malice of the Jews against me obtains its end, namely, so long as I live this mortal life. For Christ was always protected by God, and the Jews were not able to kill him in any way until he himself willed it. **56{57}[3]** *Clamabo, I will cry,* that is, at the instance of the Passion, with my mind and my mouth both praying, I cried out *ad Deum altissimum, to God the most High*: as the Apostle [Paul] acknowledged, *with a strong cry and tears* Christ poured out prayers to God;[5] *Deum qui benefecit mihi, to God who has done good to me,* that is, he has bestowed upon me many benefits, he has heard me in his kindliness, and he has filled me with as much virtue and gifts and graces of the Holy Spirit as are able to be contained within a created nature from the beginning of the creation and conception of my humanity. *For God does not give the Spirit by measure.*[6]

---

4   E. N. Christ, as God, had no need of this prayer; likewise, Christ as man enjoying the beatific vision (as *comprehensor*) had no need of this prayer. The prayer of Christ here involved only that part of his human nature that was passible and was in a wayfaring state, that is, until his resurrection.

5   Heb. 5:7a.

6   John 3:34b. E. N. Denis is not speaking here of the grace of union (which is infinite *simpliciter*), but of the Christ's habitual or sanctifying grace in Christ's human

56{57}[4] *He has sent from heaven and delivered me: he has made them a reproach that trod upon me. God has sent his mercy and his truth,*

Misit de caelo, et liberavit me; dedit in opprobrium conculcantes me. Misit Deus misericordiam suam et veritatem suam,

56{57}[5] *And he has delivered my soul from the midst of the young lions. I slept troubled. The sons of men, whose teeth are weapons and arrows, and their tongue a sharp sword.*

Et eripuit animam meam de medio catulorum leonum; dormivi conturbatus. Filii hominum dentes eorum arma et sagittae, et lingua eorum gladius acutus.

56{57}[4] *Misit de caelo, et liberavit me; he has sent from heaven and delivered me:* that is, God the Father provided help to me from above, and sent me an angel to strengthen me,[7] and in the day of the Resurrection fully delivered me from the hands of the Jews. *Dedit in opprobrium conculcantes me, he has made them a reproach that trod upon me,* that is, he has confounded my persecutors and my crucifiers, he has presented with confusion those deserving of it, he has made them contemptible in the present and in the future, depriving them of their own land and of all grace, as it was predicted of them by Jeremiah: *Bring upon them the day of affliction, and with a double destruction, destroy them O Lord our God;*[8] and with Daniel, *The city and the sanctuary* (that is, the inhabitants of Jerusalem who killed Christ, and the temple) *a people with their leader that shall come shall destroy,*[9] that is, the army of the Romans with Titus.[10] *Misit Deus misericordiam suam et veritatem suam, God has sent his mercy and his truth,* that is, the effect of his mercy and his justice has flowed over me: because in all the works of God mercy and justice are mixed. But God sent *his mercy* as the soul of Christ

---

soul. As St. Thomas says (ST IIIa, q. 7, art. 11, co.), Christ's sanctifying grace can be viewed from the perspective of Christ "according as it is a certain being" (*secundum quod est quoddam ens*) which — given the human nature of Christ's soul — is finite, since "Christ's soul is a particular creature having finite capacity." But if viewed from the perspective of the "nature of grace" (*propriam rationem gratiae*) and from the outpouring of that grace from his soul unto all mankind, and not from the perspective of Christ's human soul alone, it may be viewed as infinite.

7   Luke 22:43.

8   Jer. 17:18b.

9   Dan. 9:26a.

10   E. N. Titus (Titus Caesar Vespasianus, 39 AD–81 AD) was the general in charge of quelling the Jewish rebellion in 70 AD when Vespasian was emperor. Titus succeeded Vespasian in 79 AD

was so graciously prevented with blessings;[11] and [God sent his] *truth*, when he reunited it inseparably with the body [in the Resurrection], as the Prophets foretold. And so it continues: **56{57}[5]** *Et eripuit animam meam*, and *he has delivered my soul*, in the day of Resurrection, *de medio catulorum leonum, from the midst of the young lions*, that is, from the multitude of the proud and ferocious Jews, raising me up unto an immortal state. *Dormivi, I slept*, in death and in the grave, *conturbatus, troubled*, that is, an object of contempt, oppressed, and dead.

Filii hominum, the sons of men, not the sons of God, namely, those adversaries just discussed, *dentes eorum arma et sagittae, whose teeth are weapons and arrows*, that is, they are similar to weapons and also to arrows: for in the manner that someone is attacked by arms and wounded by arrows, so the words of the Jews, which were formed by their mouths and their teeth, assaulted me and procured wounds, saying to Pilate: *If he were not a malefactor, we would not have delivered him up to you.*[12] *Et lingua eorum gladius actus, and their tongue a sharp sword*: for they cried out, *Away with him, away with him; crucify him.*[13] For this reason, it is written, *Their tongue is a piercing arrow.*[14]

56{57}[6]   *Be exalted, O God, above the heavens, and your glory above all the earth.*

Exaltare super caelos, Deus, et in omnem terram gloria tua.

Then the Prophet perceiving Christ so trodden upon and suffering, and desiring his resurrection, ascension, and glorification: **56{57}[6]** *Exaltare, be exalted*, he says, *super caelos, Deus; above the heavens, O God*, that is, you, O Christ, true God, ascend above all the heavens: as the Apostle [Paul] said: *He that descended is the same also that ascended above all the heavens.*[15] *Et in omni terra gloria tua, and your glory above all the earth*, that is, your excellence will be proclaimed, your power will be manifested, and your knowledge will be revealed to men throughout all the earth: according to that which we read in Isaiah: *Glorify the Lord in*

---

11   Cf. Ps. 20:4a: *For you have prevented him with blessings of sweetness.* E. N. As discussed in Volume 1, footnote 17-66 the word "prevented" here means to "come before," *prae-venire.* These prevenient graces by which the human nature of Christ was graced were, as Denis has several times stated, without foreseen merits. They were entirely gratuitous.

12   John 18:30.

13   John 19:15a.

14   Jer. 9:8a.

15   Eph. 4:10.

instruction ... in the islands of the sea; from the ends of the earth we have heard praises, the glory of the Just One.[16] Hence after the Resurrection, Christ said to his disciples: *You shall be witnesses unto me in Jerusalem, and in all Judea, and Samaria, and even to the uttermost part of the earth.*[17]

56{57}[7] *They prepared a snare for my feet; and they bowed down my soul. They dug a pit before my face, and they are fallen into it.*

Laqueum paraverunt pedibus meis, et incurvaverunt animam meam. Foderunt ante faciem meam foveam, et inciderunt in eam.

56{57}[7] *Laqueum,* a snare of death, that is a death trap, the Jews *paraverunt, prepared, pedibus meis, for my feet,* that is for myself; *et incurvaverunt, and they bowed down,* that is, they humiliated and persecuted, *animam meam, my soul,* defaming it and detracting my words, works, and miracles, saying: *He seduces the people;*[18] and, *A man that is a glutton;*[19] and *He casts out devils by Beelzebub.*[20] Or [another way of seeing this], *they bowed down my soul,* that is, by praising it they sought to deflect it from the way of justice and from the truth, saying: *Master, we know that you are a true speaker.*[21] *Foderunt ante faciem meam foveam; they dug a pit before my face:* that is, they openly made preparations to destroy me by death or the suffering of the Cross; *et inciderunt in eam, and they are fallen into it:* for by putting me to death they merited to be killed by the Romans and eternally damned. For he who disposes himself to inflict harm upon another, first does injury to himself, according to this: *For your manifold wickedness ... therefore are you surrounded with snares, and sudden fear troubles you.*[22]

56{57}[8] *My heart is ready, O God, my heart is ready: I will sing, and rehearse a psalm.*

Paratum cor meum, Deus, paratum cor meum; cantabo, et psalmum dicam.

56{57}[9] *Arise, O my glory, arise psaltery and harp: I will arise early.*

Exsurge, gloria mea; exsurge, psalterium et cithara; exsurgam diluculo.

---

16   Is. 24:15–16a.
17   Acts 1:8.
18   John 7:12b.
19   Matt. 11:19a.
20   Luke 11:15a.
21   Matt. 22:16a.
22   Job 22:5a, 10.

56{57}[8] *Paratum cor meum, Deus, paratum cor meum; my heart is ready, O God, my heart is ready* to do and to endure whatever pleases you and is necessary for human redemption. And this is what Christ said to the Father: *Nevertheless, not as I will, but as you will;*[23] and again, *The chalice which my Father has given me, shall I not drink it?*[24] For *I came down from heaven,* he said, *not to do my own will, but the will of him who sent me.*[25] *Cantabo, et psalmum dicam, I will sing and rehearse a Psalm,* that is by word and deed I will praise you, and I will give you thanks. For this Psalm designates good works. **56{57}[9]** *Exsurge, gloria mea; arise, O my glory,* that is, make evident the dignity of grace and all the excellences bestowed upon my humanity, and show yourself to men by the preaching of the Apostles and the believers, since they know the glory given to me by the divinity. And so also, *exsurge, psalterium, arise psaltery,* that is, by my evangelical doctrine, whereby I exhibited the insignia of God, which doctrine sounds sweetly like a psaltery; *et cithara, and harp,* that is, by my moral doctrine and my exemplary life and suffering of death, namely, that my doctrine and life and suffering might raise up the knowledge of men, and believing them they might endeavor to follow it. For this is what Christ says through the prophet Isaiah: *I will send of them that shall be saved, to the Gentiles . . . and they shall declare my glory to the Gentiles.*[26] *Exsurgam, I will arise* from the enclosure of the sepulcher, *diluculo, early,* that is early in the morning: in accordance with this, Jesus *rising early, the first day of the week.*[27]

56{57}[10] *I will confess you,*[28] *O Lord, among the people: I will sing a psalm to you among the nations.*

Confitebor tibi in populis, Domine, et psalmum dicam tibi in gentibus.

56{57}[10] *Confitebor tibi, I will confess you* with the confession of praise, *in populis, Domine; O Lord, among the people,* namely, among the Jews, who were preached to by my very self, and praised you and honored

---

23   Matt. 26:39b.
24   John 18:11b.
25   John 6:38.
26   Is. 66:19.
27   Mark 16:9a.
28   E. N. I have replaced "give praise to you" with "I will confess you" for *confitebor tibi,* since Denis clarifies in his *Commentary* that the confession referred to here is not the confession of sin, but the confession of praise. For the two meanings of "confess," *see* footnote 27-49 in Volume 2.

you; *et psalmus, a Psalm*, that is, praise in conjunction with good works, *dicam tibi, I will sing... to you*, that is, to the honor of your name, *in gentibus, among the nations* to convert them to the faith. For as related in the Gospels, Christ, while living in the world, preached to some of the Gentiles, while he travelled through Tyre and Sidon.[29] Also, some Gentiles travelled among the Jews to [hear] his preaching, according to that written by John in the Gospel, where some Gentiles who climbing toward Jerusalem at the same time asked Phillip: *Sir, we would see Jesus*.[30] True, because Christ preached rarely and only to a few Gentiles, and because a small amount is regarded as if it were not at all, according to the Philosopher;[31] so this does not conflict with that which Christ asserted, *I was not sent but to the sheep that are lost of the house of Israel*.[32] Therefore, that which Christ now says, *I will sing a Psalm to you among the nations* was done more by his disciples than by him himself. For those to whom he said before his Passion, *Go not into the way of the Gentiles*,[33] he said after his Resurrection, *Go into the whole world, and preach the gospel to every creature*,[34] and again, *Going therefore, teach all nations*.[35]

56{57}[11] *For your mercy is magnified even to the heavens: and your truth unto the clouds.*

Quoniam magnificata est usque ad caelos misericordia tua, et usque ad nubes veritas tua.

And so, O Lord, I will confess to you, **56{57}[11]** *Quoniam magnificata est usque ad caelos misericordia tua, for your mercy is magnified even to the heavens*, that is, because the effects of your mercy were made great reaching from the earth even unto the heavenly cities, because by your grace men that are sinners are converted, and are led into the fellowship of the angels. [This is particularly the case] in the future, since at the Resurrection *they shall neither marry nor be married; but shall be as the angels of God*.[36] *Et usque ad nubes veritas tua; and your truth unto the clouds*: that is, the illumination of your truth and wisdom was made

---

29   Matt. 15:21. E. N. The towns of Tyre and Sidon were outside Israel, and were largely populated by Gentiles (*i.e.*, Syrophoenicians).

30   John 12:21b.

31   E. N. The reference is to Aristotle's *Physics*, II, 5, 197a29.

32   Matt. 15:24.

33   Matt. 10:5a.

34   Mark 16:15.

35   Matt. 28:19a.

36   Matt. 22:30.

great, reaching right up to the holy Apostles, and the preachers of the
divine word, and teachers: who are all understood [to be encompassed]
by the word clouds, for they were first and more fully enlightened by
the sun of justice and the fountain of wisdom, the Lord Jesus Christ,
than all the other foolish men on earth, just as the clouds of the air
receive the rays of the sun before the earth does. The Apostles and the
teachers are also called clouds because from them, like from the clouds,
God thunders commandments, flashes signs like lightning, and rains
down the saving message. For of them is written: *Who are these, that
fly as clouds?*[37] And again: *They shall take wings as eagles, they shall run
and not be weary, they shall walk and not faint.*[38]

56{57}[12]   *Be exalted, O God, above the heavens: and your glory above
all the earth.*

Exaltare super caelos, Deus, et super omnem terram gloria tua.

56{57}[12] *Exaltare super caelos, Deus, [et super omnem terram gloria
tua]; Be exalted, O God, above the heavens: [and your glory above].*[39] This
verse, which we have already seen explained,[40] is repeated because of
the dignity of its sentiment, and for the exaltation of Christ it expresses
the objective of all his preceding actions and sufferings.

ARTICLE XIII

TROPOLOGICAL OR MORAL EXPLANATION
OF THE SAME FIFTY-SIXTH PSALM:

56{57}[1]   *Unto the end, destroy not David, for an inscription of a title,
when he fled from Saul into the cave.*

*In finem, ne disperdas David in tituli inscriptionem, cum
fugeret a facie Saul in speluncam.*

NOW IN ACCORDANCE WITH A TROPOLOGI-
cal sense, by David fleeing from Saul into a cave is understood any
tempted Christian persecuted by the world or demons fleeing towards

---

37   Is. 60:8a.
38   Is. 40:31b.
39   E. N. The part in brackets replaces the "etc." of Denis.
40   E. N. Psalm 56:6.

Christ and hiding in his wounds in which is the greatest and most protective refuge of all the faithful, according to this: *Enter into the rock, and hide you in the pit,*[41] that is, draw near to Christ, and hide yourself in his body that was wounded for you.[42] Whence the Lord says again through Isaiah: *Go, my people, enter into your chambers, shut your doors upon yourself, hide yourself a little for a moment, until* my *indignation passes away,*[43] that is, the time of the present persecution.

56{57}[2]   *Have mercy on me, O God, have mercy on me: for my soul trusts in you. And in the shadow of your wings will I hope, until iniquity passes away.*

Miserere mei, Deus, miserere mei, quoniam in te confidit anima mea. Et in umbra alarum tuarum sperabo, donec transeat iniquitas.

56{57}[3]   *I will cry to God the most High; to God who has done good to me.*

Clamabo ad Deum altissimum, Deum qui benefecit mihi.

The Church, therefore, or any Christian striving toward the heavenly homeland through many tribulations, thinks of that which holy Job said, *Behold there is no help for me in myself,*[44] that he might invoke the divine aid, and says: **56{57}[2]** *Miserere mei, have mercy on me* a most vile sinner, *Deus, O God* most kind and conferring forgiveness; *miserere mei, have mercy on me,* filling me with grace, for I am *wretched and miserable, and poor, and blind, and naked,*[45] thinking myself to be something, when I am nothing;[46] for I belong to that number of which is written, *For you have provoked him who made you, the eternal God.*[47] *Quoniam in te confidit anima mea, for my soul trusts in you,* for you alone are able to make clean from that which is unclean[48] and to save me. For I know that truly it is

---

41   Is. 2:10a.

42   E. N. As the prayer *Anima Christi* states: *Intra tua vulnera absconde me,* "within your wounds, hide me."

43   Is. 26:20.

44   Job. 6:13a.

45   Rev. 3:17b.

46   Cf. Gal. 6:3: *For if any man think himself to be something, whereas he is nothing, he deceives himself.*

47   Baruch 4:7.

48   Cf. Job 14:4: *Who can make him clean that is conceived of unclean seed? Is it not you who only are [able]?*

written: *Cursed be the man that trusts in man, and makes flesh his arm, and whose heart departs from the Lord.*[49] For with respect to those who place their hope in created things and in transitory goods it is written in Isaiah: *They trust in mere nothings, and speak vanities.*[50] And the prophet Amos says: *Woe ... you that rejoice in a thing of naught: you that say: Have we not taken unto us horns by our own strength?*[51] For in comparison to the immensity of God, all created things are as nothing and inane, according to that which is said by Isaiah of the sublime and blessed God: *He stretches out the heavens as if [they were] nothing.*[52]

See how fruitful, sweet, and salubrious this little verse is, and how incessantly it ought to be revolved in our mind and by our mouth. Let us say it with a full and loving trust because the more we strive to trust the more undoubtedly we will receive and will be heard, praying: *Let your mercy, O Lord, be upon us, as we have hoped in you.*[53]

Et in umbra alarum tuarum, and in the shadow of your wings, that is, in your protection, *sperabo, donec transeat iniquitas; I will hope, until iniquity passes away,* that is, as long as we are in this life, in which one cannot live without sin, especially since the just man falls seven times a day,[54] I will have persevered. For since we are placed in the midst of snares, we ought never to feel secure, nor to despair, but we ought unceasingly to place ourselves under the wings of divine goodness, and always to hope in the Lord God, as in a most merciful and most affectionate father. **56{57}[3]** *Clamabo, I will cry,* not with a loud voice, but rather with great affection, *ad Deum altissimum, to God the most High,* invoking his grace both day and night; *Deum qui benefecit mihi, the God who has done good to me,* conferring on me many good things, namely the gifts of nature and the largesse of grace; and because he has thus far done me good, I trust that from now one he will also do me good.

56{57}[4] *He has sent from heaven and delivered me: he has made them a reproach that trod upon me. God has sent his mercy and his truth,*

Misit de caelo, et liberavit me; dedit in opprobrium conculcantes me. Misit Deus misericordiam suam et veritatem suam,

---

49   Jer. 17:5.
50   Is. 59:4b.
51   Amos 6:3a, 14.
52   Is. 40:22b.
53   Ps. 32:22.
54   *Cf.* Prov. 24:16.

56{57}[5] *And he has delivered my soul from the midst of the young lions. I slept troubled. The sons of men, whose teeth are weapons and arrows, and their tongue a sharp sword.*

Et eripuit animam meam de medio catulorum leonum; dormivi conturbatus. Filii hominum dentes eorum arma et sagittae, et lingua eorum gladius acutus.

And so his benefits are more fully set forth. For **56{57}[4]** God the Father *misit de caelo, has sent from heaven* his only-begotten Son, *et liberavit me, and he has delivered me,* [that is,] the Father [has delivered me] through the Son, or the Son [has delivered me] by his Passion and his Blood, from original sin and eternal death. This is what was prayed for by Isaiah: *Send forth, O Lord, the lamb, the ruler of the earth, from Petra of the desert, to the mount of the daughter of Sion;*[55] and again: that is, *Drop down dew, you heavens, from above, and let the clouds rain on the just: let the earth be opened, and bud forth a Savior.*[56] All of this was fulfilled and is set forth by the evangelist John: *By this has the charity of God appeared towards us, because God has sent his only begotten Son into the world, that we may live by him.*[57] For which reason also Peter wrote: *You were not redeemed with corruptible things as gold or silver, from your vain conversation of the tradition of your fathers, but with the precious blood of Christ, as of a lamb unspotted.*[58] *Dedit in opprobrium conculcantes me, he has made them a reproach that trod on me:* that is, the Son of God, the Savior of the world, has driven away and subdued my adversaries, namely, the world and the devil. For he — as is written in the Gospel — bound the armed man, that is, the devil, and his vessels,[59] that is, sinners snatched away from his hand. For this reason, Christ said: *Now shall the prince of this world be cast out,*[60] that is, he will be cast out of the minds of men. For that Christ vanquished the world accords with that which he said to his disciples: *In the world you shall have distress: but have confidence, I have overcome the world.*[61] For Christ by his manner of living and his Passion merited grace for us, and he showed us the means of overcoming all the delightful things and the terrible things of the world, lest worldly prosperity delight us

---

55   Is. 16:1a.
56   Is. 45:8a.
57   1 John 4:9.
58   1 Pet. 1:18–19.
59   *Cf.* Mark 3:27: *No man can enter into the house of a strong man and rob him of his goods, unless he first bind the strong man, and then shall he plunder his house.*
60   John 12:31b.
61   John 16:33b.

and adversity deter us, but imitating in all things the footsteps of Christ, we might advance in the royal way,[62] of which is written: *This is the way, walk in it: and go not aside neither to the right hand, nor to the left.*[63]

Misit Deus misericordiam suam et veritatem suam, God has sent his mercy and his truth, that is, his Son, which is to say, the Mercy of God, as far as the Gentiles to whom only mercy is given; and the Truth, as far as the Jews to whom it was given by promise: and so there might be considered to be in this a certain explanation of justice, that he came down to the Jews.[64] Or [it might be viewed] thus: *God has sent his mercy,* that is, he has infused his copious grace into men, most especially during the time of the evangelical law; *and his truth,* that is, as it was foretold in the Old Law, so it was fulfilled by Christ, according to that which is written: *The law was given by Moses; grace and truth came by Jesus Christ.*[65] **56{57}[5]** *Et eripuit, and he has delivered,* [that is,] God, the Father, by his beloved Son [has delivered] *animam meam de medio catulorum leonum, my soul from the midst of the young lions,* that is, from the army of demons: of which besides Peter addressed, *Your adversary the devil, as a roaring lion, goes about seeking whom he may devour.*[66] For when we are delivered from sin, we are freed from the midst of the devil, since it is the same thing to serve sin as it is a devil. But Christ redeemed us from all the stain of sin, according to this: *The Lord has laid upon him the iniquity of us all.*[67] *Dormivi conturbatus, I slept troubled:*

---

62   E. N. The *regia via* (or *via regia*), the "royal way" is a classic description of the Christian *conversatio* or manner of life, especially the monastic life. "The *viator* is dedicated to his *via*; ideally the *via regia*. The notion of *via regia* emerges from a fusion of Num. 20:17 and Num. 21:22 ["we will go to the king's highway (*via regia*) till we be past your borders"]. The royal way is the highway that goes straight through the country to the royal capital. This meaning is reappropriated in the allegorical interpretation of *via regia* as the straight way to the celestial kingdom reigned over by Christ, merging with the point that it is the way that has been shown by Christ in an association of *via regia* with Jn 14:6's declaration that Christ is the way." Mette B. Bruun, "Bernard of Clairvaux and the Landscape of Salvation," *A Companion to Barnard of Clairvaux* (Boston: Brill, 2011), 269 (ed. Brian Patrick McGuire) (citing Jean Leclerq, "La voie royale," *Supplément de la vie spirituelle* 7 (1948), 339).

63   Is. 30:21b.

64   E. N. Because the Messiah was promised to the Jews through the Prophets and the truth of his coming was given them (something the Gentiles did not have), it was fitting that Christ should come down first to the Jews. The Jews are the recipients of prophetic promise (truth) and prophetic fulfillment (mercy); however, the Gentiles, to whom the prophets were not sent, are only the recipients of mercy.

65   John 1:17.

66   1 Pet. 5:8.

67   Is. 53:6b.

that is, before I received the grace of Christ, I was subjected to sin, and I was interiorly disordered: for sleep betokens death. Because of this, the Apostle exclaims to such sleepers, namely, those remaining in vice: *Rise you that sleep, and arise from the dead: and Christ shall enlighten you.*[68] Christ sets forth the sense of this verse with Hosea, saying: *I will deliver them out of the hand of death. I will redeem them from death.*[69]

Filii hominum, the sons of men of those persecuting the Church, dragging down the just, or teaching falsely; *dentes eorum, whose teeth*, that is, their evil speech, are *arma, weapons*, by which they battle against the elect, *et sagittae, and arrows*, by which they blacken their reputation, and desire to injure souls; *et lingua eorum, and their tongue*, that is, perverse doctrine, *gladius actus, a sharp sword*, even piercing through into the interior, separating the soul from God, and killing it spiritually. For, as the Apostle attests, such speech *spreads like cancer.*[70]

56{57}[6] *Be exalted, O God, above the heavens, and your glory above all the earth.*

Exaltare super caelos, Deus, et in omnem terram gloria tua.

56{57}[6] *Exaltare super caelos, Deus;* be exalted, O God, above the heavens, that is, by you exalting and honoring all heavenly citizens. This the Church says, not merely praying, but rejoicing in the divine blessedness,[71] conforming its affection to the blessed in heaven. *Et in omni terra gloria tua, and your glory above all the earth.* Properly speaking, glory is defined as clear knowledge with praise.[72] The just man therefore prays that God might be known by all clearly on earth through faith and he might be praised by charity: that he might especially see fulfilled at the time of Christ, as we read in Isaiah: *The earth is filled with the knowledge of the Lord.*[73]

---

68   Eph. 5:14.
69   Hosea 13:14a.
70   2 Tim. 2:17a.
71   E. N. The Church does not pray for the blessed in heaven, but rejoices in their state. Nor does the Church pray for the damned. The Church only prays for those *in via* and those souls suffering in Purgatory. "There is no restriction by Divine or ecclesiastical law as to those of the dead for whom private prayers may be offered — except that they may not be offered either for the blessed in heaven or for the damned." P. Toner, "Prayers for the Dead," Catholic Encyclopedia (New York: Robert Appleton Co., 1908), Vol. 4, 656. The blessed do not need our prayers, and the damned are not aided by them.
72   E. N. For this definition of glory as the "clear knowledge with praise" (*clara cum laude notitia*) and its Augustinian origins, *see* footnote 28-15 in Volume 2.
73   Is. 11:9b.

56{57}[7] *They prepared a snare for my feet; and they cast down*[74] *my soul. They dug a pit before my face, and they are fallen into it.*

Laqueum paraverunt pedibus meis, et incurvaverunt animam meam. Foderunt ante faciem meam foveam, et inciderunt in eam.

56{57}[7] *Laqueum paraverunt pedibus meis, they prepared a snare for my feet.* This is what Christ said to his disciples in their person to the entire Church: *If they have persecuted me, they will also persecute you,* for *the servant is not greater than his master.*[75] Invisible enemies prepare snares, that is, deceptions, for our feet, that is, our works and our desires. For the devil *goes and takes with him seven other spirits more wicked than himself,*[76] and they will dwell in the human heart if they are allowed to enter. *Et incurvaverunt, and they cast down* from the way of justice *animam meam, my soul,* or at least they tried to cast it down from the right way of God. Or [alternatively], *They cast down,* that is, they caused affliction, as the Apostle attests to: *we are cast down, but we perish not.*[77] *Foderunt ante faciem meam foveam, they dug a pit before my face,* that is, they openly lay in wait for me, and they visited me with defamation and injury; *et inciderunt in eam, and they are fallen into it,* that is, they hurled themselves down into the pit of fault and the death of the soul. For all things that are difficult and evil *work together unto good* to the elect;[78] but the evil persecuting them harm themselves and obtain the pit of infernal damnation.

56{57}[8] *My heart is ready, O God, my heart is ready: I will sing, and rehearse a psalm.*

Paratum cor meum, Deus, paratum cor meum; cantabo, et psalmum dicam.

56{57}[8] *Paratum cor meum, Deus, paratum cor meum. My heart is ready, O God, my heart is ready.* This is what we say daily in the Lord's Prayer: *Thy will be done on earth as it is in heaven.*[79] Whence the Apostle said: *Not with sadness, or of necessity: for God loves a cheerful giver.*[80] This

---

74   E. N. I have changed the Douay Rheims "they have bowed down" for *incurvaverunt* to "they have cast down," as it fits better with Denis's *Commentary* and is an equally acceptable translation.
75   John 15:20.
76   Luke 11:26.
77   2 Cor. 4:9b.
78   Rom. 8:28.
79   Matt. 6:10.
80   2 Cor. 9:7.

holy preparation of the heart causes the denial of one's own will, true obedience, and fervid charity. Let us therefore endeavor, most beloved, to have a heart ready for doing and suffering all things that are pleasing to God; let us not carry something that comes upon us with annoyance, but let us offer, commend, and abandon ourselves purely and with integrity to the divine will. For we cannot venerate God in any greater way than in this manner: indeed, as we do this more perfectly, that much all the more we obtain merit, and make ourselves more dear to God and more perfect in all virtue. For let us fulfill that which the Apostle delivered to the Romans: let us demonstrate *what is the good, and the acceptable, and the perfect will of God.*[81]

56{57}[9] *Arise, O my glory, arise psaltery and harp: I will arise early.*

Exsurge, gloria mea; exsurge, psalterium et cithara; exsurgam diluculo.

56{57}[10] *I will confess you,*[82] *O Lord, among the people: I will sing a psalm to you among the nations.*

Confitebor tibi in populis, Domine, et psalmum dicam tibi in gentibus.

56{57}[9] *Exsurge, gloria mea; arise, O my glory,* that is, my soul, marked with the image of the Trinity: arise, I say, from the bed, from sin, from sluggishness, and all sloth, and do that which Jeremiah admonishes: *Arise, give praise in the night, in the beginning of the watches:*[83] *pour out your heart like water before the face of the Lord.*[84] And Isaiah also: *Shake yourself from the dust, arise, sit up, O Jerusalem,*[85] that is, O holy soul. For it is first necessary that the soul shake itself from inferior things and things of this earth, and then raise itself toward the heavenly and highest things, and so abide in quiet contemplation. Or [we can understand it

---

81   Rom. 12:2b.

82   E. N. I have replaced "give praise to you" with "I will confess you" for *confitebor tibi,* since Denis clarifies in his *Commentary* that the confession referred to here is not the confession of sin, but the confession of praise. For the two meanings of "confess," *see* footnote 27-49 in Volume 2.

83   E. N. This recalls what St. Josemaría Escrivá called *el minuto heroico,* the "heroic minute." "It is the time fixed for getting up. Without hesitation: a supernatural reflection and . . . up! The heroic minute: here you have a mortification that strengthens your will and does no harm to your body." St. Josemaría Escrivá de Balaguer, *The Way,* No. 206 (New York: Image, 2005), 33.

84   Lam. 2:19a.

85   Is. 52:2a.

in this way], *Arise, O my glory*, that is, all my glorification, and ascend upwards in God, so that I might not glory in myself, but I might give acquiesce to the admonishment of the Apostle: *He that glories, may he glory in the Lord.*[86] Whence also with the prophet Isaiah we read: *And the meek shall increase their joy in the Lord, and the poor men shall rejoice in the Holy One of Israel.*[87] Or [yet another way to understand it], *Arise, O my glory*, that is, the grace bestowed upon me, and all habitual perfection infused by God in me in Baptism or given afterwards, [and may it] proceed in act and work efficaciously, in the manner that the Apostle [Paul] commands: *Neglect not the grace that is in you, which was given you*, etc.[88] *Exsurge, psalterium, arise psaltery*, that is, may the praise of psalmody be roused in me; *et cithara, and harp*, that is, sweet and sonorous deeds before God, as the exercise of piety is *profitable to all things.*[89]

Exsurgam, I will arise from imperfection to the more perfect life, *diluculo, early*, that is, from the time the splendor of your grace, O Lord, will have radiated in me. And, literally speaking, I will rise up in the dawn in praise of the Most High, in accordance with this, *The just man will give his heart to resort early to the Lord that made him*;[90] and this, *My soul has desired you in the night: yea, and with my spirit within me in the morning early I will watch for you.*[91] **56{57}[10]** *Confitebor tibi in populis, Domine; I will confess you, O Lord, among the people*, that is, in the midst of my brothers and neighbors and the faithful I will praise you: as the Apostle [Paul] said: *With one mind, and with one mouth, you may glorify God*;[92] *et psalmum dicam tibi in gentibus, and I will sing a Psalm to you among the nations*, recounting to them your praise, and returning thanks to you for their conversion, encouraging them also to praise you publicly. The rest is clear from the preceding exposition.

See we have heard this truly sweet, noble, and igniting Psalm, whose power the lover and the pure praiser ardently relish. Let us conform our life, therefore, to the sense of this Psalm, so that that which is said in it might be truly said about us; let not ever our soul withdraw from the wings of divine defense, saying to God with holy Job: *Set me beside you, and let any man's hand fight against me.*[93]

---

86   1 Cor. 1:31b.
87   Is. 29:19.
88   1 Tim. 4:14a.
89   1 Tim. 4:8a.
90   Ecclus. 39:6a.
91   Is. 26:9a.
92   Rom. 15:6a.
93   Job 17:3.

PRAYER

AVE MERCY, O GOD, TO THOSE IN THE shadow of your wings, O Lord, upon those hoping in you, and those crying out to you, God most High; send your mercy and your truth which remove from us the disgrace of our enemies who are purposed to trample upon us, so that, snatched away from their midst, we might magnify the glory of your power in perpetuity.

In umbra alarum tuarum, Domine, sperantibus, et ad te Deum
altissimum clamantibus, Deus, miserere; mitte misericordiam
tuam et veritatem tuam, quae auferant a nobis
opprobrium hostium conculcare nos volentium:
ut erepti de medio eorum, gloriam
potentiae tuae magnificemus
in perpetuum.

Psalm 57

ARTICLE XIV

EXPOSITION OF THE FIFTY-SEVENTH PSALM, IN THE PERSON OF CHRIST TO THE UNFAITHFUL JEWS: *SI VERE UTIQUE IUSTITIAM LOQUIMINI.* IF IN THE VERY DEED YOU SPEAK JUSTICE.

57{58}[1] *Unto the end, destroy not David, for an inscription with title.*

In finem, ne disperdas David, in tituli inscriptione.

OW THE TITLE OF THIS PSALM IS: **57{58}[1]** *In finem, ne disperdas David, in tituli inscriptione. Unto the end, destroy not David, for an inscription with title.* All the words in the title to this Psalm are contained in previous ones, and so they are to be understood as they are explained there.

57{58}[2] *If in very deed you speak justice: judge right things, you sons of men.*

Si vere utique iustitiam loquimini, recta iudicate, filii hominum.

57{58}[3] *For in your heart you work iniquity: your hands forge injustice in the earth.*

Etenim in corde iniquitates operamini; in terra iniustitias manus vestrae concinnant.

Christ, therefore, upbraiding the unbelieving Jews says: **57{58}[2]** *Si vere utique iustitiam loquimini, if in very deed you speak justice:* that is, if you truthfully read, understand, and praise the Law and the Prophets, and if (as you say) you truly expect and desire Christ, and if, moreover, you call me Rabbi[1] from the heart and maintain to teach the way of God in truth; then *recte iudicate, judge right things,* that is, pay heed and discern me to be the Messiah King from the Law and the Prophets, O you Jews—who are so according to the origin of the flesh, but not according to the imitation of God, *filii hominum, you sons of men,* that is, of those living in this world in a reasonable manner, namely in

---

1 Matt. 22:16.

the manner of the Prophets and the Patriarchs. Yet Christ exhorts the Jews to right judgment in the Gospel, saying: *Judge not according to the appearance, but judge just judgment.*[2] But you, O Jews, judge erroneously, and the reason for this is given in the words which follow. 57{58}[3] *Etenim in corde iniquitates operamini in terra, for in your heart you work iniquity*: that is, you conjure up deceit and evil against me and you propose to persecute and kill me. Whence in Mark it is written: *Why think you these things in your hearts?*[3] And again he said to them: *Inwardly you are full of hypocrisy and iniquity;*[4] and elsewhere, *Now you seek to kill me, a man who has spoken the truth to you.*[5] *Iniustitias, injustice*, that is, evil words, *manus vestrae concinnant, your hands forge*, that is, they gather together and accumulate, for that which you have conceived in your heart you have led to effect, persecuting me, keeping close watch over me, deriding me, and slaying me.

57{58}[4]   *The wicked are alienated from the womb; they have gone astray from the womb: they have spoken false things.*

Alienati sunt peccatores a vulva; erraverunt ab utero, locuti sunt falsa.

57{58}[4] *Alienati sunt peccatores a vulva, the wicked are alienated from the womb*: that is, the Jews just identified were averse to God from the beginning of their birth, not that they sinned in the state of being born, but because they were foreseen to sin, and they were foreknown to die [spiritually], and they were hated before birth, in the way that Malachi said: *I have hated Esau.*[6] In accord with this sense, *erraverunt ab utero, they have gone astray from the womb*, for they were foreseen by God to deny Christ, the ultimate Truth. For this reason, Christ said to

---

2   John 7:24.
3   Mark 2:8b.
4   Matt. 23:28b.
5   John 8:40a.
6   Mal. 1:3a. *E. N.* In his *Commentary on Malachi*, Denis observes that this verse is invoked in Romans where the apostle Paul handles the issue of predestination, election, and the grace of God. These three things, Denis observes, "do not arise from our works or our merits. As [St. Paul] says, *For when the children were not yet born, nor had done any good or evil (that the purpose of God, according to election, might stand,) not of works, but of him that calls, it was said to her [their mother, Rebecca]: 'The elder shall serve the younger.'* [Gen. 25:23] As it is written: *'Jacob I have loved, but Esau I have hated'* [Rom. 9:10–12]." Doctoris Ecstatici D. Dionysii Cartusiani, *Opera Omnia*, Vol. 10 (Montreuil: 1900), 692.

them: *You are of your father the devil, and the desires of your father you will do;*[7] and, therefore *You hear not* [the words of God], *because you are not of God.*[8] *Locuti sunt falsa,* they have spoken false things, for they accused me of being a liar: as Jeremiah wrote about them: *They have denied the Lord, and said, It is not he.*[9] And elsewhere: *I redeemed them,* he says, *and they have spoken lies against me.*[10] Whence concerning them it is also written: *They have forsaken the Lord, they have blasphemed the Holy One of Israel, they are gone away backwards.*[11]

57{58}[5] *Their madness is according to the likeness of a serpent: like the deaf asp that stops its ears.*

Furor illis secundum similitudinem serpentis, sicut aspidis surdae et obturantis aures suas.

57{58}[6] *Which will not hear the voice of the charmers; nor of the wizard that charms wisely.*

Quae non exaudiet vocem incantantium, et venefici incantantis sapienter.

57{58}[5] *Furor illis secundum similitudinem serpentis, their madness is according to the likeness of a serpent.* For as an angry serpent pours forth venom and kills, so the Jews raving against Christ vomited forth the venom of their envy, procuring against him a judgment of death, and crucifying him. The patriarch Jacob can be seen to have foretold this Jewish furor against Christ when he said: *Cursed be their fury, because it was stubborn: and their wrath because it was cruel.*[12] These words may be said to apply literally against Levi and Simeon, but it can also be received as applying to the priests and the Pharisees who were descended from their stock.[13] *Sicut aspides surdae et obturantis aures suas, like the deaf asp that stops its ears*: that is, the malice of the Jews against Christ was such as to liken the vileness of a snake before a snake charmer. For in the manner that an asp covers one ear with its tail and the other by the earth so that it does not

---

7   John 8:44a.
8   John 8:47b.
9   Jer. 5:12a.
10   Hosea 7:13b.
11   Is. 1:4b.
12   Gen. 49:7a.
13   E. N. Jacob said these words to his sons Simeon and Levi. While the stock of Simeon played little role in the time of Christ, the stock of Levi formed the core of the Jewish priesthood. Denis includes those Pharisees who were Levites in this prophecy.

perceive the voice of the enchanter,[14] so the Jews closed their ears — one ear through avarice, the other ear by envy — so that they might not hear the preaching of Christ and his disciples. For this reason, it is written: *Many of them said: He has a devil, and is mad: why hear you him?*[15] And elsewhere: *The Pharisees, who were covetous, heard all these things: and they derided him.*[16] **57{58}[6]** *Quae,* which asp, which we have seen is similar to the Jews, *non exaudiet vocem incantantium et venefici incantantis sapienter; will not hear the voice of the charmers, nor of the wizard that charms wisely,* according to the principles of their artistry: for it will not come out of its cavern. In this, therefore, the Jews conformed themselves to vipers. Whence John the Baptist said to them: *You brood of vipers, who has showed you to flee from the wrath to come?*[17] And so also Christ himself: *You serpents, generation of vipers, how will you flee from the judgment of hell?*[18]

57{58}[7] God shall break in pieces their teeth in their mouth: the Lord shall break the grinders of the lions.

Deus conteret dentes eorum in ore ipsorum; molas leonum confringet Dominus.

57{58}[7] *Deus conteret dentes eorum in ore ipsorum, God shall break in pieces their death in their mouth,* that is, he will throw back upon them the evil of words which they said against Christ, and they will obtain death for themselves through their own words, in the manner that occurred when they said: *His blood be upon us and our children.*[19] For from that point *the wrath of God is come upon them to the end,* according to the Apostle [Paul].[20] *Molas leonum confringet Dominus, the Lord shall break the grinders of the lions:* that is, the threats, words, and harassment of the ferocious Jews inflicted against Christ, the Lord swiftly caused it to stop, raising Christ unto immortal life. For this reason, Christ in the Last Supper said: *For the things concerning me have an end.*[21]

---

14   E. N. The reference is to St. Isidore of Seville's *Etymologies,* XII, 4:12–16. Therein, St. Isidore states that when a snake charmer seeks to coax an asp (*aspis*) from its cave, the asp avoids the charm by pressing one ear on the ground and covering its other ear with its tail, thus escaping the effects of enchantment.

15   John 10:20.

16   Luke 16:14.

17   Matt. 3:7b.

18   Matt. 23:33.

19   Matt. 27:25b.

20   1 Thess. 2:16b.

21   Luke 22:37b.

57{58}[8] *They shall come to nothing, like water running down; he has bent his bow until they be weakened.*

Ad nihilum devenient tamquam aqua decurrens; intendit arcum suum donec infirmentur.

57{58}[9] *Like wax that melts they shall be taken away: fire has fallen on them, and they shall not see the sun.*

Sicut cera quae fluit auferentur; supercecidit ignis, et non viderunt solem.

57{58}[8] *Ad nihilum devenient tamquam aqua decurrens; they shall come to nothing, like water running down.* For the unbelieving Jews were destroyed by Titus and Vespasian.[22] They also spiritually came to nothing because they completely lost all grace and the being of grace. *Intendit arcum suum donec infirmentur, he has bent his bow until they be weakened*: that is, God prepared the weapons of the Roman army against the Jews until they were entirely debilitated, in the manner that Christ predicted to them: *For the days shall come upon you, and your enemies . . . shall encompass you . . . on every side, and they shall straiten you, . . . and beat you flat to the ground.*[23] **57{58}[9]** *Sicut cera quae fluit, auferentur; like wax that melts they shall be taken away.* For the Jews were removed from their land quickly and unexpectedly. They *shall be taken away* also in the day of judgment from the land of the living; and now they *shall be taken away* daily from the flock of the faithful and the fellowship of the elect. *Supercecidit ignis, et non viderunt solem; fire has fallen on them, and they shall not see the sun.* It is customary in Scripture to designate some kind of great tribulation by fire. And so it is in this sense: There came and rushed in upon the unfaithful Jews a great tribulation through the Romans because of the sin they had committed in Christ; not however, that they judged themselves to suffer in this manner because of the killing of Christ, nor did they recognize Christ to be the sun of justice by the punishment, but [because] they remained hardened and in the darkness of disbelief, according to that attested to by Isaiah: *The people are not returned to him who has struck them, and have not sought after the Lord.*[24] And through Amos, the Lord said: *I struck you [with a burning wind, and with mildew, the palmerworm has eaten up your many gardens, and your vineyards: your olive groves, and fig groves:] yet you returned not to me.*[25]

---

22   E. N. *See* footnote 56-10 as to Titus and Vespasian.
23   Luke 19:43–44a. E. N. Denis edits and re-orders these verses for his own use, without however any substantial change in meaning.
24   Is. 9:13.
25   Amos 4:9. E. N. The portion in brackets replaces the "etc." in Denis's text.

57{58}[10] *Before your thorns could know the brier; he swallows them up, as the living, so in his wrath.*

Priusquam intelligerent spinae vestrae rhamnum, sicut viventes sic in ira absorbet eos.

57{58}[10] *Priusquam, before,* O incredulous Jews, *intelligerent spinae vestrae, your thorns could know,* that is, the punishments inflicted upon you and the remorse of your consciences [could know], *rhamnum, the brier,* that is, the devil inciting you to evil, or the suggestions of the devil and vices, for which you have suffered; *sicut viventes, sic*[26] *in ira absorbet eos; he swallows them up, as the living, so in his wrath:* that is, in the way the living wicked men, who suppose that they will live a long time quickly die, and as the angry man suddenly swallows him with whom he is angry;[27] so God swallows, has swallowed, and will swallow you. For it has already been made clear how many were lost, and in what manner they are said to be reduced to nothing. Hence, the Lord by the prophet Amos says of the final rejection of the Jews: *The end is come upon my people Israel: I will not again pass by them anymore.*[28] It is fitting for the devil, concupiscence, or sin to be understood by the word brier. For brier is a plant that is in the beginning soft and supple; but when it grows and becomes mature, it pricks most severely, because it then acquires most sharp spines: so the devil, concupiscence, and sin in the beginning offer delights, and they are ingested as if they were a sweet and supple herb, but they lead altogether to the most bitter punishments.

57{58}[11] *The just shall rejoice when he shall see the revenge: he shall wash his hands in the blood of the sinner.*

Laetabitur iustus cum viderit vindictam; manus suas lavabit in sanguine peccatoris.

57{58}[12] *And man shall say: If indeed there be fruit to the just: there is indeed a God that judges them on the earth.*

Et dicet homo: Si utique est fructus iusto, utique est Deus iudicans eos in terra.

57{58}[11] *Laetabitur iustus cum viderit vindictam, the just shall rejoice when he shall see the revenge:* not indeed out of a zeal of vengeance but

---

26   E. N. The editor notes an alternative reading for *sicut* "as," being *sic*, "thus."
27   E. N. The angry man figuratively swallows, that is, absorbs the one with whom he is angry, since the object of his anger is internally consumed by him.
28   Amos 8:2b.

out a love of justice. For in the way that (as it is written) *God made not death*, yet inasmuch as there is death, he did not directly intend it, and *neither has he pleasure in the destruction of the living*[29] inasmuch as it is something evil, but [he does take pleasure in it] inasmuch as it is the effect of justice (in accordance with what Isaiah said: *Ah! I will comfort myself over my adversaries: and I will be revenged of my enemies*, said the Lord; and elsewhere, *I will accomplish my fury, and will cause my indignation to rest upon them, and I will be comforted*).[30] In a similar way, a just man rejoices when he sees the vindication of an injury caused not by him, but by God, and insofar as vengeance is a certain good of divine justice, but not insofar as it results in the perdition of the neighbor. Yet although the just man rejoices in the vindication of evil in this world insofar as the vindication in this manner is for the usefulness of the Church, or presents more favorable conditions of its disappearance; so in the day of judgment and in the heavenly homeland he will rejoice more in the divine vengeance because then it will be perfectly in conformance with, and inseparably united to, divine equity, and he will most fully be pleased with whatever accords with divine justice. For this we read in the book of Job: *The just shall see, and shall rejoice, and the innocent shall laugh them to scorn.*[31] And in other place: *How long, O Lord (holy and true) do you not judge and revenge our blood on them that dwell on the earth?*[32] Moreover, regarding this we ought not to desire absolutely the vengeance of the ungodly, except at the chance that in the present age they might be corrected so that they might not be damned (or that they might be less tormented) in the future,[33] in the manner that the Apostle [Paul] writes about a certain sinner: I delivered *such a one to Satan for the destruction of the flesh* (namely, that he might be excommunicated from the Church), *that the spirit may be saved in the day of our Lord.*[34]

---

29 Wis. 1:13.

30 Ez. 5:13a.

31 Job 22:19.

32 Rev. 6:10b.

33 E. N. "The Union Councils of Lyons and of Florence declared that the souls of the damned are punished with unequal punishments. . . . This is probably intended to assert not merely a specific difference in the punishment of original sin (*poena damni*) and of personal sins (*poena damni* and *poena sensus*), but also a difference in the degree of punishment for personal sins [*cf.* here Matt. 11:22, Luke 20:47]. . . . St. Augustine teaches 'In their wretchedness the lot of some of the damned will be more tolerable than that of others.' Justice demands that the punishment be commensurate with the guilt." Ludwig Ott, *Fundamentals of Catholic Dogma* (Rockford, IL: TAN Books 1974), 482 (trans., Patrick Lynch, ed. James Canon Bastible).

34 1 Cor. 5:5.

For in the early Church the excommunicated were sensibly punished or also struck down by demons, because of the confirmation of the faith.[35]

Manus suas lavabit, he shall wash his hands, that is, the just man shall cleanse his works, *in sanguine peccatoris, in the blood of the sinner*, that is, in consideration of the misery and the punishment inflicted upon the sinner. For from this consideration he will lament his own imperfections and will be rendered fearful and more cautious. For happy are they who are made expert by others' punishments. Hence Solomon asserts: *The wicked man being scourged, the fool* (that is, the sinner) *shall be wiser.*[36] This also is said to blessed Job about the devil: *When he shall raise him up, the angels shall fear, and being affrighted shall purify themselves.*[37] 57{58}

[12] *Et dicet homo, and man shall say*, [a man] wise in his heart: *Si utique est fructus iusto, if indeed there be fruit to the just*, that is, if reward awaits from God for doing good, *utique est Deus iudicans, there is indeed a God that judges* a judgment of damnation and reprobation, *eos, on them*, namely, sinners, *in terra, on the earth*, that is, in the body, for he will cast their body and soul into hell; or [alternatively], *on the earth*, for in the valley of Josaphat all will be adjudged; or [in the further alternative], *on the earth*, in the way in which they handle their stay [here on earth], for the damnation of the ungodly is already incipient, and it will be completed in the future. For they who are now deprived of the light of grace will also, in the future, [be deprived] of the light of glory.

---

35   E. N. "Many commentators ... are of the opinion that in Apostolic times the delivering to Satan implied much more than the spiritual punishment of excommunication. They maintain that persons thus punished were handed over to Satan in much the same way as Job, and consequently they were subject to corporal vexations and torments inflicted by the evil one." Francis Edward Hyland, *Excommunication: Its Nature, Historical Development, and Effects* (Washington, DC: Catholic University of America, 1928), 21. "Let us explain the words of Paul," said St. Ambrose, "and what was the reason that he said that he had delivered him to Satan for the destruction of the flesh, for our tempter is the devil. For he brings weakness to each of our members and sets in motion sickness on our whole bodies. And so he struck holy Job with evil sores from the feet even unto the head, because he had received the power of destroying his flesh, God having said: 'Behold he is in your hand, but yet save his life.' (Job 2:6)." *De Poenitentia Lib. Duo*, I, 13, 62, PL 16, 485.

36   Prov. 19:25a.

37   Job. 41:16. E. N. In his *Commentary on Job*, Denis observes that this is said about Leviathan, that great sea beast that is a symbol of the Devil. "This is said, therefore, not of any ordinary sea creature which might be regarded as important as the death of a flea," but "of the devil, indeed the prince of all demons, from whose unseating or expulsion from the heavenly throne at one time terrified the holy angels with a fear of admiration of the divine power and a reverential trembling." The salutary lesson is that we ought to learn from the devil's ruin and the angelic terror.

But spiritually one can apply this to Christ, so that it reads in this sense: *The just shall rejoice*, that is, the Christian people, *when he shall see the revenge* of the Jews that denied Christ; *he shall wash his hands in the blood of the sinner*: for from consideration of the reprobation of the Jews, the Christian people efficaciously believing in Christ will more perfectly adhere to Christ. *And man shall say: if indeed there be fruit to the just* for him who is converted to Christ, then it follows that *there is indeed a God that judges them*, namely, the unbelieving Jews, *on the earth*, [that is, in the land] *of promise*, in which he judged them and condemned them, delivering them over into the hands of their adversaries. Whence, the Lord said of these people: *I*, he says, *will contend with you in judgment, because you have said: I have not sinned;* [38] and again, *According to my desire I will chastise them.* [39]

Finally, that said of the just man, *he shall wash his hands in the blood of the sinner*, can be understood in another way, so that it applies to the blessed in the heavenly homeland; and so it will be in this sense: *his hands*, that is, the actions of their most blessed life, *shall wash*, not from the stain of fault, but with the water of consolation, and the refreshment of joy, *in the blood of the sinner*. For the blessed in heaven rejoice in surveying the punishment of the reprobate: first, because the injury to God is vindicated; secondly, because the order of justice is observed; and third, because the wisdom of God does not leave anything disordered in the entire universe untouched; fourth, because they have avoided such a great danger.

ARTICLE XV

TROPOLOGICAL CLARIFICATION OF
THE SAME FIFTY-SEVENTH PSALM,
IN THE PERSON OF THE CHURCH
TO ALL IMPENITENT SINNERS

57{58}[2] *If in very deed you speak justice: judge right things, you sons of men.*
    Si vere utique iustitiam loquimini, recta iudicate, filii hominum.

HE HOLY CHURCH, THEREFORE, BEING TROU-
bled by the reign of her Spouse being diminished by the ungodly either in word or by deed denying Christ their Savior and Judge, says to

---

38 Jer. 2:35b. *E. N.* That is, they maintain their innocence, their sinlessness, in denying the Christ.
39 Hosea 10:10a.

those persevering in evil in this way: **57{58}[2]** *Si vere utique iustitiam loquimini, if in very deed you speak justice*: that is, if your life accords with your words, and you acknowledge Christ, whom you confess with your lips, truly as the Savior of the world, and if you believe the doctrine of Christ to be true, as you say; then *recte iudicate, judge right things*, O *filii hominum*, O *sons of men*: that is, judge well between the highest and divine and immutable Good and created, transient, and inferior goods, turning your hearts away from vain and illicit things, and turning yourselves completely to the sovereign and immutable Good, loving him, hoping in him, and always referring the final intention,[40] love, honor, and glory to him. Yet there is a certain kind of judgment that Christ prohibits: *Judge not, that you may not be judged*,[41] namely, let us not judge others, especially in doubtful things and those things which are able to be taken in a good way. But now we are commanded rightly to judge ourselves, and what deeds have been committed by us, and our manifest works, and, most of all, that we might truly discern between the uncreated Good and created goods: which is done by the gifts of the Holy Spirit, namely, by the gifts of knowledge and counsel.[42]

Finally, many things are required for a right and worthy judgment. First, that the prelate or judge live justly. For, according to the Philosopher [Aristotle], a judge ought to be like a certain living law (*vivens lex*) and animate justice (*animata iustitia*), and a model of equity (*aequitatis regula*),[43] so that he never sways from the way of equity (*via aequitatis*). Second, that the order of right (*iuris*) be observed, and that he proceeds according to the statutes of right (*iuris*). Whence the Lord says of those who are ignorant of, and those who desert, the way of right (*iuris*): *The shepherds themselves*

---

40   E. N. As Giles of Rome (*ca.* 1243–1316) says rather circularly: *[I]lle plus diligitur in quo finalis intentio ponitur. Et in illo finalis intentio quod in infinitum amatur.* "That thing in which the final intention is placed is most loved. And in that final intention [one will find] that which is loved unto infinity." Aegidii Romani, *Opera Omnia* (Florence: Olschki 1998), Vol. 1, 367.

41   Matt. 7:1.

42   E. N. In his Tracts on the Holy Spirit, Denis defines the gift of knowledge (*scientia*) "is a simple light received or infused by God directly, in which the reasons of the pertinent things to be done in human life are seen.... [T]his knowledge is a certain simple likeness of divine justice, in which the mind sees the divine reasons of those things to be done by us which pertain to the light of merit and holy living." The gift of counsel (*consilium*) is the gift "of infused supernatural light, directing in great or arduous things, in which man is incapable without special aid ... Whence this counsel does involve all things, but concerns itself with those things where we are in need of a special divine directing light." Doctoris Ecstatici D. Dionysii Cartusiani, *Opera Omnia*, Vol. 35 (Montreuil: 1908), 251, 252.

43   E. N. See *Nichomachean Ethics*, V, 4, 1132a20 *ff. See also* ST IaIIae, q. 95, art. 1, ad 1.

knew no understanding: all have turned aside into their own way.[44] Third, he ought not to give in to the multitude or the clamor of many, according to this: *You shall not follow the crowd to do evil: neither shall you yield in judgment, to the opinion of the multitude, to stray from the truth.*[45] Fourth, he should inquire well into the cause and examine it, just like Job did: *The cause which I knew not, I searched out most diligently.*[46] Fifth, he should not be a respecter of persons, as the Lord says through Moses in Deuteronomy: *You shall hear the little as well as the great,*[47] that is, you will hear the poor as you do the wealthy. Sixth, he ought not to back away from right judgment because of fear. For which reason it is stated in Ecclesiasticus: *Seek not to be made a judge, unless you have strength enough to extirpate iniquities: lest you fear the person of the powerful.*[48] Seventh, he should not feel excessive pity, as it is written: *You shall not favor a poor man in judgment.*[49] Eighth, he should hate avarice, and disdain gifts, for they *pervert the words of the just.*[50] Ninth, he should never receive entreaties from one party to the prejudice of the other party. And tenth, and, what takes the greatest effort, we must abandon any self-love and deep-rooted hate. For love and hate pervert all judgment.[51] Whence, according to the Philosopher [Aristotle], a man is not a good judge of himself, because he loves himself too much; nor [is he a good judge] of his enemy, because he hates him.

57{58}[3]   *For in your heart you work iniquity: your hands forge injustice in the earth.*

Etenim in corde iniquitates operamini; in terra iniustitias manus vestrae concinnant.

But you, O sons of men, living life not in a human fashion, but irrationally, do not judge right things. The reason for this is: **57{58} [3]** *Etenim in corde iniquitates operamini in terra, for in your heart you work iniquity,* that is, with purpose and affection of your heart you think

---

44   Is. 56:14b.

45   Ex. 23:2. *E. N.* I have changed "crowd" to "multitude" for *turbam,* and "of the most part" by which the Douay Rheims translates *plurimorum,* to "of the multitude."

46   Job 29:16b.

47   Deut. 1:17: *There shall be no difference of persons, you shall hear the little as well as the great: neither shall you respect any man's person, because it is the judgment of God.*

48   Ecclus. 7:6.

49   Ex. 23:3.

50   Ex. 23:8: *Neither shall you take bribes, which even blind the wise, and pervert the words of the just.*

51   *Amor et odium pervertunt omne iudicium. E. N.* Probably a reference to Aristotle's *Politics,* VII, 7, 1328a15, 16.

about and engage in useless and harmful as well as prohibited things. For conceiving evil in the heart and consenting to it is — from God's perspective — reckoned as a deed.[52] But you who work this evil on earth with your body — for you walk according to the flesh[53] and long to attain its disordered desires, and like the meek will possess the world with their bodies[54] — so your bodies will be possessed by the earth. Whence of you it is written: *Woe to you that devise that which is unprofitable, and work evil in your beds.*[55] *Iniustitias manus vestrae concinant, your hands forge injustice in the earth*: in the manner that is stated in Ecclesiasticus: *The sinner will add sin to sin.*[56] And as is also said by the prophet Isaiah, *You draw iniquity . . . as a long cord.*[57] For not only does the sinner not lament daily the evil he has committed, but he gathers up iniquity like he might a bouquet of flowers. And so the Apostle [Paul] speaks of such men in a most terrible fashion to the Romans: *Do you despise the riches of God's goodness, and patience, and longsuffering? Do you not know that the benignity of God leads you to penance? According to your hardness and impenitent heart, you treasure up to yourself wrath, against the day of wrath, and revelation of the just judgment of God.*[58] All they, therefore, who consent in their heart to evil or perform illicit acts do not truly, but falsely and wretchedly, judge, for though they may with their mouths pronounce truths, yet they contradict it with their works. For also according to the Philosopher [Aristotle], no one is prudent unless

---

52   E. N. "With regard to evil thoughts, there may be a twofold delusion. God-fearing souls who have little or no gift of discernment, and are inclined to scruples, think that every wicked thought that enters their mind is a sin. This is a mistake, for it is not the wicked thoughts in themselves that are sins, but the yielding or consenting to them. The wickedness of mortal sin consists in the perverse will that deliberately yields to sin with a complete knowledge of its wickedness with full consent. And therefore St. Augustine teaches that when the consent of the will is absent, there is no sin." St. Alphonsus Liguori, *The School of Christian Perfection* (Boston: Mission Church Press, 1910).

53   Cf. 1 Cor. 3:3: *For, whereas there is among you envying and contention, are you not carnal, and walk according to man?*

54   Matt. 5:4 E. N. After the general resurrection, the meek shall inherit the earth with their glorified bodies (which will enjoy the properties of impassibility, subtlety, agility, and clarity); on the other hand, the exact opposite will happen to the evildoers whose bodies will not enjoy these properties and will hence be a burden for them by which they will suffer the pain of sense.

55   Mal. 2:1a.

56   Ecclus. 3:29b.

57   Is. 5:18. E. N. Denis's text departs from the Sixto-Clementine. Denis states *velut longam restem*, "as a long cord," whereas the Sixto-Clementine reads *quasi vinculum plaustri*, as a "rope of a cart."

58   Rom. 2:4–5.

he is virtuous: and to judge is an act of prudence.⁵⁹ For this reason, it is
written of sinners: *Woe to you . . . who have turned judgment into bitterness,
and the fruit of justice into wormwood.*⁶⁰ That is stated even more plainly
and explained elsewhere by the holy prophet Isaiah saying: *Woe to you
that call evil good, and good evil: that put darkness for light, and light for
darkness: that put bitter for sweet, and sweet for bitter.*⁶¹

57{58}[4]   *The wicked are alienated from the womb; they have gone
            astray from the womb: they have spoken false things.*

*Alienati sunt peccatores a vulva; erraverunt ab utero, locuti
sunt falsa.*

57{58}[4] *Alienati sunt peccatores a vulva; [erraverunt ab utero, locuti
sunt falsa]; the wicked are alienated from the womb [they have gone astray
from the womb: they have spoken false things].*⁶² The sense of this verse
can be gathered from the preceding exposition. Yet one should consider
that often speech seeming to exceed due measure is without prejudice
to the truth because he who speaks knows to what extent it will be
believed. Now this is so where something is more seriously and more
evidently put forth. And this way we read in the Gospel: *Many other
things . . . Jesus did; which, if they were written every one, the world itself, I
think, would not be able to contain the books that should be written.*⁶³ And
so also it now says, *The wicked are sinners from the womb, they have gone
astray from the womb:* [it says this] not that they sinned before the use
of reason and from the beginning of their birth they unceasingly went
astray; but this is said to express how perseveringly and pertinaciously

---

59   E. N. "True virtue cannot exist without prudence." *Nicomachean Ethics*, VI, 13,
2 [1144b13] (Cambridge, MS: Harvard 1956), 371 (trans., H. Rackham). "Prudence
is the virtue that disposes practical reason to discern our true good in every circumstance and to choose the right means of achieving it; 'the prudent man looks
where he is going.'. . . Prudence is 'right reason in action,' writes St. Thomas Aquinas,
following Aristotle." CCC § 1806. "No dictum of traditional Christian moral doctrine
strikes such a note of strangeness to the ears of contemporaries, even contemporary
Christians, as this one: that the virtue of prudence is the mold and 'mother' of all
the other cardinal virtues, of justice, fortitude, and temperance. In other words,
none but the prudent man can be just, brave, and temperate, and the good man is
good insofar as he is prudent." Josef Pieper, *The Four Cardinal Virtues* (New York:
Harcourt, Brace & World, 1965), 3.
60   Amos 6:1a, 13b.
61   Is. 5:20. E. N. Things that ought to be good (judgment/justice) are become
evil and bitter (like wormwood).
62   E. N. The "etc." has been replaced with the remainder of the verse in brackets.
63   John 21:25.

many sinners offend God. Of such Solomon said: *The children of men commit evils without any fear.*[64] In an opposite way the just are also said to convert to God from the womb, and to be with virtue from the womb, whether because of divine choice, or good inclination to virtues, or because the strong and stable adherence with which they hold onto God. And so holy Job said: *From my infancy mercy grew up with me: and it came out with me from my mother's womb.*[65]

57{58}[5]   *Their madness is according to the likeness of a serpent: like the deaf asp that stops its ears.*

Furor illis secundum similitudinem serpentis, sicut aspidis surdae et obturantis aures suas.

57{58}[5]   *Furor illis secundum similitudinem serpentis, their madness is according to the likeness of a serpent.* For in the way serpents are enemies of men and their venom poisons and kills, so pestilential and impious men by their words of madness inflame their neighbors with the venom of anger, poison them with bad example, and kill them through seducing them by means of praising, or threatening, or by other means. For this reason, Moses [said]: *Depart from the tents of these wicked men, and touch nothing of theirs, lest you be involved in their sins.*[66] *Sicut aspides surdae et obturantis aures suas,* like the deaf asp that stops its ears. All those who spurn the word of God and reject religious instructors or admonishers become like asps with stopped ears. Of such men the Savior says: *My word has no place in you.*[67] Let us not, therefore, shut our ears to a word of salvation, to admonishment of life, and to saving doctrine. For *blessed are they who hear the word of God and keep it.*[68] We also know because *He that is of God, hears the word of God.*[69] But of the sinner neglectful of the word of God is written: Everyone *that commits sin is of the devil,*[70] *and has not known [God].*[71] This therefore is a sign of predestination and grace: to hear the word of God with affection and cheerfully. For which reason in another place is written of the reprobate: *They are of the world: therefore of the world they speak,*

---

64   Eccl. 8:11b.
65   Job 31:18.
66   Num. 16:26.
67   John 8:37b.
68   Luke 11:28b.
69   John 8:47a.
70   1 John 3:8a.
71   1 John 3:6b.

and the world hears them.[72] Whence John the Baptists attests: *He that is of the earth, . . . of the earth he speaks.*[73]

57{58}[7][74] *God shall break in pieces their teeth in their mouth: the Lord shall break the grinders of the lions.*

Deus conteret dentes eorum in ore ipsorum; molas leonum confringet Dominus.

57{58}[8] *They shall come to nothing, like water running down; he has bent his bow until they be weakened.*

Ad nihilum devenient tamquam aqua decurrens; intendit arcum suum donec infirmentur.

57{58}[7] *Deus conteret dentes eorum in ore ipsorum*, God shall break in pieces their death in their mouth, that is, he will condemn the proud and ungodly speech of evil men, and he will hinder and restrain them from their effect, in the manner that the most proud king of the Assyrians predicted: *When you were mad against me, your pride came up to my ears: therefore I will put a ring in your nose, and a bit between your lips.*[75] **57{58}[8]**[76] *Ad nihilum devenient tamquam aqua decurrens*, they shall come to nothing, like water running down. Sin is nothing,[77] and he who sins perishes unceasingly, and is regarded as nothing by God, and he is spurned, because he is emptied of all divine, grace, and meritorious being.[78] Hence in the book of Wisdom it is said of the reprobate: *We being born, forthwith ceased to be: and have been able to show no mark of virtue: but are consumed in our wickedness.*[79] In the way, therefore, that water flows quickly downwards and is no longer seen; so sinners daily flow downwards and in the hour of death are condemned, in the last judgment, perishing

---

72 1 John 4:5.

73 John 3:31b.

74 E. N. Denis skips over Ps. 58:6.

75 Is. 37:29a.

76 F. N. Denis skips over the rest of Ps. 58:7.

77 E. N. St. Augustine famously understood sin as a privation of good (*privatio boni*), so that sin pertains to a deficiency or lack and not an efficiency or positive thing, the will being defective and not effective. So to try to find a reason for the sin is *sis quisquam velit videre tenebras vel audire silentium*, "like one desiring to see darkness or hear silence." City of God, XII,8, PL 41, 355.

78 E. N. That is, the soul in mortal sin is bereft of uncreated grace (the indwelling of the Trinity), of created sanctifying grace, and of the supernatural life and ability to merit.

79 Wis. 5:13.

in both soul and body, to be annihilated from all the blessed.[80] *Intendit arcum suum donec infirmentur, he has bent his bow until they be weakened*: that is, the threats and punishments God prepares for the iniquitous while they revolt with the resolution of sinning and fall into the eternal miseries of hell. Whence, the Lord threatens horribly transgressors by the prophet [Amos], and says: *Behold, I will screak under you as a wain screaketh that is laden with hay; and flight shall perish from the swift, and the valiant shall not possess his strength, neither shall the strong save his life.*[81]

57{58}[9] *Like wax that melts they shall be taken away: fire has fallen on them, and they shall not see the sun.*

Sicut cera quae fluit auferentur; supercecidit ignis, et non viderunt solem.

57{58}[9] *Sicut cera quae fluit, auferentur; like wax that melts they shall be taken away.* A later Psalm makes this [verse] more evident: *As wax melts before the fire, so let the wicked perish at the presence of God.*[82] For in the way the heat of fire softens and destroys wax, so the anger of divine justice removes sinners from the present life and repulses them from the future blessed life: and so in either event they are taken away and spiritually destroyed. For this reason, the Lord says through Hosea: *I will meet them as a bear that is robbed of her whelps, ... and I will devour them there as a lion.*[83] For also sinners sinning deserve the shortening of the present life, in the manner that the Lord says to the avaricious rich

---

80   E. N. Denis is not saying that the body or soul will be annihilated, but that any supernatural being in the soul will be annihilated. As St. Augustine said, "the human soul is truly asserted to be immortal, but it also has its own death of a certain kind." The doctrine of annihilationism (that the damned soul is annihilated) is heretical because it contradicts the Church's teaching that the soul is immortal and the punishment in hell is eternal. As the Catechism says "The Church teaches that every spiritual soul ... is immortal: it does not perish when it separates from the body at death, and it will reunited with the body at the Final Resurrection." CCC § 366. "The teaching of the Church affirms the existence of hell and its eternity." CCC § 1035. However, though the body and spiritual soul of the damned will have an eternal natural existence, the souls of the damned enjoy no supernatural life. "The death, therefore, of the soul occurs when God deserts it, [like the death] of the body when the soul deserts it.... For in that ultimate and everlasting punishment ... is rightly called the death of the soul, because it does not live with respect to God (*ex Deo*)." *City of God*, XIII, 2, PL 41, 377.

81   Amos 2:13–14. E. N. The first verse might be translated: "I will squeak under you as a wagon squeaks that is laden with hay."

82   Ps. 67:3b.

83   Hosea 13:8.

man: *Fool, this night do they require your soul of you.*[84] And Solomon: *Let it not be well with the wicked, neither let his days be prolonged, but as a shadow let them pass away that fear not the face of the Lord.*[85]

Supercecidit ignis, et non viderunt solem; fire has fallen on them, and they shall not see the sun: that is, the infernal fire shall fall upon the wicked, and they shall not see God: *for neither wisdom, nor knowledge, nor work, nor reason shall be in hell.*[86] Or [alternatively]: *Fire has fallen,* that is, the heat of desire and the fervor of passion, such as are the inflammation of anger, the glow of avarice, the flame of envy descended upon sinners, for the deeds of the flesh they did not in any way mortify, nor did they subject their sensuality to reason; and they did not see the sun, that is, they did not give consideration to Christ, the sun of justice, truth, and wisdom; they did not conform themselves to his precepts: for the fires of their passions burned up reason, extinguished charity, and chased away grace. And too late did they confess: *We have erred from the way of truth, and the light of justice has not shined unto us, and the sun of understanding has not risen upon us.*[87] Or [understood yet another way]: *Fire has fallen on them,* that is, tribulation has rushed upon the evil in this age. For *to the sinner* God *has given vexation and superfluous care.*[88] And *they shall not see the sun,* that is, they did not repent, nor did they turn to God, but they became impatient and obstinate, in the manner we read in Revelation: *They blasphemed the God of heaven, because of their pains and wounds, and did not penance for their works ... to give him glory.*[89]

57{58}[10]   *Before your thorns could know the brier; he swallows them up, as the living, so in his wrath.*

Priusquam intelligerent spinae vestrae rhamnum, sicut viventes sic in ira absorbet eos.

57{58}[10] *Priusquam intelligerent spinae vestrae rhamnum, before your thorns could know the brier:* that is, before the worms of your conscience and the pricks of your internal disorders would make you reflect on the enormity of sin and the gravity of the torments prepared for you in hell; *sicut viventes, sicut in ira absorbet eos; he swallows them up, as the living, so*

84   Luke 12:20a.

85   Eccl. 8:13.

86   Eccl. 9:10b. E. N. Denis has changed the order from the original "neither work, nor reason, nor wisdom, nor knowledge shall be in hell."

87   Wis. 5:6.

88   Eccl. 2:26a.

89   Rev. 16:11, 9b.

in his wrath, that is, God will quickly take you up, overwhelm you, and condemn you, just as the living who anticipated living a long time, but who suddenly die, are taken from this life. Although they have remorse of conscience and perceive the pricks of interior disorder because the disordered spirit is itself its own punishment;[90] still they do not wish to turn their attention to the disorder in this life nor to consider the future torments: and so God comes upon them when they are unready, and he quickly *swallows them up* and damns them, as we have already discussed. Moreover, this verse is more fully explained in the preceding exposition. The rest, which is now also omitted, is plentifully explained there.

Let us all take great care to judge justly, to discern correctly, and to subordinate and conform our life and morals to just judgment, and to direct it according to the tenor of the divine law, knowing most certainly because there will be reward for our work[91] and the ungodly will not escape just punishment. Hence, the most wise Solomon in Ecclesiastes provides witness to it: *Though a sinner do evil a hundred times, and by patience be borne withal, I know from thence that it shall be well with them that fear God, who seek his face.*[92]

PRAYER

WE BESEECH, O LORD GOD, GIVE US always truly to speak, love, and follow your justice; and you, who make the vile and false to be precious, grant us not to engage in iniquities on earth, so that, justified with the assistance of your compassion, we might in the just judgment be able to be numbered among the saved.

Da nobis, quaesumus, Domine Deus, vere iustitiam tuam semper
loqui, diligere et sectari; et qui vile et reprobum efficis
pretiosum, fac nos iniquitates in terra non operari:
ut ope miserationis tuae iustificati, salvandis
in iudicio iustis possimus aggregati.

---

90   E. N. On the disorder in the soul consequent to sin being its own punishment, see footnote 54-61.

91   Cf. Jer. 31:16a: *Let your voice cease from weeping, and your eyes from tears: for there is a reward for your work, says the Lord.*

92   Eccl. 8:12. E. N. Denis has *quaerunt*, "seek," instead of *verentur*, "dread," thus departing from the Sixto-Clementine text.

Psalm 58

ARTICLE XVI

EXPOSITION OF THE FIFTY-EIGHTH PSALM:
ERIPE ME DE INIMICIS MEIS.
DELIVER ME FROM MY ENEMIES.

58{59}[1] *Unto the end, destroy not David for an inscription of a title, when Saul sent and watched his house to kill him.*

In finem, ne disperdas David in tituli inscriptionem, quando misit Saul, et custodivit domum eius, ut eum interficeret.

HIS IS THE TITLE ASSIGNED TO THE PSALM now being explained: 58{59}[1] *In finem, ne disperdas. David in tituli inscriptionem, quando misit Saul, et custodivit domum eius, ut eum interficeret; unto the end, destroy not David for an inscription of a title, when Saul sent and watched his house to kill him.* In the first book of Samuel, we read that while David was singing before Saul, the same Saul sought to thrust a lance through holy David, who fled to his home. But Saul sent his guards, ordering them to guard the house of David that night, in order that when morning came, they might capture and kill David.[1] But Michal, the daughter of Saul, informed her husband [David] of this, and he was placed in a basket; and in this manner David escaped. Therefore, David wrote this Psalm on the occasion of this salvation. Many expound this Psalm of David literally, applying this Psalm literally to the historical situation just mentioned. Although another method [of interpretation] is possible, nevertheless, as will become clear, this Psalm has many things which are explained highly improperly of David. It is therefore more fitting and more true to expound of those things signified by the things done than the things done themselves. For David is a figure of Christ; also, the home of David, signifies Christ's sepulcher; but Saul [signifies] the kingdom of the Jews. And so, therefore, the sense of the title is: *Unto the end*, that is, this Psalm directing us to Christ, deals or is written [to remind us], *destroy not David*, that is, destroy not the honor and reign of Christ, which is the Church, *for an inscription of title*, by evil words or acts negating Christ to be the true Savior; *when Saul sent*, that is, the kingdom

---

1 1 Sam. 19:9–12.

145

of the Jews, *and watched his house*: because the Jews sent soldiers to guard
the sepulcher of Christ, to affix a seal on the stone and to keep watch
over it;[2] *to kill him*: that is, the Jews, therefore, caused the sepulcher of
Christ to be guarded, that they might blot out the name and the memory
of him, in the manner that Jeremiah sets forth in their person: *Let us cut
him off from the land of the living, and let his name be remembered no more*.[3]
Whence in an earlier Psalm Christ also says: *My enemies have spoken evils
against me: when shall he die and his name perish?*[4]

58{59}[2] *Deliver me from my enemies, O my God; and defend me
from them that rise up against me.*

*Eripe me de inimicis meis, Deus meus, et ab insurgentibus
in me libera me.*

58{59}[3] *Deliver me from them that work iniquity, and save me from
bloody men.*

*Eripe me de operantibus iniquitatem, et de viris sanguinum
salva me.*

And so while still passible and the Passion being imminent, Christ,
desiring to rise again to immortal life, prays: **58{59}[2]** *Eripe me de
inimicis meis, deliver me from my enemies* who are envious, detracting, and
contriving evil, namely, the Jews, of whom the Gospels say, *for the Jews had
already agreed among themselves, that if any man should confess him to be
Christ, he should be put out of the synagogue;*[5] *Deus meus et ab insurgentibus
in me, O my God and . . . from them that rise up against me*, that is, from
the cohort and tribune and ministers of the Jews, who approached and
cast hands upon Jesus, and captured him and bound him up, *libera me,
defend me*, by a rapid resurrection and by not holding me in death more
than three days. **58{59}[3]** *Eripe me de operantibus iniquitatem; deliver me
from them that work iniquity*, that is, from the Jews who afflicted me all
night: as is contained in Luke, *And the men that held him, mocked him,
and struck him, and they blindfolded him, and smote his face*,[6] and *they spit
upon him*.[7] *Et de viris sanguinum salva me, and save me from bloody men*,
that is, from them who in the Day of Preparation (*Parasceves*) either by

---

2   Matt. 27:66.
3   Jer. 11:19b.
4   Ps. 40:6.
5   John 9:22b.
6   Luke 22:63, 64a.
7   Matt. 26:67a.

tongue or by hand persecuted me even unto the effusion of blood and death, lacerating my body with a scourge, piercing my head with thorns, and ramming heavy nails through my hands and feet.[8] Christ prayed to be delivered and saved from this, not that he might not suffer, but so that he might be raised again from death, made illustrious in the world, and might be glorified in body. For this reason, he said to the Father, *Father, the hour is come, glorify your Son.*[9] And also elsewhere: *Father*, he said, *save me from this hour.*[10]

58{59}[4] *For behold they have caught my soul: the mighty have rushed in upon me.*

Quia ecce ceperunt animam meam; irruerunt in me fortes.

58{59}[5] *Neither is it my iniquity, nor my sin, O Lord: without iniquity have I run, and directed my steps.*

Neque iniquitas mea, neque peccatum meum, Domine; sine iniquitate cucurri, et direxi.

With merit, O eternal Father, I pray this: **58{59}[4]** *Quia ecce ceperunt, for behold they have caught,* [that is,] the aforementioned Jews with the aid of their ministers [have caught], *animam meam, my soul,* that is, my bodily life so that they might extinguish it; or [alternatively], *my soul,* that is, myself, so that they might kill me. For often in Scripture a part is used to signify the whole, as [for example] where [it says]: *And the Word was made flesh.*[11] See how this does not properly relate to David.[12] For he was never captured by Saul and his partisans, nor was he seized. *Irruerunt in me, they have rushed in upon me,* Christ, your Son, holy and innocent, *fortes, the strong* in evil, namely, the chiefs of the priests, the condemning Pilate, and the deriding Herod. **58{59}[5]** *Neque iniquitas mea, neither is it my iniquity* against God, *neque peccatum meum, nor my sin* against my neighbor, *Domine, O Lord* God: that is, through no fault of my own did I deserve this suffering, but *I paid that which I took not away,*[13] and I endured

---

8   Matt. 27:39, 35.

9   John 17:1a.

10   John 12:27b.

11   John 1:14. *E. N.* That is, the Word not only became flesh, but it became man, both body (flesh) and soul, since both body and soul were hypostatically united to the Word in the Incarnation.

12   *E. N.* Suggesting what Denis stated in the beginning, that this Psalm is more fittingly applied literally to Christ than David.

13   Ps. 68:5b. *E. N.* As Denis later explains with respect to this verse, "'that which I took not away,' that is, the fault that I had not contracted, the evil that I did not do,

all this for the sin of the whole world, as it is written: *I lay down my life for my sheep.*[14] Whence Isaiah said: *The Lord has laid on him the iniquity of us all.*[15] *Sine iniquitate cucurri, without iniquity have I run,* by the way of your commandments and the theatre of this age: as it is stated in an earlier Psalm, *He has rejoiced as a giant to run the way* of your commandments.[16] Whence Christ asserts: *As the Father has given me commandment, so do I.*[17] *Et direxi, and [I have] directed* all my human manner of living in this world according to the divine will, and not once have I gone astray in anything. This also does not properly or satisfactorily apply to David. Though he may not have deserved to be killed by Saul, he nevertheless had not run and directed [his life] completely without sin. For *if we say we have no sin, we deceive ourselves.*[18] And *nobody is free from sordidness on earth, not even the infant who is but a day old.*[19] For this reason, Solomon asserts: *There is no just man upon earth, that does good, and sins not.*[20] It is not seemly that David would presume to justify himself in this manner before God.

58{59}[6]   *Rise up to meet me, and behold: even you, O Lord, the God of hosts, the God of Israel. Attend to visit all the nations: have no mercy on all them that work iniquity.*

Exsurge in occursum meum, et vide: et tu, Domine Deus virtutum, Deus Israel, intende ad visitandas omnes gentes; non misearis omnibus qui operantur iniquitatem.

58{59}[6] *Exsurge in occursum meum, rise up to meet me:* that is, you, O Lord Father, rise up with me going forth to the site of Calvary, carrying on my own shoulders the Cross, that is, reach forth as one rising up and running and meeting another does, assisting, cooperating, and

---

'then I did pay': for without my own fault I suffered punishment. Yet punishment is what is due fault, as also death is the punishment for sin. Therefore, the Savior lived most entirely free from all sin, and nevertheless he endured a most bitter death, and so it follows that he paid what he did not take away."

14   John 10:15b.
15   Is. 53:6b.
16   Ps. 18:6b. E. N. In his interpretation of Ps. 18:6, Denis suggests that the "giant" in Psalm 18:6 is the Word incarnate born of the Blessed Virgin May. *See* Volume I, Article XLV (Psalm 18:6).
17   John 14:31b.
18   1 John 1:8a.
19   *Cf.* Job 15:14 (LXX). E. N. The Latin translation of the Septuagint differs from the Sixto-Clementine which states: *What is man that he should be without spot, and he that is born of a woman that he should appear just?*
20   Eccl. 7:21.

helping my humanity in all things. For all the efficacy of the merits of the humanity of Christ was through divine virtue. Meet me also during my soul leaving from my body and entering into limbo,[21] and—joined again with my body—ascending into heaven, leading it and embracing it in all things. For Christ prayed for this, saying: *Father into your hands I commend my spirit.*[22] *Et vide, and behold* with eyes of goodness and justice, how much I endured for your honor and the redemption of the world; and seeing this, grant me accidental reward and to those detained in limbo essential reward, and convert all the world to the right faith.[23]

Et tu, Domine; even you, O Lord of the universe, *Deus virtutum, the God of hosts* of heaven, namely, of the angels, *Deus Israel, the God of Israel,* that is, of the spiritual man contemplating you by faith—you who literally were specifically the God of holy Jacob, who was named Israel, and the people of the Jews, who are often named Israel in Scripture;[24] *intende ad visitandas omnes gentes; [non miserearis omnibus qui operantur iniquitatem]; attend to visit all the nations: [have no mercy on all them that work iniquity].*[25] Sometimes, the visitation of God in sacred Scripture is taken in a good sense, namely, for divine pity and assistance, in the manner that we have presented in Luke: *Through the bowels of the mercy of our God, in which . . . he has visited us.*[26] But sometimes it is taken in a

---

21   E. N. A reference to the *limbus partum,* the "limbo of the fathers," also known as "Abraham's bosom," where the souls of the righteous tarried pending the redemptive death of Christ and his victory over death.

22   Luke 23:46b.

23   E. N. Jesus in his humanity had the beatific vision—which is the essential reward of the elect—from the first instant of his conception, and so his only rewards are denominated "accidental," and involve the resurrection, glorification, and ascension unto glory of his human nature. On the other hand, those detained in limbo would receive their essential reward—the beatific vision. For more on this issue, *see* Article XII (Psalm 2:5) and Article XXIV (Psalm 7:13) and footnote 2-23 in Volume I.

24   E. N. Denis is blissfully unaware of the so-called "scandal of particularity," that is, the notion that the universal God, the Creator of the universe, could have deigned to have revealed himself in so concrete and exclusive a manner—as the God of Jacob, as the God of one man, and the God of a small tribe in one small area of the world at one particular time and place of history. The scandal would be even more particularized when that God became incarnate in one *man,* Jesus, a scandal of particularity that scandalized even the Jews, who themselves were a scandal of particularity to the world. *Cf.* 1 Cor. 1:23. More scandalous than the "scandal of particularity" is that—modernly—Christians, infected by religious indifferentism or universalism, appear scandalized by that scandal of particularity presented by Jesus Christ, who manifestly revealed himself as *the* way, *the* truth, and *the* life, *the* only means for salvation, and *the* only way to God the Father.

25   E. N. That part in brackets replaces the "etc." in the Latin text.

26   Luke 1:78.

bad sense, namely, as divine vengeance, as we find when the Lord speaks through Zephaniah: *I will visit in that day upon every one that enters arrogantly.*[27] And so also is it understood with Isaiah, where we read of the devils and the damned: *And they shall be gathered together as in the gathering of one bundle into the pit, and they shall be shut up there in prison: and after many days they shall be visited.*[28] Origen, however, believed that the visitation in this place was to be taken in a good sense: and it is for this reason that he said that ultimately the damned would be saved.[29]

According to this twofold visitation, therefore, this part can be explained in two ways. The first in this way: *Attend, O Lord, to visit all the nations,* that is, visit with your just judgment the sinners living among the nations, withdrawing from them grace in the present and glory in the future, and in both places inflicting upon them deserved punishments. And so there follows, *have no mercy on all them that work iniquity:* which is said rather as a foretelling than an imprecation, understood as pertaining only to those persevering in sin, and with one's affection conforming to the divine justice. It must not be understood as meaning as if God in no way takes pity upon the damned: for in the present they are abandoned less than they deserve because their angels divert from them many evils; and also in the future they will be punished less than they deserve.[30] Yet God is said not to have mercy upon them because he does not in the end save them and because the divine justice is reflected in them to a greater extent and more evidently than is [divine] mercy. And so James says: *Judgment without mercy to him* will be done *that has not done mercy.*[31] The second [way of understanding this section] is

27   Zeph. 1:9a. E. N. The verse as a whole allows us to understand the entire context: *I will visit in that day upon every one that enters arrogantly over the threshold: them that fill the house of the Lord their God with iniquity and deceit.*

28   Is. 24:22.

29   E. N. This is a reference to the notion of *apokatastasis,* or universal restoration of all of creation (including Satan and his demons), which Origen appears to have held. Certainly, Denis is not advocating it, but is merely mentioning it *obiter dicta.* Any interpretation of Isaiah 24:22 in this manner would be implicitly condemned by the Church, which has clearly rejected Origen's notion as heretical at the Synod of Constantinople (543 AD) "If anyone says or holds that the punishment of the demons and of impious men is temporary and that it will have an end at some time, that is to say, there will be a complete restoration (ἀποκατάστασιν/*apokatastasin*) of the demons or impious men, let him be anathema." DS 411. This error is specifically discussed in the *Summa Theologiae. See* ST IIIa (Supp.), q. 99, art. 2, co.

30   E. N. See ST IIIa (Supp.), q. 99, art. 2, ad 1.

31   James 2:13a. E. N. One might also recall here the Parable of the Ungrateful Servant, where Christ tells us in no uncertain terms how God the Father will respond to those who do not forgive their brother's trespasses from their heart. Matt. 18:21–35.

thus: *Attend to visit all the nations,* so that you might illuminate them with your grace, convert them to the faith, and lead them upon the paths of justice so that they all might be blessed in Christ: according to that often promised to Abraham in Genesis, *In your seed shall all nations be blessed.*[32] *Non miserearis omnibus qui operantur iniquitatem, have no mercy on all them that work iniquity,* that is, do not spare them in the present life, but censure them and chastise them, and requite [their evil] now, so that you might not punish them in a more serious way later.

58{59}[7] *They shall return at evening, and shall suffer hunger like dogs: and shall go round about the city.*

Convertentur ad vesperam, et famem patientur ut canes; et circuibunt civitatem.

58{59}[8] *Behold they shall speak with their mouth, and a sword is in their lips: for who has heard?*[33]

Ecce loquentur in ore suo, et gladius in labiis eorum: quoniam quis audivit?

58{59}[9] *But you, O Lord, shall laugh at them: you shall bring all the nations to nothing.*

Et tu, Domine, deridebis eos; ad nihilum deduces omnes gentes.

58{59}[7] *Convertentur ad vesperam, they shall return at evening.* This also can be understood two ways. First, of the Gentiles. *They shall return at evening,* that is, the Gentiles will be converted to Christ in the sixth and last age,[34] according to that which John says in his epistle: *It is the last hour;*[35] and Paul, We are the ones *upon whom the ends of the world are come.*[36] *Et famem patientur ut canes, and shall suffer hunger like dogs,* that is, they shall hunger and thirst for justice, and they shall avidly hear the word of God, as Luke recalls of the Thessalonians in the Acts of the Apostles: These are they *who with all eagerness, received the word of God,*

---

32 Gen. 22:18a; *see also* Gen. 12:3; 18:18.
33 E. N. I have modified the Douay Rheims from "who, say they, has heard us?" to "for who has heard?" which is closer to the Sixto-Clementine's *quoniam quis audivit?*
34 E. N. The "sixth age" is the age that Christ returns in glory, the end of human history as we know it, and which will usher in the "seventh age." This is a reference to St. Augustine's theory of history. For more information, *see* footnote 11-1 in Volume 1.
35 1 John 2:18a. E. N. The entire verse gives a better context: *Little children, it is the last hour; and as you have heard that Antichrist comes, even now there are come many Antichrists: whereby we know that it is the last hour.*
36 1 Cor. 10:11b.

daily searching the scriptures, whether these things were so.[37] *Et circuibunt civitatem, and shall go around about the city,* that is, the militant Church, in order that they might hear from those preaching the word of salvation which they desire. Of this conversion and hunger of the Gentiles, Amos says: *Behold the days come, says the Lord, and I will send forth a famine into the land: not a famine of bread, nor a thirst of water, but of hearing the word of the Lord. And they shall move from sea to sea,*[38] that is, they shall surround the Church, which will extend the length and width of the world's globe. **58{59}[8]** *Ecce loquentur in ore suo, behold they shall speak with their mouth:* that is, the Gentiles shall be converted to the faith not only with the heart, but also with the mouth, declaring the marvels of Christ, singing divine praises, and courageously and publicly confessing God by word and deed: as the Apostle [Paul] says, *With heart, we believe unto justice; but, with the mouth, confession is made unto salvation.*[39] *Et gladius in labiis eorum, and a sword is in their lips,* that is, the preaching of the Gospel will be in their mouth. For this preaching is called a sword, according to that Apostle: *And the sword of the Spirit, which is the word of God.*[40] And Christ in Isaiah, speaking of God the Father: *He has made,* he says, *my mouth like a sharp sword.*[41] For the words which the preachers speak, dreadfully inveighing against the world, are like a sharp two-edged sword. *Quoniam quis audivit? For who has heard?* That is, because few are they who obey the faith and morals of the Gospel of Christ. *For many are called, but few chosen.*[42] Whence Isaiah says: Lord *who has believed our report?*[43] **58{59}[9]** *Et tu, Domine; but you, O Lord,* O just judge, almighty God, holy and true, *deridebis eos, shall laugh at them,* that is, the called and the many, contradicting the Gospel of Christ by word and deed, *ad nihilum deduces omnes gentes, you shall bring all the nations to nothing,* that is, the way of living of the nations, depriving them of all spiritual things and being capable of merit, and finally condemning them, and reckoning them as nothing [in the supernatural life].

Secondly, it can be explained of the Jews, in this way: *They shall return at evening,* that is, at the end of the world and at the end of this last agent, they will be converted to Christ, in the manner one reads prophesied in Hosea:

37 Acts 17:11b. E. N. Denis slightly rearranges the verse, without any change in meaning.
38 Amos 8:11–12a.
39 Rom. 10:10.
40 Eph. 6:17b.
41 Is. 49:2a.
42 Matt. 20:16b.
43 Is. 53:1a.

The children of Israel shall sit many days without king, and without prince, and without sacrifice, and without altar, and without ephod, and without theraphim; and after this . . . they shall return, and shall seek the Lord their God, and David their king (that is, the Messiah, as all understand [this verse to mean]), *and they shall fear the Lord, and his goodness in the last days.*[44] Then what was foretold in Ezechiel will obviously be fulfilled: *I will save my flock,* says the Lord, *and my servant David* (that is, Christ) *their prince.*[45] Whence also the Apostle [Paul] says: When *the fullness of the Gentiles* has come in, then will *all Israel be saved.*[46] This does not disagree with that which Christ stated in the Gospel, *Elijah, when he comes . . . shall restore all things;*[47] and again, *There shall be one fold and one shepherd.*[48] For the Jews will be converted by the preaching of Elijah according to that which the Lord said to the Jews through Malachi: *Behold I will send you Elijah the Tishbite, before the coming of the great and dreadful day of the Lord.*[49] *Et famem patientur ut canes, and shall suffer hunger like dogs:* because then the Jews will most avidly hear the word of God. *Et circuibunt civitatem, and shall go round about the city,* that is, the Church of Christ, the congregation of Gentiles, which earlier they disdained, they then will visit reverently and with faith, as they accept being formed by the evangelical law. *Ecce loquentur in ore suo, [et gladius in labiis eorum: quoniam quis audivit?] Behold they shall speak with their mouth, [and a sword is in their lips: for who has heard?]*[50] This verse will be fittingly applied to the Jews then converting, as it is now declared to be fittingly applied to the Gentiles converted to the faith. But it can also be explained as applying to the Jews that spurned and killed Christ who was present before them. As in this sense: *Behold* the Jews during the time of Christ, *shall speaking with their mouth* detractions and crimes and blasphemies against Christ; *and*

---

44 Hosea 3:4–5. E. N. The ephod was a priestly sleeveless vestment, similar to a fiddleback chasuble, worn by Jewish priests (*e.g.,* Ex. 28:4 *ff.*). In his *Commentary on Hosea,* Denis describes it as "a priestly vestment which might appropriately be called a superhumeral," *i.e.,* worn over the shoulders. According to Denis, the theraphim were images of the Cherubim and Seraphim "which were in the temple, and which ceased to exist together with the temple." Doctoris Ecstatici D. Dionysii Cartusiani, *Opera Omnia,* Vol. 10 (Montreuil: 1900), 232.

45 Ez. 34:22a, 24b.

46 Rom. 11:25b, 26a.

47 Mark 9:11a.

48 John 10:16b.

49 Mal. 4:5. E. N. Denis's text which describes Elijah by the demonym Tishbite is based upon the Latin translation of the Septuagint which departs from the Sixto-Clementine Vulgate, which reads "Elijah the prophet." Elsewhere, Elijah is identified as being from Tishbe in Gilead. (1 Kings 17:1).

50 E. N. The words in brackets replace the "etc." in the Latin text.

a sword, that is, the speech of persecution and the sentiment desirous of death, *in labiis eorum, is in their lips*. For they said before Christ: *We have a law; and according to the law he ought to die, because he made himself the Son of God.*[51] *For who has heard?* That is, the Jews discussed among themselves whether to charge Christ with this crime and to inflict its punishment upon him, for they thought to hide their deliberations of Christ, lest someone apart from them perceive their malice. For they wanted to kill him without the crowd being present. For they said: *Not on the festival day, lest perhaps there should be a tumult among the people.*[52] *Et tu, Domine, deridebis eos; but you, O Lord, shall laugh at them*, delivering them into the hands of the Romans. And in the hour of their death, you laughed at them. And in the final judgment you will also laugh at them, showing them to have erred and to have lived in a manner worthy of derision: as is said in an earlier Psalm, *He that dwells in heaven shall laugh at them.*[53] And in the book of Proverbs we also read: *I also will laugh in your destruction, and will mock when that shall come to you which you feared.*[54]

58{59}[10] *I will keep my strength toward you: for you, O God, are my protector.*

Fortitudinem meam ad te custodiam, quia, Deus, susceptor meus es.

58{59}[11] *My God, his mercy shall prevent me.*

Deus meus, misericordia eius praeveniet me.

58{59}[10] *Fortitudinem meam ad te custodiam, I will keep my strength toward you*. These are the words of Christ to the Father. These accord with those stated in the Gospel: *The Son cannot do anything of himself, but what he sees the Father doing;*[55] and again, *I cannot of myself do anything.*[56] And so, therefore, it is in this sense [that it is to be understood]: All my strength, perfection, and power *toward you*, that is, to your honor and praise, O Father, *I will keep*, that is, I will observe and ordain, lest in any manner I go astray, ascribing anything to myself when I have received everything from you. And not only does Christ refer to the Father all his created power and human fortitude, but also the divine and uncreated

---

51 John 19:7.
52 Matt. 26:5.
53 Ps. 2:4a.
54 Prov. 1:26.
55 John 5:19a.
56 John 5:30a.

[power], openly confessing that it also was received from the Father. For this reason, he said: *That which my Father has given me is greater than all*,[57] that is, the divine essence which I receive from my Father [is greater than all]. For by this he shows himself to be the true God: for he adds, *I and the Father are one*.[58] Yet Christ refers his uncreated power back to the Father, as to its origin, not as to its end.[59] Or [one can understand it] thus: *My strength*, whereby my adversaries are able suddenly and in various torments to weaken, destroy, and extinguish, *I will keep . . . toward you*, that is, I will restrict and hold in reserve according to your will, O Father God, and not immediately avenge myself, but I will concede to them a time for repentance. For this I said to Peter: *Think you that I cannot ask my Father, and he will give me presently more than twelve legions of angels?*[60] For also when with words alone, at the start of the Passion, by saying, *I am he*, he caused his enemies to fall to the ground restraining their strength and then causing them to stand up again.[61]

Quia Deus susceptor meus es, for you, O God, are my protector: that is, the Word of God assumed my humanity unto his personality. God [the Father], also the Trinity, is the protector of Christ the man, for he heard all of his prayers, he received him who rose again and ascended, and sat him at his right hand. Whence, about Christ, God the Father says through Isaiah: *Behold my servant, I will uphold him*.[62] **58{59}[11]** *Deus meus, misericordia eius praeveniet me; My God, his mercy shall prevent me*.[63] God did not prevent any other creature whatsoever—indeed

---

57 John 10:29a.

58 John 10:30.

59 E. N. Denis is making it clear that there is no "causal" connection between the Father and the Son because it would imply a difference in essence (and hence deny consubstantiality) between the Father and the Son; hence, the Father is said to be "the origin of the Son." *See*, e.g., St. Thomas Aquinas, *Contra errores Graecorum*, *pars 1 cap. 1*, where St. Thomas states that the relation between the Father and the Son cannot be understood as causal, and so it is improper to speak of there being a relation of formal, material, efficient, or final causality. Thus, in speaking of the relation between the Father and the Son we should use "words connoting origin together with a kind of consubstantiality, such as fount, head, and others of that kind."

60 Matt. 26:53.

61 John 18:5–6.

62 Is. 42:1a.

63 E. N. The word "prevent" here does not mean to keep something from happening; rather, it means to go before someone, to be in front, or to anticipate. The word prevent is derived from Latin *prae-venire* (to come before). Although the use of prevent in this sense is somewhat archaic, a residuum of such sense is still found, for example, in the notion of *prevenient* grace (a grace that comes before), or a preventative remedy (a remedy that is taken before the disease).

not even all other [creatures] together—as he did Christ the man. For only through the goodness and the grace of God was the human nature of Christ assumed by the Word—for no merits had preceded [that assumption of the human nature by the Word,] but in that one and same instant it [Christ's human nature] was both created and united to God.[64]

58{59}[12] *God shall let me see over my enemies: slay them not, lest at any time my people forget. Scatter them by your power; and bring them down, O Lord, my protector.*

Deus ostendet mihi super inimicos meos; ne occidas eos, nequando obliviscantur populi mei. Disperge illos in virtute tua, et depone eos, protector meus, Domine.

58{59}[13] *For the sin of their mouth, and the word of their lips: and let them be taken in their pride. And for their cursing and lying they shall be talked of,*

Delictum oris eorum, sermonem labiorum ipsorum; et comprehendantur in superbia sua. Et de execratione et mendacio annuntiabuntur.

58{59}[14] *When they are consumed: when they are consumed by your wrath, and they shall be no more. And they shall know that God will rule Jacob, and all the ends of the earth.*

In consummatione, in ira consummationis; et non erunt. Et scient quia Deus dominabitur Iacob, et finium terrae.

58{59}[12] *Deus ostendit mihi super inimicos meos; God shall let me see over my enemies,* that is, he will reveal to me as man of that which follows regarding the Jews. *Ne occidas eos, slay them not,* that is, do not, O Christ, beloved Son, completely eradicate from the earth your crucifiers and their posterity, but pray for them, for their good, saying: *Father, forgive them.*[65] [Pray] that they not all be destroyed, but that some of them also remain in the memory and testimony of the truth of the Gospel. And so it continues: *nequando obliviscantur populi mei, lest at any time my people forget,* that is, lest at some future time Christians

---

64   E. N. Since Christ's human nature did not exist prior to it being hypostatically united to the Word, it follows it could not have been the subject of any meritorious actions. Thus, the grace of union was entirely a sheer act of grace arising from the benignity and mercy of God. This is a central doctrine in Denis's understanding of the Incarnation. *See, e.g.,* Article XXI (Psalm 5:8) in Volume I.

65   Luke 23:34a.

may consign me and my law to oblivion, not believing that there were some Jews who presumed to perpetrate such a crime; but seeing the Jews abiding amongst them, they might unceasingly be mindful of me, even eliciting proof of their faith from the rejection, dispersion, and the dereliction of the Jews. From this the reason is drawn why the Jews are not to be killed, unless they have deserved it by a specific sin.[66]

Then Christ says to the Father: *Disperge illos, scatter them* throughout the whole world, so that they are *wanderers among the nations*:[67] as was foretold by Hosea; *in virtute tua, by your power* [which is] almighty, by which all things are easy for you, by which also you employed the Roman power in dispersing the Jews. *Et depone eos, and bring them down* from prosperity and temporal glory, from kingdom, from priesthood, and from all honor of the law of their fathers, *protector meus, my protector*, that is, of my humanity, *Domine, O Lord* Father: *bring them down*, I say, not by excusing them, but by impeding their effect. **58{59}[13]** *Delictum oris eorum, for the sin of their mouth*, that is, *the words of their lips*, by which they said before Pilate: *If he were not a malefactor, we would not have delivered him up to you*;[68] and elsewhere: *Sir, we have remembered, that that seducer said, while he was yet alive: After three days I will rise again.*[69] *Et comprehendantur in superbia sua, and let them be taken in their pride*, that is, let them die in their sin: in accordance with this Christ told the Jews: *You shall die in your sin*,[70] which Christ said more as foretelling rather than imprecating. Or [alternatively], *Let them be taken*, that is, let them be detained, captured, and seized in the city of Jerusalem by the army of the Romans, as also Christ predicted.[71] Or [yet another interpretation], *Let them be taken in their pride*, that is, let them be confounded by the Apostles of Christ instructing, demonstrating, and publicly establishing the words and the miracles of the Resurrection of Christ.

---

66   E. N. Denis is referring to the Catholic doctrine regarding the treatment of the Jews which first finds its papal origins in the letter *Sicut Iudaeis* by Pope St. Gregory the Great (r. 590-604) to the Bishop of Naples. This teaching ultimately reached the status of a Papal Bull when Pope Calixtus II (r. 1119–1124) issued his bull with the same name. It was repeatedly re-promulgated by numerous popes between Eugenius III (r. 1145-1153) and Nicholas V (r. 1447–1455). Considered a sort of "bill of rights" of the Jews, it provided that the Jews were not to be killed unless they were found guilty of a particular criminal offense.

67   Hosea 9:17b.

68   John 18:30b.

69   Matt. 27:63.

70   John 9:21b.

71   Luke 19:43–44.

Et de execratione, and for their cursing, that is, for their abomination, by which they defamed Christ, and spurned him, saying, *A man that is a glutton, a friend of publicans;*[72] *and lying,* because they spoke against Christ saying, *He seduces the people;*[73] and that the disciples had stolen him from the tomb;[74] *annuntiabuntur, they shall be talked of,* that is, they will be refuted by Christ the judge, *in consummatione, when they are consumed,* that is, in the end of the world and the final judgment. Of which consummation Christ in the Gospel says: *So shall it be at the end of the world.*[75] For then *they shall look on him whom they pierced.*[76] Hence it is more clearly stated next: *in ira consummationis, when they are consumed by your wrath,* that is, in the divine vengeance and rebuke which will be in the day of judgment they will be refuted by Christ, for at that time he will tell them: *Depart from me, you cursed, into everlasting fire.*[77] *Et non erunt, and they shall be no more* in the number of the elect nor [among those] in glory: according to this, *Let the ungodly be removed so that he does not see the glory of God.*[78] *Et scient, and they shall know,* in the last day, by undergoing punishment and by looking upon the bodily presence of Christ, *quia Deus, that God,* that is Christ, *dominabitur Iacob, will rule Jacob,* that is, the true Israel, namely the people of the Jews believing in Jesus Christ, *et finium terrae, and all the ends of the earth,* that is, all the Gentiles believing in him. For the God Christ after the final judgment will have dominion over these persons in the Church triumphant, as he also has dominion of all the faithful in the Church militant.

58{59}[15] *They shall return at evening and shall suffer hunger like dogs: and shall go round about the city.*

> *Convertentur ad vesperam, et famem patientur ut canes; et circuibunt civitatem.*

58{59}[15] *Convertentur ad vesperam, [et famem patientur ut canes; et circuibunt civitatem meos];* they shall return at evening [and shall suffer hunger like dogs: and shall go round about the city].[79] This verse, which the Prophet [David] takes up again to console himself over the destruction

---

72   Matt. 11:19.
73   John 7:12.
74   Matt. 28:13.
75   Matt. 13:49a.
76   John 19:37b; Rev. 1:7a. *E. N.* Denis seamlessly combines these two biblical sources.
77   Matt. 25:41b.
78   Is. 26:10 (LXX); *E. N.* For how this verse varies from the Sixto-Clementine Vulgate, *see* Article LXXV (Psalm 36:7) and footnote 36-38 in Volume 2.
79   *E. N.* The words in brackets replace the "etc." in the Latin text.

of his people, has already been expounded upon once before.[80] Consoling himself, therefore, he suggests that a remnant will be saved, in the manner that Isaiah and Paul attest: *For if your people, O Israel, shall be as the sand of the sea, a remnant of them shall be converted.*[81]

58{59}[16] *They shall be scattered abroad to eat, and shall murmur if they be not filled.*

Ipsi dispergentur ad manducandum; si vero non fuerint saturati, et murmurabunt.

58{59}[16] *Ipsi dispergentur ad manducandum,* they shall be scattered abroad to eat: that is, the Jews converting at the end of this age will come from all sides to virtuous men, so that they might acquire the bread of life and of understanding, knowing and observing the doctrine of Christ; and so they might eat the food of obedience, of which Christ asserted: *My meat is to do the will of him that sent me.*[82] *Si vero non fuerint saturati, and . . . if they be not filled* with the aforementioned bread, that is, with the justice that they most greatly shall desire, then *et murmurabunt, they shall murmur,* not against God, but against themselves, blaming themselves in that they converted so late, and that they will not be able to make progress in accordance with their desire. Or [alternatively]: *They shall be scattered abroad to eat* the Body and Blood of Christ: which certainly then they will most devoutly consume, as they will most fully believe in it; indeed they will most devoutly embrace the Sacrament of the Altar, as did the early Church, which (as Luke affirms) they persevered *in the communication of the breaking of bread.*[83] *And . . . if they be not filled* with sacramental grace, namely, with the effects of this superlatively most worthy Sacrament, *and they shall murmur:* according to the understanding to which they have been led.

58{59}[17] *But I will sing your strength: and will extol your mercy in the morning. For you are become my protector,*[84] *and my refuge, in the day of my trouble.*

Ego autem cantabo fortitudinem tuam, et exsultabo mane misericordiam tuam; quia factus es susceptor meus, et refugium meum in die tribulationis meae.

---

80 E. N. See the discussion above regarding Psalm 58:7.
81 Is. 10:22a. *Cf.* Rom. 9:27.
82 John 4:34a.
83 Acts 2:42b.
84 E. N. I have replaced "support" in the Douay-Rheims with "protector" for the Latin *susceptor.*

58{59}[17] *Ego autem, but I, O God, cantabo fortitudinem tuam, will sing your strength,* that is, before my disciples I will praise your power by which you raised me from the dead; *et exsultabo, and I will extol,* that is, exultantly and joyfully I shall make known and shall announce, *mane, in the morning,* on the first day of the week, when I appeared to Mary Magdalen,[85] *misericordiam tuam, your mercy,* that is, the grace whereby you so quickly raised me from the dead, and that you deigned, through me, to give to those detained in limbo and the whole world. For Christ after the Resurrection preached the power of God, when (as Luke memorializes) by *appearing for forty days* to the disciples, [and remained for a time], *speaking to them of the Kingdom of God.*[86] *It is not,* he said, *for you to know the times or moments, which the Father has put in his own power.*[87] He also exulted *in the morning,* that is, during the time of the evangelical law and grace, in the mercy of God, when he told his disciples: Whoever *believes and is baptized shall be saved;*[88] and again: *Receive the Holy Spirit; whose sins you shall forgive, they are forgiven them,* etc.[89] *Quia factus es, for you are become,* O Father God, *susceptor meus, my protector:* according to the sense already stated; *et refugium meum in die tribulationis meae, and my refuge in the day of my trouble,* that is, during the entire time of my life in the world, which was full of trouble. For also as the Passion drew nigh, Christ found refuge with the Father praying and saying: My *Father, if you will, remove this chalice from me.*[90] And dying, he also exclaimed: *Father, into your hands I commend my spirit.*[91] And this was fitting for Christ to the degree he was passible and in a certain aspect a wayfarer.

58{59}[18]   *Unto you, O my helper, will I sing, for you are God my defense: my God my mercy.*

Adiutor meus, tibi psallam, quia Deus susceptor meus es; Deus meus, misericordia mea.

58{59}[18] *Adiutor meus, tibi psallam; unto you, O my helper, will I sing.* In all things God was the helper of Christ, the man, in accordance with that in the prophet Isaiah: *The Lord God is my helper, therefore I am not confounded.*[92] And in the Gospel it says: *The Father who abides in me, he*

---

85   Mark 16:9.
86   Acts 1:3.
87   Acts 1:7.
88   Mark 16:16a.
89   John 20:22b, 23a.
90   Luke 22:42a.
91   Luke 23:46a.
92   Is. 50:7a.

does the works.[93] Christ by himself and through his faithful sings to this helper, praising him with words and deeds. *Quia Deus susceptor meus es, Deus meus, misericordia mea; for you are God my protector, my God, my mercy.* Christ as man calls God his mercy, not because he concedes [he is due] any punishment or personal fault; but because he so graciously anticipated (*praevenit*) and filled him with all blessing of sweetness and preserved him from all sin. For he filled his soul with incomparable grace, making him a face-to-face beholder of the divine essence in a most excellent way, from the first beginning of its creation.

ARTICLE XVII

TROPOLOGICAL OR MORAL EXPOSITION
OF THE SAME FIFTY-EIGHTH PSALM.

58{59}[2] *Deliver me from my enemies, O my God; and defend me from them that rise up against me.*

Eripe me de inimicis meis, Deus meus, et ab insurgentibus in me libera me.

MORALLY, THIS PSALM FITTINGLY APPLIES to the Church of Christ and any individual afflicted Christian when confronting troubles. The faithful, therefore, surrounded by temptations and various adversities may cry out to God with all their heart: 58{59}[2] *Eripe me de inimicis meis, Deus meus; deliver me from my enemies, O my God,* that is, save me from those eyeing me with evil intent and secretly and industriously striving to harm me. This also pertains especially to invisible enemies. Hence, let us ardently have recourse to the help of God, that is, with discernment of the spirits, or the illumination of the Holy Spirit, to recognize the snares of the demons, so that we might be able to say with the Apostle [Paul]: *We are not ignorant of his devices.*[94] *Ab insurgentibus in me, from them that rise up against me,* that is, from the clear intruders and persecutors, *libera me, defend me,* lest my soul be led astray into impatience or other vices, or confront greater injury or wounds that is expedient to the soul. For here the Apostle pleads his disciples: *Pray that we may be delivered . . . from evil and importunate men.*[95]

---

93 John 14:10b.
94 2 Cor. 2:11b.
95 2 Thess. 3:2a.

58{59}[3] Deliver me from them that work iniquity, and save me from
bloody men.

*Eripe me de operantibus iniquitatem, et de viris sanguinum
salva me.*

58{59}[3] *Eripe me de operantibus iniquitatem, deliver me from them that
work iniquity*, that is, from all those living evil lives, even if they are not
my rivals: indeed, from family members, those close to one, neighbors,
and [religious] brothers leading evil lives; and we are especially in need
to be helped lest *with the perverse we are perverted* and consent with them
to evil,[96] and lest any proximity of nature, place, or social interaction
gives rise to an occasion of perverse imitation.[97] *Et de viris sanguinum,
and . . . from bloody men*, who through affection or deed kill their neighbor
either in the flesh or in the heart. For he who induces another person
to sin mortally spiritually kills him. And *whosoever hates his brother is a
murderer*.[98] From this, O Lord, *salva me, save me*, lest I become like them.

Finally, the first verse can be appropriately explained in this manner:
Deliver me from my enemies, O my God, that is, set me free from evil
habits and vicious practices within, latent, or in some way inactive in me,
eradicating such from my heart completely by grace, and by producing
opposite habits of virtue. *And . . . from them that rise up against me*, that
is, from actual vices, from impetuous passions, from inordinate movements, *free me*, in order that by your grace I might steadily cast them
aside, vanquish them, and from day to day less and more rarely feel them.

58{59}[4] For behold they have caught my soul: the mighty have rushed
in upon me.

Quia ecce ceperunt animam meam; irruerunt in me fortes.

58{59}[4] *Quia ecce, for behold*, O Lord, these aforesaid adversaries
ceperunt animam meam, have caught my soul, that is, they have bound it

---

96 Ps. 17:27b.
97 E. N. Denis is referring to "occasions of sin." These are "[a]ny person, place,
or thing that of its nature or because of human frailty can lead one to do wrong,
thereby committing sin. If the danger is certain and probable, the occasion is proximate; if the danger is slight, the occasion becomes remote. It is voluntary if it can
easily be avoided. There is no obligation to avoid a remote occasion unless there is
probable danger of its becoming proximate. There is a positive obligation to avoid
a voluntary proximate occasion of sin even though the occasion of evildoing is due
only to human weakness." John A. Hardon, *Catholic Dictionary* (New York: Image,
1980), 342 (s.v. "occasion of sin").
98 1 John 3:15a.

by the bonds of sin, drawing it into the consent to sin. Or [alternatively], *they have caught*, that is, they have besieged, invaded, and tried to take ahold of my soul, lying in wait to attack the health of the mind or the safety of the body. For our soul is surrounded on all sides by enemies, that is by attacks of the world, the flesh, and the devil. *The mighty*, that is, adversaries—namely demons, the powerful of the world, or the vice rooted within me or which I have a natural proclivity toward—*have rushed in on me*. These daily rush in upon us endeavoring to subvert our souls. And so the Lord must unceasingly be called upon by us.

58{59}[5] *Neither is it my iniquity, nor my sin, O Lord: without iniquity have I run, and directed my steps.*

Neque iniquitas mea, neque peccatum meum, Domine; sine iniquitate cucurri, et direxi.

58{59}[5] *Neque iniquitas mea, neque peccatum meum, Domine; neither is it my iniquity, nor my sin, O Lord*, that is, from no fault have I merited to suffer these scourges. These—Alas!—are the least appropriate, to them, namely, *that suffer persecution for justice's sake*, who are able to say with holy Job, *These things have I suffered without the iniquity of my hand, when I offered pure prayers to God:*[99] they, namely, who have been repaid with evil for good, who with the Apostle are able to say, *We are reviled, and we bless.*[100] Of such a kind was the most blessed David, the author of the present Psalm: he who after he had done so many good things to Saul, suffered from his hand the most heavy persecution. *Sine iniquitate cucurri, et direxi, without iniquity I have run and directed my steps*. This does not properly apply absolutely to anyone other than Christ and his glorious Mother,[101] unless it is explained in this manner: *Without iniquity*, that is, without mortal sin, *I have run* the way of exile or of commandment; and *I have directed my steps*, that is, my works, thoughts,

---

99 Job. 16:18.
100 1 Cor. 4:12b.
101 E. N. Our Lord's human nature, of course, enjoyed both sinlessness (*impeccantis*) and even the possibility of sinning (*impeccabilitas*) by reason of the hypostatic union. DS 301, 1347; Ludwig Ott, *Fundamentals of Catholic Dogma* (Rockford, IL: TAN Books 1974), 168–69 (trans., Patrick Lynch, ed. James Canon Bastible). By an act of perfect redemption, however, the Blessed Virgin Mary *by grace* was free from original sin and actual sin, both mortal and venial. "The most Blessed Virgin Mary was, from the first moment of her conception, by a singular grace and privilege of almighty God and by virtue of the merits of Jesus Christ, Savior of the human race, preserved immune from all stain of original sin." CCC § 491. "By the grace of God Mary remained free of every personal sin her whole life long." CCC § 491.

and words according to the precepts of the divine law. Or [alternatively], *Without iniquity I have run*, that is, I have not persevered in my sin and I have made satisfaction with respect to venial sins.[102] For such did the Apostle [Paul] say: *I am not conscious to myself of anything.*[103] And Job: *My heart does not reprehend me in all my life*,[104] namely, as far as mortal sins: for he was not without venial fault. On occasion, however, holy men may in practice describe and confess their own perfection without any pride for reasonable motives, namely, for the honor of God, for the edification of neighbor, or so that might give to those praying confidence, or expel faintheartedness of spirit. Whence, the most pious king Hezekiah, pleading for a great cause: *O Lord, remember how I have walked before you in truth, and with a perfect heart, and have done that which is good in your sight.*[105] Jeremiah also spoke of himself for our information saying: *I sat not in the assembly of jesters*,[106] and *I have not desired the day of man.*[107]

58{59}[6]   *Rise up to meet me, and behold: even you, O Lord, the God of hosts, the God of Israel. Attend to visit all the nations: have no mercy on all them that work iniquity.*

Exsurge in occursum meum, et vide: et tu, Domine Deus virtutum, Deus Israel, intende ad visitandas omnes gentes; non misereais omnibus qui operantur iniquitatem.

---

102   *E. N.* "Many sins wrong our neighbor. One must do what is possible in order to repair the harm (*e.g.*, return stolen goods, restore the reputation of someone slandered, pay compensation for injuries). Simple justice requires as much. But sin also injures and weakens the sinner himself, as well as his relationships with God and neighbor. Absolution takes away sin, but it does not remedy all the disorders sin has caused. Raised up from sin, the sinner must still recover his full spiritual health by doing something more to make amends for the sin: he must 'make satisfaction for' or 'expiate' his sins. This satisfaction is also called 'penance.'" CCC § 1459.
103   1 Cor. 4:4a.
104   Job 27:6b.
105   Is. 38:3; 2 Kings 20:3. *E. N.* Hezekiah was pleading to the Lord to be healed of his mortal sickness.
106   Jer. 15:17a. *E. N.* As Denis explains in his *Commentary on Jeremiah*: "'I sat not in the assembly of jesters,' that is, I did not give myself over in friendship to the vain and those playing games, in accordance with that in the Psalm, 'I have not sat with the council of vanity, etc.' 'I have hated the assembly of the malignant.' (Ps. 25:4, 5)." Doctoris Ecstatici D. Dionysii Cartusiani, Opera Omnia, Vol. 9 (Montreuil: 1900), 139.
107   Jer. 17:16. *E. N.* Denis elaborates this verse in his *Commentary on Jeremiah*: "'[A]nd the day of man,' that is, the prolongation of life, or human consolations, or the delicate life, 'I have not desired.'" *Ibid.*, 152.

58{59}[6] *Exsurge in occursum meum, rise up to meet me:*[108] that is, in every event, cause, work, or business, draw near to me, O Lord, and be present, show yourself to me, and receive me. Meet me, therefore, not by a change in place, since you are boundless and immovable; but by outlaying help and grace, for you alone are able to save me. Now sometimes the encounter of God is received in evil, namely, in the resistance and vengeance by which God impedes, punishes, and condemns the will and deeds of the sinner, by which the Lord bears witness against the sinner: *I will meet them as a bear that is robbed of her whelps.*[109] But sometimes he is received in good, as has already been noted. And so with the servant of Abraham: *O Lord,* he said, *meet me today, I beseech you, and show kindness, [to my master Abraham].*[110] We, therefore, considering that we are unceasingly in all matters needful of the help of God, ought always to say: *Rise up to meet me, O Lord.* But so that this prayer may draw down its desired effect, let us do that which Amos wrote: *Be prepared to meet your God,*[111] that is, do what is in you, and make yourself ready, so that you might worthily bring about the divine meeting (*obviatione divina*).[112] This also the Lord says through Jeremiah: *Who is this who sets his heart so as to approach me?*[113] *Et vide,* and see, that is, O Lord, mercifully consider how threatening this peril is to me, how much I need your grace, and with what affection and trust I call upon you.

58{59}[7] *They shall return at evening, and shall suffer hunger like dogs: and shall go round about the city.*

Convertentur ad vesperam, et famem patientur ut canes; et circuibunt civitatem.

58{59}[7] *Convertentur ad vesperam, they shall return at evening.* This Mother Church is able to say of those who neither in adolescence nor youth

---

108   E. N. The word used here and translated as "encounter" or "meet," are all forms of the word *occursus* except where otherwise indicated (on one occasion, *obviatione* is used). The Feast Day known as the "*Occursus Domini*," the Presentation, refers to the encounter or meeting between the infant Jesus and Sts. Simeon and Anna.

109   Hosea 13:8a. E. N. "'I will meet them,' bring forth vindication, 'as a bear that is robbed of her whelps,' that is," at least from the perspective of the sinner encountering God in this fashion says Denis in his *Commentary on Hosea*, "in an exceedingly most cruel fashion, giving them into the hands of most cruel enemies." Doctoris Ecstatici D. Dionysii Cartusiani, *Opera Omnia*, Vol. 10 (Montreuil: 1900), 31. We might call this God's "severe mercy."

110   Gen. 24:12. E. N. The parts in brackets replaces the "etc." of the Latin text.

111   Amos 4:12b.

112   E. N. This is another instance of Denis's invocation of the *Facientibus* principle. *See* footnote 55–88.

113   Jer. 30:21b.

wish to obey the exhortation to sanctity.[114] One is not to despair of such persons, for it is possible that they might convert in the third vigil or the eleventh hour,[115] *et famem, and . . . hunger* of justice *patientur ut canes, they shall suffer like dogs,* with such desire making progress that they may surpass those who converted in the morning, and so may cause it to happen that *the last be first, and the first last.*[116]

58{59}[10][117] *I will keep my strength toward you: for you, O God, are my protector.*

Fortitudinem meam ad te custodiam, quia, Deus, susceptor meus es.

58{59}[11] *My God, his mercy shall prevent me.*

Deus meus, misericordia eius praeveniet me.

58{59}[10] *Fortitudinem meam ad te custodiam, I will keep my strength toward you,* that is, I will attribute to you all my power, virtue, and grace, saying along with holy Job, *Behold there is no help for me in myself;*[118] and with the Apostle [Paul], *By the grace of God, I am what I am.*[119] And I will confess it to be true that which you, O Lord, say through your holy prophet [Hosea]: *Destruction is your own, O Israel, from you; your help is only in me.*[120] If, therefore, you decide to preserve and not lose the eminent strength God furnished to you, all that you are, all that you are able to do, and all that you in fact do, ascribe to God, and say this: *O Lord, my might, and my strength, and my refuge.*[121] *Quia Deus susceptor meus es; for you, O God, are my protector.* God, the Son of God, is the protector of our nature through the Incarnation; and God the Trinity is our protector of our desires in prayer, of our penance in justification, of our obedience in his goodness, of our soul in glorification, and of our body in the Resurrection. Indeed, the

---

114   E. N. The division of man's life was generally seen as six-fold in Latin: *infantia, pueritia, adolescentia, iuventa (iuventute), senecta (senectute),* and *senium.* Elizabeth Sears, *The Ages of Man: Medieval Interpretations of the Life Cycle* (Princeton, NJ: Princeton University Press, 1986), 54–69, 174–83. The boundaries between these were flexible.

115   L. *tertia vigilia,* the "third vigil," refers to the Roman method of keeping time in the evening. The evening was divided into four vigils or "watches." The *tertia vigilia* was the third watch. The fourth watch was just before dawn. The term "eleventh hour" references Matt. 20:9, the Parable of the Workers in the Vineyard.

116   Matt. 20:16a.

117   E. N. Denis skips here verses 58:8 and 58:9.

118   Job 6:13a.

119   1 Cor. 15:10a.

120   Hosea 13:9a.

121   Jer. 16:19a.

most good Lord our God unceasingly is ready to receive back, to cherish, to protect, and to save us with the arms of his paternal love, as the prophet [Jeremiah] says to the sinning soul: *You have prostituted yourself to many lovers; nevertheless return to me,*[122] and *I will not turn away my face from you;*[123] and again: *You would not blush; therefore at least at this time call to me: You are my Father.*[124] And through Ezechiel he says: At whatever hour the sinner laments, *all his iniquity . . . I will not remember* any more.[125] **58{59} [11]** *Deus meus, misericordia eius praeveniet me;* my God, his mercy shall prevent me. This is a word of good faith, and it is implicitly a fervent prayer. For the faithful says this, not presuming, but hoping and desiring. *For the Lord has heard the desire of the poor,*[126] even before it breaks forth formally or in vocal prayer. Now unless the mercy of God had prevented us,[127] we would not have been saved, for we do not merit condignly the first grace:[128] it is necessary, therefore, that the grace of God prevent us, conserve us, lead us, and perfect us. Therefore Christ says: *Without me you can do nothing.*[129]

58{59}[12]   *God shall let me see over my enemies: slay them not, lest at any time my people forget. Scatter them by your power; and bring them down, O Lord, my protector.*

Deus ostendet mihi super inimicos meos; ne occidas eos, nequando obliviscantur populi mei. Disperge illos in virtute tua, et depone eos, protector meus, Domine.

58{59}[13]   *For the sin of their mouth, and the word of their lips: and let them be taken in their pride. And for their cursing and lying they shall be declared,*[130]

Delictum oris eorum, sermonem labiorum ipsorum; et comprehendantur in superbia sua. Et de execratione et mendacio annuntiabuntur,

---

122   Jer. 3:1a.
123   Jer. 3:12a.
124   Jer. 3:3, 4.
125   *Cf.* Ez. 13:21b; Ez. 13:22a.
126   Ps. 9:38a.
127   E. N. On this use of "prevent" (from Latin *prae-venire*) as "to come before," to anticipate," "to precede," *see* footnote 17-66.
128   E. N. "It is manifest," says St. Thomas Aquinas, "that no one is able to merit for himself the first grace (*primam gratiam*)." ST IaIIae, q. 114, art. 5, co. Since grace is the principle of merit (*see* footnote 36-2, Volume 2), it is clearly impossible to merit the first grace.
129   John 15:5b.
130   E. N. In this article, I have changed the translation of *annuntiabuntur* from "they shall be talked of" to "they shall be declared."

58{59}[14] *When they are consumed: when they are consumed by your wrath, and they shall be no more. And they shall know that God will rule Jacob, and all the ends of the earth.*

In consummatione, in ira consummationis; et non erunt. Et scient quia Deus dominabitur Iacob, et finium terrae.

58{59}[12] *Deus ostendit mihi super inimicos meos; ne occidas eos, etc.* **God shall let me see over my enemies; slay them not, etc.** The Church says this, as also does Christ, of the Jews living among the Christians: whom one is not to kill for the reasons explained in the preceding exposition.[131] It can also be understood as referring to all enemies, so that it reads in this sense: *God shall let me see over my enemies*, that is, Christ has commanded me with respect to my adversaries: *slay them not, lest at any time my people forget*, that is, lest the neighbor be scandalized in your vindictiveness, and imitate your deeds, and forget my precepts that I have taught: *Love your enemies: do good to them that hate you: and pray for them that persecute and calumniate you.*[132]

Doing this, the Church therefore prays: *Disperge illos in virtute tua, scatter them by your power*, that is, you who alone are able to make the unclean clean, separate them from malice, *et depone, and bring them down* from their evil designs. Bring them down also, that is, be forbearing and blot out,[133] **58{59}[13]** *delictum oris eorum, the sin of their mouth*, namely, the illicit *sermonem labiorum ipsorum, word of their lips*, by which they sinned either against you or against their neighbor; *et comprehendantur in superbia sua, and let them be taken in their pride*, that is, by the scourge of your paternal correction let their pride be confined and restrained, so that — humbled by punishment — they may cease their proud life. *Et de exsecratione, and for their cursing*, by which they deprecate the just and scorn the way of God, *et mendacio annuntiabuntur, and their lying shall be declared*, that is, they shall be accused and contradicted by the preachers of Christ in this age on a daily basis: [preachers] whose office is to instruct the errant, to denounce the sinner, and in no way being soft on sin. They shall also be declared **58{59}[14]** *in consummatione, when they are consumed*,[134] that is, when they are made perfect in doctrine

---

131   *E. N. See* footnote 58-66 on the treatment of the Jews living in Christian Europe and the papal doctrine known by the name *Sicut Iudaeis.*

132   Matt. 5:44.

133   *E. N.* Denis skips over *protector meus, Domine*, "O Lord, my protector," directly into 58:13.

134   *E. N.* There is a rich subtlety playing off the various meanings or shades of meaning of the Latin word *consummatio.* The Latin *consummatio* can mean: (a) an

or they are become accomplished in the good; *in ira consummationis, when they are consumed by your wrath,* that is, in charitable rebukes by those endeavoring towards a virtuous consummation. For out of charity proceeds a zealous anger by which the preacher and just men denounce and castigate the ungodly, in the manner that the Apostle [Paul] said: *Rebuke them sharply.*[135] *Et non erunt, and they shall be no more,* that is, sinners after the declaration and consummation just discussed will not be the same as they were before: for they shall forsake themselves, and they will live, now not them, but Christ in them.[136] Whence Solomon admonished: *Turn the wicked, and they shall not be.*[137] *Et scient, and they shall know,* by the knowledge of the mercy of God that is exhibited toward them, *quia Deus dominabitur Iacob, that God will rule Jacob,* that is, [God will rule over] the supplanters of vices,[138] namely, the just, *et finium terrae, and all the ends of the earth,* that is, also those full of faults, provided they wish to convert to him. For in this way he shall reign in them by faith and grace, making them efficacious servants for himself.

58{59}[17]   *But I will sing your strength: and will extol your mercy in the morning. For you are become my protector,*[139] *and my refuge, in the day of my trouble.*[140]

Ego autem cantabo fortitudinem tuam, et exsultabo mane misericordiam tuam; quia factus es susceptor meus, et refugium meum in die tribulationis meae.

---

adding together or a reckoning, a summing up, (b) the accumulation or ensemble of that addition (the sum total), (c) an achievement or accomplishment, especially of something great, (d) the completion, conclusion, end, or consummation of something, and (e) the consumption or destruction of something (by, for example, eating or being burnt). Relying on these various meanings, Denis is suggesting that the evil in the one who turns to God is eaten (consumed), and is then replaced by faith and grace in Christ (and his great achievement or consummation on the Cross — *consummatum est!* — John 19:30), and thereby supplanted by good, which is gradually added together (*con-summare*) in a way of life striving to perfection (the law of gradualism), which ultimately is brought to fruition or consummation at the end of one's life at the final judgment.

135   Titus 1:13a.

136   Cf. Gal. 2:20a: *And I live, now not I; but Christ lives in me.*

137   Prov. 12:7a.

138   E. N. The name Jacob is understood as "supplanter," and metaphorically it applies to someone who supplants his sinful nature. "The faithful, therefore, who supplants sin, is Jacob," says Denis in Article XXXV (Psalm 13:7) in Volume I.

139   E. N. I have replaced "support" with "protector" for the Latin *susceptor.*

140   E. N. Denis skips verses 15 and 16.

58{59}[17] *Ego autem, but I,* O God, *cantabo fortitudinem tuam, will sing your strength,* that is, I will praise your power over me, by which you have delivered me from the mouth of the devil, and from my impiety rendered me just, and led me towards a praiseworthy life. I will also praise your omnipotence which you most greatly manifest in sparing [sinners] and having mercy; by which you created, conserve, and govern heaven and earth; by which you do *great and incomprehensible and marvelous things without number.*[141] *Et exsultabo, and I will extol,* that is, with great rejoicing I will announce, *mane, in the morning,* that is immediately at the very beginning, namely before I am occupied with anything: according to that written by Matthew: *Seek first the kingdom of God;*[142] or [alternatively], *In the morning,* that is, your grace arising and radiating in me; *misericordiam tuam, your mercy,* that is, your mercy itself and the effects of your mercy, confessing your benefits mercifully bestowed upon me: in the manner that the angel Raphael rejoiced: *Bless the God of heaven, give glory to him in the sight of all that live, because he has shown his mercy to you.*[143] *Quia factus es, for you are become,* without any change in you, *susceptor meus, my protector,* converting my heart to you. For God becomes our support not by changing himself, but by altering our heart by his grace. *Et refugium meum in tribulationis meae, and my refuge in the day of my trouble,* for you give me the grace by which in all necessities I seek refuge in your goodness.

58{59}[18] Unto you, O my helper, will I sing, for you are God my
protector:[144] my God my mercy.

Adiutor meus, tibi psallam, quia Deus susceptor meus es; Deus
meus, misericordia mea.

58{59}[18] *Adiutor meus, tibi psallam; unto you, O my helper, will I sing,* that is, with painstaking praise, namely in life and by voice, I will praise you, *quia Deus susceptor meus es, for you are God my protector:* for this reason, I do not have the ability satisfactorily to praise you. *Deus meus, misericordia mea; my God, my mercy.* Why am I not able to do so most merciful One? For no other reason than that so great and so immeasurable, ineffable, and infinite is the mercy of God over us, that it

---

141 Job 9:10. Denis's version departs slightly from the Sixto-Clementine text.
142 Matt. 6:33a.
143 Tob. 12:6.
144 E. N. I have translated *susceptor* in this verse as "protector," just like it was translated in 58:17.

is more suitable to say in the abstract "Our mercy" (*Nostra misericordia*) than to say the concrete, "our Merciful one" (*Miserator noster*). For we are accustomed to say such of that which we ardently love: "You are my love" (*amor meus*).[145] And so you, O Lord, my God, are my mercy. Others may define or describe you as they wish; I more fittingly cannot describe you other than, my God, my mercy. Aristotle said: God is pure act.[146] Plato said: God is goodness itself. Avicenna[147] said: God is pure goodness. I in eternity will declare: my God, my mercy. For I am created by your goodness, deified by your Incarnation,[148] sanctified by your manner of life, redeemed by your Passion, glorified by your Ascension.[149]

---

145   E. N. Denis says that it is more fitting to use the abstract statement "Our Mercy," *nostra Misericordia*, rather than the concrete "Our Merciful One," *Miserator noster*, in reference to God, since it is a language more akin to what lovers use. (We don't call the one we love "my lover," *amator meus*, but rather "my love," *amor meus*. "We are familiar with the tendency," Ralph McInerny said in his book *St. Thomas Aquinas*, "when speaking of God, to use abstract terms almost in preference to concrete ones. God is being, in the sense of a being, yes, but better to say that he is existence, beingness.... If we should say of a woman that she is beautiful and then, pained by the inadequacy of the remark, say that she is beauty... we would seem to be recognizing that simply to say that one is beautiful ... allows for the fact that the one we are speaking of does not exhaust the meaning of beauty.... The concrete term has the merit that its mode of signification suggests subsistence, but the defect that a limitation of the perfection by which the thing is designated is also suggested. The abstract term has the merit of expressing a perfection as unlimited, but the defect that its mode of signifying does not suggest that it can directly apply to a subsistent thing. That is why both concrete and abstract terms are inadequate when applied to God. Still, there is an especial attraction in abstract terms, ... though we are conscious that our language is being strained to the utmost when we do this...." Ralph McInerny, *St. Thomas Aquinas* (Notre Dame, IN: University of Notre Dame Press, 1982).

146   E. N. Aristotle, *Metaphysics*, XII (L), 7, 1072a25–26; 1072b26–27. Aristotle sees God as *energeia* (ἐνέργεια) without *dynamis* (δύναμις), act without any potentiality, or pure act. "God is pure act without any potentiality." ST, Ia, q. 3, art. 2, co. *See also* ST Ia, q. 2, art. 3, co.

147   E. N. The Persian Muslim philosopher known as Abu Ali Sina (*ca.* 980-1037).

148   "The Word became flesh to make us 'partakers of the divine nature': 'For this is why the Word became man, and the Son of God became the Son of man: so that man, by entering into communion with the Word and thus receiving divine sonship, might become a son of God.' 'For the Son of God became man so that we might become God.' 'The only-begotten Son of God, wanting to make us sharers in his divinity, assumed our nature, so that he, made man, might make men gods.'" CCC § 460 (quoting 2 Pet. 1:4, St. Irenaeus, *Adv. Haeres.* 3, 19, 1, PG 7/1, 939, St. Athanasius, *De inc.* 54, 3, PG 25, 192B, and St. Thomas Aquinas, *Opusc.* 57, 1–4).

149   E. N. In reading this, one cannot help but think of the "Memorial" of Blaise Pascal, who so forcefully distinguished between the God of the philosophers — here Aristotle, Plato, and Avicenna — and the God of Abraham, Isaac, and Jacob. While

Further, why is it notably said in this Psalm so often these words already mentioned, *my God* and *my protector?* And isn't God the God of all in heaven, earth, and hell? Why therefore, *my God?* It is not for all to say: *my God.* For God receives a name from causality and providence. But every single one of us calls "god" the highest thing that is loved and worshipped by him. Therefore, the belly is god of the glutton, gold [the god] of the avaricious. They, therefore, truly and properly can say, *my God* who alone worship and fervently love him, and of whom God also has a special providence, preserving them from evil, and causing them to advance in the good. For here that great and divine Areopagite Dionysius did not presume to say absolutely, *my God;* but wrote in his book in this manner: *God,* and if it is proper for me to say, *my.*[150]

Let us gather together, therefore, and establish all our affection in God, absolutely not loving in creatures anything except in him and for his sake alone. And let us finally, purely, and properly love him, for in him is simply infinite fulness of all goodness, beauty, and that which is desirable.

PRAYER

VISIT US, O LORD, WITH THE GRATUITOUS gift of goodness, and be our refuge in the day of tribulation, delivering us from the rising forces of our enemies, so that drawn away from all the assaults of our enemies, we may sing in an unceasing manner to you, our helper.

Visita nos, Domine, gratuito benignitatis munere, et esto refugium nobis in die tribulationis, eripiens nos ab insurgentibus inimicis nostris: ut ab omnibus subducti hostium incursibus, tibi adiutori modo indefessi psallamus.

---

giving a nod to the God of the philosophers, as preambular to the faith, Denis catapults to the God of faith who has made himself known in Jesus Christ, the Incarnate Word, as *my God, my mercy.* Like Pascal's "Memorial," this section of Denis's *Commentary* may be said to be an "analogy... of the event which separated human history into an *ante-* and *post-Nativitatem Domini."* Like Pascal, one detects in Denis here his "staggering discovery," one that "makes him stammer with joy." Romano Guardini, *Pascal for our Time* (New York: Herder & Herder, 1966) (trans., Brian Thompson).
150   *E. N. See* Article XXV (Psalm 7:2), where Denis mentions this also.

Psalm 59

ARTICLE XVIII

EXPOSITION OF THE FIFTY-NINTH PSALM:
DEUS, REPULISTI NOS.
O GOD, YOU HAVE CAST US OFF.

59{60}[1] *Unto the end, for them that shall be changed, for the inscription of a title, to David himself, for doctrine,*

In finem. Pro his qui immutabuntur, in tituli inscriptionem ipsi David, in doctrinam,

59{60}[2] *When he set fire to Mesopotamia of Syria and Syrian Zobah and Joab returned and slew the Edomites in the vale of the saltpits, twelve thousand men.*

Cum succendit Mesopotamiam Syriae, et Syriam Sobal, et convertit Ioab, et percussit Idumaeam in valle Salinarum duodecim millia.

HE TITLE OF THIS PSALM IS [AS STATED above]. According to a literal understanding, the sense of this title arises out of the historical books of Samuel and Chronicles.[1] David literally wrote this Psalm about the state of the reign of Israel, lamenting its miseries, and praying for its restoration. For we read in the second book of Samuel the way that Hanun, son of Nahash, the king of the Ammonites, insulted the servants of David:[2] that having been done, he, fearing David, hired some men from Mesopotamia and some from Syria and other places whose people had been defeated by David to help him. This, therefore, is the sense of the title: This Psalm directs us *in finem, unto the end,* namely, unto Christ, who is the end of all divine Scripture; it was written literally *for them that shall be changed, for the inscription of a title, to David himself,* that is, for the people of Israel, who had David as their king who had been chosen by God,[3] as also the title says: for God foretold that David was to be named king of Israel.[4] The Psalm, I say, was written for that occasion,

---

1 2 Sam. chp. 10; 1 Chr. chp. 19.
2 E. N. Hanun did so by shaving off half their beard and cutting their garments.
3 2 Sam. 5:1–3.
4 1 Sam. 16:1, 11–12.

when David *set fire to Mesopotamia of Syria and Syrian Zobah*: as the prior history clearly relates; *and Joab returned,* that is, did battle, *and slew Edom,* that is, the Idumeans, *in the vale of the saltpits.*

59{60}[3]   *O God, you have cast us off, and have destroyed us; you have been angry, and have had mercy on us.*

    Deus, repulisti nos, et destruxisti nos; iratus es, et misertus es nobis.

59{60}[4]   *You have moved the earth, and have troubled it: heal the breaches thereof, for it has been moved.*

    Commovisti terram, et conturbasti eam; sana contritiones eius, quia commota est.

59{60}[5]   *You have shown your people hard things; you have made us drink wine of sorrow.*

    Ostendisti populo tuo dura; potasti nos vino compunctionis.

Speaking, therefore, in the person of the kingdom of Israel, David says: **59{60}[3]** *Deus, repulisti nos; O God, you have cast us off* from your defense, *et destruxisti nos, and have destroyed us,* permitting enemies to cross our borders and to ravage our cities and to kill our men. *Iratus est, you have been angry* against us because of our sins. For at the time the Kingdom of Israel was afflicted with many trials. Whence the first book of Samuel says that there was *no blacksmith* found *in the land of Israel.*[5] For they had to defend against the Philistines, and the Hebrews were unable to make spears or swords, so that they were not able to fight. *Et misertus es nobis, and you have had mercy on us,* not completely destroying us, and not afflicting us as fully as we deserved. **59{60}[4]** *Commovisti terram, you have moved the earth,* that is, the inhabitants of our land, permitting us to be defeated and uprooted from the land. For the Philistines drove out the Hebrews and dwelt in their cities.[6] *Et conturbasti eam, and have troubled it,* that is, by the terror of their adversaries you have permitted them to be confounded. *Sana contritiones eius, heal the breaches thereof,* that is, repair their downfall and afflictions, *quia commota est, for it has been moved,* that is, may your kindliness be moved to show mercy upon us and to provide us aid because of these

---

5   1 Sam. 13:19a.
6   1 Sam. 31:7. E. N. After the Philistines had defeated Saul and the men of Israel at Mount Gilboa, the Philistines inhabited the Israelites' land.

our miseries that have been mentioned. 59{60}[5] *Ostendisti populo tuo dura, you have shown your people hard things,* that is, you have introduced diverse scourges upon us; *potasti nos vino compunctionis, you have made us drink wine of sorrow,* that is, you have filled us with compunction or grief and with great sorrow of mind, as a man drinking wine is filled with drink: in the way we read in Jeremiah: *Behold I will feed them with wormwood, and will give them gall to drink* says the Lord.[7]

59{60}[6] *You have given a warning to them that fear you: that they may flee from before the bow: That your beloved may be delivered.*

Dedisti metuentibus te significationem, ut fugiant a facie arcus; ut liberentur dilecti tui,

59{60}[7] *Save me with your right hand, and hear me*

Salvum fac dextera tua, et exaudi me,

59{60}[6] *Dedisti metuentibus te significationem, you have given a warning to them that fear you,* that is, understanding, *ut fugiant a facie arcus, that they may flee from before the bow,* that is, from the menace of the divine judgment. For by present chastisements God enlightens the human heart, so that it might fear the future punishment. This is why we have in Jeremiah: *You have chastised me, and I was instructed.*[8] But this you have done, O Lord, *ut liberentur dilecti tui, that your beloved may be delivered,* namely, the children of Israel whom you loved according to this, *Israel was a child, and I loved him;*[9] and this, *I have loved you with an everlasting love; therefore have I drawn you and taken pity on you.*[10] 59{60}[7] *Salvum fac, save me* who pray, and those from whom I pray, *dextera tua, with your right hand,* that is, by your favorable hand, namely by your kindly assistance, favorable presence, and gracious clemency; *et exaudi me, and hear me* the one entreating.

59{60}[8] *God has spoken in his holy place: I will rejoice, and I will divide Shechem; and will mete out the vale of Tabernacles.*

Deus locutus est in sancto suo: laetabor, et partibor Sichimam; et convallem Tabernaculorum metibor.

---

7   Jer. 23:15a.
8   Jer. 31:18a.
9   Hosea 11:1b.
10 Jer. 31:3b.

59{60}[8] *Deus locutus est in Sancto suo, God has spoken in his holy place,* that is, by his holy Prophets, namely, Samuel,[11] or Nathan,[12] both of whom he revealed the future prosperity that would exist with the kingdom of Israel during the time of David. But God spoke the truth in that which follows: *Laetabor, I will rejoice,* that is, that I, David, will have rejoiced in him as the God of my salvation; *et partibor Sichimam, and I will divide Shechem,* that is, I will divide the spoils of the land of Shechem with my servants and helpers, and I will restore its inhabitants, all of which things were accomplished by David. *Et convallem Tabernaculorum, and out of the vale of the Tabernacles,* that is, the place next to the Jordan, which Jacob called Succoth,[13] that is, tabernacles,[14] where — when returning from Mesopotamia and having differences with this brother Esau — he pitched his tents. *Metibor, I will mete out,*[15] this valley, therefore, I will divide among the children of Israel according to each one's due measure, casting out the Philistines who possessed them at the time unjustly.

59{60}[9]   *Gilead is mine, and Manasseh is mine: and Ephraim is the strength of my head. Judah is my king;*

Meus est Galaad, et meus est Manasses; et Ephraim fortitudo capitis mei. Iuda rex meus;

59{60}[10]   *Moab is the pot of my hope. Into Edom will I stretch out my shoe: to me the foreigners are made subject.*

Moab olla spei meae. In Idumaeam extendam calceamentum meum: mihi alienigenae subditi sunt.

And I also acted as the helper of my people, especially with those who were more warlike and were more powerful. Of which he mentions: **59{60}[9]** *Meus est Galaad, Gilead is mine,* that is, the people having the land of Gilead in the Transjordan in their possession: who were renowned because of the strength of Jair and Jephthah;[16] *et meus est*

---

11   1 Sam. 16:1.

12   2 Sam. 7:4–17.

13   E. N. This is the place where the patriarch Jacob built himself a house and two booths (tabernacles) for his livestock. Gen. 33:17. Some of the battles between David and Saul occurred in this vicinity. 1 Sam. 17:1.

14   E. N. The Hebrew word Succoth (*Sukkot*—סֻכּוֹת) means tabernacle, or tent, or booth.

15   E. N. Mete means to measure out or dispense.

16   Judges 10:3; 11:1. E. N. Jephthah, the son of Gilead, was a great warrior. Judges

Manasses, and Manassas is mine, that is, the people from the tribe born of Manasseh, which was famous because Gideon came forth from that branch.[17] *Et Ephraim, and Ephraim,* that is, the people born of the tribe of Ephraim, *fortitude capitis mei, is the strength of my head,* that is, the strength of my reign, of the principal power and in a certain way also the capital.[18] For there the people at the northern end of the kingdom of Israel dwelt,[19] just as the people of Judah dwelt in the southern end.[20] *Iuda rex meus, Judah is my king:* because the kings were born from the tribe of Judah, and it was the people of Judah that were its defenders and the custodians of the kingdom of Israel.[21] **59{60}[10]** *Moab,* that is, the land and the people of the Moabites, is *olla spei meae, the pot of my hope:* that is, by their help I hope to receive and to possess and use as freely as the head of a family uses a pot in assuaging his hunger in his home. *In Idumaeam, into Edom,* in which Esau lived,[22] *extendam calceamentum meum, I will stretch out my shoe,* that is, with shodden feet I went through it, making it my tributary. *Mihi alienigenae, to me the foreigners,* namely, the Philistines and other surrounding inhabitants,[23] *subditi sunt, are made subject* to obedience and to paying tribute.

59{60}[11] *Who will bring me into the strong city? Who will lead me into Edom?*

Quis deducet me in civitatem munitam? Quis deducet me usque in Idumaeam?

59{60}[12] *Will not you, O God, who has cast us off? And will not you, O God, go out with our armies?*

Nonne tu, Deus, qui repulisti nos? Et non egredieris, Deus, in virtutibus nostris?

11:1. Jair was a Gileadite who judged Israel for twenty-two years. Judges 10:3–4.

17 Judges chps. 6–8. E. N. Gideon was a renowned military leader, judge, and prophet who came from the tribe of Manasseh.

18 E. N. The land occupied by the tribe of Ephraim housed many of the capital cities founded by the Kingdom of Israel: Shechem, Penuel, Tirzah, and Samaria.

19 Joshua 16:1–18.

20 Joshua 15:1–11. E. N. This was while the Kingdom of Israel and Judah were unified during the reigns of Saul, David, and Solomon. Subsequently, the joint kingdom split into the Kingdom of Israel and the Kingdom of Judah during the reign of Solomon's son, Rehoboam.

21 Gen. 49:10; Deut. 33:7.

22 Gen. 36:8.

23 2 Sam. 8:1–14.

59{60}[13]   *Give us help from trouble: for vain is the salvation of man.*

Da nobis auxilium de tribulatione, quia vana salus hominis.

59{60}[14]   *Through God we shall do mightily: and he shall bring to nothing them that afflict us.*

In Deo faciemus virtutem; et ipse ad nihilum deducet tribulantes nos.

Moreover, so that David may express himself regarding these things and not presume on his own powers, but on the divine strength, he adds: **59{60}** [**11**] *Quis deducet me in civitatem munitam, who will bring me into the strong city* with walls and gates? *Quis deducet me usque in Idumaeam, who will lead me into Edom,* so that they will be subject to me? And he responds: **59{60}** [**12**] *Nonne tu, Deus, qui repulisti nos, will you not, O God, who has cast us off* sometimes? But at other times your anger changes into mercy. *Et non egredieris, Deus, in virtutibus nostris? And will not you, O God, go out with our armies?* This question [is asked] as if to say: Indeed, you will march out in our strength, that is, with our armies, and you will be the leader of war and the helper, in the manner that is written of our army: *The Lord its God is with it, and the sound of the victory of the king in it.*[24] And elsewhere we read: *God is the leader of our army.*[25] Or [we can understand it this way]: *And you will not . . . go out with our armies* in our powers, but yours, for you protect us by your power. **59{60}[13]** *Da nobis, give us,* O Lord, *auxilium de tribulatione, help from trouble,* that is, that we might be delivered from persecution; *quia vana salus hominis, for vain is the salvation of man.*[26] For *cursed is he who puts his trust in man, and makes flesh his arm.*[27] **59{60}[14]** *In Deo faciemus virtutem, through God we shall do mightily,* that is, by divine might we shall prevail and will do virtuous works; *et ipse ad nihilum deducet tribulantes nos, and he shall bring to nothing them that afflict us.* For God during the time of David obliterated the adversaries of Israel.

---

24   Num. 23:21. *E. N.* The verse refers to Jacob (Israel), but since it is here used for the army, I have changed the pronouns from masculine to neuter.

25   2 Chr. 13:12a.

26   *E. N.* The text has *et vana salus hominis,* "and vain is the salvation of man," but the editor appears to suggest that *quia vana salus hominis,* "for vain is the salvation of man" is proper.

27   Jer. 17:5. *E. N.* As Denis construes the latter part of this verse in his *Commentary on Jeremiah:* "'And makes flesh his arm,' that is, his strength is placed in his bodily strength rather than in the help of grace. And so Judas [Maccabeus] most forcefully said: 'The success of war is not in the multitude of the army, but strength comes from heaven' [1 Macc. 3:19]." Doctoris Ecstatici D. Dionysii Cartusiani, *Opera Omnia,* Vol. 9 (Montreuil: 1900), 149.

ARTICLE XIX

TROPOLOGICAL OR MORAL ELUCIDATION
OF THE SAME FIFTY-NINTH PSALM.

59{60}[1]   *Unto the end, for them that shall be changed, for the inscrip-*
tion of a title, to David himself, for doctrine,

In finem. Pro his qui immutabuntur, in tituli inscriptionem
ipsi David, in doctrinam,

59{60}[2]   *When he set fire to Mesopotamia of Syria and Syrian Zobah*
and Joab converted and slew the Edomites in the vale of the
saltpits, twelve thousand men.[28]

Cum succendit Mesopotamiam Syriae, et Syriam Sobal, et
convertit Ioab, et percussit Idumaeam in valle Salinarum
duodecim millia.

OW, ACCORDING TO THE MYSTICAL SENSE,
the names of this title are interpreted based upon the power which
they have, so that it is in this sense: **59{60}[1]** *In finem, unto the end,*
that is, this Psalm leads us unto Christ, and it is written *pro his qui com-*
mutabuntur, for them that shall be changed, that is, that will be converted
from the old life to a Christiform manner of life,[29] *in tituli inscriptione, for*
the inscription of a title, acknowledging Christ by his word and works to
be the king of the Jews, in the way the title [atop the Cross] declared:[30]
but they shall wholly change *to David himself,* that is, to Christ himself,
so that they might live *not unto themselves,* but unto the Lord Savior,[31]
59{60}[2] *cum succendit Mesopotamiam Syriae, when he set fire to Mes-*
opotamia of Syria, that is, during the time Christ by his humility and
holiness ignited the world with the fire of divine love to consider the

---

28   E. N. I have translated the Latin *convertit* as "converted" from the Douay Rheims's
"returned" so as to better fit with the Commentary.
29   E. N. Nicolas of Cusa, Denis's contemporary and correspondent, states in a sermon:
"The rational soul, which is clothed in a Christiform obedience, merits to be exalted
also to the glory of eternal happiness. Elsewhere, Paul commands us to put off the old
man and to put on the new. The old man is Adam, 'of earth from earth,' the new [man]
is Christ, 'of heaven from heaven.'" Sermon 201, "Let us put on the Lord Jesus Christ,"
Nicolai de Cusa, *Opera Omnia* (Hamburg: Felix Meiner Verlag, 2005), Vol. 18, 443.
30   John 19:19–22.
31   *Cf.* 2 Cor. 5:15: *And Christ died for all; that they also who live, may not now live*
to themselves, but unto him who died for them, and rose again.

sublime. For Mesopotamia is interpreted as meaning "high calling."[32] *Et Syriam Sobal, and Syrian Zobah*, that is, the height of vain antiquity. For Zobah is explained as meaning antiquity.[33] *Et convertit Ioab, and Joab converted*, that is, Christ converted the people of the Jews; *et percussit Edom in valle Salinarum, and slew Edom in the vale of the saltpits*, that is, with holy fear he slew the earthly world and the vices that are full of blood, converting them to the faith: but he slew *duodecim milla, twelve thousand men*, that is, all men in all four ends of the earth. For the number twelve is the number of perfection, which stands for wholeness.

59{60}[3]   *O God, you have cast us off, and have destroyed us; you have been angry, and have had mercy on us.*

   Deus, repulisti nos, et destruxisti nos; iratus es, et misertus es nobis.

59{60}[4]   *You have moved the earth, and have troubled it: heal the breaches thereof, for it has been moved.*

   Commovisti terram, et conturbasti eam; sana contritiones eius, quia commota est.

59{60}[5]   *You have shown your people hard things; you have made us drink wine of sorrow.*

   Ostendisti populo tuo dura; potasti nos vino compunctionis.

And the Church therefore says: **59{60}[3]** *Deus, repulisti nos; O God, you have cast us off* by permitting us to be devastated by enemies of the faith or by not hearing our prayers. For sometimes for a period of time God appears to be rejecting his people, not, however, that he completely abandons them. For this reason, the Apostle [Paul] says: *Has God cast away his people? God forbid.*[34] And in a Psalm below we also have: *For the Lord will not cast off his people.*[35] *Et destruxisti nos, and have destroyed*

---

32   E. N. The word Mesopotamia comes from Greek (*mesos* + *potamos*), and it means "between two rivers," namely the region between the Tigris and the Euphrates. It was the translation for the Hebrew Aram-Naharaim (אֲרַם נַהֲרַיִם). However, the deacon St. Stephen notes that it was there, "when he was in Mesopotamia," that the "God of glory appeared to our father Abraham." Acts 7:1–2. Moreover, etymologically, Aram stems from the verb רוּם (*rum*), "to be high." https://www.abarim-publications.com/ Dictionary/r/r-w-mfin.html#.X3xyo2hKiUk. As St. Augustine notes in his *Enarrationes in Psalmos* in discussing this verse, Mesopotamia means "high calling." PL 36, 715.
33   E. N. This is consistent with St. Augustine who says: "Zobah is interpreted as the 'vain antiquity.' Thanks be to Christ who set it afire." PL 36, 715.
34   Rom. 11:1a.
35   Ps. 93:14a.

us bodily, allowing us to be killed by unjust men: which the Church can say in the persons of the martyrs; or [this can be understood] spiritually as the hardening of our hearts or the withdrawing of grace on account of our sins. For we are destroyed if we exist without charity and grace and become nothing, for according to the Apostle [Paul]: *If I should distribute all my goods to feed the poor, and if I should deliver my body to be burned, and have not charity, it profits me nothing.*[36] For charity is the life of the soul.[37] *Iratus es, you have been angry* with your servants and your faithful in the way that a father is angry with a sinning son, whom he whips so that he may sin no more: and so you have afflicted us in the present, both within and without, with various punishments of body and soul; *et misertus es nobis, and have had mercy on us,* because by these temporal chastisements you have forgiven our sins, infused grace, and made us more cautious in the future. **59{60}[4]** *Commovisti terram, you have moved the earth,* that is, the Church militant travelling about the earth, which you permit to be attacked by many, and to be troubled by many disturbances, so that *it never continues in the same state;*[38] *et conturbasti eam, and you have troubled it,* because of the magnitude of the persecution menacing it.[39] **59{60}[5]** *Ostendisti populo tuo dura, you have shown your people hard things* so that by experience it learns compassion through that by which it was persecuted and from that which it has suffered. *For all that will to live godly in Christ, shall suffer persecution;*[40] and *through many tribulations we must enter into the kingdom of God.*[41] This the Lord said to Jeremiah: *I will chastise you in judgment, that you may not seem to yourself innocent.*[42] And in revelation: *Such as I love, I rebuke and chastise.*[43]

59{60}[6] *You have given a warning to them that fear you: that they may flee from before the bow: That your beloved may be delivered.*

Dedisti metuentibus te significationem, ut fugiant a facie arcus; ut liberentur dilecti tui,

---

36 1 Cor. 13:3.
37 E. N. *Caritas est vita animae,* "charity is the life of the soul, according to this. [1 John 3:14: He that loves not abides in death]." St. Thomas Aquinas, *De virtutibus,* q. 2 a. 12 s. c. 4.
38 Job 14:2b.
39 E. N. Denis skips over the final phrase of Ps. 59:4.
40 2 Tim. 3:12.
41 Acts 14:21b.
42 Jer. 30:11b.
43 Rev. 3:19a.

59{60}[7]   *Save me with your right hand, and hear me*
Salvum fac dextera tua, et exaudi me,

59{60}[6] *Dedisti metuentibus te significationem, you have given a warn-ing to them that fear you,* that is, through the temporal evils inflicted upon them you have warned them, *ut fugiant a facie arcus, that they may flee from before the bow,* that is, from the perpetual punishment of the divine vengeance, namely, that they may joyfully and with equanimity endure all the adversities of the present life, in order that they might be found worthy to avoid eternal torment. Whence understanding the significance of this, the prophet Jeremiah desires to be chastised in this life: *Correct me, O Lord, but yet with judgment: and not in fury, lest you bring me to nothing.*[44] Let us not grumble because of the hard things that God sets forth before us, therefore, but let us do that which that holy prophet of God Micah says: *I will bear the wrath of the Lord, because I have sinned against him.*[45] *Ut liberentur dilecti tui, that your beloved may be delivered,* namely, Christians in both reality and in name, of which the Savior says: *The Father himself loves you.*[46] And in his first epistle, John says: *Beloved, let us . . . love God, because God has first loved us.*[47] **59{60}[7]** *Salvum fac dextera tua, save me with your right hand,* that is, with the hand of your favor, so that I might reside in your right hand in heaven, that is, among your preferable and heavenly goods as Christ promised: *To him that shall overcome, I will give to sit with me in my throne: as I also have overcome, and am set down with my Father in his throne.*[48]

59{60}[8]   *God has spoken in his holy place: I will rejoice, and I will divide Shechem; and will mete out the vale of Tabernacles.*

Deus locutus est in sancto suo: laetabor, et partibor Sichimam; et convallem Tabernaculorum metibor.

59{60}[8] *Deus locutus est in Sancto suo, God has spoken in his holy place,* that is, by the Father *has spoken to us by his Son,* who is the Saint of Saints.[49] Also from that which follows it is possible for it to be the

---

44   Jer. 10:24.
45   Micah 7:9a.
46   John 16:27a.
47   1 John 4:19.
48   Rev. 3:21. *E. N.* Note that Denis does not address last phrase of Ps. 59:7.
49   *E. N.* On the expression "Saint of Saints," *Sanctus Sanctorum,* see footnote 3-26, Volume I. The Latin *sancto* could be either neuter or masculine, and so it could mean "holy place," as the Douay Rheims translates or "saint" as Denis understands it.

words of God the Father, or of Christ, or of the Church. The Father therefore says: *I will rejoice* in you, O elect ones, since I will do them good in the way I promised, saying *I will give them one heart , . . . and I will rejoice over them* for I will do them good.[50] *Et partibor Sichimam, and I will divide Shechem,* that is, I will divide the Gentiles, converting some and deserting some, *for all men have not faith.*[51] For by Shechem, in which pagans dwelt, is meant the Gentiles.[52] *Et convallem Tabernaculorum, and . . . the vale of tabernacles,* that is, the people of the Jews, *metibor, I will mete out,* receiving some of them and abandoning some of them. This also is fittingly applied to Christ, as it is to God the Father. Whence in the Last Supper, he said: *I speak not of you all: I know whom I have chosen.*[53] And the Apostle [Paul] also [said] to the Romans: *See then,* he says, *the goodness and the severity of God: towards them indeed that are fallen, the severity; but towards you, the goodness of God, if you abide in goodness.*[54]

59{60}[9] *Gilead is mine, and Manasseh is mine: and Ephraim is the strength of my head. Judah is my king;*

Meus est Galaad, et meus est Manasses; et Ephraim fortitudo capitis mei. Iuda rex meus;

59{60}[10] *Moab is the pot of my hope. Into Edom will I stretch out my shoe: to me the foreigners are made subject.*

Moab olla spei meae. In Idumaeam extendam calceamentum meum: mihi alienigenae subditi sunt.

59{60}[9] *Meus est Galaad, Gilead is mine,* that is, the congregation of martyrs, who offered the shedding of blood to Christ and in testimony of the faith, For Gilead is interpreted as heap of testimony,[55] by which is indicated the martyrs. For martyr is the word in both Greek and Latin by which a witness is called. *Et meus est Manasses, and Manasseh*

---

50 Jer. 37:39a, 41a.

51 2 Thess. 3:2b.

52 E. N. Denis follows very closely St. Augustine's *Commentary* on this Psalm and the interpretation of the words Shechem, Ephraim, Gilead, Manasseh, and Ephraim. The tie to the Gentiles arises from the fact that Jacob buried his idols there. Gen. 35:2, 4. "If [this verse] by its reference to Shechem refers to the history where the idols were hidden, it signifies the Gentiles." PL 36, 718.

53 John 13:18a.

54 Rom. 11:22.

55 E. N. Gen. 31:48: *And Laban said: This heap shall be a witness between me and you this day, and therefore the name thereof was called Gilead, that is, "the witness heap."*

is mine: that is, people forgetting the past, and stretching forth to those things that are ahead them belong to the number of my elect. Indeed, Manasseh is understood as meaning forgetfulness. We ought therefore to forget about those things which are temporal, or sensual, or inferior, and to remember constantly those things that are eternal and divine, so that, as the Apostle says, we might behold *the glory of the Lord with open face.*[56] *Et Ephraim, and Ephraim*, that is, the people rich and fertile with good works, are *fortitudo capitis mei, the strength of my head*, that is, the firm support of Christ, whose head I am, and who is the head of the Church, Now the people this speaks of are called the firm support of Christ because by them Christ conserves and firms up others in faith and grace. The Father also calls Christ his head because the Father established Christ as head of all the elect. And Ephraim is interpreted to mean fruitfulness or growing. *Iuda, Judah*, that is, the people of confession, who by life and doctrine confess the Lord, and announce the saving proclamation to others, just like *every scribe instructed in the kingdom of heaven;*[57] *rex meus, is my king*: that is, this people is at the head of the Church, for by them those under them are governed, in the manner that is stated by the prophet: *And I will give you pastors according to my own heart, and they shall feed you with knowledge and doctrine.*[58] **59{60}[10]** *Moab olla spei meae, Moab is the pot of my hope*. Let us see how this may be understood:[59] For Ruth — from whose seed was born David,[60] as was also Christ — was a Moabite; and so Moab, that is, Christ sprung from Ruth the Moabite, is called the pot of hope of God the Father because in him, like a pot or a vessel, God the Father gave us the fullness of hope to obtain possession of the divine goods, according to that which the Apostle [Paul] said: *He spared not even his own Son, but delivered him up for us all, how has he not also, with him, given us all things?*[61] For he gave those believing in Christ the power and the hope *to be made the sons of God.*[62] Let us not perceive Christ as signified by Moab to be

---

56   2 Cor. 3:18a.

57   Matt. 13:52a. E. N. In his *Commentary on Matthew*, Denis provides greater elaboration: "Every scribe instructed in the kingdom of heaven,' is any preacher or prelate, especially a bishop, in the militant Church." Doctoris Ecstatici D. Dionysii Cartusiani, *Opera Omnia*, Vol. 11 (Montreuil: 1900), 171.

58   Jer. 3:15.

59   E. N. Denis does not follow St. Augustine in this. One of the etymologies of Moab, one which Denis draws from, is that it means "from the father."

60   Ruth 4:17.

61   Rom. 8:32.

62   John 1:12a.

silly. For Moab is interpreted as meaning "from the father": by which Christ—who said of himself, *I came forth from the Father*[63]—can be signified. And if this does not please one, it can be explained in this way: *Moab*, that is, Ruth the Moabite, is the *pot of my hope*, because in her womb as in a vessel she carried Obed the grandfather of David,[64] from whom was born Christ, who is the hope of the Father, for the Father gave him to us so that he might be our hope and our Savior.[65]

These also can be the words of the Church, as in this sense: *God has spoken in his holy place*, namely, that *I*, the Church, *will rejoice in God my salvation, and I will divide Shechem, and will mete out the vale of Tabernacles*. For the early Church, namely the Apostles of Christ and their disciples, converted some to the faith, both from the Gentiles and from the Jews, and some remained in their disbelief. And the people designated by Gilead, Manassas, Ephraim, and Judah are of the Church, both as its members and its children.

Then Christ says: *Into Edom*, that is, the land of the Gentiles, *I will stretch out my shoe*, that is, my human nature, which was as it were the shoe of divinity. For while Christ endeavored to preach the Gospel throughout all the earth, he extended his shoes in Edom, for he manifested his Incarnation and humanity to men, and brought them to believe in him. For which reason he adds: *To me the foreigners*, that is, the Gentile nations, *are made subject* by faith and obedience, as was discussed about them in a Psalm above: *A people, which I knew not, have served me: at the hearing of the ear they have obeyed me.*[66] For this Balaam prophesied of Christ: *A star shall rise out of Jacob, and a man shall spring up from Israel, . . . and he shall possess Edom.*[67] Other writings have: *And all the world will be his possession.*[68] But because Christ as man does not do this, but [rather does this] by his divine power, therefore it adds: **59{60}[11]** *Quis deducet me in civitatem munitam? Who will bring me into the strong city?* By this one can understand the city of Rome, which then was the head and mistress of the world. Of this Isaiah foretold: *The high city he shall lay low.*[69] In this city, God the Father introduced

---

63   John 16:28a.
64   Ruth 4:17.
65   Matt. 1:21; Luke 2:11.
66   Ps. 17:45. *E. N. See* Article XLIII (Psalm 17:45) in Volume I.
67   Num. 24:17a, 18a.
68   *E. N.* This is not a citation to Scripture, but is a sort of summary of Scriptures prophetic utterances of Christ's reign used liturgically in antiphons, responsories, and motets.
69   Is. 26:5a.

Christ through the preaching of Peter and Paul:[70] without divine power this would not have been able to have been done. For this reason Christ responds: **59{60}[12]** *Nonne tu, Deus, qui repulisti nos? Will not you, O God, who has cast us off?* That is, [who has cast off] my Mystical Body, regarding whose persecution I told Paul: *Why do you persecute me?*[71] Or [we can understand it this way], *who has cast us off,* that is, you have permitted my body and soul to be afflicted with much sorrow. Whence I cried out on the Cross: *My God, my God, why have you forsaken me?*[72] *Et non egredieris, Deus, in virtutibus nostris; and will you not, O God, go out with our armies,* that is, these things that have been just mentioned you will not do with the natural power of my body or soul, but with the divine power. For God is said "to go out," not with reference to place, but operation, namely because he proceeds by act.

And so this [verse] can also be fittingly applied to the Church, because it stretches out its shoe in Edom, sowing the word of God throughout all the world, and foreigners are made subject to it, because the prelates of the Church are resolved to convert the Gentiles.

59{60}[13] *Give us help from trouble: for vain is the salvation of man.*

Da nobis auxilium de tribulatione, quia vana salus hominis.

59{60}[14] *Through God we shall do mightily: and he shall bring to nothing them that afflict us.*

In Deo faciemus virtutem; et ipse ad nihilum deducet tribulantes nos.

59{60}[13] *Da nobis auxilium de tribulatione, give us help from trouble* by which we might be freed from all danger, persecution, and temptation. **59{60}[14]**[73] *In Deo faciemus virtutem, through God we shall do mightily.* For *not that we are sufficient to think anything of ourselves, as of ourselves: but our sufficiency is from God.*[74] *Et ipse ad nihilum deducet tribulantes nos; and he shall bring to nothing them that afflict us:* for lest they repent, they will be eternally damned. For during the present age they often will treat with contempt the divine power: in the manner we see done by the most cruel tyrants, persecutors of the holy martyrs, who not so long

---

70 Acts 28:17–31.
71 Acts 9:4.
72 Matt. 27:46.
73 E. N. Denis does not address the last half of Ps. 49:13.
74 2 Cor. 3:5.

ago were reduced to nothing, and the Church of Christ rests in peace. For this reason he promised to it elsewhere: *Your hand shall be lifted up over your enemies, and all your enemies shall be cut off.*[75]

PRAYER

LORD, SOLACE OF THE AFFLICTED, GIVE us help in all tribulation, and heal our sorrows, and forgive us our sins: so that bringing to nothing those afflicting us, we may perform virtues of piety in you.

Solatium afflictorum, Domine, da nobis auxilium in omni tribulatione, et sana contritiones nostras, atque peccata dimitte: ut tribulantibus nos ad nihilum deductis, in te faciamus virtutes pietatis.

---

75 Micah 5:9.

Psalm 60

ARTICLE XX

DECLARATION OF CHRIST OF THE SIXTIETH PSALM:
EXAUDI, DEUS, DEPRECATIONEM MEAM
HEAR, O GOD, MY SUPPLICATION.

60{61}[1] *Unto the end, in hymns, a psalm for David.*

In finem. In hymnis, psalmus David.

RITTEN IN FRONT OF THIS PRESENT PSALM
is this title: 60{61}[1] *In finem, in hymnis, psalmus David; unto
the end, in hymns, a Psalm for David*: that is, this Psalm is written by
David, and by David fittingly signifies Christ, directing us *unto the end,*
that is, unto God, *in hymns*, so that might we venerate God with praise,
and we give thanks and sing hymns to God for the universal benefits
from the man Christ, and through him to all the human race collectively.

60{61}[2] *Hear, O God, my supplication: be attentive to my prayer.*

Exaudi, Deus, deprecationem meam, intende orationi meae.

Christ, therefore, in praise of the most high Godhead because of the
benefits granted to his humanity begins by prayer, and says: 60{61}[2]
Exaudi, Deus; hear, O God Father, or holy Trinity, *deprecationem meam,
my supplication*, which for myself, namely, I pray for the resurrection and
glorification of my body, saying: *Father, save me from this hour.*[1] *Intende
orationi meae, be attentive to my prayer*, which I pray for my Mystical
Body, namely for the salvation of the Church, saying: *Father, . . . Sanctify
them in truth. Your word is truth. . . . Holy Father, keep them in your name.*[2]

60{61}[3] *To you have I cried from the ends of the earth: when my
heart was in anguish, you have exalted me on a rock. You
have conducted me,*

*A finibus terrae ad te clamavi, dum anxiaretur cor meum;
in petra exaltasti me. Deduxisti me,*

---

1 John 12:27a.
2 John 17, 1a, 17, 11b.

60{61}[4] *For you have been my hope; a tower of strength against the face of the enemy.*

Quia factus es spes mea, turris fortitudinis a facie inimici.

60{61}[3] *A finibus terrae ad te clamavi; to you have I cried from the ends of the earth.* By the ends of the earth is not only meant its outermost parts, but also its higher and its lower parts. For the surface of the body can be said to be its ends. And so in this sense: *from the ends,* that is, from the higher parts or superficially, *of the earth,* Israel, in which I lived among men, *to you* God my Father, *I have cried,* with highest affection praying to you and saying: *Father, if you will, remove this chalice from me.*[3] *Dum anxiaretur cor meum, when my heart was in anguish,* that is, at the approach of the Passion, when my natural appetite and sensitivity naturally shrank from death, when I began to sorrow and be struck with fear, and when I was in agony, I prayed to you most extensively, and it came to be that my *sweat became as drops of blood.*[4] *In petra exaltasti me, you have exalted me on a rock,* that is, in yourself as in the highest and most strong firmament, or in your grace and your virtue and the gift of fortitude, by which I courageously approached and suffered the dangers of death, you raised me above all inordinate fear and dejection of soul. Or [alternatively], *You have exalted me,* glorifying my name throughout the whole world, and giving to me *a name which is above all names, so that in my name every knee should bow,* ... *and every tongue should confess that Jesus Christ is in the glory of God the Father.*[5] Of this exaltation, the Lord said through Isaiah: *Behold my servant shall understand, he shall be exalted, and extolled, and shall be exceeding high;* ... *kings shall shut their mouth at him.*[6]

Deduxiste me, you have conducted me **60{61}[4]** *quia factus es spes mea, for you have been my hope.* For God directed the humanity of Christ in all his works, and he led Christ the man in the way of this present age without complete ruin or stain. He even led him while still an infant into Egypt, and from there led him back [to Nazareth],[7] as is also witnessed by Hosea: *I called my son out of Egypt.*[8] He led him to the Cross, for *he delivered him up for us all.*[9] He led him also to the

---

3   Luke 22:42a; Matt. 26:39.
4   Matt. 26:37; Mark 14:33; Luke 22:43–44.
5   Phil. 2:9b, 10a, 11.
6   Is. 52:13, 15a.
7   Matt. 2:14.
8   Hosea 11:1b.
9   Rom. 8:32a.

limbo of hell,[10] and from this world into the heights of heaven. And this God did, for he was the hope of Christ, that is, because Christ hoped to obtain through prayer this good from God. For God was the hope of Christ to the extent that he was mortal and not yet glorified of body. *Turris fortitudinis a facie inimici, a tower of strength against the face of the enemy*: that is, as a strong tower protects those living within it from the spears of the enemy; so you, O God, in all things protected me who was confident in your help, and dwelt in you immovably.

60{61}[5]   *In your tabernacle I shall dwell forever: I shall be protected under the covert of your wings,*

Inhabitabo in tabernaculo tuo in saecula; protegar in vela-mento alarum tuarum.

60{61}[6]   *For you, my God, have heard my prayer: you have given an inheritance to them that fear your name.*

Quoniam tu, Deus meus, exaudisti orationem meam; dedisti haereditatem timentibus nomen tuum.

60{61}[5] *Inhabitabo in tabernaculo tuo in saecula, in your tabernacle I shall dwell forever,* that is, in the Church militant, according to that which is written in the Gospel: *Behold I am with you all days, even to the consummation of the world.*[11] Or [alternatively], *in your tabernacle,* that is, I will abide in the hearts of the elect, by faith and grace. For the elect are the tabernacle of God, as the Apostle says about them: *You are the temple of the living God,*[12] as the Lord said: I will dwell with them, and I will walk with them, and I will be their God.[13] Or [yet another way], *In your tabernacle I shall dwell forever,* that is, I will eternally remain in the Church triumphant in the empyreal heaven,[14] in the way that the Apostle [Paul] attests, *Not into the holies made with hands did Jesus enter, ... but into heaven itself.*[15] *Protegar in velamento alarum tuarum, and I shall be protected under the covert of your wings,* that is, I will be secure under the protection

---

10   E. N. This is not the hell of the damned, but the "limbo of the fathers," the *limbus patrem,* where the justified souls resided temporarily pending the redemptive death of Christ and the "harrowing" of hell, that is, their release from limbo.

11   Matt. 28:20b.

12   2 Cor. 6:16a.

13   *Cf.* Lev. 26:12: *I will walk among you, and will be your God, and you shall be my people.*

14   E. N. For the meaning of "empyreal heaven," *see* footnote 19-11, Volume 1.

15   Heb. 9:24.

of your goodness and your power. This is what Christ said through Isaiah: *In the shadow of his hand he has protected me.*[16] **60{61}[6]** *Quoniam tu, Deus meus; for you, my God,* who are in a most singular way my God, most supremely and uniquely loving me, and also most supremely loved by me, *exaudisti orationem meam, have heard my prayer,* in the manner I confessed: *Father, I give you thanks because you have heard me, and I know that you hear me always.*[17] *Dedisti hereditatem timentibus nomen tuum, you have given an inheritance to them that fear your name,* that is, by the merit of my Incarnation and Passion you have bestowed upon those fearing you a filial and chaste fear, so that they are your adopted sons; and *if sons, heirs also; heirs indeed of God, and joint heirs with Christ.*[18] For this inheritance is the participation in the grace and glory of Christ, of eternal life, which the Father gives us now in hope, to be given us afterwards in reality. Now also he gives it inchoatively by the infusion of internal consolations, divine intimacy, and daily grace. For *the grace of God is eternal life,* according to the Apostle [Paul].[19] And the Savior also said: *He who hears my word, and believes him that sent me, has life everlasting.*[20] And in the future God will give him this heredity in a full and final way, when we shall see him face to face and as he is, knowing as we are known.[21]

60{61}[7] *You will add days to the days of the king: his years even to generation and generation.*

 Dies super dies regis adiicies; annos eius usque in diem generationis et generationis.

60{61}[7] *Dies super dies regis adiicies, you will add days to the days of the king:* that is, you will add days of blessed immortality and of a serene eternity to your Son, O God the Father, to the temporal days

---

16 Is. 49:2a.

17 John 11:41b-42a.

18 Rom. 8:17. E. N. Drawing on the deeply Scriptural notion of us being "sons in the Son," *filii in Filio,* St. John Paul II in a Homily on December 31, 1996, covered this principle succinctly: "The Only-Begotten Son, one in being with the Father, comes into the world so that through sanctifying grace all people may be born again, for they have been called to the lofty privilege of being *filii in Filio,* sons in the Son, by divine adoption. https://w2.vatican.va/content/john-paul-ii/en/homilies/1996/documents/hf_jp-ii_hom_19961231.html

19 Rom. 6:23a.

20 John 5:24a.

21 *Cf.* 1 John 3:2b: *We know, that, when he shall appear, we shall be like to him: because we shall see him as he is.* 1 Cor. 13:12: *We see now through a glass in a dark manner; but then face to face. Now I know in part; but then I shall know even as I am known.*

of my mortal life, for I am the Messiah of whom we read in Zechariah: *Shout for joy, O daughter of Jerusalem: Behold your king will come to you, the just and Savior.*[22] And Isaiah said: *The Lord is our judge, the Lord is our lawgiver, the Lord is our king; he will come and he will save us.*[23] God adds these eternal days to Christ's temporal days as his years during even in the day of generations and generations, that is, even unto the day of eternity, inclusive of and exceeding all generations. The days, therefore, that God adds to Christ's days are days of eternity; these can be called many days and years, not that they run and flow by succession of time, but because they encompass and encircle all time. Whence of them is said in Isaiah: *There shall be month after month, and sabbath after sabbath.*[24] And yet, these days are more appropriately called one day, than many days: for they are not interrupted by any night. But most exactly, they are not really called a day, but an aeviternity (*aevum*), or a participated eternity.[25]

60{61}[8] *He abides forever in the sight of God: his mercy and truth who shall search?*

Permanet in aeternum in conspectu Dei: misericordiam et veritatem eius quis requiret?

And because these days of eternity are directed to Christ, therefore, 60{61}[8] *Permanet in aeternum in conspectus Dei*, he abides forever in the sight of God in heaven, where he sits at the right hand of the Father, making intercession and appearing now in the presence of God for us, according to the Apostle [Paul].[26] *Misericordiam et veritatem eius*, his mercy and truth, that is, the grace and the justice of Jesus Christ, *quis requiret, who shall search* in this present life, imploring the grace of remission [of sins], observing the commandments of Christ, and imitating his way? It is as if he were saying:[27] "Few are they who search for these things from their

---

22   Zech. 9:9a.

23   Is. 33:22.

24   Is. 66:23a.

25   E. N. St. Thomas: "[A]eviternity (*aevum*) will be nothing other than a participation in eternity (*aeternitatis participatio*) so that it is evident that essential eternity is attributed to God himself, but aeviternity is like a participated eternity (*participata aeternitas*) by spiritual substances, which exist beyond time." *Quodlibet* V, q. 4 co.

26   *Cf.* Rom. 8:34b: *Christ Jesus ... who is at the right hand of God, who also makes intercession for us. Cf.* Heb. 9:24: *For Jesus is not entered into the holies made with hands, the patterns of the true: but into heaven itself, that he may appear now in the presence of God for us.*

27   E. N. In other words, this is asked rhetorically, the implied answer being "few," *pauci.*

heart.[28] For the elect are few, and *all seek the things that are their own."*[29] Or [alternatively]: Who will seek after *his mercy and truth* in the future life? It is as if he were saying: No one. For mercy is necessary for those who are wretched; and truth concerns the fulfillment of a promise. But in heaven no one is wretched, and the divine promises have been fulfilled in them, because having possession of joy sempiternal, they do not pray for more of it for themselves, at least as it regards essential reward.[30] And so, the Savior speaking to the Apostles: *You now indeed have sorrow,* he said, *but I will see you again, and your heart shall rejoice; and your joy no man shall take from you; and in that day you shall not ask me anything.*[31]

60{61}[9] *So will I sing a Psalm to your name for ever and ever: that I may pay my vows from day to day.*

Sic Psalmum dicam nomini tuo in saeculum saeculi, ut reddam vota mea de die in diem.

60{61}[9] *Sic,* so, that is, because it is so, I, Christ, *Psalmum dicam nomini tuo, will sing a Psalm to your name,* that is, to you, God, the Father, by myself and through my ministers in heaven and earth,[32] *in saeculum saeculi, for ever*

---

28   Cf. Matt. 20:16b: *For many are called, but few chosen.*

29   Cf. Phil. 2:21: *For all seek the things that are their own; not the things that are Jesus Christ's.* E. N. "Very many writers appear to hold that the number of the reprobate very far exceeds the number of the saved ... [I]n their view, the question is narrowed to adult Catholics, and of these, perhaps most writers venture to say that only a minority are saved. Recupitus, the Jesuit, in his treatise on the Number of the Predestinate, enumerates ... Denys the Carthusian ... as holding this opinion, together with most of the Fathers of the Church." Frederick William Faber, O. C., *The Creator and the Creature: or, the Wonders of Divine Love* (Baltimore, Murphy & Co., 1857), 311–12.

30   E. N. The "essential reward" is the beatific vision of God. There remain certain other so-called "accidental rewards" in heaven (*e.g.,* at the time of the Final Judgment and Resurrection of the dead, the soul saved in heaven will then enjoy the "accidental reward" of being joined with his glorified body. For more on this topic, *see* footnote 1-48, in Volume 1.

31   John 16:22–23a.

32   E. N. "The intercession of the saints. 'Being more closely united to Christ, those who dwell in heaven fix the whole Church more firmly in holiness. ... They do not cease to intercede with the Father for us, as they proffer the merits which they acquired on earth through the one mediator between God and men, Christ Jesus. ... So by their fraternal concern is our weakness greatly helped.'" CCC § 956 (quoting VII, LG 49 and referring to 1 Tim. 2:5). "In the age of the Church, Christian intercession participates in Christ's, as an expression of the communion of saints. In intercession, he who prays looks 'not only to his own interests, but also to the interests of others,' even to the point of praying for those who do him harm.'" CCC § 2634 (citing to Phil 2:4; Acts 7:60; and Luke 23:28, 34).

and ever, praising you without end; *ut reddam vota mea, that I may pay my vows*, that is, that I may offer to you my prayers and desires for the Church militant, for which in your presence as man I make intercession,[33] *de die in diem, from day to day*, that is, unceasingly even until the end of time. For Christ shows his side and his wounds to the Father for us, and he is the Angel bringing up our sacrifice upon the sublime altar of God,[34] making it to be acceptable to God. Whence John: *We have an advocate*, he says, *with the Father, Jesus Christ the just; and he is the propitiation for our sins.*[35]

ARTICLE XXI

TROPOLOGICAL OR MORAL EXPOSITION OF THE SAME SIXTIETH PSALM.

60{61}[2] *Hear, O God, my supplication: be attentive to my prayer.*

Exaudi, Deus, deprecationem meam, intende orationi meae.

IT CANNOT BE DENIED BUT THAT THIS Psalm can be literally explained in reference to David. But because such an exposition contains little of devotional use and sweetness, and because it differs little from the tropological exposition, it will be left alone and I will follow the tropological sense, [that is,] the manner in which this Psalm conveniently relates to any one Christian, or to the Church as a whole, praying to God and giving him thanks, saying: 60{61} [2] *Exaudi, Deus, deprecationem meam; hear, O God, my supplication*, graciously and quickly giving to me the effect of my prayers, whereby I pray for indulgence and grace in the present; *intende orationi meae, be attentive to my prayer*, whereby I pray that I might obtain glory in the future: that is, consider how much affection, what amount of trust, and with what intention and end I call out to you.

---

33 Cf. Rom. 8:34.

34 *E. N.* This is a reference to the *Supplices te rogamus* in the Canon of the Mass: *Supplices te rogamus, omnipotens Deus: iube haec perferri per manus sancti Angeli tui in sublime altare tuum, in conspectu divinae maiestatis tuae.* "We humbly beseech you, Almighty God: command these [offerings] be brought to your sublime altar by the hands of your holy Angel, in the presence of your divine majesty." As Denis says in his Exposition on the Mass, one can understand the "holy Angel" as a reference to Christ, who is known as the "angel of good counsel," Is. 9:6 (LXX), and that the "sublime altar" is Christ. *See* Doctoris Ecstatici D. Dionysii Cartusiani, *Opera Omnia*, Vol. 35 (Tournai: 1908), 373.

35 1 John 2:1b-2a.

60{61}[3]   *To you have I cried from the ends of the earth: when my heart was in anguish, you have exalted me on a rock. You have conducted me,*

A finibus terrae ad te clamavi, dum anxiaretur cor meum; in petra exaltasti me. Deduxisti me,

60{61}[4]   *For you have been my hope; a tower of strength against the face of the enemy.*

Quia factus es spes mea, turris fortitudinis a facie inimici.

60{61}[3] *A finibius terrae, from the ends of the earth,* that is, from all parts and all climates of the world, *ad te clamavi; to you have I cried* in prayers poured out to you, or in giving thanks and praise through which I praised you in adversity. *Dux anxiaretur cor meum, when my heart was in anguish,* that is, [when my heart was] disturbed and afflicted with fear of imminent dangers to it, and also in sorrow because of its daily defects and negligences, namely, because it does not make headway in accordance with its desires, nor does it honor you as it desires; or [we can see it this way], *when [my heart] was anguished* by the temptations of a demon, and the persecutions of men, and the movements of passion; *in petra exaltasti me, you have exalted me on a rock,* that is, you have raised me up in Christ from the imperfection of nature unto the loftiness of grace, and from the inferior and earthly things to those things heavenly and divine. Any one of us is able to say: *From the ends of the earth,* that is, from the surface, the land in which I dwell, bounded by the heights, *to you have I cried,* according to the sense just stated. Or [alternatively], *from the ends of the earth,* that is, from the boundaries of my body, in which, as if it were the earth, dwells my soul, indeed from all my members and my senses, *to you have I cried* in the manner that was said above [in an earlier Psalm]: *All my bones shall say: Lord, who is like to you?*[36] Let us accustom our souls, therefore, in all distress to cry out to God with all confidence the way that the prophet Jonah did it saying: *I cried out of my affliction to the Lord, and he heard me ... When my soul was in distress within me, I remembered the Lord.*[37]

Deduxisti me, you have conducted me in the present exile by the way of your commandments, showing me by the light of your grace the right way *wherein I might walk.*[38] For without your grace I am blind in mind,

---

36   Ps. 34:10a.
37   Jonah 3:3a, 8a.
38   Ps. 142:8b.

and I walk in ways that are not good,[39] and are vicious and slippery, and in which I would gravely and incessantly sin, unless you lead my soul on the way to the heavenly homeland, from hardship to reward, from the creature to the Creator. For this is what you say through Isaiah: *I am the Lord your God teaching you profitable things, governing you in the way that you walk.*[40] And elsewhere is written: *The Lord conducted the just through the right ways, and showed him the kingdom of God.*[41] And Tobias said: *May God be with you in your way, and his angel accompany you.*[42] But *you have conducted me, O Lord,* **60{61}[4]** *quia factus es spes mea, for you have been my hope,* that is, you are that good in which I finally place my hope, and that I desire to receive at the end, and by whose help I trust to receive you yourself. But God is our hope because he makes us to hope in him.[43] He is also for me *turris fortitudinis, a tower of strength,* that is, a robust protection and a most sublime defender, *a facie inimici, against the face of the enemy,* whoever they may be, that is, from all the hostile incursions, in the way that we read with Solomon: *The name of the Lord is a strong tower: the just runs to it, and shall be exalted.*[44] And with the prophet Habakkuk: *The Lord God is my strength: and he will make my feet like the feet of harts.*[45] What is able to cast him down, what is able to harm him who dwells in such a high and impregnable tower? Whence the blessed Job says: *Who will grant me that I might know and find him, and come even to his throne?*[46] For of such inhabitants in such tower of strength, that is, of those leaning upon divine help, it is written: *God with his right hand will cover them, and with his holy arm he will defend them.*[47]

39　Cf. Is. 65:2: *I have spread forth my hands all the day to an unbelieving people, who walk in a way that is not good after their own thoughts.*

40　Is. 48:17b.

41　Wis. 10:10.

42　Tob. 5:21b.

43　E. N. One must not forget that hope — the *theological virtue* of hope — is a gift; it is not something we engender or elicit from nature. It is a gift of God, along with faith and charity. "Hope is a gift of God. We must ask for it." Pope Francis, Homily, Nov. 6, 2016, http://www.vatican.va/content/francesco/en/homilies/2016/documents/papa-francesco_20161106_giubileo-omelia-carcerati.html.

44　Prov. 18:10.

45　Hab. 3:19a. E. N. As Denis says in his *Commentary* on Psalm 17:34 (Article XLIV) in Volume I, "like a hart runs quickly and ascends to the heights," so our souls should run the way of God's commandments towards God.

46　Job. 23:3.

47　Wis. 5:17b.

60{61}[5] *In your tabernacle I shall dwell forever: I shall be protected under the covert of your wings,*

> *Inhabitabo in tabernaculo tuo in saecula; protegar in velamento alarum tuarum.*

60{61}[6] *For you, my God, have heard my prayer: you have given an inheritance to them that fear your name.*

> *Quoniam tu, Deus meus, exaudisti orationem meam; dedisti haereditatem timentibus nomen tuum.*

60{61}[5] *Inhabitabo in tabernaculo tuo, in your tabernacle I shall dwell:* that is, I, the Church militant, hope to attain to the fellowship of the Church triumphant, and trustingly I say that I will live in it in the empyreal heaven after I take leave from this present life *in saecula, forever,* that is, without end, in the manner that Christ promises the faithful, saying, *I go to prepare a place for you;*[48] and, *I will come again, and will take you to myself.*[49] Or [another interpretation]: I, a member of the Christian faithful, dwell in your tabernacle, that is, in the unity of the Church, in undivided charity, holy obedience, and the Catholic Faith. *Protegar, I shall be protected* from all danger of soul, *in velamento alarum tuarum, under the covert of your wings,* that is, under the protection of your mercy and your power. **60{61}[6]** *Quoniam tu, Deus meus; for you, my God,* in whom alone I trust, whom alone I desire, in whom I place all my salvation, *exaudisti orationem meam, have heard my prayer,* as I hope. For you said: *Whatsoever you shall ask the Father in my name, that will I do.*[50]

60{61}[7] *You will add days to the days of the king: his years even to generation and generation.*

> *Dies super dies regis adiicies; annos eius usque in diem generationis et generationis.*

60{61}[8] *He abides forever in the sight of God: his mercy and truth who shall search?*

> *Permanet in aeternum in conspectu Dei: misericordiam et veritatem eius quis requiret?*

60{61}[7] *Dies super dies regis adiicies, you will add days to the days of the king,* that is, after this life, to the days of this brief life, you will add days of eternal blessedness: *days,* I say, *of the king,* that is, of the ruler

---

48 John 14:2b.
49 John 14:3b.
50 John 14:13b.

and the victor of the world, the flesh, and the devil, who has power over his soul, and has defeated them. Whence the Apostle [Paul] says: *That which is at present momentary and light of our tribulation, works for us above measure exceedingly an eternal weight of glory.*[51] For this reason, a later Psalm says: *I will fill him with length of days.*[52] **60{61}[8]** *Permanet in aeternum in conspectus Dei, he abides forever in the sight of God,* that is, the Church will persist in the faith even until the end of time, like the Lord to Peter in the person of the Church: *I have prayed for you,* he said, *that your faith fail not.*[53] And this life having run its course, it will arrive to the king in his glorious aspect in the way that is written in Isaiah: *His eyes shall see the king in his beauty.*[54] And so the just man remains in eternity before the sight of God, saying always with holy Elijah, *As the Lord lives…, in whose sight I stand* today;[55] and with holy Job, *My justification, which I have begun to hold, I will not forsake.*[56] *For no man putting his hand to the plough, and looking back, is fit for the kingdom of God;*[57] *but he that shall persevere unto the end, he shall be saved.*[58]

60{61}[9] *So will I sing a Psalm to your name for ever and ever: that I may pay my vows from day to day.*

Sic Psalmum dicam nomini tuo in saeculum saeculi, ut reddam vota mea de die in diem.

60{61}[9] *Sic Psalmum dicam nomini tuo in saeculum saeculi, so will I sing a Psalm to your name for ever and ever,* that is, I will praise you incessantly in life and in word: as is said by Ecclesiasticus: *I will give glory to you, O Lord, O King, and I will praise you, O God my Savior;*[59] and again, *My soul shall praise the Lord even to death.*[60] *Et reddam vota mea de die in diem: that I may pay my vows from day to day,* that is, that I may daily fulfill all the promises that I may have made to you at the reception of Baptism, or sacred Orders, or as a Religious. Or [alternatively], *that I may pay my vows,* that is, that I might purify my

---

51   2 Cor. 4:17.
52   Ps. 90:16a.
53   Luke 22:32a.
54   Is. 33:17a.
55   1 Kings 17:1a.
56   Job 27:6a.
57   Luke 9:62.
58   Matt. 10:22b.
59   Ecclus. 51:1.
60   Ecclus. 31:8.

desires, and show them always to you; as a Psalm above says: *Lord, all my desire is before you.*[61]

See, we have heard this brief, beautiful, delightful, and rich Psalm, which so perfectly applies as much to Christ as it does to his faithful; [a Psalm] in which we begin with a devout prayer, and after which we are introduced into a saving doctrine, and thereafter the divine benefits are fervently recalled, and finally by the words of good hope our pious resolution is inflamed. Let us therefore conform our affections to the sentiments of this Psalm, and let us most assiduously bring to mind its benefits, and endeavor to fulfil that which we say: *So I will sing a Psalm to your name, now and forever.* For this — to sing to God, and to praise, magnify, and with one's entire affection to extol him — is a most divine, most salubrious, and most sweet exercise of the present life, just as it is written in Ecclesiasticus: *Blessing the Lord, exalt him as much as you can: for he is above all praise.*[62]

PRAYER

O LORD GOD, OUR HOPE AND TOWER OF our strength, protect us under the shadow of your wings, so that constantly serving you in fear of you, and made to conform to your glory, we might, by the offering of our spiritual promises, be found worthy to sing to your name forever.

Domine Deus, spes nostra et turris fortitudinis nostrae, protege nos sub umbra alarum tuarum: ut in timore tuo tibi iugiter servientes, et conformes facti gloriae tuae, mereamur in spiritualium oblatione votorum psallere nomini tuo in saecula.

---

61   Ps. 37:10a.
62   Ecclus. 43:33.

Psalm 61

ARTICLE XXII

EXPOSITION OF THE SIXTY-FIRST PSALM:
NONNE DEO SUBIECTA ERIT ANIMA MEA?
SHALL NOT MY SOUL BE SUBJECT TO GOD?

61{62}[1] *Unto the end, for Idithun, a Psalm of David.*

In finem, pro Idithun. Psalmus David.

RITTEN BEFORE THIS PRESENT PSALM IS this title: **61{62}[1]** *In finem, pro Idithun. Psalmus David. Unto the end, for Idithun, a Psalm of David.* That is, this Psalm written by David, has as its end Christ to which it directs us, and was delivered by Idithun, that is, for men that are on earth only transiently and for a short while, and who desire finally only heavenly things. The title can also be explained that David wrote this Psalm for Idithun, that is, so that it might be especially sung by the singers or Levites constituted under Idithun, who was one of the principal singers of the temple.[1]

61{62}[2] *Shall not my soul be subject to God? For from him is my salvation.*

Nonne Deo subiecta erit anima mea? Ab ipso enim salutare meum.

Man raising himself therefore towards the divine, and considering the innumerable delusions, vanities, and lies of the world, says: **61{62}[2]** *Nonne Deo subiecta erit anima mea,* shall not my soul be subject to God, adhering faithfully to him, and ordering everything under his precepts? Indeed. It is as if he was saying: "some are subject to the desires of the flesh, some to the princes of the world, some to the suggestions of demons, some to all the variety of sins. But I and my soul shall obey the Lord."[2] For *no one can serve two masters* who approve contrary things.[3]

---

1 1 Chr. 25:1.
2 E. N. In other words, the question asked in Ps. 61:2 is rhetorical. *Of course a soul ought to be subject to God!*
3 Matt. 6:24a.

For this reason we cannot obey God and the world. Whence regarding the disobedient, we find written in Jeremiah: *You have broken my yoke, you have burst my bands, and you have said: I will not serve.*[4] To the contrary, Christ instructed us: *Take my yoke upon you.*[5] Therefore, my soul shall be subject to the Lord. For Solomon said: *The mind of the just man studies obedience.*[6] Also the reason for subjection then follows: *Ab ipso enim salutare meum, for from him is my salvation,* that is, all my salvation and all my happiness proceeds to, depends upon, and makes progress by God. This is why the Lord said through Hosea: *And my people shall long for my return.*[7] Or [we can understand it in this fashion]: *From him,* that is, from God the Father is my salvation, that is, his Son and my Savior. For *God so loved the world that he gave his only begotten Son.*[8]

61{62}[3]   *For he is also my God and my Savior: he is my protector, I shall be moved no more.*

Nam et ipse Deus meus et salutaris meus; susceptor meus, non movebor amplius.

61{62}[3] *Nam et ipse* est *Deus meus, for he is also my God,* that is, the cause, governor, and creator of my nature and of its natural gifts, *et salutaris meus, and my Savior,* that is, my justifier[9] and giver of grace; *susceptor meus, my protector,* that is, the hearer of my prayers, always ready to embrace me, the penitent, and me, the one turning to him, with his arms of mercifulness; and he is working within me to draw and unite me to him: just like it is said, *If a man turn his heart to God he shall draw his spirit and breath unto himself.*[10] When therefore I do so, *non movebor amplius, I shall be moved no more* from the beginning

---

4   Jer. 2:20a.
5   Matt. 11:29a.
6   Prov. 15:28a.
7   Hosea 11:7a.
8   John 3:16.
9   L. *iustificator,* is one who justifies, or makes just, another; that is makes righteous before God. The word is actually coined by St. Augustine according to Fr. Joseph Christopher. *The First Catechetical Instruction* (Westminster, MD: Newman Press, 1962), 108, n. 83 (trans. Rev. Joseph P. Christopher, PhD). Augustine uses it in his exposition of Psalm 97[98]:5: *Nos ergo impii, ille iustificator, quando et ipsam iustitiam ipse in nobis fecit qua illi placeamus, ut ad dexteram nos ponat, et non ad sinistram.* "He is the justifier of us ungodly men, when also he causes in us his justice wherein we please him, so that he places us at his right, and not at his left." *Enarr. in Ps.,* PL 37, 1264.
10   Job. 34:14.

of the path of virtue, from the good purpose, from the divine law; nor will I fall back from my God by aversion of mind, but I will immovably adhere to him. Yet I, a wayfarer in passing, say this not presumptuously or with certainty, but with humility and in trust, unless perchance from a divine revelation one knows himself to be confirmed in the good.[11] Or this is said to indicate that which applies to the virtuous man, insofar as he acts likewise. For in the way that passions and vices are the cause of instability, distractions, and aversion [to divine things], so virtue or grace produces the basis of interior stability. For this reason, Solomon states: *The just is as an everlasting foundation.*[12] And in the book of Job: *If you will put away from yourself the iniquity that is in your hand, . . . you shall be steadfast and shall not fear.*[13]

61{62}[4] *How long do you rush in upon a man? You all kill, as if a leaning wall and a tottering fence.*[14]

Quousque irruitis in hominem? Interficitis universi vos, tamquam parieti inclinato et maceriae depulsae.

61{62}[4] *Quousque,* how long, O evildoers, *irruitis in homine,* do you rush in upon a man that is, the just and innocent man, persecuting him as if pursuing justice? *Interficitis universi vos,* you all kill, that is, O all of you [how long] do you purpose to kill him out of hate? This is the way raised in the book of Wisdom: The ungodly said: *Let us oppress the just man . . . because . . . he is contrary to our doings.*[15] Or [alternatively], *You*

---

11 E. N. "For just as no devout man should doubt God's mercy, Christ's merit, and the power and efficacy of the sacraments; so also, whoever considers himself, his personal weakness, and his lack of disposition may fear and tremble about his own grace, since no one can know with a certitude of faith that cannot be subject to error that he has obtained God's grace." DS 1534 (Council of Trent). "[N]o one, so long as he lives in this mortal condition, ought to be so presumptuous . . . as to determine with certainty that he is definitely among the number of predestined, as if it were true either that the one justified cannot sin anymore, or that, if he sins, he should promise himself an assured repentance. For without special revelation it is impossible to know whom God has chosen for himself." DS 1540 (Council of Trent).
12 Prov. 10:25b.
13 Job 11:14–15.
14 E. N. The Douay Rheims translates this verse: "as if you were thrusting down a leaning wall, and tottering fence." However, the verbal phrase "you were thrusting down" is not in the Latin, but the translator has implied it to solve the issue that Denis raises in his *Commentary.*
15 Wis. 2:10a, 12a. E. N. The Sixto-Clementine Vulgate reads *opprimamus pauperem iustum,* "let us oppress the just poor," but Denis's version quote reads *opprimamus virum iustum,* "let us oppress the just man."

all kill, that is, you all kill yourselves: for when you afflict the just you kill your own souls by sin. Whence John: *Whosoever hates his brother, he says, is a murderer:*[16] either because he spiritually kills his own soul, or because by desire he kills another, or because before God he incurs the penalty of homicide.[17] *Tanquam parieti inclinato et maceriae depulsae, as if a leaning wall and a tottering fence.* There is something implied here, [so it ought to be understood] in this sense: to act adversely to a just man in this manner is like confronting a leaning wall ready to collapse, or a tottering fence in terms of its ability to repel. For consider that as such a wall is deprived of a foundation, and is easily cast down, so, if the just man does not have God as defender and helper, by your evildoing you are able to oppress him; and since you kill him, and you regard him to be entirely destroyed, you are not attentive that God may restore him to glory nor [are you attentive] to the punishment that menaces you. In this regard it is written: *The just perish, and no man lays it to heart, and men of mercy are taken away, because there is none that understands.*[18]

61{62}[5] *But they have thought to cast away my price; I ran in thirst: they blessed with their mouth, but cursed with their heart.*

Verumtamen pretium meum cogitaverunt repellere; cucurri in siti; ore suo benedicebant, et corde suo maledicebant.

61{62}[5] *Verumtamen,* but, that is, all this notwithstanding, *pretium meum cogitaverunt repellere, they have thought to cast away my price,* that is, they purposed themselves to subvert, to make vanish, and to impede

---

16 1 John 3:15a.

17 E. N. "The fifth commandment forbids direct and intentional killing as gravely sinful. The murderer and those who cooperate voluntarily in murder commit a sin that cries out to heaven for vengeance. Infanticide, fratricide, parricide, and the murder of a spouse are especially grave crimes by reason of the natural bonds which they break.... The fifth commandment forbids doing anything with the intention of indirectly bringing about a person's death. The moral law prohibits exposing someone to mortal danger without grave reason, as well as refusing assistance to a person in danger. The acceptance by human society of murderous famines, without efforts to remedy them, is a scandalous injustice and a grave offense. Those whose usurious and avaricious dealings lead to the hunger and death of their brethren in the human family indirectly commit homicide, which is imputable to them. Unintentional killing is not morally imputable. But one is not exonerated from grave offense if, without proportionate reasons, he has acted in a way that brings about someone's death, even without the intention to do so." CCC §§ 2268–69 (footnotes omitted).

18 Is. 57:1a.

from its reward my righteousness or my virtuous works and laudable life. For good works are called "price" because by them one merits eternal life.[19] *Cucurri in siti, I ran in thirst,* that is, with great desire I hurried toward the heavenly homeland: as is stated in a Psalm above, *My soul has thirsted after the strong, living God.*[20] Or thus: *I have run the way of your commandments* with the thirst for perfection, namely thirsting for greater justice, and with great affection desiring to attain the peak of perfection.[21] *Ore suo benedicebant, et corde suo maledicebant; they blessed with their mouth, but cursed with their heart.* These things subverters of souls, the flatterers, the double-tongued, and the dissemblers do: to those that they are not able openly to pervert, they seek to deceive by flattering and by suggesting evil things under the guise of good. For this reason, we read in Jeremiah about these sorts of people: *With his mouth one speaks peace with his friend, and secretly he lies in wait for him.*[22]

---

19   E. N. "If anyone says that the good works of the justified man are the gifts of God in such a way that they are not also the good merits of the justified man himself; or that by the good works he performs through the grace of God and the merits of Jesus Christ (of whom he is a living member), the justified man does not truly merit ... eternal life, and (provided he dies in the state of grace) the attainment of this eternal life ... let him be anathema." DS 1582 (Council of Trent). "The merit of man before God in the Christian life arises from the fact that God has freely chosen to associate man with the work of his grace. The fatherly action of God is first on his own initiative, and then follows man's free acting through his collaboration, so that the merit of good works is to be attributed in the first place to the grace of God, then to the faithful. Man's merit, moreover, itself is due to God, for his good actions proceed in Christ, from the predispositions and assistance given by the Holy Spirit." CCC § 2008.

20   Ps. 41:3a.

21   E. N. As the Council of Trent made clear, once justified, the Christian can increase in justice or righteousness. "[T]he justified become both 'friends of God' and 'members of his household" [John 15:15, Eph. 2:19]; 'they go from strength to strength' [Ps. 84:7], 'renewed (as the apostle says) every day' [2 Cor. 4:16], that is 'by putting to death the members of their flesh' [*cf.* Col 3:5, Vulg.] and using them 'as instruments of righteousness' [*cf.* Rom. 6:13, 19] unto sanctification by observing the commandments of God and of the Church. When 'faith is active along with works' [*cf.* James 2:22], they increase in the very justice they have received through the grace of Christ and are further justified [cann. 24 and 32], as it is written: 'Let he who is just still be more justified' [Rev. 22:11]; and again 'Fear not to be justified until you die' [Sir. 18:22, Vulg.]; and again 'You see that a man is justified by works and not by faith alone' [James 2:24]. It is for this increase in faith that the holy Church asks when she prays 'Give us, O Lord, an increase of faith, hope, and charity,' *Da nobis, Domine, fidei, spei, et caritatis augmentum."* DS 1535 (Council of Trent); *see also* DS 1574, 1582.

22   Jer. 9:8b.

61{62}[6] *But be you, O my soul, subject to God: for from him is my patience.*

Verumtamen Deo subiecta esto, anima mea, quoniam ab ipso patientia mea.

61{62}[6] *Verumtamen Deo subiecta esto, anima mea; but be you, O my soul, subject to God:* that is, do not be disheartened, do not withdraw from the law of God, and do not grumble against God because of persecutions, temptations, and tribulations inflicted unjustly upon you, but rather be subject to him; *quoniam ab ipso patientia mea, for from him is my patience* by which I will prevail in adversity, suffering without sadness all things. For God confers patience just as he does the other infused virtues.[23] Now on occasion a man may tend to glory vainly and to vaunt his own patience when he finds himself in adversity, since he has done something of such great difficulty and he has excellently followed the footsteps of Christ; but such a one does not think his patience is from God, for he glories in himself as if he had not received it.[24] Let our soul, therefore, be subject to God in all things, namely, not only in this — that it endures with equanimity adverse things — but also in this — that it does not rejoice in its own patience as having come itself, but it attributes it to God.

61{62}[7] *For he is my God and my Savior: he is my helper, I shall not be moved.*

Quia ipse Deus meus et Salvator meus, adiutor meus, non emigrabo.

61{62}[8] *In God is my salvation and my glory: he is the God of my help, and my hope is in God.*

In Deo salutare meum et gloria mea; Deus auxilii mei, et spes mea in Deo est.

---

23   *E. N.* Although there is some controversy about it, St. Thomas Aquinas seems to have believed that patience was both a moral (acquired) virtue and also an infused virtue. Craig Steven Titus, *Resilience and the Virtue of Fortitude* (Washington, DC: Catholic University of America Press 2006), 326. *See* ST IIaIIae, q. 136. Denis clearly accepts the notion of infused patience. "What is the essence of the virtue of patience? The essence of patience consists in supporting, for the sake of the future life, all the troubles that come to us unceasingly in the present life, whether they be caused by life's own whims or by the actions of others in their dealings with us." R. P. Thomas Pègues, O. P., *Catechism of the Summa Theologica* (New York: Benziger Bros., 1922).
24   *Cf.* 1 Cor. 4:7: *For who distinguishes you? Or what have you that you have not received? And if you have received, why do you glory, as if you had not received it?*

And so I acknowledge my patience to be from God, **61{62}[7]** *Quia ipse est Deus meus, for he is my God*, from whom all good proceeds, and from whom all my sufficiency flows,[25] *et Salvator meus, and my Savior*: because by him alone is true beatitude bestowed. In one way it is fitting for Christ to be Savior, inasmuch as he is God; and in another way, inasmuch as he is man. For, as God, he is called Savior by authority, since he is the creator and giver of grace in the present just as he is of glory in the future; but inasmuch as he is man, he is called Savior instrumentally, since he is the satisfier (*satisfactor*) for the fault of the human race, [and he is mankind's] reconciler and mediator. For God is Savior according to his divinity, because he alone forgives sins,[26] he alone justifies,[27] he alone creates and infuses grace, and he alone is the giver of beatitude. Indeed, it is proper to God to be Savior in this way, according to that prophecy: *I am the Lord: and there is no Savior besides me.*[28] And God is also *adiutor meus, my helper* cooperating with me and strengthening me by grace in all my good works. *Non emigrabo, I shall not be moved* from the unity of the Church and the flock of the elect to those averse to God and the society of the perverse, because **61{62}[8]** *In Deo salutare meum, in God is my salvation*, that is, my salvation consists in this, that I may not move away from him, *et gloria mea, and my glory*: for true and rightful glorying is had only in God, in the manner that the Apostle [Paul] said: *He that glories, may he glory in the Lord.*[29] And Habakkuk: *I will rejoice in the Lord: and I will have joy in God my Jesus.*[30] *Deus auxilia mei, the God of my help*, that is, upon him depends and from him derives all my help: as is said by Hosea: *Destruction is your own, . . . your help is only in me.*[31] *Et spes mea in Deo est, and my hope is in God*: for it relies upon the divine kindness and it has God for its immediate object and cause since it is a theological and infused virtue.[32] See how excellent and splendid and most sweet this verse is, more sweet and tasty to the devout mind than *honey and the honeycomb.*[33]

---

25 E. N. 2 Cor. 3:5: *Not that we are sufficient to think anything of ourselves, as of ourselves: but our sufficiency is from God.*

26 Mark 2:7b: *Who can forgive sins but God only?*

27 Rom. 8:30b: *And whom he called, them he also justified. And whom he justified, them he also glorified.*

28 Is. 43:11.

29 1 Cor. 1:31.

30 Hab. 3:18.

31 Hosea 13:9.

32 E. N. ST IIaIIae, q. 17, art. 5, co. (hope has God as its object and is a theological virtue), ad 1 (God is the first efficient cause of hope).

33 Ps. 18:11b.

61{62}[9] *Trust in him, all you congregation of people: pour out your hearts before him. God is our helper forever.*

Sperate in eo, omnis congregatio populi; effundite coram illo corda vestra; Deus adiutor noster in aeternum.

61{62}[9] *Sperate in eo, omnis congregatio populi; trust in him, all you congregation of people,* that is, the whole Church; *effundite coram illo corda vestra, pour out your hearts before him,* that is, your prayers, desires, needs, anxieties, dangers, and sins, and whatever is present in your minds expose it before God, and set it forth into the light, show it to him, and discuss it before him: as Jeremiah exhorts, *Pour out your heart like water before the face of the Lord your God.*[34] Whence, holy Hannah attests in the first book of Samuel: *I have poured out my soul before the Lord.*[35] *Deus adiutor noster in aeternum, God is our helper forever,* that is, as long as we exist: because he conserves and he favors us with grace along the way on pilgrimage, and in the heavenly fatherland by glory, which includes confirmation in the good.[36]

61{62}[10] *But vain are the sons of men, the sons of men are liars in the balances: that by vanity they may together deceive.*

Verumtamen vani filii hominum, mendaces filii hominum in stateris, ut decipiant ipsi de vanitate in idipsum.

61{62}[10] *Verumtamen vani filii hominum, but vain are the sons of men,* speaking of the sons of men in the way of those that Moses speaks of when he said, *the sons of God seeing the daughters of men:*[37] those, plainly, who live without charity and grace. Such sons of men, therefore, are vain, because they do not refer their works and present life to what one is destined to in the end, namely, eternal life, but instead place their end in created things, attaching themselves more to creatures rather

---

34   Lam. 2:19a.

35   1 Sam. 1:15b. E. N. Hannah, one of the wives of Elkanah. Hannah was without child for a long time but eventually gave birth to Samuel, the famous judge, priest, and prophet.

36   E. N. ST Ia, q. 62, art. 1, s.c. (to be confirmed in the good is of the nature of beatitude).

37   Gen. 6:2a. E. N. Denis is saying that the use of "sons of men" by the Psalm is used in the same manner as "sons of God" is used by Moses (as the author of Genesis), namely, as a euphemism for rational creatures (men) who are living without charity and grace, without a *fides formata caritate*, a faith informed by charity. In Ps. 61:10, such are driven by lies; whereas in Gen. 6:2, they are driven by lust. Neither of these desires are consonant with a life of sanctifying grace.

than to the Creator. *Mendaces filii hominum in stateris, the sons of men are liars in the balances*: for they harbor unjust thoughts or they judge mendaciously, preferring the evil and the false to the good and the true. Regarding which the Lord said through Moses: *Do not any unjust thing in judgment, in rule, in weight, or in measure; let the balance be just and the weights equal, the bushel just, and the sextary equal.*[38] *Ut decipiant ipsi de vanitate in id ipsum, that by vanity they may together deceive*, that is, they together dupe themselves by vain, temporal, and fleeting things.

61{62}[11] *Trust not in iniquity, and cover not robberies: if riches abound, set not your heart upon them.*

Nolite sperare in iniquitate, et rapinas nolite concupiscere; divitiae si affluant, nolite cor apponere.

Therefore, the holy Prophet [David] counsels the opposite: **61{62}** **[11]** *Nolite, do not*, he says, *sperare in iniquitate, trust in iniquity*: as it is written of the ungodly, *they trust in a mere nothing.*[39] For sin is nothing:[40] therefore, do not place trust in sin as if you are able to save yourself or prosper by injustice or evildoing. *Et rapinas nolite concupiscere, and cover not robberies*: that is, do not rob another person of his things by hand or desire, and do not make common cause with plunderers, for not only are they who do such things *worthy of death, but also those that consent.*[41] *Divitiae, riches* [that are] exterior, *si affluent, if they abound* copiously, *nolite cor apponere, set not your heart on them*, that is, do not inordinately affix your will on them, do not inordinately love them, clutch them, or seek to increase them, and do not unnecessarily occupy yourself with them, namely, by acquiring them with exertion, possessing them with fear, and losing them with sorrow. Riches, however, are not to be blamed, but the inordinate affection [of them is blameworthy]. For the riches to be kept, loved, or collected are those that are necessary to spiritual goods, such as being content and at peace with food and clothing[42] and so that we

---

38 Lev. 19:35-36. E. N. The word "sextary" translates the Latin *sextarius* which is a Roman measure of liquid volume, being one sixth of a congius, which itself was 1/8 of an amphora quadrantal. (It was about equal to a pint.) The Latin word *sextarius* translates the Hebrew *hin* (הין) or the Septuagint's χοῦς (*chous*).

39 Is. 59:4a.

40 E. N. As St. Thomas puts it: *Augustinus dicit: peccatum enim nihil est, et nihil fiunt homines cum peccant.* "Augustine says: for sin is nothing, and men accomplish nothing when they sin." *Super II Cor.*, cap. 5, l. 4.

41 Rom. 1:32b.

42 1 Tim. 6:8: *But having food, and wherewith to be covered, with these we are content.*

might engage in almsgiving.[43] Yet it is difficult for the affluent not to place their hearts on riches according to that which Christ asserts in the Gospel: *With what difficulty shall they that have riches enter into the kingdom of God!*[44] Nevertheless, unless their powers are abused, *God does not cast away the mighty, since he himself is also mighty;*[45] in the same manner, unless they have abused their abundance of riches, God does not reject the rich, since he himself is rich. The holy Job did not set his heart upon his riches, as he said: *If I have rejoiced over my great riches.*[46] And elsewhere, when all was taken away: *The Lord gave* (he said), *and the Lord has taken away; as it has pleased the Lord, so is it done: blessed be the name of the Lord.*[47]

61{62}[12]   *God has spoken once, these two things have I heard, that power belongs to God,*

Semel locutus est Deus; duo haec audivi: quia potestas Dei est,

61{62}[13]   *And mercy to you, O Lord; for you will render to every man according to his works.*

Et tibi, Domine, misericordia: quia tu reddes unicuique iuxta opera sua.

61{62}[12] *Semel, once,* that is, without retraction, indeed, unalterably, firmly, and most certainly, *locutus est Deus, God has spoken,* in his very self now incarnate, and by the Prophets and the Apostles. *Duo haec audivi, these two things have I heard,* in that hidden and secret utterance, namely, in that illumination supernaturally accomplished by the Holy Spirit. Now what these two things are immediately follows: *quia potestas Dei est, that power belongs to God,* that is, just power in the punishment of the iniquitous; **61{62}[13]** *et tibi, Domine, misericordia; and mercy to you, O Lord* by crowning the good beyond what they are worthy (*ultra condignum*). And that this is in fact so, arises from this: *quia tu reddes unicuique iuxta opera sua, for you will render to every man according to his works* as the most just Judge. We read about this in the book of Job: *Far*

---

43   Luke 11:41a: *But yet that which remains [after necessities are met], give alms.*
44   Luke 18:24b.
45   Job 36:5a.
46   Job 31:25a. E. N. This statement is made when Job defends himself to his friends, and he undergoes a sort of *examen* of conscience. The implication of this scrutiny is that Job did not rejoice over, that is, did not have inordinate affection for, his great riches.
47   Job 1:21b.

from God be wickedness, and iniquity from the Almighty; for he will render to a man his work, and according to the ways of everyone he will reward them.[48] But it seems this power is received for the sake of justice, for to exercise justice it is especially necessary to have power. Whence of God it is written elsewhere: *For your power is the beginning of justice.*[49] And so these two [justice and mercy] are most especially attributed to God because all the things that divine Scripture affirms of God, especially in comparison to creatures, can be reduced to these two. For this reason, it is said in an earlier Psalm: *All the ways of the Lord are mercy and truth.*[50] Moreover, as mentioned, that which was said — *God has spoken once* — is not a reference to number, since *at sundry times and in diverse manners* he has spoken to us,[51] but in reference to steadfastness.[52] It is according to this sense that the book of Job says: *God speaks once, and repeats not the selfsame thing the second time.*[53]

EXPOSITION WITH SPECIFIC REFERENCE TO CHRIST

NE SHOULD NOTE ALSO THAT THIS PSALM is able most fittingly to be expounded of Christ, because his soul was always most perfectly subject to God, as he himself testified: *As the Father has given me commandment, so do I;*[54] and elsewhere, *I do always the things that please him.*[55] For all the well-being (*salus*) of the soul of Christ was created by God, and God was the salvation (*salutaris*) of, that is, the one who blessed, the soul of Christ.[56] For this reason, John [the Baptist] stated, *A man cannot receive anything, unless it be given him*

---

48   Job 34:10b–11.
49   Wis. 12:16a.
50   Ps. 24:10a. E. N. Truth is here equated with justice.
51   Heb. 1:1a.
52   E. N. "Through all the words of Sacred Scripture, God speaks only one single Word, his one Utterance in whom he expresses himself completely: 'You recall that one and the same Word of God extends throughout Scripture, that it is one and the same Utterance that resounds in the mouths of all the sacred writers, since he who was in the beginning God with God has no need of separate syllables; for he is not subject to time.'" CCC § 102 (citing Heb. 1:1-3 and quoting St. Augustine, *Enar. in Ps. 4, 1, PL 37, 1378*).
53   Job. 33:14.
54   John 14:31b.
55   John 8:29b.
56   E. N. As Denis makes clear a few sentences later, his understanding of Psalm 61's terms salvation and savior *when interpreted with reference to Christ* have a very restricted, limited meaning. They are not to be understood as suggesting that Christ's human nature needed redemption or salvation in the ordinary sense.

from heaven.[57] But that there is appended **61{62}[3]** *I shall be moved no more*[58] is explained of Christ thus: After the resurrection I would suffer no longer, but I will be immovable (that is impassible) in life. **61{62}[4]** *How long, O unbelieving Jew, do you rush in upon a man,* namely, upon me, the Son of Man whom you had purposed to kill? When he said to the Jews: *You are of your father the devil, and the desires of your father you will do.*[59] And again he said to them: *Why do you seek to kill me?*[60] *You all kill,* that is, [you all kill] your souls by not believing in me. Christ said this in a literal way to the [unbelieving] Jews: *You shall die in your sin.*[61] **61{62}[5]** *But they have thought to cast away my price,* that is, they had desired to shed my blood fruitlessly. For they desired to obliterate the name and the memory of Christ and to divert all men from having faith in him, and by this to see that this shedding of blood would be without profit. *I ran in thirst,* that is, I went through life in this world with a great desire for human salvation. For this reason I said at the Last Supper: *With desire I have desired to eat this Pasch with you before I suffer.*[62] And hanging upon the Cross, *I thirst.*[63] *They blessed with their mouth,* [that is,] the Jews saying to me: *Master, we know that you are true, and that you teach the way of God in truth.*[64] *But cursed with their heart:* for such things they said so that they might elicit an opportunity for killing me from my words. And so God is said to be the savior of Christ, that is, the resuscitator from death and the one who glorified him, not [however in the sense of being] the redeemer from sin.[65] Now the rest [of the Psalm] applies to Christ in this same fashion as that which was made known in the preceding discussion.

See how ineffable and how admirable the beauty and the sentiments of this Psalm are: in which the fiery words of divine love so fully embrace the devout soul, and so often take hold of it again, setting it all afire;

---

57   John 3:27.
58   Ps. 61:3.
59   John 8:44a.
60   John 7:20a.
61   John 8:21a.
62   Luke 22:15.
63   John 19:28.
64   Matt. 22:16a.
65   E. N. In other words, the words of Psalm 61:7, *He is my God and my savior,"* and 61:8, *In God is my salvation,"* savior and salvation when applied to Christ (specifically, to Christ's human nature) are not meant to be taken in the way that they apply to the rest of mankind, but in a very restricted sense. Obviously, as Redeemer and Savior of the human race, Christ's human nature needed neither to be redeemed nor to be saved from sin, the thrall of the devil, and the wrath of God.

in which obedience is commended, a most moral and saving instruction set forth, the ungodly rebuked, and at its end God most beautifully praised. Let our souls therefore always be subject to God, and let us do so reverently and with pure attentiveness, so that the loving words of this present Psalm may be pronounced ardently and with relish; let the heart before its God confidently pour itself out,[66] let the heart not set before itself exterior things, but let it elevate itself by, let it singularly focus upon, and let it affix itself entirely in God.

PRAYER

GOD OF VIRTUE, FROM WHOM COMES all the virtues of the Saints, God of help and of the hope of our glory, we pour out our hearts before you; be our helper, God, who are eternally loving, so that, working along with you, we might possess our souls in patience.[67]

Deus virtutum, a quo est omnis virtus Sanctorum, Deus auxilii et spei gloriae nostrae, corda nostra effundimus coram te; esto adiutor noster, Deus in aeternum pius: ut te cooperante, animas nostras in patientia possideamus.

---

66 Lam. 2:19a: *Pour out your heart like water before the face of the Lord.*
67 Luke 21:19: *In your patience you shall possess your souls.*

Psalm 62

ARTICLE XXIII

EXPOSITION OF THE SIXTY-SECOND PSALM:
DEUS, DEUS MEUS, AD TE DE LUCE VIGILO
O GOD, MY GOD, TO YOU DO I WATCH AT BREAK OF DAY.

62{63}[1] *A Psalm of David when he was in the desert of Edom.*

Psalmus David, cum esset in deserto Idumaeae.

HE TITLE OF THIS PSALM IS: **62{63}[1]** *PSAL-mus David, cum esset in desesrto Idumaeae; a Psalm of David when he was in the desert of Edom*: that is, this Psalm applies to the Church or to the faithful signified by David, when the Church is in the desert of Edom, that is, in its present exile and in this valley of tears,[1] full of vices and hardships, and removed or forsaken from the good.

62{63}[2] *O God, my God, for you do I watch at break of day. For you my soul has thirsted; for you my flesh, O how many ways!*

Deus, Deus meus, ad te de luce vigilo. Sitivit in te anima mea; quam multipliciter tibi caro mea!

The Church, therefore, or any just man, experiencing afflictions in the present time, and urgently seeking divine consolation, says: **62{63} [2]** *Deus, Deus meus; O God, my God,* that is, you, O almighty Creator, who are the God of all things by reason of your creation and your governing: but especially my God, because of your special providence over me by which you protect me from evil, spur me toward the good, and lead me to the ultimate end; and also because of the singular love and respect by which I love and worship you alone; *ad te de luce vigilo, for you do I watch at break of day,* that is, steadfastly when the splendor of your grace will fill my soul, I arise with you, and raise the mind with heartfelt affection to you, contemplating, loving, adoring, worshiping, and serving you. [This is to be understood] also literally, *at the break of*

---

1 E. N. On the expression "valley of tears," *see* footnote 17-147 in Volume I.

215

day, that is, early in the morning we ought to be wakeful and to arise to the worship and praise of God by praising and invoking God with a sober spirit, so that, as our external eyes are bathed with the splendor of the sun, we might so illuminate our interior eyes with the light of grace. Thus Isaiah: *In the morning early*, he says, *I will watch for you.*[2]

Sitivit in te anima mea, for you my soul has thirsted. This is the same as what is said in an earlier Psalm, *My soul has thirsted for the strong living God.*[3] For the thirst of the soul is the strong desire for a good not yet attained.[4] And so [it is understood] in this sense: *My soul*, that is, my intellectual appetite, namely, the will,[5] *has thirsted in you*, that is, with an intellectual and great desire I have longed to attain you, to acquire your consolation, to be saved from present evils, and to be led to you, fountain of universal beatitude: as Tobias said, *O Lord, do with me according to your will, and command my spirit to be received in peace.*[6] And Isaiah: *Your name*, he said, *and your remembrance are the desire of my soul. My soul has desired you in the night, but also by spirit within me [in the morning early I will watch for you.]*[7] This thirst burned the mind of Paul, who said: I have *a desire to be dissolved, and to be with Christ.*[8]

Quam multipliciter tibi caro mea! For you my flesh, O how many ways [has it thirsted for you]! That is, with how many sighs and various sentiments have I thirsted for you, that is, to your glory, *my flesh*, that is, the inferior sensitive appetite! This verse suggests the flesh is more variously moved towards God than is the soul: and this must be understood correctly. For whether the flesh is taken to be the body alone, or whether as the sensitive longing, it is not fitting for it to thirst for God directly, properly, and immediately. For since God is immaterial and simple, only an immaterial longing can reach towards him, just like he can only be contemplated with the intellectual eye. For the flesh of itself is not fit for the desire [for God], but only insofar as it is informed by the soul; and the desire is better said to belong to the whole composite [of body and soul] or to the soul [alone] than it is the flesh [alone]. That here the

---

2   Is. 26:9a.

3   Ps. 41:3a.

4   E. N. The definition is Augustinian. "This lack is good, for it indicates a desire for the good not yet attained, but most avidly and most vehemently desired." St. Augustine, *Enar. in Ps.*, 118, 18, PL 37, 1557.

5   E. N. The intellectual appetite (*appetitus intellectualis*) is equivalent to the will (*voluntas*). ST Ia, q. 82, art. 2, ad 3.

6   Tob. 3:6a.

7   Is. 26:8b–9a. E. N. The part in brackets replaces the "*etc.*" in the Latin text.

8   Phil. 1:23.

flesh is said to thirst in God, therefore, can be understood in two ways. First, because it is the occasion for the soul thirsting in God. Indeed, *the corruptible body is a load upon the soul;*[9] and the soul is burdened by many necessities, demands, afflictions, and miseries from its union with the body. For *the earthly habitation presses down the mind that muses upon many things.*[10] Therefore, the flesh here is said to thirst in many ways for God, in more ways even than the soul, because with the soul, many more causes and incitements for thirsting for God arise from the body than from the soul itself. For there are as many reasons for desiring God as there are obstacles [arising from the body] that the soul experiences as impediments that keep it away from him or draw it away from him. Thus the Apostle [Paul] exclaims to the Romans: *Unhappy man that I am! Who shall deliver me from the body of this death?*[11] In a similar sense, the flesh is said to desire against the soul, not that the flesh of itself desires, but because it is the occasion of the soul desiring against itself. For the soul according to its sensitive appetite desires against itself insofar as its intellectual appetite.[12] Secondly, it can be understood thus: that the flesh, that is, the sensitive appetite, thirsts for God, not directly or immediately, as if God is the object of its desire, but because that which it desires is in accordance with a desire for God, namely, it is in accordance with the rule of reason and the directions of moral virtues: and it thirsts in many more ways for God than does the superior appetite, because man on the part of the sensitive appetite suffers many punishments, faults, and miseries than on the part of his intellective appetite, especially since the passions of the soul, which for us are the origins of sinning, are founded in the sensitive appetite.

62{63}[3]   *In a desert land, and where there is no way, and no water: so in the sanctuary have I come before you, to see your power and your glory.*

In terra deserta, et invia, et inaquosa, sic in sancto apparui tibi, ut viderem virtutem tuam et gloriam tuam.

---

9   Wis. 9:15a.
10   Wis. 9:15b.
11   Rom. 7:24.
12   E. N. Consistent with St. Thomas, Denis divides up the appetite into a lower and a higher appetite, into a sensitive appetite and an intellectual appetite. *See* ST Ia, q. 80, art. 2, co. "Because, therefore, there is a generic difference between what is apprehended by the intellect and what is grasped by the senses it follows that the intellectual appetite (*appetitus intellectivus*) is a different power from the sensitive [appetite]." There can thus be a battle of appetites within the soul.

62{63}[3] *In terra deserta et invia et inaquosa, in a desert land, and where there is no way, and no water,* that is, in this corruptible body, made a desert by original sin, prone to errors, and in and of itself destitute of all grace. For *the flesh profits nothing.*[13] And the Apostle [Paul says]: *For I know,* he says, *that there dwells not in me, that is to say, in my flesh, that which is good.*[14] In this earth, therefore, I go about as if I were dwelling in a jail, *sic in sancto apparui tibi, so in the sanctuary have I come before you,* that is, I have presented myself before your sight in a holy sentiment and with a desire for heaven, pouring out my heart before you, and measuring myself always before your scrutiny. And so, notwithstanding the burden of the body, we aspire to heavenly things, and with a clean heart we attempt to show ourselves before God, so that we can truly say that which the blessed Apostle [Paul] said: *Though we walk in the flesh, we do not war according to the flesh.*[15] Or [alternatively] thus: *In a desert land, and where there is no way, and no water,* that is, in this wretched age which is bereft of virtues, and the wide way is leading to death,[16] a *desert land* also, that is, unfruitful and arid. Of this land Christ in the Gospel said: *When the unclean spirit is gone out of a man, he walks through places without water (loca inaquosa).* So *in the sanctuary have I come before you,* because in this world I did not live in a worldly fashion, nor did I follow the ways of sinners, but I served you in holiness and justice. And this, *ut viderem, to see* in the heavenly homeland face to face, *virtutem tuam, your power,* that is your almightiness, by which you dispose of all things in heaven and on earth, and by which you confirm most powerfully the blessed in heaven in the good; *et gloriam tuam, and your glory,* that is, your blessedness, since I will enter *into the joy* of my *Lord,*[17] and I will have sight of all his excellences in heaven. Or [we can understand it] thus: *to see,* O eternal Father, your power and your glory, that is, Christ, your Son, *who is the power of God and the wisdom of God* according to the Apostle [Paul].[18] For if, as the Scripture attests, *a wise son is the glory of the father,*[19] how much more can be said that Christ, the only-begotten of God, who is

---

13   John 6:64a.

14   Rom. 7:18a.

15   2 Cor. 10:3.

16   *Cf.* Matt. 7:13: *Enter in at the narrow gate: for wide is the gate, and broad is the way that leads to destruction, and many there are who go in thereat.*

17   Matt. 25:23.

18   1 Cor. 1:24b.

19   Prov. 10:1a. E. N. Denis's version departs from the Sixto-Clementine. His version reads *filius sapiens est gloria patris,* "the wise son is the glory of the father," and not *filius sapiens laetificat patrem,* "a wise son makes the father glad."

the eternal, unbounded, and uncreated Wisdom of the Father, is his [the Father's] glory? And so in both ways [of understanding this verse] by the virtue and glory of God is understood God himself, sublime and glorious. For we ought to do all that we can to work toward the vision of God face to face, as it is the ultimate, final, and consummate reward. For this reason the Savior said: *Now this is eternal life: That they may know you, the only true God, and Jesus Christ, whom you have sent.*[20] And Moses said to the Lord: *Show me your glory.*[21]

62{63}[4] *For your mercy is better than lives: you my lips shall praise.*

Quoniam melior est misericordia tua super vitas, labia mea laudabunt te.

62{63}[5] *Thus will I bless you all my life long: and in your name I will lift up my hands.*

Sic benedicam te in vita mea; et in nomine tuo levabo manus meas.

And so this I pray, 62{63}[4] *Quoniam melior est misericordia tua,* for *your mercy is better,* that is, the presence of your grace or the godly manner of life, by which you conserve a man in a spiritual and grace-filled existence, *super vitas, is better than lives,* that is, exceeds all kinds and manner of natural life. Indeed, much more excellent are the holy gifts (*munera*) of grace than the gifts (*donis*) of nature; and one would be better off not to exist or to live a natural life subject to sin than to be without charity and grace, in the manner Truth testified of Judas: *It were better for him if that man had not been born.*[22] Therefore, we ought

---

20 John 17:3.
21 Ex. 33:18.
22 Matt. 26:24b. *E. N.* The point being made here is that, without dying in a state of sanctifying grace (and therefore enjoying a supernatural existence in heaven), one would be better off not having had a natural existence subject to sin at all. Even without the supernatural life of grace, the natural life of the soul is eternal. The whole purpose of the natural life is to receive the supernatural life. In Sermon 81 on the Song of Songs, St. Bernard of Clairvaux (1090–1153) speaks of the fate of a human soul that dies without a supernatural life of grace: "For certainly by nature [the soul], even though it does not live spiritually [*i.e.,* does not enjoy the supernatural life of grace], necessarily lives immortally. Yet what sort of life is it in which it would be better not to have been born, than not to be able to die? Death is better; and it is more cruel since it comes from sin [either original or actual], and not of nature. 'For the death of the wicked is very evil.' [Ps. 33:22a] And so the soul that lives according to the flesh is dead while living; indeed, it would be good for it not

rather choose not to live at all unless it be to live well; and we ought to prefer more not to be at all than to lack the mercy of God. *Labia mea laudabunt te, you my lips shall praise* because of the benefits doled out to me and to others through your mercy. **62{63}[5]** *Sic bendicam te in vita mea, thus will I bless you all my life long,* that is, during the whole time I exist and remain in this life, I will bless you, that is, I will say good things about you, glorifying your goodness, and exalting you above everything else, and giving thanks to you for it. As is said in an earlier Psalm, *I will bless the Lord at all times.*[23] And Tobias said: *Bless God at all times: and desire of him to direct your ways.*[24] Or [we can look at it in this way], *I will bless you all my life long,* that is, I will live in such a manner that my manner of living will be a kind of blessing to your name, for I will order all my life to the honor, praise, and glory of your name. For God is no less blessed by a just life than he is by a sonorous voice. *And in your name,* that is, in you and to your honor, *I will lift up my hands,* [that is my] bodily [hands] to heaven, so that the spirit is more prompt to be moved to the Creator. For bodily ceremonies dispose not a little to internal devotion. Or [alternatively], *I will lift up my hands,* that is, I will raise up and confirm my desires and works in you as my last end: as Jeremiah admonishes, *Let us lift up our hearts with our hands to the Lord in the heavens.*[25] Also the Apostle [Paul]: *I will,* he said, *that men pray in every place, lifting up pure hands, without anger and contention.*[26]

62{63}[6] *Let my soul be filled as with marrow and fatness: and my mouth shall praise you with joyful lips.*

Sicut adipe et pinguedine repleatur anima mea, et labiis exsultationis laudabit os meum.

62{63}[6] *Sicut adipe et pinguedine, as with marrow and fatness* is filled, is fattened, and is nourished flesh, so *let my soul be filled* with internal consolation, ardent charity, and spiritually fattening grace: according to that which the Apostle [Paul] said, *Be zealous for the better gifts.*[27] *Et,* and then *labiis exsultationis laudabit os meum, my mouth shall praise you*

---

to live at all rather than to live so [without the supernatural life of grace]." *Sermones in Cantica,* LXXXI, 4, PL 183, 1173.

23   Ps. 33:2a.
24   Tob. 4:20a.
25   Lam. 3:41.
26   1 Tim. 2:8.
27   1 Cor. 12:31a.

with joyful lips: that is, my mouth will praise you with exulting lips, so that I will rejoice in your praise, and I will be moved to praise you from internal joy, and I will exhibit signs externally of mental joyfulness. For it is delightful for the lover to be engrossed with praise of the beloved; and the more we grow higher in the grace of God, the more happily we praise him; and it is a sign of great love to exult in the praise of God.

62{63}[7] *If I have remembered you upon my bed, I will meditate on you in the morning.*

Si memor fui tui super stratum meum, in matutinis meditabor in te.

62{63}[8] *Because you have been my helper. And I will rejoice under the covert of your wings.*

Quia fuisti adiutor meus, et in velamento alarum tuarum exsultabo.

62{63}[9] *My soul has stuck close to you: your right hand has received me.*

Adhaesit anima mea post te; me suscepit dextera tua.

62{63}[10] *But they have sought my soul in vain, they shall go into the lower parts of the earth.*

Ipsi vero in vanum quaesierunt animam meam: introibunt in inferiora terrae.

62{63}[11] *They shall be delivered into the hands of the sword, they shall be the portions of foxes.*

Tradentur in manus gladii; partes vulpium erunt.

62{63}[7] *Si*, if, that is because, *memor fuit tui*, I have remembered *you*, meditating, praying, lamenting, *super stratum meum*, *upon my bed*, that is, in my evening berth during the night, *in matutinis meditabor in te*, *I will meditate on you in the morning*, that is, I will contemplate you in the hour and during office of Matins,[28] and I will think upon those things that are pleasing to you. For the consequence is that he who is not forgetful of God in his bed will be able to recollect him outside of bed during the time of divine worship: and, lying in our bed, we ought

---

28   E. N. The canonical office of Matins (analogous to what in the Liturgy of the Hours called the "Office of Readings") was celebrated between 2:00 a.m. and dawn, prior to the office of Lauds. The word Matins is derived from the Latin *matutinus*, an adjective meaning pertaining to, or associated with, the morning.

to be entirely mindful of God, placing ourselves in our berth, as if in a tomb. Or [we can understand it] thus: *If I have remembered you upon my bed*, that is, in stillness and prosperity, *in the morning*, that is, with the rays of your grace illuminating me, *I will meditate upon you*, and recollect your goodness and infinite benefits. **62{63}[8]** *Quia fuisti adiutor meus, for you have been my helper*, strengthening the weakness of my nature with your grace:[29] for *by the grace of God, I am what I am.*[30]

Et in velamento alarum tuarum exsultabo, and I will rejoice under the covert of your wings: that is, I will not be secure in my own strength, nor will I rejoice in myself; but full of joy will I rest under the protection of your power and your mercy, and in repose and in safety will I rejoice. For, as it is written, God *having granted peace, who is there that can condemn?*[31] For here the Spouse [in the Song of Songs] says: *I sat down under his shadow, whom I desired: and his fruit was sweet to my palate.*[32] **62{63}[9]** O Lord, *adhaesit anima mea post te, my soul has stuck close to you*, that is, by charity it has clung to you, it is striving to come towards you, it stretches forth ahead, following the pathways of Christ, crying with the Spouse: *Draw me: we will run after you to the odor of you ointments.*[33] Our peace and our entire salvation consists in this attachment. For this reason, Jeremiah said to the Lord: *I am not troubled, following you for my pastor.*[34] This attachment produces and strengthens an ardent love of the Creator. *Me, me* the penitent, praying, confessing, and praising you, *dextera tua, your right hand*, that is, the favor of your grace, or the goodness of your presence, which so lovingly prevents me,[35] mercifully preserves me, and benignantly leads me to my consummation, *suscepit, has received* and heard. **62{63}[10]** *Ipsi vero in vanum quaesierunt animam mea, but they have sought my soul in vain*: that is, because the right hand of God received and sustained me, therefore my visible and invisible enemies have endeavored without effect to extinguish my spiritual life, to seduce my soul, or in some other way to harm it. *Introibunt, they shall go into*, because of their sins, *in inferiora terra, into the lower*

---

29   E. N. As St. Thomas enunciates a fundamental principal of Catholic doctrine: *Gratia non tollat naturam, sed perficiat*, "Grace does not do away with nature, but perfects it." ST Ia, q. 1, art. 8, ad 2.

30   1 Cor. 15:10a.

31   Job. 34:29a.

32   Songs 2:3b.

33   Songs 1:3a.

34   Jer. 17:16a.

35   E. N. The word "prevents" here means to anticipate, come before, *prae-venire*, as in prevenient grace. In this context, it does not mean to stop or hinder. For more on this, *see* footnote 17-66, Volume I.

parts of the earth, that is, in the pit of hell, about which elsewhere is written: *But yet you shall be brought down to hell, into the depth of the pit.*[36] 62{63} [11] *Tradentur in manus gladii, partes vulpium erunt; they shall be delivered into the hands of the sword, they shall be the portions of foxes*, that is, they will share in the punishment of lying men and deceitful devils.

62{63}[12]   *But the king shall rejoice in God, all they shall be praised that swear by him: because the mouth of them that speak wicked things is stopped.*

   Rex vero laetabitur in Deo; laudabuntur omnes qui iurant in eo, quia obstructum est os loquentium iniqua.

62{63}[12] *Rex vero, but the king*, that is, one ruling himself by reason and belonging to the royal priesthood of Christ,[37] *laetabitur in Deo, shall rejoice in God*, in whom alone is true and pure joy. For this reason we read in the book of Job: *If you will return ... then you shall abound in delights in the Almighty, and shall lift your face to God.*[38] But this joy in God cannot be had by the hypocrites and the deceitful, as Job says: *Will God hear the voice of the hypocrite? Or can he delight himself in the Almighty?*[39] *Laudabuntur omnes, all they shall be praised*, that is, they will be approved by God and all the saints, *qui iurant in eo, that swear by him* with appropriate virtuous works surrounding them. For to swear, under the appropriate circumstances, and done in an orderly fashion, is an act of virtue, namely of latria.[40] For it is written, *You shall perform your oaths to the Lord;*[41] and again, *You shall swear by his name.*[42] Now that which the Savior said,

---

36   Is. 14:15.

37   E. N. "Christ, high priest and unique mediator, has made of the Church 'a king-dom, priests for his God and Father.' The whole community of believers is, as such, priestly. The faithful exercise their baptismal priesthood through their participation, each according to his own vocation, in Christ's mission as priest, prophet, and king. Through the sacraments of Baptism and Confirmation the faithful are 'consecrated to be ... a holy priesthood.'" CCC § 1546 (quoting Rev. 1:6 and LG 10, § 1).

38   Job 22:23a, 26.

39   Job 27, 9a, 10a.

40   E. N. If not abused, an oath is an act of religion, and therefore is an act of virtue, even an act of worship. ST IIaIIae, q. 89, art. 4, co. *Latria*, a Latin term derived from the Greek λατρεία (*latreia*) meaning service or worship, is the theological term applied to the highest level of worship or veneration or adoration reserved for God alone, as distinguished from lower levels of respect or veneration, such as hyperdulia (reserved for the Virgin Mary) and dulia (reserved for the saints, angels, etc.).

41   Matt. 5:33.

42   Deut. 6:13b.

I say to you not to swear at all,[43] is not stated as an absolute prohibition, but [is to be understood in the sense] that we ought not swear habitually without necessity. Or [another interpretation of this part of the verse is this], *all they shall be praised that swear by him*, that is, all who strongly set forth or promise the good and faithfully follow and fulfill it. *Quia obstructum est os loquentium iniqua, because the mouth of them that speak wicked things is stopped*. It is already stopped by divine prohibition; and also in the day of judgment it will be obstructed by eternal condemnation. Nevertheless, the reprobate speak evil things in eternity: for even in hell they will blaspheme God, because he has such power by which he thus afflicts them, and prevails over them.

ARTICLE XXIV

ALLEGORICAL DECLARATION OF THE SAME SIXTY-SECOND PSALM ABOUT CHRIST.

NOW BECAUSE BLESSED DAVID REMAINED IN the desert when fleeing from the face of Saul,[44] this prefigures that which the evangelist John relates of Christ: The Jews *devised*, it says, *to put him to death. Wherefore Jesus walked not more openly*, but he was in a desert place *with his disciples*, next to *a city that is called Ephrem*.[45] Christ, therefore, as man spending time in exile, said to God the Father or to the entire blessed Trinity, the one true and most-high God.

62{63}[2] *O God, my God, to you do I watch at break of day. For you my soul has thirsted; for you my flesh, O how many ways!*

Deus, Deus meus, ad te de luce vigilo. Sitivit in te anima mea; quam multipliciter tibi caro mea!

62{63}[2] *Deus, Deus meus; O God, my God*, who is in a most special way *my God*, inasmuch as I am man, for he is most highly honored and beloved by me, *ad te de luce vigilo, to you do I watch at break of day*, that is, I always direct myself to you, with my soul infused by the splendor of the divine light. For from the beginning of its creation, the soul of Christ

---

43   Matt. 5:34a.
44   1 Sam. 23:14.
45   John 11:53b, 54b.

possessed not only the light of grace, but also the most excellent light of glory through which he unceasingly kept watch for God, loving him and looking upon him. For neither sleeping, eating, drinking, preaching, or any other occupation whatsoever hindered the soul of Christ from the actual contemplation of God in any manner; but he attended to God continually without any intermittent period. *Sitivit in te anima mea, for you my soul has thirsted*: to the extent of that [part of Christ's human nature] which was wayfaring and passible. For the soul of Christ, with respect to its superior powers that were directed toward in God, was always in the enjoyment of the blessedness of God: so he did not in a strict sense thirst in God, since thirst is the desire of an absent good; rather, he loved and embraced God himself. But in regard to his lower powers, the soul of Christ was a way-farer and passible: and so it thirsted in God, desiring accidental rewards and the delivery from all passibility. Whence also he said to his disciple: *If you loved me, you would indeed be glad, because I go to the Father.*[46] *Quam multipliciter tibi caro mea! For you my flesh [desires you], O how many ways!* For the body of Christ was subjected to many more sufferings than the soul, since it was mortal, and not glorified: and in many ways he thirsted in God, desiring resuscitation, ascension, and glorification: for which he also frequently prayed, saying, *Father, save me from this hour;*[47] and *Father, . . . glorify your son.*[48] Did not surely the body and soul of Christ thirst for God when he said: *O incredulous generation, how long shall I be with you? How long shall I suffer you?*[49] And in another place, *My God, my God, why have you forsaken me?*[50] Now, in what way the body can be said to thirst in God has been stated in the preceding exposition.[51]

62{63}[3] *In a desert land, and where there is no way, and no water: so in the holy have I come before you, to see your power and your glory.*[52]

In terra deserta, et invia, et inaquosa, sic in sancto apparui tibi, ut viderem virtutem tuam et gloriam tuam.

---

46 John 14:28b. *E. N.* His disciple would be glad because he would recognize that Christ's body would be resurrected, glorified, and made impassible; that is, it would receive the accidental rewards of Christ's obedience to the Father.

47 John 12:27b.

48 John 17:1b.

49 Mark 9:18.

50 Matt. 27:46b.

51 *E. N.* Article XXIII (Psalm 62:2).

52 *E. N.* I have changed "in the sanctuary," or "in the holy [place]" (*in sancto*), to a generic "in the holy," since Denis will apply "holy" as an adjective of desire (*desiderio*).

62{63}[3] *In terra deserta et invia et inaquosa, in a desert land, and where there is no way, and no water,* that is, in this vicious, error-filled, and [supernaturally] unfruitful world, *sic in sancto, so in the holy* desire *apparuit tibi, have I come before you.* For Christ was unacquainted with the vices of men while living among men;[53] but the divine vision always showed itself in the holy desire wherein he most ardently wished the honor of God the Father and sought the salvation of the world. *Ut viderem virtutem tuam, to see your power,* that is, that I might come to regard by experience your power by which through me and my Passion you decreed to destroy both the prince of this world and death. For Christ vanquished the devil and redeemed the world by divine power. *Et gloriam tuam, and your glory,* that is, that I might see you dispense, through my merits, the excellence of grace in the present and glory in the future to the elect. Christ most greatly desired this glory of God in the elect, for he deigned to die for it. Or [alternatively, it can be understood] thus: *to see,* not only spiritually and interiorly, but also with the bodily eye of the glorified body, your power and your glory after the Ascension into heaven: understanding by power and glory the effect of the divine power in which the power and glory of God shines forth. For, in part, the accidental reward consists of such a bodily vision.[54] Whence after the day of judgment, the heavenly bodies and [their] components will be more splendid than now, so that the blessed will delight in their bodily vision, and they will admire in themselves the divine power and glory.[55] To be sure, often in the divine Scriptures by the power and glory of God are understood the effects of the divine power, as when Christ said to Martha: *If you believe, you shall see the glory of God,* that is, the

---

53   E. N. Not that he did not know about the existence of evil, or ignored it in other men, but that he never knew them in the sense of having performed any evil, since he was sinless.

54   E. N. On the distinction between accidental reward (*e.g.,* the resurrection of the body, its glorification, the salvation of the elect) and substantial or essential reward (the vision of God), *see* footnote 1-48 in Volume 1.

55   E. N. Denis has a robust understanding of the Christian dogma of the resurrection of the dead, which is in accord with the Church's teaching. With respect to the resurrected body, the Sixteenth Synod of Toledo stated, based upon Christ's resurrected body: "[W]e believe at all times that at the close of this age we too will be resurrected, not as thin air or some shadowy phantasm, as the condemnable opinion of some affirms, but in the substance of the real flesh in which we now are and live...." DS 574. "The integrity of the body after its resurrection also demands the organs of vegetative and sensitive life, including the differences between the sexes." Ludwig Ott, *Fundamentals of Catholic Dogma* (Rockford, IL: TAN Books 1974), 491 (trans., Patrick Lynch, ed. James Canon Bastible).

glorious resurrection of her brother.[56] And in the book of Chronicles: *O Juda, and Jerusalem: fear you not, nor be you dismayed: tomorrow you shall go out against them, and the Lord will be with you,* that is, you will see the work of the great power of God.[57]

62{63}[4]   *For your mercy is better than lives: you my lips shall praise.*

Quoniam melior est misericordia tua super vitas, labia mea laudabunt te.

62{63}[5]   *Thus will I bless you all my life long: and in your name I will lift up my hands.*

Sic benedicam te in vita mea; et in nomine tuo levabo manus meas.

62{63}[4] *Quoniam melior est, for . . . better is,* O Father God, *misericordia tua, your mercy,* that is, the grace by which you prevented me,[58] filled me up, and perfected me, *super vitas, than lives,* that is, above all the life of nature, and of the grace and glory of all the elect. For much more worthy and better was the grace aggregated in Christ that the grace of all the intellectual creatures [put together], for *God does not give the Spirit by measure* to Christ as man.[59] *Labia mea laudabunt te, you my lips shall praise.* With the interior lips, that is, with the intellect, the memory, and the affections the soul of Christ unceasingly and without any interruption praised God as the blessed in heaven do. Also he praised him with bodily lips, in every opportune place and time. *Whence, I confess to you, O Father,* he said, that is, I praise you.[60] **62{63}[5]** *Sic benedicam te in vita mea, thus will I bless you all my life long.* Indeed, Christ by word and by deed most perfectly blessed God. For which reason he stated: *I honor my*

---

56   John 11:40b.

57   2 Chr. 20:17. E. N. God won the battle on behalf of Judah by having the Ammonites and Moabites fight against the inhabitants of Mount Seir (that is, the Edomites), and they destroyed each other, so that Judah defeated its enemies without even having engaged them in battle.

58   E. N. For the precise notion of "prevent" as coming before, anticipating, *prae-ve-nire, see* footnote 17-66

59   John 3:34b. E. N. "Since Christ as God is equal to the Father in all things, the Father loves Him infinitely and beyond measure; while as man He loves His Son and esteems Him more than all creatures put together." Franz Unolt, S. J., *The Christian's Model* (New York: Benziger Bros., 1895), Vol. 1, 137 (J. Allen, D. D., trans.).

60   E. N. For the Augustinian difference between the confession of sin and the confession of praise, *see* footnote 27-49 in Volume 2.

Father, . . . and *I don't seek my own glory.*[61] *Et in nomine tuo, and in your name*, that is, in your power, or to the honor of your name, *levabo manus meas, I will lift up my hands*, that is, I will direct all my desires and my deeds to you, God most high, and I will order them toward the heavenly beatitude of those others who, because of me, will be found worthy of [enjoying]. Or [alternatively,] *I will lift my hands*, my bodily [hands], to you in prayer which I poured when my Passion drew nigh, and on the Cross, when I offered myself to you *an acceptable, well-pleasing sacrifice.*[62]

62{63}[6] *Let my soul be filled as with marrow and fatness: and my mouth shall praise you with joyful lips.*

Sicut adipe et pinguedine repleatur anima mea, et labiis exsultationis laudabit os meum.

62{63}[6] *Sicut adipe et pinguedine repleatur anima mea, let my soul be filled as with marrow and fatness* with the joy of accidental reward, especially the salvation of the elect. Now Christ did not pray for an increase of grace, habitual grace, or essential reward because in such things he was perfect from the beginning and he was not able to increase in such things. *Et labiis exsultationis laudabit os meum, and my mouth shall praise you with joyful lips*, that is, with joyful mouth and a jocund heart I will give thanks to you for all the aggregate benefits of my elect, and I will with great exultation praise, O God, your goodness.

62{63}[7] *If I have remembered you upon my bed, I will meditate on you in the morning.*

Si memor fui tui super stratum meum, in matutinis meditabor in te.

62{63}[8] *Because you have been my helper. And I will rejoice under the covert of your wings.*

Quia fuisti adiutor meus, et in velamento alarum tuarum exsultabo.

62{63}[9] *My soul has stuck close to you: your right hand has received me.*

Adhaesit anima mea post te; me suscepit dextera tua.

62{63}[7] *Si memor fui tui super stratum meum, if I have remembered you upon my bed*: that is, because upon the Cross in which I was

---

61   John 8:49b, 40a.
62   Phil 4:18.

weakened and upon which I died, I remembered you, saying, O Father, *Why have you forsaken me?*[63] And *Father, forgive them;*[64] and *Father, in your hands I commend my spirit;*[65] *in matutinis, in the morning,* that is, at the time of the Resurrection, *meditabor in te, I will meditate on you.* For then [after his Resurrection] Christ without sorrow will recall the goodness and benefits of the Father and His own Passion, saying to his disciples: *Ought not Christ to have suffered these things?*[66] **62{63}[8]** *Quia fuisti adiutor meus, because you have been my helper,* cooperating with me in the redemption of the human race and raising me up again from death. *Et in velamento alarum tuarum exsultabo, and I will rejoice under the covert of your wings,* that is, I will always rejoice in your protection. For with respect to this Christ said to the Jews: The Father *has not left me alone.*[67] **62{63}[9]** *Adhaesit anima mea post te, my soul has stuck close to you,* for it always loved you with all its heart, all its strength, and all its mind, and it fulfilled perfectly in this life the precepts of charity — something that is not possible to any existing wayfarer. *Me suscepit dextera tua, your right hand has received me* in the Ascension, when you placed me at your right hand in heaven.[68] Or [alternatively], *your right hand has received me,* that is, the Word, or your Son, assumed my human nature. For in the way that the Holy Spirit is called the finger of God,[69] because it shows and teaches God and hidden things by illumination; so the Son is called the arm and the right hand of the Father because he is the power of God,[70] and he upholds *all things by the word of his power,*[71] according to his Apostle.

62{63}[10] But they have sought my soul in vain, they shall go into the lower parts of the earth.

Ipsi vero in vanum quaesierunt animam meam: introibunt in inferiora terrae.

---

63   Matt. 27:46b.
64   Luke 23:34a. E. N. Denis's version states *ignosce illis* instead of the Sixto-Clementine's *dimitte illis,* but without great change in meaning.
65   Luke 23:46a.
66   Luke 24:26a.
67   John 8:29a.
68   *Cf.* Mark 16:19.
69   Luke 11:20a: *But if I by the finger of God cast out devils; doubtless the kingdom of God is come upon you.*
70   *Cf.* 1 Cor. 1:24: *But unto them that are called, both Jews and Greeks, Christ the power of God, and the wisdom of God.*
71   Heb. 1:3b.

62{63}[11] *They shall be delivered into the hands of the sword, they shall be the portions of foxes.*

> *Tradentur in manus gladii; partes vulpium erunt.*

62{63}[10] *Ipsi vero,* but they, namely, the unbelieving Jews, *in vanum, in vain,* that is, against the salvation of their souls, *quaesierunt animam meam, sought my soul,* [my] corporal [soul],[72] so as to extinguish it. *Introibunt, they shall go into,* because the sin committed against me, *in inferiora terrae, into the lower parts of the earth,* that is, into deep hell;[73] **62{63}[11]** *tradentur in manus gladii,* they shall be delivered into the hands of the sword, that is, in the power of the swords of the Romans, namely, Titus and Vespasian, who will annihilate them with fire and sword; *partes vulpium erunt,* they shall be the portions of foxes, that is, the portion and possession of the most deceptive demons: for not believing in Christ, they have become sons of demons, belonging to their portion. For this reason Christ said to them: *You are of your father the devil.*[74] And literally also the [bodies of the] Jews became parts of foxes since their unburied cadavers were handed over to foxes, wild beasts, and birds to be devoured.[75]

62{63}[12] *But the king shall rejoice in God, all they shall be praised that swear by him: because the mouth of them that speak wicked things is stopped.*

> *Rex vero laetabitur in Deo; laudabuntur omnes qui iurant in eo, quia obstructum est os loquentium iniqua.*

62{63}[12] *Rex vero,* but the king, namely, Christ, of whom we read in Revelation: *And his name is called the Word of God, . . . and he has on his garment and on his thigh written, King of kings, and Lord of lords.*[76] This king *laetabitur, shall rejoice* unceasingly *in Deo, in God,* as was spoken

---

72   E. N. This is an unusual expression; presumably, by "corporal soul," *anima corporalem,* Denis means the soul of Christ to the extent it is the animating force, the form, of his body and its separation from his body, resulting in his death. Or perhaps he is referring to Christ's soul in terms of its vegetative and sensitive functions. Denis would recognize that the rational soul, in and of itself, is naturally a spirit and therefore not subject to being put to death by the unbelieving Jews.

73   E. N. By "deep hell" Denis refers to the hell of the damned.

74   John 8:44a.

75   E. N. This description is probably based upon Flavius Josephus, *The Wars of the Jews,* V, 12, 3, 523, where he describes the scene during the Siege of Jerusalem.

76   Rev. 19:13b, 16.

about in a Psalm above: *In your strength, O Lord, the king shall joy; and in your salvation he shall rejoice exceedingly.*[77] *Laudabuntur omnes qui iurant in eo,* all they shall be praised that swear by him: according to the sense proposed in the preceding exposition. In the manner that they swore, the second book of Chronicles says: *With all their heart they swore, and with all their will they sought him, and they found him.*[78] *Quia obstructum est os loquentium iniqua,* because the mouth of them that speak wicked things is stopped. Now, of course, the Lord Jesus stopped the mouth of the Jews in blaspheming and seeking to destroy him. For they said: Lest at any time *the Romans will come and take away our place and nation.*[79] They desired also totally to erase the name and memory of Jesus. And yet behold: God caught the crafty *in their craftiness,*[80] because he caused exactly the opposite to befall them. For they lost that very place or birthland and people [they sought to protect by killing him], and the name of the Lord Savior after the Passion was much more widely glorified than before.

See how most sweet and with such affection this Psalm is, whose virtue and sweetness the devout and loving mind savors. Let us endeavor, therefore, always mentally to watch for the Lord, as the Apostle said to Timothy: *But be vigilant, labor in all things, . . . Be sober.*[81] And Christ to his disciples: *Watch,* he said, *and pray, that you do not enter into temptation.*[82] Our soul is sated by God: and *we walk in the flesh,* but we do not live life in a carnal way;[83] rather, let us wait upon the Lord our God in holy desire, and let us be most concerned with him; indeed, let us always remain firm in the grace of God, and let us desire rather not to be than to be without any of God's mercy, than to be without charity and without grace. Let us praise God at all times, in all places, and in our life, and let us lift up pure hands unto him, and let us always endeavor to advance in the divine love.

---

77   Ps. 20:20. *E. N. See* Article XLVIII (Psalm 20:2), Volume 1: "For Christ . . . insofar as he was man, he did not rejoice in himself, but in God."

78   2 Chr. 15:15.

79   John 11:48b.

80   Job. 5:13.

81   2 Tim. 4:5.

82   Matt. 26:41a.

83   *Cf.* 2 Cor. 10:3: *For though we walk in the flesh, we do not war according to the flesh.*

PRAYER

GOD, OUR GOD, MAKE US TO WATCH FOR you and to thirst for you in the prayer of the light of your Spirit, so that, having been granted your grace, our soul may be filled as with the marrow and fatness of virtues, and which adhering to you, it may be received in heaven by your right hand.[84]

Deus, Deus noster, fac nos in oratione de luce Spiritus tui ad
te vigilare, ac in te sitire: ut tua praestante gratia, adipe
et virtutum pinguedine repleatur anima nostra, quo
tibi adhaerentem eam in caelestibus suscipiat
dextera tua.

---

84   Luke 21:19: *In your patience you shall possess your souls.*

Psalm 63

ARTICLE XXV

EXPOSITION OF CHRIST OF THE SIXTY-THIRD PSALM: *EXAUDI, DEUS, ORATIONEM MEAM, CUM DEPRECOR.* HEAR, O GOD, MY PRAYER, WHEN I MAKE SUPPLICATION TO YOU.

63{64}[1] *Unto the end, a Psalm for David.*

  In finem. Psalmus David.

OW THE TITLE OF THIS PRESENT PSALM IS: 63{64}[1] *In finem, Psalmus David; unto the end, a Psalm for David:* that is, this Psalm, directing us to the ultimate end, pertains to Christ who is prefigured by David.

63{64}[2] *Hear, O God, my prayer, when I make supplication to you: deliver my soul from the fear of the enemy.*

  Exaudi, Deus, orationem meam cum deprecor; a timore inimici eripe animam meam.

Therefore, Christ as a passible, wayfaring man, now close to his Passion, said to God, the Father: 63{64}[2] *Exaudi, Deus, orationem meam cum deprecor; hear, O God, my prayer, when I make supplication to you:* or with respect to myself, as when I said: *Father, if you willed it to be, remove this chalice from me; yet not my will . . . be done;*[1] and again, Father *glorify you me . . . with the glory which I had before the world was.*[2] Or [it can be understood in this manner], for my Mystical Body, as when I said: *I have prayed for you, Peter, that your faith fail not;*[3] and again, *Holy Father, keep them in your name who you have given me.*[4] *A timore inimici eripe animam meam, deliver my soul from the fear of the enemy.* Christ who came to die for the world, and who was confirmed in good, did not pray absolutely that he might not be killed, or that he might not through inordinate terror fall into vice. Why then did he pray saying,

1 Luke 22:42a.
2 John 17:5.
3 Luke 22:32a.
4 John 17:11b.

233

deliver me from the fear of the enemy? [He did so] for no other reason
than either that the natural fear of death recede from him, or that he
might be raised up unto the impassible life in which no one would be
able to cause him dread or persecute him. For then — when he rose up
into an immortal state — he would be secured from all fear of adversaries.

63{64}[3] *You have protected me from the assembly of the malignant;
from the multitude of the workers of iniquity.*

*Protexisti me a conventu malignantium, a multitudine ope-
rantium iniquitatem.*

63{64}[3] *Protexisti me a conventu malignantium, you have protected
me from the assembly of the malignant,* that is, from the false counsel of
the Jews, who frequently tested me so that they might ensnare me and
accuse me.[5] God protected Christ from this throng, for by the infused
wisdom in his soul he was able to respond to them in a blameless manner,
so that even his adversaries said: *Never did man speak like this man.*[6] *You
also protected me, O Lord Father, a multitudine operantium iniquitatem,
from the multitude of the workers of iniquity,* that is, from the Jews wishing
to throw me off the high ridge,[7] and stone me at Solomon's porch:[8] for
these men I was able to avoid by divine power, for I was made invisible
to them.[9] Whence John said: *But Jesus hid himself;*[10] and again, *They
sought therefore to take him; and he escaped out of their hands.*[11] For Jesus
was able to render himself invisible, if he so desired, to others.

63{64}[4] *For they have whetted their tongues like a sword; they have
bent their bow a bitter thing,*

*Quia exacuerunt ut gladium linguas suas; intenderunt arcum
rem amaram,*

63{64}[5] *To shoot in secret the undefiled.*

Ut sagittent in occultis immaculatum.

---

5 Matt. 22:15: *Then the Pharisees … consulted among themselves how to ensnare
him in his speech.*
6 John 7:46b.
7 Luke 4:29: *And they rose up and thrust him out of the city; and they brought him to
the brow of the hill, whereon their city was built, that they might cast him down headlong.*
8 John 10:31: *The Jews then took up stones to stone him.*
9 Luke 4:30: *But he passing through the midst of them, went his way.*
10 John 8:59b.
11 John 10:39.

63{64}[6] *They will shoot at him on a sudden, and will not fear: they are resolute in wickedness. They have talked of hiding snares; they have said: Who shall see them?*

Subito sagittabunt eum, et non timebunt; firmaverunt sibi sermonem nequam. Narraverunt ut absconderent laqueos; dixerunt: Quis videbit eos?

63{64}[4] *Quia exacuerunt, for they have whetted,* [that is,] the unfaithful Jews [have whetted], *ut gladium linguas suas, their tongues like a sword,* saying things against me with deadly words, namely: *Away with him, away with him, crucify him.*[12] *Intenderunt arcum rem amaram, they have bent their bow a bitter thing,* that is, they have prepared deceitful and insidious things for me, saying: *Not on the festival day, lest perhaps there should be a tumult among the people.*[13] And also: He was sold and betrayed by his disciple, he was condemned by the governor [Pilate], he was killed by his soldiers; *let us do all this, and let it appear we have done nothing.*[14] Yet this they did, **63{64}[5]** *ut sagittent in occultis immaculatum, to shoot in secret the undefiled,* that is, so that they might harm and destroy in secret — that is, hiddenly, with others unaware of their cunning — Christ, the lamb without the stain [of sin]. For so did the chiefs of the priests with their followers desire to kill Christ, that neither Pilate nor others would know the false machinations against Christ, and so that Christ also might be seized by them in an unforeseen manner, for they supposed him not to know of their counsel. **63{64} [5]** *Subito sagittabunt eum, they will shoot at him on a sudden,* that is, they will kill Christ suddenly. For they had not seized him and bound him for a long time before they directly handed him over bound before Pilate, and on that very day crucified him.[15] *Et non timebunt, and they will not fear* God in such a wicked action. For *they were blinded* and were made obstinate *by their own malice.*[16] For this reason, follows with: *Firmaverunt sibi sermonem nequam, they are resolute in wickedness,* that is, they pertinaciously sought to kill Jesus by the governor [Pilate]. Whence Luke says: *But they were instant with loud voices, requiring that he might be crucified; and their voices prevailed.*[17] For how much did Pilate do so

---

12   John 19:15a.
13   Matt. 26:5.
14   *E. N. Nos totum faciamus, et nihil fecisse videamur.* This is a quote from St. Augustine's *Exposition on the Psalm* 63:9. PL 36, 765.
15   Matt. 27:2, 31.
16   Wis. 2:21b.
17   Luke 23:23.

that he might release him! But they reaffirmed their evil words saying: *If you release this man, you are not Caesar's friend.*[18] When he heard this, Pilate, fearing man more than he did God, sat down in the judgment seat and condemned the Saint of Saints to death.[19]

Narraverunt, they talked, that is, among themselves they discussed, *ut absconderent laqueos, of hiding snares,* so that the procedures and the snares of the death may appear hidden to Christ. And so early in the morning in the day before the Passover *they brought him into their council, saying: If you be the Christ, tell us:*[20] and hearing his response, they accused him before Pilate. And also in the same manner they said: *We have a law; and according to the law he ought to die, because he made himself the Son of God.*[21] *Dixerunt, they have said* among themselves: *Quis videbit eos? Who shall see them?* That is, who will recognize our fraudulent machinations against this Jesus? For as it turned out, they did not reckon their malice to be manifest to all. For we read in the Acts of the Apostles, that they desired to excuse themselves of the death of Christ, saying to the Apostles: *Behold, you have filled Jerusalem with your doctrine, and you have a mind to bring the blood of this man upon us.*[22]

63{64}[7] *They have searched after iniquities: they have failed in their search. Man shall come to a deep heart:*

Scrutati sunt iniquitates; defecerunt scrutantes scrutinio. Accedet homo ad cor altum:

63{64}[7] *Scrutati sunt iniquitates, they have searched after iniquities:* that is, with great deliberation and industry they have thought about the ways and means by which they would kill Christ, in the way that John says: *The chief priests therefore, and the Pharisees, gathered a council, and said: What do we, for this man does many miracles?*[23] And Matthew: *And they consulted together,* he says, *that by subtilty they might apprehend Jesus, and put him to death.*[24] *Defecerunt, they have failed,* that is, their longed for effects were frustrated, *scrutantes scrutinia, in their search,* that is, in the searching by the council of the Jews for the manner to get rid of Christ. And they did so for these reasons: they killed him so that the

---

18   John 19:12b.
19   John 19:13, 16.
20   Luke 22:66b.
21   John 19:7.
22   Acts 5:28b.
23   John 11:47.
24   Matt. 26:4.

Romans would not come and take away their place and nation;[25] and they wanted not only to kill Jesus, but to *condemn him to a most shameful death*[26] in order that his name and memory would be entirely lost to posterity, in the way we read in Jeremiah: *Let us cut him off from the land of the living, and let his name be remembered no more.*[27] And see the very opposite [of what they planned] happened. For they either were killed by the Romans, or they were driven out and deprived of all the glory of the paternal law. But Christ bore much fruit from his Passion, for he merited the conversion of the whole world to the faith. For this reason he said: *Unless the grain of wheat falling into the ground die, it remains alone; but if it die, it brings forth much fruit.*[28] Indeed, he compares himself to a grain of wheat, because he was the grain of wheat killed by the malice of the Jews and multiplied by the conversion of the Gentiles.

Accedet homo et cor altum, man shall come to a deep heart, that is, the man Christ, by means of his deep and most wise heart, shall proceed to the Passion willingly, as an earlier Psalm says: *Burnt offering and sin offering you did not require; then said I, Behold I come.*[29] And the witness John said: *No man takes my soul away from me: but I lay it down.*[30] *He was offered because it was his own will.*[31] So by that which is said — *a man shall come to a deep heart* — the same thing is signified.[32] In the same manner it is elsewhere written, *And I and my soul will rejoice in him:*[33] not that a man and a soul are two diverse [objects] rejoicing; but because the soul is the proximate cause of joy, for by it man is made glad if he lives and reasons by it. What is just now said — *man shall come to a deep heart* — is said in the same way. For the heart, that is, the intellect, is the cause of man assenting to those things that are pleasing to God, for the intellect directs human acts. Others have [this understanding]: *man shall come to a deep heart,* that is, Christ by contemplation shall come to the profound contemplation and mystical counsel of God, pondering, namely, the manner it was decreed by the sovereign Trinity to

---

25 John 11:48: *If we let him alone so, all will believe in him; and the Romans will come, and take away our place and nation.*

26 Wis. 2:20.

27 Jer. 11:19b.

28 John 12:24b-25a.

29 Ps. 39:7b-8a.

30 John 10:18a.

31 Is. 53:7a.

32 E. N. In other words, a man with a deep heart signifies a man that acts voluntarily to undertake a magnanimous act.

33 Tob. 13:9.

save the world through his Passion. For to this heart Christ drew near, when praying he said: *But not my will be done, but yours;*[34] and again, for *thus it is written, and thus it behooved Christ.*[35]

63{64}[8]   *And God shall be exalted. The arrows of children are their wounds:*

Et exaltabitur Deus. Sagittae parvulorum factae sunt plagae eorum:

63{64}[9]   *And their tongues against them are made weak. All that saw them were troubled:*

Et infirmatae sunt contra eos linguae eorum. Conturbati sunt omnes qui videbant eos:

63{64}[10]   *And every man was afraid. And they declared the works of God: and understood his doings.*

Et timuit omnis homo. Et annuntiaverunt opera Dei; et facta eius intellexerunt.

63{64}[8] *Et exaltabitur Deus, and God shall be exalted,* that is, Christ, who approached the Passion as man, was recognized in the Resurrection to be God [and thus exalted]. For God is exalted not that his divinity is made more perfect or more sublime, but because he is raised up to sublime heights in the created minds, when they who before did not know him or did not fear him begin to know, adore, and worship him. And so in the Resurrection the Lord Jesus was exalted, in the manner the Apostle [Paul] states: *We see Jesus . . . for the suffering of death, crowned with glory and honor.*[36] Or [we can understand this verse] thus: *God shall be exalted,* that is, God the Trinity approached by Christ [the man] with a deep heart, will be glorified by the same Christ, and will be made illustrious to the whole world, where he will be held in honor. For this reason Christ was made incarnate and suffered, so that God would be known and honored by the whole world. For which reason he said in John: *Just Father, the world has not known you; but I have known you, . . . and I have made known your name to them.*[37] And in his first epistle, John openly speaking says: *We know that the Son of God is come, and he has given us understanding, that we may know the true God.*[38]

---

34   Luke 22:42b.
35   Luke 24:46b.
36   Heb. 2:9a.
37   John 17:25a, 26a.
38   1 John 5:20a.

Sagittae parvulorum factae sunt plagae eorum, the arrows of children are their wounds. This can be understood in many ways. The first way is this: *The arrows of children,* that is, the snares and the persecutions brought against Christ by the Jews, *are their wounds* because by them they deserved to be killed by the Romans and to be eternally damned: indeed, they spiritually killed themselves. Now the Jews are called children not because of their humility, but because of their envy, for every envious person makes one a child, according to this: *Anger indeed kills the foolish, and envy slays the child.*[39] For the envious person, by the very fact that he envies another, is diminished, and shows himself to be lacking the good of another: because envy is sadness of another's good, according to which one estimates his own excellence to be less, as the Philosopher says.[40] 63{64}

[9] *Et infirmatae sunt contra eos linguae eorum, and their tongues against them are made weak,* that is, the speech, accusations, and the counsel of the Jews were deprived of their intended effect (as has already been made clear): and this *against them,* that is, to their evil, because the evil that they had prepared for Christ, found its way back to them, and the words by which they said, *His blood be upon us and our children,*[41] obtained for them an abject death. The second [way of understanding these words] is thus: *the arrows of children,* that is, the preaching and the words of the humble Apostles of Christ, *are their wounds,* namely of the Jews. For by the preaching of the Apostles, Christ was made illustrious, and the Jews were confused, subdued, and sent into exile. *And . . . against them are made weak,* namely, the Apostles of Christ and other believers, *their tongues,* namely, [the tongues] of the Jews. For they were unable to resist the words and miracles of the disciples of the Lord Savior. Whence it is written: The chiefs of the priests *seeing the constancy of Peter and of John, understanding that they were illiterate and ignorant men, they*

---

39 Job 5:2. E. N. I have replaced "little one" in the Douay Rheims with "child" for the Latin *parvulum,* so that it ties into Denis's *Commentary.* In his *Commentary on Job,* Denis explains (drawing upon Pope St. Gregory the Great) that envy, which is opposed to charity, slays the envious person who is made a child by the envy: "He who is [spiritually] killed by envy is a child because he is revealed to be so by his own testimony, since he is smaller than the one by whom he is tormented." Doctoris Ecstatici D. Dionysii Cartusiani, *Opera Omnia,* Vol. 13 (Montreuil: 1897), 375. So envy both makes a man a child (less in stature than the one he envies) and then spiritually kills him by slaying sanctifying grace and charity in his soul.

40 E. N. Aristotle defines envy (φθόνος *phthonos*) as the pain caused by the good fortune of others which necessarily means one views oneself as deficient or possessing less of the good possessed by the one envied. *Eth. Nich.,* II.7, 1108b; *see also Rhet.* II.9, 1386b.

41 Matt. 27:25b.

wondered;[42] and again, *They were not able to resist the wisdom and the Spirit that spoke* through Stephen.[43] The third [way of understanding this] is thus: *The arrows of children are their wounds*, that is, the wounds that the Jews inflicted upon Christ were similar to the arrows of children because as the arrows of children are insubstantial and do not inflict injury, and if they injure at all the wound inflicted is quickly healed, so the wounds suffered by Christ from the Jews were in vain and were unable to detain him in death, but Christ was able to rise on the third day healed of all injuries and immortal. *And their tongues against them are made weak*: that is, the Jews were unable to prove or defend their own assertions. For as we read, when the guards of the sepulcher stated what they had seen, namely, the shaking of the earth and the angel descending, the Jewish leaders gave them much money so that they would say that Jesus was stolen away by the disciples while they slept.[44] Now this artifice is easily disproved. For if the guards had slept they would not have been able to know by which means the body of Christ had been taken. Nor does it have the appearance [of veracity] that the disciples — who fled from their Master while he was still alive — would return now that he was dead in the midst of armed soldiers. And finally it is well-nigh impossible that they slept so deeply that the rotation of the stone from the monument would not have resulted in their arousal. For it was a very great stone,[45] diligently sealed, and forcibly impressed,[46] for which reason without it would not be able to have been removed without great noise.

Conturbati sunt, they were troubled, that is, [they were troubled] with compunction and moved to repentance, *omnes qui videbant eos, all that saw them*, that is, all who recognized that the Jews by killing Christ had so direly sinned by shedding innocent blood. For this the centurion in the Gospels said, in seeing that Jesus had breathed his last, he greatly feared, and giving glory to God said: *Indeed this was the Son of God.*[47] And Luke says: *All the multitude of them that were come together to that sight, and saw the things that were done, returned striking their breasts.*[48] Also, after the Resurrection, through the preaching of Peter, hearts were

---

42   Acts 4:13a.
43   Acts 6:10. E. N. Stephen being the deacon Stephen, the *protomartyr*, who was "full of grace and fortitude," and "did great wonders and signs among the people." Acts 6:8.
44   Matt. 28:11–13.
45   Mark 16:4b.
46   Matt. 27:66.
47   Matt. 27:54b.
48   Luke 23:48.

stung with remorse, and eight thousand Jews converted to Christ.[49] For at that time was fulfilled that which Christ before the Passion had predicted: *When you shall have lifted up the Son of man, then shall you know, that I am he.*[50] **63{64}[10]** *Et timuit omnis homo, and every man was afraid*: not in a strict sense every man, but as applied to the kinds of individuals,[51] for some of all kinds of men converted to Christ and feared God. *Annuntiaverunt opera Dei, and they declared the works of God,* that is, some of those Christians that have been mentioned praised, and some of them announced the works and the miracles of Christ, especially the Apostles of whom this is especially said. Of whom is also added: *et facta eius, and his doings*, namely [the doings] of Christ, *intellexerunt, they understood*, by the illumination of the Holy Spirit, in particular after the day of Pentecost when Christ fulfilled that which he had promised to them: *I*, he said, will send *the promise of my Father upon you*;[52] and again, *When he, the Spirit of truth, is come, he will teach you all truth.*[53]

63{64}[11] *The just shall rejoice in the Lord, and shall hope in him: and all the upright in heart shall be praised.*

> *Laetabitur iustus in Domino, et sperabit in eo; et laudabuntur omnes recti corde.*

63{64}[11] *Laetabitur iustus, the just shall rejoice* — justified by the grace of Christ and redeemed by his Blood — *in Domino, in the Lord*, not in unlawful and fleeting things, as the Apostle said: *Rejoice in the Lord always; again, I say, rejoice.*[54] *Et sperabit in eo, and they shall hope in him*, that is, in the mercy of God, and not in their own justice, hoping by the merits of Christ to be led into blessed immortality; *et laudabuntur, and . . . shall be praised* by Christ the Judge, *omnes recti corde, all the upright in heart*, who in holiness and justice served God.[55] For Christ will say to them: *Come, you blessed of my Father, [possess the kingdom prepared for you from the foundation of the world].*[56]

---

49   Acts 2:37, 41; 4:4.
50   John 8:28.
51   *E. N. distributio pro generibus singulorum*: a distribution of the genera (kinds) of each individual. It means at least some of every kind of men feared God and became Christian.
52   Luke 23:48a.
53   John 16:13a.
54   Phil. 4:4.
55   *Cf.* Matt. 25:34–40; Luke 1:75,
56   Matt. 25:34b. *E. N.* The parts in brackets substitutes for the "etc." contained in the Latin text.

ARTICLE XXVI

TROPOLOGICAL OR MORAL EXPOSITION
OF THE SAME SIXTY-THIRD PSALM:

IN THE WAY THAT SOME CATHOLIC TEACH-ers, among whom is Cassiodorus,[57] expound the third penitential Psalm[58] literally as referring to holy Job, so some literally expound this present Psalm as referring to Daniel,[59] imitating in this (as they put it) the ancient Hebrew teachers. But, like the third penitential Psalm is fittingly explained to apply to any true penitent, so this present Psalm equally may be explained as applying to any just man facing afflictions, especially in the persons of martyrs, any one of whom can say:

63{64}[2] *Hear, O God, my prayer, when I make supplication to you: deliver my soul from the fear of the enemy.*

Exaudi, Deus, orationem meam cum deprecor; a timore inimici eripe animam meam.

63{64}[2] *Exaudi, Deus, orationem meam cum deprecor; hear, O God, my prayer, when I make supplication to you,* that is, when I pray with the most heartfelt affection. The Roman translation has, "when I am afflicted (*cum tribulor*)." For we most especially are in need to be heard and to be kept safe when suffering afflictions. So he who thus prays to God will certainly be heard, in the way that Moses said: *When you shall seek there the Lord your God, you shall find him: yet so, if you seek him with all your heart, and all the affliction of your soul.*[60] *A timore inimici eripe anima meam, deliver my soul from the fear of the enemy:* not so that I may not be tempted by demons nor that I may not sustain persecution in the world, since *through many tribulations we must enter into the kingdom of*

---

57   E. N. Flavius Magnus Aurelius Cassiodorus (*ca.* 485–*ca.* 585) was a Roman Senator who wrote a commentary on the Psalms, *Expositio Psalmorum.* These have been translated from Latin to English by P. G. Walsh, and published in three volumes by the Paulist Press.

58   Psalm 37(38).

59   E. N. The prophet Daniel is the protagonist of the biblical Book of Daniel, among other things famous for interpreting the dreams of the Babylonian king Nebuchadnezzar, surviving being thrown into a fiery furnace with his companions Shadrach, Meshack, and Abednego by Nebuchadnezzar, and being thrown in a lion's den by king Darius.

60   Deut. 4:29.

God;[61] but that I will not fear with inordinate anxiety the enemies of my soul, and that I might fulfill that which you, O Lord Jesus, command: *Be not afraid of them who kill the body;*[62] and: *In the world you shall have distress: but have confidence, I have overcome the world.*[63] In this regard we read in Isaiah: *Fear not the reproach of men and . . . their blasphemies.*[64]

63{64}[3] *You have protected me from the assembly of the malignant; from the multitude of the workers of iniquity.*

> *Protexisti me a conventu malignantium, a multitudine operantium iniquitatem.*

63{64}[3] *Protexisti me a conventu malignantium, you have protected me from the assembly of the malignant,* so that their wicked counsel was not harmful to me, nor did my heart correspond to their malignancy. God in this way protected the holy martyrs who unconquerably held out before tyrants and who were protected from all their deceit. *You have protected me* also *a multitudine operantium iniquitatem, from the multitude of the workers of iniquity,* that I would not be perverted by the perverse,[65] or would not be overcome with fear from their sheer number. This also can be said to apply to someone who strongly resists the temptations of demons and — protected by God — victoriously evades their snares: but also [it can be said] especially of those that are cloistered and who, on account of Christ, have forsaken the world and all things that are in the world, and effectively perform their service to God in a monastery; they are able to say this verse, giving thanks to God. For God truly protects those *from the assembly of the malignant,* that is, from the tumults of neighbors and friends living in carnal ways and dismissive of the cloistered way of life. They are also protected from the *multitude of the workers of iniquity,* that is, from worldly men. Of these sorts of persons John in his first epistle says: *Whatever is in the world, is the concupiscence of the flesh, and the concupiscence of the eyes, and the pride of life.*[66] They are also protected from these things, not that they are absolutely secure, but because they already have one foot in paradise: for of them the Savior said: *Every one that has left [house, or brethren, or sisters,] or*

---

61 Acts 14:21b.
62 Luke 12:4a.
63 Luke 12:4b.
64 Is. 51:7b.
65 Cf. Ps. 17:27: *And with the elect you will be elect: and with the perverse you will be perverted.*
66 1 John 2:16.

father, or mother, [or wife, or children, or lands for my name's sake, shall receive an hundredfold, and shall possess life everlasting].[67]

63{64}[4] *For they have whetted their tongues like a sword; they have bent their bow a bitter thing,*

> *Quia exacuerunt ut gladium linguas suas; intenderunt arcum rem amaram,*

63{64}[5] *To shoot in secret the undefiled.*

> *Ut sagittent in occultis immaculatum.*

63{64}[6] *They will shoot at him on a sudden, and will not fear: they are resolute in wickedness. They have talked of hiding snares; they have said: Who shall see them?*

> *Subito sagittabunt eum, et non timebunt; firmaverunt sibi sermonem nequam. Narraverunt ut absconderent laqueos; dixerunt: Quis videbit eos?*

63{64}[4] *Quia exacuerunt, for they have whetted,* [that is,] the unfaithful Jews [have whetted], *ut gladium linguas suas, their tongues like a sword,* saying things against me with deadly words, namely: *Away with him, away with him, crucify him.*[68] *Intenderunt arcum rem amaram, they have bent their bow a bitter thing,* that is, they have thought up fraudulent traps, **63{64}[5]** *ut sagittent in occultis immaculatum, to shoot in secret the undefiled,* that is, since they secretly afflict, injure, malign, and destroy the innocent man walking in the law of the Lord. **63{64}[6]** *Subito sagittabunt eum, they will shoot at him on a sudden,* that is, they will lead him to an unexpected harm. Hence Christ said to his disciples: *If they have persecuted me, they will also persecute you,* for *the servant is not greater than his master.*[69] *Et non timebunt, and they will not fear* God: for sometimes they so blind themselves with envy and with malice that they do not see themselves

---

67   Matt. 19:29. E. N. I have added the part in brackets in part to supplant Denis's "*etc.*" "As a way of showing forth the Church's holiness, it is to be recognized that the consecrated life, which mirrors Christ's own way of life, has an objective superiority. Precisely for this reason, it is an especially rich manifestation of gospel values and a more complete expression of the Church's purpose, which is the sanctification of humanity. The consecrated life proclaims and in a certain way anticipates the future age, when the fullness of the Kingdom of Heaven, already present in its first fruits and in mystery, will be achieved and when the children of the resurrection will take neither wife nor husband, but will be like the angels of God." Pope St. John Paul II, *Vita Consecrata*, 32.

68   John 19:15a.

69   John 16:20; *cf.* John 13:16.

as sinning, so that the Lord declares: *The hour comes, that whosoever kills you, will think that he does a service to God.*[70] *Firmaverunt sibi sermonem nequam, they are resolute in wickedness,* not willing to heed threats or being led to piety and truth; but they busy themselves to produce the effects of that which they have conceived in their mind. *Narraverunt ut absconderent laqueos, they have talked of hiding snares:* that is, such evil men, as well as demons, discuss among themselves the manner by which they might spread the ways of perdition among good men and hurl them down into the pit of sin, death, and damnation. For incessantly they — especially the demons — endeavor to harm in a hidden manner by proposing evil things under the guise of the good, and (as the Apostle says) they transform themselves into angels of light.[71]

63{64}[7] *They have searched after iniquities: they have failed in their search. Man shall come to a deep heart:*

Scrutati sunt iniquitates; defecerunt scrutantes scrutinio. Accedet homo ad cor altum:

63{64}[8] *And God shall be exalted. The arrows of children are their wounds:*

Et exaltabitur Deus. Sagittae parvulorum factae sunt plagae eorum:

63{64}[9] *And their tongues against them are made weak. All that saw them were troubled:*

Et infirmatae sunt contra eos linguae eorum. Conturbati sunt omnes qui videbant eos:

63{64}[10] *And every man was afraid. And they declared the works of God: and understood his doings.*

Et timuit omnis homo. Et annuntiaverunt opera Dei; et facta eius intellexerunt.

63{64}[7] *Scrutati sunt iniquitates,* they have searched after iniquities: that is, they have traced out diligently the ways to harm, as is written in Micah: *Every one hunts his brother to death.*[72] *Defecerunt scrutantes scrutinia,* they have failed in their search: because they were unable to

---

70   John 16:2b.
71   *Cf.* 2 Cor. 11:14: *And no wonder: for Satan himself transforms himself into an angel of light.*
72   Micah 7:2b.

divert those who are just by faith and truth in the manner that Christ in the Gospel promises the just: *I will give you a mouth and wisdom, which all your adversaries shall not be able to resist and gainsay.*[73] Finally, do not tyrants who strive to stamp out altogether the name of Christians completely fail? For the more horrible the torments inflicted upon the martyrs the more excellently has the glorious and mighty God made wonderful his saints;[74] and so the Catholic faith increases much more amply within a time of torment than during a time of peace: in which, of course, the almighty power of Christ and the truth of the faith are most brightly vindicated, since so experientially is the work of the Divinity made manifest.

Accedet homo, man shall come, a faithful contemplative man [shall come], *ad cor altum, to a deep heart,* that is, to profound considerations, gazing upon the marvels of the law of God,[75] and how *God has chosen the foolish things of the world that he may confound the wise, and God has chosen the weak things of the world that he might confound the strong;*[76] and how also God in this world permits the reprobate to prosper, yet the elect to suffer in so many ways, just as he decreed to save the world by the Incarnation and death of his only-begotten Son. In these things men truly come upon a deep heart, **63{64}[8]** *Et exaltabitur Deus, and God shall be exalted:* for out of such contemplation we regard with wonder the divine wisdom, we fear divine justice, and we chose to revere the divine majesty. Whence the divine word says: *Therefore men shall fear him, and all that seem to themselves to be wise, shall not dare to behold him;*[77] and again, *Behold, God is high in his strength, and none is like him among the lawgivers.*[78]

---

73   Luke 21:15.

74   Cf. Ps. 15:3: *To the saints, who are in his land, he has made wonderful all my desires in them.* E. N. This brings to mind the clarion-call of Tertullian in his *Apology: Plures efficimur, quotiens metimur a vobis: semen est sanguis Christianorum.* "We become all the more, as often as we are mowed down by you: the blood of Christians is a seed." *Apol.,* L, 13, PL 1, 535. Tertullian's sentiments are popularly expressed as "the blood of martyrs is the seed of the Church." "Martyrdom, suffering for the truth," stated Pope Benedict XVI, "is in the end victorious and more efficient than the cruelty and violence of totalitarian regimes." General Audience, May 30, 2007, http://www.vatican.va/content/benedict-xvi/en/audiences/2007/documents/hf_ben-xvi_aud_20070530.html.

75   Cf. Ps. 118:18: *Open my eyes: and I will consider the wondrous things of your law.*

76   1 Cor. 1:27a. E. N. I have re-arranged the verse some to make the text flow more naturally.

77   Job 37:24.

78   Job 26:22.

Sagittae parvulorum factae sunt plagae eorum, *the arrows of children are their wounds.* As this verse is explained three ways in the preceding article, with respect of Christ and of the Jews; so now it can be explained by comparison to the tyrants and the holy martyrs or just persons suffering affliction. For the tyrants and persecutors of the just condemn and spiritually kill themselves with the arrows and the wounding which they inflict upon virtuous men. Also, the *arrows of children*, that is, the preaching and the responses of just men and martyrs, are the wounds of the ungodly, for they have filled the world with faithful believers, destroying idolatry, and prevailing over persecutors. Additionally, the persecutors are often most severely tormented by the responses of the martyrs of Christ, as we read about in the legends of saints Vincent, Agatha, and others.[79] *Conturbati sunt, they were troubled* to repentance *omnes qui videbant eos, all that saw them*, that is, those who considered the ruin and the eternal damnation of the ungodly men just mentioned; *et timuit, and afraid*, from their punishments was, *omnis homo, every man* living in accordance with right reason, lest the same should befall him if he will have offended God. The rest [of this verse] is clear from the previous exposition.

See how full of mystery and beauty is this present Psalm in which the mysteries of Christ are contained. Therefore let us all labor to follow our Head,[80] desiring to partake in his sufferings,[81] to be unacquainted with the present worthless age and to be purified by its various tribulations: so that this deceitful and slippery life once complete, we may straightaway be found worthy to be embraced and crowned by the Lord Christ, by whom we will more highly be lifted up the more we now deny ourselves and the more we humbly lower ourselves for love of him. This is why the Savior said: *For that which is high to men, is an abomination before God.*[82]

---

79   E. N. According to Jacob de Voragine's *Golden Legend*, St. Vincent, a deacon and the proto-martyr of Spain, infuriated Dacian, the Roman governor of Spain, who subjected him to the most horrendous tortures and was tormented by St. Vincent's equanimity through his ordeal. Similarly, St. Agatha opposed herself to the provost of Sicily, one Quintianus, who desired to violate her and then sought to get her to deny the Christian faith. Like St. Vincent, St. Agatha bore her tortures with remarkable courage which tormented her persecutor.

80   Cf. Eph. 4:15: *But doing the truth in charity, we may in all things grow up in him who is the head, even Christ.*

81   Cf. 1 Pet. 4:13: *But if you partake of the sufferings of Christ, rejoice that when his glory shall be revealed, you may also be glad with exceeding joy.*

82   Luke 16:15b.

PRAYER

OD, BENIGNANT AND SOVEREIGN power, deliver our souls from the fear of our enemies, so that they who do not cease to search after iniquities against our salvation, by your insuperable deterring arm, will fail against us in their search.

Benigna et summa potestas, Deus, a timore inimicorum eripe animas nostras: ut qui scrutari iniquitates contra salutem nostram non cessant, tuo insuperabili abacti brachio, deficient a nobis scrutantes scrutinia.

Psalm 64

ARTICLE XXVII

LITERAL EXPOSITION OF THE SIXTY-FOURTH PSALM:
TE DECET HYMNUS, DEUS, ETC.
A HYMN, O GOD, BECOMES YOU, ETC.

64{65}[1] *To the end, a Psalm of David, the canticle of Jeremiah and Haggai, of the word of pilgrimage, when they began to leave.*[1]

In finem, Psalmus David, canticum Ieremiae et Aggaei, de verbo peregrinationis, cum inciperent profiscisci.

![T]HE PSALM WE ARE PRESENTLY EXPLAINING has this title: **64{65}[1]** *In finem, Psalmus David, canticum Ieremiae et Aggaei, de verbo peregrinationis, cum inciperent profiscisci; to the end, a Psalm of David, the canticle of Jeremiah and Haggai, of the word of pilgrimage, when they began to leave.* This present Psalm was written by David about the return of the Jews from their Babylonian captivity and the rebuilding of the temple.[2] Whence, the title of this Psalm is plain according to the literal sense. For it should be understood in this way: This *Psalm* about holy *David, to the end,* that is, is directing us to Christ, is *a canticle,* that is, an exultation or a giving of thanks, *of Jeremiah and Haggai,* the prophets: *a canticle,* I say, speaking *de verbo peregrinationis, of the word of pilgrimage,* or the people of the migration, or, as others [that is, other versions of the Scriptures], *when they began to leave* from Babylon towards Judea. For this Psalm addresses the pilgrimage and migration and return of the Jews. And it is called the canticle of Jeremiah or Ezechiel, and Haggai, not that they composed this Psalm, but because it is ascribed to them from the fact that Jeremiah and Ezechiel predicted the return of the Jews from Babylonia;[3] but Haggai upon the return prophesied of the rebuilding of the temple,[4]

---

1 E. N. Denis's version of 65:1 departs from the Sixto-Clementine Vulgate, which reads: *In finem. Psalmus David, canticum Jeremiae, et Ezechielis, populo transmigrationis, cum inciperent exire.* "To the end, a Psalm of David. The canticle of Jeremiah and Ezechiel to the people of the captivity, when they began to go out."

2 Ezra chp. i.

3 Jer. 50:28; Ez. 39:25–28.

4 Haggai 1:1–11.

as did also Zechariah.[5] Because of this (as will be seen) the title "canticle of Zechariah" can be placed on this Psalm just as well as [canticle] of Haggai or Jeremiah, especially since all these words, namely, *the canticle of Jeremiah* and so on even unto the end [of the verse], are certain expository added glosses: for they are not found in the Hebrew, nor are they in Jerome's translation according to the Hebrew.[6]

64{65}[2] *A hymn, O God, becomes you in Sion: and a vow shall be paid to you in Jerusalem.*

Te decet hymnus, Deus, in Sion, et tibi reddetur votum in Ierusalem.

64{65}[3] *O hear my prayer: all flesh shall come to you.*

Exaudi orationem meam; ad te omnis caro veniet.

64{65}[4] *The words of the wicked have prevailed over us: and you will pardon our transgressions.*

Verba iniquorum praevaluerunt super nos, et impietatibus nostris tu propitiaberis.

David speaking, therefore, in the person of the people returning with great joy from the previously mentioned captivity, said: **64{65}[2]** *Te decet hymnus, a hymn . . . becomes you,* that is, a divine praise with song, *O Deus in Sion, O God in Sion,* that is, in the place where the temple was located at the time of the Babylonian dispersion, for God had chosen this place for his worship, in the way that is expressed in the book of Chronicles;[7] *et tibi reddetur votum, and a vow shall be paid to you,* that is, the promise of being released or the holy desire that they would offer, *in Ierusalem, in Jerusalem:* for it was the temple that had been constructed where they offered that which by vow they owed to the Lord. **64{65}[3]** *Exaudi orationem meam, O hear my prayer* which I pour forth for the restoration of the city and the temple; *ad te omnis caro veniet, all flesh shall come to you,* that is, when the temple is restored some of all nations shall come to you so that they may adore you in it. For also many Gentiles assembled at it, as we read in the book of Acts regarding the eunuch of Queen Candace.[8] And in the book

---

5   Zech. 1:16.
6   E. N. The translation from the Hebrew by Jerome reads simply *Victori Carmen David Cantici,* "A poem of victory, a canticle of David."
7   2 Chr. 7:12–16.
8   Acts 8:27. E. N. The reference is to the highly placed eunuch of Queen Candace of Ethiopia who had come to Jerusalem to adore, and who was in his chariot reading the prophet Isaiah when he was approached by the Apostle Philip.

of the Maccabees we find that the temple was most famous all over the world, so that Seleucus, the king of Asia, provided it *with very great gifts.*[9] 64{65}[4] *Verba iniquorum praevaluerunt super nos, the words of the wicked have prevailed over us,* that is, the words and the deeds of the Babylonians oppressed us because of our sins; *et impietatibus nostris tu propitiaberis, and you will pardon our transgressions,* remitting them in the manner that you said by Jeremiah, that you would lead us back and rebuild the temple and the city of Jerusalem after *seventy years* had expired.[10]

64{65}[5]   *Blessed is he whom you have chosen and taken to you: he shall dwell in your courts. We shall be filled with the good things of your house; holy is your temple,*

Beatus quem elegisti et assumpsisti: inhabitabit in atriis tuis. Replebimur in bonis domus tuae; sanctum est templum tuum,

64{65}[6]   *wonderful in justice. Hear us, O God our Savior, who are the hope of all the ends of the earth, and in the sea afar off,*

mirabile in aequitate. Exaudi nos, Deus, salutaris noster, spes omnium finium terrae, et in mari longe.

64{65}[7]   *You who prepares the mountains by your strength, being girded with power:*

Praeparans montes in virtute tua, accinctus potentia:

64{65}[8]   *Who troubles the depth of the sea, the noise of its waves. The Gentiles shall be troubled.*

Qui conturbas profundum maris, sonum fluctuum eius. Turbabuntur gentes.

64{65}[5] *Beatus,* blessed now in hope *quem elegisiti et assumpsisti,* is he *whom you have chosen and taken to you,* so that you might return him to the land of Judaea, and you might cause him to serve you and to dwell therein. For this reason Baruch said: *My children, suffer patiently the wrath that is come upon you.... for he that has brought evils to you shall bring you everlasting joy again with your salvation.*[11] *Inhabitabit in atriis tuis, he shall dwell in your courts,* that is, in the place and the homes situated

---

9   2 Mac. 3:2–3. E. N. King Seleucus IV Philopator (*ca.* 218–175 BC) ruled the Seleucid Empire between 187 BC and 175 BC

10   Jer. 25:12a: *And when the seventy years shall be expired, I will punish the king of Babylon, and that nation, says the Lord, for their iniquity.* E. N. The third person plural "us" (*nos*) is used by Denis in his paraphrase of Jer. 25:12a, though it seems a bit jarring.

11   Baruch 4:25a, 29.

around the temple, in which sacrifices, prayers, and lessons of the law were done. *Replebimur in bonis domus tuae, we shall be filled with the good things of your house*: with the temporal and spiritual goods bestowed by your return from Babylon; also by the ministers of the temple from the oblations that they maintained in great abundance. *Sanctum est templum tuum, holy is your temple*, the material [temple], that is, appointed for holy worship; **64{65}[6]** *mirabile in aequitate, wonderful in justice*: for in it the priests judged doubtful and difficult causes just as Moses ordered.[12] Or [we might understand it thus]: *holy is your temple*, that is, the congregation of your people whom you brought back to your land is holy and wonderful in justice: for in it were the most holy and the most just men, namely, Ezra, Nehemiah, and many others.

Exaudi nos, Deus salutaris noster; hear us, O God our Savior, so that this second temple surpasses in glory the first temple constructed by Solomon: as Haggai promised, *Great shall be the glory of this last house*, he said, *more than of the first.*[13] *Spes omnium finium terrae, who are the hope of all the ends of the earth*, that is, the hope of all men living throughout the whole world, *et in mari longe, and in the sea afar off*: for one does not place hope in anything except God; and he who places it elsewhere errs. **64{65}[7]** *Pareparans montes in virtute tua, you who prepares the mountains by your strength.* It is as if it were saying: "You, O Lord God—who are of such power that you are preparing, that is, founding, preserving, and by your will disposing, the mountains of the earth, some of which are marvelously high—are able to hear us, and to fulfill easily the good promises to Israel." And this you do by means of your own power, not [power] obtained from elsewhere: *for your power is at hand when you will.*[14] Whence a later Psalm says: *The mountains ascend, and the plains descend into the place which you have founded for them.*[15] *Accinctus potentia, being girded with power.* This is said of God metaphorically. For God is himself his own power, in God all things—to be, to be able, to do—are the same.[16] Therefore, God is

---

12   Deut. 17:18: *If you perceive that there be among you a hard and doubtful matter in judgment between blood and blood, cause and cause, leprosy and leprosy: and you see that the words of the judges within your gates do vary: arise, and go up to the place, which the Lord your God shall choose.*

13   Haggai 2:10a.

14   Wis. 12:18b.

15   Ps. 103:8.

16   E. N. Compare St. Thomas Aquinas's *Compendium of Theology*, where God's being (*esse*), power or what he is able to do (*posse*), or his actions (*agere*) are identical to his essence. [A]*pparet quod in Deo nullum accidens esse potest. Si enim in eo omnes perfectiones sunt unum, ad perfectionem autem pertinet esse, posse, agere, et omnia huiusmodi, necesse est omnia in eo idem esse quod eius essentia. Nullum igitur*

said to be *girded with power*, that is, adorned and clothed with absolute power and omnipotence: because as a man is girded with armaments so that he might be strong in battle and ready for its exercise, so God in himself, or of his own power which is consubstantial to him, is strong so as to prevail against any adverse power and might, and to perform any operation that pleases him promptly and expeditiously. **64{65}[8]** *Qui conturbas profundum maris, who troubles the depths of the sea,* stirring upon it various tempests; *sonum fluctum eius, the noise of its waves:* that is, you increase and decrease the overflowing and crashing rage of the ocean over nature at the command of your own will. For this reason, a later Psalm states: *You rule the power of the sea: and appease the motion of the waves thereof.*[17] And in another place: *But the Lord sent a great wind into the sea: and a great tempest was raised in the sea.*[18] Whence the Evangelist said of the Lord Jesus: *Rising up, he rebuked the wind, and said to the sea: Peace, be still. And the wind ceased: and there was made a great calm.*[19]

64{65}[9]   *And they that dwell in the uttermost borders shall be afraid at your signs: you shall make the outgoings of the morning and of the evening to be joyful.*

Et timebunt qui habitant terminos a signis tuis; exitus matutini et vespere delectabis.

64{65}[10]   *You have visited the earth, and have plentifully watered it; you have many ways enriched it. The river of God is filled with water, you have prepared their food: for so is its preparation.*

Visitasti terram, et inebriasti eam; multiplicasti locupletare eam. Flumen Dei repletum est aquis; parasti cibum illorum; quoniam ita est praeparatio eius.

64{65}[11]   *Fill up plentifully the streams thereof, multiply its fruits; it shall spring up and rejoice in its showers.*

Rivos eius inebria, multiplica genimina eius; in stillicidiis eius laetabitur germinans.

---

eorum in eo est accidens. "It is clear that no accidents can be in God. For if in him all perfections are one, and if to be, to be able to, to act, and all things of this kind [i.e., attributes] pertain to perfection, it is necessary that all things in him are the same as his essence. Therefore, none of them is an accident in him." *Compendium theologiae*, lib. 1 cap. 23.

17   Ps. 88:10.
18   Jonah 1:4a.
19   Mark 4:39.

64{65}[9] *Turbabuntur gentes, et timebunt qui habitant terminos, a signis tuis; and they that dwell in the uttermost borders shall be afraid at your signs,* that is, all those abiding on the earth's globe will regard with wonder and will be struck with terror because of the marvels which you do at sea and upon the earth: as also there frequently was done by earthquakes, tempests, and other prodigies. *Exitus matutini et vesperi delectabis, you shall make the outgoings of the morning and of the evening to be joyful:* that is, the immolations of sacrifice that are offered in the morning and that which are offered in the evening you will cause to be acceptable to you and to be delightful to your faithful. For this reason, it is written in Ezra that, the temple having been rebuilt, they *offered in it a holocaust to the Lord morning and evening.*[20]

Consequently, the blessed David prophesied on the fruitfulness of the earth after the return from the predicted captivity: of which fruitfulness also Jeremiah[21] and Ezechiel[22] clearly prophesied. For they spoke of the future by means of the past because of the unshaken certitude of the prophecy:[23] 64{65}[10] *Visitasti terram, you have visited the earth* of Judah, giving to it plentiful fruit; *et inebriasti eam, and you have plentifully watered it,* that is, you have watered it with copious and opportune rains: in the way that Isaiah sets forth: *The rain and the snow come down from heaven, and return no more there, but soak the earth, and water it.*[24] *Multiplicasti locupletare eam, you have many ways enriched it,* that is, in many ways you have enriched the earth: because artificial riches are procured and augmented from the natural riches obtained from the things born of the fertility of the earth.[25]

Flumen Dei repletum est acquis, the river of God is filled with water, that is, the Jordan river abounds with water. Now the Jordan river is called the *river of God* because of the marvels which God accomplished in it, drying up its channel, and making its waters upriver to mount up to the height

---

20   Ez. 3:3b.

21   Jer. 31:12: *And they shall come, and shall give praise in mount Sion: and they shall flow together to the good things of the Lord, for the corn, and wine, and oil, and the increase of cattle and herds, and their soul shall be as a watered garden, and they shall be hungry no more.*

22   Ez. 28:25–26: *When I shall have gathered together the house of Israel out of the people among whom they are scattered. . . .they shall dwell therein secure, and they shall build houses, and shall plant vineyards, and shall dwell with confidence.*

23   E. N. Denis has before noted the custom of prophecy at times being written in the past tense to refer to a future event. *E.g.,* Articles XVI and XVII (Psalm 3:8) in Volume 1.

24   Is. 55:10.

25   E. N. Drawing from Aristotle (Politics I.3 [1256a35–1256b]), St. Thomas distinguishes between natural wealth (*divitiae naturales*), such as food and shelter, and artificial wealth (*divitiae artificiales*), which was man-made (*e.g.,* money) and so finds wealth to be two-fold (*duplices*). ST IaIae, q. 2, art. 1, co.

of a tower and so remain while Israel crossed it, as we read in the book of Joshua.[26] *Parasti cibum illorum, you have prepared their food,* that is, you have prepared the meals of the returning Jews by making fertile the land; *quoniam ita est praeparatio eius, for so is its preparation,* that is, because the filling up of the Jordan brings about the fruitfulness of the earth and the preparation of food. **64{65}[11]** *Rivos eius inebria, fill up plentifully the streams thereof,* that is, make the streams of the Jordan to produce bountiful produce; *multiplica genimina eius, multiply its fruits.* This is explained in the exposition of the preceding words: for the multiplication of fruits or the products of the earth is [the same in meaning as] the filling up of streams. Or [alternatively], *fill up plentifully the streams thereof,* that is, abundantly increase and fill. *In stillicidiis eius laetabitur germinans, it shall spring up and rejoice in its showers,* that is, the earth rejoices in the drops of the waters of the Jordan raining down from the skies, that is, it glorifies those that dwell by it. Or [yet another alternative], *it shall . . . rejoice* metaphorically, as when we assert that a meadow laughs.

64{65}[12] *You shall bless the crown of the year of your goodness: and your fields shall be filled with plenty.*

Benedices coronae anni benignitatis tuae, et campi tui replebuntur ubertate.

64{65}[13] *The beautiful places of the wilderness shall grow fat: and the hills shall be girded about with joy,*

Pinguescent speciosa deserti, et exsultatione colles accingentur,

64{65}[14] *The rams of the flock are clothed, and the vales shall abound with corn: they shall shout, yea they shall sing a hymn.*

Induti sunt arietes ovium, et valles abundabunt frumento; clamabunt, etenim hymnum dicent.

64{65}[12] *Benedices coronae, you shall bless the crown,* that is, the circuitousness or circular course, *anni benignitatis tuae, of the year of your goodness,* that is, of the time of your mercy, giving those things that are needed for the production of fruit. For God is said to bless the times when he blesses those things which are done or occur in time, that is, applies some grace or goodness to it. *Et campi tui, and your fields,* that is, the fields cultivated by the Jews, *replebuntur ubertate, shall be filled with plenty* of diverse fruits. **64{65}[13]** *Pinguescent speciosa deserti, the beautiful places of the wilderness shall grow fat,* that is, the fertile pastures

26   Joshua 3:16–17.

will bring forth the fodder for animals; *et exsultatione colles accingentur, and the hills shall be girded about with joy,* that is, men shall be made full everywhere with delightful fruit or offspring. **64{65}[14]** *Induti sunt arietes ovium, the rams of the flock are clothed,* with abundant wool so that there will be no lack of clothing; *et valles abundabunt frumento, and the vales shall abound with corn:* for the valleys of that land are said to be promising so that good grain may be sown in them. *Clamabunt, etenim hymnum dicent; they shall shout, yea, they shall sing a hymn.* Now inanimate things, such as those things spring forth from the soil and the like, are said to bless and cry out materially to God because they provide the matter and the occasion where men may be spurred to divine praise, and their beauty, fecundity, and arrangement lead us, if we consider it well, to crying out to and blessing the Lord. For this reason we read in Ecclesiasticus: *O how desirable are all his works! . . . And who shall be filled with beholding his glory?*[27] Here surely — as with Daniel — all creatures, even those that are inanimate, are an invitation to bless the Creator.[28]

ARTICLE XXVIII

TROPOLOGICAL OR MORAL EXPOSITION
OF THE SAME SIXTY-FOURTH PSALM:

64{65}[1] *To the end, a Psalm of David, the canticle of Jeremiah and Haggai, of the word of pilgrimage, when they began to leave.*[29]

In finem, Psalmus David, canticum Ieremiae et Aggaei, de verbo peregrinationis, cum inciperent proficisci.

OW THE PREVIOUSLY STATED TITLE IS explained morally in this fashion: **64{65}[1]** *In finem, Psalmus*

---

27   Ecclus. 42:23a, 26b.

28   Dan. 3:57–90. *E. N.* This is a reference to the Canticle of Daniel or the Canticle of the Three Young Men. From Daniel's *Benedicite, omnia opera Domini, Domino* of this Canticle to David's *Laudate Dominum de caelis* of Psalm 148, to St. Francis's *Altissimo, onnipotente bon Signore* of his Canticle of the Creatures, to the "Glory be to God for dappled things . . ." of Gerard Manley Hopkins's poem "Pied Beauty," the beauty of nature has always been a sounding board for the praise of God the Creator, for "He fathers-forth whose beauty is past change: Praise him."

29   *E. N.* Denis's version of 65:1 departs from the Sixto-Clementine Vulgate, which reads: *In finem. Psalmus David, canticum Ieremiae, et Ezechielis, populo transmigrationis, cum inciperent exire.* "To the end, a psalm of David. The canticle of Jeremiah and Ezechiel to the people of the captivity, when they began to go out."

David, unto the end, a Psalm of David, that is, this Psalm aiming at Christ, speaks of David, that is, of the Church militant now on pilgrimage and aspiring to the heavenly fatherland; and also any member of the faithful, returning from Babylonia, that is, from the confusion of vice, to the land of Judah and Sion, that is, to confession, praise, and divine contemplation. And this Psalm is *canticum Ieremiae et Aggaei, de verbo transmigrationis; the canticle of Jeremiah and Haggai, of the word of pilgrimage*, that is, it treats of the thing signified by migration and return of the Jews from Babylonia, namely of our return from the captivity of vices and the devil to the peace of the Church and the liberty of the sons of God.[30] For he who serves vices is captured by demons, as the Apostle [Paul], speaking of sinners, says: *They may recover themselves from the snares of the devil, by whom they are held captive at his will.*[31] And in the Gospel the scripture says: *Whosoever commits sin is the servant of sin.*[32] Therefore, for us, to return means to turn from confusion to order, from fault to grace, from the reign of the devil to the reign of Christ. And so returning, let us say with heartfelt joy:

64{65}[2]   *A hymn, O God, becomes you in Sion: and a vow shall be paid to you in Jerusalem.*

Te decet hymnus, Deus, in Sion, et tibi reddetur votum in Ierusalem.

64{65}[3]   *O hear my prayer: all flesh shall come to you.*

Exaudi orationem meam; ad te omnis caro veniet.

64{65}[2]   *Te decet hymnus, Deus, in Sion; a hymn, O God, becomes you in Sion*, that is, in the holy and militant Church, in which we ought unceasingly to praise and honor God, fulfilling that which the Apostle [Paul] says: *To the king of ages, immortal, invisible, the only God, be honor and glory.*[33] By Sion is meant contemplation, by which is meant the Church which already faithfully contemplates Christ. *Et tibi reddetur votum, and a vow shall be paid*, that is, a promise to you will be fulfilled perfectly, *in Ierusalem, in Jerusalem*, [meaning] that *Jerusalem which is above, . . . which is our mother* and is the triumphant Church.[34] For when we renounced the devil and all his works in sacred Baptism by

---

30   E. N. Cf. Rom. 8:21: *Because the creature also itself shall be delivered from the servitude of corruption, into the liberty of the glory of the children of God.*

31   2 Tim. 2:26.

32   John 8:34b.

33   1 Tim. 1:17.

34   Gal. 4:26. E. N. That is, the Church in heaven, the heavenly Jerusalem.

a promise of fidelity, we offered to God our body and soul, dedicating ourselves totally to his worship, firmly taking hold of our life so that all our thought, speech, and work would always be directed to God, always speaking of and venerating God: in which consists the perfect fulfillment of the precept of charity. But in the present life we are not able to fulfill this perfectly, but in the heavenly fatherland we will be able to fulfil it perfectly: for then the body will not hold back the soul.

64{65}[3] *Exaudi orationem meam, O hear my prayer, O Lord,* so that in this age and in the Church militant I might praise you with beautiful and devout hymns, in order that I might happily render to you in that supernal Jerusalem without end that which I am unable now perfectly to accomplish. *Ad te omnis caro veniet, all flesh shall come to you,* that is, every man, especially in the final judgment, when all peoples shall assemble before the Son of Man.[35] This is said so here as placing a part for the whole, namely, the flesh for the entire composite [of man, namely body and soul],[36] as in Genesis and Exodus Jacob is said to have descended into Egypt with seventy souls.[37] But are these [souls] not to be understood as flesh, [seeing that] the horses and mules [that carried them into Egypt] were flesh? And is it not written truly, *Egypt is a man and not God, and their horses, flesh, and not spirit?*[38] Shall also therefore the brute animals come before Christ in the day of judgment? To respond to this, [flesh] is used here as genus for species,[39] namely [the general term] flesh for human flesh. Or [alternatively], as the name of Prophet refers to David antonomastically,[40] so flesh in and of itself is used [antomastically] for human flesh, which is most noble.

---

35   Matt. 25:32.

36   E. N. Using the word "flesh" as a synecdoche (using part to refer to the whole) so that by "flesh" the Psalm means the whole man, a composite of body and soul. For more on Denis's understanding of synecdoches, see Article IV in Volume 1 and footnote 29-66 in Volume 2. Denis uses the "seventy souls" as an example where part is used to refer to the whole man also. Since the horses and mules are flesh, it follows that the "seventy souls" who rode them into Egypt were flesh, and therefore the "seventy souls" means seventy men of body and soul.

37   Gen. 46:27; Ex. 1:5.

38   Is. 31:3a.

39   E. N. Genus for species is a kind of synecdoche. Commonly, six types are identified: (i) *pars pro toto* (part for the whole), (ii) *totum pro parte* (the whole for the part), (iii) *genus pro specie* (a general term meaning a more specific one), (iv) *species pro genere* (a specific term meaning a more general one), (v) *plurale tantum* (using a singular to refer to a plural, and (vi) *pluralis pro singulari* (using a plural to refer to a singular).

40   E. N. Antonomasia (from Greek verb ἀντονομάζειν (*antonomazein*) meaning "to name differently") is a figure of speech where an epithet is used in place of a proper

64{65}[4] *The words of the wicked have prevailed over us: and you will pardon our transgressions.*

Verba iniquorum praevaluerunt super nos, et impietatibus nostris tu propitiaberis.

64{65}[4] *Verba iniquorum praevaluerunt super nos, the words of the wicked have prevailed over us.* Sometimes in holy Scripture a word is accepted for a deed, as David said: *What is the word that has come to pass?*[41] And Zechariah the prophet: *These then are the words which you shall do.*[42] And therefore it is in this sense: *the words of the wicked,* that is, the persecutions of sinners and the temptations of demons, have prevailed over us, that is, have led us away from the path of justice, and have cast us down into a great misery. Or [alternatively]: *the words of the wicked,* that is, the suggestion of the devil, tempting our first parents,[43] the convincing also of Eve,[44] who corrupted her man, and the excuse of Adam,[45] blaming the woman for his sin, *have prevailed over us,* because they expelled us from Paradise,[46] and a heavy yoke is upon all the children of Adam,[47] and original justice was withdrawn, and we are born *children of wrath,*[48] that is, in original sin. *Et impietatibus nostris tu propitiaberis, and you will pardon our transgressions,* that is, you will mercifully forgive us who are repentant from the actual sins which we incur from [the weakness we suffer because of] original sin, giving us the time and place to do penance: in the way that Isaiah says, *Therefore the Lord waits that he may have mercy on you.*[49] Or [alternatively]: *our transgressions,* of which as Psalm above states, *Behold I was conceived in iniquities,*[50] *tu,* you, only-begotten of God, *will pardon,* having mercy,

---

name, *e.g.,* "the Philosopher" is used to refer to Aristotle, "the Prophet" to refer to David, and "the Apostle" to refer to Paul.

41   2 Sam. 1:4. *E. N.* The translator of the Douay-Rheims has taken this into account, and so translates *Quod est verbum . . .* as "What is the matter. . . ," rather than "What is the word . . ." Hence, I did not follow the Douay-Rheims here.

42   Zech. 8:16a. *E. N.* Similar to 2 Sam. 1:4, the translator of the Douay-Rheims has taken this into account and so translated *Haec sunt ergo verba quae facietis* as "These then are the things which you shall do," and not "These are the words which you shall do." Likewise, I did not follow the Douay-Rheims here.

43   Gen. 3:4-5.

44   Gen. 3:6.

45   Gen. 3:12.

46   Gen. 3:23-24.

47   Ecclus. 40:1a.

48   Eph. 2:3b.

49   Is. 30:18a.

50   Ps. 50:7a.

providing aid, and making satisfaction for us: for this we are unable to do for ourselves. Here, the Lord says through Isaiah: *You have made me serve with your sins, you have wearied me with your iniquities.*[51]

64{65}[5]   *Blessed is he whom you have chosen and taken to you: he shall dwell in your courts. We shall be filled with the good things of your house; holy is your temple,*

Beatus quem elegisti et assumpsisti: inhabitabit in atriis tuis. Replebimur in bonis domus tuae; sanctum est templum tuum,

64{65}[6]   *wonderful in justice. Hear us, O God our Savior, who are the hope of all the ends of the earth, and in the sea afar off,*

mirabile in aequitate. Exaudi nos, Deus, salutaris noster, spes omnium finium terrae, et in mari longe.

64{65}[7]   *You who prepares the mountains by your strength, being girded with power:*

Praeparans montes in virtute tua, accinctus potentia:

64{65}[8]   *Who troubles the depth of the sea, the noise of its waves. The Gentiles shall be troubled.*

Qui conturbas profundum maris, sonum fluctuum eius. Turbabuntur gentes.

64{65}[9]   *And they that dwell in the uttermost borders shall be afraid at your signs: you shall make the outgoings of the morning and of the evening to be joyful.*

Et timebunt qui habitant terminos a signis tuis; exitus matutini et vespere delectabis.

64{65}[5] *Beatus quem elegisti et assumpsisti, blessed is he whom you have chosen and taken to you.* Properly understanding election, every one of the elect is taken [into heaven]: for only the predestinate are called the elect. But sometimes also election is commonly understood as the calling of someone to grace, whether he is led to glory or not: and so [understood in this way] not all of the elect are taken [into heaven], as the Savior said of the traitor Judas: *Have not I chosen you twelve; and one of you is a devil?*[52] And so it says: *Blessed is he whom you have chosen* from eternity, and *taken to you* in time, giving to him grace in the present and glory in the future. Whence also Baruch says: *We are happy . . . because the*

---

51   Is. 43:24b.
52   John 6:71.

things that are pleasing to God, are made known to us.[53] *Inhabitabit in atriis tuis, he shall dwell in your courts*: that is, now he remains in the Church militant spread throughout the whole world, and afterward he will dwell in the Church triumphant. Now the Church militant and triumphant is said to have many courts (*atria*) because of its most ample capacity and its plenitude of all good, in accordance to this: *O Israel, how great is the house of God, and how vast is the place of his possession! It is great and has no end: it is high and immense.*[54] Or the Church triumphant is called courts (*atria*) because of the diverse mansions in the manner that Christ attests: *In my Father's house there are many mansions.*[55]

Replebimur in bonis domus tuae; sanctum est templum tuum, **64{65} [6]** *mirabile in aequitate; We shall be filled with the good things of your house,* **64{65}[6]** *holy is your temple.* First, this verse can be understood as dealing with the Church militant, [so that it reads] in this sense: *We shall be filled with the good things of your house,* that is, in the riches of the Church, which are the sacraments, virtues, and multiform graces which already fill and fatten the devout daily in so many ways, as it says in a Psalm above: *They who fear him lack nothing.*[56] And Christ: *All things,* he says, *whatsoever you ask when you pray, believe that you shall receive; and they shall come unto you.*[57] *Holy is your temple,* that is, those consecrated in your name. Or [alternatively], *Holy is your temple,* that is, men who are holy, in whose hearts you dwell by faith and grace. *For the temple of God is holy, which you are, says the Apostle.*[58] *Wonderful in justice.* For great and wonderful is the holiness and justice of the saints in this life: who in the flesh and the world do not live carnally or worldly, but spiritually and divinely according to the perfect doctrine of Christ, which in every way is exceedingly just and marvelous, and which makes its followers wonderful. Second, this verse can be explained regarding the Church triumphant. *We shall be filled with the good things of this house,* that is, in the blessedness of the heavenly homeland. For with the essential beatitude, which is the vision of God, all the blessed will be filled, because they will see God as clearly as they desired. Also they will be filled with great accidental rewards after the day of judgment, when their holy souls will

---

53   Baruch 4:4.
54   Baruch 3:24–25.
55   John 14:2a.
56   Ps. 33:10b. E. N. Denis's version departs from the Sixto-Clementine. He states *Nihil deest timentibus eum,* whereas the Sixto-Clementine has *non est inopia timentibus eum,* "there is no want to them that fear him."
57   Mark 11:24.
58   1 Cor. 3:17b.

be united with their glorified bodies, and they will be made happy not only in intellectual virtues, but also in their sensitive powers. Whence Isaiah says: *The eye has not seen, O God, besides you, what things you have prepared for them that wait for you.*[59] The Apostle [Paul] has made this more clear in saying: *Eye has not seen, nor ear heard, neither has it entered into the heart of man, what things God has prepared for them that love him.*[60] Of this [subject matter] also earlier Psalms set forth: *You shall fill me with joy with your countenance;*[61] and, *I shall be satisfied when your glory shall appear.*[62] *Holy is your temple,* that is, the Church triumphant. For no imperfection or stain will be able to exist in the heavenly homeland, where all the blessed will be immediately joined to the fountain of purity.[63] *Wonderful in justice.* And however much all our justices in our wayfaring state are *as the rag of a menstruous woman,*[64] yet the justice of the blessed in the heavenly homeland will be perfect and wonderful: because whatever they receive from God, he will offer to them most fully, and they will unceasingly and completely stand attentive to God, turned toward him, immersed in him, and absorbed in him.

Exaudi nos, Deus salutaris noster; Hear us, O God our Savior (salutaris), that is, our Savior (*salvator*),[65] without whose help we have no power, you who are *spes, the hope,* that is, the cause and the object of hope, *omnium finium terrae, et in mari longe; of all the ends of the earth, and in the sea afar*

---

59   Is. 64:4b.

60   1 Cor. 2:9.

61   Ps. 15:11a.

62   Ps. 16:15b.

63   E. N. Cardinal Newman's version of *Adoro te devote* has these lines in the sixth verse: *O fons puritatis, Iesu Domine, / Me immundum munda tuo sanguine, / Cuius una stilla salvum facere / Totum quit a omni mundum scelere. Fountain of purity, Jesus Lord / Wash me, filthy, with your blood / Of which one drop can save / The whole world of all its sins.* See St. John Henry Newman, ed., *Hymni Ecclesiae et Breviarior Parisiensi* (Oxford: J. H. Parker 1838), 98. Newman's version replaces *Pie pelicane* (Good Pelican) with *O fons puritatis.*

64   Is. 65:6a.

65   E. N. Denis defines the word "*salutaris*" with "*salvator*," though both are translated by the English "Savior." The Latin words *salutaris* and *salvator,* both meaning Savior, were used to translate the meaning of the name Jesus, though the Latin word *salvator* was a Christian neologism. "Jesus," the Christian Cicero Lactantius (*ca.* 250–*ca.* 325) says, "which in Latin is stated *salutaris* or *salvator.*" *Div. Inst.,* 4, 12, 1, PL 6, 479 (*Iesus, qui latine dicitur salutaris, sive salvator.*) St. Augustine explains: "This [*salvator*] is Jesus in Latin. Let not grammarians seek for what is proper in Latin, but let Christians seeks for what is true. For *salus* is a Latin word. *Salvare* and *salvator* were not Latin [words] until the Savior [*salvator*] came; when he came to the Latins, he made those [words] Latin, too." Uwe Michael Lang, *The Voice of the Church at Prayer: Reflections of Liturgy and Language* (San Francisco: Ignatius 2012), 43.

off, that is, of all the faithful residing in the entire world and islands of the sea: for in you alone dwells the true salvation of all men, you who spoke through the Prophet of the Lord, *Be converted to me, and you shall be saved, all you ends of the earth.*[66] **64{65}[7]** *Praeparans montes, you who prepares mountains*, that is, the holy angels:[67] of whom a later Psalm contains this: *I have lifted up my eyes to the mountains;*[68] and again, *Mountains are round about it* [Jerusalem].[69] *In virtute tua, by your strength*, because with your own power you dispose that all things are done to your pleasure, in the Church governance, in the bridling of the devils, in the keeping and the spurring forward of men. Or [alternatively]: *You who prepares mountains by your strength*, that is, by your omnipotence by which you bring about the life and sublime doctrine of the holy Apostles and all others so that they might instruct, rule, and lead others to you who are the final end of all things. *Accinctus potentia, being girded with power.* We have seen this satisfactorily explained in the preceding article about God. But of the incarnate Christ it should be especially explained, so that it says: "You, O Christ, although by your human and natural powers you are not able to do these things, yet you are able to do these things since you are girded with power, that is, armed and girded with divine power so as to be suited to do this work." For this reason you most truly said: *Whatever the Father does, these the Son does in a like manner.*[70] **64{65}[8]** *Qui conturbas, who troubles*, that is, you strike with fear, you turn toward repentance, *profundum maris, the depth of the sea*, that is, worldly evils, or the vicious heart immersed in the bitterness of sin.[71] Now you also disturb *sonum fluctuum eius, the noise of its waves*, that is, the proud and impetuous contradictions of the worldly princes, some of whom were troubled unto salvation, that is, were moved to repentance. *Turbabuntur gentes* **64{65}[9]** *et timebunt qui habitant terminus, a signis tuis; the Gentiles were troubled* **64{65}[9]** *and they that dwell in the uttermost borders shall be afraid of your signs.* This was

---

66   Is. 45:22a.

67   E. N. St. Augustine likens the "mountains" in the Psalms as a reference to angels in the sense of messengers of God, including both the angelic spirits and the apostles or preachers who announce the Gospel. "By the name of mountain is signified the sublimeness of the angels." *Enarr. in Ps.* 89.3., PL 37, 1142. "Some mountains, therefore, are lovely, high mountains, preachers of the truth, whether Angels, or Apostles, or Prophets. These are [the mountains] around Jerusalem." 124.4, PL 37, 1650.

68   Ps. 120:1a.

69   Ps. 124:2a.

70   John 5:19b.

71   E. N. There is a play on words here relating to the Latin word for see (*mare*) and the similarly-sounding Hebrew name *Miriam* (מרים) which had been interpreted as meaning "sea of bitterness."

especially fulfilled in the time of the Apostles, when, because of their most excellent miracles, men living all over the world in great part converted to Christ, being troubled by the consideration of their vices present in them and fearing infernal punishment. *Exitus matutini et vesperi delectabis, you shall make the outgoings of the morning and of the evening to be joyful:* that is, you will cause the conversion or repentance both of those who leave vices from their youth and find refuge with God and of those who are converted in old age to be received [into heaven], and you will make the angels rejoice. *For at whatever hour a sinner is converted, you will immediately forget all his iniquities.*[72] *And joy exists with the angels of God upon one sinner doing penance.*[73] This is what Christ said in the Gospel: *And if he shall come in the second watch, or come in the third watch, and find them so, blessed are those servants.*[74] Or [we can understand it] thus: *the outgoings of the morning,* that is, the conversion of those who in the time of prosperity—which might be compared to the morning and the light, *come to you, and of the evening,* that is, the conversion of those who proceed to you in times of adversity, *you shall make . . . to be joyful.* Whether during the time of abundance or prosperity or a time of need and adversity, he who converts to the Lord will be mercifully received by him, in the manner that Christ has acknowledged: *him that comes to me, I will not cast out.*[75]

64{65}[10] *You have visited the earth, and have plentifully watered it; you have in many ways enriched it. The river of God is filled with water, you have prepared their food: for so is its preparation.*

Visitasti terram, et inebriasti eam; multiplicasti locupletare eam. Flumen Dei repletum est aquis; parasti cibum illorum; quoniam ita est praeparatio eius.

64{65}[10] *Visitasti, you have visited,* with a benign visitation, *terram, the earth,* that is, the inhabitants of the earth, namely, men sending the Apostles throughout the whole world, saying to them: *Go into the whole world, and preach the Gospel to every creature.*[76] *Et inebriasti eam, and have*

---

72   Cf. Ez. 18:21–22: *But if the wicked do penance for all his sins which he has committed, and keep all my commandments, and do judgment, and justice, living he shall live, and shall not die. I will not remember all his iniquities that he has done: in his justice which he has wrought, he shall live.*

73   Luke 15:10.

74   Luke 12:38. E. N. The Romans divided the night into four watches. The fourth watch was just before dawn.

75   John 6:37b.

76   Mark 16:15.

plentifully watered it, that is, you have exuberantly filled with spiritual gifts those who converted to the faith, you have changed them from whom they were by divine love, and you have given them drink with the sober intoxication of the spirit.[77] For this reason the Apostle [Paul] says: *I give thanks to my God always for you, for the grace of God that is given you in Christ Jesus, that in all things you are made rich in him.*[78] *Multiplicasti locupletare eam, you have in many ways enriched it*, that is, in many ways you have enriched it with charismatic and divine gifts. For *to one is given* (as the Apostle says) *the word of wisdom, to another the word of knowledge, to another the grace of healing, to another the working of miracles, [to another prophecy, to another the discerning of spirits, to another diverse kinds of tongues, to another interpretation of speeches].*[79] And again: *Everyone has his proper gift from God.*[80] Or [we can look at it] thus: *You have visited the earth*, that is, the early Church, sending to it on the day of Pentecost the Holy Spirit in a visible sign; and have *plentifully watered* it with the ardor of charity and the light of wisdom, and with knowledge of all languages, so that the incredulous Jews would say: *These men are full of new wine.*[81] *You have in many ways enriched it*, for by grace those you have gathered have also enriched others. Whence the Lord: *Fear not*, he says, *O Jacob, my servant... I will pour out my spirit upon your seed, and my blessing upon your stock.*[82] And in Joel we read: *I will pour out my spirit upon all flesh: and your sons and your daughters shall prophesy.*[83] Hence truly the time of the evangelical law is called the time of grace.

Flumen Dei repletum est aquis, the river of God is filled with water: that is, the Baptismal fount is full of the gifts of the Holy Spirit, absolving and sanctifying those reborn in it. Or this fountain is said to be filled with water because in Jerusalem it first began to be applied, and now it is increased, applied, and consecrated over the whole world. Of this

---

77 E. N. The oxymoron sober intoxication (*sobria ebrietate*) appears to have arisen originally with Philo Judaeus (*ca.* 25 BC–*ca.* 50 AD) (νηφάλιος μέθη / *nēphalios methē*) and was translated as *sobria ebriatas* by St. Ambrose. It was commonly used to describe the state of mystical contemplation. St. Augustine uses it in his work *The Christian Struggle*: "'While we are in the body, we are absent from the Lord,' [2 Cor. 5:6], may we not taste how sweet the Lord is, for he 'has given us the pledge of the Spirit' [2 Cor. 5:5] in which we sense his sweetness, and we desire him, the fountain of life, where we are inundated and watered in sober intoxication (*sobria ebrietate*)." PL 40, 296.

78 1 Cor. 1:4–5a.

79 1 Cor. 12:8–10. E. N. The parts in brackets replace the "*etc.*" in the Latin text.

80 1 Cor. 7:7a.

81 Acts 2:13b.

82 Is. 44:2–3.

83 Joel 2:28a.

fountain or river is written in another place: *A fountain shall come forth of the house of the Lord, and shall water the torrent of thorns*,[84] that is, it will wash the hearts of sinners, as is more openly recalled in Zechariah: *In that day there shall be a fountain open to the house of David, and to the inhabitants of Jerusalem: for the washing of the sinner, and of the unclean woman.*[85] *Parasti cibum illorum, you have prepared their food*, that is, you have prepared spiritual food for the faithful, namely, the Sacrament of the Body and Blood of Christ: of which is said in an earlier Psalm, *You have prepared a table before me against them that afflict me.*[86] *Quoniam ita est praeparatio eius, for so is its preparation*, that is, because this food is not given to anyone but him who is born again in the Baptismal fount: whose figure was that the Hebrew people did not come upon manna except after they had crossed the Red Sea. For in the manner that the Red Sea is a type of Baptism, so manna was a figure of the Eucharist. For this reason, the Apostle [Paul] said: *And all in Moses were baptized in the cloud and in the sea: and did all eat the same spiritual food.*[87] These were baptized figuratively; but we are baptized in truth. They also ate the same food spiritually or significatively, and so they drank the same spiritual drink spiritually; we eat and drink the same food and the same drink essentially, namely, the Body and Blood of the Savior.

64{65}[11]   *Fill up plentifully the streams thereof, multiply its fruits; it shall spring up and rejoice in its showers.*

Rivos eius inebria, multiplica genimina eius; in stillicidiis eius laetabitur germinans.

64{65}[11] *Rivos eius inebria, fill up plentifully the streams thereof*, that is, in the early Church those individuals drawn to Baptism flowed like a stream pouring forth from a fountain: these streams intoxicated, so tha, they everywhere increased and were filled with sacramental graces. *Multiplica genimina eius, multiply its fruits*, that is, insofar as many were reborn by the Baptism in Christ, and so the Church was filled with faithful. *In stillicidiis eius, it shall spring up*, that is, in the sprinkled waters of Baptism falling upon the head of the person being baptized while he was being baptized, *laetabitur germinans, shall rejoice in its showers*, that is, the Holy Mother Church obtaining and procreating new children in Christ.

---

84   Joel 3:18b.
85   Zech. 13:1.
86   Ps. 22:5a.
87   1 Cor. 10:2–3.

64{65}[12] *You shall bless the crown of the year of your goodness: and your fields shall be filled with plenty.*

Benedices coronae anni benignitatis tuae, et campi tui replebuntur ubertate.

64{65}[12] *Benedices, you shall bless,* that is, you will give the gift of grace, *coronae, the crown,* that is, the people fleeing everywhere to you in a kind crown[88] or circle: as a Psalm above states it, *And a congregation of people shall surround you.*[89] And with respect to God a Psalm below sets forth: *Great and terrible above all them that are about him.*[90] You will bless, therefore, the crown *anni benignitatis tuae, of the year of your goodness,* that is, of the time of your mercy or your grace. It is as if he were saying: "You bless the Christian people during the time of the evangelical law." For the year of divine goodness began at first with Christ's advent, and lasts even until the end of the world: and during this time God blesses his people more copiously than during the time of the natural and written law;[91] for this reason the time of grace is called the year of divine goodness.[92] *Et campi tui, and your fields,* that is, the hearts of the faithful, which you cultivate, fatten, and make fruitful with the seeds of the word,[93] *replebuntur ubertate, shall be filled* with plenty of divine gifts, holy works, and spiritual increase.

---

88 E. N. The Latin word *corona* means a garland, wreath, or crown. The interpretation Denis espouses is visually more appealing if one looks at a people or congregation as a sort of garland or circle of people around God rather than a metal crown.

89 Ps. 7:8a.

90 Ps. 88:8b.

91 E. N. In other words prior to the law of Moses and after the law of Moses.

92 E. N. In a sermon attributed (uncertainly) to Hugh of St. Victor (*ca.* 1096–1141) it states: "The year of divine goodness is the universal time of grace, which is from the Incarnation of the Lord even until the end of the world. For there were two prior times, namely the time of the natural law, which was from Adam until Moses, and time of the written law, which was from Moses until Christ." Sermon 72 (Feast Day of St. John the Baptist), PL 177, 1126.

93 E. N. The term "seeds of the word," *semina verbi*, is the Latin translation of St. Justin Martyr's (*ca.* 100–*ca.* 165) concept of *ta spermata tou logou* (τὰ σπέρματα τοῦ λόγου), "seeds of the reason," or "seeds of the logos," or "seeds of the word." See, *e.g.*, Apology II.8.1; 13.5. As the historian on the natural law, H. R. Rommen, succinctly put it, the Stoic notions of the natural law and the 'seeds of the Word' were used by the Church Fathers, and in particular St. Justin Martyr, "to proclaim the Christian doctrine of the personal Creator-God as the Author of the eternal law as well as of the natural moral law which is promulgated in the voice of conscience and in reason." Heinrich Rommen, *The Natural Law: A Study in Legal and Social History and Philosophy*, (Indianapolis: Liberty Fund 1998), 31 (Thomas R. Hanley, O. S. B., Ph.D., trans.).

64{65}[13] *The beautiful places of the wilderness shall grow fat: and the hills shall be girded about with joy,*

Pinguescent speciosa deserti, et exsultatione colles accingentur,

64{65}[14] *The rams of the flock are clothed, and the vales shall abound with corn: they shall shout, yea they shall sing a hymn.*

Induti sunt arietes ovium, et valles abundabunt frumento; clamabunt, etenim hymnum dicent.

64{65}[13] *Pinguescent speciosa deserti, the beautiful places of the wilderness shall grow fat*: that is, the souls of sinners abandoned of grace, and yet still marked and adorned with a natural image of the most-high Trinity will abound in spiritual goods by conversion to the faith and obedience of Christ. Whence also he says: *The Son of man is come to seek and to save that which was lost.*[94] And as the Apostle [Paul] said, *where sin abounded, grace did more abound.*[95] Indeed, to whom more is given, the more he loves.[96] *Et exsultatione colles accingentur, and the hills shall be girded about with joy*. In the way that the name of mountain is understood as meaning Apostle, so the name of hills, which are smaller than mountains, are understood to be perfect men, followers of the apostolic life, and most especially martyrs, who have followed not only the life of the Apostles, but also their suffering and death. Such as these, therefore, shall be girded about with joy, that is, a spiritual joy, receiving in this life internal consolations, but in the future perfect beatitude. **64{65}[14]** *Induti sunt arietes ovium, the rams of the flock are clothed*, that is, the leaders of the flock of Christ, namely the prelates, pastors, and teachers, are clothed with the fortitude, wisdom, and justice of the Holy Spirit, so that they might vigorously feed, correct, instruct, and confirm others. And true and worthy prelates of the Church are clothed so as to the lead the way in life, doctrine, and every perfection. Of rams so clothed the Lord says through Jeremiah: *And I will give you pastors according to my own heart, and they shall feed you with knowledge and doctrine.*[97] *Et valles, and the vales*, that is, their subjects and subordinates, *abudabunt frumento, shall abound with corn*, that is, the seeds of the word which they hear from their superiors will be diligently made to flourish so that they are enriched with the fruits of eternal life. *Clamabunt, they*

---

94 Luke 19:10.
95 Rom. 5:20b.
96 *Cf.* Luke 7:47: *Wherefore I say to you: Many sins are forgiven her, because she has loved much. But to whom less is forgiven, he loves less.*
97 Jer. 3:15.

shall shout, praying with affection, and confessing the benefits of God; *etenim hymnum dicent*, yea, *they shall sing a hymn* to the Lord giving thanks for all his benefits and praising him unceasingly for his goodness, in the way the Lord says through Isaiah: *Behold my servants shall praise for joyfulness of heart.*[98]

See the marvelous charm that runs through this resplendent Psalm, in which God, blessed and holy, is beautifully praised, affectionate prayers are expressed, and the divine goodness recalled. Let us endeavor, therefore, with all our strength, to lead such a stainless and holy life, so that we might praise God with all affection, we might take delight in celebrating him, we might invoke him with our hearts, and we might never be unmindful of his benefits; but let us sing to him in the present hymns, so that passing through here [on earth], we might praise him in the heavenly Jerusalem without end.

PRAYER

GOD, FATHER OF MERCY, HOPE OF ALL the ends of the earth and in the sea afar off, forgive our impieties, we beseech you; and let not the words of the iniquitous prevail eternally over us nor your unconquerable protection forsake us.

Deus, Pater indulgentiae, spes omnium finium terrae et in mari longe, impietatibus nostris, quaesumus, propitiare; et ne verba iniquorum super nos in aeternum praevaleant, tua nos invicta tuitio non derelinquat.

---

98 Is. 65:14b.

Psalm 65

ARTICLE XXIX

ELUCIDATION OF THE SIXTY-FIFTH PSALM:
IUBILATE DEO, OMNIS TERRA, ETC.
SHOUT WITH JOY TO GOD, ALL THE EARTH, ETC.

65{66}[1] *Unto the end, a canticle of a Psalm of the resurrection. Shout with joy to God, all the earth,*

In finem. Canticum psalmi resurrectionis. Iubilate Deo, omnis terra,

65{66}[2] *Sing a Psalm to his name; give glory to his praise.*

Psalmum dicite nomini eius; date gloriam laudi eius.

HE TITLE OF THIS PRESENT PSALM IS AS follows: **65{66}[1]** *In finem. Canticum psalmi resurrectionis; unto the end, a canticle of a Psalm of the resurrection*: that is, this Psalm—treating of the spiritual resurrection of the faithful and directing us unto the end, which is eternal life—is a canticle, that is, a great rejoicing of the this resurrection.

The Prophet [David] speaking in the person of the Church or any one member of the faithful, says: *Iubilate Deo, omnis terra; shout with joy to God, all the earth.* A jubilant shout (*iubilus*) is a joy (*gaudium*) that is unable to be completely held back because of its exuberance, nor can it be entirely expressed: there is more jubilancy in the mind than there is in the voice. And so it says: *Shout with joy,* that is, exult in an ineffable way unto God, that is, in God and to the glory of God, from the contemplation of his divine goodness and out of the consideration of his promised benefits: and let *all the earth* do this, that is, all the world or all its inhabitants, not only in Judea, but all nations that have converted to the faith and that have attained hope through Christ in the future resurrection. To which also Isaiah says, *Give praise, O you barren that bear not: sing forth praise and make a joyful noise, that you did not travail with child:*[1] [this is said] because the people of the Gentiles were formerly barren, but now in Christ they are said to be fecund, as the Apostle [Paul] teaches.[2] **65{66}[2]** *Psalmum dicite nomini eius, sing*

---

1 Is. 54:1a.
2 Gal. 4:27. E. N. St. Paul quotes Isaiah 54:1 and applies it to the Gentiles and Christ.

a Psalm to his name. A Psalm signifies a good deed. What else is it to sing to God, except to praise him by voice and by deed? For he who magnifies God with words yet dishonors him in his deeds contradicts himself: indeed, because works preponderate over words, he more dishonors him than honors him. *Date gloriam laudi eius, give glory to his praise,* that is, make illustrious the divine praise with words and deeds, teaching or exhibiting how excellently God is to be praised. Indeed, glory is defined as a brilliant knowledge with praise.[3] Therefore, during the time that one teaches how great and incomparable praise is due to God, he is then giving glory to his praise, that is, he glorifies the praise of God.

65{66}[3] *Say unto God, how terrible are your works, O Lord! In the multitude of your strength your enemies shall lie to you.*

Dicite Deo: Quam terribilia sunt opera tua, Domine! In multitudine virtutis tuae mentientur tibi inimici tui.

65{66}[3] *Dicite Deo, say unto God,* confessing his magnificence and praising his majesty: *Quam terribilia sunt opera tua, Domine! How terrible are your works, O Lord!* For the works of divine justice which occurred at the beginning of the world, namely, the condemning the whole human race because of the sin of the first parents,[4] destroying the whole earth by flood,[5] and drowning the Egyptians in the Red Sea,[6] and others that Sacred Scripture has memorialized are terrible. And also greatly to be feared are the works of God with respect to the evildoer, whom he will eternally damn. Whence it is written: *The Lord shall be terrible upon the ungodly.*[7] And elsewhere: *There is one most high, Creator Almighty, and a powerful king and greatly to be feared.*[8] *In multitudine virtutis tuae mentientur tibi inimici tui, in the multitude of your strength your enemies shall lie to you,* that is, confronted by your many wonders and miracles, they will not convert to you, humbly revering your power: for though they confess by their words your works, yet they deny them by their deeds.[9] It is in this way that the Jews who ascribed his miracles to the devil lied about Christ, saying, *He casts out devils by Beelzebub, the prince*

---

3   E. N. On this definition, which comes from Augustine, *see* footnote 8-22, Volume 1.
4   Rom. 5:12–19.
5   Gen. 7:21–23.
6   Ex. 14:27–28.
7   Zeph. 2:11a.
8   Ecclus. 1:8a.
9   *Cf.* Titus 1:16: *They profess that they know God: but in their works they deny him; being abominable, and incredulous, and to every good work reprobate.*

of devils;[10] and, *This man is not of God;*[11] and, *A Prophet does not arise from Nazareth.*[12] So likewise did Ananias and his wife lie to God, Peter telling Ananias, *You have not lied to men, but to God.*[13]

65{66}[4] *Let all the earth adore you, and sing to you: let it sing a Psalm to your name.*

> *Omnis terra adoret te, et psallat tibi; Psalmum dicat nomini tuo.*

65{66}[4] *Omnis terra adoret te,* let all the earth adore you, that is, let all men dwelling on the earth offer to you alone the cult of adoration (*latriae*),[14] rejecting false gods, and venerating you in all things and above all things. For adoration properly understood is the cult of latria which is owed to God alone inasmuch as he is the almighty Creator of all things, the most high Principle, the true, live, triune, and simple God. Whence, the sublime God states through Isaiah: *I the Lord, this is my name: I will not give my glory to another, nor my praise to graven things.*[15] This is also what the Prophet [David] says, *Let all the earth adore you,* O God, implicitly prophesying that the whole world would be converted to the adoration of the most high God, as occurred with the Apostles of Christ. For this reason, it states in Isaiah: *Your Redeemer, the Holy One of Israel, shall be called the God of all the earth;*[16] and in Zechariah: *In that day there shall be one Lord, and his name shall be one.*[17]

---

10 Luke 11:15b.

11 John 9:16a.

12 Cf. John 1:46a. E. N. The quote is miscited to John 1:46a; it is actually a cite to John 7:52b. However, the point is also implied in the question asked by Nathanael in John 1:46: *Can anything good come from Nazareth?* Presumably, this was the common, though disputed, view that Nathanael had accepted until he was disabused of it by Jesus. *See also* John 7:41: *Others said: This is the Christ. But some said: Does the Christ come out of Galilee?* Nicodemus was challenged by his fellow Pharisees: *Art you also a Galilean? Search the scriptures, and see, that out of Galilee a prophet does not arise.* John 7:52b.

13 Acts 5:4b.

14 E. N. Unfortunately, the word "cult" has pejorative associations attached to it. The word cult translates the Latin *cultus,* which means care or caretaking (e.g., agriculture is "taking care" or cultivating fields and crops). It is the word used to refer to the care owed to God, specifically, the duty of worship. The Pagan Cicero, for example, defined *religio* (religion) as the *cultus deorum,* the cultivation of the gods. *See* Cicero's *De Natura Deorum (On the Nature of the Gods),* II, 71–72. *Latria* is the highest form of veneration which is reserved to God alone. For more on *latria* see footnote 62-40.

15 Is. 42:8.

16 Is. 54:5b.

17 Zech. 14:9b.

Et psallat tibi, and sing to you, mentally praising you with their minds: as the Apostle [Paul] said, *making melody (psallentes) in your hearts to the God always.*[18] *Psalmum dicat nomini tuo, let it sing a Psalm to your name,* praising you with mouth or voice: as the Apostle said, *Speaking to yourselves in Psalms and hymns, and spiritual canticles.*[19]

65{66}[5]   *Come and see the works of God; who is terrible in his counsels over the sons of men.*

Venite, et videte opera Dei; terribilis in consiliis super filios hominum.

65{66}[5] *Venite, come* to hear the word of God, come to the Church, come not so much with bodily steps but rather in the walk of faith, by an increase in contemplation, and by turning back interiorly; *et videte, and see* by an internal contemplation, by the light of faith, through enlightening of the Holy Spirit, *opera Dei, the works of God,* who is *terribilis in consiliis super filios hominum, who is terrible in his counsels over the sons of men.* These works, in which God shows himself so fearfully, are especially the effects of divine predestination and reprobation, wherein none are elect except by the mercy of God, but the rest, by the demands of justice, are predestined [to reprobation].

Further, we are able to direct ourselves to how terrible God is in the counsels over the sons of men if we diligently examine the testimony of divine Scripture. See what the Lord says through Ezechiel: *Return and live, for I desire not the death of the sinner,*[20] *but that he turn from his way and live.*[21] With this the Apostle [Paul] agrees, saying: *God wills all men to be saved, and to come to the knowledge of truth.*[22] And nevertheless we read in the Acts of the Apostles: *They were forbidden by the Holy Spirit to preach the word of God in Asia, and . . . the Spirit of Jesus permitted them not.*[23] In what manner, therefore, does God will to convert all when he himself prohibits preachers to instruct certain peoples? But perchance some will say that this is not a great marvel, and that from this fact God does not show himself terrible in the counsels over the sons of men; and they will assert that the Holy Spirit prohibited Paul from informing the

---

18   Eph. 5:19b.
19   Eph. 5:19a.
20   Ez. 18:32. E. N. Denis has taken liberty with the verse. It reads: *For I desire not the death of him that dies, says the Lord God, return and live.*
21   Ez. 33:11a.
22   1 Tim. 2:4.
23   Acts 16:6b, 7b.

Asians, for he foresaw that they would not believe and so would not be suited to mercy, and hence the word of God was not preached to them. But have there not been many others to whom the Gospel of Christ has been preached by the holy Apostles who not only did not receive it and who were in all ways unworthy of it? And so the more likely reason is that which the Lord said through Ezechiel: *Son of man, go to the house of Israel.... for you are not sent to a people of profound speech, and of an unknown tongue, ... and if you were sent to them, they would hearken to you; but the house of Israel will not hearken you, because they will not hearken to me.*[24] See, he did not send a holy prophet to those who he knew would listen if a prophet were sent to them, but he sent them to those whom he knew would not listen. Isn't this counsel of God terrible? Terrible is also that counsel of God that Paul, speaking of Jacob and Esau, brings to mind to the Romans [in his epistle to them]: *For when the children were not yet born, nor had done any good or evil (that the purpose of God, according to election, might stand), not of works, but of him that calls, it was said to her: The elder shall serve the younger. As it is written: Jacob I have loved, but Esau I have hated.*[25]

There are many other incidents in the divine Scriptures in which God shows himself to be terrible in counsel over the sons of men: yet they do not call for scrutinization, but piety and a sober faith. For which reason, Solomon bears witness: *As it is not good for a man to eat much honey, so he that is a searcher of majesty, shall be overwhelmed by glory.*[26] But it ought to be observed that counsel properly understood is not suitably said of God. For counsel properly speaking is said to be the questioning of what to do, and so it presupposes doubt. For this reason, the Damascene:[27] Counsel, he says, is something found in ignorant natures. While counsel is ascribed to God, this counsel is to be understood as that which is of perfection in it apart from all of its imperfection.[28]

---

24 Ez. 3:4-7.
25 Rom. 9:11–13. *Cf.* Mal. 1:2–3.
26 Prov. 25:27.
27 E. N. St. John of Damascus (*ca.* 575-749) was born in Damascus. He took the vows of a monk, eventually dying in Jerusalem. A Doctor of the Church and a fierce defender of Icons, St. John of Damascus wrote many works, but is perhaps best known for his works *Against Heresies* and *Exposition of the Orthodox Faith*. In this instance, Denis is referring to the Damascene's *On the Orthodox Faith*, II, 22.
28 E. N. In other words, the word "counsel" when used of God, is used analogously, and not univocally (in the exact same sense) as used with humans. Yet it is not for all that used equivocally (completely differently). The perfection suggested in "counsel" (lack of ignorance through reasoned activity and knowledge) is to be made eminent

65{66}[6] *Who turns the sea into dry land, in the river they shall pass on foot: there shall we rejoice in him.*

Qui convertit mare in aridam, in flumine pertransibunt pede; ibi laetabimur in ipso.

65{66}[6] *Qui convertit mare in aridam, who turns the sea into dry land.* God literally did this with respect to the Red Sea and the Jordan River.[29] But spiritually speaking, by sea is understood sinners submerged in the waves of vices: these God converts into dry land, when the vicious billowing of the soul is extinguished through the grace of God and it begins to dry up with the fire of love and starts to thirst for justice. *In flumine, in the river,* that is, in the world, which is compared to a great sea and a river; or [alternatively], *in the river* of present mortality, or [in the further alternative], *in the river* of temptation and adversity; *pertransibunt, shall pass on* good men, *pede, on foot* of holy desires, sighing for the heavenly homeland, and spurning all prosperity of the world for love of eternal life, and also strongly enduring all its adversities, in the manner that the Apostle [Paul] admonishes: *Laying aside every weight and sin which surrounds us, let us run by patience to the fight proposed to us, looking on Jesus, the author and finisher of faith.*[30] *Ibi laetabimur in ipso, there shall we rejoice in him,* that is, in the aforementioned transition of the way to the heavenly homeland, from the world to heaven, from the billowing of vices to a restful and secure port, let us rejoice with spiritual joy, as one is to rejoice in all virtuous acts in him of whom it further states:

65{66}[7] *Who by his power rules for ever: his eyes behold the nations; let not them that provoke him be exalted in themselves.*

Qui dominatur in virtute sua in aeternum, oculi eius super gentes respiciunt; qui exasperant non exaltentur in semetipsis.

65{66}[7] *Qui dominator, he who... rules,* in heaven and on earth and all abysses, *in virtute sua, by his power,* consubstantial, coeternal, and personal to him, not obtained from another or from elsewhere, *in aeternum, forever,* without end, as it is written of God: He does according to his will, as well with the powers of heaven, as among the inhabitants

---

(*via eminentiae*), and any imperfection suggested in "counsel" (ignorance) is to be removed (*via remotionis*).

29   Ex. 14:21; Joshua 3:16–17.

30   Heb. 12:1b–2a.

of the earth: *and there is none that can resist his hand.*[31] *His power is an everlasting power, and his kingdom is to all generations.*[32] *Oculi eius super gentes respiciunt, his eyes behold the nations,* that is, the divine intellect looks upon and weighs all the works of men, so that he will rearrange all things to each as he deserves. Whence the Lord himself said: *Shall a man be hid in secret places, and I not see him?*[33] And elsewhere: *O Lord God whose eyes are open upon all the ways of the children of Adam, to render unto every one according to his ways.*[34] *Qui exasperant, let them . . . that provoke him,* that is, they who provoked God to anger out of pertinacity and pride in sinning, *non exaltentur in semetipsis, not . . . be exalted in themselves,* that is, let them not find improvement within themselves, but let them be destitute of all grace and go to ruin, as the Scripture says: *The soul that commits anything through pride, . . . because he has been rebellious against the Lord, he shall be cut off from among his people.*[35] Now this is said by the Prophet [Moses] not as an imprecation, but as a foreannouncing, or by conforming himself to the divine justice.[36] And because (as the Lord frequently asserts through Ezechiel) the house of Israel was provoking in this way,[37] and so it was that they were not exalted, but because of their iniquities committed against Christ, they were humiliated, oppressed, and cast down.

65{66}[8] *O bless our God, you Gentiles: and make the voice of his praise to be heard.*

Benedicite, gentes, Deum nostrum, et auditam facite vocem laudis eius.

65{66}[9] *Who has set my soul to live: and has not suffered my feet to be moved.*

Qui posuit animam meam ad vitam, et non dedit in commotionem pedes meos.

---

31 Dan. 4:32b.
32 Dan. 4:31b.
33 Jer. 23:24a.
34 Jer. 32:19.
35 Num. 15:30.
36 E. N. This explanation is the standard one given by Denis with respect to these imprecatory statements by prophets. *See, e.g.,* Article LXI (Psalm 27:4), Article LXIII (Psalm 34:1) and footnote 27-16 in Volume 2. *See also* Article LVI (Psalm 24:4) and footnote 24-14 in Volume 1.
37 Ez. chps. 2, 3, 12, 17, 44 *passim.*

65{66}[8] *Benedicite, gentes, Deum nostrum; O bless our God, you Gentiles* praising him, *et auditam facite vocem laudis eius, and make the voice of his praise to be heard* glorifying him before others, and drawing in all men, as much as you are able, to praise him. **65{66}[9]** *Qui posuit animam meam ad vitam, who has set my soul to live* spiritually, delivering me from the death of sin, and vivifying it with the gift of grace: as the Apostle [Paul] says: *God, who is rich in mercy, for his exceeding charity wherewith he loves us, even when we were dead in sins, has brought us to life together in Christ, by whose grace you are saved.*[38] *Et non dedit in commotionem pedes meo, and has not suffered my feet to be moved*: that is, he has not allowed my desires and my works to be unstable, wandering, and uncertain; but he confirmed and fixed my heart in him, so that I would not be able to be separated from his love and his service, neither by the temptations of the devil, nor by the blandishments, nor by the adversities of this world: indeed, perseverance has been bestowed upon me. In this way the feet of the Apostle was planted firmly, saying: *For I am sure that neither death, nor life, nor angels, nor principalities, . . . nor any other creature, shall be able to separate us from the love of God.*[39]

65{66}[10] *For you, O God, have proved us: you have tried us by fire, as silver is tried.*

Quoniam probasti nos, Deus; igne nos examinasti, sicut exa-minatur argentum.

65{66}[10] *Quoniam probasti nos, Deus; for you, O God, have proved us* through adversity and prosperity, both by you yourself effectively (*effective*) and by the adversaries of our salvation permissively (*permissive*).[40] For indeed God proves men in order that it may become known, not to God himself, but to others, whether they truly fear God, not departing

---

38   Eph. 2:4–5. E. N. I have changed the Douay-Rheims' "quickened," as the trans-lation of *convivicavit*, "has brought us to life" due to modern unfamiliarity with the word "quickened" and the need to emphasize them of this part of the *Commentary* which is the vivifying unto a supernatural, grace-filled life.

39   Rom. 8:38–39.

40   E. N. Denis seizes on the well-known distinction between God's effective will (sometimes called indicative will or decretive will) and God's permissive will and their relationship to good and evil, testing or temptation (both methods of proving us), and man's freedom. In his free acts, man relies upon the effective will of God for all that is good. In other words, God is effectively, affirmatively, actively behind the good. What about the evil man confronts? What about those Denis identifies as "enemies of man's salvation"? These act in accord with God's permissive will, so that God is in no way the source of temptation or the cause of evil.

from his precepts because of those things which tend to divert one from the good. And this God does sometimes effectively (*effective*) by himself or through his ministers, by not immediately hearing the prayers of the one praying, suspending grace, or inflicting deprivation or sickness.[41] Thus Moses: *You shall remember*, he said, *all the way through which the Lord your God has brought you . . . to afflict you and to prove* (tentaret) *you, and that the things that were in your heart might be made known, whether you would keep his commandments or not.*[42] But sometimes God proves us permissively (*permissive*) through the temptations of the devil or the persecutions of men in accordance with this: *As gold in the furnace the Lord has proved them.*[43] *Igne nos exaministi, you have tried us by fire,* that is, you have struck us with acute tribulations to see if we would be faithful adherents to you, *sicut examinatur argentum, as silver is tried,* that is, in the manner that whether something is true silver is examined by fire. For this is said in the book of Job: *God knows my way, and he has tried me as gold that passes through the fire.*[44]

65{66}[11] *You have brought us into a net, you have laid afflictions on our back.*

Induxisti nos in laqueum; posuisti tribulationes in dorso nostro.

65{66}[12] *You have set men over our heads. We have passed through fire and water, and you have brought us out into a refreshment.*

Imposuisti homines super capita nostra. Transivimus per ignem et aquam, et eduxisti nos in refrigerium.

65{66}[11] *Induxisti nos in laqueum, you have brought us into a net.* A net of deception and of fault is one thing; but a net of probation and punishment is another. God leads us into the first kind of net

---

41   E. N. "God does not desire physical evil, for example, suffering, illness, death, that is, not for the sake of the evil or as an aim. Wis. 1:13 *et seq.* 'For God has not made death: neither hath He pleasure in the destruction of the living. For He created all things that they might be.' However, God wills physical evil, natural evil as well as punitive evil, *per accidens,* that is, as a means to a higher end of the physical order (for example, for the acquisition of a higher life), or of the moral order (for example, for punishment or for moral enlightenment). Ecclus. 1:14: 'Good things and evil, life and death, poverty and riches are from God.' *Cf.* Ecclus. 39:35 *et seq.;* Am. 3:6." Ludwig Ott, *Fundamentals of Catholic Dogma* (Rockford, IL: TAN Books 1974), 45–46 (trans., Patrick Lynch, ed. James Canon Bastible).

42   Deut. 8:2.

43   Wis. 3:6.

44   Job 23:10.

permissively while by his just judgment allows us to be tempted, to be separated, and to fail.[45] But in the second kind of net, he often leads us effectively, but sometimes, however, permissively. *Posuisti tribulationes in dorso nostro, you have laid afflictions on our back.* By the word "back" one is to understand the whole man, for frequently the soul and the body are afflicted. For in the manner that burdens are placed upon and taken off the bodily back, so various afflictions fall upon and must be borne by man as a whole. **65{66}[12]** *Imposuisti homines super capita nostra, you have set men over our heads,* that is, over ourselves and over our own liberty and reason: so that we do not presume to follow our own ideas or presume to follow our own will.[46] This God sometimes does efficaciously, as when he causes good men to preside; but at other times permissively, as when evil men are given precedence. Whence we have written in Job: *God makes a man that is a hypocrite to reign for the sins of the people.*[47] And the Lord says through Isaiah: *And I will give children to be their princes, and the effeminate shall rule over them.*[48] While, therefore, the unworthy and the impious preside, we ought patiently to bear the rule of those whose whom we are unable to become free of, reasoning that this calamity has happened because of our sins; we ought not to resist with force regardless of how apparent and great the iniquity of him who presides over us is, provided his directive relates to those things to which we are subject to him, and so long as they do not oppose the divine honor and our salvation.

Transivimus per ignem et aquam, we have passed through fire and water, that is, through contrary punishments, bearing up with opposing afflictions, as are excessive heat in the air or in the body and excessive cold. Or [we can understand it thus], *through fire and water* as if through two extremes, which are to be understood all kinds of intermediate tribulations by which the elect in this world are cleansed, in the manner that is written: *Blessed is the man whom the Lord corrects.*[49] *Et eduxisti nos in refrigerium, and you have brought us out into a refreshment.* For God will not permit us to be tempted above that which we are able,[50] nor

---

45   E. N. The editor suggests that instead of *separari* (to be separated), Denis intended *superari* (to be overcome).

46   E. N. Denis is not saying that we lose our reason and will, but that it will be constrained (for good or for evil) depending upon our rulers and the pedagogy of our laws.

47   Job 34:30.

48   Is. 3:4.

49   Job 5:17a.

50   Cf. 1 Cor. 10:13: *Let no temptation take hold on you, but such as is human. And*

customarily [does he permit] the tribulation to be continuous; but, on the contrary, God both consoles and alleviates his faithful, in the way it is written: *Refuse not . . . the chastising of the Lord, because he wounds, and cures; he strikes, and his hands shall heal.*[51] And elsewhere: *But this every one is sure of that worships you, O Lord, that his life . . . be under tribulation, it shall be delivered . . . because after a storm you make a calm, and after tears and weeping you pour in joyfulness.*[52] And so, if in this life he does not give you refreshment, in the future he certainly will give it, and it will be all the more abundantly the more it has at the present time been denied.

65{66}[13] *I will go into your house with burnt offerings: I will pay you my vows,*

Introibo in domum tuam in holocaustis; reddam tibi vota mea,

65{66}[14] *Which my lips have uttered, And my mouth has spoken, when I was in trouble.*

Quae distinxerunt labia mea; et locutum est os meum, in tribulatione mea.

65{66}[15] *I will offer up to you holocausts full of marrow, with burnt offerings of rams: I will offer to you bullocks with goats.*

Holocausta medullata offeram tibi, cum incenso arietum; offeram tibi boves cum hircis.

65{66}[13] *Introibo in domum tuam, I will go into your house,* that is, into my soul which is the home and the temple of its Creator provided it lives justly, examining, judging, and exercising myself: the way it is written, *Return, you transgressors, to the heart;*[53] and elsewhere, *Consider yourself.*[54] Or [alternatively], *I will go into your house,* namely, the Church militant, remaining in ecclesiastical unity with faith and works. Or [yet another alternative is], *I will go,* that I might trust, after this life, *into your house,* that is, into the Kingdom of Heaven or the Church triumphant, as you, O Lord Jesus, said: *Father, I will that where I am, they also whom*

God is faithful, who will not suffer you to be tempted above that which you are able: but will make also with temptation a way out, that you may be able to bear it.

51 Job 5:17b–18.
52 Tob. 3:21–22.
53 Is. 46:8b.
54 *Cf.* Gal. 6:1: *Brethren, and if a man be overtaken in any fault, you, who are spiritual, instruct such a one in the spirit of meekness, considering yourself, lest you also be tempted.*

you have given me may be with me.[55] In whatever of those houses that I will go into *in holocaustis, with burnt offerings,* that is, with a fervid oblation of my own self, offering and holding myself open entirely to your will, holding nothing back for myself. For the holocaust was the name given to the sacrifice offered to the divine majesty that would be totally consumed to his honor, as a sign that man ought to abandon himself entirely to him [God], and to surrender himself entirely with ardent love to the divine honor. Therefore, this is the way that we devote ourselves to God, proceeding into his house, being made one with God, and remaining in him. *Reddam tibi vota mea, I will pay you my vows,* that is, I will discharge my promises which I have promised either in Baptism,[56] or in Orders, or in the undertaking of the religious life.[57] Regarding this Solomon commands: *If you have vowed anything to God, defer not to pay it: for an unfaithful and foolish promise displeases him.*[58] Or [we can also look at it this way], *I will pay you my vows,* that is, to you alone I will offer all my desires, desiring nothing outside of you, before you, against you, but gathering all my affections in you: as it is said in a Psalm above, *Lord all my desire is before you.*[59] **65{66}[14]** *Quae,* which promises or desires *labia mea distinxerunt, my lips have uttered,* that is, pronounced distinctly and in an orderly fashion. For if something illicit were promised, it is not to be fulfilled.[60]

Et locutum est os meum, and my mouth has spoken with words of promise and of prayer, *in tribulatione mea, when I was in trouble.* For men tend to engage in prayers and make promises when they are placed in troubling situations so that they may be delivered [from them]. **65{66}[15]**

---

55   John 17:24a.

56   E. N. In the traditional rite of Baptism these include: (a) to renounce Satan, (b) all of his works, and (c) all his pomps; and (d) to believe in all the articles of the Creed. These promises are of ancient, even apostolic, pedigree. See Apostolic Constitutions, VII, 41, PG 1, 1042 (late 4th century): "I renounce Satan, and his works, and his pomps, and his cults, and his angels, and his inventions, and all things that are under him. . . . and I ascribe myself to Christ, and believe, and am baptized into one Unbegotten, the only true God Almighty, the Father of Christ, the Creator and Maker of all things, from whom are all things; and into the Lord Jesus Christ, His only begotten Son, the First-born of all creation. . . ."

57   "As Christians, we are not surprised by such a vow-desire. In the light of the gospel of charity, it makes perfect sense, because, as Balthasar says, 'every true love has the inner form of a vow.'. . . That is why all Christian life stands under vow — whether of Baptism, Marriage, or the Consecrated Life." John Saward, *The Beauty of Holiness and the Holiness of Beauty* (Brooklyn, NY: Angelico Press, 2021), 131–32.

58   Eccl. 5:3a.

59   Ps. 37:10a.

60   E. N. Unlawful or immoral vows or promises are not binding.

Holocausta medullata, *holocausts full of marrow*, that is, good and fat [sac-
rifices], namely, myself inflamed with the fire of love, and with a body
and soul ready to do your will, *offeram tibi*, *I will offer up* to you, O Lord
God, *cum incenso arietum*, *with burnt offerings of rams*, that is, with the
prayer of the leaders of the Lord's flock, namely, of the prelates of the
Church, since by their intercession my offering will become acceptable.
Offeram tibi boves, *I will offer to you bullocks*, that is, the teachers and
the preachers of the word of God, *cum hircis*, *with goats*, that is, with
repentant sinners, so that all these might pray for me. Now by holocausts
full of marrow is rightly understood the loving offering of one's body and
soul: because marrow, which is the fat in the bone, represents devotion
and love of the heart. Now rams are said of the prelates, because as
the ram is the leader of sheep, so they are leaders of others. And also
bullocks (as the Apostle [Paul] attests) are figures of preachers,[61] for
they cut at the hearts of their audiences with their preaching to goad
them that they might be fruitful with the seed of the word. Now a goat,
which is a vile and filthy animal, signifies sinners.

65{66}[16] *Come and hear, all you that fear God, and I will tell you
what great things he has done for my soul.*

*Venite, audite, et narrabo, omnes qui timetis Deum, quanta
fecit animae meae.*

65{66}[17] *I cried to him with my mouth: and I extolled him with my tongue.*

Ad ipsum ore meo clamavi; et exaltavi sub lingua mea.

65{66}[16] *Venite*, *come* with the affection of mind, and if it involves
a work, also with the steps of body, and gather yourselves together into
the house of discipline;[62] *audite*, *hear* with the ears of the flesh and the
heart, *et narrabo omnes qui timetis Deum*, and I will tell all *you that fear
God* with a chaste and filial fear. Now such things [that are to be told
to the chaste with filial fear] are hidden and special gifts of the Creator,
and are not to be told to the impenitent and the perverse, according to
that which the Savior said: *Give not that which is holy to dogs; neither*

---

61   *Cf.* 1 Cor. 9:9: *For it is written in the law of Moses: You shall not muzzle the
mouth of the ox that treads out the corn. Does God take care for oxen?* E. N. In arguing
that the people should support those preaching to them, St. Paul uses the ox as a
symbol of the preacher: like the working ox, the preacher ought not be muzzled
by the lack of sustenance.
62   Ecclus. 51:31b.

cast you your pearls before swine.[63] For that which he desires to speak is stated thereafter: *quanta fecit animae meae, the great things he has done for my soul,* that is, how many kind and sweet benefits he has bestowed upon me, preserving me from evil and conserving me in the good. And every person should diligently ponder upon the special benefits of God that have been shown him, especially that he exists thanks to God. It also comes to light from this that occasionally others are to be told of special benefits received from God to the glory of God and the edification of the hearers, as Christ in the Gospel said to someone: *Go and tell of the great things God has done for you.*[64] Now this sort of speaking is especially rightful for the prelates and to those persons who have overcome the temptation of vainglory; with others, it does not seem very safe unless it is required by the edification of neighbor. For this reason, Christ in the Gospel said to someone: *See you tell no man.*[65] And Isaiah: *My secret to myself,* he said, *my secret to myself.*[66] **65{66}[17]** *Ad ipsum ore meo clamavi, I cried to him with my mouth,* that is, praising and calling out to God, *et exsultavi sub lingua mea, and I extolled him with my tongue,* that is, that certain delight I experience in conscience from that praise and calling out to the most High. Now this delight of the mind is sometimes so great, that it overflows into the body, and it causes delight or exultation in the mouth.

65{66}[18]   *If I have looked at iniquity in my heart, the Lord will not hear me.*

Iniquitatem si aspexi in corde meo, non exaudiet Dominus.

65{66}[19]   *Therefore has God heard me, and has attended to the voice of my supplication.*

Propterea exaudivit Deus, et attendit voci deprecationis meae.

65{66}[20]   *Blessed be God, who has not turned away my prayer, nor his mercy from me.*

Benedictus Deus, qui non amovit orationem meam, et misericordiam suam a me.

65{66}[18] *Inquitatem si adspexi in corde meo, if I have looked at iniquity in my heart,* by approval or consent to sin, *non exaudiet Dominus,*

---

63   Matt. 7:6a.
64   Luke 8:39a. *E. N.* The Gerasene demoniac whom Christ exorcised.
65   Matt. 8:4a. *E. N.* A man cured of leprosy.
66   Is. 24:16a.

the Lord will not hear me. For he who is conscious of mortal sin in him, with the purpose of remaining in sin, is not heard, in the way it is written: *God will not cast away the simple, nor reach out his hand to the evildoer.*[67] And in the Gospel one reads: *We know that God does not hear sinners.*[68] **65{66}[19]** *Propterea,* therefore, that is, because I am not conscious of being in mortal sin, *exaudivit Deus, et,* God has heard me, and for this he *attendit voci deprecationis meae,* has attended to the voice of my supplication.[69] This is what is written in the book of Job: *If you will beseech the Almighty, if you will walk clean and upright, he will pres-ently rouse himself for you;*[70] and elsewhere, *If a man be a server of God and does his will, him he hears.*[71] Yet those praying with the purpose of persevering in sin, the Lord says through Jeremiah: *Why do you cry for your affliction? Your sorrow is incurable.*[72] It is necessary, therefore, that we must be diligent to conform life to prayers, proposing always with our whole heart improvement in all.

Finally, the holy man gives thanks to God for so many benefits. **65{66} [20]** *Benedictus Deus,* blessed be God, that is, blessed be, and may he be praised and blessed by all, *qui non amovit orationem meam, et misericor-diam suam a me;* who has not turned away my prayer, nor his mercy from me, but he has kindly received and has mercifully fulfilled them.

See with what brilliancy our spirit is lit in divine praise in this Psalm; by it the recollection of divine benefits is recalled, by it our intellect is informed how much it behooves the elect to suffer in this present life, by it good purpose is strengthened with the doing of good. Therefore, with all cheerfulness, fervor, compunction, and purity let us sing this Psalm, glorying in intimate divine praise, opting to bless and honor the sublime God apart from all things, recalling with great affection his benefits, enduring with great willingness all things contrary to his love, and giving thanks to him finally in all things.

---

67   Job 8:20.
68   John 9:31a.
69   E. N. The Latin text has *indendit* (reached forth, bent down) and not *attendit* (attended); however, the editor has suggested *indendit* may be an error and *attendit* is correct.
70   Job 8:5b–6.
71   John 9:31b.
72   Jer. 30:15a. The verse continues: *for the multitude of your iniquity and for your hardened sins I have done these things to you.*

PRAYER

GOD, CREATOR OF ALL THINGS, WHO rule by your power forever, we beseech you, look over us always with the eyes of your clemency; set our soul in the path toward the life of good deeds, and may you never withdraw your mercy from us.

Deus conditor universorum, qui dominaris in virtute tua in aeternum, oculis clementiae, quaesumus, super nos semper respice; pone animam nostram ad bonae actionis vitam, et nunquam amoveas a nobis misericordiam tuam.

Psalm 66

ARTICLE XXX

EXPOSITION OF THE SIXTY-SIXTH PSALM:
DEUS MISEREATUR NOSTRI, ETC.
MAY GOD HAVE MERCY ON US, ETC.

66{67}[1] *Unto the end, in, hymns, a Psalm of a canticle for David.*

In finem, in hymnis. Psalmus cantici David.

BOVE THIS PSALM IS THIS TITLE: **66{67}[1]** *In finem, in hymnis, psalmus cantici David; unto the end, in, hymns, a Psalm of a canticle for David*: that is, this Psalm directing to *the end* or to Christ, is *a Psalm of a canticle*, that is, of spiritual joyfulness, and it applies to David, that is, to the faithful, *in hymns*, that is, in the showing of praise to God. This Psalm literally is the invocation of thanksgiving for Christ's Incarnation at one time expected in the future, but now in the past.

66{67}[2] *May God have mercy on us, and bless us: may he cause the light of his countenance to shine upon us, and may he have mercy on us.*

Deus misereatur nostri, et benedicat nobis; illuminet vultum suum super nos, et misereatur nostri.

66{67}[3] *That we may know your way upon earth: your salvation in all nations.*

Ut cognoscamus in terra viam tuam, in omnibus gentibus salutare tuum.

Therefore, it says: **66{67}[2]** *Deus misereatur nostri, may God have mercy on us*, taking away our faults, and removing all impediments to the coming by Christ, *et benedicat nobis, and bless us*, that is, that he might expend upon us the gift of grace and multiply the same in us abundantly. For the Creator blesses rational creatures by sanctifying them through grace. And the creature also blesses the Creator, praising him and attributing to him all good. *Illuminet vultum suum super nos, may he cause the light of his countenance to shine upon us*, that is, may he make his understanding to shine upon us: as a Psalm above says, *Make your face* *to shine upon your servant.*[1] God therefore shines his face upon us when, by wisdom infused upon us by him, he makes us contemplators of the divine knowledge while he regards favorably our prayers and deeds. *Et misereatur nostri, and may he have mercy on us,* preserving us from future evil, so we might not be found unworthy at his coming by losing our former grace. **66{67}[3]** *Ut cognoscamus, that we might know,* O God, O Father, *in terra, on earth,* that is, in our present exile, *viam tuam, your way,* walking in the precepts of the divine law; or [alternatively], *your way,* that is, Christ, who said of himself, *I am the way, the truth, and the life.*[2] *In omnibus gentibus salutare tuum, your salvation in all nations*: that is, for this I desire there to be mercy, that we might see all nations converting to Christ, who is their salvation: of whom Simeon said, *Because my eyes have seen your salvation.*[3] The faithful person, therefore, prays in this verse for the enlightening of the Holy Spirit, that he not depart from the way of life in the present, but that by working he might recognize, and by recognizing he might walk in the way of the Lord, of which the Savior in the Gospel says: *How narrow is the gate . . . which leads to life! And how few there are that find it.*[4] Whence we find in Tobit: *Desire of God to direct your ways.*[5] Also in this that he says — *your salvation in all nations* — one prays that Christ may be known and honored by all nations.

66{67}[4] *Let people confess to you, O God: let all people give praise to you.*

Confiteantur tibi populi, Deus, confiteantur tibi populi omnes.

Consequently, for the benefits of the Incarnation of Christ and the conversion of the world, he gives thanks: **66{67}[4]** *Confiteantur tibi populi, Deus; let people confess to you, God,* with the confession of your praise and of their own fault, glorifying you and accusing themselves; *confiteantur tibi populi omnes, let all people give praise to you,* recollecting and preaching your benefits, and giving infinite thanks to you for the Incarnation of Christ and their own conversion: in the way it is written in Isaiah: *I will remember the tender mercies of the Lord, the praise of the Lord for all the things that the Lord has bestowed upon us, and for the multitude of his good things . . . which he has given them according to his kindness.*[6]

---

1   Ps. 30:17a.
2   John 14:6a.
3   Luke 2:30.
4   Matt. 7:14.
5   Tob. 4:20a.
6   Is. 53:7.

66{67}[5] *Let the nations be glad and rejoice: for you judge the people with justice, and direct the nations upon earth.*

Laetentur et exsultent gentes, quoniam iudicas populos in aequitate, et gentes in terra dirigis.

66{67}[5] *Laetentur, let them be glad* with interior gladness, *et exsultent, and let them rejoice,* with outward signs expressing their internal rejoicing, *gentes, the nations* called to the faith of Christ,[7] *quoniam iudicas populos in aequitate, for you judge the people with justice.* For at present God daily judges the people with the judgment of discretion: of which the Savior said: *Now is the judgment of the world.*[8] For God gives faith and grace without respect of persons to all who are so disposed and who do that which is within them, and he forsakes all others: and so now he separates by promise and merit the elect from the reprobate. But in death [he will separate] every single person at the end of the world with the judgment of reward, by which the good and the evil will be separated by place and reward.[9] Yet because, as the Apostle [Paul] attests, *It is a fearful thing to fall into the hands of the living God,*[10] it might appear astonishing why the Prophet [David] exhorts the people to rejoice, and rather not to have great fear, because God judges the people in equity. [This astonishment persists] unless [we understand that] he is speaking to those persons of which it was said before: *Let the people confess to you, O God.*[11] For they who now praise God and accuse and correct themselves may anticipate that they will be secure in the future judgment, and can deservedly rejoice in its coming, because then they will receive blessed immortality and complete blessedness. For this reason Christ exhorts his disciples: *But when these things begin to come to pass, look up, and lift up your heads,*

---

7   E. N. By the expression faith of Christ, the genitive is objective, not subjective; that is, the object of faith is Christ himself. We are not speaking of the faith *of* Christ, for Christ did not have the virtue of faith since he enjoyed the beatific vision. We are speaking of faith *in* Christ.

8   John 12:31a.

9   E. N. Denis distinguishes between the judgment of discretion (*iudicium discretionis*) and the judgment of remuneration, reward, or retribution (*iudicium remunerationis*). He describes these two judgments in Article XXVIII (Psalm 9:1) in Volume 1: "The first is the judgment of discretion, by which someone is called by mercy, but another is relinquished to justice. The second is also the judgment of examination and retribution, which will occur at the end of time, which, although it will be open and visible, yet the day and time are hidden." By "place," Denis means heaven or hell. By "reward" he means the beatific vision or the punishments of hell.

10   Heb. 10:31.

11   E. N. In other words, the words are directed not to the reprobate, but to the elect: those who confess the Lord with praise and with confession of sins.

that is, with exhilarated hearts, because your redemption is at hand.[12] And so especially the people should rejoice because *gentes in terra dirigis, you direct the nations upon earth,* directing them by your grace and angelic aid in the way of eternal salvation.[13] For we are greatly in need of such direction, according to that which Jeremiah says: *I know, O Lord, that the way of a man is not his: neither is it in a man to walk, and to direct his steps.*[14]

66{67}[6]   *Let the people, O God, confess to you: let all the people give praise to you.*

Confiteantur tibi populi, Deus, confiteantur tibi populi omnes.

66{67}[7]   *The earth has yielded her fruit. May God, our God bless us!*

Terra dedit fructum suum: benedicat nos Deus, Deus noster!

66{67}[8]   *May God bless us: and all the ends of the earth fear him.*

Benedicat nos Deus, et metuant eum omnes fines terrae.

66{67}[6] *Confiteantur tibi populi, Deus, confiteantur tibi populi omnes; let the people, O God, confess to you: let all the people give praise to you.* This verse is repeated because of the joyfulness and the fruitful sweetness of its sentiment. 66{67}[7] *Terra dedit fructum suum, the earth has yielded her fruit,* that is, the Virgin Mary birthed Christ. Of this earth it is written: *Let the earth be opened, and bud forth a Savior.*[15] And of the fruit of this earth we are informed by Isaiah: *In that day the bud of the Lord shall be in magnificence and glory, and the fruit of the earth shall be high.*[16] Now morally speaking the earth gives fruit when the holy Church spiritually instructs, perfects, and conserves her sons, and when our body lives soberly, being zealously devoted to improving the soul in

---

12   Luke 21:28.

13   E. N. Fr. John A. Hardon, S. J. notes that it is both permissible and pious to believe and to put into practice such belief that "not only individuals have their own guardian angels, but societies, cities and states and whole nations have their own distinctive guardian spirits. So too it may be held that parishes and dioceses, religious institutes and the whole Catholic Church have a multitude of angels who are selectively appointed to direct and protect their collective charges." http://www.therealpresence.org/archives/Angelology/Angelology_027.htm. Deut. 32:8 (in the Septuagint translation) reads: *When the Most High divided the nations, when he separated the sons of Adam, he set the bounds of the nations (εθνῶν / ethnōn) according to the number of the angels of God (αγγέλων θεού / angelōn theou).*

14   Jer. 10:23.

15   Is. 45:8b.

16   Is. 4:2a.

all things. *Benedicat nos Deus, Deus noster! May God, our God, bless us!*
66{67}[8] *Benedicat nos Deus; may God bless us.* Although this prayer
can be directed to the entire superlatively most blessed Trinity as well
as the singular Persons, it can nevertheless also be explained in this way:
May God the Father through his Son bless us: in the manner that the
Apostle said: *Blessed be the God and Father of our Lord Jesus Christ, who
has blessed us with spiritual blessings in heavenly places, in Christ* Jesus.[17]
May our God bless us, that is, the incarnate Son of God, who in a special sense is called our God, according to this, *This is the name that they
shall call him: the Lord our just one;*[18] and this, *They shall call his name
Emmanuel, which being interpreted is, God with us.*[19] May God, that is,
the Holy Spirit, bless us. *Et metuant eum, and may they fear him,* namely,
the God one in essence and three in persons, *omnes fines terrae, all the
ends of the earth,* that is, all men dwelling throughout the whole earth:
may these fear God with a holy and filial fear.[20] According to Catholic
teachers, from the fact that the word God is here named three times,
and after this there is repeated just one time the word Him, the Trinity
in persons and the unity in nature is intimated, in the same manner as
Isaiah relates of the Seraphim: *They cried one to another, and said: Holy,
holy, holy, the Lord God of hosts.*[21] *And the Lord* in Zechariah *said to
Satan: The Lord rebuke you, O Satan: and the Lord . . . rebuke you.*[22] Even
the Jews affirm that in such places of Scripture God is said three times
for reasons of greater expression, such as we find in Jeremiah: *O earth,
earth, earth, hear the word of the Lord.*[23]

See this Psalm is brief but also most full of all manner of fervor and
devotion. Let us conform the affection of our hearts, therefore, to the
most sacred words of this present Psalm, and from the depths of our
marrow let us beseech the divine mercy in all things, so that with vices
beat back, we might be enriched with the blessings of Christ, and we
might be instructed by the light of the divine countenance. And so let us,
with most sincere hearts, beseech God on behalf of the common good
of all and the salvation of the whole world, so that all might confess
the Lord and render him honor. For whenever we assimilate the love of
the divine mind in this sort of prayer, we are followers of our heavenly

---

17   Eph. 1:3.
18   Jer. 23:6b.
19   Matt. 1:23b; *cf.* Is. 7:14b.
20   E. N. For a discussion of the different species of fear, *see* footnote 18-42.
21   Is. 6:3a.
22   Zech. 3:2.
23   Jer. 22:29.

Father, who wills that all men might be saved,[24] and *makes his sun rise on the good and the evil.*[25] Whence the divine Apostle [Paul] said: *I desire, first of all, that supplications, [prayers, intercessions, and thanksgivings] be made for all men, for kings, [and for all that are in high station,] that we may lead a quiet and a peaceable life in all piety.*[26]

PRAYER

O GOD, MERCIFUL TO ALL, O GOD, LIGHT of light and fount of brightness, shine upon us the countenance of your mercy, bless us, and make us to know on earth your way so that walking, rejoicing, and exulting without stumbling, we might arrive to the eternal dwelling, where you, O God, live and reign in Trinity.

Deus miserator omnium, Deus lux lucis et fons luminis, illumina super nos vultum tuae miserationis, benedic nos, et fac cognoscere in terra viam tuam: ut in hac inoffense ambulantes, laetantes et exsultantes, ad mansionem pertingamus aeternam, qui in Trinitate vivis et regnas, Deus.

---

24   *Cf.* 1 Tim. 2:4.
25   Matt. 5:45a.
26   1 Tim. 2:1–2. The phrases in brackets replace the "etc." of the Latin text.

Psalm 67

ARTICLE XXXI

EXPOSITION OF THE SIXTY-SEVENTH PSALM:
EXSURGAT DEUS, ETC.
LET GOD ARISE, ETC.

67{68}[1] *Unto the end, a Psalm of a canticle for David himself.*
In finem. Psalmus cantici ipsi David.

HE TITLE OF THE PSALM NOW BEING explained is: **67{68}[1]** *In finem. Psalmus cantici ipsi David; unto the end, a Psalm of a canticle for David himself:* that is, this Psalm raising us up to Christ, *is of a canticle,* that is, of spiritual exultation, for it fully and clearly handles the mysteries of our reparation:[1] and it relates to the prophet David its author, yet he who is signified by David, namely, Christ, coincides as its subject. And so this present Psalm literally speaks of Christ and his mysteries: for the Apostle [Paul] full of the Holy Spirit explained this Psalm as written about the mission of the Holy Spirit: *But to every one of us,* he says, *is given grace, according to the measure of the giving of Christ:* wherefore he says, *Ascending on high, he led captivity captive; he gave gifts to men.*[2] And he adds: *Now that he ascended, what is it, but because he also descended first into the lower parts of the earth?*[3] See, by this scripture, [that is, this Psalm,] the Apostle [Paul] proves the Ascension of Christ. But such proof [from Scripture] is not strong unless it comes from its literal sense, as Augustine has attested to.[4]

67{68}[2] *Let God arise, and let his enemies be scattered: and let them that hate him flee from before his face.*

Exsurgat Deus, et dissipentur inimici eius; et fugiant qui oderunt eum a facie eius.

---

1 E. N. The word *reparatio,* reparation, is here used as a synonym for *restitutio* (restitution), *instauratio* (renewing), and *restoratio* (restoration), namely, the reconciliation of mankind unto God.
2 Eph. 4:7–8.
3 Eph. 4:9.
4 E. N. This rule is from St. Augustine of Hippo's epistle 93 against Vicentius the Donatist. Denis mentions it in various places, including Article IV and Article XII (Psalm 2:1) in Volume I.

67{68}[3] *As smoke vanishes, so let them vanish away: as wax melts
before the fire, so let the wicked perish at the presence of God.*

*Sicut deficit fumus, deficiant; sicut fluit cera a facie ignis, sic
pereant peccatores a facie Dei.*

Therefore, it says: **67{68}[2]** *Exsurgat Deus, let God arise*, that is, let
Christ, who is the true God, rise again from the dead; *et dissipentur
inimici eius, and let his enemies be scattered*, that is, let the Jews who killed
him be scattered, dispersed, and struck down. For this came upon them
in the avenging of the blood of Christ by Titus and the Romans, in the
manner that is foretold in Daniel: *And a people with their leader that
shall come, shall destroy the city and the sanctuary.*[5] *Et fugiant qui oderunt
eum, a facie eius; and let them that hate him flee from before his face*, that
is, the unbelieving among the Jews, of whom Christ in the Gospel says,
Now they have willingly both seen and hated both me and my Father:[6] these
flee from before his face, that is, from the appearance or the reproach of
vindication which Christ will administer upon them through the Romans.
Of which vindication Christ said through Isaiah: *The day of vengeance
is in my heart, the year of my redemption is come.*[7] For before the siege
of the Jews by the Romans, all the Jews fled into Jerusalem for fear of
them. **67{68}[3]** *Sicut deficit fumus, deficiant; as smoke vanishes, so let
them vanish away.* For like smoke vanishes when fire is removed, so the
aforementioned Jews withdrew [from the city of Jerusalem] when food
was entirely consumed, and they were compelled to turn themselves over
to their enemies. Also, they gradually withdrew [from there] during that
time [and remain away] even unto the present, not only by number and
in favor, but in power, kingdom, priesthood, and all honor of the law of
their fathers. *Sicut fluit cera a facie, as wax melts before the face*, that is,
the presence and influence, *ignis, the fire, sic pereant peccatores, so let the
wicked perish*, that is, the forementioned Christicides,[8] *a facie Dei, at the
presence of God*, that is, from the sight and the infliction of divine vengeance: not that he would destroy their essence, but that he would withdraw all grace from them, and in the present life they would be variously

---

5   Dan. 9:26b.
6   John 15:24b.
7   Is. 63:4.
8   L. *Christicidiae*, a combination of *Christi* ("of Christ") and *cidium* (a suffix, derived
from *caedere*, meaning "to kill," indicating the act of killing or the person so doing). "True,
the Jewish authorities and those who followed their lead pressed for the death of Christ
[John 19:26]; still, what happened in His passion cannot be charged against all the
Jews, without distinction, then alive, nor against the Jews of today." VII, *Nostra aetate*, 4.

oppressed, and in the future age they would eternally be tormented.

Now this part [of the Psalm] can be understood as pertaining to the invisible enemies of Christ, so that it reads in this sense: *Let God arise* (as has been stated), *and let his enemies be scattered*: that is, let the power and the wickedness of the devils who seek to harm men be crushed. For Christ bound up the strong man,[9] and through the merit of his Passion he exceedingly weakened the power of the devils. *And let them that hate him*, that is, let the demons be cast out from the heart of the sinner and the body of those obsessed, *from before his face*, that is, by virtue of the presence of Christ who is at work everywhere. Whence, at the instance of the Passion, he said: *Now shall the prince of this world be cast out.*[10] And also after the Resurrection he told the Apostles: *These signs shall follow them that believe: In my name they shall cast out devils.*[11] *As smoke vanishes, so let them vanish away*: that is, let the worship of demons or idolatry be expelled by the ministers of Christ, and let the devil himself be fully overcome by the Apostles of Christ and their successors, and let Christ alone be worshipped as God in eternity. Whence it says in Isaiah: *The Lord alone shall be exalted in that day, and idols shall be utterly destroyed.*[12] Hence also the Savior said: *Behold, I have given you power to tread . . . upon all the power of the enemy: and nothing shall hurt you.*[13] *As wax melts before the fire, so let the wicked perish*, that is, the devils obstinate in evil, *at the presence of God*: for at the end of the world they will be thrust down back into hell. According to what we read in the Gospel this was fulfilled also in Jesus Christ in a literal sense when he was still walking about in the world: *As many as had evils, and the unclean spirits, when they saw Jesus, they fell down before him: and they cried saying: You are the Son of God.*[14] And again: *What have we, they said, to do with you, Jesus Son of God most high? Have you come here to torment us before the time?*[15]

This part can also be explained in a more general sense and so understood as dealing with God according to his divine operations, in this way: *Let God arise*, not by movement or by place, but through operation so that the good might be assisted, the ungodly might be resisted, and so let

---

9   Cf. Luke 11:21–22: *When a strong man armed keeps his court, those things are in peace which he possesses. But if a stronger than he comes upon him and overcomes him; he will take away all his armor wherein he trusted, and will distribute his spoils.*

10   John 12:31b.

11   Mark 16:17.

12   Is. 2:17b–18.

13   Luke 10:19.

14   Mark 3:10b–12a.

15   Matt. 8:29.

him hold himself out like someone rising up, as is said in a Psalm above: *Arise, O Lord, help us.*[16] *And let his enemies be scattered,* those who do not want to convert, namely, heretics, schismatics, pagans, Jews, and the hardened. *And let them that hate him flee from before his face,* that is, let such persons be scourged by God so that they might desire to hide themselves, though that is something not possible, because God is everywhere. Whence Scripture says: *The kings of the earth, and the princes, and tribunes, and the rich, and the strong . . . hid themselves in the dens and in the rocks of the mountains, saying Fall upon us, and hide us from the face of him that sits upon the throne and from the wrath of the Lamb.*[17] *As smoke vanishes,* so let them vanish away, lest they seek to fulfil evil works and to harm the holy. For the ungodly are incessantly in revolt, *for they shall shortly wither away as grass.*[18] *As wax melts before the fire,* [*so let the wicked perish at the presence of God*].[19] This is what is written in Isaiah: *As the tongue of the fire devours the stubble, and the heat of the flame consumes it: so shall their root be as ashes, and their bud shall go up as dust.*[20]

The Church, as does any member of the faithful, also prays this not out of the zeal of vindictiveness, but for the love of justice, conforming themselves to the divine justness. Or it prays that in the present age they might be punished so that they might not be condemned eternally. But they can also [pray] this for the dissipation, flight, disappearance, and perishing of the sinner, understood in a good sense, namely, that we might pray not nature or grace to dissipate, flee, disappear, and perish, but rather that malice do so. Yet anyone who is tempted can say these verses for the dispersing, expulsion and victory over the devil, namely, that God may come to his aid, and so by the power of the grace of God the tempting demons might be dissipated, made to flee, disappear, and perish.

67{68}[4]   *And let the just feast, and rejoice before God: and be delighted with gladness.*

> *Et iusti epulentur; et exsultent in conspectu Dei, et delectentur in laetitia.*

67{68}[4] *Et iusti epulentur et exsultent in conspectu Dei, et delectentur in laetitia;* and let the just feast and rejoice before God: and be delighted with gladness. This can be literally undestood as applying to the holy Apostles

---

16   Ps. 43:26a.
17   Rev. 6:15–16.
18   Ps. 36:2a.
19   E. N. The part in brackets replaces the "etc." in the Latin text.
20   Is. 5:24a.

and the early Church first gathered in Jerusalem. Of this is written in the Acts of the Apostles: *They were persevering in the doctrine . . . and in the communication of the breaking of bread, and in prayers.*[21] And again: *All they that believed, were together, and had all things in common;*[22] *and they took their meat with gladness and simplicity of heart.*[23]

But, in a general sense, this can be explained in this way: *And let the just feast,* now by faith with divine contemplation and refreshing *with the bread of life and understanding . . . and the water of wholesome wisdom,*[24] that is, with charity and grace and the gifts of the Holy Spirit, and especially the Sacrament of the Body and Blood of Christ. Also, in the future they will banquet with the angels, feasting upon bread in the Kingdom of God,[25] that is, they will blessedly enjoy the exceedingly most blessed Godhead, which is the refreshment of all the blessed [in heaven]. Of this spiritual banquet Solomon says in the Song of Songs: *Eat, O friends, and drink, and be inebriated, my dearly beloved.*[26] And the Son of God said to his own: *I dispose to you . . . a kingdom, that you might eat and drink at my table in my kingdom.*[27] *Et exsultent in conspectu Dei, and rejoice before God,* that is, the just will rejoice before God, as the Apostle [Paul] said: *He that glories, let him glory in the Lord.*[28] For in the present life, to exult before God or in the sight of God is to rejoice of those things and in those things that are pleasing to God, and to place oneself before God, and in the serenity of holy conscience to rejoice in virtuous acts and the divine honor. For in the heavenly homeland, the Saints exult in the sight of God, that is, of that vision of the divine essence, for they will see him as he is.[29] For this reason it is said in a Psalm above: *You shall fill me with the joy of your countenance.*[30] *Et delectentur in laetitia, and be delighted with gladness,* which God gives to them. Whence it is written of the Christians of the early Church: *They rejoiced for the consolation.*[31] For the intellectual powers, namely, the reason and the will, reflect upon their own acts: and so the mind is able to take delight of its own joy.

---

21 Acts 2:42.
22 Acts 2:44.
23 Acts 2:46b.
24 Ecclus. 15:3a.
25 Luke 14:15: *When one of them that sat at table with him, had heard these things, he said to him: Blessed is he that shall eat bread in the kingdom of God.*
26 Songs 5:1b.
27 Luke 22:29–30a.
28 2 Cor. 10:17.
29 *Cf.* 1 John 3:2b.
30 Ps. 15:11a.
31 Acts 15:31b.

67{68}[5] *Sing to God, sing a Psalm to his name, make a way for him who ascends upon the west: the Lord is his name. Rejoice before him: [but the wicked] shall be troubled at his presence,* [32]

Cantate Deo, Psalmum dicite nomini eius; iter facite ei qui ascendit super occasum. Dominus nomen illi; exsultate in conspectu eius. Turbabuntur a facie eius,

67{68}[6] *Who is the father of orphans, and the judge of widows. God in his holy place:*

Patris orphanorum, et iudicis viduarum; Deus in loco sancto suo:

67{68}[7] *God who makes men of one manner to dwell in a house: Who brings out them that were bound in strength; in like manner them that provoke, that dwell in sepulchers.*

Deus qui inhabitare facit unius moris in domo; qui educit vinctos in fortitudine, similiter eos qui exasperant, qui habitant in sepulchris.

67{68}[5] *Cantate Deo, sing to God,* with heart and voices praising him; *Psalmum, a Psalm,* that is, the words and the praises of the Psalms, *dicite nomine eius, sing to his name:* for God is most beautifully praised in the Psalms. Or [alternatively]: *a Psalm,* that is, a good work, [33] *sing to his name,* not only by word, but also preaching him through actions, just as Christ exhorted: Let them see, he said, *your good works, that they may glorify your Father who is in heaven.* [34] For it is not to be forgotten that this book [of the Psalms] is for this reason called the Psalter, because David was accustomed to sing Psalms using an instrument that is called a psaltery, singing with his mouth and playing with his hands, as in this day and age the Church does on an organ. But in a proper sense a psalm was said to be that sound or melody of the instrument that is called a psaltery: and so the songs contained in this book are called the Psalms, because when they were sung they were accompanied by such a melody. Hence by psalter one can understand a good work exhibited to the praise of God or that praise expended to God.

Iter facite ei qui ascendit super occasum, make a way for him who ascends upon the west, that is, prepare the way to Christ, by which route he comes

---

32   E. N. The Douay Rheims has expressed the implied subject of the verb *turbabuntur,* "they shall be troubled," so the words "but the wicked" are not found in the Latin text.

33   E. N. "Mystically and according to the Gloss, a Psalm signifies a good work." St. Thomas Aquinas, *In Psalmos Davidis Exp., super Psalmo* 4 n. 1.

34   Matt. 5:16.

to dwell in your hearts, for his *delights* are *to be with the children of men.*[35]
For what else anyhow is it to make a way to God except to dispose oneself
to be able to have the grace of God: to remove obstacles [to that grace],
abandoning sinful intentions, being sorrowful for past evil done, and
striving toward the obedience of the divine precepts? For here John the
Baptist drawing upon the words of Isaiah said: *Prepare the way of the Lord,*
make straight his paths.[36] And so to prepare the way to God is nothing
other than that which the prophet Amos commanded: *Be prepared to meet*
your God, O Israel.[37] Therefore, make the way to him who *ascends upon*
the west, that is, to Christ, who transcended all mortality, passibility, and
defectability in the Resurrection,[38] for, as the Apostle [Paul] has attested,
Christ rising again from the dead, dies now no more.[39] Now it is befitting
diligently to pay attention here that in this place where the words *upon*
the west (super occasum) [are used in the Vulgate], the Hebrew in truth
has the word Arabot which according to the Hebrews is the proper noun
that refers to one of the seven heavens.[40] And therefore according to them,
this is the true message: "Make way for him who ascends into heaven":
which is properly referable to Christ, who gloriously ascended into the
empyrean heaven, which without the addition is antonomastically called
heaven.[41] And so [the verse] can be reduced so that it says, *upon the west.*
For the Jews adored facing the west so as to distinguish themselves from

---

35   Prov. 8:31.
36   Luke 3:4b; Is. 40:3.
37   Amos 4:12b.
38   E. N. Christ's Resurrection has overcome death, suffering, and sin. Pope Benedict XVI: "The Resurrection, then, is not a theory, but a historical reality revealed by the man Jesus Christ by means of his 'Passover,' his 'passage,' that has opened a 'new way' between heaven and earth.... If we take away Christ and his Resurrection, there is no escape for men.... *Resurrectio Domini, spes nostra!* The resurrection of Christ is our hope!" http://www.vatican.va/content/benedict-xvi/en/messages/urbi/documents/hf_ben-xvi_mes_20090412_urbi-easter.html.
39   Rom. 6:9a.
40   E. N. According to the Babylonian Talmud, Chagigah 12b, ערבות (*araboth* or *aravot*) is the highest of seven heavens. Referring to this verse, the Talmud states: "There, in the firmaments, are the *ofanim*, the seraphim, the holy divine creatures, and the ministering angels, and the Throne of Glory. The King, God, the living, lofty, exalted One dwells above them in *Aravot*, as it is stated: 'Extol Him Who rides upon the skies [*Aravot*], Whose name is God.'" https://www.sefaria.org/Chagigah?lang=bi.
41   E. N. Antonomasia is a rhetorical device where a proper name is replaced by an epithet or a phrase (*e.g.,* "the Philosopher" as a reference to Aristotle). Denis is saying that the proper noun Arabot, which is the empyreal heaven or the seventh heaven, is through antonomasia frequently just referred to as plain and simple "heaven." On the medieval notions of heaven, specifically the empyrean or empyreal heaven, *see* footnote 19-11, Volume I.

the Gentiles, all of whom prayed toward the east out of reverence to the sun: and so by the fact that Christ is said to have ascended *upon the west* it is given to understand that he ascended above the place of human ado-ration, to the place of angelic dwelling, namely, to the empyrean heaven.

Dominus nomen illi, the Lord is his name. By this the Prophet [David] shows Christ to be the true God, because the Lord is the proper name to [refer to] God, according to this: *I the Lord, this is my name;*[42] and this, *He who calls the waters of the sea, and pours them out upon the face of the earth: The Lord is his name.*[43] For although this name — the Lord — may befittingly be used to refer to others by reason of participation and in an imperfect sense, yet it is proper to God by reason of his own nature, and according to universal plenitude, because *all things* are *under* his *power.*[44] Whence in Isaiah it says: *I am the Lord, and there is no other.*[45] It is fitting to use it also with respect to Christ according to his human nature, being that he is the ruler and Lord of all things, according to what he himself said: *The Father loves the Son: and he has given all things into his hand;*[46] and elsewhere, *All power is given to me in heaven and in earth.*[47] But this power is fittingly applied to him, inasmuch as he is man, not by nature, but by grace.[48]

---

42   Is. 42:8a.
43   Amos 5:8b.
44   Esther 13:9a.
45   Is. 45:18b.
46   John 3:35.
47   Matt. 28:18b.
48   E. N. Specifically and most notably, the "grace of union" or the "hypostatic union," a grace only found Jesus Christ. "The Hypostatic Union is a unique work of grace. The Grace of Union is the most precious that can be bestowed upon a creature. . . . It communicates the Divine Substance itself; it anticipates all possible merit on the part of the human nature, because human nature derives its subsistence — the first and most essential condition of meritorious acts — from the Logos. Besides, the Grace of Union is superior to all others in this, that it constitutes the personality of Christ, and thus makes all the privileges which it contains Christ's own personal and natural property." "The names 'God,' 'Lord,' and 'Holy' connote here a glory communicable to creatures. . . . Now the fact that Christ is placed above all other gods, lords, and saints, in a manner proper to the true God alone, shows that His participation in the Divine glory is not merely extrinsical and accidental as in other creatures, but intrinsical and substantial: He is not a simple image, but the perfect likeness of God; He is the Lord, sitting at the right hand of the Father, on the same throne, and exercising the same power. Just as in the constitution of Adam — created to the image and likeness of God — the foundation was laid for his natural glory and dominion over the world, so in the constitution of Christ — the consubstantial image of God (that is, who subsists in a Divine Person) — the foundation is laid for His Divine Glory and Power." Joseph Wilhelm and Thomas B. Scannell, *A Manual of Catholic Theology based on Scheeben's 'Dogmatik'* (New York: Benziger Brothers 1906), 101–02, 115–16.

Exsultate in conspectu eius, rejoice before him. This repeats that which is said immediately above — *let the just feast, and rejoice before God. Turbabuntur a facie eius,* **67{68}[6]** *patris orphanorum et iudicis viduarum; [but the wicked] shall be troubled at his presence,* **67{68}[6]** *who is the father of orphans, and the judge of widows,* that is, the unbelieving Jews and all the perverse shall be troubled by the appearance or vengeance of Christ, who is the father of orphans and the judge of widows. For the Jews were troubled when they were devastated by the Romans. And also all those who have been malicious will be troubled in the last judgment, as is written in the book of Wisdom: *These seeing it shall be troubled with terrible fear, . . . groaning for anguish of spirit.*[49]

Deus in loco sancto suo, God in his holy place. The holy place in which God is said particularly to dwell is the pure soul, in the manner that is written, the soul of the just man is the seat of Wisdom;[50] or [this can be said to refer to] the empyreal heaven in which the Godhead works in a most eminent manner and shines in a most brilliant way: for this reason it states in Isaiah: *Heaven is my throne;*[51] or [yet another way to look at it], the Church militant and triumphant, both of which are called the temple, house, and place of God: whence also elsewhere, *The Lord is in his holy temple;*[52] and again, the Lord has borne witness, *Where there are two or three gathered together in my name, there am I in the midst of them.*[53] **67{68}[7]** *Deus qui inhabitare facit unius moris in domo, God who makes men of one manner to dwell in a house.* By this *house* we are able to understand the Church militant and any devout congregation of men. For God by faith, charity, and grace causes his servants to be of one will, and of the same rite and custom. Whence in the Acts of the Apostles we

---

49   Wis. 5:2a, 3a.

50   *Cf.* Wis. 7:27b: Wisdom *renews all things, and through nations conveys herself into holy souls, she makes the friends of God and prophets.* E. N. The phrase itself used by Denis — *anima iusti sedes est Sapientiae* — is not found in Scripture, but is a paraphrase drawn from a variety of Scriptural sources and probably derived from St. Augustine. See Anne-Marie La Bonnardière, *Anima iusti sedes sapientiae* dans l'œuvre de saint Augustin: Epektasis (FS Jean Daniélou), eds. Jacques Fontaine and Charles Kannengiesser (Paris: 1972), 111-120. An example of St. Augustine's use of this: "'The soul of the just is throne of Wisdom.' This is a great thing, a great thing is this saying: 'the throne of Wisdom is the soul of the just'; that is, Wisdom sits as it were in her chair, as if on her throne in the soul of the just man. . .'[T]he soul of the just man is the seat of wisdom.' Who are the seats? Those of heaven. Who are those of heaven? Heaven. What is heaven? He to whom the Lord says: Heaven is my seat. And these just men are the seats." St. Augustine, Psalm 121,9 (Ps. 121:5) *Enarr. in Psalmos,* 37 PL 1626.

51   Is. 66:1a.

52   Ps. 10:5a.

53   Matt. 18:20.

read of the early Church: *The multitude of believers had but one heart and one soul.*[54] For this reason, the Apostle [Paul] said: *I beseech you, brethren, by the name of our Lord Jesus Christ, that you all speak the same thing, and that there be no schisms among you.*[55] Therefore the vice of singularity is to be greatly avoided, especially in monasteries, where the one fixed thing is the rule.[56] Nevertheless, because (as the Apostle [Paul] attests) *every man abounds in his own sense,*[57] there cannot be a perfect conformity of life in all things during this present life, just as there cannot be perfect charity or grace. But the more charity and grace are ample, that much more commendable will be the conformity of life: and so what it says — he *who makes men of one manner to dwell in a house* — is especially true of the citizens of the Church triumphant, for in it there is the highest concord, full conformity, consummated grace, and perfect charity.

Qui, *who*, namely, Christ, *educit vinctos, brings out them that were bound*, that is, the fathers and the just of all ancient times at one time held in limbo,[58] *in fortitudine, in strength* of the divinity himself. For Christ immediately after his Resurrection led out of the limbo of the fathers the saints and those captive in it, so that Zechariah speaking to Christ said: *You also by the blood of your testament have sent forth your prisoners out of the pit, wherein is no water.*[59] But because what is brought forth here is more clearly written of below,[60] so the aforesaid words are more fittingly expounded upon in another fashion here, in this way: *He who brings out them that were bound*, that is, sinners entangled in the fetters of vice, and subject to the yoke of demons, by

---

54   Acts 4:32a.

55   1 Cor. 1:10a.

56   E. N. The Abbot of Liesse, Louis de Blois (1506–1566) writes: "Diligently avoid all faulty singularity. This vice of singularity is especially to be shunned by those who dwell in monasteries, and are bound to live according to a common and approved rule." Louis of Blois, *Spiritual Works* (ed., John E. Bowden) (New York: Benziger Bros. 1903), 136.

57   Rom. 14:5b.

58   E. N. This is the limbo of the fathers (*limbus partum*) where the souls of the just prior to Christ's sacrificial death on the Cross resided, and who were released in the so-called "harrowing of hell" on Holy Saturday. Gerard Manley Hopkins wrote of this harrowing in his poem "O Death, Death": O Death, Death, He is come. / O grounds of Hell make room. / Who came from further than the stars / Now comes as low beneath. / Thy ribbèd ports, O Death / Make wide; and Thou, O Lord of Sin, / Lay open thine estates. / Lift up your heads, O Gates; / Be ye lift up, ye everlasting doors / The King of Glory will come in. Gerard Manley Hopkins, *The Poems of Gerard Manley Hopkins* (Oxford: Oxford University Press, 1961), p. 277.

59   Zech. 9:11.

60   E. N. See *Commentary* pertaining to Psalm 67:19.

his almighty and divine *fortitudine, strength.* For it is proper to God alone to remit sins, to bestow grace, and to justify the ungodly: and, according to Augustine, it is a greater and more powerful work to justify the ungodly than to create heaven and earth.[61] Christ leads out those victorious from death unto life, from fault to grace, from the state of damnation unto salvation.

Similiter eos qui exasperant, in a like manner them that provoke: that is, those God also brings out in the manner described, those who not only sin, but also do battle against the faith; these are rebels against God, and they provoke him. Among these was Saul, to whom Christ said: *Saul, Saul, why do you persecute me?*[62] *Qui habitant in sepulchris, that dwell in sepulchers.* For those who provoke the divine majesty dwell in sepulchers, that is, in a most grave practice, in a most deep pit of misery, under heavy burden of vicious habits. To these men what is said in Proverbs is fitting: *The wicked man when he is come into the depth of sins, is disdainful.*[63] With such persons, therefore, the divine power which brings them out [from evil] or converts them shines forth in a greater way than in the justification of a sinner that is not hardened, who is not so accustomed to vice. But some [commentators] in a satisfactory way fittingly distinguish that which is said here—*in like manner them that provoke*—from that which is said thereafter—*that dwell in sepulchers*—so that [God] not only brings out those who are habituated in vice, but also those who have died in mortal sin, resurrecting them to the natural and meritorious life, as clearly happened with the young man

---

61   E. N. In his Tractates on the Gospel of John, St. Augustine implies this as he reflects on John 14:14: *[I]ntellegat qui potest, iudicet qui potest, utrum maius sit iustos creare quam impios iustificare. Certe enim si aequalis est utrumque potentiae, hoc maioris est misericordiae.* "Let him who is able understand, and let him who is able judge, whether it is a greater thing to create the just than to justify the ungodly. For surely if the power is the same with both, in this [the justification of the ungodly] mercy is greater." *In Evang. Ioan. Tract.,* 72, 3., PL 35, 1823. The negative corollary of this is famously stated by St. John Henry Newman: "The Church. . . .regards this world, and all that is in it, as a mere shade, as dust and ashes, compared with the value of one single soul. . . . She holds it better for the sun and moon to drop from heaven, for the earth to fail, and for all the many millions who are upon it to die of starvation in extremest agony, as far as temporal affliction goes, than that one soul, I will not say, should be lost, but should commit one single venial sin, should tell one willful untruth, though it harmed no one, or should steal one poor farthing without excuse." John Henry Newman, *Lectures on Certain Difficulties Felt by Anglicans in Submitting to the Catholic Church* (London: Burns & Lambert, 1850), 199.

62   Acts 9:4b.

63   Prov. 18:3a. E. N. I have replaced the Douay-Rheims "contemneth," which translates *contemnit,* with "is disdainful."

that was raised by John the Evangelist,[64] and also of the dead man who had hung himself whom St. Martin resuscitated:[65] and in this is most greatly declared the omnipotence of the Creator.

67{68}[8] *O God, when you did go forth in the sight of your people, when you did pass through the desert:*

Deus, cum egredereris in conspectu populi tui, cum pertransires in deserto,

67{68}[9] *The earth was moved, and the heavens trickled down at the presence of the God of Sinai, at the presence of the God of Israel.*

Terra mota est, etenim caeli distillaverunt, a facie Dei Sinai, a facie Dei Israel.

Consequently, the Prophet [David] sets forth an example or — better said — an argument by example through received truths: **67{68}[8]** *Deus cum egredereris in conspectu populi tui; O God, when you did go forth in the sight of your people,* leading the children of Israel out of Egypt; *cum petransires in deserto, when you did pass through the desert,* leading them toward mount Sinai. Now God is said to go forth and to pass through, not by a movement of place, since he subsists uncircumscribably and unchangeably; but [he is said to do so] because during the day he showed the way to his people by a column of cloud, and at night by a column of fire.[66] Secondly, by reason of protection and providence by which he mercifully protected and graciously provided for them. *For here Moses said to the Lord: If you yourself do not go before, bring us not out of this place.*[67] Third, God is then said to go forth and to pass through in the sight of his people because his messenger, namely the angel appearing and speaking in the person of God, went before them

---

64   E. N. Probably a reference to the young man Satheus whom St. John raised from the dead as related in the *Golden Legend* of Jacobus Voragine. Satheus, an unbeliever who died in mortal sin, was raised from the dead and suffered temporarily the pains of hell, which he described as including: *vermes et umbrae, flagellum, frigus et ignis, daemonis aspectus, scelerum confusio, luctus:* "worms and darkness, scourges, cold and heat, sight of devil, confusion of sins, and wailing." https://sourcebooks.fordham.edu/basis/goldenlegend/GoldenLegend-Volume2.asp#John%20the%20Evangelist

65   E. N. In the *Life of St. Martin of Tours* (316–397 AD), written by the chronicler Sulpicius Severus (*ca.* 363–*ca.* 425 AD), the resurrection of the servant of Lupicinus who had hung himself is retold. *De Vita Beati Martini*, PL 20, 165. This appears to be the miracle referred to by Denis.

66   Ex. 13:21.

67   Ex. 33:15.

according to what the Lord told Moses: *Behold I will send my angel, who shall go before you, and keep you in your journey, and bring you into the place that I have prepared.*[68] **67{68}[9]** *Terra mota est, the earth was moved.* For then mount Sinai was seen to move and to shake.[69] Or, *the earth was moved,* that is, the inhabitants of the land, and the men in the fields were moved, as we read in Exodus: *Then were the princes of Edom troubled, trembling seized on the stout men of Moab.*[70] *Etenim caeli distillaverunt a facie Dei Sinai, a facie Dei Israel; and the heavens trickled down at the presence of the God of Sinai, at the presence of the God of Israel:* that is, then winds of the heavens poured forth rain at the presence of God, made apparent by subject creation,[71] and by the presence of God to Israel, that is, to the people that stemmed from Jacob. For then *very thick clouds* covered mount Sinai,[72] and from the cloud that rain poured forth: and the manna descended from heaven by means of a light drizzle.[73]

Finally, this can all be explained in a mystical sense, in this way: *God,* the Only-Begotten of God, *when you did go forth* from the most secret bosom of God the Father, appearing in the world by the flesh you assumed, going forth *in the sight of your people,* namely, of the Apostles and the other believers, among whom you deigned to dwell; *when you did pass through the desert,* that is, in the world full of vice and derelict of good; or [alternatively], *in the desert,* sending the Apostles to the people who were at one time deserted and sterile. *The earth was moved:* that is, worldly men and sinners were converted to the faith and to penance; *and the heavens,* that is, the holy Apostles, *trickled down* the water of saving wisdom and the rain of heavenly grace, *at the presence of the God of Sinai,* that is, by the gracious presence of God, who gave the law at mount Sinai. In this way, the Apostles and holy preachers watered those who converted to the faith; for this reason the Apostle [Paul] said: *I have planted, Apollo watered.*[74]

---

68 Ex. 23:20.

69 Ex. 19:18: *And all mount Sinai was full of smoke: because the Lord was come down upon it in fire, and the smoke arose from it as out of a furnace: and all the mount was terrible.*

70 Ex. 15:15a.

71 E. N. Denis says *apparentis per creaturam subiectam,* meaning that God made himself known by assuming the form of a creature or a part of creation that was subject to him. Thus, God might show himself through angels, through cloud and fire, through thunder and lightning, *etc.*

72 Ex. 19:16.

73 Ex. 16:14.

74 1 Cor. 3:6a.

67{68}[10]   *You shall set aside for your inheritance a free rain, O God:*
and it was weakened, but you have made it perfect.

Pluviam voluntariam segregabis, Deus, haereditati tuae; et
infirmata est, tu vero perfecisti eam.

Now, out from the first and literal sense of these two [previous] verses,
the Prophet [David] concludes: **67{68}[10]** *Pluviam voluntariam segregabis,*
Deus, haereditati tuae; you shall set aside your inheritance a free rain, O God.
It is as if he were saying: "If you bestowed upon the Israelites in the desert
and on mount Sinai such great graces, giving them manna and the law by
the coming down of an angel upon mount Sinai, then you certainly much
more amply will give your people by your Ascension into heaven." Therefore
it says: *a free rain*, that is, the dewfall of your grace, the flowing of doctrine,
and various graceful watering and spontaneous pouring of the Holy Spirit,
you have set aside, that is, you will give them as you see fit and specially, *for*
your inheritance, that is, for your chosen Christian people whom you have
freed with your own Blood. This Christ did often from time to time and
in the day of Pentecost. *Et infirmata est, and it was weakened*: that is, the
Church which is your inheritance, in and of itself is not sufficient, since it
does not have the power either by nature to save or otherwise merit. *Not*
that we are sufficient to think anything of ourselves, as of ourselves: but our
sufficiency is from God.[75] And so he adds: *tu vero perfecisti eam, but you*
have made it perfect, conferring to it by grace that which it does not have
by nature. For this Christ after his Resurrection told his disciples: *Stay in*
the city until you be endued with power from on high.[76] Moreover, literally the
Church of God is also often weak, by the coldness of the charity of many,[77]
and because of the various persecutions of tyrants. But God perfects it, by
renewing grace, and by destroying adversaries.

67{68}[11]   *In it shall your animals dwell; in your sweetness, O God, you*
have provided for the poor.

Animalia tua habitabunt in ea; parasti in dulcedine tua pau-
peri, Deus.

67{68}[12]   *The Lord shall give the word to them that preach good tidings*
with great power.

Dominus dabit verbum evangelizantibus, virtute multa.

---

75   2 Cor. 3:5.
76   Luke 24:49b.
77   Matt. 24:12: *Because iniquity has abounded, the charity of many shall grow cold.*

67{68}[**11**] *Animalia tua, your animals*, that is your Christian people, who are your sheep, *habitabunt in ea, in it shall ... dwell*, that is, [shall dwell] in the Church by faith and obedience remaining in ecclesiastical unity. *Parasti in dulcedine tua, in your sweetness ... you have provided*, that is, with your sweet goodness and kind clemency [you have provided] *pauperi, Deus; O God, for the poor*, that is, for the Christian people who are poor in spirit, who in the early Church were [physically also] poor and abject: this people you have provided with sufficient temporal goods, according to this, *Seek ... first the kingdom of God, and his justice, and all these things shall be added unto you.*[78] You have also provided the superlatively most noble food and drink for them, your Body and Blood, contained under sacramental forms. But you have also provided to us grace, internal consolation, and an abundance of divine gifts which you promised, saying *Whatsoever you shall ask the Father in my name, that will I do.*[79] 67{68} [**12**] *Dominus dabit verbum, the Lord shall give the word*, that is, a ready and prudent sermon, *evangelizantibus virtute multa, to them that preach good tidings with great power*, that is, the holy Apostles and those that followed them, who preached in a powerful manner, confirming their doctrine with miracles and the pouring out of their own blood. For in the Gospel Christ said to them: *For I will give you a mouth and wisdom, which all your adversaries shall not be able to resist and gainsay.*[80]

67{68}[**13**] *The king of powers is of the beloved, of the beloved; and the beauty of the house shall divide spoils.*

Rex virtutum dilecti, dilecti; et speciei domus dividere spolia.

67{68}[**13**] *Rex virtutum dilecti dilecti; the king of powers is of the beloved, of the beloved.* This verse is intricate and obscure. But sometimes one translation explains another, and so it was helpful to make a number of translations. So the translation by Jerome from the Hebrew has this: *The king of the armies will be leagued together.* For through the teaching of the Apostles, many kings, princes, noblemen, and potentates were made unanimous in Christ by love, faith, and worship.[81] Now, therefore, it says:

---

78   Matt. 6:33.

79   John 14:13.

80   Luke 21:15.

81   E. N. As heirs of Christ, we are ennobled in a spiritual sense: "'Christ,... in the very revelation of the mystery of the Father and of his love, makes man fully manifest to himself and brings to light his exalted vocation.' It is in Christ, 'the image of the invisible God,' that man has been created 'in the image and likeness' of the Creator. It is in Christ, Redeemer and Savior, that the divine image, disfigured in

the king of powers, that is, powerful kings, understanding the singular to stand for the plural, such as the Lord says to Pharaoh in Exodus: You still hold back my son (that is, the sons of Israel)?[82] And so [by *the king of powers*] is to be understood powerful kings have been made, *dilecti, of the beloved*, that is, of friends, *dilecti, of the beloved*, that is, of Jesus Christ, of which the Father says: *This is my Son, my beloved.*[83] Or [we can understand it] thus: *the king of powers*, that is, God the Father, who is the king of angels, who are called the heavenly powers, and they are *of the beloved*, that is of Christ himself, who is the most beloved Son of God. For all the holy angels are of Christ himself, as they are servants of his dominions. Whence Christ in the Gospel asserts of himself: *The Son of man shall send his angels.*[84] Yet it repeats *of the beloved*, and it follows with *et specie domus dividere spolia, and the beauty of the house shall divide spoils*: that is, Christ, who is the beloved of God the Father, is also the beloved insofar as he is man, he is also chosen to separate the spoils, that is, to distinguish, by diverse graces or status, those men that he redeems from the mouth of the enemy and delivers from death giving them different gifts of grace in the way that the Apostle [Paul] asserts, saying: *Some [God] has set in the Church: first the Apostles, secondly the Prophets, third the doctors:*[85] and this is the *beauty of the house*, that is, the ornament of the Church. For such distinction of ecclesiastical persons are equivalent to the ornament of the Church.

67{68}[14]   *If you sleep among the midst of lots, you shall be as the wings of a dove covered with silver, and the hinder parts of her back with the paleness of gold.*

Si dormiatis inter medios cleros, pennae columbae deargentatae, et posteriora dorsi ejus in pallore auri.

Then holy David speaks to the faithful, saying: **67{68}[14]** *Si dormiatis inter medios cleros, if you sleep among the midst of lots*, that is, if you rest with tranquil conscience between the two inheritances or between the two kinds of divine allotted goods, that is, between the temporal goods of this present life and the spiritual goods of the future life, thus

---

man by the first sin, has been restored to its original beauty and ennobled by the grace of God." CCC § 1701 (quoting GS 22, Col 1:15, 2 Cor. 4:4).

82   *Cf.* Ex. 4:23a: *I have said to you: Let my son go, that he may serve me, and you would not let him go.*

83   Matt. 3:17.

84   Matt. 13:41a.

85   1 Cor. 12:28a.

stepping beyond temporal goods so that you might not lose the eternal [goods]; then *pennae columbae, wings of a dove*, that is, the virtues and the good works of the Church, will be and are *deargentatae, covered with silver*, that is, with purity and without stain when temporal things are not inordinately desired, but only as they are necessary or useful so as to receive celestial goods; *et posteriora, and the hinder parts*, that is, the highest works, *dorsi eius, of her back*, that is, of the shoulders of the dove of the Church, which has taken upon herself to carry the yoke of the Lord, *in pallore auri, with the paleness of gold*, that is, they will find themselves completed in the fervor of perfect charity, which is designated by gold. For *charity never falls away*,[86] but that which is now imperfect will in the heavenly homeland be made perfect, provided that we remain at rest *among the midst of lots*, as is said: because *he that shall persevere unto the end, he shall be saved*.[87] And so by *lots (cleros)* we understand inheritances, because κλῆρος [*klēros*] in Greek is translated a lot or a share (*sors*); now, lots (*sortes*) obtained out of divine promise are called portions of inheritances. The Church also is called a dove on account of the innocence and cleanliness of life. But gold signifies charity, according to this: *I counsel you to buy of me gold fire tried*.[88]

67{68}[15] *When he that is in heaven appoints kings over her, they shall be whitened with snow in Zalmon.*

Dum discernit caelestis reges super eam, nive dealbabuntur in Selmon.

67{68}[15] *Dum discernit caelestis reges super eam*, when *he that is in heaven appoints kings over her*, that is, when Christ, who in a singular way is said to be in heaven, indeed of whom is written, *He that comes from heaven, is above all*:[89] when, therefore, this heavenly king judges, that is, he discerns and wisely disposes, *kings over her*, that is, rulers, namely, the Apostles and their successors, over the Church, giving them the

---

86   1 Cor. 13:8a.
87   Matt. 10:22b.
88   Rev. 3:18a. In his *Commentary on Revelation*, Denis explains this verse: "'I counsel you to buy of me' from the most opulent fountain of all good, 'gold fire tried,' that is, fervent charity, commended by divinity, exercised in all adversities, true and not false, and approved by all truly wise men. This charity exceeds all other virtues: it colors, shines, and adorns the inner room of the mind in the manner that gold, the most excellent among all metals, adorns bodily structures." Doctoris Ecstatici D. Dionysii Cartusiani, *Opera Omnia*, Vol. 14 (Montreuil: 1901), 255.
89   John 3:31b.

assignment to teach all nations throughout all the earth;[90] *nive dealba-buntur in Selmon; they shall be whitened with snow in Zalmon,* that is, the faithful in the shadow of grace shall be purified above [the purity of] snow. For understood one way Zalmon is as a proper noun, [that is, the name] of a certain mountain; in another way it is as a common noun signifying obscurity, and accepted in this [latter] manner, it can designate the grace of the way (*gratiam viae*), which is obscure by comparison of the grace of the heavenly fatherland (*gratiam patriae*).[91] Or we can also understand it in this way: The nations which before conversion to the faith or grace were in the obscurity and darkness *shall be whitened with snow.*

67{68}[16] *The mountain of God is a fat mountain. A curdled mountain, a fat mountain.*

Mons Dei, mons pinguis. Mons coagulatus, mons pinguis:

67{68}[17] *Why do you suspect curdled mountains? A mountain in which God is well pleased to dwell: for there the Lord shall dwell unto the end.*

Ut quid suspicamini montes coagulatos? Mons in quo beneplaci-tum est Deo habitare in eo; etenim Dominus habitabit in finem.

And because such faithful are made clean, therefore **67{68}[16]** *mons Dei, the mountain of God,* that is, the Church militant, of which is said in Isaiah, *There shall be prepared the mountain of the house of the Lord on the top of mountains.*[92] For the Church is called a mountain because of the height of the grace of God and the sublimeness of life of the faithful contemplating heavenly things. And so here the mountain of God is

---

90   Matt. 28:19.

91   E. N. This distinction is found in ST IaIIae, q. 113, art. 9. The *gratia viae*, or the grace of the wayfarer is distinguished from the *gratia patriae*, the grace of those in heaven. The obscurity Denis speaks of for those in the wayfaring state relative to the state of those enjoying the vision of God in heaven arises from the fact that sanctifying grace is not something experienced or sensed by the five senses while in the pilgrim state; nor is it something necessarily confirmed by religious experience or emotional states. Without special revelation, therefore, we have no absolute certainty we are in a state of grace while in a wayfaring state; at most, we can have but a moral certainty and so there is always a certain obscurity. "Q. Can you feel sanctifying grace in your soul? A. No, because sanctifying grace is completely spiritual. It is impossible to experience something spiritual, such as grace, a soul, or an angel with one of the five senses. Q. Does a religious feeling indicate sanctifying grace in the soul? A. No, nor does the absence of such a feeling indicate the absence of sanctifying grace." William J. Cogan, *A Brief Catechism for Adults* (Charlotte, NC: TAN 1993).

92   Is. 2:2a.

mons pinguis, a fat mountain, that is, abounding in spiritual goods out of the infusion of the gifts of the Holy Spirit. And so it also is this, *mons coagulatus, a curdled mountain*, that is, joined together in the manner of cheese, a collection out of diverse persons, namely, out of the simple, the poor, those cast aside; *mons pinguis, a fat mountain*: because it has within it many spiritually noble persons, as are orthodox men, that is, those with a glorious faith, fattening others by word and example. Since, therefore, the Church is one, outside of it there is no salvation; it is just like outside the ark of Noah there was no one that was saved.[93] *Ut quid suspicamini montes coagulatos? Why do you suspect curdled mountains?* That is, why do you regard separate churches or places of salvation outside of the Catholic and Apostolic Church? This [Church] is 67{68} [17] *mons in quo beneplacitum est Deo habitare in eo, a mountain in which God is well pleased to dwell*. For this mountain is the congregation of the elect, of which uncreated Wisdom says in Proverbs: *My delight is to be with the children of men*;[94] and in Revelation, *Behold the tabernacle of God with men, and he will dwell with them*.[95] *Etenim Dominus habitabit in finem, for there the Lord shall dwell unto the end*: not in the sense of a particular hour or a measure of time, but even until the end of the age, indeed he shall dwell forever with the Church of the elect, dwelling in them by faith and grace, in the manner that Christ promised, saying: *Behold I am with you all days, even to the consummation of the world*.[96]

67{68}[18]   *The chariot of God is attended by ten thousands; thousands of them that rejoice: the Lord is among them in Sinai, in the holy place.*

Currus Dei decem millibus multiplex, millia laetantium; Dominus in eis in Sinai in sancto.

---

93   *Cf.* 1 Pet. 3:20. "We cannot forget that the Church is not merely a way of salvation; it is the only way. This is not a human opinion, but the express will of Christ: he who believes and is baptized will be saved; but he who does not believe will be condemned. This is why we assert that the Church is a necessary means of salvation. . . . Let no one deceive himself: outside of this house, that is outside of the Church, no one will be saved. Of the deluge, Saint Cyprian says: If someone had escaped outside of Noah's ark then we would admit that someone who abandoned the Church might escape condemnation." *Extra Ecclesiam, nulla salus.* That is the continual warning of the Fathers. Outside the Catholic Church you can find everything except salvation." St. Josemaría Escrivá, *In Love with the Church*, No. 24 (Kiribita: Scepter Books, 1989), 28.

94   Prov. 8:31b.

95   Rev. 21:3.

96   Matt. 28:20b.

67{68}[19] *You have ascended on high, you have led captivity captive;*
you have received gifts in men. Even those not believing, to
dwell the Lord God.[97]

> *Ascendisti in altum, cepisti captivitatem, accepisti dona in*
> *hominibus; etenim non credentes inhabitare Dominum Deum.*

67{68}[18] *Currus Dei decem millibus multiplex, the chariot of God is*
attended by ten thousands. The verse is first of all explained by reference
to the holy angels. For the Prophet [David] invites the angels to show
their fellowship with the ascending Christ, because the magnificence of
a king is befitting of a large retinue, according to this: *In the multitude*
of people is the dignity of the king: and in the small number of people the
dishonor of the prince.[98] To achieve his purpose, the Prophet [David] sets
forth that certain example of the multitude of angels assisting in the
giving of the Mosaic law, in accordance with that which we see written
in Deuteronomy: *The Lord came from Sinai, and from Se'ir he rose up to*
us: he has appeared from mount Paran, and with him thousands of saints,[99]
no doubt composed of the holy angels. Therefore he says: *the chariot of*
God, that is, the number of angels taking back, reporting, and carrying
to human minds the knowledge of God, *attended by ten thousands,* that
is, containing ten thousand of angels within it: not that we here have
expressed a certain number of holy angels; but rather a finite number is set forth as an endless number, or a determinate amount for an
indeterminate. For by the number one thousand, which is a number of
perfection, multiplied by ten there is insinuated an inestimable multitude of holy angels. For in the manner that Dionysius [the Areopagite]
teaches, a multitude of holy angels incomparably exceeds all material
and sensible multitudes.[100] And this accords with what is written in

---

97   E. N. This verse is not only difficult in the Hebrew, but equally difficult in
the Latin. W. H. McClellan and William McClellan, *Obscurities in the Latin Psalter*
XI, The Catholic Biblical Quarterly, Vol. 3, No. 3 (July 1941), p. 260. I have tried
to adapt the Douay-Rheims translation to Denis's *Commentary.*

98   Prov. 14:28.

99   Deut. 33:2

100   E. N. See ST Ia, q. 112, art. 4, ad 2. "Dionysius states (in chapter 14 of his
Celestial Hierarchies) that the multitude of angels transcends all material multitudes."
Pseudo-Dionysius: "I think we also ought to reflect on the tradition in scripture
that the angels number a thousand times a thousand and ten thousand times ten
thousand [Dan. 7:10; Rev. 6:11]. These numbers, enormous to us, square and multiply themselves and thereby indicate clearly that the ranks of the heavenly beings
are innumerable." *Pseudo-Dionysius: The Complete Works* New York: Paulist Press
1987), 181 [321A] (trans., Colm Luibheid).

Daniel: *Thousands of thousands ministered to him.*[101] *Millia laetantium, thousands of them that rejoice,* that is, the multitude of angels rejoicing in God contains an indeterminate amount of thousands, as Daniel adds: *Ten thousand times a hundred thousand stood before him.*[102] *Dominus in eis, the Lord is among them,* that is, he was in association with them, *in Sinai, in sancto; in Sinai, in the holy place,* that is, on mount Sinai, which is a holy mountain and a holy place. For the angel who spoke to Moses had God assisting him; and all the angels assisting in the giving of the law had God presiding over them, as Moses said: *All the saints are in his hand.*[103] And from this the Prophet concludes that there ought to have been a greater multitude of angels associating themselves to the ascending Christ, adding: **67{68}[19]** *Ascendisti, you have ascended,* O Christ, *in altum, on high,* that is, into the empyreal heaven; *cepisti captivitatem, you have led captivity captive,* that is, before you ascended you had delivered those detained and caught up in limbo and those sufficiently cleansed in Purgatory, and you brought them with you; *accepisti dona in hominibus, you have received gifts in men:* that is, you, O Christ, inasmuch as you are man, received from God the Father or from all the superlatively most happy Trinity, the gifts or the graces to be conferred upon men. The soul of Christ received these gifts from the first instant of his creation, for Christ was always *full of grace and truth,* and *of his fulness we have all received.*[104] For in Christ there was not only the grace of personal union, but all the grace of the head which he was able to pour out upon all his members or upon the whole the Church, and to enrich all, in the manner that he said after the Resurrection, *All power is given to me in heaven and in earth.*[105] Not that it was then that for the first time that this power was given to him, but because at that time it started to be known that all things are subject to Christ. So now the Prophet said of Christ, *you have ascended on high, you have accepted gifts in men:* not that you received for the first time the gifts of grace to distribute to men in the Ascension, but because from that time Christ most clearly began to appear to be full of all blessedness and the plenitude of the Holy Spirit. Whence, as a sign of the perfect glorification of Christ, the Holy Spirit was given after the Ascension by means of a visible sign.[106] For this

---

101   Dan. 7:10a.
102   *Ibid.*
103   Deut. 33:3a.
104   John 1:14b, 16a.
105   Matt. 28:18b.
106   Acts 2:1–4.

reason it is written in John: *For as yet the Spirit was not given, because Jesus was not yet glorified.*[107] *Etenim non credentes inhabitare Dominum Deum; even those not believing, to dwell the Lord God*: that is, you, O Christ, received this gift, namely those who did not believe, that is, the infidels, to dwell [in] the Lord. For Christ is given through the merits of his Passion, that the infidels may be converted to the faith by him, and so God may dwell in them in whom before the devil dwelt.

Moreover, the Apostle [Paul] mentioning this scripture introduces a sense upon it greater than the words. Wherefore he says: *Ascending on high, he led captivity captive; he gave gifts to men.*[108] For Christ and the Evangelists and the Apostles, in customarily using the scriptures of the Old Testament as proof, are more mindful of the meaning [of the scripture] than the mere words. This is not something to be marveled at because they knew most clearly the mind of the Prophets, and they considered this more than they did the mere words.

It therefore follows from what has been said that in this place through the word *chariots* or *of chariots* there is understood the God-bearing angels who are called the thrones of God. And so is the word chariots understood where the Lord says to the Synagogue or to the men of Israel: *I will send of them that shall be saved . . . into Africa, and Lydia, . . . into Italy, and Greece; . . . And they shall bring all your brethren out of all nations for a gift to the Lord, upon horses, and in chariots, and in litters, and on mules.*[109] For these vehicles are explained in a spiritual sense because they are understood as referring to the ministries of the holy angels, which worked in conjunction with the Apostles in the conversion of the Jews and the Gentiles.

But that which is said — *the chariot of God is attended by ten thousands* — can be explained in a second way as applying to holy men. For above this verse it says, *a mountain in which God is well pleased to dwell*: and this mountain is called a chariot, for the faithful carry God in them, as the Apostle [Paul] says, *Glorify and bear God in your body*; or [it can also be viewed in this manner] because God directs them as a charioteer does a chariot.[110] Whence Elisha called Elijah the chariot of Israel and

---

107   John 7:30b.

108   Eph. 4:8. *E. N.* In his epistle to the Ephesians, St. Paul, under the inspiration of the Holy Spirit, brings forth Psalm 67:19, and provides a further gloss on it.

109   Is. 66:19a, 20a.

110   1 Cor. 6:20. *E. N.* Denis appears to argue that the chariot of Ps. 67:18 can be equated to the mountain of 67:17 because both are symbols of men in the state of grace, symbols of places where God dwells.

its charioteer.[111] For as a shepherd carries and directs his sheep, so Elijah carried and directed the children of Israel. Also, in a similar way, the king of Israel [Jo'ash] told the dying Elisha: *O my father, my father, the chariot of Israel and the guider thereof.*[112] And so, *the chariot of God*, that is, the faithful people, *is attended by ten thousands*, that is, consists in, and is an aggregate of, innumerable peoples, languages, and tribes: for the Church of Christ is assembled out of all kinds of men. But most especially by the *chariot of God* is understood the Apostles and their successors, who have carried the name of the Savior throughout the whole world,[113] as the Savior said of Paul: *This man is to me a vessel of election, to carry my name before the Gentiles, and kings, and the children of Israel.*[114] And this chariot is *tens of thousands*, that is, multiplied by the innumerable thousands of believers. For someone is said to multiply through the multiplication of those whom he spiritually or carnally generates. Whence the Lord said to Jacob: *I will cause you to increase and multiply.*[115] *Thousands of them that rejoice*, that is, many and innumerable are the thousands of faithful men who glory in the Lord in the present age out of the contemplation of his goodness and his benefits, and also from the hope of future good, and for every spiritual progress of his neighbor. *The Lord is among them.* For by charity and grace he dwells in them: and this, *in Sinai*, that is, in the mandate or the observation of the commandments furnished at Sinai. For the word Sinai is interpreted as meaning mandate. *In the holy place*, because holiness is the reason for which God remains in us.[116] For God is in the man — he remains and dwells in the man — who obeys his commandments, as Christ asserts: *If any one love me, he will keep my word, and my Father will love him, and we will come to him, and will make our abode with him.*[117]

You have ascended, O Lord Jesus, *on high*, in the manner that is said of you in Acts: *while they looked on, he was raised up: and a cloud received him out of their sight;*[118] and in another place, *Lifting up his hands, he*

---

111 2 Kings 2:12a: *And Elisha saw him [Elijah], and cried: My father, my father, the chariot of Israel, and the driver thereof.*
112 2 Kings 13:14b.
113 Cf. Ps. 18:5: *Their sound has gone forth into all the earth: and their words unto the ends of the world.*
114 Acts 9:15.
115 Gen. 48:4a.
116 Rom. 7:12: *Wherefore the law indeed is holy, and the commandment holy, and just, and good.*
117 John 14:23.
118 Acts 1:9.

blessed them, and ... was carried up to heaven.[119] *You have led captivity captive,* that is, you have delivered from the hand of the devil, with all that is in you, the whole world, which beforehand he held captive because of the guilt of sin; but he was cast out by you who affirm: *I, if I be lifted up from the earth, will draw all things to myself.*[120]

ARTICLE XXXII

CONTINUATION OF THE EXPLANATION
OF CURRENT SIXTY-SEVENTH PSALM.

67{68}[20]   *Blessed be the Lord day by day: the God of our salvation will make our journey prosperous to us.*

Benedictus Dominus die quotidie: prosperum iter faciet nobis Deus salutarium nostrorum.

67{68}[20] *Benedictus Dominus die quotidie, blessed be the Lord day by day.* Here the Prophet [David] deals with the progress of the Church. It is as if he said: "Praised be God, and let him be glorified by all day by day, because of the previously-mentioned benefits bestowed to us, and also because of benefits of being gathered together." For *prosperum iter faciet nobis, he will make our journey prosperous for us*: that is, he will show us the blessed and secure way to arrive at eternal life, illuminating our hearts, and directing our words unto the last end, in the ways he said: *I will cause you to walk in my commandments, and to keep my judgments, and do them.*[121] For man is not able to advance in the right way without being led by grace.[122] For this reason Solomon said: *The heart of man disposes his way: but the Lord must direct his steps.*[123] Whence the Apostle also entreats: May God himself *direct your hearts,*[124] and your *minds,*[125] that your *whole spirit ... may be preserved blameless in the*

---

119   Luke 24:50b–51.

120   John 12:32.

121   Ez. 36:27b.

122   E. N. ST IaIIae, q. 109, art. 4, c. "[I]n the state of corrupted nature man is not able to fulfil all the divine commandments without healing grace (*sine gratia sanante*)."

123   Prov. 16:9.

124   2 Thess. 3:5: *And the Lord direct your hearts, in the charity of God, and the patience of Christ.*

125   Phil. 4:7: *And the peace of God, which surpasses all understanding, keep your hearts and minds in Christ Jesus.*

coming of our Lord Jesus Christ.[126] And so, *Deus salutarium nostrorum,* *the God of our salvation,* that is, the author and end of our salvation or beatitude,[127] will make our journey prosperous for us. For the Beatitudes, which Christ enumerates in Matthew, are eight in number;[128] and he bestows salvation to so many of us, deigning to save us from so many sins and dangers: and all our salvation depends upon him. And so this verse is followed with this:

67{68}[21]   *Our God is the God of salvation: and of the Lord, of the Lord are the exits from death.*[129]

Deus noster, Deus salvos faciendi; et Domini, Domini exitus mortis.

67{68}[21] *Deus noster,* our God, that is to say, Christ Jesus, or the Holy Trinity, is *Deus salvos faciendi, the God of salvation,* that is of saving. And so it is stated in the Gospel: *The Son did not come so as to judge the world, but that the world may be saved by him.*[130] And it is reserved to God alone to save, according to this: *I am the Lord ... and there is no Savior beside me.*[131] It also states, *our God is the God of salvation,* because *he wills that all men be saved, and come to the knowledge of the truth,*[132] in the manner it is also stated in the book of Tobit: *You are not delighted in our being lost.*[133] And in the Gospel the Savior says: *It is not the will of your Father ... that one of these little ones should perish.*[134] *Et Domini, Domini exitus mortis; and of the Lord, of the Lord, are the exits from death.* Twice are the words "of the Lord" stated; this is done for the sake of increased expression; and [it is to be understood] in this sense: *the exits of death,* that is, the release from the death of sin and from Gehenna is of the Lord as creator, justifier, and redeemer because

---

126   1 Thess. 5:23: *And may the God of peace himself sanctify you in all things; that your whole spirit, and soul, and body, may be preserved blameless in the coming of our Lord Jesus Christ.*

127   E. N. Cf. Heb. 12:2: *Looking on Jesus, the author and finisher of faith, who having joy set before him, endured the cross, despising the shame, and now sits on the right hand of the throne of God.*

128   Matt. 5:3–10.

129   E. N. I have replaced "issues from death," which the Douay-Rheims has, with "exits from death."

130   John 3:17b.

131   Hosea 13:4.

132   1 Tim. 2:4.

133   Tob. 3:22a.

134   Matt. 18:14.

he alone can forgive sins,[135] and release from eternal punishments, and infuse grace. Or by this that is said — *and of the Lord, of the Lord are exits from death* — all doubts [that the Lord is not in control of the exits of death] are dissolved. But it is possible that someone may ask, "If God is the God of salvation, why therefore do we die?" To which the reply is: this is not incomprehensible, for even by the Lord himself, namely, by Jesus Christ, was the exit of death [suffered], for he by death departed from this world, and suffered a most bitter death. God is the *God of salvation* is said, therefore, because he delivers from the death of fault or of soul and will free from bodily mortality in the last day, *when this mortal has put on immortality.*[136] Therefore, he says through Hosea, *I will deliver them out of the hand of death. I will redeem them from death.*[137]

67{68}[22]   *But God shall break the heads of his enemies: the hairy crown of them that walk on in their sins.*

Verumtamen Deus confringet capita inimicorum suorum, verticem capilli perambulantium in delictis suis.

Following a strong literal sense to the best of our ability, that which follows is explained as follows: 67{68}[22] *Verumtamen Deus,* but God, that is, although God is a saving God, as far as is in his power, yet he does not save all men because of their malice, but *confringet capita, he shall break the heads,* that is, the leaders and chiefs *inimicorum suorum, of his enemies,* namely, the chiefs of the priests. These [malicious men] God shall break, taking away from them all spiritual being,[138] blinding them, and damning them eternally. *Verticem capilli perambulantium in delictis suis, the hairy crown of them that walk on in their sins:* that is, through the Roman army God will shatter and destroy the city of Jerusalem, which was a city *of them that walk on in their sins,* that is, the dwelling of the Jews who killed, persecuted Christ and Prophets and Apostles,[139] as [the deacon and proto-martyr] Stephen told them: *Which of the prophets have not your fathers persecuted?*[140] Now Jerusalem is called *the hairy crown,* that is, a head full of hairs, because of the towers and walls surrounding

---

135   Mark 2:7b: *Who can forgive sins but God only?*
136   1 Cor. 15:54a.
137   Hosea 13:14a.
138   E. N. The words "spiritual being" are synonymous with the supernatural life, i.e., the gift of sanctifying grace. Denis is not suggesting that God will take away their natural spiritual life. Denis is not advocating any form of annihilationism.
139   Matt. 23:37.
140   Acts 7:52a.

it appeared to be impregnable, just as head of much hair is robust.[141] Nevertheless it was overcome in the manner that Christ foretold: For [your enemies] *shall beat you flat to the ground . . . and they shall not leave in you a stone upon a stone.*[142]

67{68}[23] *The Lord said: I will turn them from Bashan, I will turn them into the depth of the sea:*

Dixit Dominus: Ex Basan convertam, convertam in profundum maris;

67{68}[24] *That your foot may be dipped in the blood of your enemies; the tongue of your dogs be red with the same.*

Ut intingatur pes tuus in sanguine, lingua canum tuorum ex inimicis, ab ipso.

67{68}[23] *Dixit Dominus: Ex Basan convertam; the Lord said: I will turn them from Bashan.* The land of Basham neighbored Judea on one side; and the Mediterranean Sea was on the other side of Judea. But Vespasian and Titus were sent by the Emperor against Judea (whose capital city was Jerusalem), and from both places or sides they assembled the army so as to destroy Jerusalem. So it is therefore in this sense [that the verse may be understood]: *the Lord said,* because the destruction of Jerusalem was accomplished as a result of divine ordinance in revenge for the blood of Christ: *from Bashan,* that is, from that place, *I will turn* the army upon Judea. *Convertam in profundum maris, I will turn them into the depth of the sea,* that is, I will direct the Roman army to the sea, so that then they might obtain the needed help, and so combined into one, prevail over Judea. 67{68}[24] *Ut instingatur per tuus, that your foot may be dipped,* O inhabitant of Jerusalem, or Roman soldier, *in sanguine, in the blood* of those killed, for so many thousands were killed that they were able to dip their feet in the blood that flowed just by walking. *Linguam canum tuorum, the tongue of your dogs,* were also able to dip *ex inimicis ab ipso, in the blood of your enemies,* that is, by the overflowing blood of the enemies of Christ that were killed, so that dogs were able

---

141   E. N. Nicholas of Lyra (*ca.* 1270–1349 AD) had a similar take on this verse, observing that it referred to the "city of Jerusalem, which was the head of the kingdom of Judaea, and it is called the head of hair, that is, with much hair, because, on account of its walls and towers surrounding it, appeared impregnable as the hairy head is said to be strong." *Biblia Sacra cum Glossa Interlineari Ordinaria . . . et Nicolai Lyrani Postilla* (Venice: 1588), III, 179.

142   Luke 19:44.

to drink to satiety that blood. Indeed, as Josephus wrote in the book of the *Jewish Wars*, from the beginning of the siege until its end one million were killed.[143]

67{68}[25] *They have seen your goings, O God, the goings of my God: of my king who is in his sanctuary.*

Viderunt ingressus tuos, Deus, ingressus Dei mei, regis mei, qui est in sancto.

67{68}[26] *Princes went before, joined with singers, in the midst of young damsels playing on timbrels.*

Praevenerunt principes coniuncti psallentibus, in medio iuvencularum tympanistriarum.

And so the Prophet sets forth the cause of such dejection. **67{68}[25]** *Viderunt ingressus tuos, Deus; they have seen your goings, O God:* that is, the unbelieving and perverse Jews saw your works, your manner of living, and your miracles, O Lord Jesus Christ, and they heard you preach; but they were contemptuous [toward your exhortation] to convert or to believe; and so they deserved to be destroyed and to be overthrown. And this is what you affirm in the Gospel: *If I had not come, and spoken to them, they would not have sin; but now they have no excuse for their sin.*[144] And again: *If I had not done among them the works that no other man has done, they would not have sin; but now they have both seen and hated both me and my Father.*[145] They have seen, therefore, *ingressus Dei mei, regis mei, qui est in sancto; the goings of my God, of my king who is in his sanctuary,* that is of Christ, the only-begotten of God the Father, who is my God and my king. See in this verse is declared most openly the Incarnation of God and the true divinity of Christ. **67{68} [26]** *Praevenerunt principes coniuncti psallentibus, princes went before joined with singers,* that is, those at the forefront among the Christians, namely, the holy Apostles or their successors, who conjoined by mind and body with other Christian singers or praisers of God, *in medio iuvencularum tympanistriarum, in the midst of young damsels playing on timbrels,* [in

---

143 "Now the number of those that were carried captive during this whole war collected to be ninety-seven thousand; as was the number of those that perished during the whole siege eleven hundred thousand." Flavius Josephus, *The Judean War,* VI, 9, 3 [420], *The Works of Flavius Josephus* (London: Chatto & Windus 1897), II, 464 (trans., William Whiston).

144 John 15:22.

145 John 15:24.

the midst] of consecrated virgins. For from the beginning of the Church there were virgins that were in a manner consecrated to God, and they are called timbrels, not because they used material timbrels, but because they insisted in praising the Creator along with the Apostles.[146] And so the princes joined with the singers in the midst of virgins *went before* and came out of the aforementioned siege of Jerusalem. For as is written in ecclesiastical history, through the warning of an angel they departed Jerusalem and Judea and entered into the kingdom of Agrippa, who was a confederate of the Romans.[147]

67{68}[27] *In the churches bless God the Lord, from the fountains of Israel.*

In ecclesiis benedicite Deo Domino de fontibus Israel.

67{68}[27] *In ecclesiis, in the churches,* that is, in your congregations, O Christian faithful, *benedicite Deo, bless God,* praising him, *Domino de fontibus Israel, the Lord from the fountains of Israel,* that is, bless your Lord himself from the Apostles, that is, because of that grace-filled benefit that he gave to the Apostles and by them to you. For the illumination and grace bestowed upon them is the salvation of the world. And the Apostles are called the fountains of Israel because from them the Church received its rivers of doctrine and the origin of virtue and grace: and as Christ said to them, *You are the light of the world,*[148] and so they can be called the fountains of the Church.

67{68}[28] *There is Benjamin a youth, in ecstasy of mind. The princes of Judah are their leaders: the princes of Zebulon, the princes of Naphthali.*

Ibi Beniamin adolescentulus, in mentis excessu; principes Iuda, duces eorum; principes Zabulon, principes Nephthali.

146   E. N. "From apostolic times Christian virgins, called by the Lord to cling only to him with greater freedom of heart, body, and spirit, have decided with the Church's approval to live in a state of virginity 'for the sake of the Kingdom of heaven.' [Matt. 19:12; *cf.* 1 Cor 7:34–36.]" CCC § 922.

147   E. N. This is a reference to the "Flight to Pella" described in the histories of Eusebius (*ca.* 260/65–*ca.* 339/340 AD) and Epiphanius of Salamis (*ca.* 310-320–403 AD) who state in their historical chronicles that the Christians in Jerusalem were miraculously warned to flee to the city of Perea or Pella four years prior to the siege and destruction of Jerusalem in 70 AD. See Eusebius, *Ecclesiastical History,* III, 5, 3 and Epiphanius *Panarion* XXIX, 7, 7 and XXX, 2, 7; *see also* Epiphanius's *Treatise on Weights and Measures,* 15. The Agrippa mentioned is Herod Agrippa II (*ca.* 27/38–*ca.* 92 or 100 AD).

148   Matt. 5:14a.

67{68}[28] *Ibi, there,* namely, in the Church, *Beniamin adolescentulus, is Benjamin a youth,* that is, Paul born of the tribe of Benjamin, as he himself revealed to the Romans,[149] who in the flower of his age was converted to Christ, that is, shortly after the killing of Stephen.[150] Or the word "a youth" is said because he was the last, in comparison to the other Apostles, to come to the faith. *In mentis excessu, in ecstasy of mind.* For he was in Damascus three days and three nights, neither eating nor drinking,[151] seeing that he was caught up even up to the third heaven, where he heard *secret words:*[152] hence, he was pulled away from the exercise of all external senses, especially when he was caught up in that rapture where he thought he had seen the divine essence. *Principes Iuda, the princes of Judah,* that is certain of the Apostles descended from the tribe of Judah, *duces eorum, are their leaders,* that is, they acted as leaders and princes of men converted to the faith of Christ. For as Christ according to his humanity was from the tribe of Judah, so John and James the Greater, and also James the lesser, Simon and Judas, sons of the sister of the glorious Virgin, are believed to have been born of the tribe of Judah. And these, inasmuch as they were Apostles, were leaders of the Christians. *Principes Zabulon, the princes of Zebulon,* and *principes Nepthali, the princes of Naphthali,* that is, some sprung from the tribe of Zebulon and Naphthali were leaders of the Christian people. For we find in the book of Joshua that the parts given to the tribes of Zebulon and Naphthali were in large part derived from the lands in Galilee,[153] which lands many of the Apostles and disciples of Christ were from. For this reason, they were called Galileans, as when the angel said to them: *You men of Galilee, what do you marvel at?*[154]

---

149   Rom. 11:1.

150   Acts chps. 7–9. E. N. St. Stephen, the first martyr of the nascent Church, died somewhere around 33 through 36 AD. Traditionally, the conversion of Paul is dated around 34 through 37 AD. If Paul was born somewhere around 5 BC, then he would have been around 39 to 43 at his conversion. Denis uses the word *iuvenis,* a word of relatively broad range, and it could mean a youth or someone who is in the flower of his age (older than an adolescent and younger than a senior).

151   Acts 9:9: E. N. After the encounter with Jesus in Damascus: *And he was there three days, without sight, and he did neither eat nor drink.*

152   2 Cor. 12:4. Denis appears to conflate this event with the encounter that St. Paul had on the road to Damascus.

153   Joshua 19:10–16; 32–39.

154   Acts 1:11. E. N. The occasion was the Ascension of our Lord.

67{68}[29] *Command your strength, O God: confirm, O God, what you have wrought in us.*

Manda, Deus, virtuti tuae; confirma hoc, Deus, quod operatus es in nobis.

67{68}[30] *From your temple in Jerusalem, kings shall offer presents to you.*

A templo tuo in Ierusalem, tibi offerent reges munera.

Then the Prophet [David] speaking in the person of the early Church, prays: **67{68}[29]** *Manda, Deus, virtuti tuae; command your strength, O God,* that is, direct the angelic power that it might protect us and cause us to increase: for we do not have the strength to resist and prevail against the Jews by human power. That God heard this prayer is proved in many places in the Acts of the Apostles. For an angel freed Peter from prison.[155] And of the chief priests it is written: *They put them in a common prison; but an angel of the Lord by night opening the doors of the prison led them out.*[156] *Confirma hoc, Deus, quod operatus es in nobis; confirm, O God, what you have wrought in us,* that is, confirm the apostolic teaching by miracles, and strengthen the hearts of believers with the Holy Spirit, and direct that the Church increase and become perfect, so that the works of faith that operate in us may be perfected, that is, by us. **67{68}[30]** *A templo tuo in Ierusalem, from your temple in Jerusalem*: for the Apostles publicly preached that Christ had risen in that temple; or [the verse can be understood in this manner], *from your temple in Jerusalem,* that is, from the congregation of the faithful, who first were gathered together in Jerusalem. And also in this sense: Confirm the works of faith that you began at that very temple in order that the faith which began there would spread throughout the whole world. For here [is the voice of] the early Church: *Lord,* it said, *behold their threatenings,* namely, that of the Jews, *and grant unto your servants, that with all confidence they may speak your word. And when they had prayed, the place was moved wherein they were … and they were all filled with the Holy Spirit, and they spoke the word of God with great confidence.*[157] *Tibi offerent reges munera, kings shall offer presents to you.* Many kings were converted to the faith, not only did they present themselves to Christ, but also gave abundant presents toward the support of the poor and the increase of the Church.

---

155   Acts 12:7–10.
156   Acts 5:18–19.
157   Acts 4:31.

67{68}[31]   *Rebuke the wild beasts of the reeds, the congregation of bulls with the cows*[158] *of the people; who seek to exclude them who are tried with silver. Scatter the nations that delight in wars.*

Increpa feras arundinis; congregatio taurorum in vaccis populorum; ut excludant eos qui probati sunt argento: dissipa gentes quae bella volunt.

In addition, the Prophet [David] prays for the destruction of the adversaries of the Church. **67{68}[31]** *Increpa,* rebuke, O Lord, destroy and punish, *feras arundinis, the wild beasts of the reeds,* that is, the cruel tyrants and heretics which spread about all sorts of vice and *wind of doctrine*[159] like reeds shaken by the wind:[160] These are called wild beasts because of their cruelty, since they tear their own souls and those of others apart. But these wild beasts were especially the Roman emperors, namely, Nero, Domitian, Diocletian, Decius, and many others, who endeavored to eradicate completely the faith of Christ. *Congregatio taurorum, the congregation of bulls,* that is, the multitude or the herd of the proud, and of the untamable heretics, or those who have no fear of God is retarded and is *in vaccis populorum, with the cows of the people,* that is, among lascivious and inconstant men. For as the prince is, so are also his ministers; and as the teacher is, so also are his disciples.[161] Or [alternatively], *with the cows of the people,* that is, among uneducated and simple men whom they endeavored to subvert. And so there follows, *ut excludant,* who seek to exclude from the faith and the kingdom of Christ, *eos qui probati sunt argento, those who are tried with silver,* that is, learned with the divine speech, believing and obeying the words of Christ. For the word silver indicates divine speech, as an earlier Psalm states: *The words of the Lord are pure words: as silver tried by the fire.*[162]

Dissipa gentes quae bella volunt, scatter the nations that delight in wars: that is, destroy the previously mentioned tyrants and heresiarchs, and all persecutors of good men who incite strife and disturbances within the Church of God, impeding their effect in doing evil works, and providing peace to the Church. This we nowadays see fulfilled because we see tyrants and heresiarchs currently at rest.

---

158   E. N. I replaced the word "kine" in the Douay-Rheims with "cows." I am sure that no one will object.

159   Eph. 4:14a.

160   Cf. Matt. 11:7.

161   Cf. Ecclus. 10:2: *As the judge of the people is himself, so also are his ministers: and what manner of man the ruler of a city is, such also are they that dwell therein.*

162   Ps. 11:7a.

67{68}[32] *Ambassadors shall come out of Egypt: Ethiopia shall anticipate her hands to God.*[163]

Venient legati ex Aegypto; Aethiopia praeveniet manus eius Deo.

67{68}[32] *Venient legati ex Aegypto,* ambassadors shall come out of Egypt. Literally, many of the converted Egyptians approached the Apostles in Jerusalem and in Rome, so as to obtain greater instruction from them, as Dionysius writes about.[164] But some explain [this verse] as applying to Philo, by whom the book of Wisdom was written, who with his companions was sent from Alexandria in Egypt to Rome to the emperor Caludius, and there he spoke with blessed Peter, and became friends with him.[165] Hence, referring to the Alexandrian Church of Mark the evangelist and the disciple of Saint Peter, he magnificently honored it and wrote a laudatory book of it. All this is fully narrated in the book of St. Jerome entitled *On Illustrious Men.*[166] *Aethiopia praeveniet manus eius, Ethiopia shall anticipate her hands,* namely, [she shall anticipate] Egypt, *Deo, to God,* that is to the glory of God. For Ethiopia converted to the faith before Egypt did, when the evangelist Matthew raised from the dead the son of the king of Ethiopia. From this fact, he converted and baptized the king with his son and daughter and a large part of the people, and he filled Ethiopia with churches.[167]

---

163   E. N. I have changed the Douay-Rheims from "shall soon stretch out her hands," which translates *praeveniet manus eius,* to "shall anticipate her hands," since the *Commentary* makes a point that Ethiopia converted prior to Egypt.

164   E. N. I could not locate this reference.

165   E. N. In his *Ecclesiastical History,* Eusebius mentions a meeting of the Jewish Platonic philosopher Philo of Alexandria (*ca.* 20 BC–*ca.* 50 AD), who was Egyptian by birth, with Peter in Rome. *Hist. Eccl.* II, 17, 1-2. Eusebius misunderstood Philo's reference to the *Therapeutae* in his *De Vita Contemplativa* to refer to a Christian monastic community in Egypt. And through this misunderstanding a legend arose — the legend of *Philo Christianus,* of Philo being a crypto-Christian — since, as Eusebius stated it, Philo "venerated and extolled, the apostolic men of his time." Eusebius, *Ecclesiastical History, Nicene and Post-Nicene Fathers, Second Series* (New York: Christian Literature Co. 1890), Vol, 1, 117. (ed., Philip Schaff and Henry Wallace). Philo was included in St. Jerome's *De Viris Illustribus (Lives of Illustrious Men),* where mention is made of Eusebius's report.

166   E. N. Thus St. Jerome: "Philo the Jew, an Alexandrian of the priestly class, is placed by us among the ecclesiastical writers on the ground that, writing a book concerning the first church of Mark the evangelist at Alexandria, he writes to our praise, declaring not only that they were there, but also that they were in many provinces and calling their habitations monasteries. From this it appears that the church of those that believed in Christ at first, was such as now the monks desire to imitate." St. Jerome, *Lives of Illustrious Men, Nicene and Post-Nicene Fathers, Second Series* (New York: Christian Literature Co. 1892), Vol. 3, 365.

167   E. N. A description of this event can be found in Jacob de Voragine's *Golden*

67{68}[33] *Sing to God, you kingdoms of the earth: sing to the Lord: Sing to God,*

> *Regna terrae, cantate Deo; psallite Domino; psallite Deo,*

67{68}[34] *Who ascends above the heaven of heavens,*[168] *to the east. Behold he will give to his voice the voice of power,*

> *Qui ascendit super caelum caeli, ad orientem: ecce dabit voci suae vocem virtutis.*

67{68}[35] *Give glory to God over Israel, his magnificence, and his power is in the clouds.*

> *Date gloriam Deo super Israel; magnificentia eius et virtus eius in nubibus.*

After this, a proclamation is exhorted by Prophet [David] to the whole world to reach for Christ. **67{68}[33]** *Regna terrae, you kingdoms of the earth,* that is, the people of all kingdoms, *cantate Deo, sing to God,* that is, to Christ, who is the Creator of all things, and is the true God, and is eternal life; *psallite Domino, sing to the Lord* Christ, all governors and all princes. *Psallite Deo, sing to God,* **67{68}[34]** *qui ascendit, who ascends* on the fortieth day after the Resurrection, *super caelum caeli, above the heaven of heavens,* that is, above the highest heaven which is contained in the heavens. For Christ ascended even up to the extremities of the empyreal heaven. *Ad orientem, to the east,* that is, even unto the right hand of the Father, which is the super-most-splendid East, the fountainlike and easternmost source of all light.[169] Or [an alternative

---

Legend, where the story of King Egippus is told. The Apostle Matthew is also said to have resided in Ethiopia for thirty-three years and converted virtually all of Ethiopia to Christ. https://sourcebooks.fordham.edu/basis/goldenlegend/GoldenLegend-Volume5.asp#Matthew

168   E. N. I have replaced the Douay Rheims's "mounts above," which translates *ascendit,* with "ascends." Given the Christological nature of this Psalm and Denis's *Commentary,* such a change is warranted.

169   E. N. The title "Light of the East," *Lumen Orientale,* is an epithet for both the Lord or the Gospel which is based upon their eastern origin: "The light of the East has illumined the universal Church, from the moment when 'a rising sun' appeared above us: Jesus Christ, our Lord, whom all Christians invoke as the Redeemer of man and the hope of the world." John Paul II, *Orientale Lumen,* 1. "My gaze turns to the *Orientale Lumen* which shines from Jerusalem (cf. Is 60:1; Rev 21:10), the city where the Word of God, made man for our salvation, a Jew 'descended from David according to the flesh' (Rom 1:3; 2 Tim 2:8), died and rose again. In that holy city, when the day of Pentecost had come and 'they were all together in one place' (Acts 2:1), the Paraclete was sent upon Mary and the disciples. From there the Good News spread throughout the world because, filled with the Holy Spirit, 'they spoke the word

understanding], *to the east*, that is, from the east, namely from the mount of Olives which is in the eastern part beside Jerusalem.

Ecce dabit voci suae vocem virtutis. Behold, he will give to his voice the voice of power. That is, the words of Christ, in which he predicted his Ascension, will powerfully accomplish their effect: just like he effected what the Prophets and he himself also predicted. For he gives to his voice *the voice of power*, so that his words are completed by deed. And so, all you faithful, **67{68}[35]** *date gloriam Deo, give glory to God*, namely, to the Christ ascending *super Israel, over Israel*, that is, because of the excellent benefits furnished to the Apostles and all the faithful, who were true Israelites.[170] For glory is clear knowledge with praise.[171] For this reason to give glory to God is to give knowledge of his name to others with the profession of divine praise, as when someone preaches and extolls the goodness of God or his benefits.

Magnificentia eius et virtus eius in nubibus; his magnificence, and his power is in the clouds, that is, the great work of Christ and his power appeared in the clouds, to which he ascended before the disciples, as is stated in Acts: *While they looked on, he was raised up: and a cloud received (nubes suscepit) him out of their sight.*[172] For sometimes Scripture puts a plural for a singular, or conversely [a singular for a plural]. And so it now puts *clouds (nubibus)* [in this Psalm] for *cloud (nubes)*. And perhaps it was not only one cloud [as related in Acts 1:9]; but as he is to return in the clouds (*nubibus*), so he left in clouds, especially since it states in Acts: *he shall so come, as you have seen him going into heaven.*[173] By clouds one can also understand the holy angels who ministered to Christ when he ascended: in whom the magnificence and the power of Christ were reflected, as the magnificence and power of a king reflects in the dignity and excellence of the ministers, and because two angels stood by the Apostles and announced the magnificence and power of Christ, saying: *This Jesus who is taken up from you into heaven, shall so come.*[174] Whence Dionysius in the fifteenth chapter of his *Celestial Hierarchy* says that in the divine Scriptures we frequently understand

---

of God with boldness' (Acts 4:31). From there, from the mother of all the Churches, the Gospel was preached to all nations, many of which boast of having had one of the Apostles as their first witness to the Lord." *Ibid.*, 2. Here, Denis calls the Blessed Trinity the super-most-splendid East, *supersplendidissimus Oriens*.

170 Cf. John 1:47b: *Behold an Israelite indeed, in whom there is no guile.*

171 E. N. This definition is Augustinian; *see* footnote 28-15 in Volume 2.

172 Acts 1:9.

173 Acts 1:11b.

174 Acts 1:11b.

the word clouds to mean the holy angels. Finally, the word clouds can also be taken as meaning Apostles, of whom is written, *Who are these who fly as the clouds?*[175] And these clouds reflected the magnificence and power of Christ when after the Ascension he gave them *a mouth and wisdom*, which all their adversaries would not be able to resist,[176] especially since he sent to them in tongues of fire the Holy Spirit.[177] Therefore there follows:

67{68}[36]   *God is wonderful in his Saints: the God of Israel is he who will give power and strength to his people. Blessed be God!*

Mirabilis Deus in sanctis suis; Deus Israel ipse dabit virtutem et fortitudinem plebi suae. Benedictus Deus!

67{68}[36] *Mirabilis Deus in Sanctis suis, God is wonderful in his Saints*: because he marvelously magnifies and exalts the Apostles and other sons of the early Church, especially those one hundred and twenty who received the Holy Spirit at the same time at Pentecost. And this was a marvelous thing that they, who at the time of the Passion had fled,[178] were so strengthened at heart that they publicly proclaimed him:[179] and it was exceedingly marvelous in the prince of the Apostles, who before the Passion denied Christ because of the challenge of a maid, yet after the coming of the Holy Spirit he undauntedly told the great multitude of Jews: *The God of our fathers, has glorified his Son Jesus, whom you indeed delivered up and denied before the face of Pilate,.... and you desired a murderer to be granted unto you, ... but the author of life you killed.*[180] But *this is the change of the right hand of the most High.*[181] Therefore, it continues: *Deus Israel ipse dabit virtutem et fortitudinem plebi suae; the God of Israel is he who will give power and strength to his people*, namely, the early Church. For he gave it the power of resolutely speaking, doing miracles, and an irreproachable manner of living, and also the strength to endure all adversity not only with equanimity, but

---

175   Is. 60:8a. *E. N.* In his *Commentary on Isaiah*, Denis compares the Apostles to these clouds because like clouds they contemplate heavenly things and dissipate quickly to convert the Gentiles. Doctoris Ecstatici D. Dionysii Cartusiani, *Opera Omnia*, Vol. 8 (Montreuil: 1899), 723.
176   Luke 21:15.
177   Acts 2:3–4.
178   Matt. 26:56.
179   Acts 4:33.
180   Acts 3:13–15.
181   Ps. 76:11b.

even with exultation, in the manner that is written in the book of Acts: *The Apostles rejoicing from the presence of the council, because they were accounted worthy to suffer reproach for the name of Jesus.*[182]

Because of the grace of such great benefits that were granted to the Christian faithful, *benedictus Deus*, blessed be God in eternity, whom we are in no manner able to be worthy to repay for his goods, because *he has no need of our goods*,[183] especially since all our goods are his gifts, as David most devoutly said, *All things are yours, O Lord, and we have given you what we received from your hand.*[184] But it is incumbent upon us that we give honor and glory to God alone, most worthily venerating him, and attributing all good to him, as also the holy David did, saying: *Now therefore, our God, we give thanks to you, and we praise your glorious name.*[185] *Yours, O Lord, is magnificence, and power, and glory, and victory; yours is praise, . . . yours are riches, you have dominion over all.*[186]

THE SPIRITUAL SENSE

67{68}[22] *But God shall break the heads of his enemies: the hairy crown of them that walk on in their sins.*

Verumtamen Deus confringet capita inimicorum suorum, verticem capilli perambulantium in delictis suis.

In addition, those things that are said beginning in that place — *But God shall break the head of his enemies* [i.e., verse 22] — can be understood more spiritually or more universally in this way: **67{68}[22]** *Verumtamen*, but that is, although God is the God of salvation, he nevertheless dashes to pieces and destroys *capita inimicorum suorum*, the *heads of his enemies*. Here, a part refers to the whole, in the way that the Philistines told their king about David: *In what better way are we able to please his master but with our heads?*[187] And so it is in this sense: *God* — whether in the present or, in any event, in the future — *confringet*, shall break, now taking vengeance on their sins and striking them down, or in a short time from now condemning them. Or [it could be understood] thus: *God shall break the head of his enemies*, that is, he will

---

182   Acts 5:41.

183   Ps. 15:2b.

184   1 Chron. 29:14.

185   1 Chron. 29:13.

186   1 Chron. 29:11a-12b.

187   1 Kings 29:4b. E. N. In other words, heads are not to be understood literally, but understood to mean the whole person.

humble, overwhelm, and condemn the proud, according to that said in Isaiah: *The day of the Lord of hosts shall be upon every one that is proud and high-minded, and upon every one that is arrogant, and he shall be humbled.*[188] And by another prophet: *I will visit in that day upon every one that enters arrogantly.*[189] God also shall break *verticem capilli, the hairy crown*, that is, the pride of their thought, *perambulantium in delictis suis, of them that walk on in their sins*, that is, those men persevering in sins. Whence elsewhere it is written: *Woe to you that reflect upon that which is unprofitable.*[190] And Isaiah says: *The loftiness of men shall be bowed down, and the haughtiness of men shall be humbled.*[191] Thus God shall break not only the proud in action, but also the haughty of thought, in the way Wisdom states, *By my power I have trodden under my feet the hearts of all the high and low.*[192] Another scripture also says this: *Why does your heart elevate you, and why do you stare with your eyes, as if they were thinking great things? Why does your spirit swell against God?*[193] Now thoughts are signified by the word "hairy" because as hair springs forth from the head and adheres to it, so thoughts proceed from the heart and also adhere to the same.

67{68}[23]   *The Lord said: I will turn them from Bashan, I will turn them into the depth of the sea:*

Dixit Dominus: Ex Basan convertam, convertam in profundum maris;

67{68}[23] *Dixit Dominus*, the Lord said, that is, he immovably decreed within himself, and has spoken through his servants, *For the Lord God does nothing without revealing his secret to his servants the prophets.*[194] *Ex Basan*, from Bashan, that is, from the filth of life and the mixing with sin, *convertam*, I will turn sinners, since those who before lived unseemly and disorderedly will begin to implement that stated by the Apostle: *But let all things be done decently, and according to order in you.*[195] For the name "Bashan" is understood to mean turpitude or

---

188   Is. 2:12.
189   Zeph. 1:9a.
190   Micah 2:1. E. N. I have replaced "devise" of the Douay-Rheims with "reflect upon" in translation of *cogitatis*.
191   Is. 2:17a.
192   Ecclus. 24:11a.
193   Job 15:12–13a.
194   Amos 3:7.
195   1 Cor. 14:40.

confusion. *Convertam in profundum maris, I will turn them into the depth of the sea*: that is, the grace of conversion that I will send at this time shall be good for nothing in an obstinate heart, in those peoples formerly submerged under a flood of vices. For this reason Peter says: *You were not redeemed ... from the vain manner of life of the tradition of your fathers ... with the precious blood of Christ, as a lamb unspotted.*[196] And Paul speaks more openly, saying: *God indeed not having regarded the times of* prior *ignorance, now declares unto men, that all should everywhere do penance.*[197] Whence also the Savior himself prophesied of it: *For God sent not his Son into the world, to judge the world, but that the world may be saved by him.*[198]

67{68}[24] *That your foot may be dipped in the blood of your enemies; the tongue of your dogs be red with the same.*

Ut intingatur pes tuus in sanguine, lingua canum tuorum ex inimicis, ab ipso.

67{68}[24] *Ut intingatur pes tuus in sanguine, that your foot may be dipped in the blood*: that is, to this God will convert you, O man, that your desire or your action is the result of the effect or the fruit of the Blood of Christ, so that you might be saved by the merits of the Passion of Christ, united — indeed, soaked — with the blood of Christ by faith and charity. Whence the Apostle [Paul] said: *you who some time were afar off, are made nigh by the blood of Christ.*[199] *Lingua canum tuorum ex inimicis ab ipso, the tongue of your dogs be red with the same*: that is, through the formed speech received from those who preached to you, you were converted from the unbelievers and Gentiles to the faith; and that this occurred is through Jesus Christ, the Savior of all men, whose kindness and grace has made friends out of enemies. Indeed many peoples that were once opposed to Christ, having received the faith, became most powerful preachers, as did Dionysius [the Areopagite], Pope Clement, the divine Ignatius, and the great Polycarp.[200] Now

---

196 1 Pet. 1:18–19. I have changed "conversation" in the Douay-Rheims to "manner of life" for the Latin *conversatione*.

197 Acts 17:30. E. N. I have replaced "having winked" in the Douay-Rheims, which translates *despiciens*, with "not having regarded."

198 John 3:17.

199 Eph. 2:13b.

200 E. N. Denis, of course, is referring to St. Dionysius the Areopagite (*fl.* 1st cent. AD), the disciple of St. Paul mentioned in Acts 17:34, who was a judge at the Areopagus Court in Athens, converted to the faith, and subsequently became

such as these are said to be enemies according to their present evil, or by the requirements of their merits; but according to eternal predestination, they were always friends, for Christ says of these: *Greater love than this no man has, that a man lay down his life for his friends.*[201] And the Apostle [Paul] said: *When we were still enemies, we were reconciled to God by the death of his Son.*[202] In different respects, therefore, they were friends and enemies.

67{68}[25] *They have seen your goings, O God, the goings of my God: of my king who is in his sanctuary.*

Viderunt ingressus tuos, Deus, ingressus Dei mei, regis mei, qui est in sancto.

67{68}[26] *Princes went before joined with singers, in the midst of young damsels playing on timbrels.*

Praevenerunt principes coniuncti psallentibus, in medio iuvencularum tympanistriarum.

67{68}[25] *Viderunt ingressus tuos, Deus; they have seen your goings, O God:* that is, the faithful by faith have considered your manner of life, O Lord Christ, and they have followed your path either in the shedding of blood or by daily mortifying and denying themselves and carrying their cross in imitation of you.[203] For they see with the eye of contemplation your most pure goings, that is, the Incarnation by which you entered into the world, your Ascension by which you entered into heaven, and also by the appearances by which you appeared to the Apostles after the Resurrection,[204] you entering into the room though

---

the first bishop of Athens. It is this historical figure's name that an unknown cleric appropriated as a pseudonym in in the late 5th or early 6th century, who is now known as Pseudo-Dionysius, and who authored the various works upon which Denis relies so heavily in this *Commentary*. Clement refers to Pope St. Clement I (?–99 AD), the third or perhaps fourth Pope of Rome, famous for his epistles, and who is considered the first of the Apostolic Fathers of the Church. Ignatius refers to St. Ignatius of Antioch (*ca.* 50–*ca.* 98-117), the third bishop of Antioch, famous for his multiple epistles to various Churches written on his way to Rome where he suffered martyrdom. Along with Pope St. Clement, St. Ignatius is considered an Apostolic Father. St. Polycarp (69–155 AD), a disciple of the Apostle John, was the bishop of Smyrna who suffered martyrdom, and is likewise considered an Apostolic Father. All these were converts to Christianity from the unbelieving Gentiles.

201   John 15:13.
202   Rom. 5:10a.
203   Luke 9:23.
204   John 20:19, 26.

the doors that were closed and your descending into hell.[205] **67{68}[26]** *Praevenerunt principes, princes went before,* that is, the prelates of the Church preceded others in all their good works, *coniuncti psallentibus, joined with singers,* that is, praising God with the sheep committed to them, *in medio iuvencularum tympanistriarum, in the midst of young damsels playing on timbrel,* that is, [in the midst] of devout souls: of which the Song of Songs says, *of young maidens they are without number.*[206] For the souls espoused to Christ by faith and charity are called maidens because of the spiritual youth of interior reformation and of grace. Of this, the Apostle [Paul] says: *Though our outward man is corrupted, yet the inward man is renewed day by day.*[207] And they are also called timbrel players because by works of penance and mortification of their own flesh they sweetly resound in the ears of God, and they praise him most graciously, in the manner that he says to any such soul: *let your voice sound in my ears: for your voice is sweet.*[208] And so *princes went joined with singers:* and this is what the Apostle says to all prelates, *be an example of the faithful in word, in conversation, in charity, [in faith, in chastity].*[209]

67{68}[27]   *In the churches bless God the Lord, from the fountains of Israel.*

In ecclesiis benedicite Deo Domino de fontibus Israel.

67{68}[27] *In ecclesiis, in the churches,* that is, in the congregations of Catholic believers, not in the conventicles of heretics, schismatics, or the wicked, from whom all should completely flee;[210] *benedicite*

---

205   Eph. 4:9: *Now that he ascended, what is it, but because he also descended first into the lower parts of the earth?* E. N. Again, this is a reference to the limbo of the fathers, the *limbus partum,* not the hell of the damned.

206   Songs 6:7b.

207   2 Cor. 4:16.

208   Songs 2:14b.

209   1 Tim. 4:12. E. N. The portion in brackets is not in the Latin text, but it appears appropriate to include it.

210   E. N. This prohibition of *communicatio in sacris,* that is, participating in the worship of God with heretics or schismatics or other religious groups, brings to mind the reaction of the Apostle John as related by his disciple Polycarp (69–155 AD), Bishop of Smyrna, and related by St. Irenaeus (*ca.* 130–*ca.* 202 AD): "John, the disciple of the Lord, going to bathe at Ephesus, and perceiving [the Gnostic heretic] Cerinthus within, rushed out of the bath-house without bathing, exclaiming, 'Let us fly, lest even the bath-house fall down, because Cerinthus, the enemy of the truth, is within.'" Irenaeus, *Against Heresies,* III, 3, 4, *Ante-Nicene Fathers* (Edinburgh: T & T Clark 1868), Vol. I, 263 (eds., Alexander Roberts and James Donaldson).

Deo Domino de fontibus Israel; bless God the Lord from the fountains of Israel, that is, because of the founts of Israel, namely, because the grace bestowed upon the teachers and pastors of the Church: those whom God filled with the gifts of the Holy Spirit, wisdom, understanding, counsel, fortitude, knowledge, piety, and fear, so that those beneath them received and drew streams of doctrine, examples of virtue, and divine grace from these [doctors and pastors] as if they were fountains.

67{68}[28] *There is Benjamin a youth, in ecstasy of mind. The princes of Judah are their leaders: the princes of Zebulon, the princes of Naphthali.*

Ibi Beniamin adolescentulus, in mentis excessu; principes Iuda, duces eorum; principes Zabulon, principes Nephthali.

67{68}[28] *Ibi, there,* that is, in the unity of the Church, *Beniamin adolescentulus, is Benjamin a youth,* that is, son of my right hand,[211] namely, the adopted son of God, incessantly advancing in the grace of God: to whom God is favorable, that is, well disposed toward and kindly, living in him by grace. For of such a Benjamin there is written in Deuteronomy: *The best beloved of the Lord shall dwell confidently in him: as in a bride chamber shall he abide all the day long, and between his shoulders shall be rest.*[212] Such are all those who completely lean upon the grace of God, whose soul is pleasing to God: to whom applies that which the Lord said through Haggai, *I will take you, . . . my servant, . . . and will make you as a signet, for I have chosen you.*[213] *Principes Iuda duces eorum, principes Zabulon, principes Nephthali; the princes of Judah are their leaders: the princes of Zebulon, the princes of Naphthali.* Judah is interpreted as confession; but Zebulon as household of the strong; and Naphthali, as

---

211   E. N. See Gen. 35:18: *His father called him Benjamin, that is, the son of the right hand.*

212   Deut. 33:12. E. N. This was Moses's blessing to the tribe of Benjamin.

213   Haggai 2:24. E. N. In his spiritual or mystical interpretation of this verse, Denis in his *Commentary on Haggai* states: "God daily mercifully draws out by grace the elect from the foreknown ungodly and justly abandoned, and he adorns them with various gifts and virtues; he also beautifies in turn the guides of others with such a splendor of grace, that they are under merit signets thrown out to be observed and to be imitated. The Lord does all of this, for he elects those whom he takes up. For truly he loved us first without any merit on our part [1 John 4:10], he elected and predestined those whom he willed [Eph. 1:4-5], according to that said in Exodus: *I will have mercy on whom I will, and I will be merciful to whom it shall please me.* [Ex. 33:19b]" Doctoris Ecstatici D. Dionysii Cartusiani, *Opera Omnia,* Vol. 10 (Montreuil: 1900), 613.

reaching out.[214] Therefore it is in this sense [that the verse should be understood]: *Princes* of Christian confession *are their leaders*, namely, [the leaders] of the Christian people. For these princes are the prelates of the Church, but most particularly the holy martyrs, who first and most eminently have confessed the name of Christ before men: and so they are constituted leaders of others, and it is incumbent upon us to imitate their example. But also the *princes of Zebulon*, that is, the princes of spiritual strength, who are well-grounded in the virtues, and adhere inavertibly[215] to God; and *the princes of Nephthali*, that is, of reaching out, of those hearts which by charity reach out towards God and their neighbor, receiving, embracing, and holding on to God with extended arms, and also in charity providing help to their neighbor in all things. These kinds of people are leaders of the sheep of Christ. For they who are adorned with virtues are truly set over others. The confession relates to faith, fortitude to hope, and the reaching out to charity.

67{68}[29] *Command your strength, O God: confirm, O God, what you have wrought in us.*

Manda, Deus, virtuti tuae; confirma hoc, Deus, quod operatus es in nobis.

67{68}[30] *From your temple in Jerusalem, kings shall offer presents to you.*

A templo tuo in Ierusalem, tibi offerent reges munera.

67{68}[29] *Manda, Deus, virtuti tuae; confirma hoc, Deus, quod operatus es in nobis; command your strength, O God: confirm, O God, what you have wrought in us.* This is a very fine prayer which the Church and all the faithful are able to, and ought to, offer it to God, pleading that God send the angelic powers to keep watch over them, in the manner that Tobias said: *May you have a good journey, and the Lord be with you in your way, and his angel accompany you.*[216] We also ought to pray that God, in his kindliness, strengthen that good which he so graciously began in us, and that he lead us with continuous

---

214 E. N. This is a commonplace interpretation. For example, so does St. Augustine understand it in his *Commentary on the Psalms*, PL 36, 835.

215 E. N. Denis uses the Latin word *inavertibiliter* (inavertibly) often. It means so affixed that it cannot be averted, deflected, or moved.

216 Tob. 5:21. E. N. Denis's version states "the Lord be with you." The Douay-Rheims has "God be with you."

progress to a secure end. For so says Paul: *It is best that the heart be established with grace.*[217] **67{68}[30]** *A templo tuo in Ierusalem, from your temple in Jerusalem.* For God, dwelling in the heavenly Jerusalem or the triumphant Church, is working in us whatever good we do and we have, according to this: *For you have wrought all our works for us.*[218] And the Apostle [Paul]: *It is God who works in you, both to will and to accomplish, according to his good will.*[219] And God works this in us from the temple of the heavenly Jerusalem, because it is from that place that he dispatches the holy angels who carry with them the gifts of graces and raise us up toward the things that are above. *Tibi offerent reges, kings shall offer... to you,* that is, all Christians, who are a generation of kings and priests,[220] who have dominion of their own souls, and strongly pursue the empire of reason;[221] *munera, presents,* that is, sacred oblations, devout prayers, abundant alms, and voluntary service — indeed, their very selves.

67{68}[31]   *Rebuke the wild beasts of the reeds, the congregation of bulls with the cows of the people; who seek to exclude them who are tried with silver. Scatter the nations that delight in wars.*

Increpa feras arundinis; congregatio taurorum in vaccis populorum; ut excludant eos qui probati sunt argento: dissipa gentes quae bella volunt.

67{68}[33]   *Sing to God, you kingdoms of the earth: sing to the Lord: Sing to God,*[222]

Regna terrae, cantate Deo; psallite Domino; psallite Deo,

67{68}[34]   *Who ascends above the heaven of heavens,to the east. Behold he will give to his voice the voice of power,*

Qui ascendit super caelum caeli, ad orientem: ecce dabit voci suae vocem virtutis.

---

217   Heb. 13:9a.
218   Is. 26:12b.
219   Phil. 2:13.
220   1 Pet. 2:9a. E. N. All, including the lay faithful, "are in their own way made sharers in the priestly, prophetical, and kingly functions of Christ; and they carry out for their own part the mission of the whole Christian people in the Church and in the world." DS 4157 (VII, *Lumen gentium*, No. 31).
221   For the "empire of reason," see Article XLIV (Psalm 17:37) in Volume 1, Article LXII (Psalm 27:7), and footnote 27-46 in Volume 2.
222   E. N. Denis skips over 67:32 in this section.

67{68}[35] *Give glory to God over Israel, his magnificence, and his power is in the clouds.*

Date gloriam Deo super Israel; magnificentia eius et virtus eius in nubibus.

67{68}[31] *Increpa feras arundinis, etc. Rebuke the wild beasts, etc.* This verse along with part of the following verses, anyone can say according to the explanation already expressed earlier, praying for the conservation of the Church and the repression of its adversaries. 67{68}[33] *Regna terrae, cantate Deo; sing to God, you kingdoms of the earth.* To the extent it is in our power, each of us, ignited with zeal for the divine honor, ought to lead and to ardently ignite all the faithful to commend themselves to God, calling to mind his benefits: and if one is alone, he can say this in the person of the Church speaking on behalf of all the faithful; and God will look upon the goodness of his affection, and will not let them be fruitless. 67{68}[34]²²³ *Ecce dabit voci suae vocem virtutis, behold he will give to his voice the voice of power.* This can be understood of that voice by which we will all be awakened to in the last day. Of this the Apostle [Paul] says: *The Lord himself shall come down from heaven with commandment, and with the voice of an archangel, and with the trumpet of God.*²²⁴ He will give this voice the voice of power, since by it he will raise all the dead in the manner that Paul attests: *The trumpet shall sound, and the dead shall rise again incorruptible: and we shall be changed.*²²⁵ 67{68}[35] *Date gloriam Deo super Israel, give glory to God over Israel,* that is, glorify the name of the Lord because of all the good things shown and promised to the true Israelites, namely, in reality and in name to the Christians. *Magnificentia eius, his magnificence,* namely, [the magnificence] *of Christ, et virtus eius in nubibus, and his power is in the clouds* of heaven, will appear physically in the last day when (as he himself foretold) *they shall see the Son of man coming in the clouds of heaven with much power and majesty.*²²⁶

67{68}[36] *God is wonderful in his Saints: the God of Israel is he who will give power and strength to his people. Blessed be God!*

Mirabilis Deus in sanctis suis; Deus Israel ipse dabit virtutem et fortitudinem plebi suae. Benedictus Deus!

---

223 E. N. Denis skips the first half of this verse.
224 1 Thess. 4:15.
225 1 Cor. 15:52b.
226 Matt. 24:30b.

67{68}[36] *Mirabilis Deus in Sanctis suis,* God is wonderful in his Saints. For he was marvelous in his saints before the Law, as in Noah, whom he saved by the ark,[227] and in Enoch, whom he transported [into heaven],[228] and also in Abraham and Lot and many others. He was also wonderful in his people, whom he led out of Egypt,[229] for whom he appeared terribly and sublimely in mount Sinai;[230] in Joshua also, at whose command the sun and the moon stood still in the heavens for the space of a day.[231] So also he was wonderful in Elijah, Elisha and many others in the time of the law. But he was most wonderful in his Saints during the time of grace; and even now he works and dwells incomprehensibly among the Christians, especially in the Sacrament of the Altar;[232] even up to the present he deigns to work many signs by his elect.[233] And also all of the devout are able to know how wonderful God works in them every day, hearing their prayers, consoling hearts, delivering from temptation, giving spiritual perfection, and frequently lighting, increasing, and perfecting the fire of divine love in them. For there is also added [to this verse]: *Deus Israel,* the God of Israel, that is, of those persons seeing God with a contemplative eye, *dabit virtutem et fortitudinem plebi suae,* he will give power and strength to his people, giving to them by grace that which they do not have and do not see by nature. The rest [of the verses] have been satisfactorily expounded upon.

See, we have heard this glorious, wonderful Psalm, truly full of mysteries: in which are described the resurrection of Christ, the casting down of the unbeliever, the institution and advancement of the Church, the sending of the Holy Spirit, and also the ascension of Christ. Let us

---

227   Gen. 27:3.
228   Gen. 19:16–20.
229   Ex. 12:42.
230   Ex. 19:16–20.
231   Joshua 10:13.
232   "[I]n the Blessed Sacrament of the Holy Eucharist, after the consecration of the bread and wine, our Lord Jesus Christ, true God and man, is truly, really, and substantially contained under the appearances of those perceptible realities." DS 1636 (Council of Trent). "If anyone denies that in the sacrament of the most Holy Eucharist the body and blood, together with the soul and divinity, of our Lord Jesus Christ, and, therefore, the whole Christ is truly, really, and substantially contained, but says that he is in it only in a sign or figure or by his power, let him be anathema." DS 1651 (Council of Trent).
233   "If anyone says that all miracles are impossible, and that therefore all reports of them, even those contained in Sacred Scripture, are to be set aside as fables or myths; or that miracles can never be known with certainty, nor can the divine origin of the Christian religion be proved from them: let him be anathema." DS 3034 (Vatican Council I, *Dei Filius,* no. 3).

endeavor, therefore, to fulfill completely all that which is exhorted by this Psalm, namely to sing, to recite psalms to God, to recount his promises, to again prepare for his coming into our hearts, so that he might remain always in us by grace, and we remain in him always through love, in the manner that is written: *God is charity: and he that abides in charity, abides in God, and God in him.*[234]

PRAYER

LORD, KING OF POWERS, SET ASIDE FOR us your inheritance the salutary rain of compunction: so that we who are weakened by sin, receiving from you the strength of right purpose, might obtain a life pleasing to you.

Rex virtutum Domine, compunctionis pluviam salutarem segrega
nobis hereditati tuae: ut qui a peccatis infirmati sumus,
receptis a te rectae intentionis viribus, ad vitam
tibi placitam proficiamus.

---

234 1 John 4:16b.

Psalm 68

ARTICLE XXXIII

LITERAL EXPOSITION OF THE SIXTY-EIGHTH PSALM:
SALVUM ME FAC, DEUS
SAVE ME, O GOD.

68{69}[1] *Unto the end, for them that shall be changed; for David.*

In finem, pro iis qui commutabuntur. David.

HE TITLE OF THIS PSALM NOW BEING
addressed is: 68{69}[1] *In finem, pro his qui commutabuntur, ipsi David; unto the end, for them that shall be changed, for David:* that is, this Psalm directs us unto the ultimate end, who is Christ, and is written for *them that shall be changed,* that is, those who are *re-formed* in Christ—those who begin to bear the image of the second sinless and heavenly man as they had borne the first earthly and sinful man.[1] This Psalm also pertains to the prophet David himself, as its author; but it fittingly applies also to him that is signified by David as its subject, namely Christ. For one cannot be allowed to doubt that this Psalm is literally to be understood to be about Christ: this is in many ways demonstrable by the canonical scriptures of the New Testament. For that most glorious prince of the Apostles said that the words of this Psalm were fulfilled in Judas, who betrayed Christ, on account of the sin committed against the Christ. For he asserts this: *Let their habitation become desolate and let there be none to dwell therein.*[2] And so also does the apostle Paul introduce a verse [of this Psalm discussed] below—*Let the table become as a snare before them* along with the subsequent verse—which he also says was fulfilled in the Jews who killed Christ, because of the enormity perpetrated by them.[3] And also in that same epistle he says that which

---

1 Cf. 1 Cor. 15:47, 49: *The first man was of the earth, earthly: the second man, from heaven, heavenly.... Therefore, as we have borne the image of the earthly, let us bear also the image of the heavenly.*

2 Acts 1:20a. E. N. This verse from Psalm 68:26, quoted by St. Peter in Acts to supply the reasoning for appointing another apostle to replace Judas, Acts 1:20, continues *And his bishopric let another take.* The latter quote comes from Psalm 108:8.

3 Rom. 9-10: *And David said: Let their table be made a snare, and a trap, and stumbling block, and a recompense unto them. Let their eyes be darkened, that they*

it says below—*the reproaches of them that reproached you are fallen upon me*—were fulfilled in the person of Christ.[4] In the same way, that which is found in this Psalm—*the zeal for your house has eaten me up*—John the evangelist asserts was foretold of Christ and was fulfilled in him, stating the manner that Christ caused buyers and sellers to be driven out of the temple with a scourge of little cords.[5] In addition, that which this Psalm says—*They are multiplied above the hairs of my head, who hate me without cause*—Christ affirms was a foreannouncement of him, [when he said:] *that the word may be fulfilled which is written in their law: They hated me without cause.*[6] This is also manifestly said in a Psalm above, in this way: *Let not them that are my enemies wrongfully rejoice over me: who have hated me without cause, and wink with the eyes.*[7] For this reason, by this testimony of the Lord and Savior it is apparent that this Psalm was literally written of him, in such a way also here [in this Psalm 68], as it was more fully said there [in Psalm 34].

68{69}[2]   *Save me, O God: for the waters are come in even into my soul.*

Salvum me fac, Deus, quoniam intraverunt aquae usque ad animam meam.

And so Christ either approaching the Passion or already suffering it, praying to the Father, or to the holy Trinity, the one and most simple God, says:[8] **68{69}[2]** *Salvum me fac, Deus; save me, O God*, not from the evil of fault, for I am unable to sin, but from the evil of punishment, namely, from pains of body and soul being inflicted or which are to be inflicted. To this is added: *quoniam intraverunt aquae, for the waters are come in*, that is, the trials and punishments, *usque ad animam meam, even into my soul*, that is, even unto the extinction of my bodily life, namely, even unto the separation of my flesh and soul. Sometimes in sacred Scripture by water is understood consolation, as here: *you have sent forth your prisoners out of the pit, wherein is no water.*[9] But sometimes by water is understood severe persecution, as we see in the book of Job: *Did you think that you should not see darkness,*

---

may not see, and bow down their back always. This is a quote from Psalm 68:23–24.

4   Rom. 15:3: *For Christ did not please himself, but as it is written: The reproaches of them that reproached you, fell upon me.* E. N. The latter half of Rom. 15:3 is a quote from Psalm 68:10b.

5   John 2:17. E. N. John quotes the first half of 68:10.

6   John 15:25b. E. N. Jesus refers to the first half of Psalm 68:5.

7   Ps. 34:19.

8   E. N. *Deus . . . est maxime simplex*, "God is most simple," SCG, 3 cap. 118 n. 4.

9   Zech. 9:11b.

and that you should not be covered with the violence of overflowing waters?[10] Whence Isaiah more openly says: *The Lord will bring upon this people the waters of the river strong and many, the king of the Assyrians.*[11] And so in these instances by waters are designated persecutions.

68{69}[3] *I stick fast in the mire of the deep: and there is no sure standing. I am come into the depth of the sea: and a tempest has overwhelmed me.*

Infixus sum in limo profundi et non est substantia. Veni in altitudinem maris; et tempestas demersit me.

68{69}[3] *Infixus sum in limo profundi, I stick fast in the mire of the deep.* Some say this refers to Christ by reason of his sepulture, for at that time he was hidden under ground, in the way he himself foretold in the Gospel: *As Jonas was in the whale's belly three days and three nights: so shall the Son of man be in the heart of the earth.*[12] But it seems that this applies to Christ also by reason of his Incarnation, by which he descended into the world, which can be called a deep mire or muddy because of the substance of the earth, or because of the viciousness and filthiness of the carnal life of men living in the world. God in Christ stood fast because, as the Apostle [Paul] attests, *he descended . . . into the lower parts of the earth,*[13] and he spent much time in the midst of a *crooked and perverse generation.*[14] *Et non est substantia, and there is no sure standing:*[15] that is, in my body I was not in a stable and uniform state of natural life. For it is true to say about Christ, based upon the fact that he was in a certain way a wayfarer and so capable of suffering, that which is written about blessed Job: *Man born of a woman, living for a short time, is filled with many miseries, . . . and never continues in the same state.*[16] Or [we can look at it this way], *there is no sure standing,* that is, there is no subsistence or

---

10 Job. 22:11.

11 Is. 8:7a. E. N. The context is the imminent Assyrian invasion against Syria and Israel, as the Assyrian army will pour over the banks of the Euphrates from Assyria into Israel and Syria and therefore "flood" these lands with destructive violence.

12 Matt. 12:40.

13 Eph. 4:9.

14 Phil. 2:15a.

15 E. N. The Douay-Rheims translates the Latin *substantia* with the word "standing." It is not referring to a posture, but rather to something along the lines of "He has standing in the community." The word *substantia* can literally mean "substance" as in essence, but it can also mean "substance" as in fortune, property, wealth, and worldly goods, such as when we say: "He is a man of substance."

16 Job 14:1–2.

power naturally subsisting in a crucified, soul-emptied, dead, and buried body. Or [yet another alternative], *there is no sure standing*, that is, natural riches were wanting in me. For Christ did not have anywhere to lay his head,[17] and he was hung naked on the cross, and he had vinegar and gall for his food and drink.[18] Behold this King of glory — he whose realm is heaven and earth and all their adornments — deigned to suffer for us. For truly *he being rich*, for our sakes *became poor* and without standing, so that out of his *poverty* we would become *rich*.[19] *Veni, I am come* from the highest heaven and the bosom of the Father by the assumption of human nature, *in altitudinem maris, into the depth of the sea*, that is, in the depth of persecution and punishment and death; *et tempestas demersit me, and a tempest has overwhelmed me*, that is, the magnitude of the punishment inflicted upon me on the gibbet of the cross killed me: as in Lamentations is written: *Waters have flowed over my head: I said: I am cut off.*[20] Yet customarily by the word altitude (*altitudinem*) is meant depth (*profunditas*), as it is here: *the well is deep (altus).*[21]

68{69}[4]   *I have labored with crying; my throat is become hoarse: my eyes have failed, while I hope in my God.*[22]

Laboravi clamans, raucae factae sunt fauces meae; defecerunt oculi mei, dum spero in Deum meum.

68{69}[4] *Laboravi clamans, I have labored with crying.* For Christ did not journey about without labor when preaching. Whence it is written: *Jesus wearied with his journey.*[23] Also he cried out, inveighing against the Jews, instructing the people, and teaching the evangelical law. Also he

---

17   Luke 9:58.

18   Matt. 27:48, 34.

19   *Cf.* 2 Cor. 8:9: *For you know the grace of our Lord Jesus Christ, that being rich he became poor, for your sakes; that through his poverty you might be rich.*

20   Lam. 3:54.

21   John 4:11. E. N. The translators of the Douay-Rheims have already taken into consideration this custom in translating Ps. 68:3. In Latin *altitudo* means height or altitude; however, it can frequently mean depth or profundity. Another example of this use, other than in this Ps. 68:3 and John 4:11, can be found in Christ's command to Peter as a predicate to his miraculous catch: (Luke 5:4): *Duc in altum! Launch out into the deep!*

22   E. N. I have translated *fauces meae*, which the Douay-Rheims translates as "my jaws," as "my throat." The Latin word *fauces*, although it can mean throat, is plural in form, and so takes a plural verb (*sunt*). However, in English such is not possible, so I have translated *sunt* (they are) with "is."

23   John 4:6b.

most greatly labored during his Passion, when *bearing his own cross he went forth;*[24] and when he cried out while on the Cross, *Father forgive them;*[25] and *It is finished;*[26] and *Into your hands I commend my spirit.*[27] For this is written about Christ by Isaiah: *Because his soul has labored, he shall see and be filled.*[28] *Raucae factae sunt fauces meae, my throat is become hoarse.* The throat of Christ was literally made hoarse. For hoarseness is caused by the drying up of humors in the throat and windpipe. Because, therefore, in his Passion Christ shed blood abundantly, as is said in a Psalm above, *I am poured out like water;*[29] so his voice became hoarse. Now in a metaphorical sense a throat can be said to be hoarse when a sermon is delivered, and those hearing do not derive profit but remain without fruit; and so the throat of Christ was hoarse with respect to the unbelievers and the perverse: to whom he said in the Gospel, *My word has no place in you.*[30]

Defecerunt oculi mei, dum spero in Deum meum; my eyes have failed, while I hope in my God. This seems to be repugnant to that which Christ said [in a Psalm] above: *I have put my trust in the Lord and shall not be weakened.*[31] And therefore it is [to be understood] in this sense: my interior eyes, namely, contemplation and mental prayer, by which hanging on the Cross I beheld God unceasingly, appeared to have failed, that is, to be deceived, and to be deprived of their effect or assistance, at the time that God the Father delivered me over into the hands of the godless. For this reason they said: *He trusted in God; let him now deliver him if he will have him.*[32] And again: *If he be the king of Israel (or, If this is the Christ, the elect of God), let him now come down from the cross.*[33] And Isaiah: *We have thought him as it were a leper, and as one struck by God and afflicted.*[34] For Christ was accustomed to affirm something about himself, according to what was the opinion of others [and not because it was in fact so]. Whence with Jeremiah: *I was as a meek lamb, he says, that is carried to be a victim; and I knew not that they had devised counsels against me, [saying: Let us put wood on his bread*

---

24 John 19:17a.
25 *Cf.* Luke 23:34.
26 John 19:30b.
27 Luke 23:46.
28 Is. 53:11a.
29 Ps. 21:15a.
30 John 8:37b.
31 Ps. 25:1b.
32 Matt. 27:43a.
33 Matt. 27:42a; Luke 23:35. *E. N.* The version in parentheses is from Luke.
34 Is. 53:4b.

and cut him off from the land of the living, and let his name be remembered no more].[35] For the Jews supposed Christ not to know their counsels against him. Or [it can be understood] thus: *My eyes have failed me, while I hope in my God:* that is, while hanging on the Cross, I most certainly trusted that I would rise again on the third day; then my bodily eyes have failed, because they became dark and were cast down.

68{69}[5] *They are multiplied above the hairs of my head, who hate me without cause. My enemies are grown strong who have wrongfully persecuted me: then did I pay back that which I did not plunder.*[36]

Multiplicati sunt super capillos capitis mei qui oderunt me gratis. Confortati sunt qui persecuti sunt me inimici mei iniuste; quae non rapui, tunc exsolvebam.

68{69}[5] *Multiplicati sunt super capillos capitis mei, qui oderunt me gratis; they are multiplied above the hairs of my head, who hate me without cause.* By this Christ means the multitude of his Jewish adversaries who hated him gratuitously (*gratis*), that is, without reasonable cause: and possibly, in a literal sense, that the number of those hating and persecuting Christ exceed the number of hairs on his head. For there were many thousands seen among the people of whom the Evangelist stated: *And the whole people answering, said: His blood be upon us and our children.*[37]

Confortati sunt qui persecuti sunt me inimici mei iniuste, my enemies are grown strong who have wrongfully persecuted me. For all are united in evil and have caused their voices against me to strengthen, not through the use of reason, but because of the multitude [of voices].[38] The chief priests offered help to the Pharisees, who were the first to conceive a grudge against Christ. Herod and Pilate also cooperated with them, for Herod mocked him [by putting on him] a white garment,[39] but

---

35 Jer. 11:19. E. N. The part in brackets replaces Denis's "etc." For this verse's "put wood on his bread" referring to nailing Jesus, the Bread of Life, upon the wood of the Cross, *see* footnote 2-9 in Volume 1 and 34-52 in Volume 2.

36 E. N. I have departed from the Douay-Rheims's translation of *quae non rapui, tunc exsolvebam,* "then did I pay that which I took not away," which might be more forcefully translated "then did I pay back that which I did not plunder."

37 Matt. 27:25.

38 Luke 23:5, 23. *But they [the chief priests and the multitude] were more earnest, saying: He stirs up the people, teaching throughout all Judea, beginning from Galilee to this place. . . . But they were instant with loud voices, requiring that he might be crucified; and their voices prevailed.*

39 Luke 23:11.

Pilate had him flogged and condemned him.[40] And all these persecuted me unjustly, that is, [because I was] without offense and without fault; indeed, they repaid my doing good with injury and scourging, as it is said in a Psalm above, *They repaid me evil for good.*[41] This is what Christ said to the Jews in the Gospel: *Many good works I have showed you from my Father; for which of these works do you stone me?*[42] And through Jeremiah: *Shall evil be rendered for good, because they have dug a pit for my soul?*[43] *Quae non rapui, that which I did not plunder,* that is, the fault which I had not incurred, the evil that I did not do, *tunc exsolvebam, then did I pay*: because I suffered punishment not through any fault of my own. For the [just] desert of fault is punishment, just like the punishment of sin is death.[44] Because the Savior is most immune from sin,[45] yet he nevertheless endured a most bitter death, it follows that he paid for that which he did not plunder. But he made satisfaction for us, and, by the merit of his particular and temporal death, he carried off from the human race the universal and eternal death inflicted by original sin. Whence it is written: *The breath of our mouth, Christ the Lord, is captured in our sins;*[46] and again, *He was wounded for our iniquities, he was bruised for our sins.*[47] Finally, Christ most openly declared through Isaiah: *You have made me to serve with your sins, you have wearied me with your iniquities.*[48]

68{69}[6] *O God, you know my foolishness; and my offenses are not hidden from you.*

Deus, tu scis insipientiam meam; et delicta mea a te non sunt abscondita.

This verse can be explained in three ways. The first way is this: **68{69} [6]** *Deus, tu scis, etc. O God, you know, etc.*, that is, if there is in me some

---

40 John 19:1, 16.

41 Ps. 34:12a.

42 John 10:32.

43 Jer. 18:20a. E. N. I have translated *captus est* as "taken captive," and departed from the Douay-Rheims's translated, "taken in."

44 Cf. Rom. 6:23: *For the wages of sin is death.*

45 E. N. It is *de fide* (that is, of the Faith) that Christ was free from all sin — original as well as actual. It is also proximate to faith (*sententia fide proxima*) that Christ was not only sinless, but he could not sin. That is, he enjoyed impeccability (*impeccabilitas*). Ludwig Ott, *Fundamentals of Catholic Dogma* (Rockford, IL: TAN Books 1974), 169 (trans., Patrick Lynch, ed. James Canon Bastible).

46 Lam. 4:20a.

47 Is. 53:5a.

48 Is. 43:24b.

folly or some sin, as the Jews assert, accusing me of teaching false things and of blaspheming: this you know. For this is a manner of speaking to those who with a clear mind excuse themselves before God while they are being accused. It is as if they were saying: "We are not ourselves conscious of any evil; but if there is evil in us, God knows it." And in this way the patriarch Judah, excusing himself and his brothers for theft before Joseph said: *God has found out the iniquity of your servants.*[49] Secondly, it can be understood in a contrary sense, in this manner: *O God, you know* through approbation, *my foolishness,* that is, my wisdom, which is chalked up as foolishness by the Jews; *et delicta mea, and my offenses,* that is, virtues and good works, which the Jews adjudge to be sins, *are not hidden from you,* but are known to you by approbation. For because Christ taught contempt of the world and called God his Father; therefore, the Jews said: *He has a devil, and is mad;*[50] and, *Why does this man speak thus? He blasphemes;*[51] and, *Who is this who speaks blasphemies?*[52] Whence they also told Pilate: *We have a law; and according to the law he ought to die, because he made himself the Son of God.*[53] In in accordance with this manner of speaking, the Savior said: *I confess to you, O Father, . . . because you have hid these things from the wise and prudent, and have revealed them to the little ones:*[54] for according to St. Augustine, this is to be understood in a contrary sense.[55] And so Paul says: *I am become foolish: you have compelled me;*[56] and again, *We are fools for Christ's sake.*[57] Third, it may be understood as said by Christ, not on behalf of himself, but on behalf of his Mystical Body, which is the Church. And so he calls his own the foolishness and sins of his members which he has taken upon himself, and for which he has made satisfaction, as he elsewhere said: *Saul, Saul, why do you persecute me?*[58] And again: *I was hungry, and you gave me not to eat; . . . naked, and you covered me not.*[59]

---

49 Gen. 44:16a.
50 John 10:20a.
51 Mark 2:7.
52 Luke 5:21a.
53 John 19:7.
54 Matt. 11:25.
55 E. N. This may be a reference to St. Augustine's Sermon 18 where he states that the "wise and foolish" in this prayer of Jesus are really only the worldly-wise, and are those of whom St. Paul states: "Has not God made the foolish the wisdom of this world." 1 Cor. 1:20. *See Sermo* 68, 3, PL 38, 438.
56 2 Cor. 12:11a.
57 1 Cor. 4:10a.
58 Acts 9:4b.
59 Matt. 25:42–43.

68{69}[7] *Let them not be ashamed for me, who await you, O Lord, the Lord of hosts. Let them not be confounded on my account, who seek you, O God of Israel.*

Non erubescant in me qui exspectant te, Domine, Domine virtutum; non confundantur super me qui quaerunt te, Deus Israel.

68{69}[7] *Non erubescant in me, qui exspectant te; let them not be ashamed for me, who await you*: that is, the saints detained in the limbo [of the fathers], awaiting me with great desire, let them not show diffidence as if they were unsure in their hope; but as the Prophets foretold and others believed, so raise me up again, and make me to lead out the saints from limbo, so that they might be glorified to receive the fruit of faith and the effect of hope. For the saints in limbo expected both Christ and God the Father:[60] Christ, as the one who would be and the one who would come down there; but the Father, as the one who would send and the one who would spiritually console them. And so, let them not be ashamed who await you, *Domine, O Lord* of all things, *Domine virtutum, O Lord of hosts* of heaven, namely, of the angels: [God,] for whom nothing is impossible. *Non confundantur super me, qui quaerunt te, Deus Israel; let them not be confounded on my account, who seek you, O God of Israel*: that is, let not the Apostles and the other faithful seeking you by faith and good works be confounded over me, that is, over my humiliation, persecution, and death; but strengthen them so as to have confidence in me, and to imitate my way. This was fulfilled especially in the day of Pentecost, when the Holy Spirit was received.

68{69}[8] *Because for your sake I have borne reproach; shame has covered my face.*

Quoniam propter te sustinui opprobrium; operuit confusio faciem meam.

68{69}[8] *Quoniam propter te, because for your sake*, that is, for the honor of your name, which I sought first of all; or [alternatively], *for your sake*, that is, for the disposition of your wisdom, by which you decreed me to suffer: in the way Peter spoke, *They assembled together . . . against your holy child Jesus, . . . to do what your hand and your counsel decreed to be done.*[61] Or [yet another way], *for your sake*, that is, for my justice since I constantly abided by your will. *Sustinui opprobrium, I have borne*

---

60 Gen. 49:18: *I will look for your salvation, O Lord.*
61 Acts 4:27–28.

reproach of the Jews, who said, *Now we know that you have a devil;*[62] and, *Will he kill himself?*[63] *Operuit confusio faciem meam, shame has covered my face*: that is, that which generally is a cause of confusion to others rushed upon me in a multiplicity of ways in the time of Passion, when they handed me over to the guards with my hands tied, when before Pilate and Herod I responded nothing, when dressed in a white robe I was mocked, disrobed, tied to a column and struck with a scourge, crowned with thorns, and, when, carrying a cross on my own back, I was led to death, and suspended between thieves. And yet Christ did not suffer from confusion, for confusion has no place in perfect man because of virtue. Yet literally confusion covered the face of Christ when the men that held him, that mocked him, that put a robe on him, that struck his face, said: *Prophesy unto us, O Christ, who is he that struck you?*[64]

68{69}[9] *I am become a stranger to my brethren, and an alien to the sons of my mother.*

Extraneus factus sum fratribus meis, et peregrinus filiis matris meae.

68{69}[9] *Extraneus factus sum fratribus meis, I am become a stranger to my brethren,* that is, to the Jews born of the stock of Abraham with me. For Christ was a stranger to the Jews who did not believe in him, for in his heart he was far from them, even though he walked among them bodily. He was also a stranger to his brothers the Apostles, all of whom abandoned him and fled.[65] Hence, holy Job in the person — or certainly as a figure — of Christ,[66] said: *He has put my brethren far from me, and my acquaintance like strangers have departed from me.*[67] And I have become *peregrinus filiis matris meae, an alien to the sons of my mother,* that is, to the Jews, the sons of Sarah, or the Synagogue. In the way that an alien or foreigner does not stay in one place a long time, but is driven away from home; so the Jews cast aside and spurned Christ as insignificant, saying to him according to John: *We know that God spoke to Moses: but as to this man, we know not*

---

62   John 8:52a.

63   John 8:22a.

64   Matt. 26:68.

65   Matt. 26:56.

66   E. N. On Job as a figure of Christ, *see* footnote 21-95, Volume 1.

67   E. N. The sons of Sarah the wife of Abraham (*i.e.,* derived from Isaac, the son of promise), as distinguished from the sons of the slave Hagar, the slave of Abraham (*i.e.,* derived from Ishmael). Isaiah 51:2: *Look unto Abraham your father, and to Sara that bore you: for I called him alone, and blessed him, and multiplied him.*

from whence he is.[68] And the same thing attests the Evangelist: *The Jews had already agreed among themselves, that if any man should confess him to be Christ, he should be put out of the synagogue.*[69] Christ was to come and live in this world in this manner, as Jeremiah predicted with amazement: *Why will you be a stranger in the land, and as a wayfaring man turning in to lodge?*[70]

68{69}[10] *For the zeal of your house has eaten me up: and the reproaches of them that reproached you are fallen upon me.*

Quoniam zelus domus tuae comedit me, et opprobria expro-brantium tibi ceciderunt super me.

Now why Christ is worthy to suffer such things, is disclosed in what follows: **68{69}[10]** *Quoniam zelus domus tuae comedit me, for the zeal of your house has eaten me up*: that is, the ardent desire for the building, informing, and conversion of the Church, or of the faithful, or of the elect, for whose salvation I was made incarnate, and which totally inflamed, absorbed, and consumed me. For Christ preached to the Church, rebuked the Jews, and performed miracles for the sake of salvation. This zeal was publicly expressed when he cast out of the temple the buyers and sellers, saying: *Make not the house of my Father a house of traffic.*[71] This zeal also ate Christ up, that is, consumed him in death: because he gave himself over to death out of his love for us, as Paul confesses: *In the faith of the Son of God*, he says, *I live, who loved me, and delivered himself for me;*[72] and again: *Christ as the Son in his own house: which house are we.*[73] For Christ wished to construe a temple to God the Father, and a perfect Church from living stones, as was predicted by Zechariah: *Behold, a man, the Orient is his name, . . . and he shall build a temple to the Lord . . . and he shall bear the glory, and he shall sit and rule upon his throne.*[74] Christ began to build this temple, teaching and refuting the errant, in the manner that was clearly foretold about him. For the prophet Malachi said regarding the coming of Christ: *Presently, the Lord, whom you seek, . . . shall come to his temple;*[75] and to this teaching he added thereafter: *He is like a refining fire, and like the fuller's herb; and he shall sit refining and cleaning*

---

68 John 9:29.
69 John 9:22.
70 Jer. 14:8b.
71 John 2:16.
72 Gal. 2:20.
73 Heb. 3:6a.
74 Zech. 6:12b–13a.
75 Mal. 3:1a.

the silver, and he shall purify the sons of Levi.[76] And so Christ himself promised to build this temple at his coming saying through Amos the prophet: *In that day I will raise the tabernacle of David that is fallen, and I will close up the breaches of the walls thereof, and repair what was fallen: and I will rebuild it as in the days of old.*[77] James in the Acts of the Apostles asserted this was predicted of Christ.[78]

Et opprobria, and the reproaches of the Jews *exprobantium tibi, of them that reproached you,* O eternal Father, rejecting me, your Only-Begotten, and ascribing my miraculous and divine works to demons, *ceciderunt super me, are fallen upon me,* that is, they have had their way in my passible human nature: for words and injuries inflicted by the ungodly against you are not able to harm the divinity, but they have power to harm and to kill my humanity. Or [we can understand it in this sense], *they are fallen upon me,* that is, they also showed themselves hostile to me. For whoever proposes to injure one of the divine Persons proposes to injure the others. For this reason Christ asserted: *He who honors not the Son, honors not the Father, who sent him.*[79] Hence the Jews reproached God the Father, indeed, the whole Trinity, especially the Holy Spirit, when they attributed to Beelzebub the miracles of Christ that were brought about by the power of the whole Trinity. Whence, when the Scribes said, *He has Beelzebub,*[80] Christ wanting to show to them that they had been the occasion of blasphemy of the Holy Spirit said: *He that shall blaspheme against the Holy Spirit, shall never have forgiveness, but shall be guilty of an everlasting sin.*[81] And, as the Evangelist explains in what follows, this is why he said this to the Jews: *Because they said, he has an unclean spirit.*[82]

68{69}[11]   *And I covered my soul in fasting: and it was made a reproach to me.*

Et operui in ieiunio animam meam, et factum est in opprobrium mihi.

68{69}[11] *Et operui in ieiunio animam meam, and I covered my soul in fasting.* Virtuous works are called the clothing of the soul, as they are here:

---

76   Mal. 3:2b–3a.

77   Amos 9:11.

78   Acts 15:15–16: *And to this agree the words of the prophets, as it is written: After these things I will return, and will rebuild the tabernacle of David, which is fallen down; and the ruins thereof I will rebuild, and I will set it up.*

79   John 5:23b.

80   Mark 3:22.

81   Mark 3:29.

82   Mark 3:30.

I will greatly rejoice in the Lord, . . . for he has clothed me with the garments of salvation: and with the robe of justice he has covered me.[83] Now Christ fasted forty days and the same number of nights:[84] and so fasting, which is an act of temperance, covered, that is, clothed spiritually, his soul. *Et factum est in opprobrium mihi, and it was made a reproach to me*, that is, an occasion of temptation by the devil, who by this was moved to tempt me inasmuch as he proposed a kind of idolatry to me, saying: *All these will I give you, if you will bow down and adore me.*[85] Or [we can understand it] thus: *I covered my soul in fasting*, that is, I was clothed with a cloak of compassion and sadness because of the infidelity and the malice of perverse men. For this is said in Mark: Jesus *was grieved for the blindness of their hearts.*[86] For as the refreshment of Christ is the conversion of our minds to God, according to what he himself said, *If any man . . . open to me the door, I will come in to him, and I will sup with him;*[87] and thus his fasting is the aversion of our hearts to God. *Et factum est in opprobrium mihi, and it was made a reproach to me:* that is, the labor and effort by which I sweat, ran, and labored for the conversion of men was the occasion of detraction, derision, and accusations against me by the Jews. For they said: *We have found this man perverting our nation.*[88]

68{69}[12] *And I made haircloth my garment: and I became a byword to them.*

> *Et posui vestimentum meum cilicium; et factus sum illis in parabolam.*

68{69}[12] *Et posui vestimentum meum cilicium, and I made haircloth my garment*, that is, I wore rough and not soft clothing. For because Christ praised the roughness of the garments of John the Baptist,[89] and disapproved of those who wore luxurious garments, it is evident that he used rough clothing. Indeed, he *began to do and to teach.*[90] This is supported by the fact that his tunic was *without seam, woven from the top throughout,*[91] in the manner that hairshirts customarily are. Or [an

83   Is. 61:10a.

84   Matt. 4:2.

85   Matt. 4:9.

86   Mark 3:5a.

87   Rev. 3:20.

88   Luke 23:2a.

89   Matt. 11:8: *But what went you out to see? A man clothed in soft garments? Behold they that are clothed in soft garments, are in the houses of kings.*

90   Acts 1:1b.

91   John 19:23.

alternative explanation is], *I made haircloth my garment*, that is, I was clothed with mortal flesh, and covered my divinity: of which flesh and haircloth a Psalm above says, *You have cut my sackcloth, and have compassed me with gladness.*[92] *Et actus sum illis in parabolam, and I became a byword to them*, that is, in the likeness of one held in reproach and in derision, in the way is written in the Gospel: *The Pharisees . . . heard all these things: and they derided him;*[93] and: *They said: He is become mad.*[94]

68{69}[13] *They that sat in the gate spoke against me: and they that drank wine sang about me.*[95]

> *Adversum me loquebantur qui sedebant in porta, et in me psallebant qui bibebant vinum.*

68{69}[13] *Adversum me loquebantur qui sedebant in porta; they that sat in the gate spoke against me*, that is, the priests sitting by the gate of the temple and instructing the people, or the judges in the gates of the city adjudicating for its residents, in the manner decreed by Moses: *You shall appoint judges and magistrates in all your gates.*[96] All these spoke against Christ, warning the people about him to such an extent that they would ask that a murderer be released to them and that Jesus be killed.[97] *Et . . . qui bibebant, and they that drank wine*, that is, the voracious Jews, *psallebant, sang*, that is, they laughingly sang out, *in me, about me*, that is of me and against me. For they composed and resounded derisory canticles of the Lord Savior, such as these: *a glutton, a wine drinker, a friend of publicans.*[98] Whence it is said through Jeremiah: *The word of the Lord is made a reproach to me, and a derision all the day.*[99] And Christ through Hosea: *I redeemed them*, he says, *and they have spoken lies against me.*[100]

---

92   Ps. 29:12b. In his *Commentary* on this verse, Denis calls the body of Christ a "hiding place" of his divinity: "you permitted my body, the despised hiding place of my soul and divinity, to be mutilated during the Passion with many wounds."
93   Luke 16:14.
94   Mark 3:21b.
95   E. N. I have departed from the Douay-Rheims which reads "they that drank wine made me their song."
96   Deut. 26:18a.
97   E. N. Cf. Acts 3:13; Matt. 16–24, where the people preferred the release of the murderer Barabbas to the release of the innocent Christ.
98   Matt. 11:19.
99   Jer. 20:8b.
100   Hosea 7:13b.

68{69}[14] *But as for me, my prayer is to you, O Lord; for the time of your good pleasure, O God. In the multitude of your mercy hear me, in the truth of your salvation.*

Ego vero orationem meam ad te, Domine: tempus beneplaciti, Deus, in multitudine misericordiae tuae; exaudi me in veritate salutis tuae.

68{69}[14] *Ego vero orationem meam ad te, Domine;* but as for me, my prayer is to you, O Lord, O God the Father, I direct and pour myself out, praying for my persecutors, in the manner that I spoke to you through the Prophet [Jeremiah]: *Remember that I have stood in your sight, to speak good for them, and to turn away your indignation from them.*[101] And in the Gospel I said: *Father, forgive them, for they know not what they do.*[102] *Tempus beneplaciti, Deus,* for the time of your good pleasure, O God: That is, you owe it to me to hear me, O God the Father, because the time that I was in the world was a time of reconciliation and of grace. Of this the Apostle said: *Behold, now is the acceptable time; behold, now is the day of salvation.*[103] *In multitudine misericordiae tuae,* in the multitude of your mercy, that is, according to, and because of, your great mercy, *exaudi me in veritate salutis tuae,* hear me in the truth of your salvation, which I pray to you, namely, that you may give me and the Church, for whose salvation I suffer all things, true beatitude and salvation, which is granted only by you. Now salvation or beatitude is two-fold, namely, essential, which is the enjoyment of God, and accidental, which consists in created goods. The soul of Christ had beatitude from its beginning, and he never asked for it for himself, but he asked it for the Church on pilgrimage and militant. But the second beatitude, which is an accidental reward, Christ requested for himself now [in this verse] and in the verses that follow. For here Christ, praying for the salvation of the Church, asks from the Father for its essential reward, saying: *Father, those whom you have given me, I will that they be where I am, and that they may be with me, that they may see my glory which you have given me.*[104] And this vision is our whole reward.[105]

---

101   Jer. 18:20b.
102   Luke 23:34a.
103   2 Cor. 6:2b.
104   John 17:24.
105   E. N. Denis says *visio est tota merces,* "the [beatific] vision is the whole reward," which would appear to be a paraphrase of St. Augustine (*tota merces nostra visio est*), *Enarrationes in Psalmos,* 90, 13 PL 37, 1170 (Ps. 90:16): "We cannot understand how great it is that we are to see, when this vision is our complete reward."

68{69}[15] *Draw me out of the mud, that I may not stick fast: deliver me from them that hate me, and out of the deep waters.*[106]

Eripe me de luto, ut non infigar; libera me ab iis qui oderunt me, et de profundis aquarum.

68{69}[16] *Let not the tempest of water drown me, nor the deep swallow me up: and let not the pit shut its mouth upon me.*

Non me demergat tempestas aquae, neque absorbeat me profundum, neque urgeat super me puteus os suum.

68{69}[15] *Eripe me de luto, ut non infigar; draw me out of the mud, that I may not stick fast.* Mud and mire are the same thing. Now, since Christ says above, *I stick fast to the mire of the deep;*[107] in what way does he now pray that he may be drawn so that he may not be stuck fast? The answer is that Christ for a time was stuck in the mire in the sense previously mentioned;[108] but now he prays to be led out or to be drawn out, that he may not remain stuck in the mud for a long time or forever. So that [it is to be understood] in this sense: *Draw me out,* O Father God, *out of the mud,* that is, of the earthly world, from the company of evil men, and from the place of sepulture; *that I may not stick fast,* that is, that I may not remain in this mud longer than is ordained by you. Indeed, Christ desired to return to the Father from this world and to ascend to the society of angels and away from the company of evil men. Whence he said to the disciples: *If you loved me, you would indeed be glad, because I go to the Father;*[109] and, *O incredulous generation, how long shall I be with you?*[110] *Libera me ab his qui oderunt me, deliver me from them that hate me,* that is, from the Jews, raising me to an impassible state, *et de profundis aquarium, and out of the deep waters,* that is, from the fury of persecutions. **68{69}[16]** *No me demergat tempestas aquae, let not the tempest of water drown me:* that is, let me not be drowned completely by the onset of the death imposed upon me, of which I said above, *A tempest has overwhelmed me,*[111] that is, that I may not remain permanently dead even until the day of the universal resurrection, but that I might be delivered from the abyss of death on the third day. *Neque absorbeat me profundum, nor the deep swallow me up,* that is, the pit of the tomb, namely, that my body

---

106   I have changed the Douay-Rheims's "mire" (for *luto*) to "mud," since otherwise Denis's *Commentary* will not be understood.

107   E. N. Ps. 68:3a.

108   E. N. That is, as a metaphor for Christ's Incarnation prior to his glorification.

109   John 14:28.

110   Mark 9:18a.

111   E. N. Ps. 68:3b.

not remain in the sepulcher decomposing; but raise me up from the deep by an accelerated resurrection; *neque urgeat super me puteus os suum, and let not the pit shut its mouth upon me*: that is, that the limbo of the holy fathers to which I descend may not contain me long, nor may the mouth, that is, its entrance, shut or close upon my soul; but in the way that I pray that my body be led out from the enclosure of the sepulcher, so do I pray that my soul be delivered from the hell of limbo: just as it is said in the Psalm above, *Because you will not leave my soul in hell.*[112]

ARTICLE XXXIV

CONTINUATION OF THE LITERAL EXPOSITION OF THE SIXTY-EIGHTH PSALM

68{69}[17] *Hear me, O Lord, for your mercy is kind; look upon me according to the multitude of your tender mercies.*

Exaudi me, Domine, quoniam benigna est misericordia tua; secundum multitudinem miserationum tuarum respice in me.

68{69}[18] *And turn not away your face from your servant: for I am in trouble, hear me speedily.*

Et ne avertas faciem tuam a puero tuo; quoniam tribulor, velociter exaudi me.

68{69}[17] *Exaudi me, Domine; Hear me, O Lord* Father, in the prayers already dispatched, *quoniam benigna est misericordia tua; for your mercy is kind*: that is, hear me therefore, for sweet is your mercy, and so because of it hear me. For although Christ deserved to be heard by the just judgment of God through the merit of his most holy manner of life, he also prays to be heard according to the mercies of the divine goodness: first, so that he might provide an example to us who always depend upon the mercy of God, and not on our own merit; second, because the mercy of God, as the justice of the soul of Christ infinitely exceeds [any] created justice, so incomparably more proper [for him] is it to be heard by the divine mercy than any mere created justice. *Secundum multitudinem miserationum tuarum respice in me, according to the multitude of your tender mercies*, and, with the eye of paternal love, help me as I have prayed. By mercy (*miseratio*) is meant the act of mercy (*misericordiae*); and the

---

112 Ps. 15:10a.

mercy (*misericordia*) of God is one and is simple. Yet [the expression] many mercies (*misericordiae*) is also said because of the diverse effects of the mercy (*misericordiae*) of God, or, better said, because of the plenitude of the divine goodness, by which God knows, through various — indeed infinite — ways — to render aid to his own. Now, if the very act of God to the one to whom he shows mercy (*miserentis*) is called the tender mercy (*miseratio*) of God abiding in him, so in this way the tender mercy (*miseratio*) of God is one and many, just as is said of mercy (*misericordia*).[113] But if tender mercy (*miseratio*) of God refers to the effects of his mercy (*misericordiae*), so it is that the tender mercies (*miserationes*) of God are in reality many. **68{69}[18]** *Et ne avertas faciem tuam, and turn not away your face,* that is, your kindly and gracious countenance, *a puero tuo, from your servant,* that is, from me, your Only-Begotten. *Quoniam tribulor, for I am in trouble* even unto death in the day before the feast of Passover, and so *velociter exaudi me, hear me speedily,* not delaying beyond three days the glorification of my body.

68{69}[19]   *Attend to my soul, and deliver it: save me because of my enemies.*

Intende animae meae, et libera eam; propter inimicos meos eripe me.

68{69}[19] *Intende animae meae, attend to my soul,* hearing its prayers and devotions; *et libera eam, and deliver it* from the interior punishments which it had during the time of the Passion, from fear and from sadness. *Propter inimicos meos, because of my enemies* the Jews, *eripe me, save me* from the state of mortality and passibility, so that the hate and perverseness of those who are against me become for you the occasion for providing help to your beloved Son. Or [alternatively]: *Because of my enemies,* that is, for the sake of their salvation, *save me* from the sepulcher, so that they do not persist in their infidelity, but they might hear the preaching of the Gospel and convert to me, as I testified to them: *When you shall have lifted up the Son of man, then shall you know, that I am he.*[114] This was fulfilled openly in the Acts of the Apostles, where it is read that eight thousand Jews that were gathered together converted,[115] and also a great multitude of priests were said to have converted.[116]

---

113   E. N. This excursus on mercy is similar to that found in Denis's *Commentary on Psalm 50:3 in Volume II, Dominus Illuminatio Mea.*
114   John 8:28a.
115   Acts 2:41; 4:4, where, respectively, 3,000 and 5,000 Jews were converted.
116   Acts 6:7b.

68{69}[20] *You know my reproach, and my confusion, and my shame.*

Tu scis improperium meum, et confusionem meam, et reve-
rentiam meam.

68{69}[21] *In your sight are all they that afflict me; my heart has expected*
reproach and misery. And I looked for one that would grieve
together with me, but there was none: and for one that would
comfort me, and I found none.

In conspectu tuo sunt omnes qui tribulant me. Improperium
exspectavit cor meum et miseriam; et sustinui qui simul
contristaretur, et non fuit; et qui consolaretur, et non inveni.

68{69}[20] *Tu,* you, O Lord Father, *scis improperium meum,* know my
reproach, that is, the injury of the words asserted against me, *et confusio-*
nem meam, and my confusion, that is, the contempt and disparagement
of my adversaries, regarding me as a nobody; *et reverentiam meam, and*
my shame. Here this reverence is not on account of veneration, but on
account of shame or ignominy.[117] Now, properly speaking, shame is the
fear of disgrace, or the dread of foul things that are difficult to avoid.
But understanding it in this manner, it has no place in Christ. For he
knew nothing shameful was able to proceed from him; nor was he in
any manner ashamed of the injuries to which he was subjected, but
through patience he rejoiced in adversity. In what way, therefore, was
there reverence in him, that is, [reverence in the sense of] shame and
confusion? Only in those things which in others are customarily the
cause of confusion and shame which abounded in him, since he was
captured as if he were a robber, and he was spit upon, stripped naked,
and hung between thieves. **68{69}[21]** *In conspectu tuo, in your sight,*
that is, known to you, *sunt omnes qui tribulant me, are all they that afflict*
me, namely, the priests, Scribes, Pharisees, and the others; and they are
subject to your power, and you are able to me deliver from their hand
and to overthrow them.

Improperium exspectavit cor meum et miseriam, my heart has expected
reproach and misery. As the time of Passion became imminent, that much
more did Christ expect injurious words[118] and the imposition of punishments by those close by him. Hence he often predicted his Passion to

---

117   E. N. The word *reverentia* in Latin can mean *reverence;* but it can also mean
fear and even *shame.* Here, Denis clarifies that in this context *reverentia* means shame.
The translators of the Douay-Rheims have taken this into account by translating
reverentia with the word shame.

118   E. N. For "verbal injuries," *iniuria verborum,* see ST IIaIIae, art. 72.

the Apostles; and the Passion being imminent, *his sweat became as drops of blood*, because of the expectation of impending punishment, *trickling down upon the ground* so much did he greatly dread it.[119] *Et sustinui, and I looked*, that is, I expected and I considered, *qui simul contristaretur, for one that would grieve together with me*, suffering the anguish with me; *et non fuit, but there was none* who might suffer with me. And I also looked *qui consolaretur, for one that would comfort* me in my sorrow, *et non inveni, but there was none*. Christ asserts this, not that no one would suffer distress about him or desire to give him consolation, especially since it is written: *There followed him a great multitude of people, and of women, who bewailed and lamented him.*[120] And he said to his Apostles at the approach of his Passion: *You now indeed have sorrow; but I will see you again, and your heart shall rejoice.*[121] But [he said this] because they were few who sorrowed compared to the others [who did not sorrow], and that which is small is regarded as if were nothing; and so, he asserts that there was no one to console him. And in a similar way he said through another prophet [namely, Isaiah]: *I looked about, and there was none to help.*[122] For Peter who cut off the ear of Malchus helped in a minimal way.[123]

68{69}[22]   *And they gave me gall for my food, and in my thirst they gave me vinegar to drink.*

   Et dederunt in escam meam fel, et in siti mea potaverunt me aceto.

68{69}[22] *Et dederunt in escam meam fel, et in siti mea potaverunt me aceto; and they gave me gall for my food, and in my thirst they gave me vinegar to drink.* We do not read that the Jews gave gall separately to Christ being crucified, but rather vinegar mixed with gall. For the evangelist Matthew says: *They gave him wine to drink mingled with gall.*[124] And in Mark: *And they gave him to drink wine mingled with myrrh.*[125] John also: *There was a vessel set there full of vinegar.*[126] And so it says *they gave me gall for food* because none of that which they offered to Christ was fit to be solid food except for gall. Also, Christ while on the

---

119   Luke 22:44.
120   Luke 23:27.
121   John 16:22.
122   Is. 63:5a.
123   John 18:10.
124   Matt. 27:34.
125   Mark 15:23.
126   John 19:29.

Cross bodily thirsted, and upon him uttering, *I thirst*,[127] they gave him vinegar, which he also took according to John.[128] Yet Mark says that he did not take it.[129] But this is not a contradiction. For he took a little so as to taste it, and immediately ceased to drink: for this reason it is written, *And when he had tasted, he would not drink*.[130] And that Matthew affirms that it was wine that was mixed with gall, but Mark says it was mixed with myrrh is easily resolved: either because the mixture was both of myrrh and gall, or because Mark used the word myrrh to refer to the quality [of the wine], namely, that the drink was bitter, and not because it was the substance of myrrh [that was mixed with the wine].

68{69}[23] *Let their table become as a snare before them, and a recompense, and a stumbling block.*

Fiat mensa eorum coram ipsis in laqueum, et in retributiones, et in scandalum.

68{69}[23] *Fiat mensa eorum coram ipsis in laqueum, let their table become as a snare before them*: that is, let this food and this drink which in their envy they gave me be to them a cause of enslavement, and let it become for them a snare of soul and body. For because of this bitter drink of Christ, the Jews deserved to be besieged by the Romans, to suffer immeasurable hunger and thirst, and at the end to be captured. For in giving to Christ this drink, their soul was ensnared and captured by the fetter of sins and the snare of vices, according to that which is written in Proverbs: *His own iniquities catch the wicked, and he is fast bound with the ropes of his own sins*.[131] This was done to them also *in retributiones*, as a recompense of eternal damnation and of infernal torments, *et in scandalum, and as a stumbling block*, that is, in confusion. For the confusion of the Jews was great in that they killed the Messiah that had been promised them in the Law. Or [an alternate explanation might be], *and a stumbling block*, that is, as the occasion of their greater ruin, for by this table they deserved to stumble from sin to sin. Or [another alternative may be] thus: *Let their table*, that is, the Scripture of the Law and the Prophets, in which is contained refreshment of the soul, *become as a snare before them*, so that from their own books they

---

127 John 19:28.
128 John 19:29–30.
129 Mark 15:23.
130 Matt. 27:34.
131 Prov. 5:22.

might be convinced by Christians that Christ was to be killed; *and a recompense*, that is, in a more heavy condemnation. For as they thought themselves wise and set themselves against Christ so all the more gravely did they sin in that they did not recognize his presence, but denied and crucified him. For this is what Christ said to them in the Gospel: *If you were blind, you should not have sin: but now you say: We see. Your sin remains.*[132] *And a stumbling block.* For the sacred Scriptures of the Old Testament are to them a daily occasion of error. For they do not desire to believe in Christ, they twist them and explain them falsely, and by this false exposition they confirm their perfidy. And so literally the table of the Jews has become for them a snare. For before the siege by Titus, they all gathered together in Jerusalem to celebrate the Paschal festival, since it was not permitted to be celebrated outside Jerusalem. And before they were able to depart, they were besieged, punished, and confounded by the Romans. Now this and in that which follows [that is, in the next verses] is said not optatively but predictively.[133] For they are not said as a kind of prayer, so that it may occur; but as a kind of prophecy, because it will occur. This is the way that Jeremiah also prophesied: *But you, O Lord, know all their counsel against me unto death: forgive not their iniquity, and let not their sin be blotted out from your sight: let them be overthrown before your eyes, in the time of your wrath do destroy them.*[134]

68{69}[24] *Let their eyes be darkened that they see not; and bend you down always their back.*[135]

Obscurentur oculi eorum, ne videant; et dorsum eorum semper incurva.

68{69}[24] *Obscurentur oculi eorum ne videant, let their eyes be darkened that they see not:* that is, let the light of truth be deprived from the heart of the Jews, and let them be rendered entirely blind because of the sin committed against Christ. The holy Prophets predicted most abundantly the blindness of the Jews at the first coming of Christ, and most of all did the most holy Isaiah, whose testimony the Apostle abundantly cites in his epistle to the Romans.[136] Indeed, thus says the Prophet: *Who is blind,*

---

132   John 9:41.
133   E. N. In other words, it is expressed not as a wish or a desire, but rather as a matter of foretold fact.
134   Jer. 18:23.
135   E. N. I have taken the liberty of restructuring the latter half of the verse, so it departs from the Douay-Rheims.
136   Rom. chps. 9–11.

but my servant? Or deaf, but he to whom I have sent my messengers?[137] And elsewhere: Blind *is the heart of this people, and heavy their ears.*[138] And again about the people of Israel the Lord says through Isaiah: *I have spread forth my hands all the day to an unbelieving people.*[139] *Et dorsum eorum semper incurve, and bend you down always their back.* There is a certain back of the mind upon which the devout carry the yoke of the Lord or his divine precepts. This back is the will in which virtue and vice first and chiefly are found. And, therefore the sense [of this verse] is: *Bend down always,* that is, turn toward earthly and vain things, deflect to false things, and incline toward the direction of fault *their back,* that is, the will, affection, and the desire of the Jews. We see this fulfilled in the Jews [at the time of Christ] since they are avaricious, averse to the greatest good, and they are unceasingly attentive to their errors. For even at the coming of the Messiah, which they supposed would come, they expected to receive a temporal kingdom and to rule over all their enemies. Now God is said to bend down their backs, not effectively, but permissively, in the manner that he is said to have hardened Pharaoh.[140]

68{69}[25] *Pour out your indignation upon them: and let your wrathful anger take hold of them.*

   Effunde super eos iram tuam; et furor irae tuae comprehendat eos.

68{69}[26] *Let their habitation be made desolate: and let there be none to dwell in their tabernacles.*

   Fiat habitatio eorum deserta; et in tabernaculis eorum non sit qui inhabitet.

68{69}[25] *Effunde super eos iram tuam, pour out your indignation upon them,* that is, the vengeance of your justice, delivering them into the hands of the Romans; *et furor irae tuae, and let your wrathful anger,* that is, your

---

137 Is. 42:19a.
138 Is. 6:10a; *cf.* Matt. 13:15.
139 Is. 45:2a.
140 Ex. chps. 4, 7–11, 14. "[S]piritual blindness and hardness [of heart] involve two things. One of these is the movement of the human mind in adhering to evil and to be against the Divine light. And in this regard God is not the cause of spiritual blindness and hardness [of heart], just as he is not the cause of sin. Now another thing is the withdrawal of grace, from which follows that the mind is not enlightened by God to see things rightly, and the heart of man is not softened to live rightly. And in this regard God is the cause of spiritual blindness and hardness [of heart]." ST IaIIae, q. 79, art. 3, c.

most heavy vindication, *comprehendat eos, take hold of them,* namely, that even unto the end of the world they might remain in their blindness, and might be strangers among the nations, that they might unceasingly blaspheme against Christ and be oppressed by many hardships. For nothing other than *wrathful anger* of God has taken ahold of them since it would seem astonishing the way they remain so strongly blind that they would not turn from their captivity. Whence Christ says in Isaiah: *I have trampled on them in my indignation, and have trodden them down in my wrath;*[141] and in Jeremiah: *My inheritance,* namely, the house or the people of Israel, *is become to me as a lion in the wood: it has cried out against me, therefore have I hated it.*[142] This in another place he says more openly: *I hated them: for the wickedness of their devices I will cast them forth out of my house: I will love them no more.*[143] And Zephaniah most openly declares: *I will pour upon them my indignation, and all my fierce anger.*[144] **68{69}[26]** *Fiat habitation eorum deserta, et in tabernaculis eorum non sit qui inhabitet; let their habitation be made desolate: and let there be none to dwell in their tabernacles.* For the Romans completely destroyed the city of Jerusalem, the temple, and the remaining cities of Judah, as also Christ predicted: *They shall not leave in you a stone upon a stone: because you have not known the time of your visitation;*[145] and Jeremiah, *I have forsaken my house, I have left my inheritance.*[146] This also the prophet Hosea said: *The Lord my God will cast them away, because they hearkened not his voice: and they shall be wanderers among the nations.*[147]

68{69}[27]   *Because they have persecuted him whom you have smitten; and they have added to the grief of my wounds.*

Quoniam quem tu percussisti persecuti sunt, et super dolorem vulnerum meorum addiderunt.

Thereafter it sets forth the cause of such a rejection of the Jews: **68{69}[27]** *Quoniam quem tu percussisti persecuti sunt; because they have persecuted him whom you have smitten,* that is, they afflicted Jesus Christ whom you allowed to be persecuted, even unto death. For God is said

---

141   Is. 63:3a.
142   Jer. 12:8.
143   Hosea 9:15.
144   Zeph. 3:8b.
145   Luke 19:44b.
146   Jer. 12:7a.
147   Hosea 9:17. E. N. Denis's quote departs somewhat from the Sixto-Clementine Vulgate.

to have smitten Christ in the manner that Isaiah foretold: *For the wick-edness of my people have I struck him.*[148] Peter also said: you handed over Jesus to Israelite men to be killed *by the determinate counsel and the foreknowledge of God.*[149] *For God so loved the world, as to give his only begotten Son.*[150] *Et super dolorem vulnerum meorum addiderunt, and they have added to the grief of my wounds.* For the Jews, in addition to the injuries of scourging, added the injuries of words, mocking him and blaspheming him. But also, beyond the sufferings inflicted upon Christ upon his own body, they added to it by inflicting injury upon his Mystical Body, namely the early Church, which they most heavily troubled, as is made clear in the Acts of the Apostles.

68{69}[28] *Add you iniquity upon their iniquity: and let them not come into your justice.*

Appone iniquitatem super iniquitatem eorum et non intrent in iustitiam tuam.

68{69}[28] *Appone,* add, O Lord, not effectively, but permissively, *iniquitatem super iniquitatem eorum, iniquity upon their iniquity,* permitting them to fall from fault into fault. For since without the grace of God man is unable to do anything good, when God removes grace from a man insistent upon vice, that man continually falls from sin into sin. *Et non intrent in iustitiam tuam, and let them not come into your justice.* Faith is the entrance or doorway into justice. For *the just man lives by faith.*[151] For what else does *let them not come into your justice* mean except let them be deprived from the faith of Christ, and let them not submit to his commandments, but let them persevere in their destructive ways?

68{69}[29] *Let them be blotted out of the book of the living; and with the just let them not be written.*

Deleantur de libro viventium, et cum iustis non scribantur.

68{69}[29] *Deleantur de libro viventium; let them be blotted out of the book of the living.* The book of the living, or the book of life, is the predestination of the elect in the divine mind: for just like something

---

148   Is. 53:8b.
149   Acts 2:23: *This same [Jesus] being delivered up, by the determinate counsel and foreknowledge of God, you [the Jews] by the hands of wicked men have crucified and slain.*
150   John 3:16a.
151   Rom. 1:17a. Cf. Hab. 2:4:b. *The just shall live in his faith.*

366   DENIS THE CARTHUSIAN : *Commentary on the Psalms* : *Volume 3*

written in a book is fixed and lasting so also that which is decreed by the wisdom of the divine mind remains stable and is not subject to change. In what manner, therefore, does someone have the power to be deleted from the book of the living, especially since no one is written in that book except for the elect? For the book of life is the knowledge of God which predestines the elect. In response to this question, [one should keep in mind that] someone is said to be written in the book of the living in two ways. First, according to the truth: and those that are so written are not able to be blotted out. Whence Christ revealing that those who are written in the book of life cannot be lost says: *There shall arise false Christs and false prophets, and shall show great signs and wonders, insomuch as to deceive (if possible) even the elect.*[152] Second, someone is said to be written in the book of the living according to his vain hope and fallacious opinion. Written in this way were the Jews, who held the opinion that they were set apart by God, notwithstanding that they disdained and killed Christ. And in a similar way Christ in the Gospel called those that were not true sons of the kingdom children of the kingdom:[153] for *the son abides* in the house *forever.*[154] But they were children of the kingdom according to their most prideful opinion, saying to the Savior: *We have one Father, even God.*[155] Regarding this error of theirs Christ declared: *You are of your father the devil.*[156] So to be blotted from the book of life is nothing other than not to be inscribed in it, not to be contained in the memory of the divine kindness. And so, in order to explain this phrase — *let them be blotted out of the book of the living* — the verse continues: *et cum iustis non scribantur, and with the just let them not be written*: not that someone can be inscribed in the book of life again; but God is said to write those whom he finally approves in the book of life. Because the reprobate are never accepted by God or never perform meritorious works, they are said not to be written in the book of life according to the way they are.

68{69}[30] *But I am poor and sorrowful: your salvation, O God, has set me up.*

Ego sum pauper et dolens; salus tua, Deus, suscepit me.

---

152   Matt. 24:24.
153   Matt. 8:12: *But the children of the kingdom shall be cast out into the exterior darkness: there shall be weeping and gnashing of teeth.*
154   John 8:35b.
155   John 8:41b.
156   John 8:44a.

68{69}[31] *I will praise the name of God with a canticle: and I will magnify him with praise.*

> *Laudabo nomen Dei cum cantico; et magnificabo eum in laude.*

68{69}[32] *And it shall please God better than a young calf, that brings forth horns and hoofs.*

> *Et placebit Deo super vitulum novellum, cornua producentem et ungulas.*

Christ additionally says, **68{69}[30]** *Ego sum pauper, I am poor.* He chose a poor mother, he lived in poverty, and he was made most poor in the Passion, for he was suspended naked upon the Cross. For which reason he said: *The foxes have holes, and the birds of the air nests: but the Son of Man has nowhere to lay his head.*[157] *Et dolens, and sorrowful.* Christ endured many sorrows in this life, lastly in his most sorrowful Passion most of all when *from the sole of the foot unto the top of the head there was no soundness in him.*[158] *Salus tua, Deus, suscepit me; your salvation, O God, has set me up:* that is, in respect to the body, your perfect beatitude and resurrection glorified me; and so *your salvation, O God, O Father, set me up,* that is I received *your salvation,* namely, the accidental reward in the Resurrection. **68{69}[31]** *Laudabo nomen Dei cum cantico, I will magnify him with praise,* that is, if it be a deed, then with spiritual joy and internal happiness and with melodious song; *et magnificabo eum in laude, and I will praise the name of God with a canticle,* that is, by praise which I will sing to him, and offer up to him, I will praise and will make manifest that God is *a great Lord and greatly to be praised.*[159] For as we say in the Lord's prayer, *Hallowed be thy name,*[160] not that God grows in holiness because of something we do, but because by our purity of our service we prove and declare him to be holy; in a similar way we magnify him.[161] **68{69}[32]** *Et placebit Deo, and it shall please God,* this salvation and this magnifying of him, *super vitulum novellum, better than a young calf,* that is, a yearling, *cornua producentem, that brings forth horns* for the defense of his head, *et ungulas, and hoofs* for the defense of his feet. For the sacrifice of praise and of evangelical praising is more acceptable to God than sacrifice under the

---

157   Matt. 8:20b.

158   Is. 1:6a.

159   Ps. 144:3a.

160   Matt. 6:9.

161   E. N. Ps. 15:2: *I have said to the Lord, you are my God, for you have no need of my goods.*

Law, which, according to the Apostle [Paul], was unable to take away
sin, or make those approaching it perfect.[162]

68{69}[33]   *Let the poor see and rejoice: seek God, and your soul shall
             live.*

             *Videant pauperes, et laetentur; quaerite Deum, et vivet anima
             vestra.*

68{69}[34]   *For the Lord has heard the poor: and has not despised his prisoners.*

             *Quoniam exaudivit pauperes Dominus, et vinctos suos non
             despexit.*

68{69}[33] *Videant, let them see* all things now foretold, [that is,]
pauperes, the poor, that is, the humble in spirit, faithfully contemplating,
et laetentur, and let them rejoice in the Lord and in his benefits. *Quaerite
Deum, seek God,* doing all that is in you, and directly attend to him with
faith and works, *et vivet anima vestra, and your soul shall live,* that is, it
will receive grace which is the life of the soul, just as the soul is the life
of the body. This is what the prophet Isaiah said: *Seek the Lord, while he
may be found: call upon him, while he is near.*[163] And in the Gospel, Christ
says, *Seek and you shall find, knock and it shall be opened to you.*[164] **68{69}**
[34] *Quoniam exaudivit pauperes, Dominum; for the Lord has heard the
poor* in spirit, of whom [the Lord] says: *Blessed are the poor in spirit.*[165]
And Isaiah: *The Lord is sublime inhabiting eternity, . . . to revive the spirit
of the humble, and to revive the heart of the contrite.*[166] *Et vinctos suos,
and his prisoners,* that is, the sinners that are among the elect, who for
a time err, but at the end will be unable to err, *non despexit, he has not
despised:* because he freely and mercifully receives penitents, in the manner that he says through Jeremiah: *Return, . . . and I will not turn away
my face from you.*[167] Or [alternatively], *his prisoners,* that is, those who
constrain themselves with the divine law and restrain themselves from
all evil paths by the divine commandments as if they were some kind

---

162   Cf. Heb. 10:4, 1: *For it is impossible that with the blood of oxen and goats sin
should be taken away. For the law having a shadow of the good things to come, not the
very image of the things; by the selfsame sacrifices which they offer continually every year,
can never make the comers thereunto perfect.*
163   Is. 55:6.
164   Luke 11:10b.
165   Matt. 5:3.
166   Is. 57:15.
167   Jer. 3:12a.

of fetter. Or [yet another way]: *his prisoners*, that is the holy detained in limbo [of the fathers], God the Father, or Christ *has not despised*, for the Father has redeemed them through the Son. Whence God says to Christ in Isaiah: *I have given you to be a covenant to the people, that you might raise upon the earth, . . . and you might say to them that are bound, Come forth; and to them that are in darkness: show yourselves.*[168]

68{69}[35] *Let the heavens and the earth praise him; the sea, and everything that creeps therein.*

Laudent illum caeli et terra; mare, et omnia reptilia in eis.

68{69}[35] *Laudent illum caeli et terra*, let the heavens and the earth praise him, that is, the angels and men, as Moses said: *Hear, O heavens, the things I speak, let the earth give ear to the words of my mouth.*[169] Let *mare et omnia reptilia in eis; the sea, and everything that creeps therein* praise God materially, providing to men the occasion for praising the Creator reflected in creation, as the nature and perfection of the cause shines in its effect.[170]

68{69}[36] *For God will save Sion, and the cities of Judah shall be built up. And they shall dwell there, and acquire it by inheritance.*

Quoniam Deus salvam faciet Sion, et aedificabuntur civitates Iuda, et inhabitabunt ibi, et haereditate acquirent eam.

68{69}[37] *And the seed of his servants shall possess it; and they that love his name shall dwell therein.*

Et semen servorum eius possidebit eam; et qui diligunt nomen eius habitabunt in ea.

68{69}[36] *Quoniam Deus salvam faciet Sion*, for God will save Sion, that is, the militant Church, giving grace to men, *et aedificabuntur*

---

168   Is. 49:8b–9a.
169   Deut. 32:1.
170   There is no better poem expressing this principle than Gerard Manley Hopkins's "Pied Beauty": Glory be to God for dappled things – / For skies of couple-colour as a brinded cow; / For rose-moles all in stipple upon trout that swim; / Fresh-firecoal chestnut-falls; finches' wings; / Landscape plotted and pieced – fold, fallow, and plough; / And áll trádes, their gear and tackle and trim. // All things counter, original, spare, strange; / Whatever is fickle, freckled (who knows how?) / With swift, slow; sweet, sour; adazzle, dim; / He fathers-forth whose beauty is past change: / Praise him.

civitates Iuda, and the cities of Judah shall be built up, that is, the particular Churches confessing Christ. For the name Judah is interpreted as confession [of praise].[171] Or [an alternative interpretation is thus], *the cities of Judah*, that is, the hearts of the confessors which are edified by faith and charity and virtuous works, as the Apostle [Paul] says: *Keep the things that are of edification one towards another.*[172] *Et inhabitabunt ibi, and they shall dwell there*, that is, the faithful shall abide within the Church, obeying its precepts;[173] *et hereditate acquirent eam, and acquire it by inheritance*: because the Catholic faith, through which the faithful are said to dwell in the Church, will last even until the end of the world. **68{69}[37]** *Et semen servorum eius, and the seed of his servants*, that is, the spiritual children of the Apostles, namely, all believers, *possidebit eam, shall possess it*, that is, the Church, by hereditary right; *et qui diligent nomen eius, and they that love his name*, that is, God himself, *habitabunt in ea, shall dwell therein*. For love is the principle measure by which we are assessed to remain in the Church and in Christ.[174]

We see also how it is possible to exposit this as applying to the Church triumphant, which is called Sion by the Apostle [Paul]: *You are come*, he says, *to mount Sion and to the city of the living God, the heavenly*

---

171   E. N. Gen. 29:35: *Now will I praise the Lord, and for this she [Leah] called him Judah.*

172   Rom. 14:19b.

173   E. N. The commandments or precepts of the Church generally include the obligation to hear Mass on Sundays and Holy Days of obligation; to fast during those times prescribed for fasting, such as Lent and Ember Days; to confess one's sins at least once a year; to receive the blessed Sacrament at least once a year at Eastertide, that is, between Palm Sunday and the octave of Easter; to support the Church financially; to keep the laws of marriage and not solemnize marriage during forbidden times. Some authors, such as St. Antoninus of Florence (1439 AD) in his *Summa Theologica* (I, xvii, 12) include abstaining from any acts that would subject one to excommunication, avoiding associations with the excommunicated, and not attending Mass or functions celebrated by a priest living in open concubinage. Melody, J. "Commandments of the Church," *The Catholic Encyclopedia* (New York: Robert Appleton Company, 1908), Vol. 4, 154.

174   E. N. "Love is therefore, the measure of our lives. God is the measure of love. God is infinite, without measure. The measure of love is clear: it is without measure!" Valerian M. Okeke, Archbishop of Onitsha, Pastoral Letter "The Measure of Love," No. 18. https://archbishopvalokeke.org/wp-content/uploads/2020/10/THE-MEASURE-OF-LOVE-2005-2.pdf. *A la tarde te examinarán en el amor; aprende a amar como Dios quiere ser amado y deja tu condición.* "In the evening [of life], they will examine you in love; learn to love as God wants to be loved, and leave your condition." St. John of the Cross, *"Dichos de luz in amor," Obras Completas* (Madrid: Editorial de Espiritualidad 1980), 119.

Jerusalem.[175] And it will then be [understood] in this sense: *For God will save Sion,* especially in the day of judgment, when he will grant the elect salvation of the body, configuring *the body of our lowness ... to the body of his glory;*[176] *and the cities of Judah will be built up,* that is the orders of the angels will be restored, and the ruins of the heavenly Jerusalem will be reshaped by men ascending to that place:[177] so it is that *the cities of Judah,* that is, the heavenly mansions will be built by living stones.[178] *And they shall dwell there,* that is, the elect [shall dwell] in the Church triumphant; *and acquire it by inheritance,* when Christ will say to them: *Come, you blessed of my Father, possess you the kingdom prepared for you from the foundation of the world.*[179] *And the seed of his servants,* that is, the imitators of the Saints,[180] *shall possess it,* that is, the land of the living without end; *and they that love his name shall dwell therein.* For *charity never falls away,* but it produces citizens of the heavenly Jerusalem.

Yet, as has been said earlier, *Let their habitation be made desolate, etc.* can be literally explained as pertaining to the city of Jerusalem and the rest of the cities of the tribe of Judah, so that [the verses] here now discussed can be understood literally to apply to the material cities of Judah, so that [it can be understood] in this sense: *The cities of Judah shall be built up.* For Jerusalem and the other cities destroyed by the Romans were rebuilt after a while, and for a long time true Israelites and spiritual Jews dwelt in them, namely, Christians, until on account of their faults, they lost their inheritance, and they were thrown out by the Saracens.[181]

---

175   Heb. 12:22a.

176   Phil. 3:21a.

177   E. N. On the concept that the elect are to replace the number of the fallen angels, see footnote 50-126, Volume 2 of Denis's Commentary (*Dominus Illuminatio Mea*).

178   E. N. Cf. 1 Pet. 2:5a: *Be you also as living stones built up, a spiritual house.*

179   Matt. 25:34.

180   E. N. "Be imitators of me, as I am of Christ." 1 Cor. 11:1. "One cannot possibly understand the teaching of the saints unless one has a pure mind and is trying to imitate their life." St. Athanasius, *On the Incarnation* (Crestwood, NY: St. Vladimir's Seminary Press, 1998), IX, 97, 96.

181   E. N. Jerusalem eventually came to be under Christian rule (324–638 AD), though for a time it was captured by the Persians (Sassanids) in 614 AD, but the city was regained by the Byzantine empire in 629 AD; however, it was later besieged by Muslim forces, capitulating to them around 638 AD, Patriarch Sophronius surrendering then to Caliph Umar. The term "Saracens" was used as a synonym for Muslims or the followers of Islam of any race, whether Arabian, Persian, Egyptian, Turkish, or otherwise.

ARTICLE XXXV

TROPOLOGICAL OR MORAL EXPOSITION
OF THE SAME SIXTY-EIGHTH PSALM

ECAUSE, AS THE DISCIPLE WHOM JESUS loved said, *He that says he abides in him, ought himself also to walk, even as he walked*[182] *(for the servant is not greater than his Lord*[183]*)*; so it is not to be marveled at that this Psalm, which literally speaks of the humility and the Passion of Christ, can be morally expounded upon as relating to his Mystical Body, especially since the Apostle [Paul] said: *And all that will live godly in Christ Jesus, shall suffer persecution.*[184] Hence, therefore, this Psalm, which literally can be explained as being about the Passion of Christ, can also be morally elucidated of his Mystical Body, which is the Church.

68{69}[2]   *Save me, O God: for the waters are come in even into my soul.*

Salvum me fac, Deus, quoniam intraverunt aquae usque ad animam meam.

68{69}[3]   *I stick fast in the mire of the deep: and there is no sure standing. I am come into the depth of the sea: and a tempest has overwhelmed me.*

Infixus sum in limo profundi et non est substantia. Veni in altitudinem maris; et tempestas demersit me.

The Church, therefore, or any individual member of the faithful seeing himself in the middle of snares, and believing him surrounded all around by tribulations, and through experience knowing that he does not have the power of his own to be able to prevail over these, may cry out to the Lord: **68{69}[2]** *Salvum me fac, Deus, save me, O God*, from all wounds of the soul, and, if it be useful for me, also from all bodily infirmities; *quoniam intraverunt aquae, for the waters are come in*, [the waters] of the temptations of the devil, the persecutions of the world, and of the attacks of the sensitive appetites, *usque ad animam meam, even into my soul*, that is, they impose themselves upon me deeply and strongly; and I am not easily able to repulse them, *for the waters are come in even into*

---

182   1 John 2:6.
183   John 13:16a.
184   2 Tim. 3:12.

my soul, that is, even up to the level of delight or consent of the mind. Anyone who is tempted or afflicted, when he experiences himself to be heavily attacked, may cry out this [verse, *save me, O God*] with all his heart. **68{69}[3]** *Infixus sum in limo profundi, I stick fast in the mire of the deep*, that is, in fleshly desire, in this vicious and lying age, so that I am subject to vices, I take delight in foul things, and I am attentive to this world through inordinate affection; *et non est substantia, and there is no sure standing* for me, that is, virtue to evade, resist, and prevail against [such evil]. Or [alternatively], *there is no sure standing*, that is, a stable place of standing, because I am subject to vanity, a vagrant heart, and a frail mind.

Veni in altitudinem maris, I am come into the depth of the sea, that is, unto enormous adversities and great tribulations; *et tempestas demersit me, and a tempest has overwhelmed me*, that is, the strength and violence of this adversity casts me down, wounds, kills, or leads me into sin in this way [that is, as if in a storm]: as the Apostle [Paul] said, *Our spirit had no rest;*[185] and again, *We were pressed out of measure . . . so that we were weary even of life.*[186] During the time our first parents had not sinned in Paradise, it was as if they were in a tranquil port; but sin once perpetrated, they and all of their posterity were cast out *into the depth of the sea*, that is, into the deep of this world, where so many times tempests overwhelm us, where daily we give way to adversities through impatience or pusillanimity, and daily we consent to sin or are overcome by some distress. The tempests of exterior persecution overwhelm the holy martyrs in bodily death; but they overwhelm the apostates from the faith in the spiritual death of their soul. Or [we can understand it] thus: *I am come into the depth of the sea*, that is, to the grade of prelate in this world;[187] *and a tempest has overwhelmed me*, that is, the din of secular business, the need to care of temporal things, and the occupation of external situations extinguish or reduce the peace of mind, the light of devotion, and the custody of the heart in me.

---

185 2 Cor. 7:5a. The Sixto-Clementine Vulgate has *nullam requiem habuit caro nostra*, "our flesh had no rest." Denis states *nullam requiem habuit spiritus noster*, "our spirit had no rest."

186 2 Cor. 1:8b.

187 E. N. The burdens (and temptations) of the episcopal office are the fodder of many warnings by moralists and saints and poets (*e.g.*, Dante). See, *e.g.*, ST IIaIIae, q. 85, arts. 1-3. The danger to the prelate's soul is perhaps best captured by the quote popularly attributed to St. John Chrysostom (though I have not been able to find it in his writings): "The road to hell is paved with the skulls of bishops." *Se non è vero, è ben trovato.*

And so, if we wish to expound completely of this [verse] literally, it also befits those certain members of Christ, namely, the holy martyrs who are thrown into the *waters*: and some truly sink; but the souls of all of them are saved. For in this regard material waters and the elements[188] entered by the mouth even to the soul, that is, even to the interior, or even to the extinction of the bodily life. These also were stuck fast *in the mire of the deep,* that is, in muddy earth, in the depth of waters, or in damp and dirty jails, as were Jeremiah, Micah,[189] and many others. Whence Jeremiah writes about himself, that he descended in the mire of the jail even unto the lower part of his back.[190] Also, some of the just came into the depths of the sea, as is written of many of the blessed martyrs who, with a rock tied to their body, were thrown from a ship, the shore, or a cliff into the sea. Of these Jonah was one, who, thrown into the sea, was swallowed by a whale, and so he prayed from the belly of the fish: *You have cast me forth, O Lord, into the deep in the heart of the sea, and a flood has compassed me: all your billows, and your waves have passed over me; the waters have compassed me about even to the soul, the deep has closed me round about, the sea has covered my head.*[191]

68{69}[4] *I have labored with crying; my throat is become hoarse: my eyes have failed, while I hope in my God.*[192]

Laboravi clamans, raucae factae sunt fauces meae; defecerunt oculi mei, dum spero in Deum meum.

68{69}[4] *Laboravi clamans, raucae factae sunt fauces meae; I have labored with crying: my throat is become hoarse.* The Church labors lamenting her sins, doing penance, and going from place to place, teaching, reproving, attracting so as to convert others; and it cries out to the Lord for the indulgence of the vicious, for the infusion of grace, for the illumination of the errant, for the amendment of the depraved. Its voices are hoarse, while preaching to others it profits nothing, or while with difficulty or only after long delay it is heard by God, or also by the exhaustion of tears or strength from great suffering by which it has been afflicted or by the

---

188   E. N. *Elementares,* a general word meaning elements, that is: earth, water, air, and fire; in short, any created reality.

189   1 Kings 22:27: *Put this man [Micah] in prison, and feed him with bread of affliction, and water of distress, till I return in peace.*

190   *Cf.* Jer. 38:6: *Then they took Jeremiah and cast him into the dungeon of Malchiah the son of Amelech, which was in the entry of the prison: and they let down Jeremias by ropes into the dungeon, wherein there was no water, but mire. And Jeremiah sunk into the mire.*

191   Jonah 2:4, 6.

192   *See* footnote 68-22.

labor it has assumed. For this holy Job said to the Lord: *I cry to you, and you hear me not; I stand up, and you do not regard me. You are changed to be cruel toward me, and in the hardness of your hand you are against me;*[193] and again, *For the arrows of the Lord are in me, the rage whereof drinks up my spirit, and the terrors of the Lord war against me.*[194]

Defecerunt oculi mei, dum spero in Deum meum; my eyes have failed, while I hope in my God. This often applies to the weak members of the Church, while they are not heard by God as they wish, who, because of the rigor or the vehemence of temptations and tribulations, are weakened, and falter in hope, and are faint-hearted. For what is true of Job does not pertain to them: *Although he (God) should kill me, I will trust in him.*[195] Or [one can look at it in this manner]: *My bodily eyes have failed*, weeping or deeply disheartened, *while I hope in my God*, for I am dejected while incessantly hoping in him, or I die because of justice or the Catholic faith. Whence it is written of David and his companions: *They lifted up their voices, and they wept until they had no more tears.*[196] Or [as another alternative]: *My eyes* of interior knowledge *have failed while I hope in my God*, because I do not faithfully, lovingly, and unceasingly place hope in God as would be befitting.

68{69}[5] *They are multiplied above the hairs of my head, who hate me without cause. My enemies are grown strong who have wrongfully persecuted me: then did I pay back that which I did not plunder.*[197]

Multiplicati sunt super capillos capitis mei qui oderunt me gratis. Confortati sunt qui persecuti sunt me inimici mei iniuste; quae non rapui, tunc exsolvebam.

68{69}[5] *Multiplicati sunt super capillos capitis mei, qui oderunt me gratis; they are multiplied above the hairs of my head, who hate me without cause.* Many and innumerable are the enemies of the Church and the saints, namely, all the non-believers, the heretics, the schismatics, the false brothers, the detractors, the ambitious, and the envious. All these gratuitously and without reasonable cause persecute the Church.

---

193 Job 30:21–21.
194 Job 6:4.
195 Job 13:15a.
196 1 Sam. 30:4b.
197 E. N. I have departed from the Douay-Rheims's translation of *quae non rapui, tunc exsolvebam*, "then did I pay that which I took not away," which might be more forcefully translated "then did I pay back that which I did not plunder."

We also have many strong and invisible enemies. Of these the Apostle [Paul] says: *Our wrestling is not against flesh and blood; but against principalities and powers, ... against the spirits of wickedness in the high places.*[198] We also have many domestic and dangerous enemies which are our own passions and vices. The Church and any just man can say about these adversaries: *Confortanti sunt qui persecuti sunt me inimici mei iniuste; quae non rapui, tunc exsolvebam; my enemies are grown strong who have wrongfully persecuted me: then did I pay back that which I did not plunder*, that is, I did not deserve the punishments I suffered. This is most fittingly applied to the holy martyrs who died for the sake of God, for the faith, or for justice. Whence also Job says: *These things have I suffered without the iniquity of my hand, when I offered pure prayers to God.*[199] For God frequently permits his elect to suffer tribulations without their deserving it, so that he may more gloriously crown them. Yet never ought one to conclude someone [suffering tribulations] to have suffered injury in the spiritual good of sanctifying grace, unless it be by a man's own fault.[200]

> **68{69}[6]** *O God, you know my foolishness; and my offenses are not hidden from you.*
>
> *Deus, tu scis insipientiam meam; et delicta mea a te non sunt abscondita.*

And so the Church speaking in the person of her weak members, or in the name of any penitent confessing humbly his own folly and sins, says: **68{69}[6]** *Deus, tu scis insipientiam meam; et delicta mea a te non sunt abscondita; O God you know my foolishness; and my offenses are not hidden from you.* For any man who sins is foolish, *for wisdom will not enter into a malicious soul.*[201] And who is so foolish and mad not to obey the precepts nor to assent to the counsels and exhortations of eternal Wisdom? It is the greatest foolishness to serve the vices of the flesh, to neglect the health of the soul, to live in such a state in which no one ought to dare to die.

---

198   Eph. 6:12.
199   Job 16:18.
200   E. N. That is, suffering tribulations does not correlate with loss of sanctifying grace or with a punishment for sin. "Such as I love, I rebuke and chastise." Rev. 3:19a. "For whom the Lord loves, he chastises; and he scourges every son whom he receives." Heb. 12:6. "While patiently bearing sufferings and trials of all kinds and, when the day comes, serenely facing death, the Christian must strive to accept this temporal punishment of sin as a grace." CCC § 1473.
201   Wis. 1:4a.

Moreover, our sins are known to God, as he elsewhere asserts: *I know your manifold crimes, and your grievous sins.*[202] The confession of one's own foolishness and iniquity makes one worthy of the infusion of true wisdom and the justification by grace. In Isaiah is written about him who thinks himself wise: *Your wisdom, and your knowledge, this has deceived you.*[203] And again, *Woe to you that are wise in your own eyes, and prudent in your own conceits.*[204] For this reason, the Apostle [Paul] exhorts: *Be not wise in your own conceits.*[205] Let us confess, therefore, always with all humility our foolishness, for we are truly foolish, as it is written: *Every man is become a fool through his own knowledge.*[206]

68{69}[7] *Let them not be ashamed for me, who await you, O Lord, the Lord of hosts. Let them not be confounded on my account, who seek you, O God of Israel.*

Non erubescant in me qui exspectant te, Domine, Domine virtutum; non confundantur super me qui quaerunt te, Deus Israel.

68{69}[7] *Non erubescant in me, qui exspectant te, Domine; let them not be ashamed for me, who await you, O Lord.* While the Church or any just man suffers injuries, or is tempted, or is afflicted in some similar way, unless God then provides aid, it is possible that others that are awaiting God might be shamed, that is, those placing hope in him, which hope is this: that (as divine Scripture affirms) God will not abandon his Church, nor will he permit the just finally to be oppressed; but he will do that which Scripture says, *Revenge is mine, I will repay, says the Lord;*[207] and, *I have not seen the just forsaken;*[208] and, *He will not suffer you to be tempted above that which you are able.*[209] What else therefore does *let them not be ashamed for me, who await you, O Lord?* mean except, "Save me in all necessity and from all distress save me, deliver me from all persecution and temptations, and hear all of my prayers, as you in sacred Scripture have promised you would do, since others placing hope in you have been strengthened in hope, seeing the great quantity of your mercy given me." And the following verse leads to the same sense. For in this Scripture

---

202   Amos 5:12a.
203   Is. 47:10a.
204   Is. 5:21.
205   Rom. 12:16b.
206   Jer. 10:14a.
207   Rom. 12:19b.
208   Ps. 36:25b.
209   1 Cor. 10:13a.

customarily repeats using other words the same sentiment for those who are concerned of their condition. For its says: *Non confundantur super me, let them not be confounded*, that is, from my being abandoned and oppressed, *qui quaerunt te, Deus Israel, who seek you, O God of Israel*: who indeed will be confounded and scandalized unless they see me being given help and grace by you. For they would say: *He who serves God labors in vain that, and what profit is it that we have kept his ordinances?*[210]

68{69}[8]   *Because for your sake I have borne reproach; shame has covered my face.*

Quoniam propter te sustinui opprobrium; operuit confusio faciem meam.

68{69}[8] *Quoniam propter te sustinui opprobrium, because for your sake I have borne reproach*: that is, because of justice, because of faith, because of the love and honor of your name, I have suffered reproach, not because of my offense or my fault. This is the true endurance and blessed patience of which the Savior says: *Blessed are they that suffer persecution for justice's sake: for theirs is the kingdom of heaven;*[211] and again, *Blessed are you when they shall revile you, and persecute you, and speak all that is evil against you, untruly, for my sake.*[212] Some, however, endure reproach not because of God or justice, but because of themselves or from their own fault. And indeed, it is a good and meritorious thing to bear with such punishments inflicted for one's fault; but this is much less virtuous than if one endures it on account of God. For which reason, the prince of the Apostles says: *This is thankworthy, if for conscience towards God, a man endure sorrows, suffering wrongfully. For what glory is it, if committing sin, and being buffeted for it, you endure? But if doing well you suffer patiently; this is thankworthy before God.*[213] But some people assert the words of the Savior just mentioned, wherein he said, *Blessed are they that suffer persecution, etc.*, in an improper way. For while they are corrected for their deviations [from justice], they excuse themselves, and they judge themselves to be oppressed, and they console themselves and say: *Blessed are they who suffer persecution for justice's sake.* If, therefore, [it is reprehensible that] we do not patiently bear the punishments and wrongs inflicted upon us on account of God, it is an exceedingly intolerable

---

210   Mal. 3:14b.
211   Matt. 5:10.
212   Matt. 5:11.
213   1 Pet. 2:19–20.

thing if we disdain to suffer the instruction, rebuking, and punishments inflicted upon us on account of our deviations [from justice] as we read in Jeremiah about some men, *They have refused to receive correction;*[214] and elsewhere, *They have hated him that rebukes.*[215]

Operuit confusio faciem meam, shame has covered my face, that is, I am exceedingly confounded and from all sides because of you: not that a virtuous man will be ashamed or confounded because of the injuries inflicted upon him; indeed, he will rejoice in such things, in the manner that Christ exhorts, *Be glad in that day and rejoice; for behold, your reward is great in heaven;*[216] but because he will endure that of which others are customarily ashamed, namely, reproach, contempt, rejection, and similar punishments. Nevertheless, those who are weaker will be confounded in spirit and will be ashamed in appearance by such [punishments]. But we must embrace such [punishments], as they might teach us to imitate the way of Christ with joy, saying with the Apostle [Paul]: *I bear the marks of the Lord Jesus in my body.*[217]

68{69}[9] *I am become a stranger to my brethren, and an alien to the sons of my mother.*

> *Extraneus factus sum fratribus meis, et peregrinus filiis matris meae.*

68{69}[9] *Extraneus factus sum fratribus meis, I am become a stranger to my brethren,* that is, those close to me, my kindred, my friends, and my household have cast me off, spurned me, and regarded me and as if I was a foreigner. The same thing is repeated using other words: *et peregrinus filiis matris meae,* that is, I was treated by my neighbors, who are the sons of my mother, which is the Church, or Eve, or my immediate mother, as a guest who is received one night and the next day is driven off. For this is what the Lord said to his disciples in the Gospel: *And you shall be betrayed by your parents and brethren, and kinsmen and friends;*[218] and again, *You shall be hated by all men for my name's sake.*[219] Likewise, religious and those who are devout, who, in following Christ, forsake father, mother, sister, brother, or wife; they are able to say this verse.

---

214   Jer. 5:3b.
215   Amos 5:10a.
216   Luke 6:23a.
217   Gal. 6:17b.
218   Luke 21:16.
219   Matt. 10:22a.

68{69}[10]   *For the zeal of your house has eaten me up: and the reproaches of them that reproached you are fallen upon me.*

Quoniam zelus domus tuae comedit me, et opprobria exprobrantium tibi ceciderunt super me.

But the reason why this was borne patiently follows: **68{69}[10]** *Quoniam zelus domus tuae comedit me, for the zeal of your house has eaten me up*: that is, great affection of the good state of the Church, of the of divine honor, of the common good, and of the salvation of brothers absorbed me spiritually, and transformed my inmost parts in charity. For zeal is the effect of love, proceeding from intense love: by which zeal man exerts himself without fail to repel from him those things which have the consequence of impeding good choice. And as love is twofold — namely, [there is a love] of desire, which loves something because of its utility or delight to oneself, in the manner that a man loves land, clothing, or money; and [there is] the love of friendship, by which a man loves the good of the beloved, so that the beloved comes into perfection — so zeal is twofold. Namely [there is] carnal and disordered [zeal]: of which is said in a Psalm above, *Do not envy (zelaveris) them that work iniquity.*[220] *Whereas there is among you envying (zelus) and contention, are you not carnal, and walk according to man?*[221] The other kind is the divine and charitable zeal, by which, namely, a man exerts himself out of love to exclude those things that are contrary to the divine honor or to the good of the beloved brother. Elijah says about this zeal: *With zeal have I been zealous for the Lord God of hosts.*[222] Of this [good zeal] it is now said, *for the zeal of your house has eaten me up.* For one is consumed by good will if, when he sees anything wrong, he desires to correct it; and if he is unable, he endures it and laments. Many of the devout in cloisters who desire to observe strictly the rigors of their order have such a zeal. And of this zeal, Gregory says: The most acceptable sacrifice is the zeal of souls.[223]

Et opprobia exprobrantium tibi ceciderunt super me, and the reproaches of them that reproached you are fallen upon me. In the manner a stone

---

220   Ps. 36:1. *E. N. See* footnote 36-7 in Volume 2 for the relationship between a private and carnal zeal and envy or jealousy. Here one's zeal for one's fleshly and disordered desires results in envy of those that do evil.

221   1 Cor. 3:3.

222   1 Kings 19:10a.

223   *E. N.* This is a reference, though not an exact quote, to Pope St. Gregory the Great's (590–604 AD) homilies on Ezechiel. "Indeed no sacrifice is to almighty God so great as is the zeal for souls. For this is what the Psalmist says: 'Zeal for your house has consumed me.'" *Hom. in Ezech.* I, 12, 30, PL 76, 932.

hurled against a tower that is unable to break through, bounces back, and might shatter glass that is found in the opposite direction to which it falls, so blasphemies and evil words hurled towards God and his Christ do not harm them, but they may be an occasion of death or injury for the servants of God when they oppose themselves to their falsehood, and they choose to die rather than to disregard or tolerate them. For reproaches hurled against the servants of God can be called reproaches of God and inflicted against God, in the manner that the Lord says through Zechariah: *For he that touches you, touches the apple of my eye,*[224] and in the Gospel: *He that hears you, hears me; and he that despises you, despises me.*[225]

68{69}[11] *And I covered my soul in fasting: and it was made a reproach to me.*

Et operui in ieiunio animam meam, et factum est in opprobrium mihi.

68{69}[12] *And I made haircloth my garment: and I became a byword to them.*

Et posui vestimentum meum cilicium; et factus sum illis in parabolam.

68{69}[13] *They that sat in the gate spoke against me: and they that drank wine sang about me.*[226]

Adversum me loquebantur qui sedebant in porta, et in me psallebant qui bibebant vinum.

68{69}[11] *Et operui in ieiunio animam meam,* and I covered my soul in fasting, abstaining bodily so as to implore the mercy of the Creator, as he himself elsewhere admonishes: *Be converted to me with all your heart, in fasting, and in weeping, and in mourning.*[227] *Et factum est in opprobrium mihi,* and it was made a reproach to me. For perverse men interpret the good works of the saints in an evil way, and they disparage them. And good men are commonly the reproach of the wicked because they are a reproof to their depravity, and they endure abuse and derision

---

224   Zech. 2:8b.
225   Luke 10:16.
226   E. N. I have departed from the Douay-Rheims which reads "they that drank wine made me their song."
227   Joel 2:12.

from them, as Job said: *The just man is laughed to scorn.*[228] Whence
the Lord said to Ezechiel: *I have set you for a sign of things to come
to the house of Israel. Say: I am a sign of things to come to you.*[229] For
these are some of the perverse men who laugh and deride the good of
others which they neither want nor can imitate. **68{69}[12]** *Et posui
vestimentum meum cilicium*, and I made a haircloth my garment. The
Church customarily does this, especially during times of great danger:
as also in the Old Testament as Scripture frequently recalls. *Et factus
sum illis in parabola*, and I became a byword to them. For the more the
good humiliate themselves, that much more are evil men enraged against
them. For this reason the Apostle [Paul] says: *We are blasphemed, and
we entreat; we are made as the refuse of this world, the offscouring of all.*[230]
68{69}[13] *Adversum me loquebantur qui sedebant in porta; they that sat
in the gate spoke against me*, that is, they who sat in an open and public
place have spoken against me; *et in me psallebant, and they sang about
me* with derision, *qui bibebant vinum they, that drank wine*, namely, the
gluttons and the drunkards. Regarding these we find in Isaiah: *Woe to
you that rise up early in the morning to follow drunkenness, and to drink
till the evening, to be inflamed with wine.*[231] For these sorts of men condemn and deride the just and the sober who prove and condemn their
vices, saying to them that which is in Joel: *Awake, you that are drunk,
and weep, and mourn all you that take delight in drinking sweet wine.*[232]

68{69}[14]   But as for me, my prayer is to you, O Lord; for the time of
your good pleasure, O God. In the multitude of your mercy
hear me, in the truth of your salvation.

Ego vero orationem meam ad te, Domine: tempus beneplaciti, Deus, in multitudine misericordiae tuae; exaudi me in
veritate salutis tuae.

68{69}[15]   Draw me out of the mud, that I may not stick fast: deliver
me from them that hate me, and out of the deep waters.[233]

Eripe me de luto, ut non infigar; libera me ab iis qui oderunt
me, et de profundis aquarum.

---

228   Job 12:4b.
229   Ez. 12:6b, 11a.
230   1 Cor. 4:13.
231   Is. 5:11.
232   Joel 1:5.
233   I have changed the Douay-Rheims's "mire" (for *luto*) to "mud," since otherwise
Denis's *Commentary* will not be understood.

68{69}[14] *Ego vero orationem meam ad te, Domine; but as for me, my prayer to you, O Lord*, I uttered, praying for myself and my enemies as you, O Lord, commanded: *Love your enemies . . . and pray for them that persecute and calumniate you*.[234] And it is proper to you, O Lord, to hear, because *tempus, the time* of such prayers is the time *beneplaciti, of your good pleasure*, that is, the time acceptable to you, *O Deus, O God*, for in that we find that which most pleases you. For in the Gospel Christ promised to those who pray for their adversaries: *You shall be the sons of the Highest*.[235] And so their prayer is accepted, and its time is pleasing. *In multitudine misericordiae tuae, in the multitude of your mercy*, that is, because of your great clemency, *exaudi me in veritate salutis, hear me in the truth of your salvation*, giving me true salvation of mind and body, which I pray from you. 68{69}[15] *Eripe me, draw me out* by your grace, *de luto, of the mud*, of which I spoke about above, *I stick fast in the mire of the deep*, namely, of the carnal life, and this vicious and obstinate world; *ut non infigar, that I might not stick fast*, that is, that I may not be completely immersed in this mud. *Libera me ab his qui oderunt me, deliver me from them that hate me*, namely, from my invisible and visible enemies, *et de profundis aquarum, and out of the deep waters*, that is, from the magnitude of tribulations: of which is written in Lamentations, *Waters have flowed over my head*.[236]

68{69}[16] *Let not the tempest of water drown me, nor the deep swallow me up: and let not the pit shut its mouth upon me.*

Non me demergat tempestas aquae, neque absorbeat me profundum, neque urgeat super me puteus os suum.

68{69}[16] *Non me demergat tempestas aquae, let not the tempest of water drown me*, that is, let not the assault of temptation, or the din of the vicious, or the needs of worldly and temporal things drown me finally, nor let them not hold me submerged. *Neque absorbeat me profundum, nor the deep swallow me up*, that is, that desperation, obstinacy, or an evil habit cause my soul to be lost. Of this deep, Solomon said: *The wicked man when he is come into the depth of sins, contemns*.[237] From those depths, the men absorbed can be seen, of which Jeremiah says: *If the Ethiopian can change his skin, or the leopard his spots: you may also do well, when you have learned evil;*[238]

---

234   Matt. 5:44.
235   Luke 6:35b.
236   Lam. 3:54.
237   Prv. 18:3a.
238   Jer. 13:23.

and, *They have made their faces harder than the rock, and they have refused to return.*[239] *Neque urgeat super me puteus os suum,* and let not the pit shut its mouth upon me. The pit is a certain kind of deepness, and it designates the same thing [as the word "the deep" earlier in the verse]. But the mouth of the deep, or the pit, is said to shut or close over the sinner as long as a sinner with both obstinate and depraved habits adds final impenitence to those, so that he disparages confession and persists in his aversion. As Isaiah says of him: *For I knew that you are stubborn, and your neck is as an iron sinew, and your forehead as brass.*[240] And Jeremiah also: *You had a harlot's forehead, you would not blush.*[241] But he who humbly confesses his sin, steps out of the enclosure of the pit, in accordance with this: *He that hides his sins, shall not prosper: but he that shall confess, and forsake them, shall obtain mercy.*[242] Whence also holy Job asserts: *I will reprove my ways in his sight, and he shall be my Savior.*[243]

68{69}[17] *Hear me, O Lord, for your mercy is kind; look upon me according to the multitude of your tender mercies.*

Exaudi me, Domine, quoniam benigna est misericordia tua; secundum multitudinem miserationum tuarum respice in me.

68{69}[18] *And turn not away your face from your young man:*[244] *for I am in trouble, hear me speedily.*

Et ne avertas faciem tuam a puero tuo; quoniam tribulor, velociter exaudi me.

68{69}[19] *Attend to my soul, and deliver it: save me because of my enemies.*

Intende animae meae, et libera eam; propter inimicos meos eripe me.

68{69}[17] *Exaudi me, Domine; Hear me, O Lord,* not because of the righteousness of my life, but *quoniam benigna est misericordia tua, because your mercy is kind.* For you, to whose merciful kindness sinners are so sweetly invited, are truly ineffably kind and totally gracious: *Turn to the*

---

239 Jer. 5:3b.
240 Is. 48:4.
241 Jer. 3:3b.
242 Prov. 28:13.
243 Job 13:15b–16a.
244 E. N. The Douay-Rheims has "servant," which I have rendered "young man," since as the *Commentary* explains, "young man" (*puero*) commonly means "servant." The translators of the Douay-Rheims have already taken that into account, but the *Commentary* will not make sense unless I translate *puero* literally.

Lord your God: for he is gracious and merciful, patient and rich in mercy, and ready to repent of the evil.[245] *Secundum multitudinem miserationem tuarum respice in me,* look upon me according to the multitude of your tender mercies with your eyes of immense kindliness. **68{69}[18]** *Et ne avertas faciem tuam, and* turn not away your face, that is, the kind remembrance of your knowledge, singular providence, and most kind approbation *a puero tuo, from your young man,* that is, from me your servant, that I might not be consigned to oblivion by you and be found among those to whom is said, *I do not know you.*[246] Now Scripture frequently signifies servant (*servum*) with the word young man (*pueri*), in the manner that Elijah says, *and he left there his servant (puerum).*[247] Sometimes also by the word young man (*puerum*) is understood son, as is written of Christ in Acts, *For... there assembled together in this city against your holy child (puerum tuum) Jesus.*[248] And so now [in this verse] it can be received as an adoptive son of God. And so that which it says sounds charming and sweet: *And turn not away your face from your young man.* This is not to be said to all men, but to those who have merited to be members of the household of God. Christ testifies concerning these through Isaiah: *Behold I and my children whom the Lord has given me for a sign.*[249] *Quoniam tribulor, velociter exaudi me; for I am in trouble, hear me speedily.* Indeed, the elect labor under continual tribulations, for *the life of man upon earth is a warfare.*[250] **68{69}[19]** *Intende animae meae, attend to my soul* by a one-on-one custody, providing to it out of all the things necessary to eternal salvation, *et libera eam, and deliver it* from the evil of fault and of punishment. *Propter inimicos meos, because of my enemies,* that is, at the occasion of my enemies, *eripe me, save me* from all danger. For the malice of those opposed to the elect is the occasion from which God saves them. For this reason, God is most inclined to hear and render aid during the time of tribulations, especially as such prayer of the one suffering tribulation proceeds out of true charity, and not out of servile fear.

68{69}[20] *You know my reproach, and my confusion, and my shame.*

Tu scis improperium meum, et confusionem meam, et reverentiam meam.

---

245 Joel 2:13.
246 Matt. 25:12.
247 1 King 19:3b.
248 Acts 4:27a.
249 Is. 8:18a.
250 Job 7:1a.

68{69}[21] *In your sight are all they that afflict me; my heart has expected reproach and misery. And I looked for one that would grieve together with me, but there was none: and for one that would comfort me, and I found none.*

In conspectu tuo sunt omnes qui tribulant me. Improperium exspectavit cor meum et miseriam; et sustinui qui simul contristaretur, et non fuit; et qui consolaretur, et non inveni.

68{69}[22] *And they gave me gall for my food, and in my thirst they gave me vinegar to drink.*

Et dederunt in escam meam fel, et in siti mea potaverunt me aceto.

68{69}[20] *Tu scis improperium meum et confusionem meam et reverentiam meam; you know my reproach, and my confusion, and my shame.* For God knows each and every adversity or punishment that befalls a man. And a man can say this [verse] along with the next verse to summon the mercy of God, who is wont to render help to the afflicted. Whence Jeremiah: *Behold, O Lord,* he says, *for I am in distress.*[251] **68{69}[21]** *In conspectu tuo sunt omnes qui tribulant me, in your sight are all they that afflict me,* which they are unable to do unless they were permitted by you. *Improperium exspectavit cor meum et miseriam, my heart has expected reproach and misery.* This is often fittingly applicable to the man constituted just[252] and the Church who recognize themselves to be menaced by the injury of words and deeds by the ungodly. But especially does this [verse] and the following one apply to the holy martyrs, who though they may have been enclosed in jail, recognized that the following day they would be gravely vexed by words and by blows. *Et sustinui qui simul contristaretur, et non fuit; [et qui consolaretur, et non inveni]; and I looked for one that would grieve together with me, but there was none: [and for one that would comfort me, and I found none].*[253] Compassion and consolation exhibited to the afflicted proceeds out of charity. For Christ in the Gospel said to the elect, *You shall be hated by all men for my name's sake;*[254] and so it befalls upon the elect sometimes to meet with no compassion or consolation; indeed, frequently they are despised by their neighbors and friends. **68{69}[22]**

---

251   Lam. 1:20a.
252   E. N. Meaning a man in a state of sanctifying grace.
253   E. N. The part of the verse in brackets replaces Denis's "etc." in the text.
254   Matt. 10:22a.

Et dederunt in escam meam fel, [et in siti mea potaverunt me aceto]; and they gave me gall for my food, [and in my thirst they gave me vinegar to drink].[255] This literally has occurred to some martyrs. But spiritually a man who infects another through bad example gives to another gall for food and vinegar to drink, and he leads his soul to bitterness and indignation. And so Moses said: *there should* not *be among you a root bringing forth gall and bitterness.*[256] And the prophet Habakkuk: *Woe to him that gives drink to his friend, and presents him gall.*[257]

68{69}[23] *Let their table become as a snare before them, and a recompense, and a stumbling block.*

> *Fiat mensa eorum coram ipsis in laqueum, et in retributiones, et in scandalum.*

68{69}[24] *Let their eyes be darkened that they see not; and bend you down always their back.*

> *Obscurentur oculi eorum, ne videant; et dorsum eorum semper incurva.*

68{69}[25] *Pour out your indignation upon them: and let your wrathful anger take hold of them.*

> *Effunde super eos iram tuam; et furor irae tuae comprehendat eos.*

68{69}[26] *Let their habitation be made desolate: and let there be none to dwell in their tabernacles.*

> *Fiat habitatio eorum deserta; et in tabernaculis eorum non sit qui inhabitet.*

68{69}[23] *Fiat mensa eorum coram ipsis in laqueum, let their table become as a snare before them*: that is, let the evil which they have prepared for me rush back upon them, and let them be restrained and punished by their own evil-doing: in the manner that is written about in Proverbs: *The wicked man shall fall by his own wickedness, . . . and the unjust shall be caught in their own snares.*[258] For all one's own evil returns to the actor, and the opposition of the persecutor will not harm the injured party if he is not dominated by any iniquity of his own

---

255   E. N. The part of the verse in brackets replaces the "etc." in the Latin text.
256   Deut. 29:18b.
257   Hab. 2:15a.
258   Prov. 11:5b, 6b.

mind. **68{69}[24]** *Obscurentur oculi eorum ne videant, let their eyes be darkened* by the amount of torments prepared for them in eternal death, and how much happiness they may have lost.[259] **68{69}[25]** *Effunde super eos iram tuam, pour out your indignation upon them,* abandoning them to their error, as in a later Psalm you say with regard to the reprobate: *I let them go according to the desires of their heart: they shall walk in their own inventions.*[260] Of whom also Job says: *The rod of God is not upon them. . . . they spend their days in wealth, and in a moment they go down to hell.*[261] *Et furor irae tuae comprehendat eos, and let your wrathful anger take hold of them,* finally, irreparably, and eternally damning them, in the manner that we read elsewhere: *The Lord is a revenger and has wrath: the Lord takes vengeance on his adversaries.*[262] **68{69}[26]** *Fiat habitatio eorum deserta, let their habitation be made desolate.* We read that the cities and the homes of the unbelievers are often destroyed, possessed, and inhabited by the faithful: and then the tabernacles of the infidels are emptied of their original inhabitants. But spiritually-speaking the homes of the impious are deserted when their souls are separated from their bodies before their time so that they are killed or die more quickly because of their sins; or when their souls, which ought to have been seats of wisdom, the couches of God, and the homes of Christ are abandoned by grace so that they are inhabited neither by God nor formed faith:[263] as the Lord says through Ezechiel regarding the sinner: *My soul was alienated from her;*[264] and regarding the impious through Hosea: *Woe to them when I shall depart from them.*[265]

---

259   E. N. Denis skips the latter half of verse 24.

260   Ps. 80:13.

261   Job. 21:9b, 13.

262   Nahum 1:2.

263   E. N. The notion of a soul being the seat of wisdom is taken from St. Augustine: *anima iusti sedes sapientiae.* The soul as the *reclinatorium Dei,* in a more dynamic sense could be understood as the "chariot-seat of God." The *fides formata* or "formed faith," is a *fides formata caritate,* a faith informed by charity, a saving, justifying, living faith. These titles for the Christian soul are frequently applied to the Blessed Virgin Mary, who, of course, is the paradigm of the soul fully responsive to God and full of grace and faith.

264   Ez. 23:18. E. N. Ezechiel compares the disobedient soul to fornicating harlots. St. Augustine famously compared himself to this: "I committed fornication against you, and all around me thus fornicating there echoed 'Well done! Well done!' for the friendship of this world is fornication against you." *Confessions,* I, 13.

265   Hosea 9:12b.

68{69}[27] *Because they have persecuted him whom you have smitten;
and they have added to the grief of my wounds.*

*Quoniam quem tu percussisti persecuti sunt, et super dolorem
vulnerum meorum addiderunt.*

68{69}[29] *Let them be blotted out of the book of the living; and with
the just let them not be written.* [266]

Deleantur de libro viventium, et cum iustis non scribantur.

68{69}[27] *Quoniam quem tu percussisti, because . . . him whom you have
smitten* permissively, [267] *persecuti sunt, they have persecuted* with malicious,
cruel, and evil intentions. For God permits the elect to be oppressed
by the ungodly so that they might be cleansed. But the ungodly do not
oppress them for the reason that they may be cleansed, but they afflict
them invidiously. And so, in the manner that a father who corrects his
son with a rod throws the rod into the fire when the son is corrected,
so God corrects the elect by the reprobate, and after [the elect] are
amended and saved, he casts the reprobate into eternal fire. *Et super
dolorem vulnerum meorum addiderunt, and they have added to the grief of
my wounds* [heaping] upon me the grief of evil words, derision, curses, and
blasphemies. **68{69}[29]** *Deleantur de libro viventium, let them be blotted
out of the book of the living*, that is, from the fellowship of the blessed in
heaven: to whose number are reckoned also unbelievers and evil men
however much they are ignorant as to what true beatitude consists in.

68{69}[30] *But I am poor and sorrowful: your salvation, O God, has
set me up.*

Ego sum pauper et dolens; salus tua, Deus, suscepit me.

68{69}[31] *I will praise the name of God with a canticle: and I will
magnify him with praise.*

Laudabo nomen Dei cum cantico; et magnificabo eum in laude.

68{69}[30] *Ego sum pauper, I am poor*, especially in the good of grace,
in the gifts of the Holy Spirit, in spiritual and internal riches; and that
which is contained in Revelation befits me: *You are wretched, and miserable,
and poor, and blind, and naked.* [268] I am also *dolens, sorrowful*, because

---

266   Denis skips verse 28 entirely.
267   E. N. That is, by God's permissive will.
268   Rev. 3:17b.

of sins committed, and the errors of the world, and your punishments. And so *salus tua, Deus, suscepit me; your salvation, O God, has set me up,* that is, your salvific grace is infused in me, and you yourself, who are the true salvation of all the elect, have mercifully set me upright: for which reason, I give thanks back to God, and **68{69}[31]** *laudabo nomen Dei cum cantico, I will praise the name of God with canticle* of psalmody, of divine hymns, and of fervent devotions, for not clamor, but love sounds in the ears of the Almighty.[269] The rest is made clear in the preceding article.

See now we have heard this most brilliant and holy Psalm that carefully deals with the Passion of Christ, the blindness of the Jews, and the establishing of the Church in a full and clear manner. We learn, therefore, by the example of Christ, to be patient in all persecution, to stand constant against all temptations, to be strong in all adversity. In this current Psalm there is contained most devout and most ardent prayers overflowing with marvelous sweetness. For what else is so full of love and suavity as those three verses, *Hear me, O Lord, for your mercy is kind; [look upon me according to the multitude of your tender mercies. And turn not away your face from your servant: for I am in trouble, hear me speedily. Attend to my soul, and deliver it: save me because of my enemies.]*[270] And so let us sing always this Psalm with great presence of mind and great dignity and fervor.

PRAYER

GOD, TO WHOM ALL THOUGHTS ARE manifest, and from whom our sins are not hidden, look upon us in the multitude of your tender mercies, and cleanse us from the stains which offend you; attend to our soul, and free it from reproach and from eternal confusion.

Deus, cui est omnis cogitatio manifesta, et a quo delicta nostra non sunt abscondita, respice nos in multitudine misericordiae tuae, et maculas te offendentes a nobis absterge; intende animae nostrae, et libera eam ab improperio et ab aeterna confusione.

---

269   *E. N.* On this expression — *non clamor, sed amor,* "not clamor, but love," which probably comes from Thomas of Celano — *see* footnote 6-22 in Volume 1.
270   Ps. 68:17–19. The parts in brackets replace the "etc." of Denis's Latin text.

Psalm 69

ARTICLE XXXVI

ELUCIDATION OF THE SIXTY-NINTH PSALM:

DEUS, IN ADIUTORIUM, ETC.

O GOD, COME TO MY ASSISTANCE, ETC.

AND OF THE ADMIRABLE VIRTUE

OF THE FIRST VERSE OF THIS PSALM

69{70}[1] *Unto the end. A Psalm for David, in remembrance that the Lord saved him.*

In finem. Psalmus David in rememoratione, quod salvum fecit eum Dominus.[1]

HIS PSALM HAS THIS TITLE: **69{70}[1]** *IN finem. Psalmus David in rememoratione quod salvum fecit eum Dominus. Unto the end. A Psalm for David, in remembrance that the Lord saved him*: that is, this Psalm was written by David, and it directs us to our end, which is Christ. In this Psalm, I emphasize, holy David, is here speaking the person of man speaking justly, with the recollection, that is, of the remembrance, that the Lord saved him. And so David wrote this Psalm so as to recall the benefits conveyed to him by God. Nicholas of Lyra says that in the Hebrew, this Psalm is entitled in this fashion: *In recollection of the victory of David*; also the translation from the Hebrew by Jerome, is thus: *To the recollection of victory*. To this is added, *that the Lord saved him*, which he asserts was added by another expositor. For this reason he says that this Psalm is a prophecy of the future, so that he [David] foresaw in the Holy Spirit, that the beginning of this Psalm would be recalled in the beginning, or near the beginning, of all canonical hours, as is now done in the Church.[2]

---

1 E. N. Denis's version departs slightly from the Sixto-Clementine Vulgate, but without any significant change in meaning.

2 E. N. The reader is referred to that tour-de-force written about this verse by St. John Cassian (*ca.* 360–*ca.* 435 AD) in his *Conferences*, specifically, chapter 10 of his tenth conference. This is readily available online and in English translation. https://www.newadvent.org/fathers/350810.htm. Denis refers to it later in this *Commentary*. The reason why Denis says that this verse is used in the beginning or *near* the beginning is because in the hour of Matins this verse is preceded with Psalm 50:17: *V. Domine labia mea aperies, R. Et os meum anuntiabit laudem tuam.*

69{70}[2]   *O God, come to my assistance; O Lord, make haste to help me.*

Deus, in adiutorium meum intende; Domine, ad adiuvandum me festina.

The Prophet [David] speaking therefore in the person of a just man being tried and tested, says: **69{70}[1]** *Deus in adiutorium meum intende; O God, come to my assistance,* that is, have regard for me in this: that you may provide to me help. Direct your assistance toward me, and not to my abandonment, blindness, and condemnation. Think over me *thoughts of peace, and not of affliction,*[3] in the way you say about some: *Behold, I devise an evil against this family: from which you shall not withdraw your necks.*[4] But because, O Lord, I unceasingly am in need of your help, and I subsist by your conservation, and so, *Domine, ad adiuvandum me festina; O Lord make help to haste me.* For you have said: *Without me you can do nothing;*[5] and through Paul, *We are not sufficient to think anything of ourselves, as of ourselves: but our sufficiency is from God.*[6]

69{70}[3]   *Let them be confounded and be afraid that seek my soul:*[7]

Confundantur, et revereantur, qui quaerunt animam meam.

69{70}[4]   *Let them be turned backward, and blush for shame that desire evils to me: Let them be presently turned away blushing for shame that say to me: Well done, Well done.*

Avertantur retrorsum, et erubescant, qui volunt mihi mala; avertantur statim erubescentes qui dicunt mihi: Euge, euge!

69{70}[3] *Confundantur et reverantur, qui quaerunt animam meam; let them be confounded and afraid that seek my soul.* This verse, with the two verses which follow it, can be explained in two ways. In the first explanation, therefore, these verses can be explained in a good sense, and it will be in this sense: *Let them be confounded* by their sins, and from such confusion let them repent, *and let them be afraid,* that is, let them honor God and let them dread the judgment of God, [them being those] *that seek my soul,* that is, my enemies, which seek to wound or

---

3   Jer. 29:11a.
4   Micah 2:3a.
5   John 15:5b.
6   2 Cor. 3:5.
7   E. N. I have replaced the Douay-Rheims "let them be ashamed," with "let them be afraid" for the Latin *revereantur,* for as Denis says later in this commentary, the phrase "let them be ashamed" often means "let them be afraid" or "let the be awed." *See* also footnotes 34-6 and 34-73 in Volume 2.

extinguish my bodily life or to corrupt and subvert my spirit. For there
is a two-fold confusion [or shame], in the way Scripture states: *For
there is a shame that brings sin, and there is a shame that brings glory
and grace.*[8] The confusion leading to sin is a shame with respect to the
good. Whence it is written: Do not be ashamed to confess your sins.[9]
But the confusion leading to grace in the present and glory in the future
is the shame arising the evil of fault, as the Apostles speaks of some:
*What fruit therefore had you then in those things, of which you are now
ashamed?*[10] **69{70}[4]** *Avertantur retrorsum, let them be turned backward,*
that is, let them cease from evil deeds, so that they may desist from
depraved intentions, and not proceed toward, and grow in, evil; and let
them who incline toward, or opt to perform, such dishonest and vicious
acts *erubescent, blush for shame; qui volunt mihi mala, [those] that desire
evils to me,* evils of punishment or of fault which belong to an ill-will.
And so a just man will seek to avoid those most inward adversaries by
prayer. *Avertantur statim; let them be presently turned away* from their
errors, *erubescentes, blushing for shame* because of their own iniquity, for
it is dangerous for them to persevere in their guilt; *qui dicunt mihi,
Euge, euge; that say to me, Well done, well done,* rejoicing in my misery,
or stating that they rejoice in my prosperity, not in a true sense, but by
reason of flattery or derision. For a man has two enemies: invisible and
visible. If we now speak of invisible enemies, therefore, then this [verse]
can in no way be explained in a good sense, especially since these sorts
of enemies are incorrigible and obstinate.

The second way of explaining this [verse] is in an evil sense, in this
manner: *Let them* the evildoers *be confounded,* with the confusion or
divine reprobation and eternal damnation, *and be afraid,* that is, let them
be restrained in the sight of the just judgment of God from their own
will toward sin, in the manner that is written in Hosea: *Israel shall
be confounded in his own will.*[11] For at times the word "to be afraid"
(*revereri*) is understood as meaning "to be ashamed" (*verecundari*), as
also irreverent (*irreverens*) means shameless (*inverecundus*), as it is here:

---

8   Ecclus. 4:25.
9   Cf. Ecclus. 4:31: *Be not ashamed to confess your sins, but submit not yourself to
every man for sin.*
10   Rom. 6:21.
11   Hosea 10:6b. E. N. In his *Commentary on Hosea*, Denis expounds on this verse:
"*And Israel shall be confounded,* that is, any one of the faithful, *in his own will,* that
is, in the affections of his own will, following not the divine precepts, nor following
the path of him who said: *I came down from heaven, not to do my own will, but the
will of him that sent me.* [John 6:38]."

Give me not over to a shameless (irreverenti)... mind.[12] *Let them be turned backward,* that is, let them turn away from the sovereign good and adhere to transient and vain things: as the Lord said of them through Jeremiah: *They have turned their back to me, and not their face;*[13] and elsewhere, *This people... is turned away with a stubborn revolting.*[14] *And blush for shame* with the shame of damnation, not of confession, *that desire evils to me,* whether their will leads to an act or it does not. *Let them be presently turned away blushing for shame [that say to me: Well done, well done.],*[15] that is, let them be deprived of your grace, and confess your name, that they might be ashamed of the public manifestation of their vice. Whence Moses said: *The Lord your God, he is a strong and faithful God, ... repaying forthwith them that hate him, so as to destroy them, without further delay immediately rendering to them what they deserve.*[16] For in the present age he immediately takes grace and protection away from them, permitting them to fall from evil to evil: which is the greatest of all punishment.

69{70}[5] *Let all that seek you rejoice and be glad in you; and let such as love your salvation say always: The Lord be magnified.*

Exsultent et laetentur in te omnes qui quaerunt te; et dicant semper: Magnificetur Dominus, qui diligunt salutare tuum,

69{70}[5] *Exsultent, let... them rejoice,* that is, let them show a sign of joy externally, and let it spring forth out from them from an interior cheerfulness, *et laetentur, and let them rejoice* with an interior joy, *in te, in you,* and not in the vanities of the world, *omnes qui quaerunt te, all that seek you* with faith and in deed, or doing all which is in their power, so that they might acquire, preserve, and possess your grace and the contemplation and delight in your goodness. *Et dicant: semper magnificetur Dominus; and let them... say always: The Lord be magnified,* that is, let him be honored and blessed, and let him be recognized to be great by all, *qui diligent salutare tuum, such as love your salvation,* that is, the salvation of grace in the present and the blessedness of glory in the future; or [we can think of it thus], *your salvation,* meaning Christ the Savior of all.

---

12   Ecclus. 23:6b.
13   Jer. 2:27a.
14   Jer. 8:5a.
15   E. N. The part in brackets replaces Denis's "etc."
16   Deut. 7:9–10.

69{70}[6] *But I am needy and poor; O God, help me. You are my helper and my deliverer: O my God, make no delay.*

Ego vero egenus et pauper sum; Deus, adiuva me. Adiutor meus et liberator meus es tu; Deus, meus ne moreris,[17]

69{70}[6] *Ego vero egenus et pauper sum; but I am needy and poor.* We are poor because of the natural imperfections of our soul and its powers. For the rational soul is the lowest in the order of intellectual substances; and the possible intellect (*intellectus possibilis*) in its beginning is as it were a blackboard lacking any drawing.[18] Additionally, the will is naturally inclined toward evil, and the memory is prone to slip. But we are truly poor because of the imperfection of grace. For *all our justices are as the rag of a menstruous woman;*[19] and that which is good in us we receive from elsewhere, and we do not prevail in anything due to our own powers. For this reason we daily beg bread from our heavenly Father saying: *Give us this day our daily bread.*[20] And David himself said in another place: *I am a poor man, and of small ability.*[21] Since therefore I am so in need and poor, O God, *adiuva me, help me* by the infusion of grace, by the Passion of Christ, by the guardianship of a holy angel,[22] by the intercession of the Saints, by the counsels and the help of my neighbors and prelates. *Adiutor meus, my helper* in the

---

17   E. N. Denis's Latin text departs slightly from the Sixto-Clementine Vulgate; I have retained his version here. However, I have kept the word *moreris* and not used the word *tardaveris* (which has much the same meaning), since the editor has made note of that fact in the margin.

18   E. N. The Scholastics divided the intellect into *intellectus passivus* (passive intellect: the lowest level of intellect, found, for example in brute animals), the *intellectus possibilis* (potential or possible intellect: an intellect that has a potential capacity), and the *intellectus agens* (active intellect). "What ordinary mortals call 'intellect' or 'understanding,' is the 'potential intellect.' It is called 'potential' because it is open to all intellectual impressions, and, prior to experience, is void of all impression, and has no predisposition of itself to one impression rather than to another." Joseph Rickaby, S. J., *Of God and His Creatures: An Annotated Translation of the Summa Contra Gentiles* (St. Louis, MO: B. Herder 1905), 122.

19   Is. 65:6a. E. N. By imperfection of grace, Denis is not suggesting imperfection in grace qua grace; rather, he is referring to the imperfection in us in responding to, or lacking the fullness of, grace.

20   Luke 11:3.

21   1 Sam. 18:23b.

22   E. N. In his commentary on Matthew, St. Jerome says, "The dignity of souls is so great that every one of them has from the time of its birth delegated its guardian angel." *Comm. Matt.* III, 18, PL 26, 130. Quoting St. Basil, the Catechism states, "'Beside each believer stands an angel as protector and shepherd leading him to life.'" CCC § 336 (St. Basil, *Adv. Eunomium* III, I, PG 29, 656).

doing of good, *et liberator meus, and my deliverer* in turning away from evil, *es tu, are you,* and I can do nothing else unless it be done through your power. *Deus meus, O my God,* whom I in a singular way love and worship, *ne moreris, do not delay* in fulfilling these prayers.

Now this Psalm can be explained in reference to Christ. For he, as man, frequently requested the help of God: that he would be raised again from the dead, that he would be glorified in body, and that he would be made illustrious through the world. But this exposition is clearly obvious from its being often stated and taught. For also this Psalm in great part is contained in the Psalm which follows it; but it is totally contained in the thirty-ninth Psalm — [which begins with] *With expectation I have waited on the Lord* and which has already been expounded upon — beginning at that place where it says, *Be pleased, O Lord, to deliver me.*[23] Whether explained in reference to Christ or [is explained in reference] to his members, that section which says, *Let them be confounded, etc.* along with the two following verses, when it is expounded in a sense of wishing evil, can be understood three ways. The first, as a way of foreannouncement, not imprecation: as a means of pointing out what will be the future of the ungodly unless they repent. The second, as a way of declaration, expressing that which the evildoer deserves. The third, as a way of prayer, that a man might conform himself to divine justice, desiring the ungodly to suffer just punishment, either in the present (so that they do not eternally perish), or in the future (unless they forthwith convert to God and serve him). And if this verse is understood to pertain to invisible enemies, then it can be simply and absolutely understood as wishing evil.

Therefore, great and marvelous is the power of the first verse of this present Psalm: because of its merits, Mother Church, instructed through the Holy Spirit, established that these verses be said in the beginning, or close to the beginning, of each of the [canonical] Hours, since, fortified by the shield of divine help, we avoid the snares of the enemy, who certainly then strongly seeks to ensnare us, and he never ceases to oppose us, when we attend to begin the divine praises.

Besides the praise of this verse is most beautifully attended to by our most illustrious father Cassian in his first book of *Collations,* describing that which the holy anchorite Abbot Isaac taught through word of mouth. He says that to possess perpetually the mindfulness of God this verse should be unceasingly repeated in the mind: for it carries

---

23   Ps. 39:14.

with it all the affections that are implanted in human nature, and it is appropriate and fitting for any condition and all attacks. Indeed, it contains the invocation against the separation of God, it contains the humility of pious confession, it contains the vigilance of solicitude and fear, it contains the consideration of one's weakness, the trust of being heard, the confidence of present and always available assistance: for he who perpetually invokes his protector is sure to have him always present. It contains the ardor of love and charity, it contains an awareness of snares and the fear of enemies which, seeing them being around day and night, it confesses that he cannot be delivered without the help of his defender. This verse is an impregnable wall against the infestation of all vexatious demons, it is an impenetrable breastplate and a most safe shield. This verse will not allow those souls who find themselves in spiritual sloth (*acedia*) and anxiety, or sad, or depressed with whatever manner of thoughts to despair of saving remedies; it shows that he who is invoked is continually aware of our struggles, and that they will not be found wanting in beseeching him. This verse admonishes not to be elated with ourselves while enjoying the successes of prosperity or spiritual advances, but as in difficulty and in sadness, so in joy and prosperity, to stand always in need of divine help, since by it we are delivered, and through it we remain steadfast. Moreover, whatever sin we might be disturbed by, whichever passion we might be tried by, whatever adversity, wandering, aridity, and tedium we might be bothered with, the cry for us is always: *God, come to my assistance, O Lord, make help to haste me.* Let the meditation upon this verse always be mulled over without ceasing in your breast. In whatever work, ministry, and journey do not cease in singing it. Reflect upon it in going to bed or during refreshment, and during the ultimate needs of nature. For the meditation upon it not only keeps you unhurt against the attacks of devils, but also is effective in purging you from the contagion from all earthly vices, leading you to those invisible and heavenly thoughts, and carrying you up to that ineffable ardor of prayer experienced by so few. Fall asleep meditating upon this verse, until formed by incessant practice of it, you become accustomed to repeat it while you sleep. Let it be the first thing to come to you when you wake up, and may it also come before all your vain thoughts, and may it follow you at all times.

PRAYER

GOD, AUTHOR OF HUMAN SALVATION, come to our assistance against those seeking our soul, so that by their attacks towards us ceasing through you, we might magnify you, our helper and protector, without end.

Deus auctor salutis humanae, contra quaerentes animam nostrum in adiutorium nostrum intende: ut eorum per te infestatione a nobis cessante, te adiutorem et protectorem nostrum magnificemus sine fine.

Psalm 70

ARTICLE XXXVII

DECLARATION OF THE SEVENTIETH PSALM:
IN TE, DOMINE, SPERAVI, ETC.
IN YOU, O LORD, HAVE I HOPED, ETC.

70{71}[1] *A psalm for David. Of the sons of Jonadab, and the former captives. In you, O Lord, I have hoped, let me never be put to confusion.*

Psalmus David, filiorum Ionadab, et priorum captivorum. In te, Domine, speravi; non confundar in aeternum.

HE TITLE OF THIS PRESENT PSALM IS: 70{71} [1] *Psalmus David, filiorum Ionadab, et primorum captivorum; a Psalm for David, of the sons of Jonadab, and the former captives.* Jeremiah narrates the way Jonadab enjoined his sons not to drink wine, and not to reside at home, but to dwell in the tabernacle, which the sons faithfully obeyed:[1] for this reason, the Lord reproached the sons of Israel,[2] and the words of Jonadab, which the sons of Israel neglected to obey, prevailed over their own words. But the Psalm now being expounded does not deal with this history, but [it deals] of the things signified by it, namely of those who voluntarily obey the divine will: of those who were at one time captive, that is, before they were converted to God they were subject to the yoke of the devil, in the manner that the Apostle [Paul] says: *We . . . conversed in time past, in the desires of our flesh, . . . and were by nature children of wrath, even as the rest.*[3] For as long as we carried the image *of the transgression of Adam,*[4] we were held captive by the law of sin; but since we began to carry the image of Christ, imitating his path, we were delivered from the miserable captivity of fault and of the devil, and we were made children of grace and free in the Lord. For this reason the Apostle said: *The first man was of the earth, earthly; the second man, from heaven, heavenly. Such as is the earthly, such also are the earthly; and such as is the heavenly, such also are they that are heavenly. Therefore, as we have borne the image of the*

---

1 Jer. 35:14.
2 Jer. 35:14–16.
3 Eph. 2:3.
4 Rom. 5:14.

earthly, let us bear also the image of the heavenly.[5] And so the sense of this title is: this *Psalm*, which is *for* the prophet *David*, as author, published for the instruction *of the sons of Jonadab*, that is, of the sons of obedience, voluntarily subject to God, *primorum captivorum, of the former captives*, that is, of the sons who were captive in the manner just described, before they obeyed the Lord, whom to serve, is truly to reign.[6]

The prophet [David] speaking therefore in the person of a man greatly afflicted, and with absolute and complete confidence in the Lord, attributing to himself no good or perfection, says: *In te, Domine, speravi; in you, O Lord, I have hoped*: that is, by the merits of your Passion, I have trusted in your immense kindliness, in your most pure goodness, O Christ, not in view of my own merits, or in the uncertainty of riches, or in any created, transient, or vain good. And so, I pray *non confundar in aeternum, let me never be put to confusion*, that is, let me not perish eternally, nor in the day of judgment together with the reprobate hear that word of eternal confusion: *Depart from me, you cursed, into everlasting fire.*[7] Since, therefore, O Lord, in the present life I am confounded, despised, troubled by evildoers, let me not be confounded in eternity, nor let me be deprived of my hope, but, obtaining its [hope's] fruit, let me be saved, in the manner that is attested in Jeremiah of those placing hope in you: *Delivering, I will deliver you, and . . . your life shall be saved for you, because you have put your trust in me.*[8]

70{71}[2]   *Deliver me in your justice and rescue me. Incline your ear unto me and save me.*

In iustitia tua libera me, et eripe me: inclina ad me aurem tuam, et salva me.

70{71}[3]   *Be unto me a God, a protector, and a place of strength: that you may make me safe. For you are my firmament and my refuge.*

Esto mihi in Deum protectorem, et in locum munitum, ut salvum me facias: quoniam firmamentum meum et refugium meum es tu.

---

5   1 Cor. 15:47–49.

6   E. N. The saying *cui servire est regnare*, whom to serve is to reign comes from a sermon attributed to St. Augustine: *Iugum enim eius obedientiae merito est suave, cui servire est regnare.* "For the yoke of obedience to him is rightly sweet, whom to serve is to reign." PL 39, 1867. The phrase is found in the Roman Liturgy in a number of collects and prayers.

7   Matt. 25:41.

8   Jer. 39:18.

70{71}[2] *In iustitia tua libera me, et eripe me; deliver me in your jus-tice and rescue me.* The justice of God is two-fold, namely, [the first is] uncreated [justice], which is God himself. By this justice God liberates just and perfect men, who, by merit of their virtuous manner of living, deserve to be saved by the Lord. But the other justice of God is created, which can be said of all grace, virtue, and perfection conceded to us by God. For all our justice is of God, as giver, preserver, and rewarder.[9] Moreover, penance or the penitential forum — wherein justice is done after sin when it is corrected and punished — can especially be said to this [kind of created] justice. In this penitential justice, therefore, where man laments his own fault, and he turns himself toward God, the sinner strives to be delivered, and is penitent that he is not yet full of virtue or abounding with good works and merit.[10] He therefore says: *In your justice,* that is, as is demanded by your divine justice, *deliver me* from the evil of fault in this world, *and rescue me* from the evil of punishment in the world to come. For your divine justice requires this: that you might deliver those that hope in you and are penitent [for their sins]. For deliverance corresponds to an act of power. This request is not in opposition to that which is said: *In you, O Lord, I have hoped.* For this hope is principally a person's reliance upon God, though in a secondary

---

9 E. N. The justice referred to here is righteousness or being in a justified state, that is, a state of sanctifying grace. In distinguishing between uncreated and created justice, Denis is referring to the fact that our justification involves created grace (*gratia creata*) and uncreated grace (*gratia increata*). Uncreated grace is the blessed Trinity himself dwelling in the human soul, both here inchoately (through a glass darkly), but in the heavenly fatherland, face-to-face. Uncreated grace is concomitantly obtained with, and because of, created grace, which is a habitual, accidental quality (meaning it does not make our soul something other than human). It readies the soul for God's presence and the soul's divinization. Created grace is a supernatural gift or operation really distinct from God, a supernatural (yet created) gift arising out of and caused by this communication of God himself, and includes, sanctifying grace, the infused supernatural virtues, and the seven gifts of the Holy Spirit.

10 E. N. "That penance is a virtue may also be inferred from the ends which the true penitent proposes to himself. The first is to destroy sin and efface from the soul its every spot and stain. The second is to make satisfaction to God for the sins which he has committed, which is clearly an act of justice. Between God and man, it is true, no relation of strict justice can exist, so great is the distance that separates them; yet between them there is evidently a sort of justice, such as exists between a father and his children, between a master and his servants. The third (end of the penitent) is to reinstate himself in the favor and friendship of God whom he has offended and whose hatred he has earned by the turpitude of sin. The foregoing considerations sufficiently prove that penance is a virtue." *Catechism of the Council of Trent for Parish Priests* (New York: Joseph F. Wagner, 1947), 265 (trans., John A. McHugh, O. P. and Charles J. Callan, O. P.).

sense a person relies upon his own merit which he knows to have been given to him by God, for our merits are the gifts of God.[11]

Inclina ad me aurem tuam, incline your ear unto me, that is, apply to me your mercy, *et salva me, and save me*, now by grace, through virtuous works, by the beginning of future happiness, namely, by deiform contemplation and internal consolations; but in the future save me by glory. 70{71}[3] *Esto mihi in Deum protectorem, et in locum munitum; be unto me a God, a protector, and a place of strength*: that is, you who are God and preserver of all things, be thus God to me, so that you might protect and preserve me, as a man in a fortified place is protected from the spears and the snares of the enemy. Just like a man who has struck another and fears the wrath of judgment hastens quickly to a place of refuge, and is kept safe within it, so be to me, a sinner, always a way back to your clemency and security in it; *ut salvam me facias, that you may make me safe*. Hence I pray to you, *quoniam firmamentum meum, for my firmament*, that is, the cause of all my firmness and stability, *et refugium meum, and my refuge*, that is, the end to which I flee, my hope, and my sovereign good, in whom alone I place my salvation, *es tu, is you*, O Lord.

70{71}[4]   *Deliver me, O my God, out of the hand of the sinner, and out of the hand of the transgressor of the law and of the unjust.*

Deus meus, eripe me de manu peccatoris, et de manu contra legem agentis, et iniqui.

70{71}[5]   *For you are my patience, O Lord: my hope, O Lord, from my youth.*

Quoniam tu es patientia mea, Domine; Domine, spes mea a iuventute mea.

70{71}[4] *Deus meus, eripe me de manu peccatoris; deliver me, O my God, out of the hand of the sinner*, that is, from the power of the devil, lest I succumb to his attacks. In the Gospel is written about him: *He was a murderer from the beginning, and he stood not in the truth; because truth is not in him;*[12] and elsewhere, *the devil sins from the beginning.*[13] Also *deliver me* also *de manu contra legem agentis, out of the hand of the*

---

11   E. N. This splendid apothegm—that our merits are nothing but God's gifts—is Augustinian. St. Augustine states that it is by God's mercy that "he crowns you, for he crowns his own gifts, not your merits," *coronat te, quia dona sua coronat, non merita tua. Enarr. in Ps.*, Ps. 102, PL 337, 1321.

12   John 8:44b.

13   1 John 3:8a.

transgressor of the law, that is, any impious man persecuting the just man, that I not be infected or seduced by such men; *et iniqui, and of the unjust*, from him who, dissolving the bond of fraternal charity, is persecuting me without cause. Most of all, O Lord, deliver me from the hand of the sinner, that is, from my own self, a sinner, to the extent that I am impious and doing things by my own hand against the law; and turn me towards you, so that I might be not such as I was, but that I might desist from being among the unjust: in the way that it is written, *Turn the wicked, and they shall not be.* **70{71}[5]** *Quoniam tu es patientia mea, Domine; for you are my patience, O Lord*, that is, the cause, end, and reward of my patience. Whence the holy Job says: *Where is now then my expectation, and who considers my patience?*[14] You are, O Lord, my God. *Domine, spes mea a iuventute mea; my hope, O Lord, from my youth*: either bodily, because many place upon themselves the yoke of the Lord from youth and place their confidence in God, those, namely, who are converted in childhood.[15] For this reason, Jeremiah states: *It is good for a man, when he has borne the yoke from his youth;*[16] and another one [states], *I will praise your name continually, . . . and I will give you thanks . . . when I was yet young, before I wandered about, [I sought for wisdom openly in prayer].*[17] Or [alternatively it can be understood spiritually]: *from my* spiritual *youth*, that is, from that time when I began to renew the spirit of my mind,[18] stripping myself of the old man with his deeds, and putting on the new man who is renewed in the knowledge of God, according to the Apostle [Paul].[19] God is the hope of men from this youth, for no one is able to be thus renewed and in this manner turned unless by hoping in the Lord.

---

14 Job 17:15.

15 E. N. The text refers to the "first vigil" (*prima vigilia*) of life, which can be variously translated. The Romans divided their evening into four watches or vigils (*vigiliae*). The first watch (*prima vigilia*) was the first watch after nightfall. Thus it could be the "first quarter" of life. However, the expression "first vigil" was often used loosely to refer to three stages, as, for example, by the Venerable Bede, who says that the first vigil (*prima vigilia*) is childhood, the second vigil (*vigilia secunda*) is adolescence, and the third vigil (*vigilia tertia*) is old age. Hom. 78, PL 94, 466. Pope St. Gregory the Great has the same three-fold division. Hom. I, 13, PL 76, 1125. I have translated it as "childhood."

16 Lam. 3:27.

17 Ecclus. 51:15a, 17a, 18. E. N. I have added the part in brackets to emphasize that the divine author is referring to his youth.

18 Cf. Eph. 4:23: *And be renewed in the spirit of your mind.*

19 Col. 3:9–10: *Lie not one to another: stripping yourselves of the old man with his deeds, and putting on the new, him who is renewed unto knowledge, according to the image of him that created him.*

70{71}[6] *By you have I been confirmed from the womb: from my mother's womb you are my protector. Of you shall I continually sing.*

In te confirmatus sum ex utero; de ventre matris meae tu es protector meus; in te cantatio mea semper.

70{71}[6] *In te confirmatus sum ex utero, by you have I been confirmed from the womb*, that is, by your power my natural being is preserved in the womb of my carnal mother even up to the time of my birth, and continually thereafter. For unless God preserves the infant in the womb, he would not be able both to be and to remain, since without the maintenance of God nothing has the power to subsist [on its own]; and unless the infant in the womb is preserved from all danger, he frequently and easily will die in the womb. Therefore, St. Thomas and many others say that a good angel is deputed to keep custody of an infant even when dwelling in the womb.[20] *De ventre matris meae tu es protector meus, from my mother's womb you are my protector*, that is, from the beginning of my birth even unto the present, you yourself and by your holy angel have protected me. Sometimes God in his just judgment may allow someone to fall, though he so greatly protects the elect that he will not permit them to die in mortal sin or to be finally devoured by the devil: indeed, the mercy of the Creator causes even the reprobate to be kept from many evils by angelic custody. But spiritually expounded the verse reads in this way: *By you have I been confirmed*, that is, I began to be confirmed in faith and grace, *from the womb*, that is, from being taught catechism, where I have been instructed in Christian doctrine. *From my mother's womb*, that is, the womb of the Church, namely, from sacred Baptism, in which I was spiritually reborn by water and the Holy Spirit.[21] For grace, faith, hope, and charity is infused [into our soul] in Baptism. *You are my protector*, preserving in me the gift of sanctifying grace bestowed upon me at Baptism.

In te cantatio mea semper, of you shall I continually sing: that is, my vocal praise, the exaltation of heart, and the thanksgiving of my soul is such in going over your benefits and in considering your goodness, that I incessantly desire to praise you, in every place, occasion, and time. And if I happen to praise man, or some creature, I do this to your glory,

---

20 *E. N.* Denis is mistaken. St. Thomas does not teach that the child in the womb is deputed its own guardian angel while it is in the womb. St. Thomas suggests the mother's guardian angel attends to the infant before birth, and that only after birth is the guardian angel particular to the child appointed. ST Ia, q. 113, art. 5, ad 3.
21 John 3:5.

ascribing to you all good, and referring all to your honor. I praise no one in evil (as an earlier Psalm has it, *For the sinner is praised in the desires of his soul*);[22] but if I praise him, I do so because of virtues and gifts grace. In this way Paul frequently praised his disciples.[23]

70{71}[7] *I am become unto many as a wonder, but you are a strong helper.*

Tamquam prodigium factus sum multis; et tu adiutor fortis.

70{71}[7] *Tamquam prodigium factus sum multis,* I am become unto many as a wonder, that is, I am reputed as a monster (*portentum*) by many, derided and despised, because my life and their lives are found to be so dissimilar.[24] For I judge as if dung[25] carnal and delectable things which they greatly value, praise, acquire, and love, so that I might adhere to Christ with a pure and free mind; I prefer heavenly, invisible, and eternal things to the earthly, visible, and transitory; I leave father, mother, brothers, sisters, wife, close friends, lands, and all other things for the love of Christ;[26] and so they reckon my life as madness.[27] Whence also the divine Apostle: *We are made a spectacle (spectaculum) to the world, and to angels, and to men;*[28] and also to the Philippians, *I count all things to be but loss for the excellent knowledge of Jesus Christ my Lord.*[29] Ezechiel also said to his people: *Ezechiel shall be unto you a sign of things to come (portentum).*[30] *Et adiutor fortis,* but you are a strong helper: that is, you, O

---

22   Ps. 10:3a (according to the Hebrew). E. N. This is equivalent to Psalm 9:24a in the Sixto-Clementine Vulgate. Ps. 10:3 in the Sixto-Clementine Vulgate reads *For, lo, the wicked have bent their bow.*

23   Rom. 1:8: *First I give thanks to my God, through Jesus Christ, for you all, because your faith is spoken of in the whole world.* Rom. 16:4: *Who have for my life laid down their own necks: to whom not I only give thanks, but also all the churches of the Gentiles.*

24   Cf. Wis. 2:15: *He is grievous unto us, even to behold: for his life is not like other men's, and his ways are very different.*

25   Cf. Phil. 3:8b.

26   Cf. Matt. 19:29.

27   Cf. Wis. 5:4: *We fools esteemed their life madness, and their end without honor.*

28   1 Cor. 4:9b.

29   Phil. 3:8a.

30   Ez. 24:24a. E. N. The Douay-Rheims translates *portentum* as "sign of things to come," a portent or omen. *Portentum* shares the meaning of something extraordinary with four other words: *ostentum, prodigium, miraculum,* and *monstrum.* Marcus Terentius Varro (*fl.* 218–200 BC) says that *ostentum* is that which shows something to men; *portentum* is that which protects something future, *prodigium* is that which directs to something far off; *miraculum* is that which is a marvel; *monstrum* is that which warns or admonishes. Servius, *Ad Aen.* III 366. In his *Etymologies,* St. Isidore of Seville in general adopts this Varran distinction. *Etymologiarum sive originum*

Lord, have strongly assisted me and given great grace and fortitude so that even though the derision and persecutions of the wicked are not withdrawn by you, yet I have not ceased from good works, as — alas! — many are wont to do, since they abandon the life of perfection they had taken when they perceive themselves to be spurned, bothered, and disparaged by others. Against this the divine Apostle exhorts us: *Let us run by patience to the fight proposed to us, looking on Jesus, the author and finisher of faith, who having joy set before him, endured the cross, despising shame, . . . For think diligently upon him that endured such opposition from sinners against himself, that you be not wearied . . . in your minds.*[31] And again: *Let us go forth therefore to him without the camp, bearing his reproach.*[32]

70{71}[8]   *Let my mouth be filled with praise, that I may sing your glory; your greatness all the day long.*

Repleatur os meum laude, ut cantem gloriam tuam, tota die magnitudinem tuam.

Next, the just man desiring to give thanks to the Lord for such great benefits that have come upon him, prays. 70{71}[8] *Repleatur os meum laude, let my mouth be filled with praise:* that is, you, O Lord, enkindle and illumine the mind so that contemplating your goodness and benefits the mouth might be filled with divine praises. *For out of the abundance of the heart the mouth speaks.*[33] And unless you enkindle the mind with the divine heat, the mouth of the body is soon becomes weary in your praise, indeed even my spirit [becomes weary]. And so in an earlier Psalm is said: *Let my soul be filled as with marrow and fatness,*[34] namely, let my mouth praise with divine love and lips of exultation. Whence now there follows [verses that explain] why he seeks his mouth to be filled with praise: *ut cantem gloriam tuam, that I may sing your glory,* that is, so that I might proclaim your glorious renown, singing the news of your excellence, *tota die magnitudinem tuam, your greatness all the day long,* that is, always, as much as is possible in this life, I will sing of your majesty and your great dignity. This indeed is the most divine and most illustrious exercise in the present life: to take delight in, to occupy oneself joyfully

---

libri XX, XI, 3: 1–4 (Oxford: Oxford University Press, 1911). The word *portentum* is sometimes used figuratively to refer to an absurdity or a monster.

31   Heb. 12:1b–3.
32   Heb. 13:13.
33   Matt. 12:34b.
34   Ps. 62:6a.

in, and to remain most affectionately in the divine praises, saying with the most blessed Isaiah: *O Lord, you are my God, I will exalt you, and give glory to your name;*[35] and again, *Your name, and your remembrance are the desire of the soul.*[36] This is the true angelic and heaven-like life, the reward of divine glorification, as the Lord himself confirms: *Whosoever shall glorify me, him will I glorify.*[37]

70{71}[9] *Cast me not off in the time of old age: when my strength shall fail, do not forsake me.*

Ne proiicias me in tempore senectutis; cum defecerit virtus mea, ne derelinquas me.

70{71}[9] *Ne proiicias me in tempore senectutis, cast me not off in the time of old age.* In the way that we have just now ascribed youth to be twofold — spiritual and bodily — so likewise is old age: one bodily, when heat withdraws and bodily power begins to die; but another is old age of the soul, when the spiritual heat of love grows cold, when the soul is not renewed by an increase of grace, but grows old in its negligence and vices, or is oppressed by the irksomeness of persecution, or is less active in doing good. And these words — *cast me not off in the time of old age* — can be understood of both kinds of old age: that is, do not withdraw from me your grace when I grow old bodily or deficient in mind; but at such time more kindly come to my aid to the degree that you know me to be more in need of it. And so, as if expounding upon what was just said, there is added: *Cum defecerit virtutes mea,*[38] *when my strength shall fail,* [that is, when my] bodily or spiritual [strength shall fail]: which most usually occurs in the agony [of death], and in the time of great sickness; *ne derelinquas me, do not forsake me.* St. Thomas used to have a singular and special devotion to this verse, and it would reduce him to sweet tears and boundless weeping.[39] For this verse is marvelously full of affection, sweet, and effective, and it is salvific: and we have considered the manner that it is fittingly so.

---

35   Is. 25:1a.
36   Is. 26:8b.
37   1 Sam. 2:30. E. N. The verse continues: *but they that despise me, shall be despised.*
38   E. N. The Latin text has *deficiet;* however, the editor suggests *defecerit.*
39   E. N. St. Thomas "was frequently rapt in spirit whilst at Mass, when the tears would spring to his eyes, and flow copiously. This happened to him also at other times. During Compline, at the words, *Ne proiicias nos in tempore senectutis cum defecerit virtute mea,* he was frequently thus carried away." Roger Bede Vaughan, *The Life and Labours of St. Thomas of Aquin* (London: Longmans & Co., 1871), Vol. 1, 434.

70{71}[10] *For my enemies have spoken against me; and they that*
watched my soul have consulted together.

Quia dixerunt inimici mei mihi: et qui custodiebant animam
meam consilium fecerunt in unum.

70{71}[11] *Saying: God has forsaken him: pursue and take him, for*
there is none to deliver [him].

Dicentes: Deus dereliquit eum: persequimini et comprehendite
eum, quia non est qui eripiat.

With merit, O Lord, I ask these things from you, **70{71}[10]** *Quia*
dixerunt inimici mei mihi, for my enemies have spoken against me whatever
they were able so as to cause me to fall and to oppress me. For demons
offer honors, the world its riches, and the flesh its delights. *Et qui custo-*
diebant, and they that watched, that is, they that observed, *animam meam,*
my soul being deceived, *consilium fecerunt in unum, have consulted together,*
that is, they are unanimous in attaining the identical purpose and the
same end to perpetrate wrong; **70{71}[11]** *Dicentes: Deus dereliquit eum;*
Saying: God has forsaken him. Since I am to them a monster (*prodigium*),
they suppose my life not to be pleasing to the Lord, especially when they
see themselves prospering and becoming stronger in this world, but they
see me being harassed and overwhelmed by various calamities. For this is
the thought process of evil men, that when they see the just man afflicted
they praise themselves and are domineering. Whence Habakkuk says:
Because the wicked prevails against the just, therefore wrong judgment goes
forth.[40] And because they suppose me to be abandoned by God, they
think that they are doing a service to God by persecuting me;[41] and
exhorting themselves, they say: *Persequimini et comprehendite eum, pursue*
and take him, that is, do with him what you want, *quia non est qui eripiat,*
for there is none to deliver him from your hands: for he rejects human
help, and he places his trust in God. These insensitive and reprobate
men do not heed the fact that *as gold in the furnace,* so God proves the
elect;[42] and that it is fitting that *through many tribulations* we enter into
glory of God,[43] the way that we are instructed by holy Job: *For he that*
has been humbled, shall be in glory, . . . and the innocent shall be saved.[44]

---

40   Hab. 1:4b.
41   *Cf.* John 16:2b: *The hour comes, that whosoever kills you, will think that he does*
a service to God.
42   Wis. 3:6a.
43   Acts 14:21a.
44   Job. 22:29a, 30b.

70{71}[12] *O God, be not far from me: O my God, make haste to my help.*

Deus, ne elongeris a me; Deus meus, in auxilium meum respice.

70{71}[13] *Let them be confounded and come to nothing that detract my soul; let them be covered with confusion and shame that seek my hurt.*

Confundantur et deficiant detrahentes animae; operiantur confusione et pudore qui quaerunt mala mihi.

70{71}[12] *Deus, ne elongeris a me; O God, be not far from me*, delaying help, removing grace, or allowing it to be made less; but, O *Deus meus, O my God*, in whom I completely and fully trust, *in auxilium meum respice, make haste to my help*, graciously rendering aid to the degree that those with evil intent strive to overthrow me: in the manner that is written, *The Lord is good and gives strength in the day of trouble: and knows them that hope in him.*[45] 70{71}[13] *Confundantur, let them be confounded* regarding their sins, *et deficiant, and come to nothing* in the execution of their evil works, *detrahentes animae meae, that detract my soul*, desiring to blacken its good name — which mortal sin is, because a good name is much more precious and loveable, and better than all wealth, the way that is confessed by Solomon: *A good name is better than precious ointments;*[46] and Ecclesiasticus: *Take care of a good name: for this is more profitable to you than a thousand treasures.*[47] For this reason, detraction is a greater sin than theft.[48] *Operiantur confusio, let them be covered with the confusion* aforementioned, *et pudore, and shame*, which greatly works together in the confession of sin to the remission of fault and also to a degree [in the remission] of punishment, *qui quaerunt mala mihi, that seek my hurt* [that is, seek] to cause [me evil], and to lead me to sin or to afflict me in some similar unjust manner. Of this good sort of confusion we find written in Ezechiel: *Be confounded, and ashamed at your own ways*, says the Lord.[49] Now, in the explanation of the preceding Psalm how confusion, shame, and failure can be understood in different ways is discussed.[50]

---

45 Nahum 1:7.

46 Eccl. 7:2a.

47 Ecclus. 41:15. E. N. Denis departs from the Sixto-Clementine Vulgate. I have followed Denis.

48 E. N. For a greater discussion on this issue, see Volume 2, Article LXXXI (Psalm 40:14).

49 Ez. 36:32b.

50 Ps. 69:3–4.

70{71}[14]   *But I will always hope; and will add to all your praise.*

Ego autem semper sperabo, et adiiciam super omnem laudem
tuam.

70{71}[15]   *My mouth shall show forth your justice; your salvation all
the day long. Because I have not known learning.*

Os meum annuntiabit iustitiam tuam, tota die salutare tuum.
Quoniam non cognovi litteraturam.

70{71}[16]   *I will enter into the powers of the Lord: O Lord, I will be
mindful of your justice alone.*

Introibo in potentias Domini; Domine, memorabor iustitiae
tuae solius.

70{71}[14] *Ego autem semper sperabo,* but I will always hope, that is,
however many they are persecuting me with words and deed, hiddenly
or publicly, I will nevertheless incessantly have confidence in you: as
blessed Job confessed regarding himself: *Although he should kill me, I
will trust him.*[51] And Solomon: *Have confidence in the Lord with all your
heart;*[52] and, *Wait for the Lord and he will deliver you.*[53] *Et adiiciam
super omnem laudem tuam,* and I will add to all your praise: that is, I
will confess that all praise by which I am able to venerate you, or by
which you are praised by others, is beneath your dignity, and infinitely
lacking in the public praise of which you are worthy because of the
thoroughly immense fullness of your goodness. And so, to the degree
that it is possible for me, I will always try to praise you with new
hymns, to extol you with more perfect praise, and never to cease from
praising you. 70{71}[15] *Os meum annuntiabit, my mouth shall show
forth,* praising you with it, and preaching about you before all, *iustitiam
tuam, your justice,* by which you reward everyone with that which he
deserves, and which you effect without any respect of persons.[54] Therefore, I do justice to you, O Lord, I make myself good by your justice,
but I accuse myself and condemn myself. By the term justice of God,
one is also able to understand the precepts of divine justice and the
[evangelical] counsels that are contained in sacred Scripture. Whence
Wisdom states: *All my words are just, there is nothing wicked nor perverse*

51   Job. 13:15a.
52   Prov. 3:5a.
53   Prov. 20:22b.
54   E. N. That is, without any partiality. *Cf.* Acts 10:34: *And Peter opening his mouth,
said: In very deed I perceive, that God is not a respecter of persons.*

in them.[55] And so, to teach, preach, or read sacred Scripture is to announce the justice of God. My mouth will also show forth *tota die salutare tuum, your salvation all the day long,* that is, I will speak of you and I will praise you unceasingly, during all the appropriate hours of the day, O Lord Christ, the Savior of all men; or [alternatively, one can understand it in this way], *your salvation,* that is, the deliverance and salvation which you mercifully expended for us in Christ, and which you have prepared for us in heaven.

Quoniam non cognovit litteraturam, because I have not known learning. This can be explained in various ways. The first is in this way. *I have not known learning,* that is, I have not shown favor to empty philosophy and any knowledge that exalts itself *against the knowledge of God.*[56] It is not that philosophy is in itself hateful or to be avoided; but because we ought not to repose and glory it or inflate ourselves by it, but [rather we ought] to order [our lives] by the divine doctrine. Or [the second way is thus], *I have not known learning,* that is, I adjudge myself to know nothing when I set myself before the countenance of God and compare myself to his infinite knowledge. Or [the third way], *I have not known learning,* that is, any knowledge acquired by human exertion, formation, and study. This does not apply to all, but to Peter and John, of whom we read that *they were illiterate and ignorant men.*[57] This may also be fittingly said about holy David, who, we read, during his youth he shepherded sheep,[58] and did not frequent any schools, as some say; but this does not seem certain, for he composed the Psalms with poetic measure.

So because whether in this or that way, **70{71}[16]** *Introibo, I will enter* by supernatural contemplation, *in potentias Domini, in the powers of the Lord,* that is, in the perfections or the divine truths, and I will know and instruct others of them. The perfection of God is his power, and it is one and simple, indeed it is his essence; but we say powers, perfections, and virtues of God in a plural way because God in himself is the most simple,[59] yet he most eminently comprehends

---

55 Prov. 8:8.
56 2 Cor. 10:5a.
57 Acts 4:13.
58 1 Sam. 16:11; 17:15.
59 E. N. On the simplicity of God, the Dominican Pedro Lumbreras (1892–1970), commenting on the third of the "Twenty-Four Thomistic Theses" wrote: "[I]n the exclusive domain of existence itself, God alone subsists, He alone is the most simple. Everything else, which participates in existence, has a nature whereby existence is restricted, and is composed of essence and existence as of two really distinct

the perfections of all things. And these divine perfections, which are wisdom, justice, mercy, are the subject of contemplation, which does not trust in its own senses, nor lean on natural reason, but is illuminated by God. Whence Christ says in the Gospel: *I confess to you, O Father, . . . because you have hid these things from the wise and prudent, and have revealed them to the little ones.*[60] What else can *from the wise and prudent* mean except from the learned? And was not Paul, who was taught the law at the feet of Gamaliel learned?[61] What, then, does it mean that you have hidden these things from the wise, the prudent, and the learned but [that you have hidden these things] from those who vainly glory in their own wisdom and learning, judging themselves wise and learned? Such men, because of their pride, are not capable of being divinely illuminated, nor will they unless they convert and become as little children.[62] And so says the most wise Paul: *If any man among you seem to be wise in this world, let him become a fool, that he may be wise.*[63] Or [we can understand the verse] thus: *I will enter into the powers of the Lord*, that is, I will receive strong illuminations of God and great graces, by placing no hope in my own capabilities, but humbly devoting myself to God, and in this way I will contemplate and will know how powerful and glorious is my God. And then, *O Domine, memorabor iustitiae tuae solius, I will be mindful of your justice alone*, that is, I will exclusively be mindful of your justice, and I will not allege any of my justice, but I will ascribe all good, virtue, and grace to you, and I will attribute all evil, all defects, and all fault to myself, and I will say with the Apostle: *By the grace of God, I am what I am;*[64] and again, *If any man think himself to be something, whereas he is nothing, he deceives himself;*[65] and again, *They*, he says, *not knowing the justice of God, and seeking to establish their own, have not submitted themselves to the justice of God.*[66]

---

principles. If there is any being, the actuality of whose existence — for existent means actual — is not received into the potentiality of essence, such a being subsists of itself, because it is perfection without limits; it is unique, because it excludes composition of any kind; it is the most simple Being: God." *See* http://www.u.arizona.edu/~aversa/scholastic/24Thomisticpart2.htm.

60   Matt. 11:25.
61   Acts 22:3.
62   *Cf.* Matt. 18:3a.
63   1 Cor. 3:18.
64   1 Cor. 15:10a.
65   Gal. 6:3.
66   Rom. 10:3.

70{71}[17] *You have taught me, O God, from my youth: and till now I will declare your wonderful works.*

Deus, docuisti me a iuventute mea; et usque nunc pronuntiabo mirabilia tua.

70{71}[18] *And unto old age and grey hairs: O God, forsake me not, Until I show forth your arm to all the generation that is to come: your power,*

Et usque in senectam et senium, Deus, ne derelinquas me, donec annuntiem brachium tuum generationi omni quae ventura est, potentiam tuam,

70{71}[19] *And your justice, O God, even to the highest great things you have done: O God, who is like you?*

Et iustitiam tuam, Deus, usque in altissima; quae fecisti magnalia, Deus: quis similis tibi?

And as if one asked, "If, O servant of God, you do not know learning, how is it that you came to know and write such lovely lessons and sublime notions?" He answers, speaking to the Lord: 70{71}[17] *Deus, docuisti me; you have taught me, O God* by the inspirations of the Holy Spirit and by supernatural illumination, *a iuventute mea, from my youth* either bodily or spiritual, either way of [understanding it] seems satisfactory; *et usque nunc, and till now,* preserving, increasing, or perfecting your grace in me. *Pronuntiabo mirabilia tua, I will declare your wonderful works,* which you do in heaven and on earth, in the works of nature and the mysteries of grace: most of all I will declare your Incarnation, Passion, and Death, O Christ. 70{71}[18] *Et usque in senectam, and unto spiritual old age, et senium, and bodily gray hairs,* to which distinction is assigned,[67] I will declare your wonderful works. *Deus, ne derelinquas me, donec annuntiem brachium tuum; O God, forsake me not, until I show forth your arm to all generation that is to come,* that is, the majesty of your power. Or [we can understand it thus], *your arm,* that is, your only-begotten Son, who is your strength and power: of whom Isaiah said: *The Lord has prepared his holy arm in the sight of all the Gentiles.*[68] And just as the Holy Spirit is called the finger of God by reason of his effects,[69] because he reveals all things; so the Son,

---

67   E. N. Denis appears to be suggesting that the assignment of spiritual old age to the word *senectus,* and bodily old age to the word *senium* is an assigned or arbitrary distinction.

68   Is. 52:10a.

69   Cf. Luke 11:20: *But if I by the finger of God cast out devils; doubtless the kingdom*

who carries and sustains all things by *the word of his power,*[70] is called the arm of God. And so I will declare, O Lord, your arm *generationi omni quae ventura est, to all the generation that is to come* even unto the end of the world. And this the author of this current Psalm most excellently accomplishes. For by the book of Psalms, which he wrote and left us, he announces this unceasingly to the entire world: any of us who does this, to the extent possible in him, glorifies the name of God, and endeavors to increase his honor; and so after his death, the testimony of the divine law is scattered, by word, reputation, and life to be true, giving witness that affirms the Catholic faith.

I will also make known, O Lord, *potentiam tuam, your power,* which truly is immense, by which you created, preserve, and rule all things, 70{71}[19] *Et iustitiam tuam, Deus; and your justice, O God,* by which you reward every man with that which he deserves: power, I say, and your justice I will make known, not as it is in itself, because such is entirely unknown, but by comparison to its sublime effects namely, *usque in altissima, quae fecisti, magnalia; even to the highest great things you have done.* But what are these highest great things produced by God? Nothing other than the distinction of the angelic orders, the creation both visible and invisible, the justification of the ungodly, the mystery of human redemption, and all of the other prodigies, signs, and miracles of God. The justice and the marvelous power of the Creator shines forth in these effects. Since these marvels of God are so many, *O Deus, quis similis tibi; O God, who is like you?* It is as if he were saying, "No one."[71] But likeness exists in two ways, imitative or imperfect, and natural or perfect. The creature has a likeness to God according to the first way, especially man, who is made in the image and likeness of God;[72] but no creature is similar to the Creator in the second way. Whence it is said by the prophet Isaiah: *To whom then have you likened*

---

of God is come upon you. E. N. The Catechism of the Catholic Church speaks of the symbols of the Holy Spirit, and with respect to this symbol it says: "'It is by the finger of God that [Jesus] cast out demons.' If God's law was written on tablets of stone 'by the finger of God,' then the 'letter from Christ' entrusted to the care of the apostles, is written 'with the Spirit of the living God, not on tablets of stone, but on tablets of human hearts.' The hymn *Veni Creator Spiritus* invokes the Holy Spirit as the 'finger of the Father's right hand.'" CCC § 700 (quoting Luke 11:20 and Ex. 31:18 and 2 Cor. 3:3).

70   Heb. 1:3a.

71   *E. N.* A negative rhetorical question.

72   *Cf.* Gen. 1:27.

God? Or what image will you make for him?[73] And Job: *God is high in his strength, and none is like him among the lawgivers.*[74]

70{71}[20]   *How great troubles have you shown me, many and grievous: and turning you have brought me to life, and have brought me back again from the depths of the earth:*

Quantas ostendisti mihi tribulationes multas et malas! Et conversus vivificasti me, et de abyssis terrae iterum reduxisti me.

70{71}[21]   *You have multiplied your magnificence; and turning to me you have comforted me.*

Multiplicasti magnificentiam tuam; et conversus consolatus es me.

70{71}[20] *Quantas, how great, O God, tribulationes, troubles* of the world, the flesh, and the devil, *ostendisti mihi, have you shown me* by experience, *multas, many* in number, *et malas, and grievous* evils of punishment, bitter and hard, or occasioned by the determined unjust or evil intention of others! *Et conversus, and turning,* that is, being placated and taking pity on me, *vivificasti me, you have brought me to life,* the life of grace, removing from me the scourge of your anger, *iterum, again,* that is, frequently; *et de abyssis terrae, and from the depths of the earth,* that is, from being submerged in sin, and the floodwaters of the world, *reduxisti me, you have brought me back* to the state of salvation and of grace. 70{71}[21] *Multiplicasti magnificentiam tuam, you have multiplied your magnificence,* that is, you have bestowed upon me in many ways your great power, scourging me in various ways; *et conversus, and turning,* from the anger of your vengeance to the gentleness of your paternal love without you suffering alteration,[75] *consolatus es me, you have comforted me* with the infusion of interior joy, the contemplation of future felicity, or the consideration of recompense, and with the consoling words of sacred

---

73   Is. 40:18.

74   Job 36:22.

75   E. N. "God is said in turn or to repent; not in the sense that His eternal disposition has changed, but that some effect of His is changed.... Now, such a change of judgment is called God's repentance, using a metaphorical way of speaking, in the sense that God is disposed like one who repents, for whom it is proper to change what he had been doing. In the same way, He is also said, metaphorically, to become angry, in the same sense that, by punishing, He produces the same effect of an angry person." St. Thomas Aquinas, *Summa contra gentiles,* lib. 3 cap. 95, n. 21. (Notre Dame, IN: University of Notre Dame Press, 1975) (trans., Vernon J. Bourke).

Scripture, wherein it is said: *The sufferings of this time are not worthy to be compared with the glory to come, that shall be revealed in us;*[76] and, *If we suffer with him,*[77] *we shall also reign with him.*[78]

70{71}[22]   *For I will also confess to you your truth with the instruments of psaltery: O God, I will sing to you with the harp, you holy one of Israel.*

Nam et ego confitebor tibi in vasis psalmi veritatem tuam, Deus; psallam tibi in cithara, sanctus Israel.

70{71}[22]   Now the sign of my consolation is: *Nam et ego confitebor tibi, for I will also confess to you* with the confession of praise, *in vasis psalmi, with the instruments of psaltery,* that is, in the Psalms, which are vessels containing divine praises in them; or [alternatively], *with the instruments of psaltery,* that is, in devout men in whose hearts praise is contained as if in a vessel; or [understood yet another way], *with the instruments of psaltery,* that is, with the stringed psaltery, which is called the vessel of Psalms; *veritatem tuam, Deus; your truth, O God,* that is, I will confess or praise your truth handed down in the divine Scriptures, or your uncreated truth, which is fountainhead of all truth. *Psallam tibi in cithara, I will sing to you with the harp,* a spiritual [harp], namely, in the mortification of the flesh which is signified by a harp,[79] O Lord, which is *Sanctus Israel, the holy one of Israel,* that is, the Sanctifier of the people contemplating you faithfully.

70{71}[23]   *My lips shall greatly rejoice, when I shall sing to you; and my soul which you have redeemed.*

Exsultabunt labia mea cum cantavero tibi; et anima mea quam redemisti.

70{71}[24]   *Yea and my tongue shall meditate on your justice all the day; when they shall be confounded and put to shame that seek evils to me.*

---

76   Rom. 8:18.

77   Rom. 8:17b.

78   2 Tim. 2:12a.

79   E. N. Observing the harp has its hollow sound box below and the psalter its hollow sound box above, St. Augustine, in interpreting this verse, says: "And because the spirit is of above, and the flesh of the earth, it seems that the spirit is indicated by the psaltery, and the flesh by the harp." *Enarr. in Ps.,* Psalm 70, PL 36, 899.

Sed et lingua mea tota die meditabitur iustitiam tuam, cum
confusi et reveriti fuerint qui quaerunt mala mihi.

70{71}[23] *Exsultabunt labia mea,* my lips shall greatly rejoice, [that
is, my] *exterior* [lips shall rejoice], that is, they will manifest the signs
of joy, *cum cantavero tibi, when I shall sing to you*: because I will have
a joyful visage *in the sight of the sanctuary*,[80] when I will praise you by
mouth. Or [we might see it in this manner]: *My lips shall greatly rejoice,*
that is, they will have joy exuberantly, *when I shall sing to you*, that is,
when to your honor [I sing] with my interior lips, namely, my intellect
and will, which form interior words and wishes. *Et anima mea quam
redemisti, and my soul which you have redeemed* by your grace from fault,
and by the price of your Blood from Hell, will exult you by singing.
70{71}[24] *Sed et lingua mea, yea and my tongue,* [my] interior [tongue],
namely, the intellect, *tota die, all the day*, that is, at the appropriate
hours and due hours, *meditabitur iustitiam tuam, shall mediate on your
justice*, considering with it your most just law. Or [alternatively], *I shall
meditate on your justice* with my bodily tongue, that is, I will speak from
the interior thoughts. *Cum confusi, when they shall be confounded*, that is,
they will be repelled, overcome, *et reverti, and put to shame*, that is, they
will be terrified, *fuerint qui quaerunt mala mihi, that seek evils to me*, that
is, demons desiring to harm me, or evil men, at whose confusion and
repelling good men, who are loving of a tranquil life, will rejoice. But
because in this life we are unable to be fully delivered and completely
and continually to be secure of their attacks, therefore this verse can
be anagogically explained as referring to the future in the state in the
heavenly homeland. For then our interior tongue and at some point
also our exterior one, for the entire day of eternity, that is, continually
and indefatigably, will mediate upon the justice of God by a most clear
contemplation, *when they [that seek evils against me] shall be confounded
and put to shame*, for in the day of judgment all the iniquitous will be
irreparably confounded, in the manner stated in Isaiah: *The Lord shall
cast death down headlong forever, . . . and the reproach of his people he shall
take away.*[81] Whence also the Lord will say to the elect: *Fear not, for
I am with you . . . behold, all that fight against you shall be confounded.*[82]

---

80 Judith 16:24a.
81 Is. 25:8.
82 Is. 41:10a, 11a.

ARTICLE XXXVIII

ALLEGORICAL EXPLANATION OF THE SAME SEVENTIETH PSALM OF CHRIST.

70{71}[1]   . . . *In you, O Lord, I have hoped, let me never be put to confusion.*

. . . *In te, Domine, speravi; non confundar in aeternum.*

70{71}[2]   *Deliver me in your justice, and rescue me. Incline your ear unto me, and save me.*

In iustitia tua libera me, et eripe me: inclina ad me aurem tuam, et salva me.

ECAUSE THIS GLORIOUS AND DECOROUS Psalm in its beginning conforms both by words and in meaning to the thirtieth Psalm, which begins as does this one; and, because as it progresses it is similar to some of the twenty-first Psalm, which begins with the words, O God, my God, look upon me: and because both of them are explained literally of Christ, so one should strive, to the extent one is able, to explain this present Psalm of the Lord Savior. Therefore, Christ, as a passible man,[83] existing in a certain manner as a wayfarer, with the Passion approaching, prayed to the Father saying 70{71}[1] *In te, Domine; in you, O Lord* Father, *speravi, I have hoped,* that is, I have received from you all the good that I have desired and that I requested from you, not by the hope that is the theological virtue, but by a certain kind of trust. For the hope that is a theological virtue is the expectation of future beatitude. Since the soul of Christ from the beginning of its creation was blessed [with the beatific vision of God], seeing God by sight, it follows that he did not have that kind of hope; nevertheless, he had a certain kind of expectation or trust, of which is written in Proverbs, *The expectation of him that expects, is a most acceptable jewel.*[84] For the soul of Christ hoped in the glorification of the body from God and had expectancies of other accidental rewards. Because I

---

83   *E. N.* "Although human nature was united to the divine person [in our Lord], he felt the bitterness of his passion as acutely as if no such union had existed; because in the one person of Jesus Christ were preserve the properties of both natures, human and divine; and, therefore, what was passible and mortal remained passible and mortal; and again, what was impassible and immortal, that is his divine nature, continued impassible and immortal." *Catechism of the Council of Trent* (New York: Catholic Publication Society, 1829), 43. (trans. J. Donovan).

84   Prov. 17:8a.

have hoped in you, O Lord, *non confundar in aeternum, let me never be put to confusion*: that is, while I am despised and mocked now by the Jews, and also by Herod and Pilate and their soldiers,[85] yet you will not let this confusion last long, but on the third day I will be honored by you through the blessed Resurrection. 70{71}[2] *In iustitia tua, in your justice*, that is, according to your justice, and according to its demands, *libera me, deliver me* from this unfaithful and evil generation, of which is written: *How long shall I be with you? How long shall I suffer you?*[86] *Et eripe me, and rescue me* from all bodily mortality and passibility.

Inclina a me, incline . . . unto me your only and beloved Son, *aurem tuam, your ear*: I pray this, not as if uncertain as to what you will do, but because you have decreed to give me what I ask through prayer, so that I make it manifest that all the good that I have I have from you, and that I might exhibit to others the form of prayer. *Et salve me, and save me*, giving also the accidental rewards, namely, bodily glorification and ascension.

———

70{71}[3]   *Be unto me a God, a protector, and a place of strength: that you may make me safe. For you are my firmament and my refuge.*

Esto mihi in Deum protectorem, et in locum munitum, ut salvum me facias: quoniam firmamentum meum et refugium meum es tu.

70{71}[3] *Esto mihi in Deum protectorem, be unto me a God, a protector*, lest before the time that was preordained by you, I be apprehended, struck down, and wounded by the Jews who tried to throw me off a cliff and stone me, but were unable because my time had not yet come.[87] Be also to me *in locum munitum, a place of strength*, that is, my helper insofar as I am man, and from whom I seek refuge in all my necessities. For this the Savior says about himself: *I cannot of myself do anything;*[88] and again, *The Father who abides in me, he does all the works.*[89] Isaiah also: *Behold the Lord God is my helper;*[90] and Jeremiah: *The Lord is with me as a strong warrior; therefore, they that persecute me shall fall.*[91]

---

85   Matt. 26:67–68; Luke 23:11.
86   Mark 9:18.
87   Luke 4:29; John 8:59; 10:31; Luke 4:30; John 10:39; 8:20.
88   John 5:30a.
89   John 14:10b.
90   Is. 50:9a.
91   Jer. 20:11a.

70{71}[4] *Deliver me, O my God, out of the hand of the sinner, and out of the hand of the transgressor of the law and of the unjust.*

Deus meus, eripe me de manu peccatoris, et de manu contra legem agentis, et iniqui.

70{71}[5] *For you are my patience, O Lord: my hope, O Lord, from my youth.*

Quoniam tu es patientia mea, Domine; Domine, spes mea a iuventute mea.

70{71}[4] *Deus meus, O my God,* who are in a most special sense my God, *eripe me de manu peccatoris, deliver me . . . out of the hand of the sinner,* that is, from the power of Judas the betrayer, whose iniquity the heavens reveal, and *the earth shall rise up against him;*[92] *et de manu contra legem agentis et iniqui, and out of the hand of the transgressor of the law and of the unjust,* that is the Jewish people, of whom I said, *Did Moses not give you the law, and yet none of you keep the law?*[93] And again, *Why do you also transgress the commandment of God for your tradition?*[94] 70{71}[5] *Quoniam tu es patientia mea, Domine; for your are my patience, O Lord.* For all perfection of the soul of Christ was infused and bestowed by God. Christ also underwent all things for the honor of God, as it says in a Psalm above, *Because for your sake I have borne reproach:*[95] and so God was the efficient and final cause of the patience of Christ. *Domine, spes mea a iuventute mea; my hope, O Lord, from my youth.* For Christ always most certainly and unwaveringly hoped in God by the previously mentioned trust. For this reason, he said: *And I knew that you hear me always.*[96]

70{71}[6] *By you have I been confirmed from the womb: from my mother's womb you are my protector. Of you shall I continually sing.*

In te confirmatus sum ex utero; de ventre matris meae tu es protector meus; in te cantatio mea semper.

70{71}[7] *I am become unto many as a wonder, but you are a strong helper.*

Tamquam prodigium factus sum multis; et tu adiutor fortis.

70{71}[6] *In te confirmatus sum ex utero, by you I have been confirmed from the womb:* that is, in the virginal womb of my Mother, consummated

---

92   Job 20:27.
93   John 7:19.
94   Matt. 15:3a.
95   Ps. 68:8a.
96   John 11:42a.

by grace, that is, by the beatific enjoyment, I was immovable and strengthened by you, so that it was not possible ever to be diverted from you. For
not only was the soul of Christ in the womb of the Virgin sanctified by
grace, but also it was made immovable by glory. *De ventre matris meae
tu es protector meus; from my mother's womb you are my protector*: that
is, from the instant of my conception even unto my death you protected
me from the ruin of any sin, from the temptation of the devil, and from
the punishments that the Jews desired to inflict against me before the
allotted time. For Christ was confirmed in good in the womb of the Virgin, and after his birth he was by no means able to sin. This he foretold
of himself through Isaiah: *Who is my adversary? Let him come near to
me. Who will contend with me? Let us stand together.*[97] See how much
freedom from concern [Jesus possessed] because of the divine protection:
for which reason, in no way can one have the opinion that Christ was
terrified when they lead him to the ridge of the cliff in order that they
might cast him down headlong.[98] *In te cantatio mea semper, of you shall
I continually sing*: that is, you, God the Father, I always praised, I always
sought the honor of your name, and not my own glory, as I stated to
the blaspheming Jews: *I do not see my own glory, but I honor my Father,
and you have dishonored me.*[99] 70{71}[7] *Tanquam prodigium factus sum
multis, I am become unto many as a wonder,*[100] namely, by the Jews, of
whom it is written: *Many of them said: he has a devil, and is mad: why
do you hear him?*[101] And when he said regarding the daughter of the
ruler of the synagogue, *The maid is not dead, but sleeps,* they derided
him.[102] Whence in Isaiah it is foretold of Christ: *So shall his visage be
inglorious among men.*[103] *Et tu adiutor fortis, but you are a strong helper,*
because you made me constant and immoveable in all adversity.

70{71}[8] *Let my mouth be filled with praise, that I may sing your glory;
your greatness all the day long.*

*Repleatur os meum laude, ut cantem gloriam tuam, tota die
magnitudinem tuam.*

---

97   Is. 50:8. E. N. Denis changes the order of the phrases in the verse.
98   Luke 4:29
99   John 8:50a, 49b.
100   E. N. As explained in footnote 70-30 above, the word *portentum* can be wonder
or portent, but also something highly unusual, monstruous, *i.e.*, a monster.
101   John 10:20.
102   Luke 8:52–53.
103   Is. 52:14a.

70{71}[8] *Repleatur os meum laude, let my mouth be filled with praise.* In no manner did Christ increase in habitual grace; nor did he pray that it be increased. Whence, in the manner that the Saints in the heavenly homeland do not pray for the benefits of grace,[104] so neither did Christ request an increase of interior grace, so that he might break forth into the praise of God. And so when it says, *Let my mouth be filled with praise*, it seems that such can be understood as rejoicing in that which is so, rather than praying that it be so.[105] Or he prays that the soul, separated from his body at death, might be united with it anew, and so his bodily mouth closed for three days by death will be opened by the Resurrection, and it might be filled with the divine praises. *Ut cantem, that I may sing*, he says, *gloriam tuam, your glory*. For Christ, inasmuch as he was a comprehensor, with his interior mouth continually sang the glory of the entire Trinity, praising it forever and ever much more sublimely than any of the blessed in the heavenly homeland: and *tota die, all the day long*, that is, incessantly, and participating in the eternal day, which is the measure of his interior operations suitable to him as a comprehensor, he sang with an interior melody *magnitudinem, the greatness* of God, knowing him most clearly, and extolling him most worthily. And so before the Passion or after the Resurrection he sang with his bodily mouth the glory of God, namely, the doctrine of the evangelical law, in which he praised God beautifully; and all the day long, that is, always at appropriate times, he sang or preached the greatness of God either by himself or through his ministers.

---

104   E. N. "The termination of earthly life and the separation of the soul from the body also ends for us the time of meriting. For this reason, it also ends the time in which we can acquire a greater intensity of love. We know that our meritorious acts bring us an increase of sanctifying grace, and that at an equal pace with the increase of sanctifying grace, we acquire an increase of the theological virtues, especially the intensification of charity. When the capacity for meriting ceases, the capacity for acquiring a further increase of charity also terminates." Fr. Gabriel of St. Mary Magdalen, *Union with God According to St. John of the Cross* (Manchester, NH: Sophia Press, 2019), 164. "The deeper the power of divine love received in this life, that is, the deeper the *viator's* charity, the greater the *viator's* capacity for beatitude." Reinhard Hütter, *Bound for Beatitude: A Thomistic Study in Eschatology and Ethics* (Washington, DC: CUA Press, 2019), 46. Since the capacity for beatitude is fixed at the time of death, the blessed in heaven do not pray for its increase.

105   E. N. Being full of grace, Christ could not merit or increase in grace; accordingly, he could not possibly be praying (in praying this Psalm) that he might receive an increase of sanctifying grace or actual grace to praise when he said "Let my mouth be filled . . ."; rather, he was recognizing that he already had such grace.

70{71}[9] *Cast me not off in the time of old age: when my strength shall fail, do not forsake me.*

Ne proiicias me in tempore senectutis; cum defecerit virtus mea, ne derelinquas me.

70{71}[9] *Ne proiicias me in tempore senectutis, etc.; cast me not off in the time of old age, etc.* Some could say Christ prayed this verse not for himself, but for his Mystical Body, in the way that he did when he was already in an impassible state and he said to Paul: *Why do you persecute me?*[106] Especially since Christ was not acquainted with bodily or spiritual old age: for he was put to death in youth, and in his interior he lived always equally fresh and vigorous: for which reason he compared himself to green wood.[107] Nevertheless, we can say that in this place by stating *the time of old age,* we can understood the time of the Lord's Passion, in which the bodily nature of Christ, was, as it were, of an old man, falling into death in his greenness and vigor. And so, in explaining this verse with reference to Christ, it would be in this sense: *Ne proiicias me in tempore senectutis, cast me not off in the time of old age,* that is, in the time of the Passion do not take from me the present of your paternal kindness, abandoning my body in the tomb, or my soul in limbo. For Christ did not pray that he not be abandoned by God in the sense of losing grace and or glory, because he knew that he was confirmed in the good. *Cum deficiet virtus mea, when my strength shall fail* [that is, when my] bodily [strength shall fail] on the Cross; when he breathed out, bowed his head, giving up the spirit;[108] *ne derelinquas me, do not forsake me,* but hear that which I say: *Father, in your hands I commit my spirit.*[109]

70{71}[10] *For my enemies have spoken against me; and they that watched my soul have consulted together.*

Quia dixerunt inimici mei mihi: et qui custodiebant animam meam consilium fecerunt in unum.

70{71}[11] *Saying: God has forsaken him: pursue and take him, for there is none to deliver [him].*

Dicentes: Deus dereliquit eum: persequimini et comprehendite eum, quia non est qui eripiat.

---

106 Acts 9:4b.
107 Luke 23:31: *For if in the green wood they do these things, what shall be done in the dry?* E. N. Meaning if they did this to one as fully-graced as I am, what will occur to those less fresh and vigorous in grace?
108 John 19:30.
109 Luke 23:46.

With merit, O Lord, I ask these things from you, O Father, 70{71} [**10**] *quia dixerunt inimici mihi, for my enemies have spoken against me,* [that is,] the Jews, [have spoken against me] evil things they were able to come up with, that is, this: *Will he kill himself?*[110] And elsewhere, *A man that is a glutton, and a wine drinker;*[111] *He blasphemes;*[112] and many other such things. *Et qui custodiebat animam meam, and they that watched my soul,* that is, the Jews, who observed my life so that they might denounce it, in the way that is written in the Gospel, *And they watched Jesus whether he would heal on the sabbath days, that they might accuse him;*[113] *consilium fecerunt in unum, have consulted together,* that is, mutually and with equal malice, according to this: *And they consulted together, that by subtilty they might apprehend Jesus, and put him to death;*[114] 70{71} [**11**] *dicentes: Deus dereliquit eum; saying: God has forsaken him.* For the Jews were of the opinion that God had withdrawn from Jesus as he would from a sinner. Whence they said: *We know that this man is a sinner;*[115] and elsewhere, *This man is not of God, who keeps not the sabbath.*[116] *Persequimini et comprehendite eum, pursue and take him.* This is what is said by John: *The rulers and Pharisees sent ministers to apprehend Jesus.*[117] And in the night of the Last Supper the chiefs of the priests said these words to their ministers whom they sent with Judas so that they might capture him. For this read it is said by Jeremiah: *For I heard the reproaches of many, and terror on every side: Persecute him, and let us persecute him.*[118] *Quia non est qui eripiat, for there is none to deliver* him, that is, there is none who by their hands rescue Jesus, because [the Jews thought] God abandoned him. For this is what the adversaries of Christ said: *Let us examine him by outrages and tortures, . . . that we might try* what will happen to him. For this reason, Isaiah said: *We have thought of him as a leper, and as one struck by God and afflicted.*[119]

70{71}[**12**] *O God, be not far from me: O my God, make haste to my help.*

        Deus, ne elongeris a me; Deus meus, in auxilium meum respice.

---

110 John 8:22a.
111 Matt. 11:19a.
112 Mark 2:7a.
113 Mark 3:2.
114 Matt. 26:4.
115 John 9:24b.
116 John 9:16a.
117 John 7:32b.
118 Jer. 20:10a.
119 Is. 53:4.

70{71}[13] *Let them be confounded and come to nothing that detract my soul;
let them be covered with confusion and shame that seek my hurt.*

*Confundantur et deficiant detrahentes animae; operiantur confu-
sione et pudore qui quaerunt mala mihi.*

70{71}[12] *Deus, O God,* Father, *ne elongeris a me, be not far from
me,* delaying my resurrection beyond three days. *Deus meus, in auxilium meum respice; O my God, make haste to my help,* with your divine
power cooperating with my humanity in the redemption of the human
race, and delivering me from the hands of the Jews by the Resurrection to an impassible state. This is what Christ prayed for before the
Passion as it is described by John: *Now is my soul troubled. And what
shall I say? Father, save me from this hour.*[120] **70{71}[13]** *Confundantur
et deficiant detrahentes animae meae, let them be confounded and come
to nothing that detract my soul.* In many ways were the Jews that were
persecuting and killing the Lord Savior confounded and abandoned.
Were they not confounded when the sun became darkened, the earth
shook, and the veil in the temple rent in two?[121] So also when in
the day of the Resurrection the soldiers who were by the sepulcher
recounted to them what they had encountered, and in what manner
he had risen again;[122] when moreover they heard the prince of the
Apostles, the most blessed Peter say, *Jesus of Nazareth, a man approved
of God among you, by miracles, and wonders, and signs, which God did by
him, in the midst of you, . . . you have slain;*[123] when also by the hands
of the Apostles he performed great signs in Jerusalem,[124] and many
thousands converted to Christ.[125] But most confounded and utterly
abandoned were they in the siege of Titus and the Romans.[126] *Operiantur confusione et pudore, let them be covered with confusion,* that is, let
them be confounded and ashamed on all sides, inwardly with respect
to themselves, and outwardly with respect to others; *qui quaerunt mala
mihi, that seek my hurt,* that is, the Jews, who placed upon me the
evil of fault, and afflicted me with the evil of punishment. Whence
Christ said through Jeremiah: *Let them be confounded that persecute*

---

120 John 12:27a.
121 Matt. 27:45, 51.
122 Matt. 28:11.
123 Acts 2:22–23.
124 Acts 2:43.
125 Acts 2:41; 4:4.
126 E. N. A reference to the siege of Jerusalem by Titus, resulting in the destruction
of the city of Jerusalem, and great suffering by the inhabitants of the city.

me, and let not me be confounded: let them be afraid, and let not me be afraid:... and with a double destruction, namely, in the present and in the future, *destroy them*.[127] Now this was said by Christ as a foretelling rather than as calling down a curse. There are also many other ways that it can be explained, namely, by means of prayer, for good, and that the foregoing becomes known.

70{71}[14]   But I will always hope; and will add to all your praise.

Ego autem semper sperabo, et adiiciam super omnem laudem tuam.

70{71}[15]   My mouth shall show forth your justice; your salvation all the day long. Because I have not known learning.

Os meum annuntiabit iustitiam tuam, tota die salutare tuum. Quoniam non cognovi litteraturam.

70{71}[16]   I will enter into the powers of the Lord: O Lord, I will be mindful of your justice alone.

Introibo in potentias Domini; Domine, memorabor iustitiae tuae solius.

70{71}[14] *Ego autem semper sperabo*, but I will always hope. For whatever the Jews said or did to Christ, he remained steadfastly hoping in God, and with certitude expecting to be resurrected by him, to be glorified in body, and to be raised above the highest heavens. *Et adiiciam super omnem laudem tuam*, and I will add to all your praise, that is, all the praise by which in the Law and the Prophets you are praised, I will add the proclamation of the evangelical law, and the Scriptures of the New Testament: in which there is contained many more sublime divine praises than in the teachings of the Old Law. 70{71}[15] *Os meum annuntiabit iustitiam tuam*, my mouth shall show forth your justice. During the time that Christ preached in the world, he announced the justice of God, teaching that God is just, that he does not leave sin unavenged, warning even sinners, and establishing upright precepts and most saving counsels. For this reason he himself said: *I am the light of the world*;[128] and *As the Father has taught me, these things I speak*.[129] Whence regarding this we have in Joel: *Be joyful in the Lord your God:*

---

127   Jer. 17:18.
128   John 8:12a.
129   John 8:28b.

because he has given you a teacher of justice.[130] And he says through Hosea: *The time to seek the Lord is, when he shall come that shall teach you justice.*[131] I also shall show forth your justice with my mouth, O God the Father, *tota die, all the day long,* that is, so long as I am in the world, *salutare tuum, your salvation,* that is, the saving plan which you have proposed to the world through me. Now fittingly the time that Christ lived in the world is called the day, because the Sun of justice shone and appeared according that which he stated: *So long as I am in the world, I am the light of the world.*[132] And this whole day Christ announced by word and deed the salvation of God, that is, himself or the salvation by which he saved the word. And so he said in the Gospel: *I must work the works of him that sent me, while it is day.*[133] John the Baptist announced the salvation of God in this way, saying: *He that believes in the Son, has life everlasting; but he that believes not the Son, shall not see life; but the wrath of God abides on him;*[134] and [Christ stated it in this way], *I am the way, the truth, and the life; no one comes to the Father but by me;*[135] and in another place, *He that believes and is baptized shall be saved.*[136]

Quoniam non cognovit litteraturam, because I have not known learning, that is, knowledge through exertion and study or human explanation, according to this, *And the Jews wondered, saying: How does this man know letters, having never learned?*[137] Because, therefore, I did not know learning through study, but by divine illumination, so *introibo, I will enter* by perfect contemplation or fruitive and blessed vision, *in potentias Domini, into the powers of the Lord,* knowing the perfections and powers of the divine nature and his great works. For the soul of Christ from the beginning of its creation saw by sight the divine essence and its powerful perfections in no other way but through supernatural illumination.[138] *Domine, memorabor iustitiae tuae solius; O Lord, I will*

---

130 Joel 2:23b.
131 Hosea 10:12b.
132 John 9:5.
133 John 9:4a.
134 John 3:36. E. N. The Latin text erroneously has Christ, rather than John the Baptist, as the editor notes in the margin.
135 John 14:6.
136 Mark 16:16a.
137 John 7:15.
138 E. N. Christ, in his human soul, had the beatific vision (supernatural ineffable knowledge) and infused knowledge (supernatural effable knowledge); thus he had no necessity for experiential knowledge (natural effable knowledge), though he in fact experienced the latter.

be mindful of your justice alone: that is, as man, I will ascribe no good to myself as coming from me, but I will attribute all the justice of my manner of living to you, and I will teach others to do the same. This is what Christ asserted: *If I glorify myself, my glory is nothing;*[139] and, *I receive glory not from men;*[140] and: *When you shall have done all these things that are commanded you, say: We are unprofitable servants; we have done that which we ought to do.*[141]

70{71}[17]   *You have taught me, O God, from my youth: and till now I will declare your wonderful works.*

Deus, docuisti me a iuventute mea; et usque nunc pronuntiabo mirabilia tua.

70{71}[18]   *And unto old age and grey hairs: O God, forsake me not, Until I show forth your arm to all the generation that is to come: Your power,*

Et usque in senectam et senium, Deus, ne derelinquas me, donec annuntiem brachium tuum generationi omni quae ventura est, potentiam tuam,

70{71}[19]   *And your justice, O God, even to the highest great things you have done: O God, who is like you?*

Et iustitiam tuam, Deus, usque in altissima; quae fecisti magnalia, Deus: quis similis tibi?

70{71}[17] *Deus, docuisti me a iuventute mea et usque nunc; you have taught me, O God, from my youth and till now.* God the Trinity taught the soul of Christ from the first instant that he created it, giving to it manifold wisdom, namely, the wisdom of the beatific vision, by which he knew God by uncreated sight, as do also the Saints in heaven; also [giving it] infused or conferred wisdom, by which he knew all things in their proper nature through innate or concreated sight, as also the angels before their fall and confirmation knew. Christ also had (according to some) acquired or experiential knowledge,[142]

---

139   John 8:54a.
140   John 5:41.
141   Luke 17:10.
142   E. N. ST IIIa, q. 9, art. 4. "Aquinas is generally thought to have been the first thirteenth-century Scholastic doctor to posit the existence of naturally acquired human knowledge in Christ, as opposed to uniquely infused knowledge." Thomas Joseph White, O. P., "The Infused Science of Christ," *Nova et Vetera*, Vol. 16, No. 2

of which the Apostle said, *He learned obedience by the things which he suffered,*[143] And he chose there to learn by experience, because Christ learned nothing from others, but [learned experientially] by his own discovery according with the acquired knowledge placed there. It is in regard to this knowledge that one can understand that which is read in the Gospel: *Jesus advanced in wisdom and age.*[144] But because Christ from the beginning was perfectly instructed, how is it that he now states— *You have taught me, O God, from my youth and till now*—and if he himself increased in knowledge as time progressed? In response, God is said to teach the Saints in heaven and the soul of Christ always, since he unceasingly preserves the wisdom infused in them.

Pronuntiabo mirabilia tua, I will declare your wonderful works. Christ taught most hidden, most supernatural, and most thoroughly incomprehensible things, such as that God is one and three, that he was God and man in the unity of person, that our beatitude consists in the vision of the divine essence, that he himself would be raised again and would judge all the dead, and many other things: and so he himself or through his disciples declared the wonders of God. **70{71}[18]** *Et usque in senectam et senium, and unto old age and grey hairs,* that is, even unto the time of my Passion, I will declare your wonderful works. Whence in the night of the Passion he told the Jews: *Hereafter you shall see the Son of man sitting on the right hand of the power of God, and coming in the clouds of heaven.*[145] Also, before Pilate in the day of the Passion he stated: *I am a king. For this was I born, and for this came I into the world, that I should give testimony to the truth.*[146] Or [we can understand the verse thus]: *And unto old age and grey hairs,* that is, even to the last age of the world and the end of time, I will pronounce through my ministers your wonderful works. For even until the end of the world, instructed by Christ, Christians will sing of the marvels of God written in the New and the Old Testament.

Deus, O God, Father, *ne derelinquas me, forsake me not* in the tomb or limbo, *donec annuntiem brachium tuum, until I show forth your arm,* that is, your power, *generationi omni quae ventura est, to all the generation that is to come,* that is, to all men born even unto the end of the

---

(2018), 619–20. This represented a departure from his earlier opinion found in III Sent., d. 14, a. 3, as Aquinas mentions in ST IIIa, q. 12, art. 2.

143   Heb. 5:8b.
144   Luke 2:52a.
145   Matt. 26:64.
146   John 18:37.

world. We see this fulfilled in Christ because after the Resurrection he instructed his disciples, opening their understanding, so that *they might understand the Scriptures;*[147] and after fifty days he sent to them the Holy Spirit, who instructed them in all languages and in wisdom.[148] By this Christ truly revealed to them his divine power, and also taught all the generations that were to come: because through the teaching of the Apostles, he promulgated the Catholic faith, and converted the whole world. Whence also Christ in the Gospel says: *And what I say to you, I say to all.*[149] *Potentiam tuam, your power,* **70{71}[19]** *et iustitiam tuam, Deus, usque in altissima; quae fecisti magnalia; and your justice, O God, even to the highest great things you have done.* In the Incarnation, Passion, Ascension of Christ the power and justice of God most excellently shone. For that God and man are joined together in one person shows the power of God to be infinite. Similarly, that Christ was born of a Virgin and that he performed such miracles as is believed. But the justice of God shines out in this, *that he spared not even his own Son, but delivered him up for us all,*[150] so that no fault should remain unavenged. Now Christ declared this power and justice of God by word and deeds, bearing witness that he was equal to the Father,[151] the first beginning,[152] and the true God,[153] and yet nevertheless true man, less than the Father,[154] and passible. But Christ also professed the justice of the Father, when he said: *Just Father, the world has not known you; but I have known you.*[155] In such a way, therefore, Christ declared the power and the justice of God, even in the highest marvels which he performed, that is, by attaining the mysteries of human redemption, which are the highest marvels above all the natural works of the Creator. For before his Passion Christ abundantly foretold his Incarnation, Passion, Resurrection, Ascension, and the sending of the Holy Spirit.

---

147   Luke 24:45.
148   Acts 2:3–4.
149   Mark 13:37.
150   Rom. 8:32a.
151   John 10:30: *I and the Father are one.*
152   John 8:25: *They said therefore to him: Who are you? Jesus said to them: The beginning, who also speak unto you.*
153   John 10:33: *For a good work we stone you not, but for blasphemy; and because that you, being a man, make yourself God.*
154   John 14:28: *I go to the Father: for the Father is greater than I.*
155   John 17:25a.

70{71}[20] *How great troubles have you shown me, many and grievous: and turning you have brought me to life, and have brought me back again from the depths of the earth:*

Quantas ostendisti mihi tribulationes multas et malas! Et conversus vivificasti me, et de abyssis terrae iterum reduxisti me.

70{71}[21] *You have multiplied your magnificence; and turning to me you have comforted me.*

Multiplicasti magnificentiam tuam; et conversus consolatus es me.

70{71}[20] *Quantas ostendisti mihi tribulationes multas et malas; how great troubles have you shown me, many and grievous*, that is, you have permitted persecutions and various punishments to be inflicted upon me in the way that Isaiah foretold: *The Lord was pleased to bruise him in infirmity;*[156] and *The Lord has laid on him the iniquity of us all.*[157] And Peter said: *Those things which God before had showed by the mouth of all the Prophets, that his Christ should suffer, he has so fulfilled.*[158] Whence he says by Jeremiah: *You, O Lord, have shown me, and I have known; you showed me their doings.*[159] *Et conversus, and turning*, that is, reconciled to the world through my Passion, *vivificasti me, you have brought be to life*, resurrecting me from the dead on the third day; *et de abyssis terrae, and from the depths of the earth*, that is, from the sepulcher and hell,[160] and *iterum reduxisti me, you have brought me back again* in the day of the Resurrection. 70{71}[21] *Multiplicasti magnificentiam tuam, you have multiplied your magnificence*, gloriously and powerfully resurrecting me. *For the angel of the Lord descended, and coming rolled back the stone; and the earth directly was moved, and the guards also struck with terror, and became, as it were, dismayed.*[161] And also two angels sat next to the sepulcher, one at the head, and the other at the foot.[162] *Et conversus, and turning to me* from the anger by which you were angry at men, *consolatus es me, you have comforted me*, freeing me from all suffering and sorrow which I had during the time of the Passion, and glorifying my body, and rewarding me after the Resurrection with new joy and suitable accidental reward.

---

156 Is. 53:10a.
157 Is. 53:6b.
158 Acts 3:18.
159 Jer. 11:18.
160 E. N. Again, this hell is the limbo of the fathers, not the hell of the damned.
161 Matt. 28:2, 4.
162 John 20:12.

70{71}[22]   For I will also confess to you your truth with the instruments
of psaltery: O God, I will sing to you with the harp, you Holy
One of Israel.

Nam et ego confitebor tibi in vasis psalmi veritatem tuam,
Deus; psallam tibi in cithara, Sanctus Israel.

70{71}[22] *Nam et ego,* for I also your Only-Begotten *confitebor tibi,*
will also confess, that is, I will praise you, *in vasis psalmi,* with the instruments of psaltery, that is, through devout men, containing in their hearts
your praise, I will confess *veritatem tuam, Deus;* your truth, O God, praising you through them, and inflaming them toward giving you praise, in
the way I spoke through the prophet Isaiah: *Give praise, O you heavens,*
and rejoice, O earth, you mountains, give praise with jubilation, because the
Lord has comforted his people, and he will have mercy on his poor ones.[163]
Psallam tibi in cithara, I will sing to you with the harp, that is, in my flesh
crucified and put to death for you, O Lord, who are, and whose name is,
Sanctus Israel, the Holy One of Israel: according to that written elsewhere,
Our Redeemer, the Lord of hosts, the Holy One of Israel, is his name.[164]

70{71}[23]   My lips shall greatly rejoice, when I shall sing to you; and
my soul which you have redeemed.

Exsultabunt labia mea cum cantavero tibi; et anima mea
quam redemisti.

70{71}[24]   Yea and my tongue shall meditate on your justice all the day;
when they shall be confounded and put to shame that seek
evils to me.

Sed et lingua mea tota die meditabitur iustitiam tuam, cum
confusi et reveriti fuerint qui quaerunt mala mihi.

70{71}[23] *Exsultabunt labia mea cum cantavero tibi,* my lips shall
greatly rejoice when I shall sing to you. As more amply the lips of Christ
both interior and exterior always rejoiced in delight and exultation and
in eternity rejoice in the divine praise, so more ardently did he love God
above all other things, and more clearly did he know him. Whence we
read in the Gospel: Jesus *rejoiced in the Holy Spirit, and said I confess*
to you, Father.[165] *Et anima mea, and my soul* will exult in your praise,

---

163   Is. 49:13.
164   Is. 47:4.
165   Luke 10:21a.

quam redemisti, which you have redeemed from all passibility and lowly condition, and also from all fault — not that which it had, because it was utterly free from fault, but from that fault it might have had had it not been prevented by the influence of your grace, and the hypostatic union with the Word. 70{71}[24] *Sed et lingua mea, yea and my tongue* both interior and exterior, *tota die, all the day* eternally in the heavenly home-land, *meditabitur iustitiam tuam, shall meditate on your justice,* praising and declaring it to your glory, *cum confuse et reveriti fuerint, when they shall be confounded and put to shame* with a perfect and consummated confusion, as those eternally condemned, *qui quaerunt mala mihi, that seek evils to me:* according to the sense already mentioned.

See this brilliant and resplendent Psalm full of sweetness of heavenly harmony, embracing fiery words of holy love, including most affection-ate prayers, praising must beautifully God, and repulsing all timidity; so certainly this Psalm is marvelously consoling to the attentive reader, and it can also be so appropriately explained as referring to the Lord Savior. But some expound it literally of David, which explanations I omit because of their prolixity, and because they lead to very little devotion. With great ardor, therefore, and with all fervor and custody of mind, let us endeavor to chant this Psalm that is so fulgid, especially since the persecutions and temptations of all our visible and invisible adversar-ies may be driven away, defeated, and cast down by the power of this present Psalm.

PRAYER

GOD OF INEFFABLE MERCY DO NOT withdraw from us: look with solicitude toward our aid, and do not abandon us even unto old age and grey hairs; enliven and kindly console us, and make us worthy to sing perpetually of the magnitude of your glory.

Deus misericordiae ineffabilis, ne elongeris a nobis: respice in auxilium nostrum, et ne nos derelinquas usque in senectam et senium; vivifica nos et pie consolare, et gloriae magnitudinem tuae fac nos perpetim digne decantare.

Psalm 71

ARTICLE XXXIX

LITERAL EXPOSITION OF THE SEVENTY-FIRST PSALM:
DEUS, IUDICIUM TUUM REGI DA.
GIVE TO THE KING YOUR JUDGMENT, O GOD.

71{72}[1] *A Psalm on Solomon.*

Psalmus, in Salomonem.

HE TITLE OF THIS PRESENT PSALM IS: 71{72}
[1] *In Salamonem, on Solomon.* Some assert that David wrote this
Psalm for his son, Solomon, praying for the prosperity of his reign; but
in no way can this possibly be true, because many things are contained
in this Psalm which in no way fittingly apply to Solomon, as will be
made clear. But Jerome says that this Psalm was entitled by Solomon, as
if the author, because Solomon published the present Psalm. But Augustine and Cassiodorus (whose positions we see are more in accord) say,
as do others, that this Psalm was written by David. Also, all the great
and Catholic teachers, namely, Jerome, Augustine, Cassiodorus, Hugh
[of Saint-Cher] explain this Psalm as literally referring to Christ; and
so this is the sense of the title: *On Solomon,* that is, this Psalm tends
toward and leads us to Christ, who is represented by Solomon. As all
know, Solomon is interpreted as peaceful:[1] and so Christ is the true
Solomon, reconciling the world to the Father. Of which, the Apostle
said to the Ephesians: Christ *is our peace, who has made both one, . . . by
the cross* dissolving *the enmities in himself; and coming, he preached peace
to you that were afar off, and peace to them that were nigh.*[2] And to the
Romans: *When we were still enemies, we were reconciled to God by the
death of his Son.*[3] For this reason, Zechariah said: *He shall bear the glory,
and shall . . . rule . . . and he shall be a priest . . . and the counsel of peace
shall be between them both,*[4] namely, between the divinely elect Gentiles

---

1 E. N. 1 Chr. 22:9: *The son, that shall be born to you, shall be a most quiet man: for
I will make him rest from all his enemies round about: and therefore he shall be called
Peaceable [Shelomo]: and I will give peace [shalom] and quietness to Israel all his days.*
2 Eph. 2:14a, 16a, 17.
3 Rom. 5:10a.
4 Zech. 6:13.

and Jews. Of this the Apostle says: *Unto them that are called, both Jews and Greeks, we preach Christ, the power of God and the wisdom of God.*[5] For Christ is the cornerstone by which Jews and Gentiles are connected and joined in the unity of the Church by faith and charity.[6]

71{72}[2]   Give to the king your judgment, O God: and to the king's son your justice: To judge your people with justice, and your poor with judgment.

Deus, iudicium tuum regi da, et iustitiam tuam filio regis; iudicare populum tuum in iustitia, et pauperes tuos in iudicio.

Therefore, the prophet [David] says to God, the Father, or to the entire blessed Trinity, whose gifts and works are indivisible:[7] **71{72}[2]** *Deus, iudicium tuum;* O God, your judgment, that is, your judicial power, *regi, to the king,* that is, to Christ the King of kings, and the Lord of lords,[8] *da, give,* constituting him the judge of the living and the dead; *et iustitiam tuam, and your justice,* that is, the habit of true equity by which one proceeds in all right judgment, give *filio regis, to the king's son,* that is, to Christ: who according to the divine generation is the Son of the eternal King, namely, of you; but according to the human generation, he is the son of David, an earthly king. *Iudicare populum tuum in iustitia, to judge your people with justice:* that is, he gives to Christ judgment and justice for this reason: so that he might justly judge the Christian people, dividing and separating them from the unfaithful people, and giving to everyone that of which they are deserving; so that he might also judge *et pauperes tuus, and your poor,* that is, the true and spiritual poor, of which Matthew states this: *Blessed are the poor in spirit;*[9] *in iudicio, with judgment* of discretion in the present, and in the judgment of remuneration in the future,[10] since now he may separate them from the rich and the proud by desire and merit, but in the future by place and reward.

---

5   1 Cor. 1:24.

6   Cf. 1 Pet. 2:6.

7   E. N. This refers to the Augustinian-inspired principle or maxim, *omnia opera Trinitatis ad extra indivisa sunt,* "all the works of the Trinity outside of itself are indivisible." Though not in any of his writings in so many words, it is an accurate apothegm of his doctrine. This does not refer to the relations of the Trinity of persons *ad intra.*

8   Rev. 17:14.

9   Matt. 5:3.

10   E. N. For the distinction between the judgment of discretion and the judgment of retribution, remuneration, or reward (final judgment), *see* footnote 1-39 in Volume 1.

But it seems wondrous the way the Prophet [David], who certainly was and is a member of Christ, presumed to pray for the head, namely, for Christ praying to the Father and as Christ rendering judgment and justice. To respond to this, the holy Prophet is not saying these things praying for Christ, as if Christ is lacking in his prayers, but in order to make known the affections of his heart which desired honor and glory for Christ. In just this fashion a later Psalm also says: *Not to us, O Lord, not to us, but to your name give glory.*[11] And so where it says — *your poor with judgment* — he separates and divides the poor of God from the poor of the world and of the devil. For there is the avaricious poor, and there is proud poor, and there is the involuntary poor: these are not the poor of God. For it is the poor of spirit, the poor in love, the poor in things and in the mind so that they might be empty to be free for God: and these are the poor of God. And of these the prophet Isaiah says: *The poor men shall rejoice in the Holy One of Israel.*[12]

Now the Psalmist also here says, *O God, give to the king your judgment,* like Daniel most clearly foretelling of Christ saying: *I beheld therefore in the vision of the night, and lo, one like the Son of Man came with the clouds of heaven, and he came even to the Ancient of days ... and he gave him power, and glory, and a kingdom.*[13] In the Gospel, the Savior also acknowledged this to be fulfilled in him, saying: *For neither does the Father judge any man, but has given all judgment to the Son.*[14] And Peter speaking of Christ: *He commanded us,* he said, *to testify that it is he who was appointed by God to be judge of the living and of the dead.*[15]

But this seems to be contrary to that which Christ said, *I judge not any man:*[16] and that also which the most blessed evangelist clearly stated, saying, *God sent not his Son into the world, to judge the world, but that the world may be saved by him.*[17] In considering this, we must surely keep in mind that in judgment there are two things to be recalled: the judicial authority, and the exercise of the judicial authority or the handing down of judgment. With regard to the first of these, the judgment applies to God the Father, or the whole Trinity, and not to Christ insofar as he is man. For Christ himself said: *I seek not my own glory; there is one that seeks and judges,*[18]

---

11 Ps. 113:9.
12 Is. 29:19b.
13 Dan. 7:13–14a.
14 John 5:22.
15 Acts 10:42.
16 John 8:15b.
17 John 3:17.
18 John 8:50.

namely God, the Trinity. But with respect to the second, with regard to the handing down of the sentence, it applies to Christ the man to judge, as the Gospel affirms, saying: *The Father has given him power to do judgment, because he is the Son of Man.*[19] To these both Paul briefly hints, saying: *God has appointed a day wherein he will judge the world in equity, by the man whom he has appointed.*[20] In this way, therefore, is the manner by which judgment coincides in God the Trinity and in Christ the man in different ways. Moreover, that which Christ says, *I do not judge any man*, can refer to the time of his first coming, but it will be manifested in the judgment of remuneration and vengeance. For the first coming of Christ was in humility, and he came *not to be ministered to* or to judge, *but to minister* and to be judged.[21] Whence (as we read in Luke) when John and James said to Christ, *Lord, will you that we might command fire to come down from heaven, and consume them* (namely, those who did not receive the Lord Jesus)?[22] Jesus responded to them: *You know not of what spirit you are; the Son of Man came not to destroy souls, but to save.*[23] Here also [we might consider that] he did not want to condemn the woman caught in adultery.[24] Isaiah reveals that Christ was to be so justly and judicially judging his people, saying: *He shall not judge according to the sight of the eyes, nor reprove according to the hearing of the ears; but he shall the judge the poor with justice, and shall reprove with equity the meek of the earth.*[25]

71{72}[3] *Let the mountains receive peace for the people: and the hills justice.*

Suscipiant montes pacem populo, et colles iustitiam.

71{72}[3] *Suscipiant montes, let the mountains receive*, that is, the sublime and apostolic men and great prelates of the Church, *pacem populo, peace for the people*, that is, the grace of true and internal peace toward the salvation and education of the people, so that the Apostles and their successors might obtain from God both for themselves and the flock

---

19   John 5:27.
20   Acts 17:31a.
21   Matt. 20:28.
22   Luke 9:54.
23   Luke 9:55b–56.
24   John 8:11.
25   Is. 11:3b–4a. *E. N. Christus tam iuste ac iudicialiter iudicaturus*, Christ so justly and judicially judging. As 2 Inst. 479 states, *non apparet iudicialiter ante iudicium*, something does not appear judicially before judgment. Christ does not act *judicially* until he exercises that judgment.

committed to them the stable quiet of peace. This is also fulfilled in the Apostles, when they heard from the Lord Jesus: *Peace I leave with you, my peace I give unto you;*[26] and *Into whatsoever house you enter, first say: Peace be to this house.*[27] Let also *colles, the hills* receive *iustitiam, justice,* that is, let those beneath [the prelates of the Church] receive the grace of obeying the divine precepts specified by their superiors. We find written in Joel about the fruitfulness of these mountains and hills: *In that day the mountains shall drop down sweetness, and the hills shall flow with milk.*[28]

71{72}[4]   *He shall judge the poor of the people, and he shall save the children of the poor: and he shall humble the oppressor.*

Iudicabit pauperes populi, et salvos faciet filios pauperum, et humiliabit calumniatorem.

Then the Prophet [David] shows fulfilled that which he prayed for: 71{72}[4] *Iudicabit pauperes populi, et salvos faciet filio pauperum; he shall judge the poor of the people, and he shall save the children of the poor.* For at present he judges his poor with the judgment of discretion, as has already been said; but in the last day, he will judge them with the judgment of blessed reward, in the manner that he asserted in Revelation: *Behold, I come quickly; and my reward is with me, to render to every man according to his works.*[29] *Et humiliabit calumniatorem, and he shall humble the oppressor,* that is, Christ will confound, damn, and destroy all the tyrants and tempters of the Church, the devil, and the Antichrist, in accordance with that [stated] in Isaiah: *He shall strike the earth with the rod of his mouth, and with the breath of his lips he shall slay the wicked,* namely, the Antichrist.[30] Of this we have from the same [prophet]: *Moab shall be trodden down under him.*[31] Of whom also the Apostle [Paul] said: *The wicked one shall be revealed, whom the Lord Jesus shall kill with the spirit of his mouth.*[32] Now Christ humiliates many oppressors and tyrants also

---

26   John 14:27a.

27   Luke 10:5.

28   Joel 3:18a.

29   Rev. 22:12.

30   Is. 11:4b.

31   Is. 25:10a. E. N. In his *Commentary on Isaiah,* Denis equates Moab with the Antichrist: "*And Moab shall be trodden down under him,* that is, the Antichrist shall be, *as straw is broken in pieces with heavy cart,* that is, he shall be completely destroyed and condemned, according to that said by the Apostle: *Whom the Lord Jesus will kill . . . with the brightness of his coming* (2 Thess. 2:8)." Doctoris Ecstatici D. Dionysii Cartusiani, *Opera Omnia,* Vol. 8 (Montreuil: 1899), 512.

32   2 Thess. 2:8.

in this life, depriving them of their life or their reign. But all [tyrants and oppressors] in the day of judgment will be finally humbled: for then all who then exalt themselves will be humbled, not with a virtuous humility, but with a damning degradation.

71{72}[5]   *And he shall continue with the sun, and before the moon, throughout all generations.*

Et permanebit cum sole, et ante lunam, in generatione et generationem.

71{72}[5] *Et permanebit cum sole et ante lunam, in generatione et generationem; and he shall continue with the sun, and before the moon, throughout all generations.* As by the moon one can understand the Church, so by the sun we can understand the eternal Father, who is the fountain-like light illuminating all things: and this verse can be explained in reference to both the sun and the moon. For Christ remains with the intellectual sun, namely, with God the Father, because he is co-eternal with him. In accordance with his divine nature, he abides with this sun from the part before (*a parte ante*), as *the brightness of his glory*[33] and the *brightness of eternal light*.[34] According to his human nature and divine nature, Christ also abides from the part after (*a parte post*) the same as the material sun: because as the sun is incorruptible, so also Christ persists incorruptibly.[35] And before either moon, namely, the ["moon" of the] Church and a moon of one of the planets [i.e., any material moon], Christ, according to his divine nature, abides from the part before (*a parte ante*), as Wisdom itself attests in Ecclesiasticus: *I came out of the mouth of the most High, the first-born before all creatures.*[36] And in Proverbs: *The Lord possessed me in the beginning of his ways, before he made anything from the beginning. When he prepared the heavens, I was present.... I was with him forming all things.*[37]

---

33   Heb. 1:3a.

34   Wis. 7:26a.

35   E. N. In dealing with eternity—time without beginning and without end—the Scholastics distinguished between two eternities, one looking backwards from an instant in time (*aeternitas a parte ante*) and one looking forward from an instant in time (*aeternitas a parte post*). Christ insofar as he is God is eternal *a parte ante* and *a parte post*. Christ insofar as he is man is eternal only *a parte post*, since his human nature began its existence at a point in history. In medieval cosmology, the sun, like other celestial bodies including the moon, was believed to be created incorruptible and aeviternal. *See* ST Ia, art. 6, q. 2, co.

36   Ecclus. 24:5.

37   Prov. 8:22, 27a, 30a.

See here how manifestly the divinity of Christ and his eternity is declared. For this reason, the Apostle also says: *Jesus Christ, yesterday, and today; and the same forever.*[38]

71{72}[6] *He shall come down like rain upon the fleece; and as showers falling gently upon the earth.*

Descendet sicut pluvia in vellus, et sicut stillicidia stillantia super terram.

71{72}[6] *Descendet sicut pluvia in vellus, he shall come down like rain upon the fleece.* In the Book of Judges it is related how in the instance of Gideon the fleece was rained upon or made wet with dew, though the earth remained dry, and subsequently the surrounding earth was wet, but the fleece was not dampened. So [this verse must be understood] in this sense: Christ our king descended into the womb of the Virgin, as the rain descended upon the fleece of Gideon. For in the manner that the rain descended upon the fleece so that it was not distilled by the fleece, neither did not seep out, nor did the fleece suffer any division or corruption, so the Word of God in the bosom of the Father coming to the Virgin in no way damaged or violated her: for she did not conceive through man, but became pregnant by being overshadowed by the Holy Spirit; and also the body of Christ in the womb of the Virgin was supernaturally formed,[39] in accordance with Zechariah, *Behold I will grave the graving thereof,*[40] says the Lord, that is, I will form his body. *Et sicut stillicidia stillantia super terram, and as showers falling gently upon the earth.* In the manner that raindrops softly and sweetly fall from heaven to earth and refresh and it and make it fruitful, so Christ by his Incarnation sweetly and without a sound descended in the Virgin Mother, and by her into the world. For his first coming was in humility,

---

38 Heb. 13:8.
39 Luke 1:35. *E. N.* "If anyone does not, following the holy Fathers, confess properly and truly that holy Mary, ever virgin and immaculate, is Mother of God, since in this latter age she conceived really and truly, without human seed from the Holy Spirit, God the Word himself, who before the ages was born of God the Father, and gave birth to him without corruption, her virginity remaining equally inviolate after his birth, let him be condemned." DS 503 (Lateran Synod, 649 AD). "Mary's virginity includes *virginitas mentis*, that is, a constant virginal disposition, *virginitas sensus*, that is, freedom from inordinate motions of sexual desire, and *virginitas corporis*, that is, physical integrity. The Church doctrine refers primarily to her bodily integrity." Ludwig Ott, *Fundamentals of Catholic Dogma* (Rockford, IL: TAN Books 1974), 203–04 (trans., Patrick Lynch, ed. James Canon Bastible).
40 Zech. 3:9a.

poverty, and mildness, according to that predicted by Zechariah: *Rejoice greatly, O daughter of Sion ... Behold your king shall come to you, the just and Savior, he is poor, etc.*[41] And in the Gospel, he himself confessed: *The Son of Man has not where to lay his head.*[42]

71{72}[7] *In his days shall justice spring up, and abundance of peace, till the moon be taken away.*

> *Orietur in diebus eius iustitia, et abundantia pacis, donec auferatur luna.*

71{72}[7] *Orietur in diebus eius, in his days shall ... spring up,* that is, in the first coming of Christ, *iustitia, justice,* that is, the perfection of life, or the Catholic faith. For the time of Christ is the time of grace; therefore, men who imitate the path of Christ live more perfectly and with more holiness than the Jews during the time of the law. And so Christ in the Gospel says: *Unless your justice abound more than that of the scribes and Pharisees, you shall not enter into the kingdom of heaven.*[43] So, he said, *it becomes us to fulfill all justice.*[44] For to such an extent did grace and justice abound during the time of Christ more than it did before, as it is written in John, *For as yet the Spirit was not given, because Jesus was not yet glorified:*[45] not, however, that it was not given at all before [Christ], but because it was not given in such an exuberant fashion.[46]

Et abundantia pacis, and abundance of peace. This refers to what was said in an earlier Psalm: *Come and behold the works of the Lord, what wonders he has done upon earth, making wars to cease even to the end of the earth.*[47] And Isaiah says: *Nation shall not lift up sword against nation, neither shall they be exercised any more to war.*[48] And so this abundance of peace that arose during the time of Christ is understood as pertaining to a temporal peace which existed throughout the whole world under Caesar Augustus, under whom Christ was born,[49] so that the whole world could

---

41   Zech. 9:9a.

42   Luke 9:58b.

43   Matt. 5:20.

44   Matt. 3:15b.

45   John 7:39b.

46   E. N. Denis appears to say that the "time of Christ" means *after* Pentecost, i.e., after the fulness of Christ's dispensation was received.

47   Ps. 45:9–10a.

48   Is. 2:4b.

49   Luke 2:1. E. N. This is a reference to the so-called the *Pax Romana* or *Pax Augusti,* a 200-year period of relative peace across the Roman Empire which began

be described ruled by one man. But because this peace did not last until the moon had been taken away, therefore, according to this exposition, when it says, *donec auferatur luna, till the moon be taken away*, it refers to the duration of Christian justice, which will last even until the end of the world, and not to the duration of the earlier-mentioned peace. It also appears more fitting that this abundance of peace be understood of the magnitude of internal peace located in the tranquility of conscience. Of this, the Apostle [Paul] says: *Let the peace of Christ rejoice in your hearts.*[50] And Zechariah prophesied Christ giving it to his faithful, saying: *He shall speak peace to the Gentiles.*[51] For the angels at Christ's birth announced this peace, saying: *Glory to God in the highest, and on earth peace to men of good will.*[52] This peace abounds in good men, as the Apostle prays: *And the peace of God, which surpasses all understanding, keep your hearts and minds.*[53] And because of its abundance, Christ is called the *Prince of Peace.*[54] And so this *abundance of peace* remains in the elect, *till the moon be taken away*, that is, it will never cease, just as the moon; or [we can understand it thus], *till the moon be taken away*, that is, until such a time that the Church militant is transformed into the community of the triumphant Church which is rid of all corruption and mortality. Not that it will then cease; but because it will then be perfected: and so, *Till* does not denote the end of peace, but its continuation: in the manner that Matthew says of Joseph and Mary, *He knew her not till she brought forth her firstborn son.*[55]

---

with the reign of the Caesar Augustus (27 BC–14 AD). "[T]he *Pax Christi* is not necessarily opposed to the *Pax Augusti*," said Benedict XVI. "Yet the peace of Christ surpasses the peace of Augustus as heaven surpasses the earth.... One thing is clear, though: Augustus belongs to the past, Jesus Christ on the other hand is the present and the future—he is 'the same yesterday and today and forever' (Heb. 13:8)." Benedict XVI, *Jesus of Nazareth: The Infancy Narratives* (New York: Image 2012), 77–78.

50 Col. 3:14a.
51 Zech. 9:10a.
52 Luke 2:14.
53 Phil. 4:7.
54 Is. 9:6b.
55 Matt. 1:25. E. N. Denis is referring to the Semitic idiom where the word "until" (or "till") does not imply that the action ceases (or the opposite occurs) thereafter. In his *Tract against Helvidius* defending the perpetual virginity of Mary, for example, St. Jerome gives numerous examples of this usage, such as Gen. 35:4, Deut. 34:5–6, Ps. 122:2, Is. 46:4, Matt. 28:20, 1 Cor. 15:23. *See St. Jerome: Dogmatic and Polemical Works* (Washington, DC: Catholic University of America Press, 1981), 18-20. (trans., John N. Hritzu). Just as the phrase Joseph "knew her not till she brought forth her firstborn son" does not imply he knew her thereafter, so does the phrase that peace

71{72}[8] *And he shall rule from sea to sea, and from the river unto the ends of the earth.*

Et dominabitur a mari usque ad mare, et a flumine usque ad terminos orbis terrarum.

71{72}[8] *Et dominabitur,* and *he shall rule,* [that is,] Christ [shall rule], *a mari, from sea* in the east *usque ad mare, to the sea* in the west, for *the sound* of the Apostles *has gone forth into all the earth,* and they have converted some to Christ even *unto the ends of the world;*[56] *et a flumine, and from the river* of earthly paradise, or the river Jordan;[57] or [alternatively], from any river whatsoever, namely, from all rivers, understanding the singular as a plural; *usque ad terminus orbis terrarium, unto the ends of the earth.* Whence in Zechariah is written: *His power shall be from sea to sea, and from the rivers even to the end of the earth.*[58] And this is said of Christ: First of all, because all things, even inanimate and irrational things, are subject to him, just as he says in the Gospel: *All power is given to me in heaven and in earth.*[59] Secondly, because all men existing in the entire world, whether they will or do not will it, are subject to the power of Christ, according to that which he himself said, speaking of himself to the Father: *You have given him power over all flesh.*[60] Thirdly, because in every part of the inhabitable world, there are some who have obeyed Christ by faith and works. For this reason, God the Father says to Christ in Isaiah: *I have given you to be the light*

---

shall last "till the moon be taken away" mean that there will not be peace after the final conflagration when the moon as we know it is no more. The perpetual virginity of Mary is a dogma of the faith. Mary persisted in the integrity of virginity, "before giving birth (*ante partum*), in giving birth (*in partu*), and perpetually after giving birth (*post partum*)." DS 1880 (Pius IV, *Cum quorumdam hominum,* 1555 AD). Denis himself addresses this Semitism at some depth in his discussion of Psalm 109:1 in Volume 5, and whether Christ will sit at the right hand of the Father *after* he makes his enemies his footstool: *see* Article XVII (Psalm 109:1).

56   Ps. 18:5.

57   E. N. "'Alone among all rivers,'" says St. Gregory the Theologian, "'the Jordan received the first-fruits of sanctification and blessing, and has shed the grace of baptism over the whole world, as from a source. And these things are signs of that regeneration which is effected by Baptism.' This is a very striking definition of a type, that it is an act truly accomplished, and signifying some future action. St. Gregory then alludes to the Jordan in its relation to Paradise: 'The Jordan is glorified because it regenerates men and makes them fit for God's Paradise.'" Jean Daniélou, *From Shadows to Reality: Studies in the Biblical Typology of the Fathers* (London: Burns & Oates, 1960) (trans., Dom Wulstan Hibberd), 275.

58   Zech. 9:10b.

59   Matt. 28:18b.

60   John 17:2a.

of the Gentiles, that you may be my salvation even to the farthest part of the earth.[61] And this is what the Savior told the Apostles: *You shall be witnesses unto me in Jerusalem, and in all Judea, and Samaria, and even to the uttermost part of the earth.*[62]

71{72}[9] *Before him the Ethiopians shall fall down: and his enemies shall lick the ground.*

Coram illo procident Aethiopes, et inimici eius terram lingent.

71{72}[10] *The kings of Tharsis and the islands shall offer presents: the kings of the Arabians and of Saba shall bring gifts:*

Reges Tharsis et insulae munera offerent; reges Arabum et Saba dona adducent.

71{72}[11] *And all kings of the earth shall adore him: all nations shall serve him.*

Et adorabunt eum omnes reges terrae, omnes gentes servient ei.

71{72}[9] *Coram illo procident Aethiopes, before him the Ethiopians shall fall down.* For these who have converted will humbly adore Christ according to Matthew the evangelist.[63] Now by Ethiopians can be understood the Gentiles, who before their conversion to Christ were black with the mental blindness of vice as the Ethiopians are covered with black skin.[64] *Et inimici eius, and his enemies,* those incredulous of Christ, *terram lingent, lick the ground,* that is, they are attached to things of this world, and with an inmost love they attached themselves to these things. Whence Jeremiah: *They that depart from you,* he says, *shall be written in the earth.*[65] Or [we can see it] thus: *his enemies,* that is, those who at one time opposed themselves to Christ *shall lick the ground* after their conversion, that is, they will kiss and prostrate themselves even unto the ground out of a devotion to Christ. 71{72}[10] *Reges Tharsis et insulae munera offerent: reges Arabum et Saba dona adducent; the kings of Tharsis and the islands shall offer presents: the kings of the Arabians and of Saba shall bring gifts.* This was literally fulfilled not only by the three Magi

---

61   Is. 49:6b.

62   Acts 1:8b.

63   Matt. 2:11. E. N. The reference is to the three Magi: *And entering into the house, they found the child with Mary his mother, and falling down they adored him; and opening their treasures, they offered him gifts; gold, frankincense, and myrrh.*

64   E. N. On the Ethiopians as symbolic of a soul darkened by sin, *see* footnote 17-161 in Volume I.

65   Jer. 17:13a.

offering gold, frankincense, and myrrh to Christ in the day of Epiphany, but also by many other kings and princes of these lands, who for a long time were under the Catholic faith and offered to Christ or the Church a variety of gifts, namely spiritual and bodily sacrifices. **71{72}[11]** *Et adorabunt eum omnes reges; omnes gentes servient ei. And all kings of the earth shall adore him: all nations shall serve him.* Both of these divisions here described are referring generally to some kinds of the individuals, and not universally to all individuals of the kind.[66] For also that some of all kinds of kings and peoples would adore Christ is prophesied by Daniel, who said: *All peoples, tribes and tongues shall serve him.*[67] And Micah: *He shall stand, and feed in the strength of the Lord . . . and they shall be converted, for now shall he be magnified* in the midst of all the earth.[68]

71{72}[12] *For he shall deliver the poor from the mighty: and the needy that had no helper.*

Quia liberabit pauperem a potente, et pauperem cui non erat adiutor.

Consequently, it will lead to the condition of the universal dominion of Christ. **71{72}[12]** *Quia liberabit pauperem a potente, for he shall deliver the poor from the mighty.* But what poor? There follows: *et pauperem cui non erat adiutor, and the needy that had no helper* other than God himself. Such a poor man is humble in all things, who does not lean upon his own strength, but with complete affection places his confidence in God. Now in this manner God in many ways frees the poor from the powerful, that is, from the devil, whom Christ in the Gospel calls the strong man;[69] and of whom in Job is written: *There is no power upon earth that can be compared with him who was made to fear no one.*[70] Or [alternatively], *from the mighty*, that is, from all proud and strong men who prevail as a result of natural strength or worldly power. First, Christ delivers the poor from these powerful men, giving to them patience in adversity, constancy in the good: so that malice [displayed against them]

---

66   E. N. *Pro generibus singulorum* and not *pro singulis generum*, meaning not *all* kings and not all peoples, but some of all kings and some of all peoples. See footnote 21-54.
67   Dan. 7:14. E. N. Again, meaning here that *some* of all kinds of peoples, tribes, and tongues, and not *all the individuals* of all peoples, tribes, and tongues.
68   Micah 5:4.
69   Luke 11:21: *When a strong man armed keeps his court, those things are in peace which he possesses.*
70   Job 41:24. E. N. Job is describing the power of Leviathan, that sea creature that symbolizes evil and chaos and the devil.

does not harm them, indeed it works in them to the good.[71] Second, because he causes them courageously to overcome temptations, and the more they with great eagerness purse the virtues, that much more can they fight back. Third, because he will save them eternally, from those damned in eternity. For this he says through Jeremiah: *Sing to the Lord, praise the Lord, because he has delivered the soul of the hand of the wicked.*[72] And the Lord says through Isaiah: *I the Lord will hear the needy and the poor, I . . . will not forsake them.*[73]

71{72}[13] *He shall spare the poor and needy: and he shall save the souls of the poor.*

Parcet pauperi et inopi, et animas pauperum salvas faciet.

71{72}[14] *He shall redeem their souls from usuries and iniquity: and their names shall be honorable in his sight.*

Ex usuris et iniquitate redimet animas eorum, et honorabile nomen eorum coram illo.

71{72}[13] *Parcet pauperi et inopi*, he shall spare the poor and the needy, forgiving their sins, lightening punishments, and bestowing grace. Whence he says through Malachi: *I will spare those that fear me, says the Lord . . . as a man spares his son that serves him.*[74] *Et animas pauperum salvas faciet*, and he shall save the souls of the poor, now by grace, but in the future by glory. For this reason the Apostle [Paul] said: *Their very deep poverty has abounded unto the riches of their simplicity.*[75] **71{72}[14]** *Ex usuris et iniquitate redimet animas eorum*, he shall redeem their souls from usuries and iniquity. For Christ through his ministers and vicars, namely, through the Pope and the other prelates and leaders, condemn and prohibit usury under the threat of eternal damnation. There is however also another kind of usury from which Christ saves his own, namely, the obligation of eternal punishment which follows from the perpetration of sin. For sin is, as it were, the currency of demons, and on account of it they demand from us perpetual punishment, which we have not undertaken, but must suffer, because of sin which we have contracted

---

71 E. N. Rom. 8:28: *We know that to them that love God, all things work together unto good, to such as, according to his purpose, are called to be saints.*

72 Jer. 20:13.

73 Is. 41:17b.

74 Mal. 3:17.

75 2 Cor. 8:2b.

through diabolical suggestion. Christ redeemed the poor once and for all from this usury and from all sin through the price of his Blood, and the infusion of spiritual grace which is the effect of the merits of the Lord's Passion. *Et honorabile nomen eorum coram illo, and their names shall be honorable in his sight,* that is, before God, the name of the poor of God, who are called Christians, is worthy of veneration and praise. Indeed, this is the name of which Isaiah, refuting the Jews, said: *The Lord God shall slay you, and call his servants by another name, in which he that is blessed upon the earth, shall be blessed in God. Amen.*[76] This name (as Luke recalls in the Acts of the Apostles) was first imposed upon the disciples of Christ in Antioch.[77]

71{72}[15]   *And he shall live, and to him shall be given of the gold of Arabia, for him they shall always adore: they shall bless him all the day.*

Et vivet, et dabitur ei de auro Arabiae; et adorabunt de ipso semper, tota die benedicent ei.

71{72}[15] *Et vivet, and he shall live,* that is, Christ having conquered death, shall rise again immortal and he shall live forever. *Et dabitur ei de auro Arabiae, and to him shall be given of the gold of Arabia.* For many leaders of the Christians bestowed such gold (which is honorable conduct) to Christ and his ministers toward the support of the poor, the construction of churches, and for other pious uses. But [understood] mystically, by gold is understood wisdom, and by Arabia is understood the Gentiles: and so to Christ was given the gold of Arabia, when the wise men of this world and those most learned in natural philosophy were converted to the faith of the Church, as is manifest of the divine Dionysius [the Areopagite], Augustine, and many others. But also a man gives gold from Arabia to Christ when he does not rely upon himself, but he subjects all the natural knowledge to the faith, as a creature is subject to the Creator. *Et adorabunt de ipso semper, for him they shall always adore,* that is, the faithful of Christ will always adore God, that is, out of contemplation of his goodness and benefits. For we ought always to adore and venerate God because of the benefits given to us through Christ. *Tota die, all the day,* that is, all that part of the day that is fitting and when due, *bendicent ei, they shall bless him,* that is, they will praise Christ the king.

---

76   Is. 65:15b–16a.
77   Acts 11:26.

71{72}[16] *And there shall be a firmament on the earth on the tops of mountains, above Lebanon shall the fruit thereof be exalted: and they of the city shall flourish like the grass of the earth.*

Et erit firmamentum in terra in summis montium; superextolletur super Libanum fructus eius, et florebunt de civitate sicut foenum terrae.

71{72}[16] *Et erit, and there shall be* Christ the king *firmamentum in terra, a firmament on earth,* that is, the cause of all the fixity and stability of man dwelling upon the earth, *in summis montium, on the tops of mountains,* that is, in the most profound teachings of the Prophets, confirming and illuminating his elect in the wisdom of the Scriptures, validating them in themselves, as we see in the Gospel of John: *Truth came by Jesus Christ.*[78] Whence also after the Resurrection he said to the disciples: *It is necessary that all things be fulfilled, which are written in the law of Moses, and in the prophets, and in the psalms, concerning me.*[79] *Superextolletur super Libanum fructus eius, above Lebanon shall the fruit thereof be exalted:* that is, the effect of the Passion of Christ, namely, the grace of God, or the elect themselves who are redeemed by the Blood of Christ and elevated above all the dignity and brilliance of this world. For Lebanon is interpreted as meaning whiteness, and in [that region] grow tall trees, namely, cedars [which embellish the land]. The present world is represented by this height and embellishment.

But some careful examiners of other translations have expounded sublimely and fruitfully this verse. For that place where it says here — *there shall be a firmament on earth, etc.* — the Hebrew has, *there shall be an abundance of grain;* but in Jerome's translation: *there shall be memorable wheat;* and also in the Chaldaic translation, considered authentic among the Hebrews: *there shall be a cake of wheat.*[80] And so it seems that our translation is tainted with the mistake of a scribe, and has firmament (*firmamentum*) in lieu of grain (*frumento*). And so this place can be expounded upon as referring to the Sacrament of the Eucharist, in which Christ, under the species of wheaten bread is truly contained. Therefore, holy David, speaking of Christ, says: There will be an abundance of wheat, or a memorable wheat, or a cake of wheat, because the Messiah king, Christ the Lord, under the form of wheaten bread,

---

78 John 1:17b.
79 Luke 24:44b.
80 E. N. Almost all modern translations use grain or wheat, and not firmament. The Hebrew word is בַּר (*bar*) which means grain or, more particularly, wheat. The Septuagint, however, translates the Hebrew by στήριγμα (*stērigma*), which means support.

will be gathered together in the form of a cake, will be contained and reserved in the Church:[81] and Christ himself is that grain *on the tops of mountains*, that is, above the heads of priests, in the loftiness of the raising the Victim of the altar.[82] The priests are also called mountains because of the eminence of [the sacrament] of Orders, of wisdom, and of power. Above Lebanon shall the fruit thereof be exalted, for by fruit of this Sacrament, men are raised and led to the heavenly place and the fellowship of the triumphant Church.

Et florebunt de civitate, and they of the city shall flourish, that is, the faithful of the Church [shall flourish,] *sicut foenum terrae, like the grass of the earth*. For in the way that grace during its time quickly grows and becomes beautifully green, so Christians leaving the church after Holy Communion, spiritually flourish in grace, and grow lofty in the perfect life, while they share in the assigned effect of this Sacrament, as Christ attested to: *He that eats my Flesh, and drinks my Blood, abides in me, and I in him*.[83] And again, *If any man eat of this bread, he shall live forever*.[84]

71{72}[17] Let his name be blessed for evermore: his name continues before the sun. And in him shall all the tribes of the earth be blessed: all nations shall magnify him.

Sit nomen eius benedictum in saecula; ante solem perma-net nomen eius. Et benedicentur in ipso omnes tribus terrae; omnes gentes magnificabunt eum.

Because of such great benefits of Christ, therefore, **71{72}[17]** *Sit nomen eius benedictum in saecula, let his name be blessed for evermore*, that is, let him be praised and glorified by all generations. *Ante solem permanet nomen eius, his name continues before the sun*. For Christ existed from eternity, and he eternally preceded the generation of all creatures,

---

81   E. N. "The Blessed Sacrament is to be lovingly reserved in a tabernacle 'which is the spiritual heart of every religious and parochial community.' 'Without the cult of the Eucharist, as with a beating heart, a parish becomes arid." Congregation for the Clergy: *Instruction: The Priest, Pastor and Leader of the Parish Community*, 21 (Aug. 4, 2002).

82   E. N. Using these other translations, Denis puts upon this Psalm a Eucharistic interpretation to support the priestly elevation of the Host after its consecration. As the *Missale Romanum* states: "The words of consecration being uttered, ... [the priest] elevates it as high as he conveniently can; and with his eyes fixed upon it, a thing he also he does in the elevation of the chalice, he worshipfully displays it to the people to be adored by them."

83   John 6:57.

84   John 6:52a.

as is written of him: *His going forth is from the beginning, from the days of eternity.*[85] *Et benedicentur in ipso omnes tribus terrae, and in him all the tribes of the earth be blessed.* From this it is evident that the exposition of the Apostle Paul to the Galatians — that that which God spoke to Abraham saying, *in you all kindred of the earth shall be blessed*[86] refers to Christ — is true. For this is what the Apostle asserts: *In your seed, that is, in Christ (as he interprets it), will all nations be blessed.*[87] And this is what now the Psalmist says, *And in him shall all tribes of the earth be blessed*: for not only the twelve tribes of Israel, but also all races of the world are blessed in Christ, for they are saved by him, and they receive grace now and later the glory of the blessed by the merits of the Incarnation and the manner of living of Christ. For this reason, Peter said in speaking of Christ: *To him all the prophets give testimony, that by his name all receive remission of sins, who believe in him.*[88] *Omnes gentes magnificabunt eum, and all nations shall magnify him* with praise and by deed. There is also in this verse a distribution of the kinds of each individual,[89] for from all the kinds of tribes and families some, indeed even many, will believe in Christ, in the manner that Zechariah predicted: *Sing praise, and rejoice, O daughter of Sion: for behold I come, and I will dwell in the midst of you ... and many nations shall be joined to the Lord in that day.*[90]

71{72}[**18**] *Blessed be the Lord, the God of Israel, who alone does wonderful things.*

Benedictus Dominus, Deus Israel, qui facit mirabilia solus.

71{72}[**19**] *And blessed be the name of his majesty forever: and the whole earth shall be filled with his majesty. So be it. So be it.*

Et benedictum nomen maiestatis eius in aeternum, et replebitur maiestate eius omnis terra. Fiat, fiat.

71{72}[**20**] *The praises of David, the son of Jesse, are ended.*

Defecerunt laudes David, filii Iesse.

---

85   Micah 5:2b.
86   Gen. 12:3.
87   Gal. 3:16a, 8b.
88   Acts 10:43.
89   E. N. *See* footnote 21-54.
90   Zech. 2:10-11a. E. N. Verse 11 continues, *they shall be my people, and I will dwell in the midst of you: and you shall know that the Lord of hosts has sent me to you.*

71{72}[18] *Benedictus Dominus Deus Israel, blessed be the Lord the God of Israel* bestowing such great benefits to men, *qui facit mirabilia solus, who alone does wonderful things* by his own authority and power. For although God performs miracles through the Saints, according to that which the Gospel itself states, *He who believes in me, the works that I do, he also shall do:*[91] yet this the Saints do not do except by the divine power, and God is the principal author. But there are certain marvels that can also be done by demons and the ungodly; but miracles which completely transcend the order, course, and law of created nature — such as the stopping of the sun,[92] the resurrection of the dead, the revelation of the secrets of the heart — can be done by God alone. **71{72}[19]** *Et benedictum nomen maiestatis eius in aeternum, and blessed be the name of his majesty forever,* that is, the name of the great power of God, by which he is called Omnipotent, and by which he is always praised and glorified by all; *et replebitur maiestate eius omnis terra, and the whole earth shall be filled with his majesty,* that is, all men shall be filled with the knowledge of the divine majesty, as was predicted by Isaiah: *The earth is filled with the knowledge of the Lord.*[93] And this was done throughout the whole world by the holy Apostles. Or [we can understand it in this way]: *By his majesty,* that is, the world shall be filed by the magnificence of the divine works or the glorious effects of the Creator, in the manner that occurred in the day of Pentecost[94] and thereafter, when God poured forth his Spirit upon all flesh,[95] for then the Spirit of the Lord filled the whole world,[96] and great miracles in the name of Christ began to be done in all the world. Finally, the Prophet [David], desiring with great affection to verify by his very act the predicted prophecy, added: *Fiat, fiat; So be it, so be it.*

See we have heard this Psalm truly glittering with all heavenly beauty. In it, the dual nature and one person of Christ is most clearly commended, his universal reign is described, and the institution of the Church declared. It is clear from this, that there are many things stated in this Psalm, that in no way can be truly said of Solomon.[97]

---

91   John 14:12.

92   Joshua 10:13.

93   Is. 11:9b.

94   Acts 2:17.

95   Joel 2:28a.

96   Wis. 1:7a.

97   E. N. Which is what Denis argued at the beginning: despite its title, this Psalm is not about Solomon, but about Jesus Christ. Denis does not provide commentary on Ps. 71:20.

PRAYER

O LORD, BY THE INDULGENCE OF YOUR liberality may we receive peace and justice, which with your help we might continually possess: so that, our oppressors humbled, we might magnify your blessed name for ever.

Tuae, Domine, largitatis indulgentia suscipiamus pacem et iustitiam, quam iugiter te adiutore obtineamus: ut humiliatis calumniatoribus nostris, nomen tuum benedictum in saecula magnificemus.

Psalm 72

ARTICLE XL

ELUCIDATION OF THE SEVENTY-SECOND PSALM:
QUAM BONUS ISRAEL DEUS.
HOW GOOD IS GOD TO ISRAEL.

72{73}[1] [1] *The praises or hymns of David, the son of Jesse, are found wanting, a Psalm for Asaph. How good is God to Israel, to them that are of a right heart!*

Defecerunt laudes seu hymni David filii Iesse, psalmus Asaph. Quam bonus Israel Deus, his qui recto sunt corde!

OW THE TITLE OF THE PRESENT PSALM IS: 72{73}[1] *Defecerunt laudes seu hymni David filii Iesse, psalmus Asaph; the praises or hymns of David, the son of Jesse, are found wanting, a Psalm for Asaph:* that is, after those things the prior Psalm said concerning the future were fulfilled, namely, Christ becoming Incarnate, the *praises and hymns of David, the son of Jesse,* that is, the people of Jerusalem signified by David, were *found wanting.* For these [the people of Jerusalem] were accustomed to praise God for his temporal benefits and for exterior goods; but after Christ was born, these praises were found wanting because they destroyed place and people. These praises, therefore, contained in the present Psalm, express the rectitude of the providence of God disposing all things, though to some people it seems contrary, as it is seen as imperfect when they perceive now the evil to flourish and prosper, but the good to suffer trial be to be oppressed. According to Jerome, this Psalm is also said to be of Asaph, as author, but according to Augustine [it was Asaph] as singer, so that David composed this Psalm that was sung by Asaph, who was one of the principal singers of the temple in the time of David.[2]

But first, the prophet David sets forth the principal purpose or intended conclusion [of the Psalm]: and thereafter he argues on the part of both sides. Therefore, he says: *Quam bonus Israel Deus! How good is God to*

---

1 E. N. Denis's title varies from the Sixto-Clementine Vulgate, which (translated) reads: *A Psalm for Asaph.*
2 1 Chron. 16:5; 25:1, 2.

Israel! That is, God is very good to the Christian people who contemplate the Godhead faithfully, *his qui recto sunt corde, to them that are of a right heart*, that is, the just, scheming nothing evil, but always conforming themselves to the divine law. Now God is good to all men insofar as he preserves them in being and provides to each one of them. But to the just, God is powerfully good, that is, kind, sweet, and liberal. For that which is diffusive of itself is called good. But God, as much as it is in himself, is prompt to communicate his goodness to all men; and nothing else impedes us from partaking of the divine gifts except our negligence and sins, in the manner that Jeremiah attests: *Your sins have withheld good things from you.*[3] Because therefore this impediment is removed by those with a right heart, they are worthy to accept the divine gifts. And so others, who know only in a distorted or artless way the divine goodness, will not come to know it experientially or partake in it sweetly. For this reason, God is strongly good to them [with a right heart], according to this: *The Lord is good to them that hope in him, to the soul that seeks him.*[4]

72{73}[2]   *But my feet were almost moved; my steps had well-nigh slipped.*

Mei autem pene moti sunt pedes, pene effusi sunt gressus mei.

72{73}[3]   *Because I had a zeal on occasion of the wicked, seeing the prosperity of sinners.*

Quia zelavi super iniquos, pacem peccatorum videns.

And so the Prophet [David] begins to argue the opposing part, and, speaking in the person of the weak-willed, says: **72{73}[2]** *Mei autem pene moti sunt pedes, but my feet were almost moved*: that is, my affections are as bent, and they are averse to observing the divine law fully; or [alternatively], my feet, that is, the intellect and will, because men tend toward God by these, by contemplating and loving. *Pene effuse sunt gressus mei, by steps had well-nigh slipped*: that is, my works are, as it were, emptied out, and they are deprived from reward because of my inconstancy. **72{73}[3]** *Quia zelavi, because I had zeal*, that is, by envy and irrationality was I moved, *super iniquos, on occasion of the wicked*, envying their temporal prosperity and *pacem, peace* [that is] false, carnal, and transitory [peace], *peccatorem videns, seeing the wicked*, which I was unable to endure with equanimity because of my imperfections. For man ought not to be moved in this manner, as it says in a Psalm above,

---

3   Jer. 5:25b.
4   Lam. 3:25.

Be not emulous of evildoers, nor envy them that work iniquity.[5] But if one suffers from the prosperous successes of the ungodly to the extent these oppose themselves to their salvation, this proceeds out of love [for them], and it does not pertain to the zeal of envy. But we ought not reckon that the ungodly have true peace, since peace is the tranquility of good order,[6] which the malicious lack, for sensuality prevails over the rational in them, and the flesh dominates over the spirit. Whence it is written: *There is no peace to the wicked, says the Lord.*[7] Repeatedly therefore the holy Prophets proclaim this question and the thinking of the weak, why, namely, the good are afflicted in this age, and the ungodly prosper. Here Jeremiah says: *You indeed, O Lord, are just, if I plead with you; but yet I will speak what is just to you: Why does the way of the wicked prosper, and why is it well with all them that transgress against you?*[8] And Habakkuk: *Why do you look at the disdainful, and hold your peace when the wicked man tramples upon the man that more just than himself? Your eyes are pure, you do not see evil. Why do you look upon them that do unjust things?*[9] Job also: *Is my debate against man, that I should not have just reason to be troubled? Why then do the wicked live, are advanced, and are strengthened with riches, ... and the rod of God is not upon them?*[10] But this prosperity of the evildoers does not cause the perfect and just man uncertainty or anxiety: for he is not ignorant that God *scourges every son whom he receives,*[11] and that *as gold in the furnace, he proves the elect,*[12] and that *through many tribulations we must enter into the kingdom of God.*[13]

---

5 Ps. 36:1b.

6 E. N. Denis defines peace as *tranquillitas bonae ordinationis,* the tranquility of good order, drawing from St. Augustine's famous definition of peace in Book 19.13 of the *City of God.* "Peace of mortal man and God is ordered in faith under obedience to the eternal law; the peace of men is ordered concord; household peace is the ordered concord of those living together between those ruling and those obeying; civil peace is the ordered concord between the citizens ruling and those obeying; the peace of the celestial city is the most ordered and most concordant society in enjoying God, and of one another in God. The peace of all things is the tranquility of order (*tranquillitas ordinis*). Order is the disposition of equal and unequal things, each to its own place." St. Augustine, *City of God,* XIX, 13.1, PL 41, 640.

7 Is. 57:21.

8 Jer. 12:1.

9 Hab. 1:13. E. N. Denis departs from the Sixto-Clementine Vulgate. Additionally, Denis re-arranges the verse.

10 Job 26:4, 7, 9b.

11 Heb. 12:6b.

12 Wis. 3:6a.

13 Acts 14:21b.

72{73}[4] *For there is no regard to their death, and there is strength in their stripes.*[14]

Quia non est respectus morti eorum, et firmamentum in plaga eorum.

Now why we see peace to be with the sinners is explained in what follows: 72{73}[4] *Quia non est respectus morti eorum, for there is not regard to their death*: that is, because they do not regard and do not consider death to be impending, and so they live secure, as if they will never die.[15] *Et firmamentum in plaga eorum, and strength in their stripes.* The negation at the beginning is to be resumed in that which is now expressed, in this sense: Nor is strength, that is, some virtue or a stable fortitude from penance in their stripes, that is, their life is vicious and miserable. For sin is a wound (plaga) to the soul; and as holy Job says about them who persevere in vices: *They have said to God, Depart from us, we desire not the knowledge of your ways.*[16] Isaiah also: *They say to the seers, See not; and to them that behold, Behold not for us those things that are right. Speak unto us pleasant things, see errors for us.*[17] Or [alternatively] thus: *For there is no regard in their death*: that is, they have peace in vices because God does not receive them with the eye of his clemency, as Isaiah says of the sinner, *I hid my face from you, and was angry: and he went away wandering in his own heart:*[18] and so God does not concern himself with their eternal death, for he does not

---

14   E. N. I have modified the Douay-Rheims (from "nor is their strength in their stripes [*i.e.*, wounds] to "and strength in their stripes" so that the comments of Denis in the *Commentary* on how the latter clause should be understood (which the translators of the Douay-Rheims already took into account) can be seen.

15   E. N. The *memento mori*, or recollection that one is mortal, is one of the four so-called *novissima*, or four last things (death, judgment, hell, and heaven) upon which it is spiritually useful to mediate. "In all your works remember your last end (*novissima tua*), and you shall never sin." Ecclus. 7:40. As one translation of Ecclesiasticus 41:3 put it, *O mors, bonum est consilium tuum*, "O death, your counsel is good." Pope St. John Paul II wrote in his Apostolic Exhortation *Reconciliatio et Penitentia*, No. 26: "Nor can the Church omit, without serious mutilation of her essential message, a constant catechesis on what the traditional Christian language calls the four last things of man (*quattuor novissima hominis*): death, judgment (universal and particular), hell and heaven. In a culture which tends to imprison man in the earthly life at which he is more or less successful, the pastors of the church are asked to provide a catechesis which will reveal and illustrate with the certainties of faith what comes after the present life: beyond the mysterious gates of death, an eternity of joy in communion with God or the punishment of separation from him. Only in this eschatological vision can one realize the exact nature of sin and feel decisively moved to penance and reconciliation."

16   Job 21:14.

17   Is. 30:10.

18   Is. 57:17.

obstruct it. And *there is strength*,[19] that is, strong perseverance and the hard obstinacy, in their stripes, in their interior [wounds], that is, in fault, for they do not repent. Or [yet another alternative] which is more literal, is this: *For there is no regard to their death*: that is, they do not appear to die quickly, but sometimes they live longer than the just, in the manner that is written: *A just man perishes in his justice, and a wicked man lives a long time in his wickedness.*[20] This can also refer to the condemnation of their grave offenses. But sometimes they deserve through some good work done outside of charity,[21] a prolongation of their life. And *there is strength in their stripes*: that is, if evil men have incurred some blow, they are quickly attended to and they do not last long in it, for there is much approbation and human consolation ready for them, which often the just are in need of and lack.

72{73}[5] *They are not in the labor of men: neither shall they be scourged like other men.*

In labore hominum non sunt, et cum hominibus non flagellabuntur.

72{73}[5] *In labore hominum, in the labor of men*, that is, of holy and virtuous men, *non sunt; et cum hominibus; they are not . . . like other men* truly rational in their manner of living, *non flagellabuntur, neither shall they be scourged* with the scourge of children, toward the amendment in the present life, but the scourge of the reprobate and toward the perdition in the pit of hell. But these verses here ought not to be understood as [suggesting] that sinners do not labor in this life, especially since it elsewhere says: *We wearied ourselves in the way of iniquity and destruction, and have walked through hard ways.*[22] Ecclesiastes also says: *God has given to a man that is good in his sight, wisdom, and knowledge, . . . but to the sinner he has given vexation, and superfluous care.*[23] There is therefore a

---

19 *E. N.* In this interpretation and the next, Denis does not bring forward the negative of the first clause.

20 Eccl. 7:16b.

21 *E. N.* In other words, a naturally-good work done outside of the state of grace, and therefore not in any way supernaturally meritorious. As the *Summa Theologiae* says, works done outside of charity (*extra caritatem facta*) are not condignly meritorious of either any temporal or eternal good from God." But someone "may be said to merit congruously some good through good works done outside of charity." These can include: temporal goods, a disposition to grace, and the forming of the habit of doing good (natural) works. ST IIIa (Supp.), q. 14, art. 4, c.

22 Wis. 5:7a. *E. N.* The verse continues: *But the way of the Lord we have not known.*

23 Eccl. 2:26a.

two-fold labor: penitential labor, and the labor of evil works. For in the way that from its very nature virtue is delectable, so from its nature vice is bitter, laborious, and punitive: yet often, with respect to us, the contrary occurs because of the corruption of our nature. Therefore, sinners are not found in holy and penitential labor, for they have time neither for sacred vigils, nor pure prayers, nor due discipline, nor most wholesome fasting, but they spend and waste their time in vain pursuits. Yet though their life, according to the truth, is much more laborious and punitive that the manner of living of the good, because. after all, the perverse life pleases them more, and therefore they judge themselves to live without labor, and they suppose the life of the just to be laborious, and they abhor it and disdain it. But the just have true judgment, and by experience the have come to learn how sweet it is to serve God, how delightful it is to have a serene conscience, how great is the joy of a pure souls, how truly sweet is the yoke of Christ, and light its burden.[24] According to Bernard, this verse is to no one more properly applicable than to the clergy of our time.

72{73}[6]   *Therefore pride has held them fast: they are covered with their iniquity and their wickedness.*

> *Ideo tenuit eos superbia; operti sunt iniquitate et impietate sua.*

72{73}[7]   *Their iniquity has come forth, as it were from fatness: they have passed into the affection of the heart.*

> *Prodiit quasi ex adipe iniquitas eorum; transierunt in affectum cordis.*

And so because the evildoers prosper and enjoy a leisurely life, **72{73}** [6] *Ideo tenuit eos superbia, therefore pride has held them fast,* that is, the bonds of exaltation constrict them, and they are led into the captivity and servitude of pride: indeed they have become slaves of pride according to this, *Whosoever commits sin, is the servant of sin.*[25] *Operti sunt iniquitate et impietate sua; they are covered with their iniquity and their wickedness:* that is, in the manner that perfect men are said to be covered and dressed with justice, so these are working evil everywhere, they are doers of iniquity to their neighbor and impiety toward God. **72{73}[7]** *Prodiit quasi ex adipe iniquitas eorum, their iniquity has come forth, as it were from fatness:* that is, their evil is caused by abundance and fatness or the copiousness of temporal things, because the copiousness of temporal things is the kindling for

---

24   Matt. 11:30.
25   John 8:34b.

all transgressions. And so the just man prays: *Give me only the necessaries of life.*[26] *Transierunt in affectum cordis, they have passed into the affection of the heart*, that is, they have consented to the concupiscences of the flesh and illicit desires. Against this, the Apostle [Paul] states of just men: *And they are Christ's, have crucified their flesh, with the vices and concupiscences.*[27] To which we are admonished by the prince of the Apostles, who says: *I beseech you as strangers and pilgrims to refrain yourselves from carnal desires which war against the soul.*[28]

72{73}[8] *They have thought and spoken wickedness: they have spoken iniquity on high.*

Cogitaverunt et locuti sunt nequitiam; iniquitatem in excelso locuti sunt.

72{73}[9] *They have set their mouth against heaven: and their tongue has passed through the earth.*

Posuerunt in caelum os suum, et lingua eorum transivit in terra.

72{73}[8] *Cogitaverunt, they have thought*, with mental consent, *et locuti sunt, and they have spoken*, with their bodily mouth, *nequitiam, wickedness*, that is, fraudulent and cruel words against virtuous men, whom they seek to oppress: this is most apparent in tyrants, the murderers of the blessed martyrs. Whence it is stated in Isaiah: *The vessels of the deceitful are most wicked: for he has framed devices to destroy the meek. Iniquitatem, iniquity*, that is iniquitous words, *in excelso, on high*, that is, in an exalted way, boldly, loudly, and publicly, *locuti sunt, they have spoken*: as is written elsewhere, *They have proclaimed abroad their sin as Sodom, and they have not hid it.*[29] 72{73}[9] *Posuerunt in caelum os suum, they have set their mouth against heaven*: that is, with neck erect and haughty mind they have uttered words of blasphemy against God, as is written in the book of Job: *He has run against him with his neck raised up, and is armed with a fat neck.*[30] Whence also the Pharaoh said: *I know not the Lord.*[31] And Sennacherib: *Let not your God deceive you, for he is unable to deliver you.*[32] Nero, also, Domitian, Diocletian and

---

26 Prov. 30:8b.
27 Gal. 5:24.
28 1 Pet. 2:11.
29 Is. 3:9a.
30 Job 15:26.
31 Ex. 5:2b.
32 Is. 37:10a.

many others expressed many blasphemies against Christ. *Et lingua eorum transivit in terra; and their tongue has passed through the earth*: that is, their speech clung to the things of earth, or it evolved into deed, and it exceeded the weakness of human measure.

72{73}[10]   *Therefore will my people return here and full days shall be found in them.*

Ideo convertetur populus meus hic, et dies pleni invenientur in eis.

And so the Lord says of the people that have been pre-elected: 72{73} [10] *Ideo convertetur populus meus hic, therefore will my people return here*: that is, because there is such iniquity and condemnation accompanying the temporal prosperity of the ungodly, the people who will be saved will turn to me, here, that is, in this circumstance currently being considered: for they will examine how dangerous worldly prosperity and carnal desire is; and so they will abhor them and flee them, they will no longer greatly envy the ungodly, but they will feel sorry for them, and they will give themselves over to a spiritual and arduous manner of life. *Et dies pleni, and days full* of the fruits of penance and good works, *invenientur, shall be found* by God, the judge, *in eis, in them* that have been converted to God. For the life of the saints (says Ambrose) will be fullness; but empty are the days of the evil.[33]

72{73}[11]   *And they said: How does God know? And is there knowledge in the most High?*

Et dixerunt: Quomodo scit Deus? Et si est scientia in excelso?

72{73}[12]   *Behold these are sinners; and yet abounding in the world they have obtained riches.*

Ecce ipsi peccatores, et abundantes in saeculo, obtinuerunt divitias.

72{73}[13]   *And I said: Then have I in vain justified my heart, and washed my hands among the innocent.*

Et dixi: Ergo sine causa iustificavi cor meum, et lavi inter innocentes manus meas.

---

33   E. N. The reference is to St. Ambrose's *Commentary on Luke: Plenitudinem iusti vita habet, inanes autem dies sunt impiorum,* "the life of the just will have fullness, but the days of the ungodly will be empty." PL 15, 1643.

72{73}[14] *And I have been scourged all the day; and my chastisement has been in the mornings.*

Et fui flagellatus tota die, et castigatio mea in matutinis.

72{73}[11] *Et dixerunt, and they said*, the previously mentioned weak men before they have been made perfect by converting to God [said]: *Quomodo scit Deus? How does God know* these inferior things, if he allows these things, namely, that the ungodly might prosper? *Et si est scientia in excelso? And is there knowledge in the most High?* That is, is there providence in the sublime God? Indeed, it seems that there is not: for if it were, God would have delivered to evil men the adversity and punishments they deserve, but to just men prosperity and joy. This is what is written with blessed Job: *Do you not think that God is higher than heaven . . . and he does not consider our things, and he walks about the poles of heaven?*[34] Whence, it is written in another place about those who deny divine providence: *They have counted our life a pastime, and the business of life to be gain, and that we must be acquiring every way.*[35] Now, why the weak say this is stated in what follows: **72{73}[12]** *Ecce ipsi [sunt] peccatores, et; behold these are sinners, and* nevertheless they are *abundantes in saeculo; obtinuerunt divitias; yet abounding in the world, they have obtained riches* by seizing inheritances. **72{73}[13]** *Ergo, then*, that is, when it is so, I *sine causa, in vain*, that is, without profit and reason, *iustificavi cor meum, justified my heart*, with all care keeping custody of my heart from evil thoughts, *et, and* without cause *lavi inter innocents manus meas, washed my hands among the innocent*, that is, I kept my works unstained. **72{73} [14]** *Et fui, and I have been* without cause *flagellatus tota die, scourged all the day*, that is, assiduous in exterior vigils, fasts, discipline, tears, and prayers taken up on behalf of God or undertaken for spiritual progress; *et castigatio mea in matutinis, and my chastisement has been in the mornings*, that is, the amendment by which I have reformed myself, and the holy exertions particular engaged in in the morning, by which I disciplined by body and spirit, or by which I was chastised by you, was empty.

72{73}[15] *If I said: I will speak thus: behold I should condemn the generation of your children.*

Si dicebam: Narrabo sic; ecce nationem filiorum tuorum reprobavi.

---

34   Job 22:12a, 14a.
35   Wis. 15:12. E. N. I have changed the Douay-Rheims's "must be getting every way," to "we must be acquiring every way."

Consequently, he argues in opposition: **72{73}[15]** *Si dicebam, if I said in my heart: Narrabo sic, I will speak thus*, that is, if I have thought so to feel and so to assert things about your providence and the happiness of evil men; *ecce nationem filiorum tuorum reprobavi, behold I should condemn the generation of your children*, that is, then I contradict the generation and the society of the elect, for their life would be without reward: as the Lord complains of some through Malachi: *Your words have been unsufferable to me, says the Lord. And you have said: . . . He labors in vain that serves God, and what profit is it that we have kept his ordinances, and that we have walked sorrowful before the Lord of hosts?*[36]

72{73}[16]   *I studied that I might know this thing, it is a labor in my sight.*

Existimabam ut cognoscerem hoc; labor est ante me.

72{73}[17]   *Until I go into the sanctuary of God, and understand concerning their last ends.*

Donec intrem in sanctuarium Dei, et intelligam in novissimis eorum.

72{73}[16] *Existimabam ut cognoscerem, I studied that I might know this thing*: that is, I supposed myself to have reason to question and to ascertain why the ungodly prosper and the holy are afflicted in so many ways; *hoc labor est ante me, it is a labor in my sight*, that is, to know the cause is most laborious an undertaking for me. **72{73}[17]** *Donec intrem in sanctuarium Dei, until I go into the sanctuary of God*, that is, until God reveals *the uncertain and hidden things* of his *wisdom*,[37] admitting me into the secret of his knowledge, and opening for me sacred Scripture, which is also called the sanctuary of God. For God speaks to us and responds through sacred Scripture, as God gave responses in the sanctuary of the tabernacle.[38] *Et intelligam in novissimis eorum, and I will understand concerning their last ends*, that is, I will consider what threatens the perverse at their end, what punishment and damnation looms over them, how quickly they head towards death, how severely they will be judged, and how irreparably they will be condemned. I will heed also what blessedness awaits the elect and the just, how they

---

36   Mal. 3:13–14.

37   Ps. 50:8b.

38   *Cf.* Ex. 25:22: *Thence will I give orders, and will speak to you over the propitiatory, and from the midst of the two cherubims, which shall be upon the ark of the testimony, all things which I will command the children of Israel by you.*

will be safely divided [from the reprobate], how mercifully they will be received by the Judge, and how gloriously they will be crowned. When I pay attention to these things, then assuredly I will not be moved by the prosperity of the depraved, nor will the adversities suffered by the good disturb me: because I know that God cleanses his elect here in order that they will more speedily and copiously be glorified in heaven: as is also attested to in Revelation: *Such as I love, I rebuke and chastise.*[39] Also, the careful contemplation of these last things beforehand preserves men from all ruin, according to this: *In all your works remember your last end, and you shall never sin.*[40] But because the reprobate do not think about these things, they are a nation without counsel, and without wisdom: *O that they would be wise and would understand, and would provide for their last end,*[41] as is asserted about them in Deuteronomy; and so they sin without measure and number.

72{73}[18] *But indeed for deceits you have put it to them: when they were lifted up you have cast them down.*

Verumtamen propter dolos posuisti eis; deiecisti eos dum allevarentur.

Then set forth are the torments of the depraved. **72{73}[18]** *Verumtamen,* but, O God, *propter dolos,* for deceits which the ungodly have perpetrated against neighbor, *posuisti eis, you have put it to them,* that is, to the ungodly, the end of their life being briefer than might otherwise have been the case. For often, men die untimely because of their sin, namely, when they are satiated with their iniquities. Whence in Job is written about the sinner: *Before his days shall be full, he shall perish.*[42] And again the holy Job: *Wicked men,* he says, *were taken away before their time.*[43] *Deiecisti eos dum allevarentur, when they were lifted up you have cast them down:* that is, while they were still flourishing and full of pride, you humbled the iniquitous, killing them or damning them. Obadiah asserted this: *The pride of your heart has lifted you up. But though you be exalted as an eagle, and though you set your nest among the stars, then will I bring you down, says the Lord.*[44]

---

39 Rev. 3:19a.
40 Ecclus 7:40.
41 Deut. 32:29.
42 Job 15:32a.
43 Job 22:15b–16a.
44 Obad. 3a, 4.

72{73}[19] How are they brought to desolation? *They have suddenly ceased to be: they have perished by reason of their iniquity.*

Quomodo facti sunt in desolationem? Subito defecerunt; perierunt propter iniquitatem suam.

72{73}[20] As the dream of them that awake, O Lord; so in your city you shall bring their image to nothing.

Velut somnium surgentium, Domine, in civitate tua imaginem ipsorum ad nihilum rediges.

72{73}[19] *Quomodo facti sunt in desolationem,* how are they brought to desolation, losing temporal goods and bodily health, or incurring death, in which no one has the strength to help them? *Subito defecerunt, they have suddenly ceased to be:* as is said in Job: *The praise of the wicked is short, and the joy of the hypocrite but for a moment.*[45] *Perierunt, they have perished,* eternally condemned, *propter iniquitatem suam, by reason of their iniquity:* as Scripture elsewhere testifies to, *They spend their days in wealth, and in a moment they go down to hell.*[46] 72{73}[20] *Velut somnium surgentium, Domine, in civitate tua imaginem ipsorum ad nihilum rediges. As the dream of them that awake, O Lord; so in your city you shall bring their image to nothing.* That is, in the way that a dream vanishes the moment one is awake, and it is recognized as being false, so, O Lord, you will bring to nothing, that is, you will condemn and destroy their image, that is, all the apparent happiness and glory of the reprobate you will take from them in your heavenly city, lest they see your blessedness. For here the ungodly are said to be in the day of their reprobation: *What has pride profited us? Or what advantage has the boasting of riches brought us? All those things are passed away like a shadow, and like a messenger that runs on.*[47] And again it is written in Scripture: *The hope of the wicked is as dust, ... and as a thin froth which is dispersed by the storm, ... and as the remembrance of a guest of one day that passes by.*[48] And so in the book of Job it is written: *If his pride mount up even to heaven, and his head touch the clouds, in the end he shall be destroyed like a dunghill. . . . As a dream that flees away he shall not be found, he shall pass as a vision of the night.*[49]

---

45 Job 20:5.
46 Job 21:13.
47 Wis. 5:8–9. E. N. I have replaced the Douay-Rheims's "post" with "messenger."
48 Wis. 5:15.
49 Job 20:6–8.

72{73}[21] *For my heart has been inflamed, and my reins have been changed:*

Quia inflammatum est cor meum, et renes mei commutati sunt;

72{73}[22] *And I am brought to nothing, and I knew not.*

Et ego ad nihilum redactus sum, et nescivi.

72{73}[23] *I am become as a beast before you: and I am always with you.*

Ut iumentum factus sum apud te, et ego semper tecum.

And so I say this, **72{73}[21]** *Quia inflammatum est cor meum, for my heart has been inflamed* with the zeal of justice and the fire of the Holy Spirit, and that which was said by Jeremiah has taken hold of me: *The word of the Lord ... came in my heart as a burning fire;*[50] *et renes mei, and my reins,*[51] that is, the movements and affections of my sensitive appetite, which formerly were moved according to the movements of desire, *commutati sunt, have been changed,* that is, they have been subordinated to the empire of reason.[52] This is something that cannot occur without the great grace of God.[53] **72{73}[22]** *Et ego ad nihilum redactus sum, and I am brought to nothing:* that is, before my reins were converted, when I was subject to sin and was the servant to disordered desire, I was nothing with regard to spiritual being;[54] and *nescivi, I knew not* that I was so [spiritually] annihilated,[55] because of the blindness of sin: for I regarded myself as being something, when I was nothing.[56] Or [alternatively]: *I am brought to nothing,* in considering myself; *and I knew not,* that is, I regarded myself not as wise, but as ignorant: because the Apostle says: *If any man think that he knows*

---

50 Jer. 20:8b, 9b.
51 E. N. "Reins" = "kidneys," a symbol of a man's innermost part. *See* footnote 7-10 in Volume 1.
52 *See* Article XLIV (Psalm 17:37) in Volume 1 and Article LXII (Psalm 27:6) and footnote 27-46 in Volume 2 for the "empire of reason."
53 E. N. "In the state of corrupt nature, man needs habitual grace healing of nature (*gratia habituali sanante naturam*) to the end that that he may completely abstain from sin." ST IaIIae, q. 109, art. 8, c. Sanctifying or habitual grace may be divided into two: *gratia sanans,* or curative or healing grace, which heals our post-lapsarian wounded nature, and *gratia elevans,* or elevating grace, which provides us with the supernatural virtues necessary for the supernatural life.
54 E. N. By spiritual being (*esse spirituale*), Denis means the life of sanctifying grace, a supernatural existence. For more on this, *see* footnote 27-42 in Volume 2.
55 E. N. Here, it is useful to recall the etymology of the word annihilated. It comes from the Latin to be reduced to nothing (*ad* ("to") + *nihil* ("nothing")).
56 *Cf.* Gal. 6:3: *For if any man think himself to be something, whereas he is nothing, he deceives himself.*

anything, he has not yet known as he ought to know;[57] and again, *Be not wise in your own conceits.*[58] **72{73}[23]** *Ut iumentum factus sum apud te, I am become as a beast before you*: that is, in comparison with your wisdom, I rather appear to be an irrational animal than a rational creature. Or thus [we might take it]: *I am become as a beast before you,* that is, I have placed my back under your yoke, I have obeyed your precepts so promptly, as a beast of burden, carrying his burden, obeys his master. *Et ego semper tecum, and I am always with you.* For he who humbles himself before God and submits to him unceasingly remains in him by grace.

72{73}[24] *You have held me by my right hand; and by your will you have conducted me, and with glory you have received me.*

> *Tenuisti manum dexteram meam, et in voluntate tua deduxisti me, et cum gloria suscepisti me.*

72{73}[24] *Tenuisti manum dexteram meam, you have held me by my right hand*: that is, by grace you have strengthened me and supported me, in the way one is supported by a friend who is at one's right hand; *et in voluntate tua, and by your will,* that is, by the observation of your precepts, or according to your will of good pleasure,[59] *deduxisti me, you have conducted me* in the way of pilgrimage at this exile, leading me by the right way to eternal happiness; *et cum gloria, and with glory,* that is, gloriously and powerfully, *suscepisti me, you have received me,* uniting me — whom you have snatched from the mouth of the devil and the death of sin — to you by charity. Or [alternatively], *with glory,* that is, heavenly beatitude, *you have received me,* that is, you have received me, transferring me from the wayfaring state to the heavenly homeland, and from *this body of death* to the incorruptible state,[60] especially in the day of judgment, *when this mortal will put on immortality.*[61]

---

57   1 Cor. 8:2.
58   Rom. 12:16b.
59   E. N. Denis is distinguishing here between what has been called God's sig-nified will and the will of good pleasure. "God ... manifests His will to us in two ways: by the rules He has made for us and by the various events which He causes to occur in our lives. In the former we have the signified will of God, in the latter His will of good-pleasure." Dom Vitalis Lehodey, O. C. R., *Holy Abandonment* (Dublin 1934)
60   Rom. 7:24b.
61   1 Cor. 15:53b, 54a.

72{73}[25] *For what have I in heaven? And besides you what do I desire upon earth?*

Quid enim mihi est in caelo? Et a te quid volui super terram?

72{73}[26] *For you my flesh and my heart has fainted away: you are the God of my heart, and the God that is my portion forever.*

Defecit caro mea et cor meum; Deus cordis mei, et pars mea, Deus in aeternum.

72{73}[25] *Quid enim mihi est in caelo? Et a te quid volui super terram? For what I have in heaven? And besides you what do I desire upon earth?* That is, I require nothing but you yourself, and I place my hope in, or set my happiness upon, no creature, either heavenly or earthly; but you are to me the object and cause of faith, hope, charity, and happiness. *I count all things but as dung, that I may gain Christ.*[62] Loving you, Creator, above all things, I am not able to satisfy my affection with finite goods, every creature being insufficient and inadequate for me; but I look to you alone, O eternal God, who are infinite goodness and uncircumscribed truth, to quiet, fulfill, and beatify my intellect and affection. **72{73} [26]** *Defecit caro mea*, my flesh ... *has fainted away*, that is, my lower appetites, *et cor meum*, and my heart, that is, my higher appetite, [has fainted away] in contemplation and love of the sovereign good, and of the beatitude prepared for me by God, because *eye has not seen, nor ear heard, neither has it entered into the heart of man, what things God has prepared for them that love him.*[63] *Deus cordis mei*, the God of my heart, that is, the love of my soul, its sovereign good, and God, its complete beatitude. For that which it most worships and loves is God's very self. *Et pars mea Deus in aeternum*, and the God that is my portion forever: that is, God is that good which I chose before all others, which I have loved before all things, which I intend always to hold on to, because he alone is sufficient for me, for in him I find the fulness of all good, beauty, and desirability. Whence also Isaiah, happy in this good, said: *Your name and your remembrance are the desire of the soul. My soul has desired you.*[64] And other scripture: *Let them that love you shine, as the sun shines in its rising.*[65]

---

62 Phil. 3:8b.
63 1 Cor. 2:9; Is. 64:4.
64 Is. 26:8b–9a.
65 Judges 5:31b.

72{73}[27] For behold they that go far from you shall perish: you have
destroyed all them that are disloyal to you.

Quia ecce qui elongant se a te peribunt; perdidisti omnes qui
fornicantur abs te.

72{73}[27] *Quia ecce qui elongant se,* for behold they that go far by
mortal sin *a te, from you,* Savior of all, *peribunt, shall perish,* because they
will go into everlasting fire.[66] *Perdidisti omnes qui fornicantur abs te, you
have destroyed all them that are disloyal to you:* that is, all who separate
from you with adulterous or evil thoughts and attach themselves to
transient things, you in the present ruin, withdrawing grace from them,
and in the future you will destroy them, repelling them from glory. For
it is a kind of spiritual fornication that the soul — marked with the
image of the most-high Trinity, and which ought to be a daughter to
her Creator and a bride of Christ — should make herself unfaithful to
her God, and lean upon, take delight in, and enjoy creatures more than
the Creator.[67] So the fornicators against God will be destroyed, as it is
written: *I have broken their heart that was faithless (fornicans), and revolted
from me,*[68] says the Lord. And again: *Rejoice not, O Israel, . . . for you
have committed fornication against your God.*[69]

---

66 Matt. 25:41b.
67 E. N. In Latin, the soul (*anima*) is feminine in gender, and so here is described as
a daughter (*filia*) and bride (*sponsa*) of God. In this instance, I have also used female
personal pronouns. (In the past, often the soul was referred to as "she"; however, this
practice seems to have fallen into desuetude, and the soul is generally neutered into
an "it." We ought, however, to reflect on the fact that the soul is feminine in gender in
Latin (as is *psyche* (ψυχή), the Greek word for soul), and there is no one better than
Dietrich von Hildebrand to guide us here. "In the natural order woman represents,
in contrast to the man, the receptive principle. . . . Nevertheless, here [in the spiritual
order] too the receptive principle is a formal constituent of woman and belongs, as
an element essential to its perfection, to the nature of 'femininity,' a category which
cannot be confined to the female sex. Here, where infinite and finite being, Creator
and creature, God and man, meet, the man as an individual soul is as purely receptive
as the woman. Here God alone is the giver, the creative and fertilizing principle, and
the human being, as a creature, the recipient, therefore, if you like, 'feminine.' And
this is pre-eminently true in the supernatural order of the soul as the bride of Christ
the God-man. Since woman in her receptive relation to man is the obvious natural
image of the soul as receptive or conceiving from and by Christ, and since we speak
of the soul as the bride and Christ as the bridegroom, not vice versa, it is woman, not
man, that is the natural type of that consecrated virginity, which represents precisely
the nuptial status of the soul as Christ's bride." Dietrich von Hildebrand, *In Defense
of Purity* (Steubenville, OH: Hildebrand Press, 2017), p. 88, n. 1
68 Ez. 6:9a.
69 Hosea 9:1a.

72{73}[28] *But it is good for me to adhere to my God, to put my hope in the Lord God: That I may declare all your praises, in the gates of the daughter of Sion.*

Mihi autem adhaerere Deo bonum est, ponere in Domino Deo spem meam; ut annuntiem omnes praedicationes tuas in portis filiae Sion.

72{73}[28] *Mihi autem adhaerere Deo, but . . . for me to adhere to my God* by charity and humble service, *bonum est, is good,* indeed most good, most salvific, and most worthy. For the highest nobility of the created mind is its conversion to God. *Ponere in Domino Deo spem meam, to put my hope in the Lord God* is good for me. For here the Bride says: *I to my beloved, and his turning is toward me.*[70] And Christ in the Gospel: *One thing is necessary.*[71] *Ut annuntiem, that I may declare* to all, or that by my singing to the glory of your name, *omnes praedicationes tuas, all your praises* contained in sacred Scripture, or inspired by divine influence in me, *in portis filiae Sion, in the gates of the daughter of Sion,* that is, in churches militant, who are the daughters of Sion, that is, of *the heavenly Jerusalem, who is our mother:*[72] For many are the particular churches, that is, the congregations of the faithful. Moreover, according to the venerable Hugh [of St. Cher], there are seven kinds of preaching which are designated by this verse:[73]

Sacra, fides, virtus, vitium, laus, praemia, poena.
Holy things, faith, virtue, vice, praise, reward, punishment.

For holy things are to be preached, that is: the seven sacraments of the Church;[74] faith, that is, the twelve articles of the faith;[75] virtues, that is,

---

70 Songs 7:10.
71 Luke 10:42a.
72 E. N. Gal. 4:26.
73 E. N. Hugo of St. Cher, *Commentary on the Psalms* (Lyons: Sumptibus Societatis Bibliopolarum, 1645), II, 187.
74 E. N. "Christ instituted the sacraments of the new law. There are seven: Baptism, Confirmation (or Chrismation), the Eucharist, Penance, the Anointing of the Sick, Holy Orders and Matrimony." CCC § 1210.
75 E. N. This are found in the Creed, namely: (1) I believe in God, the Father Almighty, Creator of heaven and earth; (2) And in Jesus Christ, His only Son, our Lord; (3) Who was conceived by the Holy Ghost; born of the Virgin Mary; (4) Suffered under Pontius Pilate: was crucified, dead, and buried; (5) He descended into hell: the third day He rose again from the dead; (6) He ascended into Heaven: sitteth at the right hand of God the Father Almighty; (7) From thence He shall come to judge the living and the dead. (8) I believe in the Holy Ghost; (9) The

the theological, moral, and intellectual virtues, in order that they may be acquired;[76] vices, that is, mortal sins, so that we might avoid them; praise, that is, commendation, examples, and the life of Christ and the Saints; also the rewards of the elect, and the punishments of the reprobate.

See how this Psalm is complete, most worthy of all praise, which to devout minds is most consolatory: in whose beginning is placed the word full of all sweetness, during whose progress the Prophet [David] beautifully preaches, and finally concludes with how vain and false the prosperity of the ungodly is, and how contemptible are the superfluities of the rich. For (as Jerome says) unceasing success in regard to temporal things is a certain indicator of eternal reprobation. And this is the severest wrath of God, when he permits a man to prosper temporally, he does not chastise him, but abandons him to his contrivances and desires.[77] In addition, this Psalm shows how God exercises certain and just providence over the acts of humans. It also copiously makes manifest what is the life of an elect and just man, namely, that his heart be justified, his hands be washed among the innocents, he might be scourged all day and chastised in the morning, his heart is enkindled with divine love, his flesh mortified, and he exists not in his own eyes, he confesses most humbly his lack of wisdom to the Lord, and in all things he subjects to his [the Lord's] rule as if he were a dutiful beast of burden. And then it recalls the benefits of the grace of God, and ascribes all spiritual progress to God. Finally, the soul most affectionately and most devoutly addresses God, affirming itself to strive for nothing outside of God, to desire God as its last end, and to be lacking in love and contemplation of him, either because it does not have the power to know him as clearly so as to love him as ardently as he is knowable and lovable, or because from the excess of fiery love and the rapture of contemplation he is with weak body and with a heart alienated from itself. Ultimately, he choses to forsake wholly all things, to adhere completely to God, and to only place his trust in him: and this, not as a result of his own reward, with any sort of reflection of himself, but so that he might proclaim all the praises of God. Therefore, let us think about and

---

Holy Catholic Church; the Communion of Saints; (10) The forgiveness of sins; (11) The resurrection of the body; (12) Life everlasting.

76   E. N. Theological virtues: faith, hope, charity. ST, IaIIae, q. 62, arts. 1–4. Moral or Cardinal virtues: prudence, justice, fortitude, and temperance. ST IaIIae, q. 61, arts. 1–5. Intellectual virtues are divided into speculative (understanding, science, wisdom) and practical (art and prudence). ST IaIIae, q. 57, arts. 1–6.

77   Cf. Ps. 80:13: *So I let them go according to the desires of their heart: they shall walk in their own inventions.*

chant this present Psalm with great attention in order that all mundane prosperity may be worthless to us, and that we might fully please, love, and take delight in that one thing that is alone necessary.[78]

PRAYER

O GOD OF OUR HEART, O GOD, OUR portion in eternity, through you strengthening us, let not our heart and flesh cease in doing good; make us always to hold fast on to you, and to place our hope in you, Lord God, until, you leading the way, we might be found worthy to enter into your heavenly sanctuary: where you live and rule, three and one God, for all ages.

Deus cordis nostri, Deus pars nostra in aeternum, te confortante
in bonis agendis non deficiat caro et cor nostrum; fac
nos tibi semper adhaerere, et in te Domino Deo
spem ponere, donec te praevio duce, caeleste
sanctuarium tuum mereamur introire:
qui trinus et unus Deus, vivis
et dominaris in
omnia saecula.

---

78   Luke 10:42.

Psalm 73

ARTICLE XLI

LITERAL EXPOSITION OF THE SEVENTY-THIRD PSALM:
UT QUID, DEUS, REPULISTI IN FINEM?
O GOD, WHY HAVE YOU CAST US OFF UNTO THE END?

73{74}[1] *Understanding for Asaph. O God, why have you cast us off unto the end, [why] is your wrath enkindled against the sheep of your pasture?*

Intellectus Asaph. Ut quid, Deus, repulisti in finem, iratus est furor tuus super oves pascuae tuae?

THE TITLE OF THIS PSALM NOW BEING explained is: 73{74}[1] *Intellectus Asaph, understanding for Asaph.* Asaph is interpreted as [signifying] congregation,[1] which in the Old Law was called the Synagogue, but now is called the Church. According to Jerome, this Psalm was composed by Asaph, as also the other Psalms entitled for Asaph.[2] But Augustine felt otherwise. And therefore, according to Augustine, the sense of this title is: *Understanding for Asaph,* that is, in this Psalm is treated what is understood by the Synagogue or the Church, namely, figures passed over now, and which were fulfilled by Christ, and that we ought to expect and to seek Christ, not in temporal things, but eternal things. Moreover, according to Catholic teachers, this Psalm literally speaks of the captivity and destruction of the Jews accomplished by Titus and his army.

Therefore, the Prophet [David], because of this destruction of the kingdom and people of the Hebrews, by means of expressions of admiration and of great suffering in order that he might summon forth the mercy of God quickly, says: *Ut quid, Deus, repulisti; O God, why have you cast off* the land and your people from yourself and your protection, delivering them into the hands of adversaries, *in finem, unto the end,* that is, totally and even unto the end of the world? Now some explain this Psalm as literally dealing with the Babylonian

---

1 E. N. The Hebrew verb [אסף (*asap*)] means to collect and gather together, such as a harvest or men; hence its relationship to congregation.

2 E. N. These are Psalms 49 and 72–82.

captivity:[3] but that did not last until the end; indeed God frequently through Jeremiah said that he would not give them over and utterly destroy them [as a people in the Babylonian captivity], but wanted to bring them back to their land after seventy years.[4] Therefore, it is not of that captivity that this Psalm speaks of, but rather of that [captivity] in which they are now in, because this [latter one] lasts even unto the end. This is what is contained in Daniel, *The desolation shall continue even ... to the end;*[5] and elsewhere: *The end is come upon my people Israel: I will not again pass by them anymore.*[6]

But this raises the question of how the Prophet in the subsequent verses calls the Jews unbelieving and perverse, sheep of the flock of the Lord, and the congregation of God. The answer is that they are called sheep and congregation of God in the same manner that Christ in the Gospel proclaims them *children of the kingdom,*[7] that being because they were born from the seed of the holy Patriarchs and Prophets, and they were specially called by God: for Christ in the Gospel said, *I was not sent but to the sheep that are lost of the house of Israel.*[8] Or they are called sheep of the flock of God because they were bestowed the land of promise, flowing with milk and honey,[9] and their fathers ate heavenly bread when [they roamed for] forty years in the desert.[10] But whether we explain this Psalm of the captivity caused by the Romans or the Babylonians, it remains that the Jews were wicked during that time. For during the time of the Babylonian captivity, they adored alien gods; but during the time of the captivity conducted by Titus, they had killed Christ, and they were laid waste because of his murder. This does not escape the notice of this Prophet, since he begins by means of a series of questions. He also prays for the delivery of the Jews from their present captivity, referring to their spiritual captivity by demons, and their being ensnared in the bonds of infidelity and obstinacy, rather than their expulsion from their land. For the holy Prophet [David] knew that the Jews would finally be converted to Christ. Though at various times some

---

3   E. N. The Babylonian captivity or exile occurred between 597 BC, when the Chaldeans under King Nebuchadnezzar II, conquered Jerusalem. It lasted until 538 BC, when the Persians under King Cyrus the Great overthrew the Chaldeans and conquered the city of Babylon.

4   Jer. 4:27; 25:11, 12; 29:10–14.

5   Dan. 9:27b.

6   Amos 8:2b.

7   Matt. 8:12a.

8   Matt. 15:24.

9   Ex. 3:8 *and elsewhere.*

10   Ex. 16:35.

of them have converted; yet they will not convert as a group except at the end of time. For, according to the Apostle [Paul], when the *fullness of the Gentiles* will have come in, then *all Israel* will be saved.[11] Also the devastation of the Jews by the Romans is excellently and clearly prophesied by Balaam: *They shall come in galleys from Italy, they shall overcome the Assyrians, and shall waste the Hebrews.*[12]

Iratus est furor tuus super oves pascuae tuae, your wrath is enkindled against the sheep of your pasture, that is, the sons of Israel: *for the wrath of God is come upon them according to the Apostle.*[13] And because they are so awfully and finally forsaken, they are deprived, both interiorly and exteriorly, from all the grace of God and from their land, and so the wrath of God is said to be upon them. The divine Scripture ascribes wrath and anger to God, according to that which we find written elsewhere: *The Lord is a revenger, and has wrath:*[14] not that in God there arises a new passion or change or disquiet, but because there is a similarity in operation, for it is considered to appear in the manner of wrath or anger when our sin is avenged by horrible punishments. Now that true and properly-so-called passions do not correspond to God in this manner, he himself testifies through Jeremiah: *Do they provoke me to anger, says the Lord? Is it not themselves, to the confusion of their countenance?*[15]

73{74}[2] *Remember your congregation, which you have possessed from the beginning. The rod of your inheritance which you have redeemed: mount Sion in which you have dwelt.*[16]

Memor esto congregationis tuae, quam possedisti ab initio. Redemisti virgam haereditatis tuae, mons Sion, in quo habitasti in eo.

73{74}[2] *Memor esto,* remember, O Lord, threatening mercy, not perceiving something anew, *congregationis tuae, your congregation,* that is, the Synagogue, *quam possedisti, which you have possessed* as your peculiar and chosen people, *ab initio, from the beginning,* you who spoke to their fathers, Abraham, Isaac, and Jacob, promising them that their seed would be your people: as Moses said, *The Lord has been closely joined to your fathers, and loved them and chose their seed after*

---

11 Rom. 11:25b–26a.
12 Num. 24:24a.
13 1 Thess. 2:16b.
14 Nahum 1:2a.
15 Jer. 7:19.
16 E. N. I have replaced the Douay-Rheims's "scepter" (which translates the Latin *virgam*) with "rod."

them.[17] The Prophet [David] prays, therefore, for the enlightenment of the Jews; he diligently recalls also the former benefits of God in order that God might be more easily reconciled. For it is fitting for a magnanimous person to forgive quickly the friend who has offended him because of the former familiarity and prior friendship. He therefore adds: *Redemisti virgam hereditatis tuae, the rod of your inheritance which you have redeemed,* that is, the rod that is your inheritance, namely, the Israelite people, which are called rod because by it you have corrected sinners dwelling in the land of Canaan, and because, like a rod, it was made straight through the justice of the law, and its being raised higher through faith and contemplation of future goods. In any event, sometimes in sacred Scripture a singular person is designated by a rod: in a manner that is written in Isaiah of the incomparable and Christ-bearing Virgin Mary, *And there shall come forth a rod out of the root of Jesse.*[18] But in this place "rod" signifies a congregation of people. This [people] God delivered out of the land of Egypt and Babylon, and out of many other oppressive burdens, as is made clear in the books of Judges, Maccabees, Esther, and Judith. Now what is the rod is stated by what follows: *mons Sion, mount Sion,* that is, the Synagogue, understanding the vicinity for the place, for upon mount Sion was built the temple. *In quo habitasti in eo, in which you have dwelt.* God dwelt upon this mount by means of a special grace, showing his marvels in the temple, and dwelling familiarly among his people, for he said to Moses: *I will dwell in the midst of the children of Israel;*[19] and, *The Lord your God walks in the midst of your camp.*[20] We are also able to say that God, the only-Begotten of God, the man Christ dwelt, that is, frequently and occasionally for relatively long times went to the temple or this mount, in the manner that was predicted by Malachi: *Presently the Lord, whom you seek, and the Angel of the Testament, whom you desire, shall come to his temple.*[21]

---

17   Deut. 10:15.

18   Is. 11:1a. E. N. This identification of the "rod" of Isaiah 11:1 with Mary is very ancient. For example, in his *Against the Jews (Adversus Iudaeos)*, Tertullian (ca. 155– ca. 240 AD) states: "'And there shall be born,' [Isaiah] says, 'a rod from the root of Jesse,' which is Mary — 'and a flower shall ascend from his root.... [which refers to] Christ; rightly compared to a flower indeed by his glory, from his grace; but pruned from the branch of Jesse by Mary." *Adv. Iudaeos,* IX, 26, PL 2, 623-24. St. Ambrose is succinct: "The root is the family of the Jews, the rod is Mary, the flower of Mary is Christ." *De Ben. Patriarch.,* 4, 19, PL 14, 713.

19   Ex. 29:45.

20   Deut. 23:14a.

21   Mal. 3:1. E. N. The "Angel of the Testament" is a reference to the Messiah. A. J. Mass, S. J., *Christ in Type and Prophecy* (New York: Benziger Brothers 1893), Vol. I, 437–38.

73{74}[3] *Lift up your hands against their pride unto the end; see what things the enemy has done wickedly in the sanctuary.*

Leva manus tuas in superbias eorum in finem. Quanta malignatus est inimicus in sancto.

73{74}[4] *And they that hate you have made their boasts, in the midst of your solemnity. They have set up their ensigns for signs.*

Et gloriati sunt qui oderunt te in medio solemnitatis tuae; posuerunt signa sua, signa,

73{74}[5] *And they knew not both in the going out and on the highest top. As with axes in a wood of trees,*

Et non cognoverunt sicut in exitu super summum. Quasi in silva lignorum securibus,

73{74}[6] *They have cut down at once the gates thereof, with axe and hatchet they have brought it down,*

Exciderunt ianuas eius in idipsum; in securi et ascia deiecerunt eam,

73{74}[7] *They have set fire to your sanctuary: they have defiled the dwelling place of your name in the land.*

Incenderunt igni sanctuarium tuum, in terra polluerunt tabernaculum nominis tui.

73{74}[8] *They said in their heart, the whole kindred of them together: Let us abolish all the festival days of God from the land.*

Dixerunt in corde suo cognatio eorum simul: quiescere faciamus omnes dies festos Dei a terra.

73{74}[3] *Leva manus tuas in superbias eorum in finem, lift up your hands against their pride unto the end.* The holy doctors commonly understand this in a good sense, so that it is the prayer of the Prophets for the correction of the Gentiles, from their seeing the Jews being devasted in this way. And so it will be [understood] in this sense: extend your power *against their pride*, namely, of the Romans, extinguishing in them fault, but not grace; and so destroy them in *the end*, that is, in a saving way, since by your correction they may receive eternal life. In a literal sense this also can be seen to be fittingly understood in a bad way, and so it is a prayer for the destruction of the Roman rule as it relates to the extinction of the Gentile emperors and of unfaithful people, but not as it relates to those that that were subject to Christ. And so this was fulfilled at the time of Constantine: for the Christian people began to rule from that time.

Quanta malignatus est inimicus, see what things the enemy has done wickedly, that is, how many evil deeds any particular adversary, or [specifically] Titus with his army, has done, *in sancto, in the sanctuary,* that is, in Mount Sion and in the holy city of Jerusalem, which [temple and city] were entirely devastated by the Romans! And Titus and his army are said to be wicked or malicious because they served and worshipped idols or because they destroyed the temple with unjust intention, not in vengeance of the shedding of Christ's blood, but out of the desire of domination. 73{74}[4] *Et gloriati sunt, and they . . . have made their boasts* in evil things and vices, [they, that is,] *qui oderunt te, that hate you,* namely, the just-mentioned idolaters, *in medio solemnitatis tuae, in the midst of your solemnity,* that is, in the middle of the temple, which having entered, they destroyed with laughter and exultation. Or [an alternative understanding is], *in the midst of your solemnity,* that is, in the middle of the Passover feast. For it was when the Jews had poured into Jerusalem to celebrate the Passover festivities that they were besieged by the Roman army and Titus and Vespasian. *Posuerunt, they set up,* these Romans, *signa sua, their ensigns,* that is, their own ensigns or military banners which they used during battle, namely eagles and dragons,[22] *signa, signs,* that is, as a certain indication of triumph; 73{74}[5] *et non cognoverunt, and they knew not* the true God nor his justice, because they did not think the Jews to suffer these things because of the sin committed against the Son of God, but because they supposed they had prevailed out of their own power. They supposed also their ensigns *sicut in exitu, both in the going out* as is customary during war, *super summum, and on the highest top,* that is, upon the highest place, so that it might be seen from far off.

Quasi in silva lignorum, as . . . in a wood of trees, that is, as trees are cut down in the forest, so *securibus, with axes* 73{74}[6] *exciderunt, they have cut down* and shattered to pieces *ianuas eius, its gates,* namely, of the temple and of the city of Jerusalem, *in id ipsum, in the same,* that is, with equal effort and unanimous will; *in securi et ascia, with axe and hatchet,* that is, by such instruments of carpentry, *deiecerunt eam, they have brought it down,* that is, the city and the house of God built in it. 73{74} [7] *Incenderunt igni sanctuarium tuum, they have set fire to your sanctuary,* that is, the temple dedicated to you, *in terra, in the land* of Judaea: for the flames destroyed that part that they did not otherwise destroy. Whence Daniel states: And a people with their leader that shall come, shall destroy the city and the sanctuary, and the end thereof shall be

---

22   E. N. The dragon (*draco*) was the military standard of the Roman calvary. On the other hand, the eagle (*aquila*) was the military standard of the Roman legion.

waste.[23] *Polluerunt tabernaculum nominis tui, they have defiled the dwelling place of your name*: for the Romans entered into the aforementioned temple with horses and women, which was prohibited by the [Mosaic] law; indeed, the law prohibited gentiles and the uncircumcised from entering the temple. **73{74}[8]** *Dixerunt in corde suo, cognatio eorum simul; they said in their heart, the whole kindred of them together*, that is, those living in that perverse generation, thought that which follows: *Quiescere faciamus omnes dies festos Dei a terra, let us abolish all the festival days of God from the land*, that is, let us impede, by killing men and destroying the temple, all worship of the God whom these [Jews] adore. The Romans spoke this either directly or equivalently. For if they did not say this openly, yet nevertheless they said it interpretatively or equivalently: for the destruction of the city and the temple, and the destruction of the population, necessarily was accompanied by the cessation of the feast days: and so in the first way intending [to stop the worship directly], but in the other way they also intended it, albeit indirectly.

73{74}[9] *Our signs we have not seen, there is now no prophet: and he will know us no more.*

Signa nostra non vidimus; iam non est propheta; et nos non cognoscet amplius.

Consequently, the voice of the Jews in this stated affliction is set forth, who bemoaningly and querulously say: **73{74}[9]** *Signa nostra non vidimus, our signs we have not seen*. It is as if they were saying: "Where are now those miracles which God did with our fathers, when he led them out of the land of Egypt, and led them through the Red Sea and the desert, and led them into the land of promise, and in myriad ways delivered them from the devastating powers?" In this way also Gideon is said to have written. Indeed, when the angel said to him, *The Lord is with you, O most valiant of men*, Gideon said: *I beseech you, my lord, if the Lord be with us, why have these evils fallen upon us? Where are his miracles which our fathers have told us of?*[24] *Iam non est propheta, there is now no prophet* who might console us, and who might pray for us to the Lord, and might teach us that which we ought to do. For after the Jews killed Christ and expelled his disciples,[25] they no longer had a prophet. And from this there is no

---

23 Dan. 9:26b.
24 Judges 6:12–13.
25 E. N. The Jews that accepted Christ as Messiah and God were at some point in time formally expelled from the synagogues. But it may be that this had been brewing in the minds of the Jewish leaders even during Christ's life, for as St. John says "the

doubt that this Psalm is not speaking of the Babylonian captivity. For during that time, according to St. Jerome, the Jews had true and holy prophets, since during that very time Ezechiel prophesied in Babylon and Jeremiah in Judah;[26] and he stated that each told the Jews what to do so that they might be liberated, and by this liberation they were consoled; in what a manner [they did so] can be certainly seen in their books of those prophets. *Et nos non congnoscet amplius, and he will know us no more.* The Jews during the time of the siege by Titus undertook great prayers, fasts, and sacrifices so that they might be divinely delivered. But when they did not experience the help of God, and they perceived themselves already defeated, as if hopeless they said: *He will know us no more*, that is, God now no longer attends to us, he neither accepts our works nor does he know us by approbation.[27]

73{74}[10]   *How long, O God, shall the enemy reproach? Is the adversary to provoke your name forever?*

Usquequo, Deus, improperabit inimicus? Irritat adversarius nomen tuum in finem?

73{74}[11]   *Why do you turn away your hand: and your right hand out of the midst of your bosom forever?*

Ut quid avertis manum tuam, et dexteram tuam de medio sinu tuo in finem?

Consequently, the Prophet greatly vexed by the delay of divine aid, and desiring to appeal God toward mercy, sighingly says: 73{74}[10] *Usquequo, Deus, improberabit inimicus? How long, O God, shall the enemy reproach?* That is, how long will these people from Italy, and their successors, glorying in the destruction of our lands, of our expulsion, and our oppression insult us? *Irritat adversarius nomen tuum in finem? Is the adversary to provoke your name forever?* That is, how long will this unbelieving people irritate you, blaspheming your name, and disparaging your majesty? In this regard the Prophet [David] prays that the rule of the Romans be removed from the [pagan] Gentiles, and that dominion be brought under the yoke of

---

Jews had already agreed among themselves that if any man should confess him to be Christ, he should be put out of the synagogue." John 9:22; *see also* John 12:42.
26   Ezek. 1:1, 3; 3:15; Jer. 1:2, 3 and elsewhere.
27   E. N. God knows all; however, Scholastics distinguished between the knowledge of vision (*notitia visionis*) in God, and the sort of knowledge of approval or approbation (*notitia approbationis*). Because of God's lack of approval, it is *as if* he does not see us. *See* footnote 5-11 in Volume 1.

the true Israelites, that is, of the Christians. Some explain the last part of this verse, so that it returns to the cause of the question which was presented in the first part of the verse. For it says by means of questioning, *How long, O God, shall the enemy reproach?* And it ascribes a reason in response, saying: *Is the adversary [to provoke your name forever]?* It is as if he were saying, "So long as our enemy casts reproach upon us," for the adversary — that is, the Jewish people who are adverse to Christ, who are unbelieving and obstinate, offend and blaspheme your name — vexes us, O Christ, true God, forever, that is, without ceasing, and even unto the end of the world: and so they will not be delivered by Christ, so that they might verify that which is written, *The people that shall deny him shall not be his.*[28] **73{74}[11]** *Ut quid avertis manum tuam, why do you turn away your hand,* that is, withdraw from us your power of help, abandoning the Jewish people into captivity, and this in two ways, for they were deprived of their own land and by the devil's bonds they are held fast to his will? Why, moreover, O God, do you avert *dexteram tuam, your right hand,* that is, the kind and successful prospect of your assistance, preservation, and favor, *de medio sinu tuo in finem, of the midst of your bosom forever?* The holy Prophet [David] speaks to God in a human manner, for, when man does not provide aid to one in need, he is said to restore his hand on his chest; but he is said to draw out his hand when he renders help. Because the Prophet observed that God would so finally forsake the Jews, he asked why in the end that is, in eternity, namely at the end of the world, he would draw back his hands from giving aid.

73{74}[12] But God is our king before ages: he has wrought salvation in the midst of the earth.

Deus autem rex noster ante saecula, operatus est salutem in medio terrae.

73{74}[13] You by your strength did make the sea firm: you did crush the heads of the dragons in the waters.

Tu confirmasti in virtute tua mare; contribulasti capita draconum in aquis.

73{74}[14] You have broken the heads of the dragon: you have given him to be meat for the people of the Ethiopians.

Tu confregisti capita draconis; dedisti eum escam populis Aethiopum.

---

28 Dan. 9:26a.

73{74}[12] *Deus autem rex noster ante saecula*, but *God is our king before ages*, that is, the true God, one, eternal, eternally remaining before all things, *operatus est salute in medio terrae*, has wrought salvation in the midst of the earth: because he founded, preserved, and saved our fathers in the land of Judah. 73{74}[13] *Tu confirmasti in virtute tua mare*, you by your strength did make the sea firm. Literally, God confirmed the Ocean Sea in its place,[29] so that it does not burst forth and cover the earth, as Manasseh the king of Judah said: *O Lord God, . . . you have marked the sea with your word of command, you who have confined the deep and marked it with your terrible and glorious name, and whom all men fear.*[30] The Lord also confirmed the sea with supernatural firmness when he lead Israel through the sandy bottom of the Red Sea, and there were waters on either side of the Hebrews like walls.

Contribulasti capita draconum in aquis, you did crush the heads of the dragon in the waters. The Prophet [David] asserts and calls to mind certain divine miracles done in antiquity so that he might show that God also would be able to redeem the sons of Israel out of the present captivity, removing the veil from their hearts,[31] converting them to the truth of the Christian faith. In order to show this, *you did crush*, he says, *the heads of the dragons in the waters*. By dragons we understand tyrannical princes; and by waters, tribulations or punishments. Whence, the Lord said to Pharaoh: *And you, Pharaoh . . . great dragon that lies in the midst of your rivers.*[32] And so it is in this sense [that it should be understood]: *You*, O Lord, *did crush*, wounding and killing, *the heads of the dragons*, that is head dragons, or princes and tyrants, *in the waters* of tribulation, striking them down with unforeseen and horrendous death or punishments. This is clear with respect to Og and Sihon kings of the Amorites and many others in the books of Joshua and Judges;[33] or [alternatively], *in the* material *waters*

---

29   E. N. The Romans recognized two major seas, one being the Mediterranean (the *mare mediterraneum* (which means "sea in the middle of the earth") and the *mare oceanum*, the Ocean Sea, which was the translation of the Greek Ὠκεανός (*Okeanos*) and which was originally thought to be a great salt water river or sea that encircled the earth. From a Eurocentric vantage point, the Ocean Sea was the Atlantic Ocean.
30   Prayer of Manasseh. E. N. The Prayer of Manasseh is an apocryphal ancient prayer associated with Manasseh, the king of Juda. See 2 Chr. 33:13.
31   Cf. 2 Cor. 3:15–16: *But even until this day, when Moses is read, the veil is upon their heart. But when they shall be converted to the Lord, the veil shall be taken away.*
32   Ez. 29:3.
33   Num. 21:35, 24; Joshua 12:7 *et seq.* Judges *passim*; Ex. 14 :28. E. N. During their Exodus from Egypt to the Promised Land, the Israelites encountered Sihon, an Amorite king of Heshbon, that would not let the pass through his lands. The Israelites defeated him at the battle of Jahaz and took possession of his land, which

drowning them, as occurred to Pharaoh and his princes. **73{74}[14]** *Tu confregisti capita draconis*, you have broken the heads of the dragon, that is, the power and the suggestion of the prince of demons and all other unclean spirits, giving to our fathers the power of overcoming their temptations: and so you have saved them from the powers and persecution of visible and invisible enemies. *Dediste eum, you have given him*, that is the dragon or the devil, *escam populi Aethiopum, to be meat for the people of the Ethiopians*, that is, you have converted the Gentiles to the faith. Before their conversion they were deformed with the black of vices, but after [their conversion] they were made whiter than snow by faith and grace.[34] Now the demon is said to be given as food to the faithful [in two ways]. First, because their body is reduced or made smaller. For the body of the devil is the congregation of sinners and unbelievers. Second, because the devil is in a manner devoured, consumed, and chewed upon by the just man, since he is defeated and trampled upon by the power of the Savior. Whence also Moses said to the Israelite people: *You shall consume all the people*, that is, you will vanquish and will destroy them.

73{74}[15] *You have broken up the fountains and the torrents: you have dried up the Ethan rivers.*

Tu dirupisti fontes et torrentes; tu siccasti fluvios Ethan.

73{74}[15] *Tu dirupisti fontes et torrentes, you have broken up the fountains and the torrents*, drawing from the granite rock, struck twice by Moses, such a copious flow of water,[35] so that the people and their beasts of burden might drink. And thus it says in a Psalm below: *Who turned the rock into pools of water, and the stony hill into fountains of*

Moses gave to the tribe of Gad. Num. 21:23–24; Joshua 13:24–28. Similarly, Og, the Amorite king of Bashan, was soundly routed at Edrei, the Israelites leaving no survivors. Deut. 3:1–7; Num. 21:33–35. This gave the Israelites possession of numerous walled cities and territories which Moses divided among the Israelites. These victories were part of the *mirabilia Dei*, and were memorialized in two Psalms: "He smote many nations, and slew might kings: Sihon king of the Amorites, and Og, king of Basan" (Ps. 134:10–11) and "Who smote great kings . . . Sihon king of the Amorites . . . and Og, king of Basan: for his mercy endures forever." (Ps. 135:18–20).

34   Ps. 50:9: *You shall sprinkle me with hyssop, and I shall be cleansed: you shall wash me, and I shall be made whiter than snow.* E. N. On the Biblical symbology associated with the Ethiopians, *see* footnote 17-161.

35   Num. 20:11. E. N. This is the event at Massah and Meribah recalled in the Invitatory Psalm: *Today if you shall hear his voice, harden not your hearts: As in the provocation [כִּמְרִיבָה (as in Meribah)] according to the day of temptation [מַסָּה (Masah)] in the wilderness: where your fathers tempted me, they proved me, and saw my works.* Ps. 94:8–9.

waters.[36] *Tu siccasti fluvios Ethan, you have dried up the Ethan rivers,* that is, the River Jordan, leading the sons of Israel through its dry river bed according to that which is said in the book of Joshua: *As soon as they came into the Jordan . . . the waters that came down from above stood in one place, and swelling up like a mountain, [were seen afar off from the city that is called Adam, to the place of Zarethan].*[37] The Prophet [David] calls the River Jordan with a plural noun — rivers — because its waters were divided into two parts, and so two rivers were made by that part that dried up. It is for this reason that Joshua says: *The waters that were beneath, ran down into the sea of the wilderness . . . until they wholly failed.*[38] Or [another possibility is that] he was using the plural for singular, as Scripture frequently does. For also they said to the sons of Israel, *These are your gods Israel, that have brought you out of the land of Egypt;* and yet there was but one molten calf.[39]

73{74}[16]   *Yours is the day, and yours is the night: you have made the morning light and the sun.*

Tuus est dies, et tua est nox; tu fabricatus es auroram et solem.

73{74}[17]   *You have made all the borders of the earth: the summer and the spring were formed by you.*

Tu fecisti omnes terminos terrae; aestatem et ver tu plasmasti ea.

73{74}[18]   *Remember this, the enemy has reproached the Lord: and a foolish people has provoked your name.*

Memor esto huius, inimicus improperavit Domino, et populus insipiens incitavit nomen tuum.

Consequently, the Prophet expresses the omnipotence of God by the works of creation, so that he might establish how powerful he is to deliver the children of Israel from their present captivity. 73{74}[16] *Tuus est dies et tua est nox; yours is the day, and yours is the night.* For God institutes, distinguishes, rules, and dispenses all time; and all things are obedient to him. Whence also Christ wanting to show himself to be not under the law, but the Creator, God and Lord, of all things, said: *For the Son of Man is Lord even of the Sabbath.*[40] But no one is the lord of time except God, at whose command the times run. For as the movements of the heavens obey

---

36   Ps. 113:8.

37   Joshua 3:15–16a. E. N. The part in brackets replaces the "etc." in the Latin text.

38   Joshua 3:16b.

39   Ex. 32:8b. E. N. So the plural word *gods (dii)* was used in a singular sense, since there was only one false god, the one idol of the molten calf.

40   Matt. 12:8.

only the Creator (according to the most holy Dionysius [the Areopagite] in the epistle to Polycarp),[41] so no one else has the power to change them; and so to be influenced is proper to time. *Tu fabricatus es auroram, et solem; you have made the morning light and the sun*, you who cause the morning and noon. For since God created the sun, it follows that he is the maker of light: for what is the cause of a cause is the cause of the thing caused;[42] and, according to the philosophers, the first cause influences the effect more strongly than any second cause.[43] Now by the creation of the sun is understood the creation of all the heavenly bodies brought forth by God. Of which is said through Isaiah: *He that stretches out the heavens as nothing, and spreads them out as a tent to dwell in.*[44] And along with the sun all the stars of the heaven are in all things ordered by divine command, according to the book of Job: *He commands the sun and it rises not: and shuts up the stars as it were under a seal.*[45] **73{74}[17]** *Tu fecisti omnes terminos terrae, you have made all the borders of the earth*: according to that written in Isaiah, *The Lord is the everlasting God, who has created the ends (terminos) of the earth.*[46] Whence also, the omnipotent and sublime Creator said to blessed Job: *Where were you when I laid up the foundations of the earth? Tell me if you have understanding. Who has laid the measures thereof, if you know? Or who has stretched the line upon it? Upon what are its bases grounded?*[47] *Aestatem et ver, the summer and the spring*, that is, the time of summer and of spring, *tu plasmasti, were formed by you.* For time — since it is caused by the movement of the *Primum Mobile* — is formed by God just like also the *Primum Mobile* is.[48] For four things are posited as coeval, that is, as being created simultaneously, namely: the angel, the heaven, time, and matter.[49] **73{74}[18]** *Memor esto huius, remember this*, O Lord: this, I say,

---

41   E. N. The marvels associated with the heavenly spheres related in Scripture are "possible only to Christ the cause of all, 'who does great and marvelous things without number.'" *Pseudo-Dionysius: The Complete Works* (New York: Paulist Press, 1987), 269 (trans., Colm Luibheid).

42   L. *causa causae est causa causati.*

43   L. *prima causa plus influit in effectum, quam aliqua causa secunda.* E. N. See St. Thomas Aquinas, *Super De causis*, l. 1.

44   Is. 40:22b.

45   Job 9:7.

46   Is. 40:28a.

47   Job 38:4–6.

48   E. N. In classical, medieval, and Renaissance geocentric astronomical theories based upon Ptolemy, the *Primum Mobile* (literally, "first in movement") was believed to be the outmost (tenth) sphere of the heavens that was the cause of all other movements in the celestial spheres. Beyond the *Primum Mobile* was the empyreal heavens. On the empyrean or empyreal heaven, *see* footnote 19-11.

49   E. N. St. Albert the Great (*ca.* 1200–1280 AD) wrote a short work (*De IV*

which follows. *Inimicus improperavit Domino*, *the enemy has reproached the Lord*: that is, your adversary Titus the idolater—of whom was said above, *see what things the enemy has done wickedly in the sanctuary!*—this enemy insulted the Lord, believing himself to have prevailed by the power of his gods and that the God of Israel was unable to defend the Jewish people. Perhaps he thought or said this. *Et populus insipiens, and a foolish people*, that is, the army of the Romans, lacking knowledge of the true God, and worshipping idols, *incitavit nomen tuum, has provoked your name*, that is, by the siege and destruction of Jerusalem, [the Roman army] has offended you, for they did this without right intention; but they were the rod of the Lord's anger, as were the Assyrians and the Babylonians, all of whose heart was not set on correcting [the Jews for their infidelity], but on destroying [them] in the manner that the Lord said of the king of the Assyrians through Isaiah: *Woe to the Assyrian, he is the rod and staff of my anger. . . . But he shall not take it so.*[50]

73{74}[19]   *Deliver not up to beasts the souls that confess to you: and forget not to the end the souls of your poor.*

Ne tradas bestiis animas confitentes tibi, et animas pauperum tuorum ne obliviscaris in finem.

73{74}[20]   *Have regard to your covenant: for they that are the obscure of the earth have been filled with dwellings of iniquity.*

Respice in testamentum tuum, quia repleti sunt qui obscurati sunt terrae domibus iniquitatum.

73{74}[21]   *Let not the humble be turned away with confusion: the poor and needy shall praise your name.*

Ne avertatur humilis factus confusus; pauper et inops laudabunt nomen tuum.

73{74}[19] *Ne tradas bestiis, deliver not up to beasts*, that is, to demons, tyrants, or cruel men, *animam confitentem tibi, the souls that confess to you*, that is, men that taking heed of their sins and your proclamation. For he states a part—namely, the soul—for the whole man.[51] *Et anima pauperum tuorum, and the souls of your poor*, that is, of those cast off and of

---

coaequaevis) on the four *coaequaeva* or coeval realities of creation mentioned here by Denis. Henryk Anzulewicz, "The Systematic Theology of Albert the Great," *A Companion to Albert the Great* (Boston: Brill, 2013), 42–43. (ed., Irven M. Resnick).

50   Is. 10:5, 7a.

51   E. N. In other words, the word "soul" is used synecdochally (a part of something referring to the whole) to refer to the whole man.

those needy, *ne obliviscaris in finem, you will forget not to the end*, forsaking
them in their condition and their tribulation, as if they are of no concern
to you. The Prophet prays, therefore, literally for the liberation of the
people of Israel, so that they may be delivered from the death of sin and
the captivity of the devil. 73{74}[20] *Respice in testamentum tuum, have
regard to your covenant*: that is, the law given by you, and take heed of
its testimony, for in it you promised to pardon your poor;[52] and so that
you might deign to hear more, consider the wickedness of your enemies;
*quia repleti sunt, qui obscurati sunt, terrae domibus iniquitatum; for they that
are the obscure of the earth have been filled with dwellings of iniquity*: that
is, the Italians mentioned above, darkened in their interior by their evil
and unbelief, have become rich and have filled the world with *dwellings
of iniquity*, that is, with worldly and unjust riches: of which the Savior
said, *Make unto you friends of the mammon of iniquity*. 73{74}[21] *Ne
avertatur, let not . . . be turned away* from the grace of your mercy *humilis
factus confusus, the humble with confusion*, that is the Jewish people greatly
humiliated by their present captivity; *pauper et inops, the poor and the
needy* in spirit *laudabunt nomen tuum, shall praise your name* with great
fervor and remarkable exultation, in the way Baruch states it: *The dead
that are in hell . . . shall not give glory and justice to the Lord; but the soul
that is sorrowful for the greatness of evil it has done, and goes bowed down,
and feeble . . . gives glory and justice to you, the Lord*.[53]

73{74}[22]   *Arise, O God, judge your own cause: be mindful of your
reproaches with which the foolish man has reproached you
all the day.*

*Exsurge, Deus, iudica causam tuam; memor esto improperio-
rum tuorum, eorum quae ab insipiente sunt tota die.*

73{74}[23]   *Forget not the voices of your enemies: the pride of them that
hate you ascends continually.*

*Ne obliviscaris voces inimicorum tuorum: superbia eorum qui
te oderunt ascendit semper.*

73{74}[22] *Exsurge, Deus, arise, O God*, not by changing place, but
strongly rendering aid, *iudica causam tuam, judge your own cause*, which
you have against your adversaries, and grant victory to them who have just
cause; *memor esto improperiorum tuorum, be mindful of your reproaches*, that

---

52   *Cf.* Is. 66:2b. *But to whom shall I have respect, but to him that is poor and little,
and of a contrite spirit, and that trembles at my words?*
53   Baruch 2:17–18.

is, of the assaults upon your servants and of the blasphemies against your name; *eorum, of them,* I say, of your reproaches, *quae ab insipiente sunt tota die, with which the foolish man has reproached you all the day*: because the foolish Roman people said many things against God in the aforementioned siege. The Prophet [David] prays God to be mindful of these reproaches, so that he might place upon the Jews these temporal punishments of being cast out and oppressed for their sins and convert; and that he not plead against them according to the rigor of his justice, removing grace from them in the present and glory in the future. For this reason, he adds: **73{74}[23]** *Ne obliviscaris voces inimicorum tuorum, forget not the voices of your enemies*: that is, remember their iniquitous words, so that by at that occasion you might spare the people of Israel that are so afflicted. *Superbia eorum qui te oderunt, ascendit semper; the pride of them that hate you ascends continually*: first, because they add sin to sin, according to this, *The sinner will add sin to sin*;[54] and in Revelation, *He that is filthy, let him be filthy still: and he that is just, let him be justified still.*[55] Secondly, because the exaltation of the proud tends to go higher. For which reason Isaiah says: *When you were mad against me, your pride came up to my ears, says the Lord.*[56]

ARTICLE XLII

TROPOLOGICAL OR MORAL EXPOSITION
OF THE SAME SEVENTY-THIRD PSALM.

73{74}[1] ... *O God, why have you cast us off unto the end, [why] is your wrath enkindled against the sheep of your pasture?*

> ... *Ut quid, Deus, repulisti in finem, iratus est furor tuus super oves pascuae tuae?*

ACCORDING TO THE MORAL UNDERSTAND-ing, in the present Psalm the Prophet [David] speaks in the person of the Church, or in any man on fire with fraternal charity and praying for the reformation of the Christian people. The Church or the man of virtue, therefore, seeing the persecution, lapse, and degradation of Christians with great compassion, speaks with great affection to the Lord, and pleading says: **73{74}[1]** *Ut quid, Deus;* why, O God, Trinity, glorious,

---

54   Ecclus. 3:29b.

55   Rev. 22:11a.

56   Is. 37:29a.

blessed, and happy God, *why*, that is, for what utility or for what reason, *repulisti, have you cast off* the Christian people, exposing them to such miseries, such assaults of heretics, schismatics, and unbelievers, indeed, also false brothers, who in faith are Christian, but in deed are demonic: and this, *in finem, unto the end*, that is, so perseveringly? But in a special way we can say this about the loss of the sepulcher of Christ and the Holy Lands and the city of Jerusalem.[57]

Iratus est furor tuus super oves pascuae tuae, your wrath is enkindled against the sheep of your pasture: that is, you are carrying out great revenge against your Christian people, whom you allow to be oppressed, to be tempted, to be afflicted, and to be wearied with visible and invisible attack of enemies, so that the lands of Christians are already possessed by infidels, but the hearts or souls of a great number by sin and demons. And so it is a wise, beautiful, and efficacious kind of prayer, to include in that prayer something reasonable and in some way due to him who is being prayed to, so that he may be soothed by it and he may hear [the prayer by answering it]. Now it seems entirely becoming that the Lord might be easily reconciled to his own people, who were so honored by him with many benefits. The Church or the faithful man, praying for other Christians, asserts the Christians to be the sheep of the pasture of God: which is a loving, trusting, familiar, and most sweet word, and it befits the Christians much more perfectly than it does the Jews. For they were fed with manna; but we with the Body and the Blood of Christ, prefigured by the manna.[58] By this we are daily fed, receive the multiform grace of such a great Sacrament, are incorporated into Christ, and, unless there be in us some failure [in us], we will be spiritually fattened, enriched, and perfected. For the Body of Christ is truly the grain of the elect, and his Blood is truly the wine springing forth virgins, that is chaste souls and spouses of Christ. Of this grain and wine we find written in Zechariah: *For what is the good thing of the Lord, and what is his beautiful thing, but the corn of the elect, and wine springing forth virgins?*[59]

---

57   E. N. The First Crusade with the objective of freeing the Holy Lands from the rule of the Muslims was called by Pope Urban II in 1095 at Clermont. After it had been under Muslim rule for about 450 years, the crusaders, in the First Crusade, conquered Jerusalem in 1099. It was re-captured by Saladin in 1187, whereupon it was ruled by the Muslim Ayyubid dynasty. After subsequent unsuccessful efforts to regain the city, it was ultimately regained in 1229, but was lost to in 1244 to the Khwarazmian dynasty, eventually falling under Mamluk control in 1260. The final foothold in the Holy Land was lost with the fall of Acre to the Mamluks in 1291.

58   Ex. 16:15; John 6:48–59.

59   Zech. 9:17.

73{74}[2] *Remember your congregation, which you have possessed from
the beginning. The rod of your inheritance which you have
redeemed: mount Sion in which you have dwelt.*[60]

> *Memor esto congregationis tuae, quam possedisti ab initio. Rede-
misti virgam haereditatis tuae, mons Sion, in quo habitasti in eo.*

73{74}[2] *Memor esto, remember,* O Christ the King, Savior of the
world, *congregationis tuae, your congregation,* that is, the universal Church,
renewing, protecting, increasing, and saving her throughout the whole
world; *quam possedisti, which you have possessed* by baptismal grace the
most blessed Passion by hereditary right, as the Father told you in
a Psalm above: *Ask of me, and I will give you the Gentiles for your
inheritance.*[61] And this congregation you have possessed *ab initio, from
the beginning* of the early Church, for as many as were ordained to
life everlasting, believed.[62] And as the Apostle [Paul] said, *The sure
foundation of God stands firm, having this seal: the Lord knows who are
his.*[63] Or God is said to possess the Church from the beginning, that is,
from eternity, by reason of the divine predestination according to which
he loved her from eternity. Christ also in his way possessed her from
eternity in that God (according to the Apostle) chose us and graced us
from eternity in Christ,[64] and decreed to give us the complete gift of
grace in him; indeed and gave it, according to the Apostle, who said:
*God called us by his holy calling, not according to our works, but according
to his own purpose and grace, which was given us in Christ Jesus before the
times of the world; but is now made manifest.*[65] But it must be affirmed
that this giving was before the times of the world, according to divine
predestination,[66] and not by means of actual infusion.

*Redemisti virgam hereditatis tuae, the rod of your inheritance which you
have redeemed,* that is, the Christian people, which are a kingly and priestly

---

60   E. N. I have replaced the Douay-Rheims's "scepter" (which translates the Latin
virgam) with "rod."

61   Ps. 2:8a.

62   Acts 13:48b.

63   2 Tim. 2:19a.

64   *Cf.* Eph. 1:4, 6: *As he chose us in him before the foundation of the world, that we
should be holy and unspotted in his sight in charity . . . unto the praise of the glory of
his grace, in which he has graced us in his beloved Son.*

65   2 Tim. 1:9, 10a.

66   E. N. According to divine predestination means in the divine mind. "Predestination is *not something in the predestined*; but *rather in him who predestines.* . . . Whence
it is manifest that predestination is a kind of reason of order, *existing in the divine
mind,* of some persons towards eternal salvation." ST I, q. 23, art. 2, c. Hence divine
predestination exists before the creation of the one predestined.

people, you have divinely raised up from spiritual Egypt, that is, from a worldly way of life, vicious and dark, from many errors, all sin, and the punishment of hell: and all this at a most precious price, namely, your own Blood. Whence it is written in Revelation: *He has loved us and washed us from our sins in his own Blood, and has made us a kingdom, and priests to God and his Father.*[67] And Peter in his epistle: *You were not redeemed with corruptible things as gold or silver, from your vain conversation of the tradition of your fathers, but with the precious Blood of Christ, as of a lamb unspotted and undefiled.*[68] For this reason, Christ himself declared: *I am the good shepherd; and I know mine, and mine know me . . . and I lay down my life for my sheep.*[69] Now this congregation of yours is *mons Sion, mount Sion,* that is, the Church militant, faithfully looking at God *in quo, in which* mountain *habitasti, you have dwelt* bodily and visibly when you were seen on earth and conversing with disciples.[70] For this reason, the Apostle [Paul] says: *Christ as the Son in his own house: which house are we.*[71] Presently also and even until the end of the world, Christ dwells in us, as he himself said: *I am with you all days, even to the consummation of the world;*[72] and again, *For where there are two or three gathered together in my name, there am I in the midst of them.*[73] Now Sion is interpreted as meaning the act of beholding, and so the Church is designated by it, in whose person the Apostle says: *We all beholding the glory of the Lord with open face.*[74]

73{74}[3]   *Lift up your hands against their pride unto the end; see what things the enemy has done wickedly in the sanctuary.*

Leva manus tuas in superbias eorum in finem. Quanta malignatus est inimicus in sancto.

73{74}[4]   *And they that hate you have made their boasts, in the midst of your solemnity. They have set up their ensigns for signs.*

Et gloriati sunt qui oderunt te in medio solemnitatis tuae; posuerunt signa sua, signa.

73{74}[3] *Leva manus tuas in superbias eorum in finem, lift up your hands against their pride unto the end.* The Church of God is not taught

---

67   Rev. 1:5b–6a.
68   1 Pet. 1:18–19.
69   John 10:14–15.
70   Cf. Baruch 3:38: *He was seen upon earth, and conversed with men.*
71   Heb. 3:6a.
72   Matt. 28:20b.
73   Matt. 18:20.
74   1 Cor. 5:5a.

by her teacher Christ to return evil for evil, but to overcome evil by good,[75] praying for one's enemies.[76] And this verse must be explained in a good way, so that [it is understood] in this sense: so *Lift up your hands*, that is, extend your power, *against their pride*, namely [the pride] of the enemies of the Church, who are persecuting the just, destroying in them not nature, but fault;[77] or in the present paternally and mercifully punishing them lest they perish eternally, as the Apostle delivered the Corinthian over to Satan for the destruction of the flesh, so that he might be saved in the day of the Lord.[78] But that handing over was nothing other than excommunication, which in the early Church used to be accompanied by sensible confirming signs, namely the bodily vexation of the excommunicated person by a demon, to which often used to follow by bodily death; but now with the faith confirmed, such necessary signs are no longer necessary. And that this explanation [of this verse] is apt, is evident from that which follows, *unto the end*, that is, order your correction, by which you scourge the proud, unto eternal life or true salvation.

Quanta malignatus est inimicus in sancto! See what things the enemy has done wickedly in the sanctuary! That is, how much great evil was done by the successors of Mohamed in the Holy Land, to which the people are now subject! In the manner Christ foreannounced in the Gospel: *Jerusalem shall be trodden down by the Gentiles; till the times of the nations be fulfilled.*[79] Or [alternatively], *See what thing the enemy has done wickedly,* that is, any heresiarch, tyrant, or perverted man among your holy people, beguiling them, afflicting them, or killing them! This is most clearly applicable to the Arians,[80] who, as we read in chronicles, slew innumerable Christians, poisoned emperors with the Arian perfidy, and incarcerated innumerable bishops. 73{74}[4] *Et gloriati sunt, and they ... made their boasts,* when *they have done evil ... in most wicked things,*[81] [they] *qui oderunt te, that hate you,* namely, the evildoers just mentioned, and this, *in medio solemnitatis tuae, in the midst of your solemnity,* which they frequently

---

75   Rom. 12:21: *Be not overcome by evil, but overcome evil by good.*
76   *Cf.* Matt. 5:44: *But I say to you, Love your enemies: do good to them that hate you: and pray for them that persecute and calumniate you.*
77   E. N. The prayer is for the conversion of the enemy (destruction of fault), and not the destruction of their life (nature).
78   1 Cor. 5:5.
79   Luke 21:24b.
80   E. N. "The fundamental tenet of Arianism was, that the Son of God was a creature, not born of the Father, but, in the scientific language of the times, made 'out of nothing.'" St. John Henry Newman, *Arians of the Fourth Century* (London: Longmans, Green & Co., 1919), 202.
81   Prov. 2:14.

violated. For often the perverse perform their more wicked works, as the demons in possession of their heart inspire, during the more sacred and more solemn days. *Posuerunt signa sua, they have set up their ensigns.* The Arian heretics used to carry around their banners to the derision of the Catholics; and many tyrants devastating the Church, frequently erect their banners as a sign of their victory against the Christians.

Moreover, what is said in the three following verses so often literally occurs to the Church of Christ, according to the sense just explained in the prior article, that it is not necessary to bring to mind specific examples: especially since also in our time (alas!) they are abundantly occurring in the Church, in the kingdom of Bohemia and its lands and neighboring lands,[82] by the detestable and execrable reign of those heretics, whose madness exceedingly and for too long a time (on account of our sins, and permitted by divine judgment) has raged furiously against many; but now by the grace of God it is not a little repressed and extinguished by the sword.[83]

73{74}[9] *Our signs we have not seen, there is now no prophet: and he will know us no more.*

Signa nostra non vidimus; iam non est propheta; et nos non cognoscet amplius.

But since the Christian faithful are so often attacked by scourges, persecutions, hunger, thirst, and death, what ought they to say, except that which follows? 73{74}[9] *Signa nostra non vidimus, our signs we have not seen*: that is, we have not experienced, nor do we now experience, the so greatly admirable protections of God which sometimes have appeared and were experienced by our most-Christian fathers, who — when they were but few — overthrew, by the help granted them from above, great multitudes of unbelievers: as was manifest by the most religious Theodosius, Charlemagne, Godfrey of Bouillon, and many others. But also the Apostles and their successors, often with angelic aid, were known to have been rescued from jails and chains, and from all manner of vexations by unbelievers. But now no such thing like this appears before us: for which

---

82 E. N. Denis is referring to the Bohemian Jan Hus (*ca.* 1372–1415), the Hussite Wars (1420–1434), and the so-called Bohemian or Hussite Reformation. These heretics were not fully suppressed until 1620, when the Bohemian Revolt was suppressed by King Ferdinand II, and the inhabitants of Bohemia — under the then-regnant principal, *cuius regio, eius religio* (whose realm, their religion) — were compelled to become Catholic.

83 E. N. For the reasons given, Denis skips Ps. 73:5–7; however, he also skips Ps. 73:8.

reason only patience is necessary for us with a most certain faith; and that which in the book of Maccabees is told us: *We are ready to die rather than to transgress the laws of God, received from our fathers.*[84] Therefore we ought not to violate them, for in the present we are permitted to die, knowing that which follows in this same passage states: *The King of the world will raise us up, who die for his laws, in the resurrection of eternal life.*[85] Whence elsewhere is written: *Though in the sight of men they suffered torments, their hope is full of immortality.*[86] And again: *Afflicted in few things, in many they shall be well rewarded.*[87] In a few things, he says, afflicted: why not preferably in many things, especially since (the Apostle attesting) through many tribulations we must enter into the kingdom of God?[88] For no other reason but that which the same Apostle says, *The sufferings of this time are not worthy to be compared with the glory to come, that shall be revealed in us.*[89] *Iam non est propheta,* there is now no prophet. With good reason, the Church laments its lapse, which now cools the charity of many,[90] so that graces of the Holy Spirit (which Paul enumerates:[91] *To one, he says, is given the word of wisdom, to another the word of knowledge . . . to another, the working of miracles, to another prophecy, etc.*) do not greatly manifest themselves in Christians in the fullness that they did in times past, especially as they did in the early Church, in which many were prophets; and at various times [thereafter] the prophetical grace flashed not a few times, such as it did in Anthony, Hilary, John the Hermit, Benedict,[92] and many others. But now, alas, the Church is exceedingly weak, and there is now no prophet; and so we can say

---

84   2 Mac. 7:2b.

85   2 Mac. 7:9b.

86   Wis. 3:4.

87   Wis. 3:5a.

88   Acts 14:21b.

89   Rom. 8:18. E. N. Denis is saying that relative to the glory to come, even the greatest tribulations suffered on earth can be characterized as being "afflicted in few things," thereby reconciling Wis. 3:5 and Acts. 14:21 through Rom. 8:18.

90   Cf. Matt. 24:12: *And because iniquity has abounded, the charity of many shall grow cold.*

91   1 Cor. 12:8-10.

92   E. N. St. Anthony the Great (*ca.* 251–356 AD), a Christian monk from Egypt known for his austerities, temptations, and sanctity. St. Hilary of Poitier (*ca.* 310–*ca.* 367 AD), the holy and learned bishop of Poitiers, who battled against the Arian heresy (and earned the epithet *Malleus Arianorum,* "Hammer of the Arians") and is considered a Doctor of the Church. St. John the Hermit, or St. John of Egypt (*ca.* 305–394 AD), known in particular for his prophetic gifts. St. Benedict of Nursia (*ca.* 480–*ca.* 547 AD) is, of course, the famous Father of Western Monasticism and author of the Rule of St. Benedict.

such a thing considering the current affliction: *et, and* our God *nos non cognoscet amplius, will know us no more* by approving our works. This is said not as being an assertion [of positive fact], but in a sorrowful spirit, expressing lament or because it appears to be so.

73{74}[10]   *How long, O God, shall the enemy reproach? Is the adversary to provoke your name forever?*

       Usquequo, Deus, improperabit inimicus? Irritat adversarius nomen tuum in finem?

And so the just man, or the Church, wearied by the wickedness of the enemy, says to the Lord: 73{74}[10] *Usquequo, Deus, improperabit, how long, O God, shall . . . reproach,* that is, how long shall the *inimicus, the enemy,* heresiarchs, pagans, Jews, and tyrants insult you and your servants? For he who casts reproach upon the servants of God, casts reproach upon God. For this reason, the Savior said: *He that hears you, hears me; and he that despises you, despises me.*[93] And how long, O Lord God, *irrit adversarius nomen tuum in finem, is the adversary to prove your name forever,* dishonoring you, spurning your commandments, and persecuting your ministers?

73{74}[12][94] *But God is our king before ages: he has wrought salvation in the midst of the earth.*

       Deus autem rex noster ante saecula, operatus est salutem in medio terrae.

73{74}[13]   *You by your strength did make the sea firm: you did crush the heads of the dragons in the waters.*

       Tu confirmasti in virtute tua mare; contribulasti capita draconum in aquis.

73{74}[14]   *You have broken the heads of the dragon: you have given him to be meat for the people of the Ethiopians.*

       Tu confregisti capita draconis; dedisti eum escam populis Aethiopum.

73{74}[12] *Deus autem rex noster ante saecula, but God is our king before ages,* that is, Christ before all time was eternally begotten of the Father, *operatus est salute in medio terrae, has wrought salvation in the*

---

93   Luke 10:16a.
94   E. N. Denis skips verse 11.

midst of the earth, namely, in Judaea, and on Mount Sion, reconciling us to God by his Passion and Blood.[95] For he humbled himself (as the Apostle says), *becoming obedient unto death, even to the death of the cross.*[96] Of this salvation of Christ, the eternal Father said, speaking of Christ through Zechariah: *Behold I will bring my servant, the Orient . . . and I will take away the iniquity of that land in one day,*[97] namely, the Day of Preparation. For on that day, Christ was the Lamb of God who took away *the sins of the world,*[98] as he himself said: *For the Son of Man is come to seek and to save that which was lost.*[99] 73{74}[**13**] *Tu, you* O Lord Christ, *confirmasti in virtute tua, by your strength did make firm,* that is, by your divine power; or [alternatively] by your strength, that is, in interior perfection and the Catholic faith; *mare, the sea,* that is, the Gentiles, who are indicated by the word sea, first, on account of the bitterness of the vices of the Gentiles; second, because, like water, they were restless, and they flowed from sin to sin; third, because of their multitude. Whence in another place is written: *Many waters are many people.*[100] Christ has so far confirmed this sea, that they wish to die for the truth of the Christian faith. Hence, speaking of Christ, the Lord says through Isaiah: *Behold I have given him for a witness to the people, for a leader and a master to the Gentiles.*[101] And Isaiah, speaking to the Lord, says: *Behold you shall call a nation, which you knew not: and the nations that knew you not shall run to you.*[102] This also is written in the Acts of the Apostles, that the Holy Spirit fell upon Cornelius and those who were with him, and they spoke with tongues. When this was witnessed, those that were of the circumcision were astonished, saying: *Therefore, is the grace of God poured out also to the nations.*[103]

Contribulasti, you did crush, O Lord Jesus, *capita draconum in aquis, the heads of the dragons in the waters,* that is, you have destroyed, overcome, and extinguished the malignant spirits and their pride in the fountain of Baptism: for by it men are made into children of grace from children of

---

95   Cf. Rom. 5:10: *For if, when we were enemies, we were reconciled to God by the death of his Son; much more, being reconciled, shall we be saved by his life.*

96   Phil. 2:8.

97   Zech. 3:8b, 9b.

98   John 1:29.

99   Luke 19:10.

100   Cf. Rev. 17:1b, 15: *I will show you the condemnation of the great harlot, who sits upon many waters. . . . And he said to me: The waters which you saw, where the harlot sits, are peoples, and nations, and tongues.*

101   Is. 55:4.

102   Is. 55:5a.

103   See Acts 10:44–46.

wrath, children of salvation and of the Creator from children of perdition and of the devil, for in this water all sins are forgiven, as is written of it in Zechariah: *In that day there shall be a fountain open to the house of David... for the washing of the sinner.*[104] Now just like by David is understood Christ, so by the house of David is designated the Church of Christ, which now is cleansed in the baptismal waters. **73{74}[14]** *Tu confregisti capita draconis, you have broken the heads of the dragon.* This is explained in the preceding article as the casting down of the prince of demons, which agrees with that which is recalled in Revelation: *Michael and his angels fought with the dragon, and the dragon fought and his angels; and they prevailed not, neither was their place found any more in heaven.*[105] This can also be explained as referring to the Antichrist, in this way: You, O Christ, *confregisti, that is, you shall break,* I say, the heads, that is, the principal promoters, or the dominations and powers, *draconis, of the dragon, that is, the Antichrist.* In Revelation it is written of him: *I saw a beast coming up out of the sea, having seven heads and ten horns.*[106] Christ will break and condemn this dragon and all of his splendor.

73{74}[15] *You have broken up the fountains and the torrents: you have dried up the Ethan rivers.*

Tu dirupisti fontes et torrentes; tu siccasti fluvios Ethan.

73{74}[15] *Tu dirupisti fontes et torrentes, you have broken up the fountains and the torrents:* that is, you have opened the sacred Scriptures, in which are contained the fountains of wisdom and the torrents of knowledge, and you have revealed its mysteries by the infusion of the Holy Spirit. Or [alternatively], by fountains and torrents can be understood the Apostles, who are the highest teachers of the Church, and all inferior preachers—whose hearts God shattered, and from which flow streams of holy preaching drank by the whole world to its health. *To siccasti fluvios Ethan, you have dried up the Ethan rivers.* Ethan is a Hebrew name which is interpreted as meaning "Robust." But by rivers in this place is understood doctrines, which flow from the heart of one man into the mind of another. So it has, therefore, this sense: You, O Christ, Savior of the world, dried up, made arid, and showed the doctrines of the proud glorying in their wisdom, and those strong of opinion, namely, the teachings of vain philosophy, and the various errors of idolatry and

---

104 Zech. 13:1.
105 Rev. 12:7b–8.
106 Rev. 13:1a.

of diabolical doctrine to be useless. For this reason, the Apostle [Paul] says: *Has not God made foolish the wisdom of this world?*[107] And again: *But the foolish things of the world has God chosen, that he may confound the wise.*[108]

73{74}[16] *Yours is the day, and yours is the night: you have made the morning light and the sun.*

Tuus est dies, et tua est nox; tu fabricatus es auroram et solem.

73{74}[17] *You have made all the borders of the earth: the summer and the spring were formed by you.*

Tu fecisti omnes terminos terrae; aestatem et ver tu plasmasti ea.

73{74}[16] *Tuus est dies, yours is the day,* that is, spiritual men illumined by the sun of justice and the fountain of wisdom, *et tua est nox, and yours is the night,* that is, the people living carnally. For all kinds of men are God's by right of creation and universal dominion. *Tu fabricatus es auroram et solem, you have made the morning light and the sun,* that is, the glorious Virgin and Christ the man, the Son of the Virgin, giving both whatever they have of both gifts of nature and of grace. Indeed, Mary, is called the morning light: because as the morning light precedes the day, so she [preceded] Christ. Whence in the Song of Songs we read of her: *Who is she that comes forth as the morning rising?*[109] Christ also, even as man, is called the sun: because as all the stars are thought to receive the light by the sun, so all saints are distributed the light of faith, grace, and wisdom by Christ.[110] *For of his fulness we all have received.*[111] 73{74}[17] *Tu fecisti, you have made,* that is, you have spiritual reformed and regenerated, *omnis terminos terrae, all the borders of the earth,* that is, all the elect in dwelling at the ends of the earth. *Aestatem et ver, the summer and the spring,* that is, the remuneration or reward and merit, *tu plasmasti ea, you formed.* For the trees' flowers in the spring produce fruit

---

107   1 Cor. 1:20b.
108   1 Cor. 1:27a.
109   Songs 6:9a.
110   *E. N.* It was thought that the sun was the source of light of all the heavenly bodies, both the planets and the stars. As St. Albert the Great wrote, "as the finest philosophers — Aristotle and Avicenna, Ptolemy and Messellach — say, only the sun illuminates by its own light and all the other planets and stars are illuminated by the sun, as also the moon is." H. Darrel Rutkin, "Astrology and Magic," *A Companion to Albert the Great* (Boston: Brill, 2013), 466 (ed., Irven M. Resnick).
111   John 1:16a.

in the summer: and so by summer we understand reward; by spring, merit. Now God causes in us not only reward, but also merit, according to that in Isaiah: *Lord, you will give us peace: for you have wrought all our works for us;*[112] By summer also can be understood fervid lovers of the Godhead; by spring, those new and beginning in the service of God.

73{74}[18] *Remember this, the enemy has reproached the Lord: and a foolish people has provoked your name.*

Memor esto huius, inimicus improperavit Domino, et populus insipiens incitavit nomen tuum.

73{74}[19] *Deliver not up to beasts the souls that confess to you: and forget not to the end the souls of your poor.*

Ne tradas bestiis animas confitentes tibi, et animas pauperum tuorum ne obliviscaris in finem.

73{74}[18] *Memor esto huius,* remember this of the ecclesiastical congregations: of which it is said, *inimicus improperavit Domino,* the enemy has reproached the Lord, that is, heretics and perverse men have disparaged the doctrine of Christ and the Church, saying: *Stolen waters are sweeter, and hidden bread is more pleasant;*[113] *et populus insipiens, and a foolish people,* that is, those ignorant of the true God, or showing themselves to be ignorant of him by their works, *incitavit nomen tuum, has provoked your name,* that is, they have provoked your anger: and so they will perish, as is stated of them, *The people that does not understand shall be beaten.*[114] **73{74}[19]** *Ne tradas, deliver not up,* or permit them to be delivered up, *bestiis, to the beasts,* that is, to the demons or men that are mad, *animam confitentem tibi, the souls that confess to you* their sins and your proclamation. The rest [of this Psalm] is clear from the previous explanations.

See we have heard this Psalm that is so full of meaning and affection: in which is recalled the early benefits of divine familiarity, is related the maliciousness of the persecutors of the Church, is written about the

---

112　Is. 26:12. E. N. One might here recall St. Augustine's notable observations in his dispute with the Pelagian heretics: "God crowns his gifts, not your merits; if [the merits] derive from yourself, and not from him, they are your merits. But these, if they are so, are evil; and God does not crown them. If, however, they are good, they are the gifts of God, because, as the Apostle James says, 'Every best gift, and every perfect gift, is from above, coming down from the Father of lights.'" *On Grace and Free Will,* 6, 15, PL 44, 890.

113　Prov. 9:17.

114　Hosea 4:14b.

tribulations of the just, is prayed for the correction of adversaries, and is demonstrated the divine power and its effects. In a way, therefore, it is becoming that we sing this Psalm with suitable devotion, so that we might be informed by it in all adversities and affectionately to turn and confidently to pray to God, recalling the benefits shown to our fathers, so that we might obtain similar things, and we might be delivered from all unsteadiness and difficulty.

PRAYER

CHRIST, OUR GOD AND KING BEFORE all ages, O Christ, who at the end of the age have wrought salvation by the redemption of your Church, which from the beginning you possessed in predestination, have regard for the covenant confirmed with your Blood, making the same Church to persevere as your solemnly promised one, and to stand yoked in safety: who with God the Father and the Holy Spirit live and reign, God, for ever and ever. Amen.

Deus, Rex noster ante saecula, Christe, qui in fine saeculi operatus
es salutem in redemptione Ecclesiae tuae, quam ab initio tuo
possedisti praedestinatione, respice in testamentum sanguine
tuo confirmatum, faciendo eamdem Ecclesiam tuam
devotam permanere, et in securitate iugi
consistere: qui cum Deo Patre et
Spiritu Sancto, vivis et regnas
Deus, per omnia saecula
saeculorum.
Amen.

Psalm 74

ARTICLE XLIII

DECLARATION OF THE SEVENTY-FOURTH PSALM:
CONFITEBIMUR TIBI, DEUS, CONFITEBIMUR.
WE WILL PRAISE YOU, O GOD, WE WILL PRAISE.

74{75}[1] *Unto the end, corrupt not, a Psalm of a canticle for Asaph.*

In finem, ne corrumpas. Psalmus cantici Asaph.

HE TITLE OF THIS PRESENT PSALM IS: 74{75} [1] *In finem, ne corrumpas, Psalmus cantici Asaph; unto the end, corrupt not, a Psalm of a canticle for Asaph.* Some expound upon this Psalm literally of the Jewish people returning from the Babylonian captivity, as it is a giving of thanks by the people being liberated from that place and returning to Judaea. And so the sense of this title is: *A Psalm of a canticle for Asaph, corrupt not,* that is, do not destroy, O Lord, the people of Israel, as you did in the Babylonian captivity. But it seems to me that this exposition contains little of devotion and contains but modest amount of sweetness: and this can be [adequately] touched upon briefly in this way.

74{75}[2] *We will praise you, O God: we will praise, and we will call upon your name. We will relate your wondrous works.*

Confitebimur tibi, Deus, confitebimur, et invocabimus nomen tuum; narrabimus mirabilia tua.

74{75}[2] *Confitebimur tibi, Deus; we will praise you, O God,* we returning from captivity with the permission of Darius, king of the Medes and Cyrus king of the Persians, since you have justly punished us, for we have sinned; *confitebimur, we will praise you,* since you have mercifully restored us, indeed also justly, because you promised through Jeremiah that after seventy years we would be delivered from captivity;[1] *et invocabimus nomen tuum, and we will call upon your name* for grace to avoid past sins, so that we might not fall into similar evils. *Narrabimus mirabilia tua, we*

---

1 Jer. 25:11: *And all this land shall be a desolation, and an astonishment: and all these nations shall serve the king of Babylon seventy years.*

will relate your wondrous works which we saw and recognized in Babylon, the manner, namely, you delivered the three young men from the fiery furnace,[2] and Daniel from the lions' den,[3] and Susanna from the hands of ungodly judges:[4] all these are gathered together in the book of Daniel.

74{75}[3]   *When I shall take a time, I will judge justices.*

Cum accepero tempus, ego iustitias iudicabo.

74{75}[4]   *The earth is melted, and all that dwell therein: I have established the pillars thereof.*

Liquefacta est terra et omnes qui habitant in ea, ego confirmavi columnas eius.

74{75}[5]   *I said to the wicked: Do not act wickedly: and to the sinners: Lift not up the horn.*

Dixi iniquis: Nolite inique agere, et delinquentibus: Nolite exaltare cornu.

74{75}[6]   *Lift not up your horn on high: speak not iniquity against God.*

Nolite extollere in altum cornu vestrum; nolite loqui adversus Deum iniquitatem.

Then the Prophet [David] changes person, and he says in the person of God: 74{75}[3] *Cum accepero tempus, ego iustitias iudicabo; when I shall take a time, I will judge justices,* that is, at the time foreordained and arranged by me, I will judge the justices of the elect, delivering them from the hands of the unjust, as demanded and deserved by their justices. 74{75}[4] *Liquefacta est terra, the earth is melted,* that is, Judaea is burned and destroyed by the Chaldeans, *et omnes qui habitant in ea, and all that dwell therein,* that is, who dwell in that land, for their hearts are unloosed with fear of the Chaldeans. *Ego, I, God, confirmavi columnas eius, have established the pillars thereof,* that is, I have established in good and in fortitude of unshaken spirit the princes of this people, namely Zerubbabel, the high priest and son of Jehozadak, Joshua, Zechariah, Haggai, Esdras, and Nehemiah.[5] 74{75}[5] *Dixi, I said,* that is, I God, not with words, but in deed, ordered *iniquis, the wicked,* that is, the proud Babylonians: *Nolite inique agere, do not act wickedly,* that is, do not any longer reign over and oppress foreign people, as you have hitherto done; I said *et delequentibus,*

---

2   Dan. chp. 3

3   Dan. chp. 6.

4   Dan. chps. 13, 14.

5   1 Esdras 3:2; 5:1; 7:6; 2 Esdras 7:7; Haggai 1:14; 2:5.

and to sinners, that is, the aforesaid sinners: *Nolite exaltare cornu, lift not up the horn*, that is, do not reign over or exercise kingly power. **74{75}[6]** *Nolite exaltare cornum vestrum, lift not up your horn*, commanding every kingdom and having absolute rule; *nolite loqui adversus Deum iniquitatem, speak not iniquity against God*, blaspheming the God of Israel and mocking his people, in the manner that you have heretofore done. All this God said to the Chaldeans, not by word, but by deed: because he took away from them the power of continuing evil works, transferring their kingdom to the Medes and the Persians, as we have contained in Daniel, and in Isaiah and Jeremiah, where it is admirably and most evidently foretold.[6]

74{75}[7] *For neither from the east, nor from the west, nor from the desert hills:*

Quia neque ab oriente, neque ab occidente, neque a desertis montibus.

74{75}[8] *For God is the judge. One he puts down, and another he lifts up.*

Quoniam Deus iudex est; hunc humiliat, et hunc exaltat.

74{75}[9] *For in the hand of the Lord there is a cup of strong wine full of mixture. And he has poured it out from this to that: but the dregs thereof are not emptied: all the sinners of the earth shall drink.*

Quia calix in manu Domini vini meri, plenus misto. Et inclinavit ex hoc in hoc, verumtamen faex eius non est exinanita; bibent omnes peccatores terrae.

Now why God said this to them is stated by the Prophet [David]: **74{75}[7]** *Quia neque ab oriente, neque ab occidente, neque a desertis montibus; for neither from the east, nor from the west, nor from the desert hills*, that is, because you cannot flee the divine judgment, O Babylon, in any part or side of the world: and for this reason: *quoniam Deus, for God* existing everywhere, seeing everything, and almighty, *iudex est, is the judge.* **74{75}[8]** *Hunc humiliat, et hunc exaltat; one he puts down, and another he lifts*, that is, one presses down, and one he lifts up, however pleases him and men deserve; **74{75}[9]** *quia calix in manu Domini, for in the hand of the Lord there is a cup*, that is, punishment or vengeance is in the power of God: cup, I say, *vini meri plenus mixto*, of strong wine full of mixture: that is, the punishments that God is able to pour out upon the ungodly are very bitter

---

6   Dan. 5:28; Is. 13:17; Jer. chp. 51.

and pungent, in the manner that a blend of pure wine is.[7] *Et inclinavit ex hoc in hoc, and he has poured it out from this to that*: that is, God pours out his punishment and vengeance from one people unto another, punishing the perverse successively, according to the order of his most just wisdom; *verumtamen faex eius non est exinanita, but the dregs thereof are not emptied*, that is, the bottom or the bitterness of this cup is not emptied, because the divine power does not desist in its avenging. Now all the rest that remains in the Psalm will be explained in the following article.

ARTICLE XLIV

TROPOLOGICAL OR MORAL EXPOSITION
OF THE SAME SEVENTY-FOURTH PSALM.

74{75}[1]   *Unto the end, corrupt not, a Psalm of a canticle for Asaph.
In finem, ne corrumpas. Psalmus cantici Asaph.*

NOW, ACCORDING TO THE TROPOLOGICAL sense, the previously mentioned title is explained in this fashion: 4{75}[1] *Psalmus cantici, a Psalm of a canticle*, that is, of spiritual joyfulness, because it has to do with remuneration of the just, it is *Asaph, for Asaph*, namely, for the congregation of the faithful or the Church: For Asaph is interpreted to mean congregation. The Psalm (I say) is written, *ne, that you not*, you one of the faithful, *corrumpas, corrupt yourself* by pride; and your hope, which is *in finem, unto the end*, that is, tending to Christ or eternal life, you may not empty out. Now this Psalm especially detests pride, commends humility, considers the justice of God's judgment, and declares the just renumeration of all men.

74{75}[2]   *We will confess you, O God: we will confess, and we will call
upon your name. We will relate your wondrous works.*[8]
*Confitebimur tibi, Deus, confitebimur, et invocabimus nomen
tuum; narrabimus mirabilia tua.*

---

7   *E. N.* The Greeks and Romans had pure wine (*vinum merum*) to which they typically added water so as to make it less intoxicating and palatable. The mixture was called mixed wine.

8   *E. N.* I have changed the Douay-Rheims' "praise" to "confess." As elaborated in footnote 27-49 in Volume 2, the word "confession" can be a "confession of praise" or a "confession of sin." Since Denis comments on this in the *Commentary*, I thought it fit to use the more general term "confess."

The Prophet speaking as the author of the present Psalm — whether the author was David or whether Asaph — speaks in the person of the Church and says: 74{75}[2] *Confitebimur tibi, Deus, confitebimur; we will confess you, O God, we will confess.* The repetition of words is a sign of a firm statement and of an ardent desire. Or [alternatively], that he first says, *We will confess,* it could refer to the confession of divine praise, of which the Savior says, *I confess to you, O Father:*[9] and this confession remains in the heavenly homeland, just as it is said in a Psalm below, *Confession and beauty are before him.*[10] But that it repeats a second time, *we will confess,* could refer to the confession of one's own fault, of which James says: *Confess . . . your sins one to another, and pray for one another, that you may be saved.*[11] And so, *We will confess you, O God,* that is, we will praise you, glorifying your eternal, endless, and pure goodness, with mouth and deed, recalling to mind your great and most bountiful benefits, namely, the gift of nature and of grace, and attributing it all to you. He who with blessed James exclaims — *Every best gift, and every perfect gift, is from above, coming down from the Father of lights* — confesses to God in this way.[12] For this recalling of the benefits of God certainly always applies, as that which Paul mentioned: *What have you that you have not received?*[13] And again: *Our sufficiency is from God.*[14] But that which James adds — *with whom there is no change, nor shadow of alteration* — relates to the praiseworthiness of the divine nature or goodness as it is itself. For we either praise God for himself and his own goodness or on account of his benefits: and everywhere in sacred Scripture where there is something said regarding the praise of God, it can be reduced and bought back to these two methods of confessing to the Lord with the confession of praise. *Et invocabimus nomen tuum, and we will call upon your name,* that is, you yourself with an internal affection, and we will pray with all our heart and from our most intimate core, in order that we may find grace with you and we may be preserved, advance, and be completed in the good. We praise you, therefore, for the benefits already received, and we invoke you for acquiring benefits and for obtaining promises.

Narrabimus mirabilia tua, we will relate your wondrous works written in the Old and the New Testaments, praising you the creator God for your supernatural effects. But especially ought we relate, either alone

9   Matt. 11:25a.
10   Ps. 95:6a. E. N. Again, I have changed the Douay-Rheims's translation from "praise and beauty" to "confession and beauty."
11   James 5:16a.
12   James 1:17a.
13   1 Cor. 4:7a.
14   2 Cor. 3:5b.

before God, or also if reason demands, to our neighbors, the wondrous works of God he deigns to work around every single one of us, mercifully forgiving our sins, bestowing the grace of conversion, and justifying our once-sinful souls: this is the great marvel of God because (as Augustine states) it is a greater thing to justify a sinner than to create heaven and earth.[15] Hence we read: *You may declare his virtues who has called you out of darkness into his marvelous light.*[16] But most of all we ought to declare, and we ought unceasingly to recall the marvelous works of our Lord Jesus Christ, all that which he assumed, did, and endured for our salvation: indeed, the mysteries of human Redemption, the Incarnation, the manner of living, the life, the doctrine, the signs, the Passion, the Resurrection, and the Ascension of Christ. For this is written: *Has not the Lord made the saints to declare all his wonderful works, which the Lord Almighty has firmly settled to be established for his glory?*[17]

74{75}[3]   *When I shall take a time, I will judge justices.*

Cum accepero tempus, ego iustitias iudicabo.

Now the voice of Christ is introduced: **74{75}[3]** *Cum accepero tempus, ego iustitias iudicabo; when I shall take a time, I will judge justices:* that is, when the time of the judgment of God instituted and fixed by wisdom comes, *I will judge justices.* This can be explained in two ways. The first is thus: *Justices,* that is, I will scrutinize the works that appear just to men, and I will see if they are truly just and acted with just intention. For God will scrutinize so strictly the works of the just, that Peter in his epistle said: *If the just man shall scarcely be saved, where shall the ungodly and the sinner appear?*[18] The second is thus: *I will judge justices,* that is, I will carry out just judgments, judging the elect with the judgment of approbation and the reprobate with the judgment of condemnation. For this reason, Solomon says: *He that sees into the heart, he understands, and nothing deceives the*

---

15   E. N. "Justification is the most excellent work of God's love made manifest in Christ Jesus and granted by the Holy Spirit. It is the opinion of St. Augustine that 'the justification of the wicked is a greater work than the creation of heaven and earth,' because 'heaven and earth will pass away but the salvation and justification of the elect ... will not pass away.' He holds also that the justification of sinners surpasses the creation of the angels in justice, in that it bears witness to a greater mercy." CCC § 1994 (quoting *In Jo. Ev.* 72,3, PL 35,1823). This is quoted by St. Thomas in his *Summa Theologiae.* ST IaIIae, q. 133, art. 9, c.

16   1 Pet. 2:9b.

17   Ecclus. 42:17.

18   1 Pet. 4:18.

keeper of your soul, and he shall render to a man according to his works.[19] It is necessary (according to the Apostle) for all of us to appear before the tribunal of Christ;[20] and Christ will judge every one of us one by one in the hour of our own death, but universally he will judge all men in the last day. Also, in the first coming Christ received the time of judging in a passive and merciful way, according to this: *For the Son of man is come to seek and to save that which was lost.*[21] But in the second coming he will receive the time of judging actively and for the purpose of vindication, as John says: *Behold, I come quickly; and my reward is with me, to render to every man according to his works.*[22] And Daniel: *The judgment sat, and the books were opened . . . and lo, one like the Son of Man came with the clouds of heaven.*[23]

74{75}[4] *The earth is melted, and all that dwell therein: I have established the pillars thereof.*

Liquefacta est terra et omnes qui habitant in ea, ego confirmavi columnas eius.

But how horrible will that judgment the Prophet exposes, adding: **74{75}[4]** *Liquefacta est terra, et omnes qui habitant in ea; the earth is melted, and all that dwell therein.* For before the final judgment, the earth and atmosphere will be set afire and cleansed with the flame of conflagration, and the men then living will melt like lead and be dissolved with fear, as the Savior said: *There shall be signs in the sun, and in the moon, and in the stars; and upon the earth distress of nations. . . . men withering away for fear, and expectation of what shall come upon the whole world.*[24] From this future melting of the earth in the day of judgment, of which the Prophet now speaks in the past tense, in keeping with the custom of the prophets, the most blessed Peter says: *But the day of the Lord shall come as a thief, in which the heavens* (read: the atmosphere) *shall pass away with great violence, and the elements shall be melted with heat, and the earth and the works which are in it, shall be burnt up.*[25] Isaiah also: *Behold,* he says, *the day of the Lord shall come, a cruel day, and full of indignation, and of wrath, and fury, to*

---

19 Prov. 24:12.
20 2 Cor. 5:10: *For we must all be manifested before the judgment seat of Christ, that every one may receive the proper things of the body, according as he has done, whether it be good or evil.*
21 Luke 19:10.
22 Rev. 22:12.
23 Dan. 7:10b, 13a.
24 Luke 21:25a, 26a.
25 2 Pet. 3:10.

lay the land desolate, and to destroy the sinners thereof out of it.[26] *Ego,* I, the
Lord, *confirmavi columnas eius, have established the pillars thereof:* that is, I
will confirm and preserve in grace just and perfect men who will exist at
the end of the world, during the time of the Antichrist, lest in such great
persecution and terrors they are overcome and fall by being overwhelmed.
*For there shall be then great tribulation, such as has not been from the begin-
ning of the world until now, neither shall be. And unless those days had been
shortened, no flesh should be saved: but for the sake of the elect those days shall
be shortened.*[27] Also, the word pillars can be understood as meaning the
holy Apostles, whom Christ after his Resurrection confirmed in the faith.
But perfect men, wise and holy, are called the pillars of the world and the
Church for they support others by their prayers, teaching, and example.

74{75}[5] *I said to the wicked: Do not act wickedly: and to the sinners:
Lift not up the horn.*

*Dixi iniquis: Nolite inique agere, et delinquentibus: Nolite
exaltare cornu.*

74{75}[6] *Lift not up your horn on high: speak not iniquity against God.*

*Nolite extollere in altum cornu vestrum; nolite loqui adversus
Deum iniquitatem.*

74{75}[5] I, Christ, *dixi,* said by myself, through the Prophets, by the
Apostles and other chosen men, *iniquis: Nolite inique agere,* to the wicked:
Do not act wickedly. Whence in the Gospel it is written: *Do penance: for
the kingdom of heaven is at hand.*[28] And Isaiah: *Wash yourselves, be clean,
take away the evil of your devices from my eyes.... Learn to do well: seek
judgment, relieve the oppressed.*[29] I said *et delinquentibus,* and to the sinners,
that is, those transgressing the divine law: *Nolite exaltare cornu, lift not up
the horn,* that is, do not boast of yourselves, do not inflate yourselves with
pride and resist God. Indeed, this is written: *The Lord God has sworn
by his own soul, ... I detest pride.*[30] And to these same proudful men, he
said: *Woe to those who say, Have we not taken unto us horns by our own
strength?*[31] **74{75}[6]** *Nolite extollere in altum cornum vestrum, lift not up
your horn on high:* that is, do not lift up your soul to excellence beyond

---

26   Is. 13:9.
27   Matt. 24:21–22.
28   Matt. 3:2; 4:17.
29   Is. 1:16–17a.
30   Amos 6:8a.
31   Amos 6:14b.

measure; but do that which the prince of the Apostles teaches, *Be you humbled therefore under the mighty hand of God, that he may exalt you in the time of visitation;*[32] and that which is written in Ecclesiasticus, *The greater you are, the more humble yourself in all things, and you shall find grace before God.*[33] Those to whom Moses said, *you take too much upon you, you sons of Levi,*[34] lifted their horn on high. And Micah: *Thus says the Lord: Behold, I devise an evil against this family . . . and you shall not walk haughtily, for this is a very evil time.*[35] *Nolite loqui adversus Deum iniquitatem, speak not iniquity against God,* praising, loving, and doing that which he censures, hates, and prohibits. Do not cover, excuse, or defend your sins. Do not murmur against your prelates, or deflect back your sins unto the Creator, saying that because of the constellations, or the disposition of the fates or of nature you are not able to flee sin.

74{75}[7] *For neither from the east, nor from the west, nor from the desert hills:*

Quia neque ab oriente, neque ab occidente, neque a desertis montibus.

74{75}[8] *For God is the judge. One he puts down, and another he lifts up.*

Quoniam Deus iudex est; hunc humiliat, et hunc exaltat.

74{75}[7] *Quia neque ab oriente, neque ab occidente, neque a desertis montibus;* for neither *from the east, nor from the west, nor from the desert hills* will you be able to avoid or escape, **74{75}[8]** *quoniam Deus iudex est,* for *God is the judge:* who through Jeremiah asserted about himself, *I am the judge and the witness;*[36] and elsewhere through same Prophet he confesses: *Shall a man be hid in secret places, and I not see him, says the Lord?*[37] Whence also God has spoken through Malachi: *I will come to you in judgment, and will be a speedy witness against evildoers.*[38] *Hunc,* one, that is, the proud man, God *humbles; et hunc, and another,* that is, the humble man, *exaltat, he lifts up:* as the Gospel says, *Every one that exalts himself, shall be humbled; and he that humbles himself, shall be exalted.*[39]

---

32 1 Pet. 5:6.
33 Ecclus. 3:20.
34 Num. 16:7b.
35 Micah 2:3.
36 Jer. 29:23b.
37 Jer. 23:24a.
38 Mal. 3:5a.
39 Luke 14:11; 18:14.

Besides in the present time God temporarily exalts some in their power or reign, advancing them to a sublime state, and he humbles others, depriving them of their former place: as is apparent of the Babylonians who were destroyed by the Medes and Persians,[40] who were destroyed by the Greeks, and the Greeks who were destroyed by the Romans.[41] And God, the almighty governor of all kingdoms, did this according to the order of his justice. Hence it is written in Daniel: *Blessed be the name of the Lord, for he changes times and ages, takes away kingdoms and establishes them.*[42] And in the first book of Samuel: *The bow of the mighty is overcome, and the weak are girt with strength. The Lord makes poor and makes rich, he humbles and he exalts. He raises up the needy from the dust, . . . that he may sit with princes, [and hold the throne of glory. For the poles of the earth are the Lord's, and upon them he has set the world.]*[43] And Ecclesiasticus: *God has overturned the thrones of proud princes and has set up the meek in their stead.*[44] This Nebuchadnezzar experienced, saying: *He does according to his will, as well with the powers of heaven, as among the inhabitants of the earth: and there is none that can resist his countenance.*[45]

74{75}[9]   For in the hand of the Lord there is a chalice of strong wine full of mixture. And he has poured it out from this to that: but the dregs thereof are not emptied: all the sinners of the earth shall drink.

Quia calix in manu Domini vini meri, plenus misto. Et inclinavit ex hoc in hoc, verumtamen faex eius non est exinanita; bibent omnes peccatores terrae.

74{75}[9] *Quia calix in manu Domini,* for in the hand of the Lord there is a chalice. By chalice, Scripture signifies suffering or punishment,

---

40   Cf. Dan. 5:28: *Your kingdom is divided and is given to the Medes and Persians.*
41   E. N. After suffering some defeats (Salamis and Platea), the Persian empire slid into decay. Eventually, Alexander the Great defeated Darius III in the battle of Issus (333 BC). Upon Alexander's death, Jerusalem and Judaea fell under Ptolemaic (Greek) control after the Wars of the Diadochoi (322 and 281 BC). Judaea was lost to the Seleucid Empire under Antiochus the Great (198 BC). After the Maccabean rebellion, Judaea became an independent kingdom, the Hasmonean Kingdom, which was defeated in 37 BC by Herod the Great, who served as a client to Rome. Ultimately, the region fell under direct Roman rule in 4 BC.
42   Dan. 2:20b–21a.
43   1 Sam. 2:4, 7–8. E. N. The part in brackets replaces the "etc." in the Latin text.
44   Ecclus. 10:17.
45   Dan. 4:32. E. N. Denis has *vultui eius* (his countenance) which departs from the Sixto-Clementine's *manui eius* (his hand).

such as when Christ said to the Father, *Remove this chalice from me;*[46] and to the sons of Zebedee: *My chalice you will drink.*[47] The chalice in the hand of the Lord, therefore, is the punishment resting in the divine power by which God is able to torment unjust men. Moreover, in this chalice *vini meri plenus mixto, of strong wine full of mixture,* that is, full of a variety of diverse punishments as it stated in a Psalm above: *He shall rain snares upon sinners: fire and brimstone and storms of winds shall be the portion of their chalice.*[48] By wine full of mixture is understood bitter flavor or austere taste, which the sinners feel out of the infliction of divine vengeance. But others explain it this way: *Chalice,* that is, the measure of retribution, is in the hand of the Lord, the judge of the world: *chalice,* I say, *of strong wine,* that is, a mixture of sadness and consolation as it relates to wayfarers, in whom, along with tribulations of the flesh or some other kind of punishment is mixed divinely inspired internal consolations. For in the elect there is in this age the rod and the staff of God, that is, penal correction and consoling sustenance, which are found together. Or [alternatively] the chalice means this full mixture, that is, the admixture of mercy and justice which are found mixed in all the works of God, according to this, *All the ways of the Lord are mercy and truth.*[49]

Et inclinavit ex hoc in hoc, and he has poured it out from this to that: that is, the Lord, the just judge of all, pours out his chalice from one people to another, scourging by degrees one people by another, as he scourged the Hebrews by the Chaldeans, and the Chaldeans by the Medes, and the Medes by the Greeks, and the Greeks and the Assyrians by the Italic people. Or [we can see it this way]: *He has poured it out from this to that,* that is, God from his chalice or measure of consolation pours in the chalice of affliction, and its converse; this means he mixes in consolation with temptation or affliction in the wayfarer, and vice versa. *Verumtamen faex eius non est exinanita; but the dregs thereof are not emptied:* that is, the last part of the chalice of the Lord drunk, namely, punishment without consolation, does not cease: for the punishment of hell, which lacks all relief, is also expressed by the name of dregs, and it never ends. *Omnes peccatores terrae, all the sinners of the earth,* who unless they repent, *bibent, shall drink* from these dregs, for they will be eternally condemned.

---

46 Luke 22:42.
47 Matt. 20:23.
48 Ps. 10:7.
49 Ps. 24:10. E. N. "'The world has need of that truth which is justice, and of that justice which is truth.'... St. Thomas pointed out: 'At times justice is called truth.'" Pope St. John Paul II, Address to the Tribunal of the Roman Rota, Jan. 28, 1994 (quoting Pope Pius XII, AAS 34 (1942), p. 342, n. 5 and ST IIaIIae, q. 58, art. 4, ad 1).

Whence in another place is written: *The evil man shall drink of the wrath of the Almighty.*[50] These dregs of the chalice of the Lord, are the gall and wormwood of which the Lord through Jeremiah declares, *Behold I will feed them with wormwood, and will give them gall to drink.*[51]

74{75}[10] *But I will declare forever: I will sing to the God of Jacob.*

Ego autem annuntiabo in saeculum; cantabo Deo Iacob.

And so the Church, or any just man, desiring to give thanks for his illumination and correction by the Lord, says: **74{75}[10]** *Ego autem annuntiabo*, but I will declare the benefits of God and his praises *in saeculum, forever*, that is, perseveringly, so long as I live; *cantabo*, I will sing with mental joy, *Deo Iacob, to the God of Jacob*, that is, for any vice of man supplanted. For Jacob is interpreted as meaning supplanter.[52]

74{75}[11] *And I will break all the horns of sinners: but the horns of the just shall be exalted.*

Et omnia cornua peccatorum confringam; et exaltabuntur cornua iusti.

The voice of Christ now follows **74{75}[11]** *Et omnia cornua peccatorum confringam*, and I will break all the horns of sinners, that is, all the dignities and exaltations of the proudful and the ungodly I will cast down, especially in the last day: according to what is written in Isaiah, *And I will visit the evils of the world, and against the wicked for their iniquity: and I will make the pride of infidels to cease;*[53] and with Hosea, *I will change their glory into shame.*[54] *Et exaltabuntur cornua*, but the horns . . . *shall be exalted*, that is, the virtues, high trust, and sublime contemplation *iusti, of the just*: for whatever of perfection is found in a just man, this will be exceedingly perfected after his death in the heavenly fatherland, and he will be rewarded with eternal honor; and in the day of judgment, the body and soul of the just man will be found above the height of the movable heavens.[55]

---

50   Job 21:20b.

51   Jer. 23:15a.

52   E. N. Jacob, the son of Isaac and Rebecca, is said to be a "holder of the heel" or "supplanter" because he twice deprived his twin brother Esau of the latter's birthright. *See* also footnote 43-103 and Article XXXV (Psalm 13:7) and Article XXVI (Psalm 13:7) in Volume I.

53   Is. 13:11.

54   Hosea 4:7b.

55   E. N. The lower levels of heavens were thought to be moving (with the stars

Let us do, therefore, what in the present Psalm we sing, insisting on the praise of God, bringing to mind our vices, and above all things and in all things abhorring all pride, and embracing, with unceasing effort, true humility, for *God resists the proud, and gives grace to the humble.*[56] He also is our highest and only teacher: *Learn of me,* he says, *because I am meek and humble of heart.*[57] For pride is hateful (as Scripture attests) *before God and men.*[58] Hence, the good father instructing his son says: *Never suffer pride to reign in your mind, or in your words: for from it all perdition took its beginning.*[59] And in the book of Job is said: *A vain man is lifted up into pride, and thinks himself born free like a wild ass's colt.*[60] Further, Christ himself taught us humility with his last word and deed in the Last Supper, washing the feet of his disciples, and saying to them: *He that is the greater among you, let him become as the younger; and he that is the leader, as he that serves.*[61]

PRAYER

O LORD, WITH A SINGULAR PENANCE, WE confess to you; propitiate our sins so that you might make us worthy by the mercy we have received of calling upon your holy name: so that we might sing forever to you with joy and exultation, God of Jacob, for our salvation.

Singulari poenitentia, Domine, confitemur tibi; peccatis nostris
propitiare, ut percepta indulgentia, dignos nos efficias
sancti nominis tui invocatione: ut pro salute nostra
in saeculum tibi Deo Iacob cantemus in
gaudio et exsultatione.

and planets); however, the immovable heaven above the movable heavens is the so-called empyrean heaven. In Dante Alighieri's words: "The numbers, the orders, the Hierarchies, declare the glory of the movable Heavens (*li cieli mobili*), which are nine; and the tenth announces this Unity and stability of God (*unitade e stabilitade di Dio*)." *The Banquet of Dante Alighieri* (London: George Routledge & Sons, 1887), 63. (trans. Elizabeth Price Sayer).

56   James 4:6b.
57   Matt. 11:29.
58   Ecclus. 10:7a.
59   Tobit 4:14.
60   Job 11:12.
61   Luke 22:26.

Psalm 75

ARTICLE XLV

LITERAL EXPLANATION OF THE SEVENTY-FIFTH PSALM:
NOTUS IN IUDAEA DEUS.
IN JUDEA GOD IS KNOWN.

75{76}[1] *Unto the end, in praises, a Psalm for Asaph: a canticle to the Assyrians.*

> *In finem, in laudibus.*[1] *Psalmus Asaph, canticum ad Assyrios.*

THE TITLE OF THIS PRESENT PSALM IS again: **75{76}[1]** *In finem, in laudibus. Psalmus Asaph, canticum ad Assyrios. Unto the end, in praises, a Psalm for Asaph: a canticle to the Assyrians.* According to Hebrew and Catholic teachers, the Psalm now being expounded literally speaks of the marvelous victory of the Jewish people in the time of Hezekiah, which God granted them over the Assyrians when the angel of the Lord in the Assyrian camp struck down one hundred and eighty five thousand men. Upon witnessing this, Sennacherib fled.[2] Foreseeing in the spirit this liberation, the author of the present Psalm wrote this Psalm, whose title is expounded thus: *Psalmus, a Psalm* before us, *in finem, unto the end,* that is, directing us unto Christ, *in laudibus, in praises,* because it contains the praise of God which, singing, we direct unto God, it is *for Asaph,* either as the author, according to some, or as a singer; or, Asaph, that is, Synagogue, insofar as by it is meant edification. And it is *canticum, a canticle,* that is, it includes spiritual exultation, written *ad Assyrios, to the Assyrians* who were laid waste, that is, to the Assyrians in the throes of dejection.

75{76}[2] *In Judea God is known: his name is great in Israel.*

> *Notus in Iudaea Deus; in Israel magnum nomen eius.*

And so it says: **75{76}[2]** *Notus in Iudaea, in Judea ... is known,* that is, in the land and the people of the Jews, *Deus, God:* For the worship

---

1 E. N. The editor of the Latin text suggests *laudibus* (in praises) which conforms to the Sixto-Clementine Vulgate, in lieu of Denis's *carminibus* (in songs). It also conforms to the Psalm as quoted in the body of the *Commentary.*

2 2 Kings. 19:35; 2 Chr. 32:21; Is. 37:36.

of the one, true, and most high God remains with the people of the Jews, though the other nations slouched toward idolatry. *In Israel magnum nomen eius, his name is great in Israel.* By Israel he indicates the Jews, for the Jews were the sons of Jacob, who was called Israel.[3] Or by Israel he expresses in a special way the ten tribes which during the time of Hezekiah had not been transported [into Babylon in exile]. And though they in large part had converted unto idolatry, adoring the golden calves that Jeroboam had made,[4] many among the people still remained who worshipped the true God, one of whom was Tobias, as is made clear in the book of Tobit.[5] Whence, it is written: *The Lord said to Elijah: I left me seven thousand men in Israel, whose knees have not been bowed before Baal.*[6] So, therefore, *in Judea,* that is, in the people of the tribe of Judah and Benjamin, among whom dwelt the Levites, for Jeroboam made himself priests of the lowest of the people;[7] and also, *in Israel,* that is, in the people of the twelve tribes believing in and worshipping God, *great was his name,* namely [great was the name] of God, because they knew the greatness of God, and God exhibited to them his power and magnificence by slaying the Assyrians in so marvelous a way. For the name of someone is said to be great where his power is greatly exhibited and where it is clearly recognized. And that which Moses said to his people is clearly true: *The Lord your God has chosen you, to be his peculiar people of all peoples that are upon the earth;*[8] and again: *Behold the Lord our God has shown us his majesty and his greatness.*[9]

75{76}[3]   *And his place is in peace: and his abode in Sion.*

Et factus est in pace locus eius, et habitatio eius in Sion.

75{76}[4]   *There has he broken the powers of bows, the shield, the sword, and the battle.*

Ibi confregit potentias arcuum, scutum, gladium, et bellum.

75{76}[3] *Et factus est in pace locus eius,* and his place is in peace: that is, the land of Judah, which had been attacked by the king of the Assyrians, acquired peace when the armies of the king were been killed;

---

3   Gen. 32:28.
4   1 Kings 12:28.
5   Tobit 1:5, 6.
6   1 King. 19:18; Rom. 11:4.
7   1 Kings 12:31. E. N. Jeroboam made priests from those who were not of the tribe of Levi.
8   Deut. 7:6b.
9   Deut. 5:24a.

et habitatio eius, and his abode, namely, [the abode] of God had been made to be *in Sion,* that is, in the temple built upon mount Sion.[10] For when peace had returned, the most pious king Hezekiah with the priests and the people most devoted to God returned thanks to God and served him in the temple; and so God by a great grace dwelt in his temple: in the manner that Habakkuk said, *The Lord is in his holy temple.*[11] 75{76} [4] *Ibi, there,* namely, in the land of Judah, the Lord *confregit potentias arcuum, scutum et gladium; has broken the powers of bows, the shield, and the sword,* that is, all the instruments of war of the Assyrians, *et bellum, and the battle,* that is the warriors of king Sennacherib. Or [alternatively], *the battle,* that is, his war, dissipated. For God destroyed the instruments of war, preventing them from being used in the act of the killing in war; or [in the further alternative], the Jews in large part destroyed these arms as also [they did] other spoils.

75{76}[5] *You enlighten wonderfully from the everlasting hills.*

Illuminans tu mirabiliter a montibus aeternis.

75{76}[6] *All the foolish of heart were troubled. They have slept their sleep; and all the men of riches have found nothing in their hands.*

Turbati sunt omnes insipientes corde. Dormierunt somnum suum, et nihil invenerunt omnes viri divitiarum in manibus suis.

75{76}[7] *At your rebuke, O God of Jacob, they have all slumbered that mounted on horseback.*

Ab increpatione tua, Deus Iacob, dormitaverunt qui ascenderunt equos.

75{76}[5] *Illuminans tu mirabiliter, you enlighten wonderfully,* that is, sending forth and pouring forth your light of mercy with marvelous goodness upon us, *a montibus aeternis, from the everlasting hills,* that is, from the holy angels, who are called everlasting hills because they are sublime and immortal. God marvelously showed the Jews through these [angels] because God granted this victory by the prayers and the ministry of the angels that had custody over the Jews. And so though it is written in Scripture, *An angel of the Lord departed, and slew in the camp of the Assyrians, etc.,*[12] it is also believed that individual angels having custody over individual Jews prayed to God for that triumph.

10 2 Chr. chps. 29 and 30.

11 Hab. 2:20a.

12 2 Kings. 19:35; Is. 37:36.

75{76}[6] *Turbati sunt omnes insipientes corde, all the foolish of heart were troubled*: that is, the perverse ministers and the perfidy of the king, namely, the Assyrians honoring idols, with terrified hearts were also killed bodily by the sword of the angel. Or [alternatively], all the foolish of heart were troubled because the people living around Judaea, hearing of the destruction of Sennacherib, were astonished at such an admirable blow. Whence, for a long time after had Nebuchadnezzar besieged Jerusalem, the people in the vicinity of Judaea did not reckon that Nebuchadnezzar would prevail because of the defeat of Sennacherib. For this reason, Jeremiah said in his Lamentations: *The kings of the earth ... would not have believed, that the adversary and the enemy should enter in by the gates of Jerusalem.*[13] It is said, further, that this enlightenment was done in a marvelous way, because the bodies of the Assyrians were reduced to ashes.

Dormierunt, they have slept, the Assyrians killed by divine power [have slept], *somnum suum, their sleep*, that is, the sleep of death: from which no one rises up from, except by God; *et nihil invenerunt omnes viri divitiarum in manibus suis, and all the men of riches have found nothing in their hands*: that is, none of the previously-mentioned Assyrians who were rich because of the spoils [of war], which they had collected from the many lands devastated by them, were helped or derived profit from their riches since they were killed. But their works, though not their riches, followed them;[14] and as a Psalm above says regarding riches: *For when he shall die he shall take nothing away; nor shall his glory descend with him.*[15] 75{76}[7] *Ab increpatione tua, at your rebuke*, that is, by the rigor of your vengeance, *Deus Iacob, O God of Jacob* the patriarch, to whom you said: *I am the God of Abraham, the God of Isaac, and the God of Jacob: This is my name forever, and this is my memorial unto all generations;*[16] *dormitaverunt, they have all slumbered* with the sleep of death: of which is written in the book of Job, *The rich man when he shall sleep shall take away nothing with him;*[17] and Christ [said], *Lazarus our friend sleeps.*[18]

---

13   Lam. 4:12.

14   *Cf.* Rev. 14:13: *And I heard a voice from heaven, saying to me: Write: Blessed are the dead, who die in the Lord. From henceforth now, says the Spirit, that they may rest from their labors; for their works follow them.*

15   Ps. 48:18.

16   Ex. 3:6b, 15b.

17   Job 27:19a.

18   John 11:11b.

75{76}[8] *You are terrible, and who shall resist you? From that time your wrath.*

> *Tu terribilis es; et quis resistet tibi? Ex tunc ira tua.*

75{76}[8] *Tu terribilis es, you are terrible* because of the vindication of your justice, and the inscrutable profundity of your judgment. For this reason, the holy Job said: *I have always feared God as waves swelling over me.*[19] *Et quis resistet tibi? And who shall resist you?* It is as if he were saying, "No one." In this same manner Jeremiah asserts this: *For who is like to me? And who shall abide me? says the Lord. And who is that shepherd that can withstand my countenance?*[20] *Ex tunc, from that time,* that is, from the time that you killed the Assyrians, *ira tua, your wrath,* that is, the vengeance of your justice, is evidently known.

75{76}[9] *You have caused judgment to be heard from heaven: the earth trembled and was still,*

> *De caelo auditum fecisti iudicium: terra tremuit et quievit,*

75{76}[10] *When God arose in judgment, to save all the meek of the earth.*

> *Cum exsurgeret in iudicium Deus, ut salvos faceret omnes mansuetos terrae.*

75{76}[9] *De caelo auditum fecisti iudicium, you have caused judgment to be heard from heaven*: that is, the just vengeance that you exercised upon the whole army of the Assyrians you made heard in heaven and earth, that is, by the heavenly power by which you wrought your vengeance. For as vengeance from heaven done by the ministry of an angel is said to be heard from heaven because of the heavenly power, which was the cause of the existence of that vengeance, so also is it true of the cause of the existence of the vengeance, since the cause can stand in place of its promulgation.[21] Or [alternatively] thus: *You have caused judgment to be heard from heaven,* that is, you caused to be heard by man the heavenly judgment: inasmuch as that which is said—*judgment . . . from heaven*—is as much as to say, and so is as if "heavenly judgment" was said.[22] And

---

19 Job 31:23a.
20 Jer. 49:19b; 50:44b.
21 E. N. The ministering angel's acts were heard from heaven, and since the ministering angel was sent (promulgated) by God as cause, one can say also that God caused the acts to be heard from heaven.
22 E. N. Denis is saying that "judgment . . . from heaven" (*de caelo iudicium*) is equivalent as saying "heavenly judgment" (*iudicium caeleste*), so that by the verb "heard" one understands that the judgment issued from heaven.

this was the heavenly judgment: that the Lord thrust against the king and the army of the Assyrians, killing so many troops. Or [in the further alternative] thus: *You have caused judgment to be heard from heaven*, that is, from heaven you have revealed this judgment. For God revealed to Isaiah what the future of this king and his people was; indeed, Isaiah frequently in his book of his visions foretells this. Isaiah also himself foretold it to Hezekiah.[23] *Terra tremuit, the earth trembled*, that is, the people of the Jews were in great dread because of the coming of the Assyrians. Or the earth is said to tremble because of the multitude of the Assyrian army: in the manner that is found in the first book of Maccabees, *The earth shook at the noise of the armies*.[24] *Et quievit, and was still*, that is the people of the land of Judaea ceased from their dread when the Assyrians were killed. **75{76}[10]** *Cum exsurgeret in iudicium Deus, when God arose in judgment*, that is, when he was proceeding with the act of judgment, sending his angel so that he was slaughtering the aforementioned people, *ut salvos faceret omnes mansuetos terrae, to save all the meek of the earth*, that is, so as to deliver the meek and holy king Hezekiah along with his people from the hand of the Assyrian.

75{76}[11] *For the thought of man shall give praise to you: and the remainders of the thought shall keep holiday to you.*

Quoniam cogitatio hominis confitebitur tibi, et reliquiae cogitationis diem festum agent tibi.

75{76}[11] *Quoniam cogitatio hominis, for the thought of man*, that is, the heart and the meditation of the heart of king Hezekiah and any one of his servants, following him in virtues, *confitebitur tibi, shall give praise to you* with the confession of praise, giving thanks to you for such a gracious liberation; *et reliquiae cogitationis, and the remainders of the thought*, that is, the memories of such a deed, begotten in Hezekiah and his people and in their posterity, at the first consideration of this deed, *diem festum agent tibi, shall keep holiday to you*, that is, there will be the occasion so that such a liberation might be solemnly recalled by the people of Hezekiah, indeed and by all who learn of such a marvelous work: for all of us hearing of this miracle, in some manner keep this feast, contemplating and marveling God in such an admirable work.

---

23   Is. 37:21–35.
24   1 Macc. 9:13a.

75{76}[12]   *Vow and pay to the Lord your God: all you that are round*
             about him bring presents. To him that is terrible,

             Vovete et reddite Domino Deo vestro, omnes qui in circuitu
             eius affertis munera terribili,

75{76}[13]   *Even to him who takes away the spirit of princes: to the*
             terrible with the kings of the earth.

             Et ei qui aufert spiritum principum; terribili apud reges terrae.

And so the Prophet [David] speaking of the Jewish people liberated
from the Assyrians, so that they might be thankful to God says: 75{76}
[12] *Vovete,* vow with a voluntary vow as an act of thanksgiving, *et reddite,*
and pay, that is, fulfil your vow, *Domino Deo vestro, omnes qui in circuitu*
eius affertis munera; to the Lord your God: all you that are round about
him bring him presents, that is, those from all the earth who are about
Jerusalem and encircling it and the temple in which God is asserted to
be and to dwell, assemble together so that you might immolate victims
to the Lord: to the Lord, I say, *terribili, terrible,* he is for this, 75{76}
[13] *Et ei qui aufert spiritum principum, even to him who takes away the*
spirit of princes, killing the great as if they were small, *terribili apud reges*
terrae, to the terrible with the kings of the earth, who were terrified of the
God of Israel after hearing of the destruction of Sennacherib. Whence
also Nebuchadnezzar said: *I now praise, and magnify, and glorify the*
King of heaven: because all his works are true.[25] And Darius: *Let all the*
inhabitants of the whole earth fear the God of Daniel: for he is the Savior,
working signs, and wonders in the earth.[26]

ARTICLE XLVI

MORAL EXPOSITION OF
THE SAME SEVENTY-FIFTH PSALM.

75{76}[1]   *Unto the end, in praises, a Psalm for Asaph: a canticle to*
            the Assyrians.

            In finem, in laudibus. Psalmus Asaph, canticum ad Assyrios.

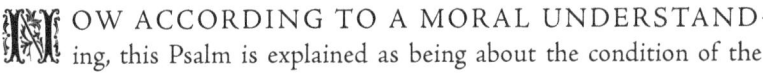 OW ACCORDING TO A MORAL UNDERSTAND-
ing, this Psalm is explained as being about the condition of the

25   Dan. 4:34a.
26   Dan. 14:42.

Christian Church, namely, of any man, people, or community of Christ's faithful, delivered from great danger, and magnificently praising God and inviting others to holy devotion and the giving of thanks to him because of this. And so the sense of the title stated above, is as follows: 75{76} [1] *Psalmus Asaph, a Psalm for Asaph,* that is, the congregation of the faithful, fittingly signified by the name Asaph, *in finem, unto the end* (who is Christ), tending and directing us *in laudibus, in praises,* so that the Church may harmoniously sing praises to God from a promptitude of will and through the impetus of holy delight, and not with sadness, or of necessity: for *God loves a cheerful giver.*[27] And this Psalm *canticum, a canticle,* that is, praise of spiritual joy, *ad Assyrios, to the Assyrians,* that is, to those to whom it is directed, they, namely, who direct their hearts to God. For Assyrians is interpreted as meaning "those directing."[28]

75{76}[2]   *In Judea God is known: his name is great in Israel.*

Notus in Iudaea Deus; in Israel magnum nomen eius.

And so it says: 75{76}[2] *Notus in Iudaea Deus, in Judea God is known.* Literally, this is unable to be accepted as pertaining to this time because the land of Judaea is inhabited (alas!) by the Saracen,[29] and the people of the Jews are unacquainted with the true God: in the manner that Christ spoke about the Jews, *Neither me do you know, nor my Father;*[30] and elsewhere, *It is my Father... of whom you say that he is your God, and you have not known him.*[31] What, therefore, is Judaea, and in what manner is God truly known, unless it be in the Christian Church, believing in God with the heart, confessing him by mouth, and honoring him with good works? Indeed, of this Judaea the most blessed evangelist John says: *We know that the Son of God is come: and he has given us understanding that we may know the true God.*[32] Whence Christ testified: *Just Father, the world has not known you; but I have known you... and I have made known your name to them, namely, those whom you gave to me.*[33] For Judaea is interpreted as meaning confession. And

---

27   2 Cor. 9:7b.
28   E. N. Compare Cassiodorus's *Commentary:* "Assyrians is interpreted as meaning "those directing," those who, already ruled by the teachings of the faith, strive to walk in the right paths." PL 70, 340.
29   E. N. In other words, by the followers of Islam.
30   John 8:19a.
31   John 8:54b–55a.
32   1 John 5:20.
33   John 17:25–26a.

the Church most truly confesses the Lord, because she alone truly knows God through the truth of the Catholic faith, acknowledging God, one and three, the Incarnate only-begotten of God, and that our beatitude is to be placed in the vision of God. *In Israel*, that is, in a man or in people, contemplating God through sincere faith, *magnum nomen eius, his name is great*, that is, he is reputed magnificent and glorious, and the name of God, or God himself, is incomparably known, who says of himself in another place: *I am a great King, . . . and my name is dreadful among the Gentiles.*[34]

75{76}[3]   *And his place is in peace: and his abode in Sion.*

            Et factus est in pace locus eius, et habitatio eius in Sion.

75{76}[4]   *There has he broken the powers of bows, the shield, the sword, and the battle.*

            Ibi confregit potentias arcuum, scutum, gladium, et bellum.

75{76}[3] *Et factus est in pace locus eius*, and his place is in peace: that is, the rational creature is disposed, accommodated to, and dignified by peace, and so that God might dwell in him, which he said about himself through Isaiah: *Over whom shall my spirit rest, unless it be the quiet and the humble?*[35] Now quiet is the same thing as peaceful, because peace is the stillness of the mind. For peace is the tranquility of a well-ordered heart: namely, [peace exists] so long as the flesh serves and is ordered by the spirit, sensuality by reason, and the reason by God, so that always the inferior promptly obeys its superior. God freely dwells in a soul that is granted such peace, of which Paul says, *God has called us to peace;*[36] and again, *God is not the God of dissension, but of peace.*[37] This peace makes men children of God, according to this: *Blessed are the peacemakers: for they shall be called children of God.*[38] God dwells in a peaceful man, therefore, just like in a beloved son: and so all Christians — but most especially the religious or the hermit — must greatly strive to possess a stable, immovable, true, and internal peace to the extent they are able. Therefore, the Apostle admonishes this: *Follow peace with all men, and holiness, without which no one shall see*

---

34   Mal. 1, 14b, 11a.

35   Is. 66:2. E. N. Denis departs from the Vulgate and quotes a Latin translation of the Septuagint version of Is. 66:2.

36   1 Cor. 7:15b.

37   1 Cor. 14:33a.

38   Matt. 5:9.

God, looking diligently . . . lest any root of bitterness spring up do hinder.[39]
And elsewhere: *If it be possible, as much as is in you, have peace with all
men.*[40] For every holy soul passing through this present exile rests in
splendid peace, according to that which the Lord asserted through Isaiah:
My people shall sit in the beauty of peace.[41] And so, that any Christian
should have great desires for this peace comes from this: that Christ,
sending forth his disciples before his Passion, commanded them that
they should pray for peace before all men: *Into whatsoever house you
enter, first say: Peace be to this house.*[42] And also after the Resurrection,
appearing to this disciples, he announced peace first of all, saying, *Peace
be with you.*[43] And also do not all the Apostles who wrote epistles, in
their greetings singularly write and wish to those whom they write
peace, saying, Grace to you and peace, or something similar? We should
therefore avoid all disturbance and discord, so that we might have among
us constantly the God of peace.

   Et habitatio eius, and his abode, namely [the abode] of God, is *in Sion,*
that is, in the Christian Church, or in any man faithfully keeping God
before his eyes. For this the Savior said in the Gospel: *I am with you
all days;*[44] and *We* (the Father and I) *will come to him and will make our
abode with him.*[45] For Sion is interpreted as meaning contemplation;[46]
and this is certain: that every contemplative is inhabited by the holy and
most high Trinity. **75{76}[4]** *Ibi, there,* namely, in the virtuous man and
in the Church, God by his grace *confregit, has broken,* destroyed, and
extripated *potentias arcuum, the powers of bows,* that is, the powers of
false suggestion of the devil, and the hidden snares of human deceit;
scutum, the shield, that is, excuses regarding one's own fault, by which
the sinner defends himself against correction; *gladium, the sword,* that is,
manifest resistance, by which man fights against God, fights against truth,
and resists his superior; *et bellum, and the battle,* that is, disobedience
or rebellion, by which the flesh desires and battles against the spirit. All
this evil God by the grace of his goodness expels from man, because it

---

39   Heb. 12:14–15a.
40   Rom. 12:18.
41   Is. 32:18a.
42   Luke 10:5.
43   Luke 24:36.
44   Matt. 28:20b.
45   John 14:23b.
46   E. N. This is the common interpretation. For example, Sts. Hilary of Poitier,
Isidore, Cassiodorus, and Augustine all interpret Sion as meaning "looking" or "contemplation" or "observation."

is proper to God to remove sins and to justify the impious, as Job says: *Who can make him clean that is conceived of unclean seed? Is it not you who only are able?*[47] By *bow* one can also understand sudden delight, which, similar to the bow, can unexpectedly attack and quickly kill; and by *shield*, a perverse will by which the unjust man arms himself for vice; but by *sword*, a vicious deed, by which man actually destroys himself; and also by *battle*, the habit of sinning, by which the sinner unceasingly fights against the divine law. For of those who are subject to these vices, it is elsewhere written: *Woe to them . . . because their hand is against God.*[48]

75{76}[5] *You enlighten wonderfully from the everlasting hills.*

Illuminans tu mirabiliter a montibus aeternis.

75{76}[5] *Illuminans tu*, you enlighten, O God, *mirabiliter, wonderfully*, that is, supernaturally, *a montibus aeternis, from the everlasting hills*, that is, by angelic spirits or by the holy angel [you enlighten] the Church militant. For in the manner that the most glorious prince of theologians Dionysius [the Areopagite] teaches,[49] God governs the ecclesiastical hierarchy or the militant Church through the angelic hierarchy, and single angels accompany, serve, and have charge over individual men. Also, archangels guard kings; and the universal Church has been given Michael, the overseer of paradise, to have as guard, in the manner that the Synagogue, whose prince was reported to be Michael.[50] By these mountains which are most copiously enlightened by the divinity, God illumines the human heart, sending to us by them the grace of his help, and the direction of the mind in all things. Whence, according to Dionysius, even before the written law, many nations were converted to the faith and to the worship of one God by angelic illumination. Others, however, have explained this verse as referring to the Apostles, by whose preaching God was marvelously illustrated to the world, converting it to the faith by many miracles. And they call the holy Apostles mountains because of their excellence of grace, the eminence of life, the height of wisdom; and they are also called eternal mountains because they are eternally reigning with Christ.

---

47 Job 14:4.

48 Micah 2:1.

49 *E. N.* The reference is to the *Celestial Hierarchy* of Pseudo-Dionysius. See *Pseudo-Dionysius: The Complete Works* (New York: Paulist Press, 1987) 170–72 (trans., Colm Luibheid)

50 Dan. 10:21.

75{76}[6] *All the foolish of heart were troubled. They have slept their sleep; and all the men of riches have found nothing in their hands.*

Turbati sunt omnes insipientes corde. Dormierunt somnum suum, et nihil invenerunt omnes viri divitiarum in manibus suis.

75{76}[6] *Turbati sunt omnes insipientes corde, all the foolish of heart were troubled,* that is, all who did not consent either to the angelic inspiration or to the apostolic preaching have fallen into disorientation and disquiet of mind, a lack of true peace, the tumult of vices, and the din of passion. For this reason, *dormierunt somnum suum, they have slept their sleep,* that is, the sleep of sin: of which the Apostle cries out, *Rise you who sleep;*[51] and again, *It is now the hour for us to rise from sleep.*[52] These [sinners] delight in, rest in, and finally persist in carnal, transitory, fleeting, and vain things. Or [another way of looking at it is] thus: *They have slept their sleep,* that is, dying in their vices, they have tasted a miserable death. Whether explained as referring to the sleep of sin or to the sleep of death, it is fitting to add [the adjective] *their,* so that it is foolish [of heart] that are said to have slumbered in sleep. For there is also a two-fold sleep of the just: namely, the sleep of holy contemplation, or of the internal repose and interior strength in the Lord: of which is said in a Psalm above, *In peace, in the selfsame I will sleep;*[53] and in Genesis, *The Lord God cast a deep sleep upon Adam.*[54] There is also the sleep of the death of the blessed, which is called the birth of the Saints:[55] and this is what is stated in the Book of Acts, since this is said of Stephen [the protomartyr who was stoned by the Jews], *he fell asleep in the Lord.*[56] *Et nihil invenerunt omnes viri divitiarum, and all men of riches have found nothing,* that is, the avaricious, *in manibus suis, in their hands,* that is, in their works: for in the hour of their death, and

---

51   Eph. 5:14a.

52   Rom. 13:11.

53   Ps. 4:9.

54   Gen. 2:21a. *E. N.* In his *Commentary on Genesis,* Denis explains: "According to Catholic teachers, this sleep [of Adam] was not a natural or bodily sleep, but rather was the numbness, quiet, ecstasy or absorption of the mind in God out of a profound and most intense contemplation of God and of his secret mysteries." Doctoris Ecstatici D. Dionysii Cartusiani, Opera Omnia, Vol. 1 (Montreuil: 1896), 81.

55   *E. N.* The *dies natalis* or birthday of the martyrs was the date of their death, and this was generally recognized as their feast day. This was extended to all saints, whether martyrs or not. All Saints Day, which in the past was celebrated within the Octave of Easter, for example, was called the *Dominica in Natale Sanctorum,* or the Sunday of the Birth (or Nativity) of the Saints, by the Würzburg *comes* or Lectionary. John Hennig, "The Meaning of All the Saints," *Medieval Studies* X (1948), 148.

56   Acts 7:59b.

also in the day of judgment, they will come to find empty and void of all good and meritorious works; then the riches, delights, and goods of this passing life will be of no profit to them. For this reason, it is said: *What has pride profited us? Or what advantage has the boasting of riches brought us? All those things are passed away like a shadow.*[57] And again it is written: *Go to now, you rich men, weep and howl in your miseries, which shall come upon you. Your riches are corrupted: and your garments are motheaten. Your gold and silver is cankered: and the rust of them shall be for a testimony against you, and shall eat your flesh like fire.*[58]

75{76}[7] At your rebuke, O God of Jacob, they have all slumbered that mounted on horseback.

Ab increpatione tua, Deus Iacob, dormitaverunt qui ascenderunt equos.

75{76}[7] *Ab increpatione tua, at your rebuke,* that is, from your chastisement or discipline, and from your exhortation, threatening, reproving, and preaching, *Deus Iacob, dormitaverunt, O God of Jacob, they have all slumbered,* that is, they have not amended [their lives], nor have they been vigilant with virtues, but they have slumbered in sin, *qui ascenderunt equos, that mounted on horseback,* that is, that delighted in temporal honors, dignities, preferments, and pomps. For God rebukes sinners by scourges and the exhortations of sacred Scripture; but some men are indeed obdurate, whence they are rightly corrected, as the Lord through Haggai says of such men: *I struck you with a blasting wind, and . . . with the mildew and with hail, yet there was none among you that returned to me, says the Lord.*[59] Or [alternatively], *that mounted on horseback,* that is, they confided more in the strength of horses than in the help of God. For this reason, Isaiah says of such men: *You have said we will flee to horses; therefore shall you flee. And we will mount upon swift ones; therefore shall they be swifter that shall pursue after you.*[60] And Hosea gives us counsel: *Return to the Lord, and say to him . . . We will not ride upon horses:*[61] not that to mount the beast that is called horse is a fault, but stiffening the neck against God is sinful, either by placing confidence in the horse or in the raising up of oneself in the height of pride.

---

57 Wis. 5:8–9a.
58 James 5:1–3a. E. N. Verse three ends: *You have stored up to yourselves wrath against the last days.*
59 Haggai 2:18.
60 Is. 30:16.
61 Hosea 14:3a, 4a.

75{76}[8] *You are terrible, and who shall resist you? From that time your wrath.*

Tu terribilis es; et quis resistet tibi? Ex tunc ira tua.

75{76}[8] *Tu terribilis es, you are terrible* in the manner that is brought out in Ecclesiasticus: *Behold the heaven, and the heavens of heavens, the deep, and all the earth, and the things that are in them, shall be moved in his sight; ... when God shall look upon them, they shall be shaken with trembling. And in all these things the heart is senseless*[62] which is not afraid of God. Job also: *Power and terror are with him, who makes peace in his high places.*[63] *Et qui resistet tibi? And who shall resist you?* Certainly, no one, for you yourself spoke through Isaiah: *My counsel shall stand, and all my will shall be done.*[64] And other scripture testifies: *God, whose wrath no man can resist, and under whom they stoop that bear up the world.*[65] For this reason, the most blessed Job says: *God is alone, and no man can turn away his thought. ... And therefore I am troubled at his presence, and when I consider him I am made pensive with fear.*[66] God will appear terrible especially in the future judgment inasmuch as the Apostle says: *It is a fearful thing to fall into the hands of the living God.*[67] *Ex tunc, from that time,* that is, from the time all foolish hearts are troubled by the just withdrawal of your grace and they have slept their sleep, etc., *ira tua, your wrath,* that is, your vengeance will begin to appear. For the most formidable wrath of God in this life is for him to abandon the sinner in his error: and so the wrath of God does not appear in the ungodly while he perseveres in vice. *For here it is written: For it is a token of great goodness when sinners are not suffered to go on in their ways for a long time, but are presently punished.*[68] Or [alternatively], from that time, that is, from the time of the last day, your perfect wrath will appear in the damned for eternity, for these are vessels of wrath, according to the Apostle.[69]

75{76}[9] *You have caused judgment to be heard from heaven: the earth trembled and was still,*

De caelo auditum fecisti iudicium: terra tremuit et quievit,

---

62   Ecclus. 16:18–20a.
63   Job 25:2.
64   Is. 46:10b.
65   Job 9:13.
66   Job 23:13a, 15.
67   Heb. 10:31.
68   2 Macc. 6:13.
69   Rom. 9:22b.

75{76}[10] *When God arose in judgment, to save all the meek of the earth.*
Cum exsurgeret in iudicium Deus, ut salvos faceret omnes
mansuetos terrae.

75{76}[9] *De caelo auditum fecisti iudicium, you have caused judgment
to be heard from heaven:* that is, from the mouth of Christ and of the
holy Apostles and of other faithful preachers, all of whom are said to
be of heaven because of their angelic life and heavenly manner of living,
you have made to hear, O God the Trinity, the judgment of discretion
by which you separate in the present the elect from the reprobate in life
and morals. For Christ and his disciples preached and taught how God
had predestined some from eternity, and others he had hated, and now
daily he discerns among them, the former mercifully considering, but the
latter justly spurning. But during the time of Christ, at the beginning
of the evangelical preaching, he began especially to make known this
judgment, for at that time he began especially to make clear who are the
elect and who are foreknown. For this reason, the Savior said: *Now is the
judgment of the world.* And this is why he adds: *Now shall the prince of
this world be cast out,*[70] namely, out of the hearts of the elect, so that it
may be clear who belongs to God. Or [alternatively]: *From heaven,* that
is, by heavenly illumination or the inspiration of the Holy Spirit, you
have heard the judgment that is in the future, at the end of the world:
for the Apostles and their successors, and their predecessors, the holy
prophets, concordantly taught and announced to men this final judgment.
Or [yet another alternative understanding]: *You have caused judgment to
be heard from heaven,* that is, you have made to be heard when the Lord
himself shall come down from heaven with commandment, and with the
voice of an archangel, and with the trumpet of God, saying: *Rise, you
dead, and come to judgment.*[71] But also when Christ himself will carry
out his sentence, saying, *Depart from me, you cursed, into everlasting fire;*[72]
and, *Come, you blessed of my Father.*[73] God the Trinity will make heard
the judgment which he conceives within himself of all men, of which
judgment Christ, as man, is executor or prolator.[74]

---

70 John 12:31.
71 1 Thess. 4:15; *see also* 1 Cor. 15:52: *In a moment, in the twinkling of an eye, at
the last trumpet: for the trumpet shall sound, and the dead shall rise again incorruptible:
and we shall be changed.*
72 Matt. 25:41a.
73 Matt. 25:34a.
74 E. N. A prolator (*prolator*) is the judicial official who delivers the sentence or
promulgates the judgment.

Terra tremuit et quievit, the earth trembled and was still 75{76}[10]
cum exsurgeret in iudicium Deus, when God arose in judgment. This can
be understood in various ways. For when Christ comes at the time of
judgment, all men living in earth will be terrified; but the good will
be quieted from this terror, because God will render judgment in their
favor. The ungodly also will be quieted from their former vices because
they will no longer be able to take delight in them. For this quieting is
foretold in Isaiah: *Keep quiet in doing perversely.*[75] Or [we can understand in this way:] the substance of the earth will then tremble, that
is, it will undergo something similar to a man quaking, because of the
fire of conflagration and the violence of waves of the sea; and it will
be quieted from this agitation, because at the time of judgment the
movements of the heavens shall cease, and the earth will be shine as if
gold.[76] So then, *the earth trembled and was still,* that is, it will tremble
and then be quiet, when God arises in judgment, that is, when Christ,
with all the worshippers of heaven, comes to judge, according to that in
Isaiah: *The Lord will enter into judgment with the ancients of his people,
and its princes;*[77] *ut salvos faceret, to save,* that is, so that he might save
from all corruption, death, and trouble, *omnes mansuetos terrae, all the
meek of the earth,* that is, meek men who bridle anger. One can also
explain this of Christ rising again from the dead. For, as Matthew said,
at Christ's Resurrection *there was a great earthquake. For an angel of the
Lord descended [from heaven, and coming, rolled back the stone, and sat
upon it].*[78] And this movement of the earth was quieted when *God arose,*
the Son of God, namely, Christ, from death in judgment, that is, so that,
in his time, he who was judged by the world, may judge the world, and
so that he might judge the Jews.

75{76}[11]   *For the thought of man shall give praise to you: and the
remainders of the thought shall keep holiday to you.*

*Quoniam cogitatio hominis confitebitur tibi, et reliquiae cogi-
tationis diem festum agent tibi.*

---

75   E. N. The Douay-Rheims has "Cease to do perversely" for *quiescete agere perverse.*
I have modified the translation so that it fits with Denis's argument. *Quiescete* is in
the imperative voice and can be translated as: rest, repose, keep quiet, be inactive,
be at peace.

76   E. N. The conflagration at the end of the world is handled in ST Suppl., q.
74, arts. 1–9.

77   Is. 3:14a.

78   Matt. 28:2. E. N. The part in brackets replaces the "etc." of Denis.

75{76}[11] *Quoniam cogitatio hominis confitebitur, for the thought of man shall give praise to you*: that is, the first occupation or the principal exercise of the heart of a virtuous man will be to praise you and to accuse himself: and so he will fulfill the Gospel: *Seek . . . first the kingdom of God*;[79] *et reliquiae cogitationis, and the remainders of thought*, that is, other meditations born from these principal occupations, *diem festum agent tibi, shall keep holiday to you*, that is, they will fill their mind with good reflections, whose intent will be to be free from care and to adhere to you solemnly, and to spend time festively and fruitfully. For when man praises God first for his benefits, and then brings to mind the sins he has done: then his soul will be filled with the splendor of grace, and man will consider how much beatitude he has allowed to slip by through sinning, how much misery he has fallen into, how much punishment he deserves, how vilely he has wasted time, how grave a sin ingratitude is, and how merciful God—who spared him for such a long time—is, and how lavish is the measure of the grace of conversion; and the many other things the soul thus speaking to itself considers.

75{76}[12] *Vow and pay to the Lord your God: all you that are round about him bring presents. To him that is terrible,*

> *Vovete et reddite Domino Deo vestro, omnes qui in circuitu eius affertis munera terribili,*

75{76}[12] *Vovete, vow*, that is, I consider that you have made a vow, or have received sacred orders, or have entered into religious life, or some other doing and giving something for the honor of God; *et reddite, and pay*, that is, I will rejoice that I may give back *Domino Deo vestro, to the Lord your God*. For to vow is a counsel, as it pertains to [the category of] supererogation.[80] But to fulfill a vow is of precept, in the manner that Moses asserted, *But that which is once gone out of your lips, you shall observe, and shall do as you have promised to the Lord your God*;[81] indeed

---

79 Matt. 6:33a.

80 E. N. "The distinction between the precepts of the Gospel and the so-called Evangelical Counsels, or counsels of perfection (vows of celibacy, poverty, obedience), is as old as the Church. It has always been Catholic teaching, (1) that there are works of supererogation, *i.e.*, good works not enjoined as a strict duty; (2) that these works are not merely good in opposition to bad, but better in opposition to good (*opera meliora*), and (3) that whereas a precept binds [all] of necessity, a counsel is a matter of free choice." Antony Koch & Arthur Preuss, *A Handbook of Moral Theology* (St. Louis, MO: B. Herder Book Co., 1918), Vol. 1, 238.

81 Deut. 33:23a.

also speedily is it to be fulfilled, according to that which is contained in Ecclesiastes: *If you have vowed anything to God, defer not to pay it: for an unfaithful and foolish promise displeases him.*[82] And so Thomas affirms that a vow obligates more than an oath.[83] And therefore it is much more perfect, and much more meritorious to do a good thing from a vow than without a vow, much like it is a greater thing to give a tree with fruit than [to give] the fruit alone. For the will is like a tree from where good and bad fruits, that is virtuous and vicious works, are born. Therefore, he who promises to God offers his will to God and obligates himself; it is clear also that such a thing is a more prompt and ardent service to God than not promising. But also the vow or promise, since it is an act of virtue that is called latria, receives a great reward: and so he who does a work from a vow is deserving of two things, namely by reason of the vow, and again by reason of the good work. Now there are also certain vows common to all, without which no one is able to be saved, such as the promises made at the Baptismal fount to believe and to renounce the works of Satan. And these [promises] fall under [the category of] precept, as does Baptism. But other vows are special, in the way that the vow of chastity, poverty, and so forth. Now these promises are of counsel; but once the vow is done, then they fall under [the category of] precept. So, therefore, *vow and pay to the Lord your God*, all you faithful, *that are around about him bring him presents*, that is, you who from all parts run toward God, and approach God encircling him, who in any event is in your midst;[84] not, however, that all men encircle God as if they enclose and circumscribe God with them, for he is boundless. The rest [of this Psalm] if clear for the preceding explanation.

See we have heard a joyful, pleasant Psalm, full of the praise of God, which teaches us to carry this out with internal sweetness, heartfelt joy, and attentive minds so that we ourselves and anything of ours may be able to be Judaea, praising to Lord with faith and deed, and to be Israel, beholding his glory with an open face:[85] and so with peaceful and sincere heart, let us prepare a dwelling for the Lord in us.

---

82   Eccl. 5:3.

83   E. N. ST IIaIIae, q. 89, art. 8, c. Thomas's reasoning is that a vow's obligation — which is a promise direct to God — stems from *fidelity* to God and also the *reverence* due him. The obligation undertaken by an oath, however, stems from the *reverence* we owe to God to make true that which is promised in his name. Since violating a vow involves both infidelity and irreverence to God, its obligation is by its nature more binding than that of an oath.

84   *Cf.* Matt. 18:20: *For where there are two or three gathered together in my name, there am I in the midst of them.*

85   2 Cor. 3:18a.

PRAYER

O GOD, SEARCHER OF REINS AND HEARTS, to whom the thoughts of all men are manifest, strengthen the weakness of our minds with the blessing of your power, so that we might think upon those things that are just and good, and by sincere devotion and living well, we might return to you our Lord God.

Deus, scrutator renum et cordium, cui omnis confitetur cogitatio
hominum, mentium nostrarum infirma benedictionis tuae
virtute corrobora: ut quae iusta et pia sunt,
cogitemus, et vota fidelia recte vivendo, tibi
Domino Deo nostro redamus.

FINIS

NDREW M. GREENWELL IS A MAR-
ried Catholic layman, with three children and four
grandchildren. He is a civil trial and appellate lawyer based
in Corpus Christi, Texas, who has written articles for Catholic Online and for a number of years wrote a blog on the
natural moral law called *Lex Christianorum*. He has translated
works from German, Latin, French, and Italian into English.
He is a member of the Latin Mass Community at St. John
the Baptist Church in Corpus Christi, Texas. Angelico Press
is publishing his translations of all of Denis the Carthusian's
works on the Mass and the Eucharist.

www.ingramcontent.com/pod-product-compliance
Lightning Source LLC
Chambersburg PA
CBHW021311070526
44553CB00068B/1239/J